THE COLONIAL LEGACY IN FRANCE

THE COLONIAL LEGACY IN FRANCE

Fracture, Rupture, and Apartheid

Edited by Nicolas Bancel, Pascal Blanchard,
and Dominic Thomas

Translated by Alexis Pernsteiner

Indiana University Press

This book is a publication of

Indiana University Press
Office of Scholarly Publishing
Herman B Wells Library 350
1320 East 10th Street
Bloomington, Indiana 47405 USA

iupress.indiana.edu

The paper used in this publication meets the minimum requirements of the American National Standard for Information Sciences—Permanence of Paper for Printed Library Materials, ANSI Z39.48-1992.

Manufactured in the United States of America

Library of Congress Cataloging-in-Publication Data
Names: Bancel, Nicolas, editor of compilation. | Blanchard, Pascal, editor of compilation. | Thomas, Dominic Richard David, editor of compilation.
Title: The colonial legacy in France : fracture, rupture, and apartheid / edited by Nicolas Bancel, Pascal Blanchard, and Dominic Thomas ; translated by Alexis Pernsteiner.
Description: Bloomington : Indiana University Press, 2017. | Includes bibliographical references and index.
Identifiers: LCCN 2017013119 (print) | LCCN 2017011782 (ebook) | ISBN 9780253026514 (eb) | ISBN 9780253026255 (cloth : alkaline paper)
Subjects: LCSH: Postcolonialism—France. | France—Colonies. | Nationalism—France. | Ethnicity—Political aspects—France. | Ethnic conflict—France. | Apartheid—France. | France—Ethnic relations. | France—Race relations. | France—Politics and government—21st century.
Classification: LCC JV1827 (print) | LCC JV1827 .C65 2017 (ebook) | DDC 325/.344—dc23
LC record available at https://lccn.loc.gov/2017013119

1 2 3 4 5 22 21 20 19 18 17

CONTENTS

xi
Note on Translation

1
Introduction: A Decade of Postcolonial Crisis: Fracture, Rupture, and Apartheid (2005–2015) / *Nicolas Bancel, Pascal Blanchard, and Dominic Thomas*

Part I. Colonial Fracture / 2005
1.1. The Emergence of the Colonial

43
1. The Republican Origins of the Colonial Fracture / *Nicolas Bancel and Pascal Blanchard*

53
2. When a (War) Memory Hides Another (Colonial) Memory/ *Benjamin Stora*

61
3. A Difficult History: A Brief Historiography of the Colonial and Postcolonial Situation / *Nicolas Bancel*

69
4. Reducing the Republic's Native to the Body / *Nacira Guénif-Souilamas*

78
5. Colonization and Immigration: "Blind Spots" in the History Classroom / *Sandrine Lemaire*

89
6. Memory Wars: A Study of the Intersection between History and Media / *Pascal Blanchard and Isabelle Veyrat-Masson*

1.2. The Return of the Colonial

115
7. The Enemy Within: The Construction of the "Arab" in the Media / *Thomas Deltombe and Mathieu Rigouste*

123
8. Islam and the Republic: A Long, Uneasy History / *Anna Bozzo*

130
9. The Republic, Colonization, and Beyond . . . / *Michel Wieviorka*

137
10. Colonial Natives and Indigents: From the Colonial "Civilizing Mission" to Humanitarian Action / *Rony Brauman*

144
11. The *Banlieues* as a Colonial Theater, or the Colonial Fracture in Disadvantaged Neighborhoods / *Didier Lapeyronnie*

153
12. The Pitfalls of Colonial Memory / *Nicolas Bancel and Pascal Blanchard*

165

13. Overseas France: A Vestige of the Republican Colonial Utopia? / *Françoise Vergès*

Part II. Postcolonial Ruptures / 2010

2.1. Debating the Colonial Legacy

175

14. Rethinking Politics in the French Overseas Departments / *Jacky Dahomay*

187

15. “Race,” Ethnicization, and Discrimination: Is History Repeating Itself or Is This a Postcolonial Peculiarity? / *Patrick Simon*

198

16. From the Empire to the Republic: “French Islam” / *Valérie Amiraux*

209

17. Immigration: From *Métèques* to Foreigners / *Yvan Gastaut*

220

18. Inequality between Humans: From “Race Wars” to “Cultural Hierarchy” / *Pascal Blanchard*

2.2. Postcolonial and Critical Gazes

233

19. The Postcolonial Challenges of Teaching History: Between History and Memory / *Benoît Falaize*

246

20. Postcolonial Studies in French Academia / *Catherine Coquery-Vidrovitch*

257
21. From Slavery to the Postcolonial / *Patrick Weil*

272
22. The Great Strip Show: Feminism, Nationalism, and the Burqa in France / *Elsa Dorlin*

285
23. From the Red Peril to the Green Peril: The New Enemy Within / *Renaud Dély*

Part III. Apartheid and the War of Identities in France / 2015
3.1. The End of the "French Model"?

303
24. From the Dakar Speech to the Taubira Affair / *Ariane Chebel d'Appollonia*

311
25. Could Islamophobia Be the Start of a New Identity-Based Bond in France? / *Rachid Benzine*

319
26. The Black Question and the *Exhibit B* Controversy / *Alain Mabanckou and Dominic Thomas*

330
27. Cultural Orientalization or Political Occidentalism? / *Nicolas Lebourg*

341
28. Faces of the Front National (1972–2015) / *Sylvain Crépon*

351
29. Infiltration of Liquid Populism / *Raphaël Liogier*

3.2. The Rejection of the Other, Identity Radicalization, and the Colonial Unconscious

363
30. Nanoracism and the Force of Emptiness / *Achille Mbembe*

368
31. Antiracism: A Failed Fight or the End of an Era? / *Emmanuel Debono*

378
32. Closing Borders against Fear: Europe's Response to the 2015 "Migrants Crisis" / *Claire Rodier*

386
33. Toward a Real History of French Colonialism / *Alain Ruscio*

395
34. Is a Colonial History Museum Politically Impossible? / *Nicolas Bancel and Pascal Blanchard*

412
35. After *Charlie*: A New Era or Unfinished Business? / *Alec G. Hargreaves*

429
Bibliography

463
Index

NOTE ON TRANSLATION

The following sections of the book were written in English:

Introduction, "A Decade of Postcolonial Crisis: Fracture, Rupture, and Apartheid (2005–2015)," by Nicolas Bancel, Pascal Blanchard, and Dominic Thomas

Chapter 26, "The Black Question and the *Exhibit B* Controversy," by Alain Mabanckou and Dominic Thomas

Chapter 35, "After *Charlie*: A New Era or Unfinished Business?," by Alec G. Hargreaves

THE COLONIAL LEGACY IN FRANCE

INTRODUCTION

A DECADE OF POSTCOLONIAL CRISIS: FRACTURE, RUPTURE, AND APARTHEID (2005–2015)

Nicolas Bancel, Pascal Blanchard, and Dominic Thomas

> Who cannot see just how disquieting ideologies of separation have become? Who has not been able to grasp the disastrous consequences of a religious worldview in which everyone is assigned a set identity defined by an innate essence? By drawing attention to the genealogy of the *regimen* and the art of governing mankind, historians have thrown a harsh light on what remains of modernity.
>
> Patrick Boucheron, "Ce que peut l'histoire," Inaugual lesson at the Collège de France, December 17, 2015.[1]

Paris, November 13, 2015 . . . one hundred and thirty dead and almost four hundred injured . . . Earlier, in January 2015, French prime minister Manuel Valls had used the word *war*, a word he has since repeated on multiple occasions along with French president François Hollande as a way of describing the November attacks: "What I want to say to the French people, is that France is at war. What happened was a systematically organized act of war."[2] A few days later, on November 16, speaking in Versailles before a joint session of parliament, François Hollande declared "This was an act of war" and went on in the following days to explain the nature of this war. Then, on November 27, at a national ceremony held at the Invalides to honor the civilian victims of the attacks, the president paid homage, stating that "We will fight to the end and we will win" and also that "France will do everything possible to destroy this army of fanatics who committed these crimes." According to the historian Patrick Garcia, the symbolic importance of the Invalides is especially significant because the "Invalides has for a very long time been a national monument for those who lost their lives for the nation, for military casualties. It is this symbolic value that is reproduced. The November 13 victims have been elevated to a rank traditionally reserved for military heroes: to that of everyday heroes. This does not mean that they are combatants as such, but there is something of that nature implied: the attacks were an act of war, we are at war, these victims are therefore war victims."[3] But what kind of "war" is it exactly?

One could very well be mistaken for thinking government officials were talking about a very *classic* kind of war, a war between two states (namely the "French state" and the "Islamic State"), two armies with a clear enemy and military objectives; in other words, a war in which an effective strategy promises to deliver a "victory." However, closer scrutiny points to a war in which one finds oneself a combatant alongside an entire nation composed of fellow combatants, a war in which all victims are honored, de facto, as soldiers. In the end, whether or not the war itself is or is not classic is secondary, since there can be no doubt that we are "at war" both *here* and *over there*.[4] A war that is somewhere between a cold war and a "clash of civilization," a war in which each individual must now choose her or his "side," a conflict one should not forget is simultaneously a political "civil war," as Prime Minister Valls warned on France Inter radio in early December 2015 in a discussion on the rise of the far-right Front National party. The word has seeped into our collective consciousness.[5] We are at war. Take note. And this war jeopardizes, first and foremost, our identity—an identity that we would like to safeguard, protect, defend; an identity our enemies are also seeking to impose on us, in our *banlieues* housing projects or in the form of attacks, the very kind that is driving Daesh.

A few months prior, in January 2015, in the aftermath of the attacks against the *Charlie Hebdo* weekly newspaper, the prime minister had evoked the existence of a "territorial, social, and ethnic Apartheid" in France. *War* and *apartheid*, two words one could not have imagined putting together a mere decade ago in France on the eve of the riots and uprisings that coincided with our collective work on the "colonial fracture."[6] At the time, the aim had been to shed light on the particular context in France in which the failure to reckon with colonial history had triggered a competing memory war that was contributing to a broader identity crisis.[7]

Every indication is that France (both mainland and overseas) finds itself today in a postcolonial crisis that can partially be explained by the profound economic, political, and social asymmetries associated with the so-called *Global South*. These conclusions were those of the contributors to both *La fracture coloniale*[8] and *Ruptures postcoloniales*,[9] several chapters from which are included here in *The Colonial Legacy in France*. Our argument is that the fracture we initially alluded to and that eventually mutated into a "rupture" is today evident and contained in an apartheid-like situation that directly contributes to the competing specificity of the *identity wars* France now finds itself engaged in.

"We Are at War"

Individual chapters seek to interrogate the *new fractures* in French society and to build connections between these and their colonial roots. *The Colonial Legacy in France* makes no claim to being exhaustive, or for that matter to providing a monolithic interpretation of the situation in France today. Quite the contrary in fact. Instead, we are trying to find ways of working together in order to improve our understanding of how we arrived at this point. How can one explain rising extremism and populism[10] and the recrudescence of hatred toward Jews and Muslims, establish connections between those who see evidence of decline and the "clash of values," address the malaise in the disadvantaged *banlieues* housing projects, gauge the effects of nostalgia and the impact of memory,[11] understand the role colonial culture plays over a longer history,[12] and analyze the kind of "institutional forgetting" that has come to characterize the art of governance in France today? In other word, our goal is to *understand*.

We also want, as indeed we had back in 2005 and 2010, to lay the groundwork for an interdisciplinary reading of events, one that would go beyond some of the early interpretations of the attacks while also countering a deep-seated denial of the historical origins to the events. *Understanding* should not be confused with *excusing*, a position at odds with Manuel Valls's comments made on January 9, 2016, on the occasion of the first annual commemoration ceremony for the attacks that had taken place at the kosher supermarket.[13] In reality, he was merely reiterating earlier comments made on November 26, 2015, at the Senate, when he said that "I've had enough of people constantly trying to provide cultural or sociological excuses or explanations for the events that have taken place," or at the National Assembly claiming that "no social, sociological or cultural excuse should be invoked." The past, social injustice, discrimination, religious adherence, or memory wars may not be able to explain everything, but they most certainly cannot be dismissed entirely. Such anti-intellectual statements signal a form of state populism overwhelmed by present circumstances. As Pascal Ory explained in an article in *Le Monde* on January 9, 2016, "France, the daughter of the Enlightenment, thought of herself for a long time as exemplary, but has found this role increasingly difficult to assume following the Vichy regime and decolonization."[14] *Understanding,* Bernard Lahire has noted, protects us from an "incredible obscurantist regression" and therefore allows us to better grasp how this French contradiction can assist us in thinking differently when it comes to the complex challenges of the day.[15] Refusing to *understand* is tantamount to believing only in what one sees, refusing to go beyond appearances, and to blindly enter into war. Only a few steps separate the refusal to understand and obscurantism. In this refusal to understand lies the impossibility of mastering one's subject and therefore of conquering it. *Understanding* the origins of contemporary events is the best way of making sure they don't happen again or, for that matter, spread exponentially, but it is also a way of resolving conflict.[16]

"The persistence of this *denial,* in France, is not without consequences," as Pascal Blanchard, Nicolas Bancel, and Sandrine Lemaire have argued, since "it introduces and stirs up conflict over memory, while also bolstering the sentiment among certain members of the population—in particular those French people that are descendants of postcolonial immigrants—that their history is ignored; this also encourages people to turn a blind eye when it comes to neocolonial policies in Africa."[17] A postcolonial interpretive grid can therefore allow for an engagement with "a range of elements defining the crisis in France today," including the identity crisis, therefore gaining a better understanding as to just what is at stake in the conjunction between war and apartheid.[18] The former brings to mind the period between 1950 and 1962 when France was at war with its empire, all the way from Algeria to Indochina, whereas the latter refers to a system in which colonial relations were expressed in their ultimate racial form in South Africa and only came to juridical end at the dawn of the 1990s. The specter of the imperial past thus finds itself haunting us on two fronts.

The year 2005 was the year in which French people discovered the colonial past in journals, magazines, special editions of academic journals, and in academic books,[19] a time in which this past was questioned but also reaffirmed by politicians who voted on such laws as the "Loi portant reconnaissance de la Nation et contribution nationale en faveur des Français rapatriés" (Law concerning the recognition of the nation and national contribution in favor of repatriated French), known as the Debré 2005-158 law (February 23, 2005) in which the "positive aspects of the French colonial experience" were invoked.[20] This thirst for knowledge was soon crushed by the concerted efforts of neoreactionary and nostalgic discourse and the deafening silence of the state on these and related issues. The colonial question as such was yet again and, for the most part, marginalized over the next decade or so. At the same time though, the migratory question became a "problem" in far-right political discourse, but it extended far beyond into mainstream politics, and in the 2007 presidential elections, identity issues were very much at stake. That same year, the place of Islam in society became a major political "issue." Thus, 2005 marked a turning point in more ways than one, and paved the way for 2015.

This period also happens to coincide with the birth of a third generation of jihadists, one that found in the urban riots and uprisings of 2005 a form of inspiration that would lead to a quite different way of conceiving of revolt in the West. After the failure of bin Laden's "world revolution," theorized by his former disciple Abu Musab al-Suri in his 2004 book *The Global Islamic Resistance Call*, a book that was widely distributed on the internet and which has heavily influenced what is today Daesh (and its founder, Abu Musab al-Zarqawi), he argued that the new global terrorism must target the West by enlisting support from marginalized youth of postcolonial immigrant background living in urban housing projects.[21] Abu Musab al-Suri is no stranger to Europe. He was educated in France, married a Spanish woman, and knows how to mobilize people from the chronological third generation of immigrants, whether through propaganda streamed over the internet or through militants operating in prisons.[22] He has taken part in all of the major global jihadist phases without being active on the ground as such. He is, in a way, a self-made "visionary" who has found an audience for his ideas in the context of the gradual demise of al-Qaeda and the ensuing chaos that resulted from US intervention in Iraq and the civil war in Syria.

Things really started to speed up in 2010, with a decree prohibiting concealment of the face in public spaces, President Sarkozy's national security speech in Grenoble, and the rise of populist parties throughout Europe. At the same time, the Arab Spring was getting underway in the Middle East and North Africa. As Gilles Kepel has shown, we are witnessing a "hystericization of the debate" on Islam for which the political elite is to be held partially responsible given their incapacity to measure the dramatic geopolitical realignments that have resulted from the Arab Spring as well as the growth of Islam in the *banlieues* neighborhoods. This is the result of "a return of colonial repression"[23] coupled with the "ethno-racial exclusion factory" the projects have become. Ahmed Dahmani, a fitness instructor who was close to an accomplice of one of the Bataclan concert hall attackers, had the following to say: "I'm not convinced the authorities really have any idea as to what is going on in these neighborhoods in which 'community harmony' or 'peaceful coexistence' doesn't exist. Young people around here are searching for an identity and values at an age when they are especially vulnerable. But they get no help. I'm quite surprised with this display of force from the authorities with no regard for the origins or root of the problem."[24] Immigration, urban violence, the emergence of a small radicalized faction in the *banlieues* projects as confirmed by the background of recent jihadists, colonial memory, chaotic political situation in parts of the Maghreb and Middle East, mobilization of international terrorist networks, and mixed Western response in international interventions: a multidimensional set of fragments that can be seen to coalesce.[25]

Understanding the "root" of this configuration is therefore key. *Understanding* that the "war" is henceforth *here*, that it is built on the failures and shortcomings of our social system, that it attracts and mobilizes a fraction of one generation and that, at the opposite end of the spectrum, a portion of public opinion—no less than seven million voters during the second round of the 2015 legislative elections—now believe that a portion of the national body has no (or no longer has) legitimate claim to the national territory.[26] A postcolonial divide between "them" and "us"—*On est chez nous* (We're in our home) has now become the slogan of the Front National—and once again the "illegitimate children"[27] of postcolonial immigration are *delinked* from the "native" population of "French stock" or, at the very least, those assimilated to this essence (notably those immigrants or repatriated families associated with European migratory flows since the mid-nineteenth century or the *pieds-noirs* that came from Algeria in the early 1960s).

The Current Crisis in Context

The context of recurring crises has contributed to the emergence of the identity component of this war, evenly spread between the prototype of the "patriot" and that of the "enemy," the "national community" and the "foreigner," who are by very definition hostile.[28] However, this foreigner can also be French or binational, which is, of course, all the more frightening and distressing. The option of stripping (foreign-born) binationals (dual citizens) of their French nationality received broad bipartisan support even if it was not ultimately voted into law.[29] This serves to underscore the degree to which identity radicalization has burgeoned in the French nation. Advocates were essentially prescribing a two-tier citizenship that would be symbolic (because generally speaking it was pointless), presented as republican (as Gérard Courtois argued in *Le Figaro* on January 9, 2016), but also embraced by the far-right who see it as *popular* (because 75 percent of people polled say they support it) when in fact it is *populist* in every sense of the term. In fact, what we have observed is a dramatic rise in suspicion toward certain segments of the French population whose genealogy is not "strictly speaking French," as is the case already for the descendants of postcolonial immigrants from the Maghreb and sub-Saharan Africa.

The reality is that one of the logical outcomes of decolonization has been the dual-based memory that defines postcolonial immigrants: they are the fruit of a history in which they are the descendants not only of migrants but also of native subjects of the empire. At the same time, they are inserted into a French society that neither recognizes this dual affiliation nor, for that matter, colonial or postcolonial history, the latter also serving to explain the physical presence of these populations and the debasing representations that cling to them. This complex relationship to history and memory, in addition to banishment in disadvantaged neighborhoods and ethno-racial–based discrimination, contributes to feelings of marginalization that are then also compounded when religious stigmatization is a factor superimposed on historical markers. In order to destabilize Western societies, Daesh's strategy has been to nurture and emphasize precisely these kinds of polarization by drawing attention to forms of historical humiliation during colonialism or in the guise of contemporary Western "imperialism" as a way of mobilizing Muslims (or future converts) in order to provoke civil wars in Europe, bolstered by the identity crisis Europe is experiencing. Likewise, antisemitism also serves as a device for mobilizing support from excluded populations in disadvantaged neighborhoods by instrumentalizing the Palestinian question.[30] From this perspective, France finds itself on the front lines because of its colonial past (with the French Mandate of Syria and Lebanon [1923–1946], colonies in Sahelian Africa, and colonies and protectorates in the Maghreb), the weight of the postcolonial migratory presence in mainland France, the social crisis in the *banlieues*, its difficult relationship with Islam since the Iranian Revolution and the strikes of 1982–1984, as well as forces of inertia to be found in colonial nostalgia and that impede any attempt to achieve a collective and shared narrative when it comes to this period in history.[31]

De facto, these identity concerns have been discussed in related ways. Caribbean authors Édouard Glissant, Jean Bernabé, Patrick Chamoiseau, and Raphaël Confiant have, for example, deployed a variety of concepts such as *antillanité* (Caribbeaness), *créolité* (Creoleness), and *le tout-monde*, a theoretical apparatus that has sought to account for France's diversity and history, much in the same way as Frantz Fanon had done previously with the colonial context in mind or Abdelmalek Sayad had done when it came to the confrontation between Maghrebi immigrants and French society.[32] These questions touch every aspect of social life, and people are bombarded with them along with a range of other issues, including the "White question"[33] or the "gender question,"[34] that until recently were relatively unexplored in France when it came to thinking about identity.

Today, we are caught in an identity maelstrom that has been handed down from imperial history, infused with cultural and economic globalization and multidirectional migratory flows, all of which were brought into the light of day during the 2015 attacks. In a book published in 2015, *Le Grand Repli*, that explored the concept of "defensive identity" in France, authors Nicolas Bancel, Pascal Blanchard, and Ahmed Boubeker argued that France was a "plural society that had never thought of itself as multicultural but that now had to in order to remedy the growing phantasm of a country lying in the path of the destructive winds of a foreign invasion, and find a way to establish conditions that will be conducive to peaceful coexistence, and in so doing decolonize existing social relations. [. . .] In other words, concentrate on peaceful coexistence and fight against misconceptions. Peaceful coexistence in the form of the right to be here and take part in the cultural, political, and social life of the country, without having to establish your credentials first. In other words, peaceful coexistence as opposed to defensive identities."[35]

How can one recapture that feeling of peaceful coexistence that illuminated France on that fateful day of January 11, 2015, when millions of people took to the streets in unity marches? Coherent answers to these and other questions can only take place in a constructive and productive manner by inscribing the situation in a much longer history, one that attempts to take into consideration the interwoven nature of several rich traditions and memories as well as the "religious fact" and its political dimension.

Grandeur and *Decline*?

The existential crisis France is undergoing is anchored in General de Gaulle's conviction that "France cannot be France without grandeur"[36] and in Charles Maurras's vision of the nation's "slow decline," albeit under the battering today of a Muslim enemy working hand in hand with various *métèques* and Jews, and, of course, considering global finance,[37] all factors that contribute in a democratic space (the Republic in this case) to the destruction of French values and traditions. These syntheses of genealogically opposed views is strikingly evident in the works of a number of contemporary authors, the most popular of which is, without a doubt, Éric Zemmour, the most politicized being Robert Ménard (now mayor of Béziers), the most complicated, Alain Finkielkraut, the most ambiguous, Laurent Bouvet, the most institutional, Pierre Nora, and the most consistent, Pascal Bruckner.

These neoreactionary interpretations of the decline of France have introduced concepts and terms such as cultural insecurity, the threat of a *grand remplacement* (great substitution or replacement), and "reverse colonization,"[38] all of which have given rise to the myth of a "great departure" (a consequence of the great substitution) of immigrants and, while we are at it, why not their descendants as well.[39] This great departure stands as the only "solution" that would give France a chance to free itself from the trap in which it finds itself caught, thereby killing two birds with one stone and ridding itself at the same time of the terrorist threat. In other words, it would be the way to definitively solve the question of fractured identities. This pretty much corresponds to the mythic portrait offered by the leaders of the Front National to their supporters[40] in the guise of posters in which the *banlieues* are represented as lawless spaces (under such catchy headings as "Choose your *banlieue*"), in their slogan *On est chez nous* (We're in our home), and of course implicit in the strong ties they maintain with the memory of the Algerian War.[41] According to Éric Zemmour in his bestseller *Le suicide français* (The French Suicide),[42] the loss of Algeria marked the beginning of France's decline, along with the women's liberation movement and the "culture of May 68." Supposedly, France, during the period between 1995 and 2015, has been experiencing a *second Algerian War* of sorts, with the Khaled Kelkal bombings all the way up until the November 2015 attacks, a period that has been witness to the Arab-African Muslim transforming into the latest incarnation of the mujahedeen,[43] a war with heavy losses that got underway right after the Évian Accords were signed, after the loss of Indochina, and the humiliation suffered at Suez in 1956. And that only worsened throughout the postcolonial era.[44] From the populist Poujade to Jean-Marie Le Pen and Marine Le Pen, one finds but one political tradition: a shared vision of the world.

The findings of a study conducted in 2015 by Ipsos on *fractures françaises* (French fractures) are extremely revealing.[45] In all, 26 percent of respondents stated that "France is in decline and that the situation is irreversible;" 70 percent agreed with the following statements: "In my daily life I seek inspiration from the past," that "Things used to be better in France," and that "We no longer feel at home in France" (a category in which respondents who also stated they were Front National supporters agreed at a level of 95 percent). Additional questions revealed that two-thirds of all respondents felt there were "too many immigrants in France."[46] Significant disparities were recorded between socialist and Front National perceptions of the difficulties facing immigrants when it came to integration, although 81 percent did agree that "Islam was a growing concern that called for serious attention." What we have, effectively, is a meeting between two ideologies, that of the "enemy within" facing off against the anxiety of "decline," almost as if France now needed a designated enemy in order to define itself.[47]

These indicators are striking, and as we have already mentioned, can be corroborated by both the quantity and the popularity of books devoted to the malaise,[48] most notably those of Éric Zemmour, but also books by Pascal

Bruckner, Alain Finkielkraut, Paul-François Paoli, Max Gallo, Alain Griotteray, Daniel Lefeuvre, and a long list of other authors. As far as Renaud Camus is concerned (an outspoken supporter of the Front National), the question is now one of decivilization, that is, a process by which the white population is gradually being supplanted by Afro-Maghrebi racial mixing and Muslim immigrants so that the time will come when native-born French people will be outnumbered.[49]

Perhaps not surprisingly, works of literature have also focused on these questions. The controversial writer Michel Houellebecq has sold almost a million copies of his novel *Soumission* (Submission) that stages the 2022 presidential elections in France and the victory of a Muslim party.[50] The novel was released in France on January 7, 2015, the same day as the *Charlie Hebdo* shootings, and its promotion had to be postponed in the immediate aftermath of those attacks. But other recent works of a quite different nature have also enjoyed critical success, highlighting the tenuous relationship between closed and open mindsets. During the autumn of 2015 alone, one could mention Mathias Énard's Goncourt prize-winning novel *Boussole,* or for that matter the two novels selected for the prestigious Académie Française prize, Boualem Sansal's *2084* and Hédi Kaddour's *Les Prépondérants,* books that examine, respectively, a journey marked by orientalism, a dictatorship, and colonial life in 1920. Let us not forget that back in 2011, Laurent Jenni's novel *L'art français de la guerre* (also the recipient of the Goncourt Prize) had inaugurated a broader debate on the concepts of memory and colonial wars.[51] In other words, a library of works that mirror the big questions of the day.

Decline, immigration, identity, conflict, terrorism—an inventory of terms that are now inseparable. In fact, a worldview that has shaped the works of the philosopher Alain Finkielkraut for the past twenty-five years.[52] According to him, France "is disintegrating. Not that long ago we were the envy of the world, but today people feel pity for us. Once an example to emulate, people are today repelled by us: the stubborn refusal we are witnessing in Eastern European countries when it comes to accepting permanent quotas of asylum seekers on their soil is because they don't want to end up like us."[53] These kinds of statements have become all too common, contaminating the field of politics in what has become a process of constant one-upmanship between the Front National (FN) and the former Union for a Popular Movement (UMP), recently renamed the Républicains (LR). In this dynamic, the right is fighting for ownership over traditional FN xenophobic and identity policies in what has become a scramble for authenticity, all in the name of upholding precious republican ideals and values, and announcing what has been described, with reference to the multiple ways in which Le Pen's far-right party is reshaping French politics, as a "lepenization" of the public domain.

France is certainly not alone in the West when it comes to the issue of defensive identities. The concern with protecting national identity in the face of challenges associated with immigration are to be inscribed in a much longer history of nationalist and racist positions—forever immortalized in the deplorable words of the conservative politician Enoch Powell whose nationalistic, glorificatory, and patriotic tone in his "Rivers of Blood" speech in 1968 warned of the deadly threat immigrants posed to British life, and echoed more recently in Germany in 2010 in Thilo Sarrazin's controversial book *Deutschland schafft sich ab* (Germany abolishes itself), in which the author established a correlation between the drop in the birth rate and the increase in Muslim immigration, bemoaning the gradual disappearance of a population of "pure German stock."[54] Evidence of the widespread appeal of such positions are to be found in recent electoral successes, such as those of the UK Independence Party (UKIP) and of course the outcome of the June 23, 2016, advisory referendum on the withdrawal of the United Kingdom from the European Union (known as Brexit), the Freedom Party in Austria, the Lega Nord for Independence (Northern League) in Italy, the Popular Association/Golden Dawn neo-Nazi party in Greece, the Swedish Democrats,[55] the Union of Center Democrats in Switzerland, the Freedom Party (PVV) in the Netherlands, Belgium's Vlams Belang, the Polish KNP (Congress of the New Right), the Bulgarian VMRO (Bulgarian National Movement),[56] and, for that matter, the disquieting positions of the right wing of the Republican Party in the United States.[57] The situation in France is thus far from being unique; rather, one finds global concern for analogous issues, including in countries that never had colonies or empires and in which there has been no migratory pressure.[58] The phenomenon of defensive identity may very well be pervasive, highlighting heightened levels of anxiety in the face of rapid globalized transformations, but the fact remains that each particular national space is confronted with a distinct set of challenges linked to specific historical experiences and trajectories. In France's case, the current crisis can be partially explained by examining its colonial history. We emphasized this point in our consideration of the colonial fracture back in 2005, right at the time when the crisis became flagrantly conspicuous in the form of riots and uprisings in the *banlieues* housing projects.[59]

From the "Revolt of the Invisibles" to "Apartheid"

In 2007, a group of artists, filmmakers, rappers, and writers got together and published a manifesto (and later a book) in which they stated that "this country, our country, has all it needs to once again be exemplary so long as it accepts itself as it is rather than as it once was."[60] The revolt that took place in the French *banlieues* in 2005 drew international attention to socioethnic and socioracial inequalities in France, under the aegis of a republic that remains according to the principles of the Constitution of 1791 "one and indivisible," a model that protects the rights of citizens but that does not address ethnicity and race.[61]

Caught in the trap of "a past that refuses to pass" as Benjamin Stora proposes, has France really failed when it comes to these questions?[62] Is the questioning of the relationship to the past not legitimate when one considers the failure of the political establishment to evaluate the impact of French imperial history on the present, a failure that extends into the domain of assimilation and integration policy and that has yielded "ethnic reservations" in "urban zones" as an outcome of policy over the past fifty years? There is not one single explanation for the current crisis, but the connection with the colonial enterprise and the impact on the present is so compelling that we firmly believe it deserves concerted scrutiny. And let's be very clear: our work on these and related questions over the past decade did not diagnose a situation of *apartheid* or announce a *war*, or for that matter point to the "lost *banlieues* of the Republic"—these words are not ours; to us, these terms are indicative of the range of ills in evidence in French society today and that we think are worthy of additional consideration.

We started to explore the contemporary configuration of these issues in *Le Grand Repli*, a book published in 2015 on the eve of the November attacks.[63] As with *The Colonial Legacy in France*, we attempted to tackle the situation from a multidimensional perspective, bringing into the conversation the work of anthropologists, (cultural) historians, political scientists, sociologists, and so on. The term *apartheid* is of course especially striking, inextricably linked to the racial separation that was institutionalized by the National Party in South Africa in 1948–1949.[64] But it is, of course, also related to a broader context, namely that of the colonial situation of the French, Portuguese, or British empires, while also, of course, reminding us of the racial segregation associated with Brazil or the United States that only came to an official end as recently as the 1960s. At first sight, such a term might even appear oxymoronic in the French republican milieu. When Manuel Valls used the word *apartheid* in 2015, he was neither referring to a "legal" apartheid (as was the case in South Africa) nor to "official segregation" (as had been the case in colonial empires or in the United States), but rather to a "situational apartheid" that had been handed down as a *heritage* and that was the outcome of a historical amalgamation of conscious and unconscious administrative and social practices that have been at work since the process of colonial independence got underway (1954–1962) and that are to be found in immigration and urban policies in France since the Fifth Republic was enacted in 1958. This postcolonial racism, which France does not want to hear about, serves to elucidate the present situation and lends credence to Manuel Valls's declaration and awareness that French society is indeed "ethnicized."[65]

On the domestic political landscape, the main themes of the far-right—obsessive fear of immigration from the former colonies,[66] the rejection and refusal of foreigners, focalization on Islam, apprehension and concern over the question of gender, and dread over the "substitution" of the white population through racial mixing—have percolated in some leftist circles and completely taken over the traditional right. This was evident in President Sarkozy's infamous speech delivered in Dakar in 2007 in which he recycled racist representations of "Africans" and revealed a colonial mindset, or in the "national identity" debate launched shortly thereafter in 2009 that asked people to think about the following question: "What does it mean to be French today?"[67] At these pivotal moments, few political leaders came out and overtly claimed to be anti-Muslim or anti-Roma; rather, instead, politicians would say they were defenders of the West or of security, including the FN who has engaged in a concerted campaign of *dédiabolisation* (de-demonization) in which they wave the flag as protectors of "national preference."[68] But when it comes down to it, behind all this rhetoric, is there not a deep-seated desire for a society in which everyone has, or knows her or his place?

This political climate, along with the apparent helplessness of the state in addressing growing difficulties in urban ghettos, French overseas departments and territories drifting deeper and deeper into decline, and in escalating unemployment numbers has resulted in large segments of the population being abandoned. This has encouraged the gradual ethnicization of a range of problems and religious radicalism, problems that have been compounded by the massive discrimination of which the residents are victims, resulting in their near-total separation and exclusion from the rest of society and, in the end, withdrawal.[69] A country associated with the invention of a "diverse society" long before others would embrace such a paradigm, admittedly of course with all kinds of contradictions and paradoxes, appears to be slowly metamorphosing into a segregationist society. Summoning the notion of "poor whites"[70] is now relatively common, another reminder of the United States and South Africa, as well as of a number of other cultures such as Narendra Modi's "new society" (overtly anti-Muslim) in India or the form of segregation found in early twentieth-century Brazilian society.

The consequence of this political polarization has been to divide French society into factions, the one in which "poor whites" now identity along those lines and vote accordingly[71] and the other that drives youth from immigrant backgrounds to "unbelong,"[72] reject France, and fabricate alternative (and often mythic) categories of identification, producing what Éric Fassin has summarized as follows: "The racialization of society no longer spares antiracism.... Two opposing ways of approaching racism now clash: on the one side those who embrace universalism and on the other the spokespersons for those racialized [*racisés*]."[73] Comparison is not always possible, but having said this, the situation today shares many points of commonality with the early 1930s,[74] a period that saw the old national parties and leagues such as Action française emerge from obscurity at the same time as other increasingly radical political movements. The nationalist Parti social français founded in 1936 by François de La Roque (with its one million militants) considered itself capable of establishing alliances with the parliamentary right, such as Jacques Doriot's Parti populaire français that signed the Front de la liberté agreement in 1937 with the Fédération républicaine, a precursor of sorts to the Rassemblement bleu Marine (RBM, the Marine Blue Gathering, a coalition of far-right, right-wing, and left-wing political and independent parties).[75] In the 1930s, ultra-right parties were so mobilized around their shared hatred of the communist and Jewish "other" that they chose Hitler over the Front populaire, a decision that resulted in Vichy France.[76]

In terms of the present situation, deep-seated frustrations have exacerbated tensions[77] and at stake we find the objective of defeating this "other," of fighting abroad (military intervention), of deporting and expelling foreigners, or at the very least, of implementing mechanisms aimed at placing these people in a juridical category at the periphery of citizenship. On one of the posters distributed by the Front National de la Jeunesse (National Front of the Youth, FNJ), we can read the slogan "Lorsque nous arriverons ... Ils partiront!" (When we are elected ... they'll leave!). No longer capable of being inclusive, in fear or terror of outsiders, the national community now excludes.[78] Will whites eventually come together in solidarity around such models?[79] And will other groups—Muslims, Jews, blacks, Arabs, Corsicans, Turks, Armenians—follow in their example?[80] Has color become the new indicator of societal fracture, including in the realm of the antiracist struggle?[81] After all, as Éric Fassin suggests, "In a society in which everyone is defined in racial terms, through no fault of their own (or not, as the case may be), well even White people become ... Whites ... And this is reason for concern today since are we not at risk of a gulf opening up between a 'White' antiracism and a 'non-White' antiracism?," and which, as he concludes, can only produce "a tension between two opposing ways of approaching antiracism that appear to be getting racialized."[82] We may not have reached this point just yet, but a cursory glance at the massive problems confronting populations in *banlieues* neighborhoods and in the overseas regions would certainly seem to indicate that we are heading down that road.

A major study, *Trajectoires et origines: Enquête sur la diversité des populations en France,* published by the Institut national d'études démographiques (National Institute for Demographic Studies, INED) in 2016, confirms these observations.[83] As Patrick Simon, one of the lead investigators, stated in an interview in *Le Monde* newspaper, "French society is in lockdown mode."[84] He goes on to explain how that study shows that "the descendants of immigrants don't feel a distance between them and the national community" or between French society's institutions. Instead, the opposite is true. It is these very same institutions that produce discrimination "forgetting that integration consists in a reciprocal exchange and permanent process of adaptation."[85] Difficulties and problems emerge when "there is a failure to recognize the status of minorities and move beyond those stereotypes responsible for discrimination and racism." And if there is anything the study serves to confirm, "it is that these very same minorities have never been treated on equal terms."[86]

Indeed, if one looks to the American context, Affirmative Action was first introduced by President Kennedy in 1961, and in the United Kingdom, the parliament established the Race Relations Act in 1976 (itself an amendment of earlier parliamentary acts) and the Commission for Racial Equality, measures whose specific objective were to target discrimination on the grounds of race. However, the French Republic remains one and indivisible as enshrined in the Constitution of 1791, a principle that underscores the commitment to protecting the rights of all citizens regardless of ethnicity, religion, or other social associations. But behind this mirage of words and grand principles, the equality of citizens simply does not exist. As the Cameroonian political scientist Achille Mbembe has argued, "The perverse effect of this indifference to differences is thus a relative indifference to discrimination."[87] The truth is that ethnic discrimination has never been taken into consideration or, for that matter, seriously combatted in France. The wake-up call has thus been all the more brutal, and the fact remains that the vast majority of French intellectuals and scholars have refused to confront this reality, without even mentioning the political elite that have basically turned their attention away from this *fracture* that has as a consequence only grown deeper.[88] There has been considerable criticism of the prime minister's recourse to the term *apartheid,* which has been deemed inappropriate given that South African apartheid was an organized system, whereas the situation in France today is the outcome of inopportune policies.

These are the circumstances in which neoconservative voices have gained prominence, in conjunction with an upsurge in support and electoral advances for the Front National, developments fueled by an irrational desire to turn back time in the face of societal transformations that appear out of control. In their thinking, immigration and racial mixing, along with a rushed and ill thought-out opening up to globalization, have together contributed to a dramatic weakening of the middle classes and to precipitating the working classes into a downward spiral toward economic destruction. These transformations have thus taken on a revolutionary scale; the resulting precariousness, apprehension, and anxiety have spawned a demand for reassurance, for protection, and for security as a logical outcome of the unremitting call for a return to the past.[89]

There is no doubt that France is undergoing rapid cultural and social transformation, on a similar scale to the kind experienced during the Roman conquest, Christianization, the waning years of the seigniories, or for that matter, during the Napoleonic era. In the face of these changes, fear is not itself an unexpected response, but the refusal to take the measure of this newfound reality is shortsighted, willful blindness even. This has coincided with the gradual disappearance of the traditional left–right divide that has underpinned French political and democratic life for almost two centuries and a palpable shift to the right (known as *droitisation*). This is the backdrop for the escalation of debates around religious or territorial identities as well as concern with ethnic factionalism, collectively forming the new frontiers of policy.[90]

A Minefield of Identity Politics

Hamstrung by alarming expressions of religious affiliation by extremists and radicals on all sides and pervasive contempt and hatred for the West, we find ourselves traversing a minefield of identity politics.[91] Neoconservatives and populists have rekindled their attachment to a mythic and glorious vision of the colonial past. No matter where one looks, or how one looks at the situation, each side continues to find inspiration in this climate. The real question, though, is whether public policies and the glaring failure of integration measures are to be understood as the mere consequence of ineffective or misguided policies or rather the fruit of nondecolonized practices that continue to be applied to today's postcolonial populations and yesterday's *native subjects of the empire*.

A number of interpretations have been put forward, and among these, the culturalist argument is the most common. It goes something like this: postcolonial immigrants may very well have been faced with obstacles and a difficult path to integration, but in the end the main issue is to be found in their incompatibility with French or European societal models, born, or at the very least influenced by, cultures that don't share the same commitment to liberty. The physical and sexual assaults and attacks that took place at the Cologne railway station (and in other German and European cities) on the night of December 31, 2015, (in Cologne alone, over eight hundred complaints were filed, half of which were for sexual assault) were a terrifying example of this exclusion and of the social maladjustment of certain immigrants. In Germany, it was mostly immigrants living on the margins of society that were implicated in the crimes committed against women, rather than refugees. They are, therefore, delinquents and not simply immigrants. For the most part, these men were Maghrebis residing in urban ghettos with almost no chance of obtaining the status of political refugee, or for that matter, of finding jobs as regular workers. They therefore find themselves excluded from integration mechanisms, language classes, and employment and survive thanks to criminal behavior or by joining organized gangs. The German authorities are, of course, well aware of this situation but absolutely refuse to legalize their status out of fear that this would be construed as an incentive, a "pull factor," to come to Germany and attract other migrants. The situation is therefore untenable for the latter, and the result is devastating, although predictable.

Living together harmoniously cannot happen overnight; it takes time and effort on both sides—on the part of the host society as much as that of immigrants themselves who have arrived from another culture and often with other codes. The Algerian author Kamel Daoud, author of the celebrated novel *Meursault, contre-enquête* (The Meursault Investigation, 2014),[92] wrote about these questions in an article in *Le Monde*, "Cologne, lieu de fantasmes," on January 31, 2016,[93] an article that was heavily criticized by a collective of specialists of the Muslim world, accusing him of "recycling Islamophobic phantasms."[94] According to Jocelyne Dakhlia, "One needs to pay attention to the emergence of new forces. The whole notion of a clash of civilizations has led us straight into the jaws of disaster, to jihadism, terrorism and war. One would be hard pressed to imagine a worse outcome. The challenge now is to find a solution and to restore the kind of political and social harmony essential for a lasting peace, and this certainly won't come from further entrenchment or by closing oneself off by reiterating the idea of a clash of civilizations."[95]

A distance has therefore emerged between "them" and "us" that can only result in a "politics of difference."[96] For if the colonial past is foreclosed, the place of the Global South (in the geographic sense of the term) remains crucial in the political and social imagination,[97] especially when it comes to the manner in which constructs and perceptions of former colonies and diasporic populations (in France and in Europe) continue to influence both domestic and foreign policy, evident, as Éric Fassin has argued, in the "political unconscious"[98] and in various forms of racism and a "State xenophobia"[99] that is the "result of rather than the cause of immigration policy."[100]

In a speech delivered in Grenoble in 2010, President Sarkozy coupled immigration with criminality and did not think twice about stigmatizing Roma populations. A few years earlier in 2007, during a campaign speech in Toulon, he had already glorified the colonial enterprise and denounced "repentance."[101] Then came the turn of Claude Guéant who, as minister of the interior, claimed in February 4, 2012, on the campaign trail, that "In view of our republican principles, not all civilizations, practices, or cultures, are equal." These statements are all connected to similar representational modes and colonial mentalities that find themselves constantly updated and adapted to new circumstances, in these instances related to ethnic and race relations and immigration, underscoring the "clash of civilizations" or explaining the current European "migration crisis" that many have either predicted or wished for. However, this so-called clash of civilizations is totally farfetched as Raphaël Liogier has convincingly demonstrated: "When one looks at current conflicts, these have nothing to do with clashes between civilizations. Instead, what we have are a combination of conflicts between States, terrorist organizations, organized crime, economic networks, and globalized positions on identity. The idea of a civilization under siege is a more typical of the kind of stance found today in a Europe that has itself become fundamentalist, in other words retracing its origins and former hegemony."[102]

According to sociologist Michel Wieviorka, we find ourselves confronted with wayward ideologies in which "scapegoating" has become ubiquitous and "populations [Muslims, populations with immigrant backgrounds] are blamed for their problems and accused of menacing society, its values, civilization. The goal is no longer to establish conditions that will allow people to succeed, to achieve inclusion in French society, but rather to rescue the latter from the supposed dangers it faces."[103] Pierre Tevanian has also underlined how official rhetoric has favored a legal and security-based vocabulary in which terms such as *insecurity* and *zero tolerance* are repeated incessantly and allied with expressions such as *national preference*,[104] what Gérard Noiriel has aptly termed a "vocabulary of threats,"[105] an identifiable pattern in which external threats (linked to clandestine or uncontrolled immigration)[106] and internal threats are associated with a French "enemy within" with an immigrant background,[107] namely those youth susceptible to starting a war against their own people, their very future, and at the same time against their own country through terrorism.

These questions were consistent with President Sarkozy's positions, as for example in the "Discours sur la nation" he gave in Caen on March 9, 2007, in which he emphasized that "being French is to feel one is the heir to a unique and shared history which one has every reason to be proud of. If one truly loves France, then one must assume responsibility for one's own history as well as that of all those French people who have made France great."[108] Having excluded and rejected a critical gaze at the colonial past, the version of history that he proposes is one from which significant segments of society (such as populations with backgrounds in postcolonial migration) are excluded.[109] The devastating impact of these repeated assaults on ethnic minorities throughout the period 2007 to 2012 has yet to be fully assessed, and there is no doubt that they have added a symbolic exclusion to existing forms of discrimination and disaffection while also accentuating identity-related tensions (a deliberate strategy of far-right conservative political advisers such as Patrick Buisson).

In contrast, Paul Gilroy drew attention to comparable issues in Great Britain during the 1980s in his influential book *There Ain't No Black in the Union Jack: The Cultural Politics of Race and Nation,* and then later in *Postcolonial Melancholia,* in which he asserted that "it has become necessary to take political discussions of citizenship, belonging, and nationality beyond the dual prescription of assimilation and immigration control. . . . All these changes can be used to point to the enduring significance of 'race' and racism and their historic place in the long and slow transformation of Britain, its changing relationships with itself, with Europe, with the United States, and the wider postcolonial world's."[110] These findings are transposable to the French context in which the collective memory of those people for whom France represents *home* must now be combined simultaneously with individuals and groups whose memory is also elsewhere.[111] These are precisely the kind of considerations that have influenced immigration policy and that are to be found in a range of mechanisms aimed, as Gérard Noiriel has shown, at "selecting immigrants on the basis of 'Republican values,'" while asserting that this "is necessary in order to protect French identity in the future, in other words to invoke these 'values' exactly as immigration experts had used race during the 1920s as way to prevent racial mixing."[112]

Return to the Colonial Past

Colonial history fashioned the representation of colonial "natives," who in turn would eventually make up the greater part of postcolonial immigration to France.[113] As we have argued for years now, this history remains relatively unknown and its impact on the very notion of republicanism underexplored.[114] The *Trente Glorieuses,* as the postwar period of economic growth is commonly known, was punctuated by revolts, racist crimes, and ineffectual policies, culminating in the "*banlieues* crisis" of 2005.[115] Yet, the weight of this history is considerable: the colonial enterprise got underway in the sixteenth century, French history was marked by slavery and the slave trade, and the French empire was the second largest when it crested with some sixty million "subjects."

Hence, discriminatory representations have endured throughout this long history,[116] literally clinging relentlessly to the skin of postcolonial immigrants who have found themselves relegated to the periphery of "Frenchness." The Chirac-Sarkozy presidencies (1995–2012), spanning almost two decades, effectively neutralized attempts at rethinking or revisiting the colonial past, except for revisionist initiatives such as the aforementioned "Law concerning the recognition of the nation and national contribution in favor of repatriated French" or the Mémorial national de la France d'Outre-mer project that aimed to provide a memorial site dedicated to the memory of those who lived and worked in French colonies during the nineteenth and twentieth centuries. François Mitterrand started in 1982, very early on, therefore, in his two-term presidency (1981–1995), the process of proscribing amnesties for the leaders of the failed coup d'état in French Algeria in 1961 (also known as the Generals' putsch) and of the Secret Army Organization (OAS) who engaged in armed struggle in an attempt to derail and prevent independence from French colonial rule. And François Hollande has been exceedingly prudent on the question, reluctantly agreeing to examine the "mistakes" of the past with "lucidity," as he stated during his inauguration on May 15, 2012, when he also paid tribute to the memory of former prime minister Jules Ferry (1832–1893), praising him for his role in making primary education mandatory, open to all, and secular, yet also recognizing his "mistakes" and misguided decisions as an advocate of colonial expansionism. He would also use the term *lucidity* again in a speech in Dakar in October 2012, and then again five days later in Paris with reference to the "bloody repression" of Algerian demonstrators that took place on October 17, 1961, and then later in July 2015 in Cameroon in relation to the war that took place there during the 1950s. This was an important departure from previous official positions, given that former prime minister François Fillon had spoken only a few years earlier at the very same site of "pure invention" on the subject of colonial conflict there. But beyond this "lucidity," there is nothing concrete or significant to mention. No *rupture* to speak of.

Our aim is not to incriminate or to make the nation feel guilty[117]—most of the contributors to *The Colonial Legacy in France* were, in fact, born after independence and are only indirectly connected to this history—but rather to take into consideration a longer history as a way of shedding light on a range of social practices that are still very much indebted to (post)colonial attitudes. The contemporary moment therefore finds itself trapped, unable to move on or at least beyond these ways of thinking that hark back to the imperial period.[118] Having said this, what is absolutely clear is that culpability toward the colonial past has stifled discussions, a process that has been further impeded by groups who have elected to exploit this feeling, often in reductive or oversimplistic terms, by engaging in memorial revenge or retaliation. Franco-Congolese writer Alain Mabanckou has not hesitated to denounce such positions: "This tireless hatred toward Whites is futile; it is as if vengeance could somehow resorb the humiliations of history and restore some kind of alleged pride that Europe had once violated. Those who blindly hate Europe are just as sick as those who cling to a blind love for an imaginary Africa of a bygone period."[119]

The most fruitful path to an open conversation on the colonial is one that puts aside incrimination and feelings of guilt, that leaves no place for self-hatred or hatred of the "other," in which there is no room for bargaining over historical facts, and in which there can be consensus when it comes to recognizing that the "end of empire" left an open wound in French nationalism. As Benjamin Stora has explained, research on the colonial past has made it possible to think additionally on "the vast discrepancy that exists between those who had no choice but to forget in order to survive, those who had to painstakingly endure the memories, and those who could no longer bear the desired or deliberate memory gaps on both sides of the Mediterranean when it came to the Algerian War."[120] Very quickly, Pierre Nora noted, polarized views came to characterize thinking on this war, and two clear "camps" or "sides" emerged, triggered by revelations of torture.[121] This was followed shortly thereafter, in the late 1990s and early 2000s, by a burgeoning interest among the "children" of African and Caribbean immigrants in the history and memorialization of slavery and colonialism, right around the time when Paul Aussaresses, a French general and intelligence officer, not only *admitted* but also *defended* the use of torture in Algeria, subsequently extending his remarks to recommend that such measures would also be appropriate in the newfound context of the fight against al-Qaeda after the dramatic attacks of 9/11.[122]

The generational change that has occurred in French politics has played a considerable role when it comes to taking into account this complex past. In the 2002 presidential elections, both candidates who made it through to the runoff stage in the two-round voting system (Jacques Chirac and Jean-Marie Le Pen) had started their political careers during the colonial era, a half-century earlier (in Algeria in the case of the former, and in Indochina and Algeria for the latter). By 2007, the two new main candidates had quite different backgrounds. Nicolas Sarkozy denounced "repentance" and gave pledges of loyalty to the "nostalgic" in various campaign speeches, whereas Ségolène Royal did not touch upon the issue during her campaign, almost as if for her this "page" had been definitively turned. Merely five years later, identity questions had swept aside any possibility of linking current problems with colonial history. Conservative advisers such as Patrick Buisson encouraged Sarkozy's UMP party to move further to the right, while Marine Le Pen asked provocatively during a stop on the campaign trail, and with reference to the Toulouse and Montauban attacks against soldiers and Jewish civilians, "How many Mohamed Merahs are arriving every day in France on boats and planes filled with migrants?" and later stated that "the problem is not about a madman; what happened is the beginning of a green invasion in our country" (March 25, 2012). As for François Hollande, who has been extremely active on the African continent since he was elected, he holds a special relationship to colonialism and to Africa.[123] His father was in favor of French Algeria and a staunch supporter of the far-right during the 1965 presidential elections. However, while a student at the École nationale d'administration (ENA), he completed an internship at the French embassy in Algiers, an experience he later wrote about in his 2012 campaign book, *Changer de destin*, as a way of better apprehending France's relationship to the nostalgia for imperial grandeur.[124] Somewhere in these new positions on memory, located as they are between nostalgia and amnesia and between factionalist memories and total negation of all commemorative processes, the current crisis set in.[125]

In actual fact, today's Republic was also built *in* the colonies and two models have always existed, opposing those who subscribed to empire (to this day, one finds politicians and scholars who are proponents of a "positive approach" to that era)[126] and those who contested it.[127] Similarly, such binary constructs are to be recorded in the glaring differences between those who believed in the right of the "superior races" over the "inferior races" (Jules Ferry) and those who did not share this belief (Georges Clemenceau), between those who dove headstrong into colonial wars (from Guy Mollet to François Mitterrand, without forgetting René Coty and just about all right-wing elected representatives) and those who considered other avenues (from Pierre Mendès-France to Michel Rocard, including Alain Savary). The collaborator/resistance fighter dichotomy has been crucial to the memorial patrimonialization of France, yet this kind of reconciliation has not taken place in relation to colonialism. To do this would be to take a step toward incorporating colonial, postcolonial, and diasporic histories into the broader fabric of the nation, thereby potentially avoiding the war of identities we have before us. French society needs to find ways to restore the imbalance, to improve its relationship to memory, to help young people rediscover their place in the national community, to overcome fear so that immigration can no longer be relegated to the margins of citizenship.[128] A cursory glance around the world provides multiple examples of other countries who have already been able to do this: South Africa ending apartheid and embracing a Truth and Reconciliation Commission, Italy recognizing "colonial crimes" in Libya, Germany acknowledging its responsibility in the massacre of the Herero people in Namibia, the British admitting to their role in repression in Kenya (even going so far as to initiate compensation), the Dutch formally apologizing for their colonial misdeeds, and the Japanese to the Korean people for their use of "military comfort women." These examples could assist France in the process of examining its past. As the socialist politician Pierre Joxe has written, "We are yet to relinquish the habit of having subjects, of coexisting with individuals of an inferior status, and of having people work for our benefit that do not all enjoy the Rights of Man and even less those of citizens."[129] What is desperately needed, he went on to argue, is a "cultural history" which thus far has been almost completely absent in political debates, when it is essential to understanding certain difficulties that we have."[130]

Contempt and Hatred of the West[131]

With all due respect to Pierre Nora, for whom only "politics" or signs of a "politicized history" are to be found in colonial historical reminiscences,[132] we cannot continue to ignore it forever and are going to have to deal with it sooner or later.[133] The fact remains that the postcolonial racism no one wants to hear about explicates the current situation.[134] There are far too many people who are the descendants of grandparents and parents who came to France and Europe during the colonial period in a spirit of adventure and discovery who only later expressed feelings of exile and nostalgia, displacements that all too often resulted in social disillusionment. For the new generation of migrants, the passage to "Fortress Europe" is complex and supplemented by a new vocabulary structured around such terms as *detention center, refugee status, detention camps, quotas,* and *clandestine.*[135]

Ethnic minorities experience this treatment on a daily basis and are permanently reminded that whether they are French of foreign origin, foreigners, undocumented, refugees, or exiles, and so on, that they will never be a part of society, in other words that "they will never be like us." Ethnic minorities experience this on a daily basis in this pristine "white" France, while at work, in their neighborhoods, or in the schools to which they are relegated and to which people of "pure French stock" do all they can to avoid sending their children. This fracture therefore touches upon every aspect of society, conditioning, as a result, a broad range of daily practices. In 2013, then minister of justice, Christiane Taubira—a black woman from the French overseas department of Guiana—was described as a "guenon" (an ape) by Anne-Sophie Leclère (a former FN candidate in the Ardennes region), when she juxtaposed the image of a baby ape with the minister of justice under the heading "Then & now." Shortly thereafter, *Minute* magazine (November 14, 2013) ran a cover with the headline, "Maligne comme un singe, Taubira retrouve la banane" (Crafty as an ape, Taubira gets her smile back). One may very well dismiss these egregious instances of racism by saying that they in no way represent mainstream French society, but the very fact that this racist unconscious can now be freely expressed or formulated in writing is cause for grave concern.

This fracture therefore touches upon every aspect of society, conditioning, as a result, a broad range of daily practices.[136] These realities offer fertile ground upon which radical jihadists can launch their fight against "whites," denounce the Republic, and accuse the West. It is not, therefore, a matter of choosing between "micro-populations" and the "people," as the philosopher Michel Onfray would have us think, or between one person's suffering and another's, but rather of assessing the *legacy* of the past in contemporary discrimination so that functioning and operative policies that promote equality can be implemented and in doing so dispose of hierarchies of exclusion. Equality is the bedrock upon which societies that wish to have a common future are built, and this is quite different from the objectives of defensive identities that reduce everything to religion or remain attached to the past. Taking a close look at discrimination does not prevent an analysis of the nation or integration policies, or subject to closer scrutiny the cultural challenges that have accompanied transformations in Western societies.

If one looks closely at the situation, a number of problems can be identified, problems that together have worked toward undermining the inclusion of ethnic minorities. In the first instance, France has clearly failed to foster a genuinely diverse society, preferring instead to uphold a model of coexistence based on moral values but without taking into consideration the complex nature of the intercommunity dynamics. Secondly, France has been incapable of explaining to native-born French people that the integration of the "other" is a lengthy, ambivalent, and potentially destabilizing process, and this shortsightedness has therefore also entailed a failure to appreciate the extent to which the fear generated by these transformations has, in the face of a wider social crisis, left mostly economically disadvantaged or vulnerable populations feeling as if they are being "racially" displaced or superseded. This is the *fracture* upon which the Front National has acted and that has permitted it to thrive,[137] expanding its support toward increasingly vast horizons. For the past three decades (at least), the political establishment has barely touched upon the question of discrimination, such that it is those very people who are discriminated against that find themselves held accountable for their circumstances and responsible for their failure to integrate.

Beyond the Identity Fault Lines

In his 1946 book *Anti-Semite and Jew: An Exploration of the Etiology of Hate,* Jean-Paul Sartre argued that "the Jewish problem is born of anti-Semitism; thus it is anti-Semitism that we must suppress in order to resolve the problem."[138]

Elsewhere, in "Orphée noir" ("Black Orpheus"), an essay in which he examined the place of the "Negro" in French society, Sartre extended his analysis stating that a Jew, "white among white men, can deny that he is a Jew, can declare himself a man among men. The Negro cannot deny that he is Negro, nor can he claim that he is part of some abstract colorless humanity: he is black."[139] Sartre's conclusions are of course open to debate;[140] however, this kind of representational logic is evident today in discussions pertaining to Muslims, for if a Muslim is defined according to purely visible criteria—such as headscarves, veils, burqas, and burkinis—this would completely ignore the fact that adherents to this faith, above and beyond the multiplicity of practices and variations of Islam, cannot be reduced to vestimentary codes or ethnic categories, to limit our observations only to the French context, for a Muslim could just as well be white or black, or be of sub-Saharan, Maghrebi, Asian, or European origin.[141] The process of prescribing religious identity labels is thus a conglomeration of cultural, political, and social projections, and the demonization and apportionment of blame to Islam also relies on phantasmatic constructs.[142]

Islam is omnipresent today in debates surrounding the migration crisis in Europe, in the attacks that took place in Paris, Lebanon, Burkina-Faso, Tunisia, and Mali (among others, of course), and Muslims have become a "global race." Republican presidential hopeful Donald Trump went so far as to call for an end to all Muslim immigration to the United States in a context in which Islam has become inseparable from jihadism, thereby further accentuating the stigmatization of the Muslim community. It has become almost impossible to be a Muslim in America without being simultaneously the object of suspicion, a situation rendered even more difficult by the near total absence of Muslims in the media, who could denounce what is done in the name of Islam.[143] And the same pretty much holds true for France and other European countries.[144]

Not long ago the danger was red (denoting communists), today it is green (for Islam). In order to protect the national community, every effort must be made to exclude this *enemy*. During the interwar years, there was general consensus that a communist could not be a full-fledged *patriot*. As things stand now, a Muslim cannot really be considered a patriot. During the 1930s, the enemy came from the East; today, it is from the South. The mere mention of his presence, hearing her name, his mere existence is enough to unleash a tirade. Even "nationals" have become suspect, especially if they are "binationals" or dual citizens. Yesterday they came with a knife between their teeth, today they wear the hijab and slippers. Yesterday the workers or union meeting announced the *grand soir* (the revolution or the "big evening"); today the daily street prayer precedes the *grande nuit* (the night of power). Yesterday the Comintern attacked French colonial territories; today global jihadism is attacking

France and countries in its francophone "sphere of influence."[145] Selecting one's enemy in this manner as a way to define and fortify oneself, an enemy who also appears perfectly legitimate in light of recent events and the international dimension of the problem, has proven highly convincing as a device for enlisting support well beyond traditional far-right constituencies.[146] Needless to say, the terrible events that France experienced in 2015 have brought these matters to the fore and further aggravated the state of affairs.

The choice of young jihadists to go down this path of no return is partially the result of bitterness, of resentment, and of a willingness to seek revenge for a rejected and stigmatized youth who, though born in France, do not feel French.[147] But these identity fault lines do not only apply to the children of immigrants or of Muslim families. More than one third of all radicals who have set off for the Middle East were *converts* who have shouldered and integrated the marginality and feelings of revolt of the descendants of postcolonial immigration. Of course, the Islamic State (Islamic State in Iraq and the Levant, ISIS) has played a role in guiding them, in training them, and in coordinating the attacks, but above all, it has *inspired* them. Having said this, one should not downplay the power of religion itself in mobilizing individuals, in this instance in the guise of sectarianism or extremism. All signs point to a "spiritual identity" that is conceived in opposition to the West. Not all revolts are social, and there exists no society in which there is unanimity when it comes to questions as fundamental as identity.

Besides, radicalism and jihadism emerged from the still-smoldering ashes of progressive movements the world over, notably the most recent postcolonial struggles in the Middle East, Africa, or in the former Soviet republics. In France, since the enactment of the Law on the Separation of the Church and State in 1905 and the devastating impact of the antisemitic Dreyfus affair, the very idea that religion could represent a political force has been widely denounced. Western zealots of ISIS adhere first and foremost to religious fundamentalism, in other words, to a worldview that promises a complete overhaul of society and of its values. A *vengeance* of sorts for those who feel, rightly or wrongly, that they are the humiliated in this long history, or at the very least the heirs of this humiliation. The attraction of fundamentalism is personified today in ISIS, as it was previously in al-Qaeda, or a quarter of a century ago now in certain Palestinian factions that found support in France via organizations such as the Mouvement des travailleurs arabes (Arab Workers Movement, MTA). But the actual identification and factors that encourage and motivate the decision to actually join up are to be found *in* France or Europe and the West, and *not* in the Middle East itself.[148] And at the other end of the spectrum, there are French people filled with hatred for the "other," riddled with anxiety, abandoned by the political elite, and with no option but to believe in the preachings of a political party born in the mid-1970s out of the ruins of the loss of French Algeria.

This is precisely why the solutions to this situation cannot be limited to "technical" responses, to merely addressing and treating the problems associated with disadvantaged *banlieues* neighborhoods, or by renovating housing projects.[149] Ghettos are the product of racial and social *fractures*, but also of mental ones that have roots in colonial practices and in forms of humiliation dating back to the nineteenth century (in the guise of the racial question)[150] or the twentieth century (with imperial history).[151] These contribute to the building of a postcolonial society in which one learns very early on to which racial category one belongs. This is how one can be born French and yet remain, because of the color of one's skin, in the name of a religion, or because of some other marker, a foreigner, an "other," in one's own country. The *fracture* is also to be found somewhere in the mind. Research on social, urban, and educational questions must focus on these issues, and the fight against discrimination and the promotion of elites stand as a priority, especially given that programs and schemes in these areas are virtually nonexistent (either for budgetary reasons, or simply because of the perception that investment would be pointless). Furthermore, unemployment levels among African immigrants is at 27 percent, compared with 15 percent for new arrivals, and 9 percent for the native-born population. What is more, things are not improving for the children of immigrants, on the contrary in fact, and the chronological third generation is facing a major crisis, analogous to the one in evidence today in the French Antilles or in Réunion where almost half the youth population cannot find work. At the same time, institutional racism has failed on these issues and the banner of secularism, French *laïcité*,[152] one of the founding pillars for coexistence in French society, is today being manipulated in order to exclude those who don't look like "us."

Political rhetoric is dominated by terms that serve to reinforce bipolarity, terms whose prevalence has been illustrated by Cécile Alduy and Stéphane Wahnich in the form of "word clouds" that include *radical, terrorist, fundamentalist, jihadist, republic, national, values, laïcité, liberty, democracy,* and *protection,*[153] delineating and defining in the process the figure of the "enemy within." These second or third generation bearers of mixed or hybrid identities are all the more threatening because of their insider status, but also because of their ubiquitous nature, linked as it is to globalization as corroborated by the circulation of the November 13, 2015, terrorists between the Middle East and Europe. This mobility now means that all migration is deemed suspect, and the determination to infiltrate terrorists and foreign fighters from Iraq and Syria (successfully according to some reports) has done little to help improve matters. There is thus a coalescence at work between exclusion and stigmatization that has introduced "a *translocal* phenomenon by which individuals raised in a local context (say, a working class neighborhood in the suburbs of Paris or London) are pushed into adopting a transnational identity and association not truly their own."[154]

This war against a part of Islam, along with various attempts at rendering the religion "invisible" in the public space—the banning of headscarves, the full-face veil, the burqa, burkinis, minarets on mosques (in France, Belgium, Switzerland, Spain, Austria, Italy, and the Netherlands), have only fueled the perception of constant persecution among Muslims (something that Daesh and its epigones have latched onto). France has also failed to rethink *laïcité* and find ways of promoting a more open society, one with which people from different backgrounds could identity without feeling they have to abandon important elements of their culture and heritage.[155] Living together in harmony is not always something that comes naturally, no matter what illustrious minds may have to say on the subject. An effort has to be made and mechanisms put in place that nurture dialogue, cultivate relations, and provide safeguards, while also promoting an environment conducive to a more permanent social equilibrium. Likewise, foreign policy and military interventions against "Islamists" or "terrorists" in France's *pré-carré africain*[156] (literally, France's neocolonial "backyard") in the Central African Republic, the Ivory Coast, and Mali, the destabilization of Afghanistan and Iraq, along with allied strikes against ISIS since 2014, have also sustained the idea and perception of a relentless assault on Islam, a religion that has been targeted and the victim of aggression over a much longer history. The Great Syrian Revolt and anticolonial insurgency of 1925,[157] the Rif War in Morocco (1921–1927), the Thiaroye massacre in Senegal in 1944, the Sétif, Guelma, and Kherrata massacres in Algeria in 1945, the Malagasy uprising of 1947, the Paris massacre of October 17, 1961, or for that matter the war in Cameroon[158] are all important reference points for another collective memory that cannot be obliterated or swept under the rug.[159]

Reconnecting with History

Our backs are up against the wall and it is no longer enough to invoke the "great values" of secularism. Concrete efforts must be made to fight against the segregation of territories and entire segments of the French population, while at the same time standing firm in opposition to all forms of radicalism.[160] We must endeavor to arrive at a national narrative that relinquishes the claim to the univocal, that does not adopt a warlike posture, and that seeks to better *understand* the situation.[161] Only then will we be able to follow the natural course of history—a common and shared history. Many thought colonial history would just go away if it was left alone, rendered invisible, and if claims for equality were ignored. But that did not happen. The war of identities was born of this silence, of this obstinate blindness.

In "A More Perfect Union," the speech given by Barack Obama in Philadelphia on March 18, 2008, the candidate for the Democratic nomination in the presidential elections recognized that "what would be needed were Americans in successive generations who were willing to do their part—through protests and struggle, on the streets and in the courts, through a civil war and civil disobedience and always at great risk—to narrow that gap between the promise of our ideals and the reality of their time."[162] There are two visions (at least) at work in France today as to how French society should look, visions that can no longer be divided along simple party lines. They pit a closed, partitioned, and claustrophobic country—moving headstrong toward a war of identities while refusing to think about recent transformations, and hiding behind the idea of a society in decline while embracing an increasingly reactionary interpretation of history—against those who believe in an open, diverse society that has renounced a monolithic view of history in order to stress points of commonality and a mutually constitutive model of citizenship, while not of course obfuscating the obvious challenges that necessarily come with the integration of diverse cultures.[163]

The dread one finds in disaffected working class communities, disproportionately impacted by globalization, is that they will end up occupying a social status they equate with immigrant populations, in other words, to end up in a position that is even "below them." Cultural insecurity has become a fashionable concept in political circles,[164] and reactionary thinkers have managed to convince large segments of French society that immigration is responsible for their deteriorating economic circumstances. The enemy within has been identified, named, and rendered visible. People are petrified of Islam, and 2015 was, because of the terrorist attacks, a landmark year in terms of the contribution it made toward channeling this fear and turning it into the most widely shared sentiment in the nation today. The stage is therefore set for an identity conflict. There are those who dream of that blessed time when the "other" knew their place, their rightful place, their correct place. It is more than time to attempt to *understand* the genealogy of this configuration and to come out of this collective denial and blindness in order to avoid an all-out *war of identities* that would be deadly for French and European society.

Nicolas Bancel is Professor at the University of Lausanne, Switzerland, and codirector of the ACHAC Research Group. He is author or coeditor of numerous influential books, including *De l'indigène à l'immigré* (1998), *La République coloniale: Essai sur une utopie* (2003), *La République coloniale* (2006), *Human Zoos: Science and Spectacle in the Age of Colonial Empires* (2008), *La France arabo-orientale* (2013), *Colonial Culture in France since the Revolution* (2014), *The Invention of Race* (2014), and *Vers la guerre des identités* (2016).

Pascal Blanchard is a historian and researcher at the Laboratoire Communication et Politique (Paris, France, CNRS), codirector of the ACHAC Research Group, and a documentary filmmaker. He is a specialist on the colonial question in France, contemporary French history and immigration, and author, coauthor, editor, or coeditor of *Human Zoos: Science and Spectacle in the Age of Colonial Empires* (2008), *Human Zoos. The Invention of the Savage* (2011), *Zoos humains et exhibitions coloniales: 150 ans d'inventions de l'autre* (2011), *Colonial Culture in France since the Revolution* (2014), *La France arabo-orientale* (2013), *Les années 30 sont de retour: Petite leçon d'histoire pour comprendre les crises* (2014), *Le Grand Repli* (2015), and *Vers la guerre des identités* (2016).

Dominic Thomas is Madeleine L. Letessier Professor and Chair of the Department of French and Francophone Studies at UCLA. Elected to the Academy of Europe in 2015, his books include *Black France: Colonialism, Immigration, and Transnationalism* (2007) and *Africa and France: Postcolonial Cultures, Migration, and Racism* (2013), and he is coauthor, editor, or coeditor of *Museums in Postcolonial Europe* (2010), *A Companion to Comparative Literature* (2011), *La France noire* (2011), *Colonial Culture in France since the Revolution* (2014), *The Invention of Race* (2014), *Francophone Afropean Literatures* (2014), and *Vers la guerre des identités* (2016).

Notes

1. See Patrick Boucheron, *Ce que peut l'histoire* (Paris: Fayard, 2016), 39.
2. Eight o'clock news on TF1, November 14, 2015.
3. Patrick Garcia, interview with Blandine Le Cain, "L'hommage aux Invalides 'élève les victimes au même rang que des héros militaires,'" *Le Figaro*, November 26, 2015.
4. The notion of "war" was already omnipresent in the work of several scholars focusing on France before the attacks. See Andrew Hussey, *The French Intifada: The Long War between France and Its Arabs* (London: Faber and Faber, 2014).
5. Samuel Huntington, *The Clash of Civilizations and the Remaking of World Order* (New York: Simon & Schuster, 1996).

6. Pascal Blanchard, Nicolas Bancel, and Sandrine Lemaire, eds., *La fracture coloniale: La société française au prisme de l'héritage colonial* (Paris: La Découverte, 2005).

7. Pascal Blanchard, Marc Ferro, and Isabelle Veyrat-Masson, eds., *Les guerres de mémoire dans le monde, Hermès,* no. 52 (October 2008); Pascal Blanchard and Isabelle Veyrat-Masson, eds., *Les guerres de mémoires: La France et son histoire* (Paris: La Découverte, 2008); and Paul Ricœur, *La mémoire, l'histoire, l'oubli* (Paris: Seuil, 2003).

8. *La fracture coloniale* brought together an interdisciplinary and international group of specialists who had been working for a long time on colonial history, immigration, and identity questions, including Nicolas Bancel, Pascal Blanchard, Sandrine Lemaire, Marcel Dorigny, Benjamin Stora, Françoise Vergès, Anna Bozzo, Sarah Frohning Deleporte, Michel Wieviorka, Olivier Le Cour Grandmaison, Marc Ferro, Achille Mbembe, François Gèze, Rony Brauman, Ahmed Boubeker, Thomas Deltombe, Mathieu Rigouste, Nacira Guénif-Souilamas, Didier Lapeyronnie, Olivier Barlet, Philippe Liotard, Patrick Simon, and Arnauld Le Brusq.

9. Nicolas Bancel, Florence Bernault, Pascal Blanchard, Ahmed Boubeker, Achille Mbembe, and Françoise Vergès, eds., *Ruptures postcoloniales: Les nouveaux visages de la société française* (Paris: La Découverte, 2010). As was the case with the book *La fracture coloniale,* published five years earlier, this book also included an interdisciplinary and international team of specialists, including Nicolas Bancel, Florence Bernault, Pascal Blanchard, Ahmed Boubeker, Achille Mbembe, Françoise Vergès, Abdelmalek Sayad, Pierre Robert Baduel, Ann Laura Stoler, François Durpaire, Anne McClintock, Patrick Weil, Ramón Grosfoguel, David Murphy, Charles Forsdick, Mamadou Diouf, Carpanin Marimoutou, Olivier Barlet, Sylvie Chalaye, Mathieu Rigouste, Nacira Guénif-Souilamas, Gabrielle Parker, Michel Wieviorka, Catherine Wihtol de Wenden, Benoît Falaize, Marie-Claude Smouts, Catherine Coquery-Vidrovitch, Benjamin Stora, Jacky Dahomay, Patrick Simon, Pascal, Valérie Amiraux, Éric Macé, Dominic Thomas, Alain Tarrius, Elsa Dorlin, and Herman Lebovics.

10. Raphaël Liogier, *Ce populisme qui vient* (Paris: Textuel, 2013).

11. Drawing a parallel between French colonial nostalgia and the American context of segregation in the South, the historian Benjamin Stora has had recourse to the term *sudiste.* Interview with Benjamin Stora by Jérôme Skalski, "La décolonisation des imaginaires n'est pas une question achevée," *L'Humanité,* January 8–10, 2015.

12. Nicolas Bancel, Pascal Blanchard, Sandrine Lemaire, and Dominic Thomas, eds., *Colonial Culture in France since the Revolution* (Bloomington and Indianapolis: Indiana University Press, 2014).

13. See Bernard Lahire, interviewed by Julie Clarini, "Comprendre le monde tel qu'il est, ce n'est pas 'excuser' les individus qui le composent," *Le Monde,* January 8, 2016. See also Bernard Lahire, *Pour la sociologie: Et pour en finir avec une prétendue "culture de l'excuse"* (Paris: La Découverte, 2016).

14. See Pascal Ory, *Ce que dit Charlie: Treize leçons d'histoire* (Paris: Gallimard, 2016).

15. Lahire, "Comprendre le monde tel qu'il est, ce n'est pas 'excuser' les individus qui le composent."

16. In late November 2015, Alain Fuchs, president of the Centre National de la Recherche Scientifique (CNRS), announced a call for projects "aimed at improving our understanding."

17. Pascal Blanchard, Nicolas Bancel, and Sandrine Lemaire, "Introduction: La fracture coloniale: Une crise française," in *La fracture coloniale,* ed. Blanchard, Bancel, and Lemaire, 14.

18. See Benjamin Stora, *Le transfert d'une mémoire: De l'Algérie française au racisme anti-arabe* (Paris: La Découverte, 1999), quoted in "Introduction: La fracture coloniale: Une crise française," Blanchard, Bancel, and Lemaire, 10.

19. These included: special editions of journals, magazines, or supplements in newspapers: *Le trou de mémoire, Hommes et Libertés,* no. 131 (2005), *Repenser le passé colonial, Nouveaux Regards,* no. 30 (July–September 2005), *La vérité sur la colonisation, Nouvel Observateur,* December 8–14, 2005, *France coloniale, deux siècles d'histoire, Histoire et Patrimoine* (2005), *La question postcoloniale,*

Hérodote, no. 121 (2006); *La colonisation en procès, L'Histoire*, no. 302 (2005), and *Colonies, un débat français, Le Monde 2* (2006). Several books, especially between 2004 and 2006: Mohammed Harbi and Benjamin Stora, eds., *La guerre d'Algérie: 1954–2004: La fin de l'amnésie* (Paris: Robert Laffont, 2004); Sylvie Thénault, *Histoire de la guerre d'indépendance algérienne* (Paris: Flammarion, 2005); Pascal Blanchard and Sandrine Lemaire, eds., *Culture coloniale* (Paris: Éditions Autrement, 2003); Pascal Blanchard and Sandrine Lemaire, eds., *Culture impériale* (Paris: Éditions Autrement, 2004); Pascal Blanchard and Nicolas Bancel, eds. *Culture postcoloniale* (Paris: Éditions Autrement, 2006); Yves Benot, *Les lumières, l'esclavage, la colonisation* (Paris: La Découverte, 2005); Marc Ferro, ed., *Le livre noir du colonialisme: XVIe-XXIe siècle: De l'extermination à la repentance* (Paris: Hachette, 2004); Olivier Le Cour Grandmaison, *Coloniser, exterminer: Sur la guerre et l'état colonial* (Paris: Fayard, 2005); Claude Liauzu, ed., *Colonisation: Droit d'inventaire* (Paris: Armand Colin, 2004); Nicolas Bancel, Pascal Blanchard, and Françoise Vergès, *La colonisation française* (Toulouse: Milan, 2007); Claude Liauzu and Gilles Manceron, eds., *La colonisation, la loi et l'histoire* (Paris: Syllepse, 2006); Sébastien Jahan and Alain Ruscio, eds., *Histoire de la colonisation: Réhabilitations, falsifications et instrumentalisations* (Paris: Les Indes savantes, 2007); Patrick Weil and Stéphane Dufoix, eds., *L'esclavage, la colonisation . . . et après?* (Paris: PUF, 2005); Nicolas Bancel, Pascal Blanchard, and Françoise Vergès, *La République coloniale* (Paris: Albin Michel, 2006); Éric Deroo and Sandrine Lemaire, *L'illusion coloniale* (Paris: Tallandier, 2006); Claude Liauzu, *Dictionnaire de la colonisation française* (Paris: Larousse, 2007); and Jean-Pierre Rioux, ed., *Dictionnaire de la France coloniale* (Paris: Flammarion, 2007).

20. "Loi portant reconnaissance de la Nation et contribution nationale en faveur des Français rapatriés" (Law concerning the recognition of the nation and national contribution in favor of repatriated French), known as the Debré 2005-158 Law, February 23, 2005, https://www.legifrance.gouv.fr/affichTexte.do?cidTexte=JORFTEXT000000444898.

21. *The Global Islamic Resistance Call* is a sixteen-hundred-page volume that was published following the 2004 Madrid attacks. Abu Musab al-Suri was arrested by the Pakistani authorities in November 2005 (right after the London attacks), handed over to the US authorities, and later to Syria. He was released from prison in 2001 and international security agencies lost track of him shortly thereafter.

22. Brynjar Lia, *Architect of Global Jihad: The Life of Al-Qaida Strategist Abu Mus'ab al-Suri* (New York: Columbia University Press, 2008).

23. Gilles Kepel, interview with Christophe Ayad, "Le logiciel du djihadisme a changé," *Le Monde*, December 26–28, 2015.

24. Quoted in *Metronews*, November 2015.

25. There are several examples that corroborate the link between the social and urban crisis and the background and training of a number of terrorists with roots in disadvantaged neighborhoods and government housing: Mehdi Nemmouche is from Trois-Ponts in Roubaix, Amedy Coulibaly grew up at the Grande Borne à Grigny, Mohamed Merah was from the Izards in Toulouse, Ismaël Omar Mostefaï from the Canal in Courcouronnes, Foued Mohamed-Aggad lived at the Meinau in Strasbourg, Hasna Aït Boulahcen at the Cité des 3000 in Aulnay-sous-Bois, Fabien Clain at the Mirail in Toulouse when he first arrived in France, Sid Ahmed Ghlam settled in the Vert-Bois neighborhood in Saint-Dizier, the brothers Kouachi resided at the Curial-Cambrai in the nineteenth arrondissement in Paris, and Samy Amimour grew up in Drancy.

26. See Olivier Roy, "Le djihadisme est une révolte générationnelle et nihiliste," *Médiapart*, December 2, 2015, and Raphaël Liogier, *Le mythe de l'islamisation: Essai sur une obsession collective* (Paris: Seuil, 2016).

27. Abdelmalek Sayad, "Les enfants illégitimes (Part I)," *Actes de la recherche en sciences sociales* 25, no. 1 (1979): 61–81 and "Les enfants illégitimes (Part II)," *Actes de la recherche en sciences sociales* 26, no. 1 (1979): 117–132.

28. Hervé Le Bras, *Le sol et le sang* (La Tour-d'Aigues: Éditions de l'Aube, 1994).

29. See Samir Khebizi's article on the perception of binationals, "Moi, Samir, binational," *Libération*, December 24, 2015.

30. Pierre-André Taguieff, *Une France antijuive?: Regards sur la nouvelle configuration judéophobe* (Paris: CNRS Éditions, 2015).

31. See Benjamin Stora, "La décolonisation des imaginaires n'est pas une question achevée," *L'Humanité*, January 8–10, 2016.

32. Édouard Glissant, *Caribbean Discourse: Selected Essays*, trans. J. Michael Dash (Charlottesville: University of Virginia Press, 1989), Jean Bernabé, Patrick Chamoiseau, and Raphaël Confiant, *Éloge de la créolité/In Praise of Creoleness*, trans. Mohamed B. Taleb-Khyar (Paris: Gallimard, 1991), Frantz Fanon, *Black Skin, White Masks*, trans. Richard Philcox (New York: Grove Press, 2008 [1952]), and Abdelmalek Sayad, *La double absence: Des illusions de l'émigré aux souffrances de l'immigré* (Paris: Seuil, 1999).

33. Sylvie Laurent and Thierry Leclère, eds., *De quelle couleur sont les Blancs?: Des petits Blancs des colonies au racisme anti-Blancs* (Paris: La Découverte, 2013).

34. Laurie Laufer and Laurence Rochefort, eds., *Qu'est-ce que le genre?* (Paris: Petite Bibliothèque Payot, 2014) and Éric Fassin, *L'inversion de la question homosexuelle* (Paris: Amsterdam, 2005).

35. Nicolas Bancel, Pascal Blanchard, and Ahmed Boubeker, *Le Grand Repli* (Paris: La Découverte, 2015), 27.

36. Charles de Gaulle, *Mémoires de guerre*. Vol. 1: *L'appel* (Paris: Plon, 1954), 1.

37. Nicolas Baverez, *La France qui tombe: Un constat clinique du déclin français* (Paris: Perrin, 2003).

38. Renaud Camus, *Le grand remplacement* (Neuilly-sur-Seine: Éditions David Reinharc, 2012).

39. Renaud Camus' comments have also been taken up in the mainstream media, notably in the *Le Figaro* newspaper. See Ivan Rioufol, "Bloc-notes: La libanisation de Marseille, première alerte," *Le Figaro*, September 13, 2013.

40. Nicolas Lebourg and Joseph Beauregard, *Dans l'ombre des Le Pen: Une histoire des numéros 2 du FN* (Paris: Nouveau Monde, 2012) and Caroline Monnot and Abel Mestre, *Le système Le Pen: Enquête sur les réseaux du Front national* (Paris: Denoël, 2011).

41. Robert Ménard had a street in Béziers previously named the Rue du 19 mars 1962—the date of the Évian accords—renamed the Rue du Commandant Denoix de Saint-Marc, a former putschist in French Algeria. See Lebourg and Beauregard, *Dans l'ombre des Le Pen*.

42. Éric Zemmour, *Le suicide français* (Paris: Albin Michel, 2014).

43. Alec G. Hargreaves, "French Muslims and the Middle East," *Contemporary French Civilization* 40, no. 2 (2015): 235–254 and "Empty Promises? Public Policy Against Racial and Ethnic Discrimination in France," *French Politics, Culture and Society* 33, no. 3 (2015): 95–113.

44. Fausto Giudice, *Arabicides: une chronique française (1970–1991)* (Paris: La Découverte, 1992).

45. Brice Teinturier and Stéphane Zumsteeg, *Fractures françaises* (Paris: Ipsos/Sopra, 2015).

46. See also the study *TeO* released by the Institut national d'études démographiques (INED) and the Institut national de la statistique et des études économiques (INSEE) in early 2016, in particular the conclusion that 29 percent of the "population . . . has a background in immigration."

47. See Juliette Rennes on the historical background to this perception, "L'argument de la décadence dans les pamphlets d'extrême droite des années 1930," *Mots* 58, no. 1 (March 1999): 152–164.

48. See Pascal Durand and Sarah Sindaco, eds., *Le discours "néo-réactionnaire": Transgressions conservatrices* (Paris: CNRS Éditions, 2015).

49. See Daniel Lindenberg, *Le rappel à l'ordre: Enquête sur de nouveaux réactionnaires* (Paris: Seuil, 2002).

50. Michel Houellebecq, *Soumission* (Paris: Flammarion, 2015); *Submission*, trans. Lori Stein (New York: Farrar, Straus and Giroux, 2015).

51. Alexis Jenni's *L'art français de la guerre* (Paris: Gallimard, 2011) stimulated discussions on memory and colonial war. This was also the subject of a more recent book. See Alexis Jenni and Benjamin Stora, *Les mémoires dangereuses: De l'Algérie coloniale à la France d'aujourd'hui suivi* (Paris: Albin Michel, 2016).

52. Beginning with his book *La défaite de la pensée* (Paris: Gallimard, 1987) all the way up until *La seule exactitude* (Paris: Stock, 2015).

53. Christian Makarian, "Alain Finkielkraut: 'La France se désintègre,'" *L'Express*, October 7, 2010.

54. Thilo Sarrazin, *Deutschland schafft sich ab: Wie wir unser Land aufs Spiel setzen* (Munich: Deutsche Verlags-Anstalt, 2010).

55. Antoine Jacob, "L'Europe du Nord gagnée par le populisme de droite," *Politique internationale* 127 (March–April 2010): 221–238.

56. Pierre-André Taguieff, ed., *Le retour du populisme: Un défi pour les démocraties européennes* (Paris: Encyclopaedia Universalis, 2004) and Philippe Vervaecke, ed., *À droite de la droite: Droites radicales en France et en Grande-Bretagne au XXe siècle* (Villeneuve-d'Ascq: Presses universitaires du Septentrion, 2012).

57. Aurélie Godet, *Le Tea Party? Portrait d'une Amérique désorientée* (Paris: Éditions Vendémiaire, 2012).

58. Jean-Yves Camus and Nicolas Lebourg, *Les droites extrêmes en Europe* (Paris: Seuil, 2015).

59. Véronique Le Goazious and Laurent Mucchielli, *Quand les banlieues brûlent... Retour sur les émeutes de novembre 2005* (Paris: La Découverte, 2006). These riots are also placed in a broader context by Stéphane Beaud and Michel Pialoux, *Violences urbaines, violence sociale: Genèse des nouvelles classes dangereuses* (Paris: Fayard, 2003).

60. "Manifeste par le collectif *Qui fait la France*," *Les inrockuptibles*, no. 614 (September 4, 2007): 18, and Karim Amellal et al., *Qui fait la France? Chroniques d'une société annoncée* (Paris: Stock, 2007). See also, three years later, a similar initiative in Lilian Thuram et al., *Appel une France multiculturelle et postraciale?* (Paris: Respect, 2010).

61. Ahmed Boubeker, *Les mondes de l'ethnicité: La communauté d'expérience des héritiers de l'immigration maghrébine* (Paris: Balland, 2003) and Loïc Wacquant, *Urban Outcasts: A Comparative Sociology of Advanced Marginality* (Cambridge, UK, and New Malden, MA: Polity Press, 2008).

62. Benjamin Stora, *La guerre des mémoires: La France face à son passé colonial: Entretiens avec Thierry Leclère* (La Tour-d'Aigues: Éditions de l'Aube, 2007) and Stora, *Le transfert d'une mémoire*.

63. Bancel, Blanchard and Boubeker, eds. *Le Grand Repli*.

64. Nicolas Bancel, Pascal Blanchard, and Dominic Thomas, "Postcolonial France: From the Colonial Fracture to Ethnic Apartheid (2005–2015)," *Occasion* 9 (2015), http://arcade.stanford.edu/sites/default/files/article_pdfs/Occasion_v09_bancel-Blanchard-Thomas_01Pass_final.pdf.

65. Jean-Loup Amselle, *L'ethnicisation de la France* (Paris: Éditions Lignes, 2011) and Etienne Balibar, "Le retour de la race," *Mouvements* 50 (March–April 2007): 162–171.

66. Laurent Gervereau, Pierre Milza, and Émile Temine, eds., *Toute la France: Histoire de l'immigration en France au XXe siècle* (Paris: Somogy, 1998) and Patrick Simon, "Les revirements de la politique d'immigration," *Les Cahiers français* 369 (2012): 86–91.

67. See, for example, Jean-Pierre Chrétien, ed., *L'Afrique de Sarkozy: Un déni d'histoire* (Paris: Karthala, 2008) and Patrick Buisson and Pascal Gauchon, *OAS: Histoire de la résistance française en Algérie* (Bièvres: Éditions Jeune Pied-Noir, 1981).

68. See Renaud Dély et al., *Les années 30 sont de retours: Petites leçon d'histoire pour comprendre les crises du présent* (Paris: Flammarion, 2014), 30.

69. See Pierre Tevanian, *La République du mépris: Les métamorphoses du racisme dans la France des années Sarkozy* (Paris: La Découverte, 2007) and Ariane Chebel d'Appollonia, *Les frontières du racisme: Identités, ethnicité, citoyenneté* (Paris: Presses de Sciences Po, 2011).

70. See Aymeric Patricot, *Les petits blancs: Un voyage dans la France d'en bas* (Paris: Plein Jour, 2013).

71. Catherine Nay, "Panique à bord," *Valeurs actuelles*, March 16, 2015, wrote that "a recent study shows that the Front National has become the party of the proletariat and poor whites in the private sector struggling to make ends meet."

72. See Salman Rushdie, *East, West* (London: Jonathan Cape Ltd., 1994), a book in which the author develops the notion of "double-unbelonging."

73. Éric Fassin, "L'antiracisme en voit de toutes les couleurs," *L'Humanité*, January 8, 2016.

74. Dély et al., *Les années 30 sont de retour* and Eugen Weber, *La France des années 30: Tourments et perplexités* (Paris: Fayard, 1996).

75. Alain Duhamel, "Marine Le Pen, retour aux années 30," *Libération*, March 31, 2011.

76. Ariane Chebel d'Appollonia, *L'extrême droite en France: De Maurras à Le Pen* (Paris: PUF, 1987).

77. Anne Zelensky, "Le concept d'équivalence des cultures serait-il un avatar de la pensée colonialiste?," *Le Monde*, February 10, 2012.

78. Richard Millet, *De l'antiracisme comme terreur littéraire* (Paris: Éditions Pierre-Guillaume de Roux, 2012).

79. Theodore W. Allen, *The Invention of the White Race* (New York: Verso Books, 2012).

80. Some have even gone so far as to argue that antiracism is *the* factor "responsible" for the rise in popularity of the FN. See, for example, Pierre-André Taguieff, *Les fins de l'antiracisme* (Paris: Michalon, 1995). Such conclusions are also to be found in what might be described as a "populist" socialist trend, as, for example, in the work of Laurent Bouvet, *Le sens du peuple: La gauche, la démocratie, le populisme* (Paris: Gallimard, 2012).

81. Emmanuel Debono, "Un nouvel antiracisme s'affirme par l'exclusion du Blanc," *Le Monde*, November 12, 2015.

82. Éric Fassin, interview with Caroline Trouillet, "Les pouvoirs publics sont responsables d'une racialisation de la société qu'ils prétendent pourtant combattre," *Afriscope* 42, September 23, 2015.

83. Cris Beauchemin, Christelle Hamel, and Patrick Simon, eds., *Trajectoires et origines: Enquête sur la diversité des populations en France* (Paris: INED, 2016).

84. Patrick Simon, interview with Marilyne Baumard, "La population française a pris conscience qu'elle vit dans une société multiculturelle," *Le Monde*, January 8, 2016.

85. Ibid.

86. Ibid.

87. Achille Mbembe, *Sortir de la grande nuit: Essai sur l'Afrique décolonisée* (Paris: La Découverte, 2010), 136.

88. Gérard Noiriel, *Le creuset français: Histoire de l'immigration (XIXe-XXe siècle)* (Paris: Seuil, 1988).

89. Louis Dumont, *Essai sur l'individualisme: Une perspective anthropologique sur l'idéologie moderne* (Paris: Seuil, 1983).

90. Gilles Finchelstein, "Quant le clivage gauche-droite s'efface, c'est l'identité qui s'impose," *Le Monde*, January 30, 2016 and *Piège d'identité: Réflexions (inquiètes) sur la gauche, la droite et la démocratie* (Paris: Fayard, 2016).

91. Éric Dupin, *L'hystérie identitaire* (Paris: Le Cherche-Midi, 2004).

92. Kamel Daoud, *Meurseault, contre-enquête* (Arles: Actes Sud, 2014); *The Meurseault Investigation*, trans. John Cullen (New York: The Other Press, 2015).

93. Kamel Daoud, "Cologne, lieu de fantasmes," *Le Monde*, January 31, 2016.

94. Noureddine Amara et al., "Nuit de Cologne: 'Kamel Daoud recycle les clichés orientalistes les plus éculés,'" *Le Monde*, February 11, 2016.

95. Jocelyne Dakhlia, "'S'enfermer dans l'idée d'un choc des cultures,' c'est la vraie défaite du débat," *Le Monde*, March 1, 2016.

96. Achille Mbembe, "L'intarissable puits aux fantasmes," in *L'Afrique de Sarkozy: Un déni d'histoire*, ed. Chrétien, 122.

97. Jean-Loup Amselle and Elikia M'Bokolo, *Au cœur de l'ethnie: Ethnies, tribalisme et état en Afrique* (Paris: La Découverte, 1985).

98. Éric Fassin, "Laïcité négative: une islamophobie sans voile," *Médiapart*, April 10, 2011.

99. Éric Fassin, *Démocratie précaire: Chroniques de la déraison d'état* (Paris: La Découverte, 2012).

100. Éric Fassin, "La conscience du préfet et l'inconscient du ministre," *Regards*, October 1, 2009. See also Dominic Thomas, *Africa and France: Postcolonial Cultures, Migration, and Racism* (Bloomington and Indianapolis: Indiana University Press, 2013).

101. In his "Discours de Toulon," February 7, 2007, Nicolas Sarkozy had described the colonial enterprise in the following terms: "The European dream needs a Mediterranean dream. It shrank when the dream that in days of yore had propelled the knights from all corners of Europe on their expeditions to the Orient [the Crusades] was broken, a dream that had drawn so many emperors of the Holy Roman Empire and so many French kings to the south, a dream that had been Bonaparte's in Egypt, Napoleon III's in Algeria, and de Lyautey's in Morocco. This dream that was not so much a dream of conquest as it was a dream of civilization. Let's not tarnish our past."

102. Raphaël Liogier, "Il n'y a pas de guerre des civilisations car il n'y a qu'une seule civilisation," *Libération*, January 10, 2016 and *La guerre des civilisations n'aura pas lieu: Coexistence et violence au XXIe siècle* (Paris: CNRS Éditions, 2016).

103. Michel Wieviorka, "Nicolas Sarkozy, sur les pentes de l'idéologie," *L'Obs*, February 2, 2012.

104. Pierre Tevanian, *Le Ministère de la peur: Réflexions sur le nouvel ordre sécuritaire* (Paris: L'Esprit frappeur, 2003).

105. Gérard Noiriel, *À quoi sert "l'identité nationale"* (Marseille: Agone éditeur, 2007).

106. Michel Agier, *Gérer les indésirables: Des camps de réfugiés au gouvernement humanitaire* (Paris: Flammarion, 2008).

107. Mathieu Rigouste, *L'Ennemi intérieur: La généalogie coloniale et militaire de l'ordre sécuritaire dans la France métropolitaine* (Paris: La Découverte, 2009).

108. Nicolas Sarkozy, "Discours sur la nation," March 9, 2007, http://sites.univ-provence.fr/veronis/Discours2007/transcript.php?n=Sarkozy&p=2007-03-09.

109. Jürgen Habermas, *L'intégration républicaine: Essai de théorie politique* (Paris: Fayard, 1998) and Abdellali Hajjat, *Les frontières de l'identité nationale: L'injonction à l'assimilation en France métropolitaine et coloniale* (Paris: La Découverte, 2012).

110. Paul Gilroy, *There Ain't No Black in the Union Jack: The Cultural Politics of Race and Nation* (Chicago: The University of Chicago Press, 1987) and *Postcolonial Melancholia* (New York: Columbia University Press, 2005), 123–124.

111. Lawrence Kritzman, "Identity Crises: France, Culture and the Idea of the Nation," *SubStance* 24, nos. 1–2, issue 76–77 (1995): 13; Dominic Thomas, *Black France: Colonialism, Immigration, and Transnationalism* (Bloomington and Indianapolis: Indiana University Press, 2007); and Michel Le Bris and Jean Rouaud, eds., *Je est un autre: Pour une identité-monde* (Paris: Gallimard, 2010).

112. Noiriel, *À quoi sert "l'identité nationale."*

113. There are several edited volumes on these questions. See Pascal Blanchard and Armelle Chatelier, eds., *Images et colonies* (Paris: Syros, 1993), Pascal Blanchard and Nicolas Bancel, *De l'indigène à l'immigré* (Paris: Gallimard, 1998), Éric Deroo and Sandrine Lemaire, *L'illusion coloniale* (Paris: Tallandier, 2005), Bancel, Blanchard, Lemaire, and Thomas, eds., *Colonial Culture in France since the Revolution*, and Didier Daeninckx, *L'école des colonies* (Paris: Hoëbeke, 2015).

114. Bernard Mouralis, *République et colonies: Entre histoire et mémoire, la République française et l'Afrique* (Paris: Présence africaine, 1999).

115. Lucienne Bui Trong, *Les racines de la violence: De l'émeute au communautarisme* (Paris: L. Audibert, 2003).

116. Alain Ruscio, *Nostalgérie: L'interminable histoire de l'OAS* (Paris: La Découverte, 2015) and Émmanuelle Comtat, *Les pieds-noirs et la politique quarante ans après le retour* (Paris: Presses de Sciences Po, 2009).

117. One critic, Laurent Fidès, in his book *Face au discours intimidant: Essai sur le formatage des esprits à l'ère du mondialisme* (Paris: Éditions du Toucan, 2014), went so far as to suggest that scholars who work on these issues "justify the violence of delinquent youth from immigrant backgrounds."

118. Philippe Bernard, "Des 'enfants de colonisés' revendiquent leur histoire," *Le Monde*, February 21, 2005.

119. Alain Mabanckou, *Le sanglot de l'homme noir* (Paris: Fayard, 2012), 11.

120. Benjamin Stora, "Guerre d'Algérie: 1999–2003, les accélérations de la mémoire," *Hommes & Migrations* 1244 (July–August 2003), 83.

121. Florence Beaugé, "Comment *Le Monde* a relancé le débat sur la torture en Algérie," *Le Monde*, March 17, 2012.

122. See Paul Aussaresses, *Services spéciaux, Algérie (1955–1957): Mon témoignage sur la torture* (Paris: Perrin, 2001).

123. See Christophe Boisbouvier, *Hollande l'Africain* (Paris: La Découverte, 2015).

124. François Hollande, *Changer de destin* (Paris: Robert Laffont, 2012).

125. Michel Wieviorka, *Le Front national entre extrémisme, populisme et démocratie* (Paris: Maison des sciences de l'homme, 2013).

126. Marc Michel, *Essai sur la colonisation positive: Affrontements et accommodements en Afrique noire (1830–1930)* (Paris: Perrin, 2009).

127. Gilles Manceron, *Marianne et les colonies: Une introduction à l'histoire coloniale de la France* (Paris: La Découverte, 2003).

128. Valérie Becquet and Chantal De Linares, eds., *Quand les jeunes s'engagent: Entre expérimentations et constructions identitaires* (Paris: L'Harmattan, 2006), Narica Guénif-Souilamas, ed., *La République mise à nu par son immigration* (Paris: La Fabrique, 2006), Patrick Weil, *La République et sa diversité: Immigration, intégration, discrimination* (Paris: Seuil, 2005), Abdellali Hajjat, *Immigration postcoloniale et mémoire* (Paris: L'Harmattan, 2005), Patrick Simon and Sylvia Zappi, "La politique républicaine de l'identité," *Mouvements* 38 (March–April 2005): 5–7, and Dominique Vidas and Karim Bourtel, *Le mal-être arabe: Enfants de la colonisation* (Marseille: Agone éditeur, 2005).

129. Pierre Joxe, *À propos de la France: Itinéraires 1: Entretiens avec Michel Sarrazin* (Paris: Flammarion, 1998), 46.

130. Joxe, *À propos de la France*, 63.

131. Gaël Brustier, *La guerre culturelle aura bien lieu... L'occidentalisme ou l'idéologie de la crise* (Paris: Mille et Une nuits, 2013).

132. Pierre Nora, "La question coloniale: Une histoire politisée," *Le Monde*, October 15, 2011.

133. Éric Savaresse, *Algérie, la guerre des mémoires* (Paris: Non lieu, 2007).

134. Éric Maurin, *Le ghetto français: Enquête sur le séparatisme social* (Paris: Seuil, 2005), Hervé Vieillard-Baron, *Les banlieues françaises ou le ghetto impossible* (La Tour-d'Aigues: Éditions de l'Aube, 1994), Jacqueline Costa-Lacoux, "L'ethnicisation du lien social dans les banlieues françaises," *Revue européenne des migrations internationales* 17, no. 2 (2001): 123–138, and Jean-Luc Richard, *Partir ou rester?: Destinées des jeunes issus de l'immigration* (Paris: PUF, 2004).

135. See Claire Rodier, *Xénophobie business: À quoi servent les contrôles migratoires?* (Paris: La Découverte, 2012) and Dominic Thomas, "Fortress Europe: Identity, Race and Surveillance," *International Journal of Francophone Studies* 17, nos. 3–4 (2014): 445–468.

136. Didier Fassin and Éric Fassin, eds., *De la question sociale à la question raciale?: Représenter la société française* (Paris: La Découverte, 2006) and Françoise de Barros, "Des Français musulmans

d'Algérie aux 'immigrés': L'importation de classifications coloniales dans les politiques du logement en France (1950–1970)," *Actes de la recherche en sciences sociales* 159 (2005): 27–45.

137. Pascal Perrineau, *La France au front* (Paris: Fayard, 2014).

138. Jean-Paul Sartre, *Anti-Semite and Jew: An Exploration of the Etiology of Hate*, trans. George J. Becker (New York: Schocken Books Inc., 1948 [1946]), 147.

139. Jean-Paul Sartre, *Black Orpheus*, trans. Samuel W. Allen (Paris: Présence africaine, 1976 [1948]), 15.

140. See Jonathan Judaken, *Jean-Paul Sartre and the Jewish Question* (Lincoln and London: University of Nebraska Press, 2006).

141. Thomas Deltombe, *L'islam imaginaire: La construction médiatique de l'islamophobie en France, 1975–2005* (Paris: La Découverte, 2010), Sadek Sellam, *La France et ses musulmans: Un siècle de politique musulmane* (Paris: Fayard, 2006), Charlotte Nordman, ed., *Le foulard islamique en questions* (Paris: Amsterdam, 2004), Claude Askolovitch, *Nos mal-aimés: Ces musulmans dont la France ne veut pas* (Paris: Grasset, 2013), and Edwy Plenel, *Pour les musulmans* (Paris: La Découverte, 2015).

142. Patrick Simon and Vincent Tiberj, *Sécularisation ou regain religieux: La religiosité des immigrés et de leurs descendants*, INED, *Document de travail*, no. 196 (July 2013).

143. Olivier Roy, *L'échec de l'islam politique* (Paris: Seuil, 2015).

144. Samir Amghar, "Les salafistes français: Une nouvelle aristocratie religieuse," *Maghreb-Machrek* 185 (Spring 2005): 13–32.

145. Arun Kundnani, *The Muslims Are Coming! Islamophobia, Extremism, and the Domestic War on Terror* (New York: Verso, 2014), Marwan Mohammed and Abdellali Hajjat, *Islamophobie: Comment les élites françaises fabriquent le "problème musulman"* (Paris: La Découverte, 2013), and Alice Géraud, "Pour beaucoup, l'islamophobie est devenu un racisme acceptable," *Libération*, September 21, 2013.

146. As Jean-Jacques Becker and Serge Berstein wrote, "Almost 90% of the French electorate rejected Bolshevism in 1919, from the extreme left to the extreme right," "L'anticommunisme en France," *Vingtième Siècle: Revue d'histoire* 21, no. 15 (July–September 1987): 18.

147. Jean-Pierre Luizard, *Le piège Daech: L'État islamique ou le retour de l'histoire* (Paris: La Découverte, 2015). See also Sylvain Brouard and Vincent Tiberj, *Français comme les autres? Enquête sur les citoyens d'origine maghrébine, africaine et turque* (Paris: Presses de Sciences Po, 2005).

148. Fouad Laroui, *De l'islamisme: Une réfutation personnelle du totalitarisme religieux* (Paris: Robert Laffont, 2015).

149. Céline Braconnier and Nonna Mayer, eds., *Les inaudibles: Sociologie politique des précaires* (Paris: Presses de Sciences Po, 2015).

150. Nicolas Bancel, Thomas David, and Dominic Thomas, *The Invention of Race: Scientific and Popular Representations* (New York: Routledge, 2014) and George L. Mosse, *Toward the Final Solution: A History of European Racism* (New York: Howard Fertig, 1997).

151. Jean-Charles Depaule, ed., *Les mots de la stigmatisation urbaine* (Paris: Unesco/Maison des sciences de l'homme, 2010).

152. Béatrice Mabilon-Monfils and Geneviève Zoïa, *La laïcité au risque de l'autre* (La Tour-d'Aigues: Éditions de l'Aube, 2014).

153. Cécile Alduy and Stéphane Wahnich, *Marine Le Pen prise aux mots: Décryptage du nouveau discours frontiste* (Paris: Seuil, 2015).

154. Loretta Bass, "What Motivates European Youth to join ISIS," *Syria Comment*, November 20, 2014.

155. Jean Baubérot, *La laïcité falsifiée* (Paris: La Découverte, 2014).

156. Boisbouvier, *Hollande l'Africain*.

157. Vincent Cloarec and Henry Laurens, *Le Moyen-Orient au 20ᵉ siècle* (Paris: Armand Colin, 2003) and James Barr, *A Line in the Sand: Britain, France and the Struggle That Shaped the Middle East* (New York: Simon & Schuster, 2011).

158. Thomas Deltombe, Manuel Domergue and Jacob Tatsitsa, *Kamerun! Une guerre cachée aux origines de la Françafrique (1948–1971)* (Paris: La Découverte, 2011).

159. Catherine Coquio, *Le mal de vérité ou l'utopie de la mémoire* (Paris: Armand Colin, 2015).

160. See Charles Robinson, *Fabrication de la guerre civile* (Paris: Seuil, 2016).

161. Didier Fassin, "La souffrance du monde: Considérations anthropologiques sur les politiques contemporaines de la compassion," *L'Évolution psychiatrique* 67, no. 4 (October–December 2002): 676–689.

162. See Tracy Denean Sharpley-Whiting, ed., *The Speech: Race and Barack Obama's* A More Perfect Union (New York and London: Bloomsbury, 2009).

163. Joël Roman, "Pour un multiculturalisme tempéré," *Hommes & migrations* 1197 (April 1996): 18–22.

164. Laurent Bouvet, *L'insécurité culturelle* (Paris: Fayard, 2015).

PART I

COLONIAL FRACTURE / 2005

1.1. THE EMERGENCE OF THE COLONIAL

1

THE REPUBLICAN ORIGINS OF THE COLONIAL FRACTURE

Nicolas Bancel and Pascal Blanchard

THE LINKS BETWEEN colonization and the Republic remain of utmost importance and relevance to contemporary debates in French society. Might colonization, in fact, represent the inevitable reverse side of what stands as a universal utopia, one that invariably becomes less and less "pure" as one moves away from the center (the metropole), and as the color of the people who are theoretically placed under its "protection" becomes darker? Such complex questions are no doubt impossible to answer definitively. However, they do have the merit of clearly setting out an issue that has, until now, often been avoided or, at times, even distorted.

In order to better understand these issues in all of their complexities, we will begin by examining an article we published in a special report devoted to the question in 2005,[1] a report in which editors Patrick Simon and Sylvia Zappi undertook a broad reflection on republican politics and identity. A diverse and balanced array of contributions served to highlight the urgency of the discussion, despite what some might call its "paradoxical" nature. In their introduction, the editors explained how

> the Republic prides itself on its emphasis on the universal citizen and its disinterest in identities, which belong to the private sphere and therefore do not concern the state or the public sphere. The very idea of identity politics is thought to be an invention of multicultural societies, which are believed to foster group membership, allegiances, labels, and emblems. For the Republic, these represent a hypertrophic expression of identity that serves to hide the issue of inequality behind a show of respect for beliefs and practices. In contrast to such displays of identity and community, the Republic asserts its credo of undifferentiated and neutralized public and political spaces. The universal citizen acts on a neutral playing field, but it has

> chosen the rules of the game to its own advantage. For although the universal promotes neutrality, it is embodied, as we all know, by historic figures that represent the dominant group. If one were to describe the ideal universal citizen in France of the 2000s, basing oneself on a sociology of its main representatives (politicians, the media, the economic elite, intellectuals, and community associations), the neutral figure would be that of a white middle- or upper-class man.[2]

And the editors go on to posit that, "On further examination, republican indifference toward identity is more than dubious. It bears a striking resemblance with an identity politics that cannot understand itself as such, precisely because it serves the interests of the ideal citizen. On the surface, the lack of differentiation acts as a guarantee of fair treatment, but in fact, through contrast, it ends up making minority identities visible."[3] We shall therefore position ourselves in a similar perspective with respect to the issue of the Republic's relationship to the "other," in this case colonized peoples. Our aim is to analyze the "first moments" of this relationship in the nascent Third Republic.

We shall first concern ourselves with the genealogy of the link between republic and colony. In this perspective, the status of the "other"—descendants of slaves, subjects, or natives[4]—is inconceivable without a broader reflection on French identity and a consideration of its evolution throughout the nineteenth century. Over the course of its slow construction, from the reincorporation of Languedoc to the annexation of Savoy, and including the progressive integration of Brittany, Moselle, and Corsica, as well as the successive back and forth over Alsace-Lorraine, the French territory was in a state of perpetual movement and transformation. In that process, the nation was an ongoing conquest, situated between two utopian references: national insularism and universal expansion.

The first conquest was that of a Carolingian Europe, which was reconstituted under the Empire (and organized into one hundred and twenty "European" departments). This Europe was federative, revolutionary, and imperial, and it began to take possession of other (non-European) worlds with the campaign in Egypt after having "sacrificed" or "lost" overseas territories such as Haiti and Louisiana. Slavery was also reinstated in 1802.[5] The second was evidenced in many regimes as early as 1830, but it became crystallized under Napoleon III—through the myth of the Arab Kingdom, policies established in Algeria, the conquest of French Cochinchina, and the disastrous Mexican experience as well as the expeditions to China—after the nation's continental borders were pragmatically "established." The Third Republic would choose to combine these two aspects, with one particularity: an integration of land and a segregation of men. From this point of view, it would show itself to be even more restrictive than the Ancien Régime, going back on "liberalities" granting citizenship prior to 1870.[6]

The Promotion of a "French Model"

The colonial epic spanning the five continents unfolded in the name of universalist values and human rights. In mainland France, it reaffirmed the republican regime—and thus the power of the state—as well as republican values, which helped bolster a national sentiment. The dynamics of "Greater France" became republican and postrevolutionary, drawing on—and deliberately constructing—a national imaginary that told a story of France's conquering destiny, beginning with the Crusades.[7] This quest for a universal destiny capable of promoting the "French model"—by definition, unique, universal, superior—was one of the era's leitmotivs. France's vocal support of equality gave it, above others, the right to colonize the world. Beginning in 1871, a wave of colonial conquests asserted a system of values, which the Republic would make its own. That system rooted itself in epics: from Clovis to Charlemagne, from Saint Louis to Joan of Arc, from Robespierre to Napoleon, from the Restoration to Napoleon III's Arab Kingdom. It formed what would be the substratum of a national identity. The successive conquests—it is often forgotten that France was in a state of almost perpetual war from 1856 to 1961—made France what it was in the twentieth century and legitimized its overseas expansionist projects in the early 1880s; they established the Third Republic as a conquering power.

It would therefore be wrong to assume that the colonial commitment of opportunistic republicans was a kind of accident or betrayal of universalist values. Neither was it—at least not exclusively—a liberty taken by colonial business circles, which were still only emerging and not yet very influential. Nor was it simply a concession to an army seeking to regild its tarnished ego after the defeat in Sedan.[8] The interest of republicans in colonial expansion, therefore, had other, more structural motives, even if satisfying the army or a fraction of the economic sphere did play a role in the dynamics of colonialism. And one should not be too quick to dissociate republican political ideology from a colonial ideology shaped by republicans themselves in the nascent Third Republic.

On the contrary, all indications suggest that the colonial project fitted perfectly with republicanism's emerging ideological system. First, because colonization was, from its inception, conceived as a collective project capable of uniting social groups and political parties—even if, in the early 1880s, it was not yet a mobilizing force and remained an important topic of debate in Parliament, notably with respect to the issue of funding these conquests (1884–1886). Second, because the colonial project was associated with essential republican values: progress—Comtian positivism was the philosophy favored by most in the republican camp—equality, and the greatness of the nation.[9]

To that end, it is important to remember the difficult context surrounding such politics. In the early 1880s, the great imperial drive came from opportunistic republicans, but this was by no means a foregone conclusion, and they had to fight for it, since a fraction of republicans and a majority of conservatives and monarchists opposed them. The first of these opponents sought to align foreign policy with the revolutionary principles that formed the foundation of the First Republic—namely, equality and liberty. The second argued against dissipating a national energy that they thought should be focused instead on reconquering Alsace and Lorraine. The parliamentary debates of December 22–25, 1885,[10] were therefore decisive, since they led to a fusion of republican and colonial visions, perpetuated over the long term with the progressive creation of a colonial consensus (1890–1910).

Jules Ferry, who served on two occasions as Prime Minister (1880–1881 and 1883–1885), presented two arguments in favor of colonization during those debates that seem crucial today. The first was that the Republic, like all great nations, needed to assert a policy of colonial strength as a way of guaranteeing its stature with respect to its European rivals (notably, England). That idea later gave rise to Napoleon's policy of expansion. The second argument was based on the belief that although the Republic's universalist principles were cited as legitimate reasons for imperialism and the desire to "civilize" natives and progressively bring them into freedom's light, the "inferior races" to be colonized could only benefit from such principles in time. There was therefore a kind of "epistemological rupture" that turned the act of conquest into a natural extension of the Republic—henceforth a colonizing Republic. It also made the distinction between "whites" and non-European populations into an essential principle of discrimination, conceived as an application of republican principles. This moment was absolutely fundamental, since it was then that racial inequality was first introduced into the heart of the republican colonial project.

Racial discourse would then go on to permeate the political body, through various channels: physical anthropology, Darwinism's influence on life sciences, sociopolitical conversions of scientific work (for example, through social anthropology), and so forth. And this discourse, which gained rational currency with thinkers at the Paris School of Anthropology, was also massively disseminated throughout popular culture, thanks to a range of novel social apparatuses: "human zoos," posters for shows, the press, and anthropological post cards.[11]

Inscribing Itself in a Republican Movement

Republican motives to civilize "natives" quickly attached themselves to the revolutionary project, in the sense that conquest became legitimized by a future horizon—a goal that "natives" could attain over the long term. That was the original principle behind the "civilizing mission," which would become the central dogma of republican colonial discourse until decolonization. As a concept, the "civilizing mission" was created out of a representation of French uniqueness and the belief in a special link between France and the world. That link was materialized both in its universal mission of "education" and in a pragmatic colonial reaction to the freedoms granted up until that point in the colonial "trading posts" (notably in the Indies and Senegal).

For republicans, the uniqueness of the nation and the special link, both of which gradually took shape in the late nineteenth century, were not simple illusions. The idea of uniqueness was first embodied in metropolitan France by a literacy and education campaign that led to the great republican law of 1880; it was then conceived as a principle to be extended to the conquered—or soon to be conquered—colonial space. Discourse on the civilizing mission also made use of positivist arguments on the role of science in progress, a pillar of republican thought—both separated from religion and enlightened—and a contrast to a mostly conservative and monarchist clergy. In the same way, the argument was relentlessly adapted for republican discourse on colonial spaces. In short, republican ideas of liberty and equality were applied to a vague future horizon, when the "savages" would at last be "civilized." This is what set French colonialism apart from the kind practiced by England and Germany.

Republican political ideology was therefore adapted to the imperial project, and this from the very beginning. This genealogy is crucial, in the sense that republicans quickly abandoned themes of essentialized racial discrimination in their discourse to legitimize conquest. In fact, racial discrimination was no longer useful to republicans as an argument, although in the late twentieth century it was the accepted explanation for colonial action. But it did inform the exceptional system, which, to different degrees and according to varying local constraints, would be installed throughout the colonial territories. One particularity of the French colonial system was precisely the variety of legal situations it applied to the "natives" and their descendants; many such legal categories were formulated over time by the successive regimes that contributed to the colonial puzzle. That was also, no doubt, what concealed an apparent contradiction between a representation of the Republic, which heralded human rights, and its colonial practices, which flouted them. In the end, the civilizing mission was a logical extension of human rights, which were promised to the "natives" just as soon as circumstances allowed, which is to say, when cultural—racial—differences could be abolished.

Such thinking could be found among ideologues of the Third Republic—Ferry and Léon Gambetta in particular. The socialist Jean Jaurès also expressed such ideas when, in 1884, he spoke of a "utopian course" for the subsequent seventy-five years:

> When we take possession of a country, we must bring the glory of France with us, and be sure to be hospitable, since France is as pure as it is great; it is imbued with justice and goodness. Without deceiving them, we can tell these people that we have never voluntarily harmed their brothers; that we were the first to extend White freedom to colored men and abolish slavery . . . That wherever France has established herself, she is loved; that wherever she has simply set foot, she is missed; that wherever her light gleams, she is beneficent; that wherever she no longer shines, eyes gaze at her long and beautiful sunset and hearts remain steadfast.[12]

Ideas developed by Jules Duval (*Les colonies et la politique coloniale de la France*, 1864), Paul Leroy-Beaulieu (*De la colonisation chez les peuples modernes*, 1874, taken from a work written in 1870), and Ernest Renan (*La réforme intellectuelle de la France*, 1871) were therefore digested, adapted, and absorbed by the most illustrious republicans, from both the left and the right—from Jules Ferry to the Prince of Arenberg, from Maurice Rouvier to Gambetta, from Théophile Delcassé to Raymond Poincaré. Despite very strong initial opposition, consensus on the colonial project emerged in the final two decades of the nineteenth century. And, after the First World War, the colonial fiction of a space where the republican ideal could be played out—a union of all men around the same utopian horizon, the abolishment of political, religious, and social divisions—functioned as the mirror of a situation for which the mainland longed, to the point of almost totally erasing the violent reality imposed upon the colonized people.

The colonies were presented as the concrete realization of the civilizing œuvre, which further reinforced consensus on the issue. The work of civilizing the "natives" was considered in pragmatic terms: economic growth, social progress, the development of bureaucratic colonial tools. In short, the colonies were portrayed in their process to "catch up" to the mainland. Moreover, the conservative and extreme right united during the 1920s around the colonial project. In the same period, the republicans and moderate left also got swept up in the imperial fervor. This concomitance of events was another source of consensus, even if debates still continued on the manner in which to govern the colonies. That is how colonization gained legitimacy in the metropole, and it held onto that legitimacy until the period of independence movements. Meanwhile, notions of the colonial and the national began to merge in the political imaginary. So much so that, in the mid-1920s, being anticolonial was synonymous with being anti-French; inversely, wanting a great France was the same as supporting "Greater France."

Indeed, and as we argued previously in *La République coloniale,* a book written with Françoise Vergès, "the active, tireless, and devoted participation of republicans in the colonial adventure in terms of the legal, cultural, and political construction of the empire—has rarely been considered in its proper dimensions. It was a constellation of networks, interests, and desires that, although at times opposed, revolved around a dream: to build a colonial empire in which republican ideals could flourish."[13] That is a crucial point since the republican desire to build an empire that differentiated itself at once from the Ancien Régime's colonial empire and its great rival, the British Empire, must be considered in all its dimensions, including its pragmatic and utopian aspects.

A "perfect" republican dream existed at that moment. It had persuaded a large portion of the French elite and established a strong following among the general public. Both the colonies and metropole were constructed hand in hand, and that reality shaped the nation just as it shaped what are today independent countries (as well as the French overseas departments and territories). The "republican citizen" could therefore be at once a colonial and affirm her republicanism; he could, in good faith, believe in the value of freedom and practice "colonial racism;" she could participate in a system of segregation overseas (and in the mainland for migrants coming from overseas) and denounce regimes practicing a similar system, such as Germany in the 1930s or the United States in the 1950s; he could strive for the universal and also circumscribe it, limiting it to whites and a minority of "colored people" through the use of well-organized "positive discrimination."[14] What seems like a contradiction today was then the norm, including for the main political players of the day, as shown, for example, in the use of doublespeak by Marius Moutet, president of the Human Rights League, defender of a number of anticolonial leaders, and minister of overseas France for the Popular Front; the position of a so-called colonial humanism, represented by Maurice Delafosse, André Demaison, Robert Delavignette, and Georges Hardy, is also a good—and still relevant—example.

Was It *Really* the Republic?

What role did the Republic really play in the fundamental process of constructing values of identification and representation for the national space, which included the colonial space? Obviously, it would be an exaggeration to assert that it was the only instigator, as if it were a living and single body. However, it is clear that the Republic did fully participate in the process. The values that lie at the core of national identity are deeply embedded in the republican heritage. Their promotion by republicans, beginning in 1880, is therefore perfectly logical.[15] It is incontestable that the Republic did contribute to politically shaping archetypes with respect to colonial populations in such a way that legitimized their long-term subordination—the *Code de l'indigénat* (1881) being the most obvious expression of this form of legalized domination. It did so according to what was, from the outset, a racial principle. The "native" became, through the Republic's cultural invention, "a human/not-human" and a "citizen/not-citizen."

The Republic also contributed to the progressive expansion of the national space into the imperial space. The republicans' obsession with challenging the monarchist right and the emerging extremist royalists, the Ultras, in the domains of patriotism and continental expansionism forced them into a twofold position: to be a "nationalist," and preferably more so than any other doctrine or trend, and also to form their own brand of patriotism, to make it noticeable and distinctive from all the others. That is why, in all the discourse propagating a faith in republican colonialism, the nation is intimately linked to the colonies.

As early as 1890, the national and colonial spaces began to blur. The republican state used its institutions to promote this confusion, particularly through its education system. The famous pink map depicting France and its empire on classroom walls is not simply an anecdotal vestige or an innocent souvenir of republican colonial ambition: it was slightly red, revolutionary, and reminiscent of the commune; and it was also slightly white, a nod to the Ancien Régime and the "forty kings who made France." In reality, it symbolized the creation of an enlarged nation—until then, all regimes in France had devoted themselves to extending the borders they had inherited—and was a concrete representation of that aim. The result was that the national territory became *colonized* by the empire.

The empire helped to "renationalize" the French space, breathing new life into it and providing it with a sense of national identity, which was threatened by revolutionary social movements. The internationalism of new revolutionary movements was, in fact, perceived as a new threat that could gain momentum with colonized populations. Such internationalism—such nascent *cosmopolitanism*—was to be fought, and the renationalization of French identity, through the empire, would help. The civilizing mission became a kind of crucible of Frenchness; French workers, unionists, feminists, priests, and socialists could all participate. It was an ideal system for giving life to new heroes of the Republic. It was France's Wild West, our virgin prairie. To be sure, it was populated with natives, but in a sense, they were simply a part of the décor.

The republican genealogy of modern colonial ideology would have an important consequence, which the opportunistic republicans did not anticipate: the perpetuation of a double colonial discourse. There was a difference between the mainland and the colonies. In the first case, republican reforms, while not leading to radical changes in the social structure—that was not, after all, their aim—did allow for a certain amount of social mobility and, at the price of regional languages and cultures, the creation of a nation-state in which French people recognized themselves. It is therefore clear that universalist republican discourse and the concrete realization, in France, of the empire were intricately linked. Of course, it was another story in the colonies and through the migration of the formerly colonized (those from overseas, to the mainland). The metropole's ability to dominate demanded large-scale means of coercion. De facto inequality between colonials and the colonized, as well as between migrants and nationals, had to be maintained.

Modern colonialism's republican genealogy can shed light on the current ways in which it has become obscured. Refusing to see the colonial period as a process that continues to affect political cultures (and particularly republicanism) in mainland France is a way of avoiding reality, perhaps in order to uphold the tenets of republican ideals and principles that we sense are under threat. Such an attitude is understandable, but it also damages a perception of the historic process that led to the colonial Republic, making it difficult to grasp the necessity of its dismantling through decolonization.

Nicolas Bancel is Professor at the University of Lausanne, Switzerland, and codirector of the ACHAC Research Group. He is author or coeditor of numerous influential books, including *De l'indigène à l'immigré* (1998), *La République coloniale: Essai sur une utopie* (2003), *La République coloniale* (2006), *Human Zoos: Science and Spectacle in the Age of Colonial Empires* (2008), *La France arabo-orientale* (2013), *Colonial Culture in France since the Revolution* (2014), *The Invention of Race* (2014), and *Vers la guerre des identités* (2016).

Pascal Blanchard is a historian and researcher at the Laboratoire Communication et Politique (Paris, France, CNRS), codirector of the ACHAC Research Group, and a documentary filmmaker. He is a specialist on the colonial question in France, contemporary French history and immigration, and author, coauthor, editor, or coeditor of *Human Zoos: Science and Spectacle in the Age of Colonial Empires* (2008), *Human Zoos. The Invention of the Savage* (2011), *Zoos humains et exhibitions coloniales: 150 ans d'inventions de l'autre* (2011), *La France arabo-orientale* (2013), *Colonial Culture in France since the Revolution* (2014),

Les années 30 sont de retour: Petite leçon d'histoire pour comprendre les crises (2014), *Le Grand Repli* (2015), and *Vers la guerre des identités* (2016).

Notes

1. Nicolas Bancel and Pascal Blanchard, "La fondation du républicanisme colonial: Retour sur une généalogie politique," ed. Patrick Simon and Sylvia Zappi, *Mouvements* 2, no. 38 (March–April 2005): 26–36.

2. Patrick Simon and Sylvia Zappi, "La politique républicaine de l'identité," *Mouvements* 2, no. 38 (March–April 2005): 5.

3. Ibid., 5–6.

4. The status of natives precedes the Third Republic, as their status officially entered French law in February 1862 with respect to Algeria, deeming local populations different from "French from France." They were therefore "nationals" without "citizenship," or in other words, "French subjects." However, the reforms of 1865 made it possible to gain access to French citizenship, which the Crémieux Decree (1870) extended to Jews. The Third Republic's segregationist reforms of 1889 later modified all such legal situations, to the point of erasing all traces of them.

5. It is often forgotten that, in addition to reinstating slavery (which had been abolished during the revolution), Napoleon Bonaparte also banned interracial marriage (and any mention of such marriages in civil records) as well as the entry of "colored people" onto "metropolitan" soil. This was when two perceptions of immigration were first established in France.

6. See Emmanuelle Saada, "Une nationalité par degré: Civilité et citoyenneté en situation coloniale," in *L'esclavage, la colonisation et après*... ed. Patrick Weil and Stéphane Dufoix (Paris: PUF, 2005), 193–226.

7. See Suzanne Citron, *Le mythe national: L'histoire de France en questions* (Paris: Les Éditions ouvrières, 1987) and Raoul Girardet, *Mythes et mythologies politiques* (Paris: Seuil, 1986).

8. Indeed, army officials, like the conservative right (to which most of the officers—aristocrats—belonged), were above all obsessed with the loss of Alsace-Lorraine and "revenge" against Germany.

9. Claude Nicolet, *L'idée républicaine en France (1789–1924)* (Paris: Gallimard, 1982).

10. See Gilles Manceron, *Marianne et les colonies: Une introduction à l'histoire coloniale de la France* (Paris: La Découverte, 2005).

11. Nicolas Bancel, Pascal Blanchard, Gilles Boëtsch, Éric Deroo, and Sandrine Lemaire, eds., *Zoos humains: Au temps des exhibitions humaines (XIXe-XXe siècles)* (Paris: La Découverte, 2002).

12. Jean Jaurès, lecture at the Alliance Française, 1884.

13. Nicolas Bancel, Pascal Blanchard, and Françoise Vergès, *La République coloniale: Essai sur une utopie* (Paris: Albin Michel, 2003), 11.

14. See Dominique Colas, *Race et racisme, de Platon à Derrida: Anthologie critique* (Paris: Plon, 2004).

15. Christophe Charle, *Les élites de la République, 1880–1900* (Paris: Fayard, 1987); Christophe Prochasson, *Les années électriques, 1880–1910* (Paris: La Découverte, 1991).

2
WHEN A (WAR) MEMORY HIDES ANOTHER (COLONIAL) MEMORY

Benjamin Stora

IN A BOOK I published in 1991, *La gangrène et l'oubli*,[1] I analyzed how a number of subtle lies and repressions, how denial and memory gaps, from across the Mediterranean, worked together to hide and distort the history of the Algerian War. Today, the memory of that war has surged to the fore massively, in both Algerian and French societies. However, behind that war hides another, even bigger piece of history, that of colonization. That "block" of history remains imposing and almost unmoving, precisely at the origin of the Algerian War; and there is still much to be explored and studied. Indeed, despite the work of historians over the past several years, French society has not really come to terms with its colonial history.[2] Proof, if indeed necessary, of the way the Algerian War has been "received" by French society.

A Peripheral Drama

More than fifty years after the beginning of the Algerian War, the groups carrying the burden of this memory in French society are fairly well known. All of its actors, approximately three million in 1962—mostly made up of soldiers (1.2 million), *pieds noirs*[3] (1 million), immigrants (400,000), and *harkis*[4] (100,000)—have had children who are now adults.[5] In French society in 1990–2000, it was that second generation that tried, in various ways, to reappropriate the memory of the Algerian War and learn more about what had really happened during the conflict. Today, of the sixty-six million or so people living in France, six to seven million are directly affected by the Algerian War. That figure may seem enormous, but it is also deceptive.

Why does a diffuse sensation persist suggesting that the rest of French society does not seem "touched" by this colonial history? Are the above-mentioned groups perhaps isolated within French society? And not just isolated within society, but isolated from one another? In truth, has not the oft-cited repression of the Algerian War been made possible precisely because the core of French society has never really accepted the colonial issue? Indeed, why is it that the Algerian War always only appears from the outside, on the periphery, in both general history and contemporary France?

In order to better understand this rejection and expulsion to the periphery, it is worth examining the way in which this war was forgotten. The amnesty laws voted with respect to the Algerian War prevented some actions from being judged. These laws of 1962, 1964, 1974, and 1982 are all still in effect, and have created a kind of amnesia. The state has hidden its "secrets." But most troubling is the realization that society has preferred not to see or admit to this war. For most French people, Algeria remained a distant territory, and relatively little was known about the populations living there. That is why, in 1931, an international colonial exhibition had to be organized, to acquaint the French with "their" colonies.

The French essentially discovered Algeria much later, during the Algerian War itself, when forces were sent there after a vote for "special powers" was taken in March, 1956. Before that, even if Algeria was considered to be French, it was not one of society's central preoccupations. The history of that southern country was not integrated into French history. France considered itself to be the center of a deeply European—Western—history; it was certainly not an active player in an African or Arab history.

The repression—or rather, the denial—of the Algerian War can in part be traced to the denial of France's colonial history. Consider cinematographic production in France: very few films have dealt with, not so much the Algerian War, but colonial history itself. History must be seized at its origins, its genesis, indeed with its genealogy. If we want to understand the Algerian War, we have to go back further in time, look at what was going on a hundred and fifty years earlier. Otherwise, we can never comprehend how cruel and harsh it really was, and how much it fit within the logic of a system. French cinema has never sought to construct sweeping historical narratives on France's colonial history. In a way, the Algerian War can be considered a part of a history external to that of France.

Images without History

It is possible to measure the peripheral character of colonial history by looking at cinematic images. French movies do show struggles against a fading colonial system, with the independence of India in 1947 and the Indochina War, with the French military disaster in Dien Bien Phu in 1954, and, of course, with the Algerian War. And the struggles against a longstanding colonial presence as well as resistance to war (Vietnam) serve to construct a singular continent, the idea of which has sometimes been neglected due to an absence of established links between these two elements.

But the "great spectacle" in terms of colonial history fell to the English and the Americans. Seeking to distance itself from exotic, "orientalist" films that led the viewer through a beautiful and mysterious world, Anglo-Saxon cinema denounced the colonial system in sometimes surprising ways. For instance, *Fifty-Five Days at Peking* (1963, directed by Nicolas Ray, and starring Charlton Heston, Ava Gardner, and David Niven) is a story about the Boxer Rebellion, when on June 20, 1900, with the blessing of the empress, an uprising took place against foreigners in Beijing who were chased out of China. In 1982, Richard Attenborough's *Gandhi*, with Ben Kingsley and Candice Bergen, tells the story of the life and struggle of one of the most important spiritual leaders of our time and for the independence of India. That historical fresco was awarded numerous Oscars.

But the colonial adventure, in terms of its injustices and unfair modes of functioning, has never really haunted Western cinema, and particularly not French cinema. Decolonization wars appear as a series of elliptical, unrelated sequences. Rarely is a genealogy of injustices offered that could allow the viewer to situate the "natives'" explosions of violence in a comprehensible narrative. The brutal occlusion of the colonial universe makes the colonial drama incomprehensible.

When it comes to colonial history, French cinema has mostly constructed a fantasy somewhere between nostalgia for the lost empire and unspoken shame for injustices committed. But what is especially striking is the degree to which *absence* characterizes the historical reality: absence of the prewar period (the colonial era), absence of the aftermath of the decolonization wars, and absence of the figure of the colonized.[6] In a sense, the colonial world has never really been made *present*. The absence of images works to dematerialize countries, which evaporate and become almost abstract.

The figure of the colonized is absent, and that lack engenders landless characters looking for ways out. Absence of anchors, of landmarks. Only crumbling shores, brief encounters, and loss. Scripts in which the goal is to find the chimerical reality of a universe that is at once lost and gestating, but never real. After Algeria's independence in 1962, Algerians had to create their own cinema, in order to make up for French cinema's amnesia with respect to the war and to colonial history generally. The task was daunting: to create an imaginary of Algeria at war, and replace all the amnesiac cinema from *before and during* the war.[7]

French fiction films on the war and during the war, are extremely rare. Claude Autan-Lara's film, *Thou Shalt Not Kill*, was filmed in 1958, but it was banned, and it was not shown until four years after the start of the war. Jean-Luc Godard filmed *The Little Soldier* in 1959. Alain Resnais's *Muriel* was filmed in 1961. French cinema was extremely late in covering the historical development of the war as it was developing in real time. The issue, of course, was one of self-censorship, the result of strong state censorship. For example, the state banned Paul Carpita's 1955 film on Indochina, *Les rendez-vous des quais*.

It should also be noted that the "colonial theater" itself posed a formidable challenge. Indeed, French colonial history can at once be read as a history of segregation and racism *and* as a French, republican history. The two histories cohabited and constantly overlapped. How can one account for the "southern" universe, which featured both segregation and contact? That is the filmmaker's challenge when trying to film this history of connection and separation. In terms of telling a "southern" history today, André Téchiné, in his film *Loin* (2001), has met that challenge for present-day Morocco, by shining light on the twofold process of separation and circulation. Of unspoken desires and divided territories. Of invisible communities and the walls put up by identity-based community groups. Between Jewish and Moroccan Muslims, and the French. *Wild Reeds*, an earlier film by André Téchiné (1994), is equally striking; it shows the history of attachment and separation between Algeria and France, with an *image* (long hidden): the burial of a young soldier. A comparison with Raoul Walsh's or John Ford's films, in terms of racism and segregation, and the paternalistic universe of that combination, might prove worthwhile. French and American cinema would also benefit from being compared to each other, especially with respect to the "south," and not just to Vietnam.

These issues were forgotten in the 1960s, just after Algeria's independence. Today, the formerly colonized and the French should take interest in understanding what happened in this history of passion, love, and hate. The rise of the Front National in France and the "problem of the *banlieues*" make these still-decisive questions about contact and the refusal to recognize the "other" all the more urgent. We are paying the price for our tardiness in addressing these questions. And the challenge of "southerliness" in French cinema has not been met, perhaps due to a fear of melancholy and nostalgia for Algeria. However, it is now time to understand how real society functioned, through a restitution of what day-to-day life was like under the colonial system. And we must avoid oversimplification. Can the young generation of filmmakers, born after the war, meet such a challenge? Obviously, those who are being devoured by this history have difficulty talking about it.

Likewise, no prewar narrative has been offered: everything begins in 1954. As if there were no past before that. What major French film tells us about the conquest of Algeria between 1830 and 1847? And yet that conquest engendered a violent seventeen-year war. The seizure of Constantinople in 1837 was, for example, recounted in François Maspero's tremendous book on the subject.[8] He detailed the life of Achilles Le Roy de Saint-Arnaud, a French officer during the conquest, from letters sent to his family, which testified to the cruel brutality of the war.

What makes the colonial world so inconceivable is, in a sense, the fact that its *beginnings*, including the hate and wars, have been erased. Given such a glaring absence, the cinema of formerly colonized countries is forced to do everything at once: legitimize a nation, construct an identity, and situate itself in the history of cinema.[9] Seeking to break with colonial cinema, in which the "native" appears as a mute person against an exotic background, this cinema is active in breathing life into the nation-state. Can new images in French cinema understand and accept such a desire to affirm a new identity? Can they account for the complex movement of a colonial universe on the verge of extinction?

The Solitude of Memory Bearers

The tardiness with which we have come to the colonial issue can also be seen in the "memory wars" related to the Algerian War, which, in a sense, obscure an overall understanding of colonial history. The difficulty with which colonial history is remembered can also explain why the Algerian War is considered an external conflict while Vichy is understood as a Franco-French drama that concerns all of French society. Algeria seems only to concern groups that must bear the memory of the distant colonial war: immigrants, *harkis*, and soldiers. Hence the perpetual feeling of solitude present within these groups. If French society voted by referendum for self-determination in 1961 and 1962, it was not, for the majority of French people, due to a sentiment of anticolonialism, but rather because they sought to rid themselves of an unruly and cumbersome "south." The strong movement for "peace in Algeria" did not appear as a way to grant southerners sovereign rights as citizens of their own country, but rather to cast off what had become burdensome populations. It is in part for that reason that, when Algerian immigration continued in the 1970s and 1980s and up until the present day, it has seemed intolerable to numerous sectors of society who have wanted to "forget" Algerian and colonial history.

Fifty years after the beginning of the Algerian War, today's difficulties with multicultural coexistence tend to be explained with religion or culture rather than history. And the link between that colonial history and the present day is weak. Yet the same groups who are nostalgic for French Algeria (some *pieds noirs* and some soldiers) have a peculiar conception of Algeria, which is thought to "contaminate" society. They nurse a desire for revenge against immigrants who continue to arrive in France. Another group poses a challenge to the traditional colonial memory, and it consists of the children of immigrants, and even the children of *harkis*. They are fighting to gain recognition for the Algerian War—and, more broadly, colonial history—in the French public sphere. They are trying to shed light on everything that happened in that colonial history: segregation, separation, as well as conviviality, failed mixing, and a common history.[10]

In the end, however, how much do these groups fighting one another over heritage really affect French society? In some ways, these debates might be seen as peripheral. Some even view this as a dispute between people with a memory of the south, people who continue to tear each other apart. Meanwhile, the rest of French society remains indifferent. This memory remains "peripheral" precisely because no consensus has been achieved concerning the memory of the Algerian War. More than fifty years later, it is not taboo for supporters of French Algeria to publicly declare their position; meanwhile, it is extremely rare to hear someone claim to be a supporter of Pétain.

War between Victims

A generational change is possible with respect to colonial memory. Consider May 1968: it is generally accepted that this event was a settling of accounts by a younger generation toward a "father" generation that collaborated and supported Vichy. A similar settling of accounts regarding what occurred fifty years ago with Algeria could come to pass. However, there is another difficulty to take into account.

In the post-1968 years, critical sentiment toward the state was strong; today it is weaker.[11] For politically engaged young people of the time, being political meant radically indicting the state. Today, a logic of victimhood has replaced research into state, or even personal, responsibility. In terms of the Algerian War, *pieds noirs* consider themselves to be the victims of General de Gaulle; the soldiers believe they were cogs in a system, the officers feel they were betrayed by politicians, Algerians feel like victims of the French, and *harkis* think they were betrayed by French authorities. A kind of compartmentalized victimhood has formed, creating a competition for the status of the greatest victim. The situation has become such that the various memory groups, who are already on society's periphery, do not hold government or political leaders responsible, but ask each other to account for the past. The intercommunitarian and factionalist competition has been aggravated by the interminable conflict between Israel and Palestine. Responsibility is always attributed to others.

Rather than questioning the state's role, communities always hold other communities and other memories responsible. The state had its reasons for abandoning these groups on society's periphery. Religion filled the void in that abandoned zone, captivating the early generation of "millennials," those who never learned about colonial history. They experience that history as a denial and an injustice. And they have had an influence on the younger members of their generation: the fifteen-to-twenty-year-olds. Communitarianism and ethnic factionalism have filled a void. In the 1980s and 1990s, the school system "spun" the history of the Algerian War, and more broadly, that of colonialism. Only today are schools beginning to wake up to the memory of the Algerian War, which is of course relatively late.[12] At the university level, the first courses on the history of colonization did not appear until the 1990s.

One might pose the question of how colonial history has been shunted onto the periphery from another angle: immigration, which has long been separated from official French history. To this day, whenever society reflects on North African immigrants in France, it does so from the perspective of novelty, as if "they" had always been foreign to French national history. And for one reason: Maghrebis belong to the unacknowledged history of colonization, a history that is nevertheless an integral part of France's history.

Benjamin Stora is Professor at the University of Paris 13 and the Institut national des langues et civilisations orientales. He is author of numerous books, including *La gangrène et l'oubli: La mémoire de la guerre d'Algérie* (1991), *Appelés en guerre d'Algérie* (1997), *Algérie, la guerre invisible* (2000), *Les trois exils: Juifs d'Algérie* (2006), *Les guerres sans fin: Un historien, la France et l'Algérie* (2008), *Le mystère De Gaulle: son projet pour l'Algérie* (2009), *Lettres et carnets de Français et d'Algériens* (2011) and, most recently, of *François Mitterrand et la guerre d'Algérie* (2012), *La guerre d'Algérie racontée à tous* (2012), *Voyages en postcolonies: Vietnam, Algérie, Maroc* (2012), and *Mémoires dangeureuses* (2016).

Notes

1. Benjamin Stora, *La gangrène et l'oubli: La mémoire de la guerre d'Algérie* (Paris: La Découverte, 1991).

2. See, for example: Jean Meyer, Jean Tarrade, Annie Rey-Goldzeiguer, and Jacques Thobie, *Histoire de la France coloniale, des origines à 1914* (Paris: Armand Colin, 1990); Charles-Robert Ageron, Jacques Thobie, Gilbert Meynier, and Catherine Coquery-Vidrovitch, *Histoire de la France*

coloniale, de 1914 à 1990 (Paris: Armand Colin, 1990); Charles-Robert Ageron and Marc Michel, eds., *L'ère des décolonisations* (Paris: Karthala, 1995); and Marc Ferro, ed., *Le livre noir du colonialisme: XVI*[e] *siècle–XXI*[e] *siècle: De l'extermination à la repentance:* (Paris: Robert Laffont, 2003).

3. Translator's note: the term *pieds noirs*, which literally means "black feet," refers to people of European origins who were born or lived in the Maghreb during the French colonial era.

4. Translator's note: the term *harkis* is generally used to designate Algerians who supported the French presence in Algeria during colonialism, and in France today are known collectively either as *Français musulmans rapatriés* (FMR) or *Français de souche nord africaine* (FSNA).

5. One might also add the *pieds rouges* (red feet) to these groups, or those who believed in the battle for Algeria's independence and returned to the country after 1962. All these groups have in common their physical link to Algeria. They all lived or were born in Algeria; they all have a physical bond with the place. One could also include those who do not have a direct physical link to Algeria, but whose lives have been affected by that country's history: such as those who fought for Algerian independence or for French Algeria, intermediaries, or advocates of French Algeria in the *métropole*.

6. On the absence of the other in colonial cinema, see: Adelkader Benali, *Le cinéma colonial* (Paris: Le Cerf, 1999); Nicolas Bancel, Pascal Blanchard, and Francis Delabarre, *Images d'empire, 1930–1960: Trente ans de photographies officielles sur l'Afrique française* (Paris: La Martinière/La Documentation française, 1996).

7. See Abderrezak Hellal, *Image d'une revolution: La révolution algérienne dans les textes français durant la période du conflit* (Algiers: OPU, 1988); and Boualem Aïssaoui, *Images et visages du cinema algérien* (Algiers: Ministère de la culture et du tourisme—Office national pour le commerce et l'industrie cinématographique, 1984).

8. François Maspero, *L'honneur de Saint-Arnaud* (Paris: Plon, 1993).

9. For a comparison with Arab cinema, see: Yves Thoraval, *Les ecrans du croissant fertile* (Paris: Séguier, 2003).

10. See Patrick Weil and Stéphane Dufoix, eds., *L'esclavage, la colonisation et après…* (Paris: PUF, 2005).

11. See Benjamin Stora, *La dernière génération d'octobre* (Paris: Stock, 2003).

12. Mohammed Harbi and Benjamin Stora, eds., *La guerre d'Algérie: 1956–2004, la fin de l'amnésie* (Paris: Robert Laffont, 2004).

3

A DIFFICULT HISTORY

A BRIEF HISTORIOGRAPHY OF THE COLONIAL AND POSTCOLONIAL SITUATION

Nicolas Bancel

WHY IS COLONIAL, and postcolonial history in particular, so marginalized in French academic research? Is such a question even legitimate today? Certainly, if we consider colonization to be one of the major historic phenomena of the past two centuries, then there can be no doubt as to the pertinence of these questions. But then what accounts for such marginalization? Admittedly, I came to this question by way of two experiences. The first was noticing how little visibility French research had in the fields of colonial and postcolonial studies,[1] and even the sometimes condescending attitude of some of our foreign colleagues who seemed bemused by a kind of "provincialization" in French research. The second was a debate that took place in a center for historical research on the legitimacy of a number of subjects, in which participants reflected on the very feasibility of producing a history of the "colonial culture" of mainland France. Is it not, participants asked, in a sense, dangerous to revive the cultural output of colonization, much of which contained violent, racist symbolism? Moreover, is this really a good time to develop a "postcolonial history" of the former metropole? Indeed, such a task could potentially stir up past constructs that shape current forms of discrimination, which primarily affect descendants of the former empire. Would not such a recollection risk further impeding the integration of such groups within French society? Would it not aggravate the postcolonial divide between those groups and society as a whole?

These experiences reveal two major issues. The first concerns the history of the institutional—academic—historian. How has colonial history unfolded? Why did it quickly recede? And how can we explain, *from an institutional perspective*, the fact that, in a sense, colonial history in France "missed the bus" on a number of historical questions that are currently being interrogated so fruitfully by contemporary research abroad, most notably in the English-speaking world? The second question might have to do with a kind of implicit consensus within the fundamentally conservative field of history in France as to how history, in terms of its discursive production, should not put into question "national unity" or cohesiveness—a discourse that genealogically belongs to the field of history itself, given that the initial function of academic history was to "create the nation."[2]

What is Colonial and Postcolonial History?

Let us first agree on the terms themselves. What do colonial and postcolonial histories cover? From the very inception of institutionalized "colonial history" within the academic discipline of history, in the very late nineteenth century, the field's epistemology has been unstable. Is it the study of European conquest? Of the administration of colonized territories? Of native societies? As Sophie Dulucq and Colette Zytnicki have shown, colonial history has hesitated over how best to determine its scope, its subjects, and even its chronology.[3] However, there is one aspect that has never, since the emergence of academic colonial history in France, been cause for debate: colonial history is first and foremost about the colonizer's actions and colonized societies. It is understandable that, in its beginnings, colonial history was unable to conceive of the ways in which mainland society would itself be affected by colonization. What is less understandable, however, is the fact that this idea has never found a legitimate place within French academia, even though, as we know, Raoul Girardet published his book *L'idée coloniale en France* in 1969 and Michel Foucault suggested imagining the effects of colonization on France as early as 1976.[4]

In fact, historical perspectives began to become more complex during the 1960s: colonial history could have been imagined as a dialectical process, one that engendered changes both in the colonies and in the metropole. A second widening of perspective could have occurred in the mid-1980s. That would have been a rethinking of the canonical chronology separating colonization from the postcolonial period. To be sure, that divide, which stemmed from political history, had already been relativized in terms of the former colonies. In the 1970s and 1980s, scholars such as Catherine Coquery-Vidrovitch, Jacques Thobie, Pierre Brocheux, and Gilbert Meynier tried to show, in numerous publications, how postcolonial societies remained deeply branded by colonization. Indeed, analyzing postcolonial situations by articulating the former colonial situation was seen as perfectly legitimate; the historian's job, after all, is to explain historic changes in time and not let him or herself be dominated by canonical chronologies. It was therefore obvious to everyone that the political independence of the former colonial nations did not miraculously wipe away the social, political, economic, and cultural effects of the colonial period.

However, the *legitimacy* of research that tries to gain insight into the connections between the colonial and postcolonial periods *in France* is in itself problematic: what we consider to be perfectly normal for formerly colonized countries becomes transgressive when applied to France, even within academic circles. And it is important to note that until the late 1990s, such inquiries did not take place within French academia, despite the fact that they were taking place in Anglo-Saxon institutions.

What happened? And is the situation more open today? As concerns this second question, current historical practice in France is telling: researchers very rarely inquire into the effects of colonization on the metropole, although there were some important exceptions in the mid-2000s.[5] But it is striking to note that there is no equivalent to Anglo-Saxon postcolonial studies in France. In fact, colonial history remains marginal, and postcolonial history simply does not exist. It is a voiceless, seemingly distant history—first of all, because it only applies to the former colonies. This history has no right or legitimacy to assimilate into the national history. That is certainly a sign of a mental block or at least indifference.

Weak Recognition for Colonial History in Academia

Genealogically speaking, colonial history has developed in the twofold context of the creation of professional historians and an instrumentalization of historical discourse for great national causes. Colonial history's main subjects of investigation have therefore been centered on the moment when France began to expand its empire in the 1830s with the conquest of Algeria, then, beginning in the 1880s, with the imperial push toward, mainly, sub-Saharan Africa. The fact that colonial history began to take shape at the same time as imperial conquest should not come as a surprise. It clearly served a double purpose, firstly of accumulating knowledge (here, historical knowledge) as a way of objectivizing conquered spaces and peoples (a tendency that can be found in all the burgeoning human sciences), and secondly of using that same knowledge in the hegemonic process underway. Indeed, the birth of colonial history also owes much to the dynamics created by the research conducted by geographical societies, research that was very much encouraged by the "colonial lobby."[6]

Several types of knowledge producers can be distinguished in the creation of colonial history: enlightened hobbyists, such as administrators, soldiers, and colonials with an interest in colonial history; there were also well-known academics who, without necessarily being specialists of the colonial, used the weight of their scientific legitimacy in collaborative publications. However, even if some dissertations on colonial history were written in the period between 1880 and 1890, the field of colonial history remained marginal within the university, and it would take a lot of pressure from the colonial lobby before, in 1893, the first chair of colonial geography was established.

The academic history of the field of colonial history was itself strongly influenced by the efforts of the colonial lobby, that worked tirelessly from the late nineteenth century until the end of the interwar years, for the discipline to be recognized. There were several efforts to create a course on colonial history, but they failed due to a lack of interest within the university. In fact, colonial history was not really taught until it was financed by the Colonial Union in 1905. The course was terminated after 1917, and it would not be revived until 1942, when the secretary of state of the colonies funded a chair in the history of colonization at the Sorbonne. Several chairs were created in provincial universities during the interwar years, and at one point such a chair existed at the Collège de France.[7] A small network gradually began to occupy a tiny space within the larger academic institution of historians. Such gains, however, were soon lost, and in 1961, the chair of colonial history at the Sorbonne, held by Charles-André Julien, was discontinued.[8] After that, colonial history almost completely disappeared from French universities—at the same time as the empire collapsed.

This brief foray reveals two crucial characteristics. The first is that colonial history was never very widespread within academia, even during the most intense periods of colonial expansion. From its origins, this history was poorly considered and little recognized within university circles. From its inception, the subject was, in a way, considered dubious, and there were several reasons for that. On the one hand, from the 1890s until the end of the Second World War, colonial history was not very rich in scope. It was essentially descriptive, at the margins of historiographical movements, and most often focused on studying French conquest and the administration of the colonized territories, in what was very often a hagiographical—or even utilitarian—optic. Colonial history therefore seemed to participate in the ideological legitimization of colonization, with a mostly conservative output, in which the colonial "gesture" was inscribed in the construction of the nation. On the other hand, academic output was very small.[9] In reality, this history was being written elsewhere: in scholarly societies, colonial institutes, and by independent researchers.

The second is that colonial history was linked to pressure from the colonial lobby, which, as we have seen, endowed the first university chairs and historical journals specialized on the colonial world (whose boards included CEOs, colonial bureaucrats, and colonial military personnel). The institutional situation of colonial history was very fragile, since it was directly associated with the evolution of the empire. When the empire collapsed, the support of the colonial lobby and the ideological raison d'être of the discipline simultaneously disappeared.

In addition to these contextual factors, there was an institutional factor: the reorganization of the human sciences after 1957, in which Fernand Braudel played an important role, and which made "cultural areas" the new field where scientific knowledge was to apply itself, and preferably in a multidisciplinary way. Colonial history no longer had a place in this new framework.[10] Amateur researchers were still interested in colonial history, but they were more or less ignored by academics precisely because they were amateurs and also because they usually had ties to the colonial apparatus itself.[11] Meanwhile, in the 1960s and 1970s the shift in focus of non-European historical studies onto "cultural areas" led to the creation of chairs dedicated to sub-Saharan Africa, Asia, and the Maghreb, as well as research centers devoted to the study of these areas.

However, it was practically impossible to make comparisons on colonization between these various areas. It therefore became even more difficult to work on the effects of colonization in France (a topic that did not generate any interest among historians before 1969). Cultural areas were introduced to academic institutions to the detriment of colonial history, and although they did help to renew historical work and generate new perspectives, they also contributed to a historiographical impasse with respect to the history of colonization.

Academic Illegitimacy of Postcolonial History?

It is clear that although colonial history was adopted very early on as a foundational saga by scholars, it remained marginalized within the academic context. Meanwhile, the idea of France as a postcolonial society is still practically unthinkable among professional historians.

Since its beginnings, colonial history has been able to occupy very little institutional space. It had virtually no legitimacy, and that is basically still the case even today. Dynamics at play within the institution therefore work against recognizing colonial and postcolonial history in academia. Change is slow within the institution and it is difficult for new historical fields to emerge and gain recognition. Unlike in the United States, where the discipline of history has constantly evolved in order to explore new subjects and focus on current social issues related to historical processes (history of minorities, racism, genre, etc.), the French university has been extraordinarily slow to change, for the most part cautious, and ultimately conservative. Today, colonial and postcolonial history is seen to possess the dangerous potential to undermine national unity and the social body—and in my opinion, such a danger reflects society's own weakness, something which introduces an entirely different debate.

In addition to the institution's structural inertia, which, as we have just seen, dates back a long time, there is reluctance based on a consensus related to the genesis of the discipline itself: constructing memory, preserving the nation. This has not been an intentional process: too many signs point in this direction. That is why it is not impertinent to suggest that there is a kind of intransigence with respect to the consideration of new issues, or the simple possibility of imagining France as a society affected by colonization and the postcolonial period. That kind of thinking—to which several chapters gathered in this book attest—can be seen as a "threat" to contemporary history such as it has been written. Such a threat risks stirring up sensitive issues such as the hidden facets of republican colonial politics, universalist discourse, the concrete policies of power and oppression in the colonial and postcolonial context, migratory policies, forms of discrimination, and racism.

In addition to that consensus and these reservations, colonial history remains inextricably connected to colonial power. In 1997, Didier Gondola published an article in which he went so far as to argue that French historians interested in Africa maintained a dominant position through the expression of a kind of external condescension toward African research and scholarship.[12] It is of course a provocative argument, but it is far from absurd to consider that this institutional history has been handed down to us: namely the repetition of an unequal situation that allows the French historian to objectivize the position of formerly colonized historians with respect to their trajectory in the postcolony; and possibly even to relativize—or downplay—the scientific quality of their work in view of their commitments (political or otherwise). Meanwhile, French historians continue to ignore their own commitments in today's French society, which is, in fact, deeply influenced by colonial history. The reluctance of some historians to develop colonial history in the metropole is perhaps also an effect of that influence.

However, that debate and those positions are hopefully falling out of fashion. Significantly, a historiography of the colonial and postcolonial periods—imagined in the context of French society—is today being developed in a variety of places. The work of several sociologists is indicative of this transformation, notably that of Didier Lapeyronnie, Ahmed Boubeker, and Nacira Guénif-Souilamas. One can also point to the innovative work of historians and political scientists such as Patrick Weil, Emmanuelle Saada, and Claire Andrieu. These scholars are also thinkers who, in their work on contemporary issues, have been breaking the fettered chronological tradition of a colonial history that, in France, is supposed to have ended in 1962. Their publications expose the hybrid lines of continuity, as well as connections between the colonial and postcolonial periods that are neither univocal nor teleonomic. And they demonstrate how such connections combine with factors relating to our modernity.

A number of other indicators of change across a diverse array of domains also point to just how impoverished the field of history remains on these issues, especially as compared to a number of academic research centers in the Anglo-Saxon world. Research centers devoted to colonial and postcolonial history in France are urgently needed, and this need is immediate. But real change will have to happen in order for the colonial phenomenon to become a legitimate topic of research in itself. Only then will we be able to make comparisons between the different zones of colonization, between French colonization and colonization by other European countries, and also to begin to understand colonization in terms of a dialectical process that had an impact on the culture, representation, categories of understanding, the history of the sciences, legal issues, forms of government, institutions, and so on in the metropole.

Postcolonial history will assert itself naturally. Indeed, the symbolic end of empire obviously makes very little sense in the long-term process I am imagining. Breathing new life into research on these issues is also an urgent social and political necessity. As other chapters in this book confirm, there is an undeniable sense of the vast field of work that remains to be done on connections between the colony and the postcolony. *The Colonial Legacy in France* also highlights how a number of urgent present-day issues can only be understood if we consider the historical field of colonial and postcolonial studies.

Nicolas Bancel is Professor at the University of Lausanne, Switzerland, and codirector of the ACHAC Research Group. He is author or coeditor of numerous influential books, including *De l'indigène à l'immigré* (1998), *La République coloniale: Essai sur une utopie* (2003), *La République coloniale* (2006), *Human Zoos: Science and Spectacle in the Age of Colonial Empires* (2008), *La France arabo-orientale* (2013), *Colonial Culture in France since the Revolution* (2014), *The Invention of Race* (2014), and *Vers la guerre des identités* (2016).

Notes

1. See Catherine Coquery-Vidrovitch, "Réflexions comparées sur l'historiographie africaniste de langue française et anglaise," *Politique africaine*, no. 66 (June 1997): 91–100.

2. See Gérard Noiriel, *Qu'est-ce que l'histoire contemporaine?* (Paris: Hachette, 2001); François Dosse, *L'histoire en miettes* (Paris: La Découverte, 1994).

3. Sophie Dulucq and Colette Zytnicki, eds., *Décoloniser l'histoire?: De l''histoire coloniale' aux histoires nationales en Amérique latine et en Afrique (XIXe-XXe siècle)* (Paris: SHOM, 2003).

4. Raoul Girardet, *L'idée coloniale en France: De 1871 à 1962* (Paris: La Table Ronde, 1972).

5. See Sylvie Thénault, *Une drôle de justice: Les magistrats dans la guerre d'Algérie* (Paris: La Découverte, 2001); Raphaëlle Branche, *La torture et l'armée pendant la guerre d'Algérie* (Paris: Gallimard, 2001); Benjamin Stora, *Le transfert d'une mémoire: De 'l'Algérie française' au racisme anti-arabe* (Paris: La Découverte, 1999); and Patrick Weil and Stéphane Dufoix, eds., *L'esclavage, la colonisation et après...* (Paris: PUF, 2005).

6. Gilles de Gantes, "De l'histoire coloniale à l'étude des aires culturelles: La disparition d'une spécialité du champ universitaire français," *Outre-Mers, Revue d'histoire* 90, nos. 388–89 (2003): 7–20; Colette Zytnicki, " 'La maison, les écuries': L'émergence de l'histoire coloniale en France (des années 1800 aux années 1930)," in *Décoloniser l'histoire?*, ed. Dulucq and Zytnicki, 9–23.

7. The relative "invisibility" of (post)colonial studies and African studies in the French academy was discussed at the colloquium organized by Franco-Congolese author Alain Mabanckou at the Collège de France on May 2, 2016, "Penser et écrire l'Afrique," where he held the chair in Artistic Creation during 2015–2016.

8. de Gantes, "De l'histoire coloniale à l'étude des aires culturelles."

9. Ibid., and Marie-Albane de Suremain's study on academic journals, "L'histoire coloniale dans le *Bulletin du Comité d'études historiques et scientifiques de l'A.O.F.-IFAN*, 1916–1960," in *Décoloniser l'histoire?*, ed. Dulucq and Zytnicki, 39–57.

10. Daniel Rivet, "Le fait colonial en nous: Histoire d'un éloignement," *Vingtième siècle*, no. 33 (January–March 1992): 127–138.

11. Henk Wesseling, "Overseas History," in *New Perspectives on Historical Writing*, ed. Peter Burke (Cambridge: Polity Press, 1991), 67–92.

12. Didier Gondola, "La crise de la formation en histoire africaine en France vue par les étudiants africains," *Politique africaine* 65 (1997): 132–139.

4

REDUCING THE REPUBLIC'S NATIVE TO THE BODY

Nacira Guénif-Souilamas

THE DAYS FOLLOWING decolonization must have surely been triumphant. At least that is what third worldism and the promises of development for all in the South and reformist unionism in a democratic world in the North would have had you believe. But these positions did not take into consideration the rush to forget it all—since it could not be erased—as soon as independence was declared. Amnesia and disillusionment were introduced into our world, which was fashioned by the dynamics of the postnational, the postindustrial, and the postcolonial. Far from stopping at the borders, these dynamics crossed through every part of France, and became inscribed in the core of people's relationships with each other and also within themselves. And it fell to individuals to wear away at their doubt and attain a state of amnesia.

That is the context in which the need to reconsider France's colonial past, in order to flush out what remains and move on, has arisen. Some French citizens are not considered to be "real" French people because of their immigrant and colonial backgrounds. Some among them have caused a scandal by choosing to speak of contemporary forms of "indigenization," even describing themselves as the "Natives of the Republic."[1] In the face of this approach, indignation is not acceptable. Just as it is unrealistic to think that we could forget without being forced at some point to remember, it is useless to try to impose rules and goals on those engaged in this work. At once personal and communal, this enterprise does not react well to prescriptions doled out by unwitting doctors. The task of "decolonizing minds" is not about obeying tacit rules shared by a society, but rather about freeing an imaginary that is all too often policed and rethinking the conditions of a real democracy, one founded on real and not official rights.

The Patriarchal Order at the Service of the Colonial Order, or the "Government of Bodies"

An essential key to understanding the provocative dimension of the movement *Indigènes de la République* (the Natives of the Republic) has to do with an obvious fact that many refuse to admit: the discrimination and frustrations that these people experience is located *in their bodies,* which are invested with phantasmagoric symbolism that is itself bound up with the alienation and subjugation imposed onto their grandparents and great-grandparents. The historic depth is here combined with an intergenerational layer; together, they show how individuals—who are sometimes unaware of a colonial history and its aftermath—can reproduce and transmit traits that were thought to have disappeared a long time ago. The idea here is not to say that the descendants of yesterday's colonized peoples have become today's "natives" in France, but to seriously examine the nature of a worldview that was born and sharpened during the colonial era, traces of which still remain palpable.

Those traces appear in a social and political world that has not relinquished a kind of *government of bodies,* which reached its height in the colonial era and has not disappeared, even a half-century after the return of France, more or less, to its hexagonal borders. The attitude continues to exist in the routine administrative management of both yesterday's and today's immigrants, as well as in social divisions and segregation. French people with colonial and immigrant backgrounds are not fascinated by the native status of their ancestors to the point of obsession; they are not interested in using that history as a way of emphasizing their own victimhood. But there are many French people who are aware of society's disparaging gaze, who are confronted with a denial of rights, and who face discrimination in ways that suggest the native is still inhabiting their bodies.

Much like the dehumanizing and destructive treatment experienced during colonial indigenization, there is today an attempt to dispossess French postcolonials against their will and at their expense. In Algeria, the first form of dispossession related to land, which was taken over, as described by Abdelmalek Sayad, by means of proletarianization and in such a way that dismantled the condition of peasants;[2] and that movement relied on the fact that the patriarchy, there as elsewhere, maintained power over bodies thanks to an asymmetry between the sexes. Colonial civilization did not have positive effects on the material condition of natives, which modernization further diminished, nor on the patriarchal hierarchy, which civilizing rhetoric did not undo.

And there was a reason for that: the myriad forms of oppression toward colonized men and the even harsher treatment of their women was not random. It was part of a system that sought to install the colonial order within a local version of patriarchal order. The fact that native women suffered a double oppression was never denounced; on the contrary, it guaranteed endogamy and minimized the risk of sexual—and therefore civilizational—deviance. In this configuration, the aim was not to uphold certain forms of contact between the dominated and the dominating, but to avoid and limit any contact whatsoever and reinforce the existing order. Contact between natives and Europeans had to follow a strict logic of servitude and service that met the economic and social needs to the colonizer. Domestic service and sexual service.

In fact, during the interwar years, after contact had inevitably been established and mixed couples produced offspring, French law invented the category *French race* in order to appropriate the children of inopportune couplings. It was another way of controlling disorder. The only aim of racial separatism was to preserve the colonizer's purity and hegemony, which could be weakened if blood was mixed with that of a native. Nevertheless, the fascination for the "wild" nature of native women and the desire to appropriate them sexually would not wane.

Only on the eve of decolonization did "enfranchising" the colonized become an issue—and more specifically, promising native women freedom through the symbolic gesture of removing their headscarves during a ceremony in Algiers, this public act becoming the ultimate sign of negated power. It was the first gender-based partition erected between natives, and would later be used and reused to separate and put the descendants of emigrants or those born in the former metropole into competition. Thus, even though it could reveal the tangible effects of oppression on the colonized, the gender variable was neutralized in such a way as to benefit the colonial order, giving free rein to alluring and awesome bodies. Indeed, the eroticized and stereotyped body of the native—both genders included—came to embody the empire's generosity and its universal good deeds, as shown in the weekly newspaper *L'Illustration*, published between 1843 and 1944, in all manner of variations on the theme of civilizing power.

The erotization and sexualization accompanying colonial history was indifferent to gender. The promoters of this kind of sexuality in conquered territories did not consider natives in terms of their gender identities; they appropriated their bodies and denied them their souls and minds. Natives were then elevated to the level of colonials or whites, who prized them and sought out their company. And the creation of a desirable body also had its effect on the other natives, who did not have a place in the sexual economy: they remained close to their native nature, which justified their subordination.

The Eternal Native

The continued sentiment of dispossession among certain populations is an extension of a process begun in the past. That process was refined over time. Today it weighs on the bodies of French people, it wears away at people's identities within a society that sometimes loses itself in the labyrinth of its own history. Current efforts aimed at advancing the *civilization process*—to borrow Norbert Elias's term—of postcolonial immigrants and their descendants no longer target work—such as was massively the case during the industrial period—but target the body—its visibility and its unruliness. The aim is to polish native bodies and, in a sense, make them invisible within the social body. Where once contact was strictly controlled, today it is prescribed and necessary—even if it still remains dubious and therefore monitored.

In a form of perfect parallelism, the words once used to speak of natives have been employed to designate successive waves of immigrants and "almost French people" coming from the former colonies. Civilizing them, therefore, consists in making them dissolve into the society in which they are now supposed to belong; the process functions as a constant reminder of their deeply uncivilized and uncivilizable nature. The idea is that they must fight their own nature in order to gain the right to citizenship, a status that is always promised and always postponed, due to continued outbursts of their true nature. Like yesterday's natives, today's immigrants—and their descendants—especially if they are Muslim, are prisoners of their own nature and are therefore condemned to the Sisyphean task of shedding that nature. The story of this failure is based on the ideal function occupied by the figure of the native: an absolute foreigner who is also domesticated; a symbol of inner alterity that can neither be expelled nor truly assimilated. Therefore, if natives continue to have a face and a body in postcolonial France, it is because their place in society, a necessary one in the order of things, is similar to that of the poor and all those "without." They are maladapted outcasts.

This internal alterity is not simply due to the dominated and fated situation occupied by their immigrant fathers—laborers—and their mothers—assigned to the maintenance and reproduction of the household. It also lets the dominant class wash its hands of any responsibility for the discrimination faced by young French descendants of colonized peoples, such as when they try to find jobs.

In the past, the supposed savagery of natives cleared the colonial order of its responsibility in the maintenance of a patriarchal order. Today, immigrants and their descendants are viewed with suspicion, particularly because of the idea that they might reproduce unacceptable codes and mores. History repeats itself as the unequal French social order accommodates discrimination and exempts itself from any political or symbolic responsibility for its relationships of domination, which are attributed to the relics of what is presented as an intangible tradition that has been imported into France by immigrants. Immigrants themselves are blamed for this situation, which is thought to be a reflection of their mental and cultural universe.

And when structural reasons are given to explain why immigrant men cannot hold jobs, it is always possible to stigmatize them for their inability to control their uncivilized nature. Recent stories of gang rape have even cast them as having repulsive sexual tendencies. Their deviance no longer resides in their social delinquency, but in their inability to internalize—within their bodies—basic rules of civility in male-female relationships. And that inability, which drives them to take advantage of their women—the exception having been held up as the rule—is brandished as the perfect illustration of their native (barbarian) tendency that was not eliminated with decolonization and emigration. Acts of sexual deviation are shown to be the true nature of these men. Meanwhile, the women are viewed as their natural victims. The overrepresentation of "Maghrebi" men in the penal system—and more specifically for sexual crimes—is viewed as irrefutable proof of their sexually deviant nature.

Imputed Sexual Roles

Descendants of "natives," therefore, necessarily have a sex, which is defined for them by others. Gender and sexuality have become totalizing traits that are used to enact sexual separatism: first, between new types of French men and French women, and second, between them and other French people. This structure is a notable departure from the colonial era, demonstrating the reversal whereby the sexualization of natives has been conceived in a new way. France is undergoing a social revolution, and natives are the products. The native, who is at once criminalized and idealized, embodies the reinvented figure of the slave who was alienated from his master. In today's gendered and sexualized division of natives, men are defined as heterosexual and violent with respect to themselves and others; meanwhile, women are placed on the open market—which is competitive and "racially" mixed—of eroticization.

A gendered division is therefore joined by a sexual division, and French people with the same colonial background are not supposed to find themselves in the same segments of the love and marriage market. A strict form of exogamy regulates and orients girls' choices toward the prescribed model, which is the subject of frequent statistical study: mixed marriages. Although mixed marriages are to be expected in an increasingly multicultural and multiethnic society, the regular publication of figures reflecting that trend is evidence of an obsession with purity—of blood and "race"—and with the idea that mixing must occur in eugenically controlled conditions.

Marriages that deviate from miscegenation norms are suspected of deviating from French mores. Yet expectations of mixing are not upheld in unions between sons of postcolonial immigrants and "white women." Such marriages are seen as threatening transgressions. That is an example of the colonial norm—in the form of segregation between natives and colonials—that is asserting itself today. On the one hand, Arab or black men are relegated to heterosexual and violent roles—roles which civilized and enlightened men disapprove—and they have to prove that they have been domesticated in order to be admitted into the dominant love market. On the other hand, girls with Arab or African backgrounds have to demonstrate their freedom by openly showing disdain for the idea of virginity and by denouncing men who seek to oppress them, force them into marriages, rape them, or genitally cut them. Since legal recourse is not sufficient, it is important to designate all those who do not *publicly* break with barbarian practices. Authorities of moral judgment abound, indicating those, who by dint of their bodies, prove unable to conform.

The attribution of gender and sexual roles to natives is not only reflective of other tendencies that deny them rights (in the workplace, for housing, as examples), but also a way of dispossessing them of themselves—self-possession being a privilege of the civilized. Since they are not considered civilized, French people with colonial backgrounds are constantly reminded of their need to conform, which is essentially evaluated according to a gendered and sexualized scale. Whereas in other domains, equality between men and women has yet to be achieved; in the case of the sons and daughters of migrants, gender is used as a way to define, hierarchize, and put them in competition with one another. Gendered and sexualized difference, such as it has been constructed with respect to natives, gets internalized by those upon whom it is imposed, and it is used to justify inequality.

When these new French people show no signs of their choices in the realm of love, their attitudes with respect to the other sex, or their sexual practices, they tend to elicit the following extreme forms of questioning: Why are they so obsessed with virginity, and why the propensity for rape? All those who do not adhere to expectations in the domains of gender and sexuality are viewed as incapable of assimilating based on ethnic, cultural, and religious criteria. The degree of legitimacy of French people with colonial backgrounds is measured according to a scale of *embodied* assimilation and animality. It would be considered contradictory for young women who seek to emancipate themselves to also express desire, pleasure, and virginal tendencies. And it would be incomprehensible not to attribute rape as a tendency among young men from the *banlieues*, especially considering they themselves claim not to understand what is so wrong with rape.

In keeping with processes that once led colonials to believe in the need to bring civilization to the natives, the division between those who are sexually desirable and those who betray an animal sexuality is effected in good conscience, since it is believed the objects of such divisions are themselves responsible for discriminatory thinking. In a way, it is believed that they should learn to behave properly. It is considered that, since sexual mores and rules for proper behavior are accessible to all, when French people with colonial backgrounds are caught transgressing them, they have no excuse. Their correction is gauged in terms of sexual civility, which is enforced, as it was in the past, with force. It did not, however, prevent colonials from raping peasant women or servants, stealing from them their virginity and reducing them to prostitution—the only option for women tainted with the shame of rape.[3]

This denial of humanity, which in the past authorized all manner of actions, now helps distinguish between the market of eroticization—believed to be the only means of accessing the marriage market which is dominated by notions of "racial" (as opposed to social) mixing—and a return to obscurantism, with female genital cutting and forced marriages. The Islamic headscarf is seen as a symbol of such acts. Behind this binary thinking and moral judgment, which erases the complex and varied worlds of French people with colonial backgrounds, one senses the trace of words that date back to the colonial empire: civilization, barbarianism, and so forth.

The emphasis on sexual behavior and the enforcement of mores is, for those to whom it is applied, an obligation, and only a degree of leniency is afforded to those who are deemed civilized. For those whose bodies show visible signs of foreignness, the rules are unbending. They have to demonstrate that they have rid themselves of two sexual traits inherited from the patriarchal order: the preservation of one's virginity and the tendency to rape. Those two practices are associated with the very character of those with colonial backgrounds. Such thinking, however, ignores the rape of "white" women and women from the middle classes, and it turns a blind eye to the use of rape—by men of all backgrounds and social classes—as a rite of passage or a test of virility.[4]

Today's Norms of Indigenization

Men of colonial backgrounds are believed to be dominated by their sex drive, incapable of controlling it and therefore unable to adapt to modern societal norms and expectations. They are condemned to being considered backward in the process of civilization. Entangled in antiquated forms of virility—forms dating back to industrial modernity and the colonial era—they are presented as incapable of behaving according to today's codified and complex rules of male-female gender dynamics. Their insistence on playing out old forms of virility, particularly with respect to the women in their entourage, is taken as a sign that they have not understood the risk of occupying the negative symbolic pole of a society in search of new norms. When they try to reduce the distance between themselves and mainstream society, they are denied access, and they are confronted with society's vision of them: natives who are dominated by savagery.

As for "native" women, they are viewed according to their colonial background and according to their need to be saved from their own communities. Mothers are considered to be oppressed by their community's patriarch. Daughters are viewed in terms of being protagonists in a civilizing drama. Their men are cast as oppressive and sexually reprehensible, and they take on corollary roles of being docile and obedient. Intellectuals bestow on themselves the responsibility to act as savior and as such try to convince these women to renounce the oppressive world from which they come. Women are also told they need to relinquish their feminine nature in order to become free, in a strange movement of oscillation between denouncing the patriarch and returning back to him—when they are tasked with educating their boys not to be oppressors.

But far from being a relic of patriarchal gender norms, this scenography betrays the powerful effects of contemporary forms of indigenization. But these people we are talking about are French, products of the French territory, and vernacular French people: men supposedly incapable of adapting to civilization; women confined by men in a well-intentioned society. They are from here. Their ancestors were from the former colonies. They represent an internal and external alterity. They are, in fact, already an integral part of a postcolonial France.

Ideal figures of French people with colonial backgrounds can be applied to all immigrants and candidates for citizenship. They are constantly evaluating and reevaluating their place in society. Meanwhile, new "lords" of the Republic are assigning them roles. Much like their ancestors, Algerian immigrants, as portrayed by Abdelmalek Sayad, are French people who are forced to prove themselves in order to gain full access to citizenship.[5] Such tests of worthiness are less demanding for other candidates who are not linked to France's colonial history, who are not stigmatized based on belonging to the Muslim religion, and who are not alienated based on their gendered and sexualized bodies. The similarities between the colonial treatment of colonized peoples and the discrimination of French people with colonial backgrounds are related to the same essentialist and normative matrix. Such a matrix is only capable of recognizing what adheres to the norm. Meanwhile, responsibility for victims or damages is rejected. The "other" is stigmatized for being indelibly different.

Nacira Guénif-Souilamas is an anthropologist and sociologist, Professeur des Universités at the University of Paris 8. A regular media commentator on immigration, ethnic minorities and discrimination, racial visibility, gender, sexism, religion, racism, and law in Muslim societies, **Guénif-Souilamas** is a member of the TERRA network and Vice President of the Islamic Cultural Center in Barbès, Paris. Notable publications include *Des "beurettes" aux descendantes d'immigrants nord-africains* (2000), *Des beurettes* (2003), *Les féministes et le garçon arabe* (2004), and *La République mise à nu par son immigration* (2006).

Notes

1. "Nous sommes les indigènes de la République! Appel pour les Assises de l'anticolonialisme postcolonial," January 11, 2005, http://indigenes-republique.fr/le-p-i-r/appel-des-indigenes-de-la-republique/.
2. Abdelmalek Sayad, *La double absence: Des illusions de l'émigré aux souffrances de l'immigré* (Paris: Seuil, 1999).
3. See Christelle Taraud, *La prostitution coloniale* (Paris: Payot, 2003).
4. See Laurent Mucchielli, *Le scandale des "tournantes"* (Paris: La Découverte, 2005).
5. Sayad, *La double absence.*

5

COLONIZATION AND IMMIGRATION

"BLIND SPOTS" IN THE HISTORY CLASSROOM

Sandrine Lemaire

LISTENING TO WHAT students say, following the news, and reviewing the results of a survey conducted in 2003, one could easily conclude that the topic of colonial history and immigration in French schools was severely underrepresented. The survey we took does indeed show a lack of understanding—or at best a very vague understanding—of colonial and immigration history, despite the fact that a real need to learn about these topics, particularly in order to better understand current events, has been expressed.

However, although the history of immigration is, for the most part, absent from the curriculum through secondary school, the history of colonization and decolonization is nevertheless featured in history textbooks, which have made a lot of progress on this issue since the 1980s. How then can we explain the feelings and frustrations revealed by our survey? These frustrations are, moreover, for the most part expressed by a fringe of the immigrant—or later-generation immigrant—population. Some seek an official acknowledgement of past events, some call for the inclusion of accomplishments of the colonized, many others take varying positions around the postcolonial anticolonialism reparations group, "*Indigènes de la République*" (the Natives of the French Republic), which was started in January 2005.[1]

It is precisely the perceived lack of a clearly defined approach to colonization and immigration that sometimes leads to radicalized discourse. Some try to fill the void in instruction by reconstructing history from the perspective of a social "fracture," or of a history of division and exclusion. This fracture is a kind of blind spot, which can be seen, for example, in the Debré Law 2005-158 of February 23, 2005 promoting "recognition for the work of France overseas."[2]

Article 4 of that law, which stated that "school programs highlight the positive aspects of the French overseas presence, notably in North Africa," was subsequently repealed in January 2006, but nevertheless proved to be particularly divisive.[3]

The school system, which is a traditional institution of socialization as well as an important mechanism of transmission, has become a core locus in various memory polemics. What role does it play in perpetuating the sentiment of fracture and how could it be used to fight discrimination and militant identity claims? Definitive solutions to reducing this fracture will no doubt be complex and multifaceted. It would seem that a better approach to this portion of national history in the school curriculum could contribute to easing tensions related to "multicultural" cohabitation.

The Textbook at the Heart of the System

The main players in the scholastic universe are, of course, teachers, who have a number of tools that are getting more and more sophisticated thanks to advanced technologies. Among these tools, the textbook remains an essential means of transmission—not the only means, but one of the most utilized. Textbooks reflect the main initiatives and axes of learning, which are decided upon by the education authorities in charge of official instruction. In truth, however, large-scale education initiatives are often localized. That is why textbooks, because they are instruments propagating an idea over generations, constitute one of historians' best means of transmitting government messages and major ideological tendencies. Textbooks synthesize discourse, inviting students into the heart of national consensus, and even the nation's mystifications.

During the colonial period, authors of textbooks were promoters of colonization. Textbooks on all manner of subjects—history, geography, literature, and philosophy—reflected the era's imperial sentiment and preached the gospel of the empire, which had already infiltrated the mainstream press. Today's perception of the history of French colonization is, in part, nourished by these teachings, particularly for those born before 1970. Indeed, imperial power is a recurring theme in the majority of textbooks from the 1920s until the 1950s. They insisted that France was a great nation because it possessed colonies, and they valorized France's victories and territorial acquisitions. Students were thus invited to explore the history of their country, which featured a glorification of colonial battles and heroes, the works of "civilization," modernization, and examples of which they could be proud.

Scholastic discourse in the colonial period was without a doubt an essential element in a strategy to promote colonial ideology throughout the social body. It was a crucial and targeted tool that sought to affirm a French identity.

History taught at school reflected an uncontested political discourse: the overwhelming majority of public opinion supported the myth of the white man's superiority. The schools were transmitting a kind of patriotic belief in the idea of the metropole's goodness from generation to generation. This history, which valorized the French, simultaneously promoted a number of stereotypes about those being colonized. Nothing interrupted this vision of history, and many French people internalized this idealized vision of the nation. The process was so successful that we can still find traces of this thinking in French society today. In the past, what children were not confronted with the struggle of good against evil in their studies? Did they not identify with the heroes fighting the bad guys? Did they not choose the side of power over the overt weakness of the "other"? Did they not associate themselves with the civilized people bringing science and progress to yesterday's "primitive and archaic natives" and today's "terrorists"?

The political, economic, and cultural landscapes have changed. There have also been important advances in the field of historiography. In today's climate, curricula and textbooks are more cautious, but major ideological debates remain, as exemplified by the law of February 2005 or the footbridge in Marseille that would have connected the National Education building and the memorial for France Overseas, had it been constructed. Still, textbooks do not account for this phenomenon in all its complexity. That is, in part, due to spatial and technical limitations for developing ideas in scholastic materials, but it is also the result of the fact that the official curriculum does not emphasize the necessity of teaching this history.

In the wake of decolonization, textbooks already reflected the difficulties involved in resolving a thorny issue: how to speak of independence, when the official discourse on France's "civilizing mission" and the supposed gratitude of colonized peoples for the colonial system had, until the last minute, remained unchanged? That, in large part, explains why textbooks remained silent on this phase of national history in the period immediately following decolonization. The history of independence was essentially bracketed—that is, when it was not recast as "cooperation"—from 1960 until 1980. Then, in the early 1980s, the caesura seemed to become more defined.

A Clean Break between National History and Colonial History

Although the colonial past is now studied in schools, its inclusion in the national history curriculum remains peripheral at the primary and secondary levels. There is a clear schism at work in the national memory between the *colonial* and the *national*, and between colonial history and national history. The scholastic approach to colonization in general—and to the Algerian War in particular—reveals how the nation-state has become separated from the empire in the present-day imagination of French history. Although the empire is often studied in relation to major crises, like the world wars or the Algerian War, it is difficult to find a general interpretation in textbooks of modern French history that takes into account the full scope of the colonial enterprise—and notably of the resulting cultural interactions, which are not always conflictual.

History programs appearing in economic, social, and literary sections during the last two years of high school introduce themes like "Europe and the dominated world" and "The Third World: independence, challenge to the world order, diversification," in a comparative approach that would not be cause for criticism except that it neglects to show the importance of the phenomena in all their complexity, nor does it speak to their national particularities. In the current framework, only a cursory notion of a few key ideas is offered. A general sense of the reasons for European colonization is provided, in which the English, French, and Belgian systems are compared and contrasted, and a few important controversies are mentioned. With the exception ofheroes of conquest or resistance, and a handful of colonial elites illustrative of a given period, a system, and a set of beliefs, people are very rarely mentioned in today's textbooks. Native populations—the colonized—are moreover completely excluded. And there is nothing about public opinion, colonial culture, or the ideological impact on the metropole's elites. This account of colonialism, as was also the case in the past, still leaves no place for the "other." There is no mention of the peoples who shared this history, except as anonymous "victims," charismatic leaders (like Gandhi), or "enemies."

Having said this, there has been marked change between the history promoted during the imperial period, which established a veritable racial hierarchy in order to justify colonial domination and its "civilizing mission," and textbooks published since the 1980s, which make no mention of such a hierarchy. But there is something dehumanized and disembodied about the new approach to this history in schools: it is not presented in a specific time or place—hence the lack of awareness displayed by those we interviewed in Toulouse, an ignorance that could be extended to the majority of French society. Rather, colonization is shown to have occupied a period from the mid-nineteenth century to 1939, and to have concerned France and Europe and, to varying degrees, different parts of world. The lack of precision becomes even more salient in the chapter on French history during the same period: nothing indicates the extent to which colonization was intrinsically linked to national history, to the same extent as the territorial space, demographics, the development of the Republic, and the First World War. Often, the schematic framework makes it difficult to understand the relationship between events.

Make no mistake: my aim is not to criticize the authors of these programs nor the related textbooks; nor do I wish to prescribe a specific or "community-oriented," multiculturalist, "reparations-based" curriculum. Those are the types of objections raised by a number of voices seeking to clear the school system of responsibility for lacunae in the curriculum. For them, it is important not to mention anything that might affect national unity. But my aim is simply for the history of France to be taught in all of its complexity, including its darker areas and contradictions, as indeed we have begun to do in the case of Vichy.

If that aim is still difficult to achieve, it is because the rupture between national history and colonial history—the relative marginalization of the colonial past in textbooks—is revealing of its absence in the national consciousness itself. It is significant, for instance, that in the 1990s, only 7 percent of French people considered the Algerian War to be one of the "main impacting events" of French history in the twentieth century. In March 2005, the journalist Philippe Bernard, discussing the historical amalgams put forth by the previously mentioned *"Appel des Indigènes de la République,"* argued that the group's demands "in any case reflect the debate on France's amnesia with respect to its colonial past and the transmission of that past for the construction of a shared history by all of the elements that make up France's population."[4]

Focus on Traumatic Episodes

For lack of a vision of colonial history in all of its complexity, French memory has focused on *traumatic* episodes. Individuals reconstruct their own colonial past around shocking events, the most emblematic of which is the Algerian War. Once presented as the "jewel" of the empire, the colonial system's "model" of success, and a true extension of France on the other side of the Mediterranean, Algeria held an important place in the school curriculum. Today, the history of Algeria maintains a certain privilege in comparison to the rest of the colonial system and the decolonization process, but more as an example of a violent war that overturned the Fourth Republic. The stakes represented by Algeria were in fact much larger than all the other parts of the colonial territory. Durably anchored in the political sphere and marking the minds of the entire population, the trauma linked to Algeria's independence—which directly impacted the metropole through the conscription of hundreds of thousands of soldiers, and also through the return of the *pieds noirs* and the *harkis,* and even through the OAS attacks—led to an almost complete eclipse of this history from textbooks for almost twenty years, before slowly being reintroduced in the 1980s, and then becoming the predominant story told in "colonial" historiography in the late 1990s.

But how do we explain the fact that many who went to school during that time—when textbooks anticipated political arguments and only began using the term *war* in the 1980s to describe a conflict that was not even officially recognized until August 10, 1999—seem ignorant of this issue? Despite having been adopted by the school curriculum, the "nameless war" is one of the rare episodes from colonial history to continue to stir up passionate debate, particularly whenever the media comes out with sensational "revelations" on the topic. The content and the place occupied by this history in the curriculum are therefore apt places to look, particularly if we also consider the difficulties inherent in teaching a history whose memory is still contested among its main actors. Textbooks are constrained by space, and therefore tend to stick to the key events; very few delve into the origins of the Algerian War (November 1, 1954, is mentioned, but never explained). With the exception of the change to the Fifth Republic in 1958, no one mentions the impact of this war on the political, economic, cultural, and social life of French people in the metropole.

Moreover, the emphasis on the Algerian War, which is presented as a violent example of decolonization, with torture shown to be the most significant manifestation, tends to reduce colonial history to this single traumatic event and to overshadow the period preceding it. Through the focus on this traumatic event, "Republican consensus" has been able to crystallize around the condemnation of the most visible and revolting aspects of colonization, while drawing a mask over the colonial system itself. This kind of reductive narrative feeds the resentment felt by French youth who—rightly or wrongly—consider themselves to be the "descendants" of the colonized, and it favors a mythology of the struggle for an idealized freedom, ignoring both abuses and manipulations.

Research in the field of history is becoming increasingly nuanced in its vision of the colonial phenomenon. However, the pieces of national history defined as official priorities to be taught in textbooks, tend to treat colonial history not as a major element of national history that can be calmly approached, but almost as a kind of epiphenomenon. Its dramatic and bloody dimension is limited to the end of a period (like Algerian decolonization); namely, the history of the world's second largest colonial empire. At the same time, students are still exposed to images that celebrate the "former metropole's" "civilizing mission," even if it is not called that anymore. Meanwhile, the fact that the colonial system of domination profited from its position is never mentioned, and students are never given the opportunity to understand the concrete aspects of a system at the hands of which the colonized experienced discrimination and racism, suffered under the *Code de l'indigénat,* held a different status within the Republic, and were exposed to economic, social, and cultural inequalities and injustices of all kinds. Furthermore, there is almost no mention of the compromises made by the colonized themselves. Students are simply not equipped to understand why colonized peoples revolted, except perhaps because of their "fanaticism" or "ingratitude." Nor are they invited to consider why France was so violently opposed to their "emancipation," as some textbooks cautiously put it.

To be sure, teachers are not obligated to transmit the messages put forth in textbooks. They are free to teach their classes as they see fit and to provide their students with all the materials for reflection that they deem worthwhile. Still, they should be made aware of new approaches to history. In fact, some advances have been made since 2004; one example is the mention of human exhibitions (the term *human zoos* is even used) showcasing specimens from across the empire and explaining how recourse was made to these display practices as a way of underlining the type of discourse constructed in the late nineteenth century around the "other." But teachers lack the elements needed to think critically about the discourse with which they grew up. The aim here is not to develop a conspiracy theory on the instrumentalization of history, but instead to point out how this problem is the result of a culture.

Gaps in Instruction: Grounds for Radicalization?

The void in instruction is, in part, responsible for the radicalization of discourse. Tellingly, a study by the Institut français d'opinion publique (IFOP) ordered by the Ministry for Urban Affairs and conducted June 12–15, 2001, surveyed 522 persons aged fifteen to fifty-five, all born in France to parents from Algeria, Morocco, Tunisia, or sub-Saharan Africa (but not Southeast Asia), and found that they were critical of French society's "capacity to integrate."[5] More than a third of those surveyed believe that the situation of youth born into immigrant families had only gotten worse over the past ten years, and their feelings of rejection were much stronger than in the overall population of young people of the same age (8 percent). For these youth, the principal place of integration remained the school: 65 percent cited it above work (48 percent) and sports (34 percent), findings which the study taken in Toulouse two years later confirmed. These findings underline the necessity of confronting and teaching this national history in order to restore a past to the entire French population.

The lack of a clear explanation of the relationship between colonization and immigration, for example, effectively denies these groups a memory. Indeed, some of these signs can be found in the two above-mentioned studies. Beyond the need for expression by more than 90 percent of those surveyed, is it not the case that racism such as it exists in France today, particularly as it is directed toward immigrants from North Africa, sub-Saharan Africa, and also toward "overseas French populations,"[6] is a legacy of this as yet unacknowledged history?

One might rightly wonder about the stakes of memory and the legacy of silence. Images and discourse were used to create a culture, and they became part of a collective memory in French society, which undoubtedly explains some of today's mental blocks. In such a context, the issues arising from the presence in France of the formerly colonized and their children are ignored, and instead immigrants are stigmatized and radical discourse has emerged from the mouths of their descendants. A growing number of deeds, words, and images have proved polarizing on the issue of integration, a situation that a fringe of the political establishment and the media have been exploiting and that has been distilled into simplistic equations, whereby immigration is perceived as a problem, and immigrants considered delinquents, and so forth. North African immigration in particular, and postcolonial immigration in general, have become a favorite issue onto which the problems of society get phantasmagorically projected, and these fears have led a number of media sources to speak in such a way as to further aggravate the situation rather than to provide real, useful information.

In the face of discrimination, French youth from immigrant families have started looking elsewhere for answers to their real or perceived feelings of rejection. Some end up feeding into French society's fantasies by falling into their assigned role of "little savages." Others, out of conviction or simply as a reaction, express nostalgia for the colonial or develop a defensive posture toward the "threat" of the "other." In any case, history is being called upon to meet a powerful cultural demand for a more expanded public. The work to be done here in no way threatens "republican ideals"—the aim is not to shake up the "scholastic sanctuary"—but rather seeks to reinforce their foundations. Although history once produced less understanding than it did group adhesion, today that is happily not the case. For example, new programs were introduced in 2004, such as an innovative and fascinating chapter titled, "Consequences and Memories of the Second World War": it takes up the intersecting interests that led to silence on the Vichy regime in postwar France, and that gave way to the construction of memory linked to an effort to preserve national consensus. For their part, students exposed to this new curriculum seem particularly interested in the ways in which history and memory are constructed.

France therefore contributes to training the critical minds of its youth, looking back on the mythology of the Resistance without any show of culpability, and without any official laws of recognition or monuments. And at no point do students, who are made aware of these lacunae, reject the Republic and its values, nor do classes become enflamed. The same pattern can be applied to colonial history: the simple fact of giving these young adults the keys to understanding could help curb the false arguments that some enjoy spreading, and it could help to "pacify" the varied and contradictory memories on this past.

Not teaching, for example, the role played by colonial troops in the liberation of the France limits students' comprehension of the former colonies' recent past and their relationship to present-day France. Similarly, overmythologizing their participation—presenting them as victims forcefully drafted into roles of "cannon fodder" or as heroic volunteers—runs the risk of stereotyping the "other" as either an eternal victim or a hero devoted to the "Mother Country." The aim is not to overstate or deform the past, but to describe and analyze it clearly, which would help students relate to different facets of our history and understand their families' history. Such an approach would at last provide them with foundations with which to better construct their identity and find their place as citizens.

Finally, when it comes to the precolonial period, one finds nothing, or almost nothing, in the curriculum that evokes the existence of non-Western empires and civilizations. Often, history begins with the arrival of Europeans, a reductive view embraced by former President Nicolas Sarkozy in the speech he delivered at Cheikh Anta Diop University in Dakar (Senegal) in July 2007. The perception that there is a fracture between two radically different worlds will only grow if these territories continue to be deprived of their history and only studied in terms of geography, as if they were simply vast regions "running" after development. The North-South divide, which students are asked to define, further aggravates this fracture since it is grounded in an age-old conception that pits a developed and opulent world—in other words a civilized world—against a world marked by poverty and a striving for development. If these are, in fact, undebatable facts, some nuance would be more than welcome, particularly to avoid reinforcing the questionable notion of a "clash of civilizations." That notion contributes to cultivating fertile ground for devaluing the "other": students and future adults unfamiliar with other cultures are then only equipped to think about otherness in terms of superficial generalizations and stereotypes.

The history of immigration is another example. An important phenomenon, migration is completely neglected in the history class and is only brought up in units on social and economic sciences in the first year of high school, in the context of a chapter on policies of cultural integration. Emphasizing the history of immigration in the history class would necessarily reduce isolationist tendencies. Explaining France's postwar needs and even going back to previous examples of migration, back to the stigmatization undergone by Italians, Polish, Spanish, and Portuguese during the first half of the twentieth century, would help students think additionally about the issue of rejection and understand the mechanics of fallacious arguments. Similarly, the history of France's overseas departments and territories is stunningly neglected in the curriculum, although these appear in geography textbooks, where they are described as "tropical France" and are often featured on tourist brochures as exotic destinations. And one wonders why these French citizens, living in France, express distress over the fact that others persist in thinking of them as foreigners.

Changes to the school curriculum could help to reduce the fractured knowledge in history and geography. Indeed, a critical analysis of prejudice, the history of colonization and immigration, an explanation of the interdependence between nations, and the contributions of myriad civilizations and cultures, via immigration, would inevitably deconstruct stereotypes and offer students a firmer, shared foundation. Again, at issue here is history, not morality. The aim is to construct a shared, unbiased history that tells how various groups have helped to build the nation. Such a history would equip students to think critically about simplistic discourse and images used, notably by the media, to propagate colonial culture. Commemorations, official recognition, laws, and museums cannot supplant the kind of education needed to think critically about information.

The aim, therefore, is to give youth straddling two different cultures—or youth lacking historical referents because they were born in France but still are confronted with discrimination—the necessary tools for understanding and situating themselves. A national consciousness must be the result of a common past integrated into the present. However, although the school system remains a pillar of transmission and of evolution in thought, it cannot by itself process this memory for society, nor can it resolve all social issues. It cannot legitimately take on everything since its educational aims are necessarily associated with a collective project that exceeds it. But it can help modify perspectives and reconstruct history.

Sandrine Lemaire holds a doctorate in history and teaches at the Lycée Jean Jaurès de Reims. Codirector of the ACHAC Research Group, her publications include *Afrique: Un continent, des nations* (1997), *La fracture coloniale* (2005), *L'illusion coloniale* (2005), *Human Zoos: Science and Spectacle in the Age of Colonial Empires* (2008), *Les tirailleurs* (2009), *Colonial Culture in France since the Revolution* (2014), as well as numerous entries in the *Dictionnaire historique et critique du racisme* (2013) edited by Pierre-André Taguieff.

Notes

1. "Nous sommes les indigènes de la République! Appel pour les Assises de l'anticolonialisme postcolonial," January 11, 2005, http://indigenes-republique.fr/le-p-i-r/appel-des-indigenes-de-la-republique/. See also Philippe Bernard, "Des enfants de colonisés revendiquent leur histoire," *Le Monde*, February 21, 2005.

2. "Loi portant reconnaissance de la Nation et contribution nationale en faveur des Français rapatriés" (Law concerning the recognition of the nation and national contribution in favor of repatriated French), known as the Debré 2005-158 Law, February 23, 2005.

3. See Thierry Le Bars and Claude Liauzu, "Et l'histoire de la présence française outre-mer?," *L'Humanité*, March 10, 2005.

4. Philippe Bernard, "Banlieues: la provocation coloniale," *Le Monde*, November 18, 2005.

5. Christine Garin, "Un regard critique sur la société française," *Le Monde*, January 30, 2002.

6. Jean-Louis Saux, "Les Français d'outre-mer se plaignent de discriminations en métropole," *Le Monde*, December 11, 2004.

6

MEMORY WARS

A STUDY OF THE INTERSECTION BETWEEN HISTORY AND MEDIA

Pascal Blanchard and Isabelle Veyrat-Masson

The very idea of "memory wars" has triggered considerable controversy, especially when it is considered in a "memorial" temporality that begins with the centennial of the French Revolution in 1889 (and on the eve of the "Dreyfus affair"), spans the twentieth century, and engages with a new century that finds itself at the intersection of several "memory wars." A trace of this "omnipresence in the present day" was evident in President Nicolas Sarkozy's speeches and ongoing "dialogue" with the past: from the "rebels of 1917" to the "memory of Vichy," and passing by way of the "speeches" in Dakar and Constantine on colonization, the homage paid to Aimé Césaire, the commemorations of 1848 (second abolition of slavery), and the "liquidation" of the legacy of 1968. Traces can also be found in debates among "specialists," whose books, essays, and pamphlets have been warning against the "abuses of memory" for the past decade or, in their pronouncements, of a clash between history and memory, or "memory's duty" as a crucible of the "end of history."

The Divide between History and Memory

Our objective is not to offer an exhaustive overview of all the works that have been published on *collective memory* since Maurice Halbwachs introduced the term, and which we do not find particularly useful for our purposes.[1] Let us recall that it was Pierre Nora's work on realms or sites of memory (*lieux de mémoire*) in the mid-1970s that marked the true renewal of historical work on these issues relating memory and that numerous studies, both critical and uncritical, have since taken up.[2]

In the late 1980s, Pierre Vidal-Naquet bemoaned the fact that so few historians had focused on "memory" to consider its relationship to representations of the past.[3] That was not the case, however, for Henry Rousso, who tirelessly pursued empirical and theoretical studies on the distinction between memory—a "lived" experience that makes memories sacred and mythologizes them—and history—a "scholarly" construction founded on a critical discourse that, to be sure, consists in "selecting facts," but also offers structure to the narrative.[4] This distinction was an effort to avoid confusion, remove prejudice, and familiarize historians with the "exercise of memory." Pierre Vidal-Naquet also reminded us that "history comes from memory" and that we should not always seek to oppose it. If only such words had been heeded, a number of pitfalls would have been avoided in the subsequent decades.

However, these two notions have continuously found themselves opposed to each other, becoming entangled in conflicts "of memory." Without a doubt, memory intersects with history, often penetrating it and introducing itself into commemoration. Today, the debate has extended beyond the muted halls of the university and into the core of our societies through wide media coverage. There are more or less two types of debate or conflict that have come to dominate the landscape: those that pit memory against history and those that support memory (against the state, against forgetting, against hegemonic memories—all of which often interact).

The opposition between history and memory has become one of the most important paradigms in intellectual debates today. It is at the center of antirepentance movements and competitions for memory. According to Enzo Traverso, if memory is "sanctified," then "mythologization and amnesia become a constant threat to history," which suggests the need for extreme vigilance.[5] For him, much of modern and contemporary historiography has fallen into that trap. Thus, Pierre Nora and his "work," which sought to reconstruct national history around "lieux de mémoire," devoted only limited attention to the question of colonial history or to the role of media. Such misunderstandings among historians led to hardened positions and "quarrels" that quickly became major conflicts.

De Bellae Memoriae

There is no doubt that history has an influence on memory and vice versa. Memory cannot exist without history, since memories are founded in (and on) acquired knowledge, and "move forward" in line with historiographical debates as well as social and generational expectations. Is it possible to imagine historical research disconnected from any social or memorial demands? When history and memory are placed in opposing camps, social advancement becomes impossible.

That notwithstanding, history and memory are not the same. Whereas a memory can be "monopublic" (blacks, Jews, women, homosexuals, regional minorities, and so on), a history cannot relinquish its "universalist duty." Nevertheless, when it comes to media coverage, the two facets of our relationship to the past are intermingled. And it is at the intersection of these antagonisms that "memory wars" appear, and in which groups seek to make themselves heard based on identity markers.

Our goal is therefore not so much to investigate the "notion of memory" and its role with respect to history. In fact, that work has already been done.[6] Several defining publications are available on the subject,[7] the "stakes of memory" are already sources of debate, and the divide between history and memory has already been sufficiently explored so as to offer readers a large body of work from which to seek answers to their questions.[8] Rather, we are more interested in focusing on the notion of memory *wars* themselves. They are at the center of our reflections, be they real or fictional, media-generated or the work of specialists, old or new. We shall explore the emergence of memory-based conflicts through the prisms of time (duration) and media (the capacity to be disseminated).

One should avoid the impetus to produce a restrictive definition of memory. Instead, what might be a conflict of memory for some may be viewed by others as a conflict of history, which implicates a number of actors, including historians; de facto, it contains a "media-related" and political dimension.[9] That observation has led us to suggest a twofold approach, by way of the subject "history-memory" and the filter "media-vector," understood in a broad sense as a "vehicle of memory" (from the monument to television).

In addition, the previously unheard of visibility of these memory conflicts in the public space coincided with the "reign of the instantaneous" ushered in by new information technology. The acceleration of learning time "weighs on our capacity to envision the future,"[10] and the media has been reframing a unilateral discourse on the past, by allowing divergent perspectives to express themselves. Moreover, the strictly "national" dimension of memory has become less and less relevant as a framework for understanding. The globalization of information has disrupted national memories with, as we have seen, the "great commemorations" of June 6, 1984, on the beaches in Normandy and of January 27, 1995, in Auschwitz; national paradigms and the legitimacy of the nation-state's memory are therefore being put into question by new, competing models. Meanwhile, the media has played a major role in this reshuffling process.

Television has quickly become a key player in this field, offering a permanent view onto the past. A few notable shows have served as landmarks in this "public history"[11]: the emblematic miniseries *Holocaust* (first airing in 1978), which Henry Rousso considers a pivotal moment,[12] as well as "special" shows dedicated to commemorations on public television. A new breed of historians act as "specialists" (we are thinking in particular of Max Gallo—presented as a "consulting historian"—who appears beside Marie Drucker in a new show on France 3, *Droit d'inventaire*), and have replaced people like Armand Jammot of *Dossiers de l'écran,*[13] as well as Alain Decaux and Léon Zitrone; they are the ones who set the tone of history being transmitted—but, as we shall see, on another scale.

At the same time, the cinema has been using the past to renew "French passions;" recently, films like *Indochine, Days of Glory, The Officers' Ward,* and *Les âmes grises* have been developed in a very different context than that of *Si Versailles m'était conté, Night and Fog,* and *Papy fait de la résistance.* They have also been major box office hits. Today, the internet has been a game changer, setting up a world in which thousands of memories interact and in which all are invited to express their ideas on the past, and contribute to the construction of a new "encyclopedia of knowledge" (Wikipedia) or devote themselves to explicit, if at times extreme, revisionist history (as on the site of the Association des Anciens Amateurs de Récits de Guerres et d'Holocaustes [Association of Former Enthusiasts of War and Holocaust Stories]).

Everyone can construct his or her own "virtual museum," activist memories, and points of view on the past, rivaling the websites of official museums or public institutions. After Pascal Bruckner's *The Tears of the White Man* and *Télévision, nouvelle mémoire,*[14] the rate of publication has sped up. Each year, pamphlets or "event-books"—we are thinking here of Pascal Bruckner's essay, *La tyrannie de la pénitence,* General Aussaresses's books, and Pierre Péan's works on Vichy and Rwanda—shake up memories and disrupt the smooth historical narrative.[15] The commemorations and memorials of those nostalgic for the colonial saga rival the plaques and exhibitions devoted to the "dark hours" of the ultramarine epic. School textbooks remain hot button issues, and we are increasingly reliant on legislators to write the past; commemorations have become major spectacles, which we have put in the hands of large advertising agencies (Havas, Publicis, Euro RSCG, Auditoire, DDB, Le Public Système, among others).[16]

In this context, professional historians have begun to worry about those who present themselves as "memory activists." A strange competition has been established between print media, with its "original" reports on the past, and people like Robert Hossein, who puts on an extremely popular historically "revisionist" show every year. Exhibitions have become showcases of "memory-based debates," as evidenced, for example, by the 2008 exhibition at the Bibliothèque

Historique de la Ville de Paris that featured color photographs of Paris during the Nazi occupation, taken by André Zucca, a photographer closely linked to the Germans. The initial title, "Les Parisiens sous l'occupation" (Parisians under Occupation), was changed to "Des Parisiens sous l'occupation" (Some Parisians under Occupation), the latter title being accompanied by an explanatory text, for those unable to understand the nuance, and several "safeguards" (there was even talk of closing the exhibition). Clearly, a review of history leads to processes (and counterprocesses) that are incredibly contemporary in scope and go beyond a simple reading of the past.

As Jean El Gammal has pointed out, the processes at work in reviewing the past and the polemics involved in historical issues are not new, as confirmed by the example of the French Revolution, a debate that has structured political life for the past two centuries and that continues to exert influence over our present day in various forms.[17] Other conflicts from the past tend to resurface in times of crisis or go through cycles, such as the Dreyfus affair, which Vincent Duclert reminds us "was interrupted during the Great War and the Union sacrée. But the conflict reemerged with renewed energy in the mid-1920s, with the rise of antisemitism and new, more extreme forms than at its previous height in 1898."[18] Memory wars need a present context as much as they do a past.

Media Coverage and "Memory Wars"

At the intersection of these diverse approaches to history and memory, we have sought to better understand the paradigms of the main memory conflicts in France that have spanned the twentieth century, to measure the part played by fantasy, ideology, political and social concerns, as well as legal and financial interests behind these fractures in the national narrative. For the most part, we found connections with the present, in the sense that these conflicts still resonate today; they demonstrate the extent to which today's society interacts with its past as well as its struggle for present meaning and its fears for the future.

All wars rely on three entities in order to exist: battlefields, people, and weapons. The primary battlefields of this century's memory wars in France could be organized around the French Revolution, the ways in which the nation's history is taught, the Dreyfus affair, the Great War, Vichy, the Shoah, May 1968, colonization (and the Algerian War), slavery (and its abolition), and immigration. To this end, the work of historians, journalists, activists, politicians, and artists can be considered relevant, in addition to various books and films, the school system, television, monuments, museums, the internet, commemorations, and academia. Likewise, the multiple ways in which these conflicts are presented in the media (as well as media and institutional "strategies") can also provide useful insights, placing such conflicts into perspective, but also compelling us to think of memory conflicts in the context of their times (as well as in the context of their collective succession and the relationships from one war to the next).

Memory wars cannot exist without transmission and mediation, or media coverage (in its widest sense). For example, a study of the evolution of history's place in television can shed light on the media-related stakes at work in this issue over the past thirty years as well as the strategies of memorial pacification (or legitimation);[19] it also allows us to compare the cycles of memory in different memory-related outlets; we are thinking notably of discussions for a museum on French history at the Invalides,[20] and of the role of historical museums, as well as of "event" books and some political declarations and grandiose commemorations, in the process of opening up some past events over the past fifty years.[21]

Important changes have taken place over the past several decades, notably with the emergence of the internet and the evolution of textbooks that are now more attentive to contemporary memorial debates,[22] as well as a shift in perspective on the commemorative past. Indeed, as Serge Barcellini explains, we have shifted from a "classical" commemoration of those who died "for" France to one that highlights those who died "because of" France (in this, 1995 was a turning point).[23] Thus, a completely new relationship to French history has emerged, making it difficult to find a form capable of unifying various passions. However, despite a social recognition of history as a social science, textbooks continue to serve as "generational smugglers," with their creation of a "new memory" for young generations, as Benoît Falaize and Françoise Lantheaume have shown.[24]

The varied perspectives trace a cartography of French memory wars, calling into question the relationship between history and memory, which informs all aspects of French society. This has led to a crisis of sorts for historians,[25] a situation of one-upmanship among politicians and essayists, and an unprecedented production of books and art. Debates on "repentance," the "rise of community-based identities," and legacies from the past have flourished in traditional circles as well as old and new media. Our object of study is clearly France, at least the "way" in which we think, see, and "manufacture" France in its relationship with the past and with the stakes of that past.[26]

Memory wars are not, as we know, specific to France. For example, a collaborative report conducted by Marc Ferro on *Les guerres de mémoires dans le monde* (Memory Wars Around the World) featured fifteen articles on the complex relationship between media and memory wars in various geographical areas and countries.[27] Memory wars, in all their diversity, act as foundational elements in debates on identity, in France as well as elsewhere in the world: from Chile to India, from Japan to Spain, from Algeria to the United States, from Eastern Europe to the Caribbean, from Australia to the Near East, and so forth.[28]

French Identity?

In many cases, these conflicts with the past are explicit reflections of the eye of the national storm. They structurally illustrate a nation's foundational past event (or a part of the country's population) that is central to "national identities." Do people need memory wars to introduce these major past events into the present? Does the acceleration of knowledge distribution and the globalization of knowledge lead to explosions of conflict? In the end, are not memory wars simply making visible phenomena that were once relegated to the antechamber of public debate?[29] Do they not give voice—through noisy media debate[30]—to the hitherto silent frustrations of "history's victims"? And do they not lead to slow changes in official memory?

Increasingly, historians have also been debating their roles in these conflicts. Nicolas Offenstadt, in the opening article of *Mediapart*'s special edition, *Usages et mésusages de l'histoire,* explains that in addition to "history as a discipline and an art, memories also speak of the past, but differently."[31] Similarly, Bernard Pudal has argued that "moments of 'enlistment' in historical work are often correlated to naively positivist conceptions of historical research, which divide the academic community and lead part of that community to assert the difference between history and memory and insist on vigilance with respect to public uses of history."[32] However, such reactions also make it harder to hear "new" memories emerging outside of the academic world.

In our opinion, it is time to agree to look at these conflicts for what they are—a reality of our times—and to ask ourselves the extent to which and in what forms they have been present throughout the twentieth century, and if, after the storm, "calm" can be regained. Resurgent memories can indeed, as Olivier Wieviorka has pointed out in the context of the Second World War's "dark years," engender new "memorial frustrations," but memorial processes also lead to new forms of balance and, as a result, a potential disequilibrium between those who consider themselves to be the natural inheritors of the past and those who are now finding a new place in the collective memory.[33]

It appears we are experiencing a surge of "memorial expectations," a phenomenon that is linked to the collapse of the nation-state's monolithic structure of history-memory. In reality, however, such expectations (though often denied or hidden from view) never really disappeared. What seems different today, is that these processes are developing more quickly. That is undoubtedly the result of new media, which accelerate the dissemination of information, debates, and conflicts. New weapons have led to new debates.

The role of the historian has not been diminished; it has simply been recast, since there can be no faithfulness to the past without truth. To be sure, the historian runs the risk of being manipulated or forced into defending uncomfortable positions, as we saw with the Cité nationale de l'histoire de l'immigration (The National Museum for the History of Immigration, CNHI), and more recently with former minister of immigration, national identity, integration, and co-development Brice Hortefeux's rather cavalier efforts to establish an Institute on Immigration and Integration (in collaboration with the High Advisory Council on integration), to be presided over by Hélène Carrère d'Encausse, and for which historians were placed into working groups without their prior consent. Paul Schor is thus rightly concerned about "the disorganization, the concerns raised by the missions, and the personalities of the institute's research directors," a combination of factors that "will further sharpen the divide between specialized researchers of these issues and a minister whose only concern is having opinion makers under his thumb."[34] The instrumentalization of history (and of historians) is also an issue in the creation of a foundation for remembering the Algerian War (announced by prime minister François Fillon on September 25, 2007). Such initiatives call into question the role of historians in the complex field of remembrance.

A Media Debate?

There is a sort of twofold issue of "too much memory": on the one hand, the state produces an "awkward" memory, and on the other hand, fragmented memories have been emerging from all manner of sources.[35] In such a context, it is important to distinguish between *necessary forgetting* (after tragic events), *perverted forgetting* (Benjamin Stora),[36] which serves to safeguard an imaginary narrative, and *media-based forgetting*, which is the immediate product of new vectors of dissemination that are related to processes going beyond traditional debates on memory. The media functions through images, places, monuments, and discourse that necessarily rely on emotions and power.

The rise of "memorial laws" has led Jean-Pierre Azéma to disparage "the rivalry and one-upmanship at work in remembrance and victimhood and that have taken teachers and citizens' historical knowledge hostage. It is a shame that lawmakers have ignored the perverse effects of memorial laws. The fact that their aims are not exempt from electioneering is disconcerting."[37] Others have deconstructed these debates (notably the historian Gilles Manceron in his response to Jean-Pierre Azéma),[38] and the parliamentary commission's manner (and conclusions) of approaching these issues should impact (or aggravate) the relationship between history and memory in the coming years. The state continually intervenes in these issues through the law as well as through traditional forms (museums), recurrent modes (textbooks and recruitment programs in universities), and through the media (public television, for example).

These various processes need to be decoded and methodologies developed for interpreting and analyzing the different modes of their dissemination, the possible forms of manipulation,[39] and the role of the media in an era when the scoop has become the most accomplished form of information. In such a context, crime, genocide, violence, and "secrets" become "memorial musts" in the media, since they are the most likely to appeal to the widest possible audience. The abundance of such topics has led to a new space of expression. History is becoming less and less dictated by winners, and reading the (monolithic and linear) past has become an inexhaustible mode of interpretation, the results of which vary from a rebalancing of memories to extremely harmful forms of political manipulation.[40] As a discipline, history must adapt; it must be open to the ever-changing landscape of memories and be capable of revising itself. It should not become a slave to memory; rather, the two modes should complement each other.

The encounter between an analysis of the media and historical contextualization makes for a particularly useful point of departure for discussion. These kinds of interactions can provide an original dimension to the relationship between the present and the past and to memory conflicts, both through the types of questions that will be asked and also through the plurality of approaches to analogous phenomena.

When we surf the internet, read debates in newspapers like *Libération, Le Monde,* or *Le Figaro,* go to the movies, do homework with our kids, listen to debates between "specialists," watch new TV shows like *Secrets d'histoire* or *Droit d'inventaire*; when we visit monument and museums, we are confronted more than ever before with constantly changing "issues of memory."[41] The hypermedia coverage of a given topic has made forgetting all but impossible. In this power struggle between *sites of memory* and *sites of forgetting,* in the transition from the past into the future, the importance of focusing on the *present of memory*—at the very moment when memory conflicts have become a fascinating and terrifying domain—seems obvious.[42]

Making the link between the domains of history and memory seems more urgent today than before. Memory and history "are not separated by insurmountable barriers; rather, they are constantly interacting."[43] The result is a privileged relationship between "strong memories" and the writing of history. And, as Philippe Artières and Michelle Zancarini-Fournel have suggested, successive memories "interact and give way to one another, over time contributing to producing another historical narrative that is at once legitimate and the source of controversy. History and memory feed off one another. The memories of the children of 1968 activists are now confronted with a historiography that, forty years later, is beginning to become more complex and increasingly appealing to readers."[44]

Over the past twenty years, the notion of "war" seems to have become explicit (and ubiquitous) in the context of the relationship between history and memory.[45] In 1985, the first issue of *Vingtième siècle: Revue d'histoire,* titled "Les guerres franco-françaises" (Franco-French Wars) already emphasized what appeared to the authors to be a French specificity, an identity founded on deep internal conflicts. In fact, the debates of the era dealt with what many other thinkers long before us (from Henry Rousso in 1985, to Daniel Lindenberg in 1994, to Benjamin Stora in 2007)[46] called French memory wars. After *lieux de mémoire* was accepted as an essential concept for doing history, it progressively became apparent that memory (especially in its plural form) led to conflicts, and was a major source of difficulty for an already fragile social harmony. Another issue of *Vingtième siècle: Revue d'histoire,* published in 1994, appeared to temporarily establish the beginning of a consciousness that memory wars were beginning to take a peculiar turn in France.

The War Becomes Visible

In that highly symbolic issue, Daniel Lindenberg contributed an enlightening article on the question.[47] The structure, contents, and contributors to the issue foreshadowed all the debates that have since emerged. A cursory overview attests to that assertion: an article by a historian of the "colonial fact," in which Charles-Robert Ageron critiques Mohand Hamoumou's work on *harkis,*[48] insisting that it was not "a shameful page of our history"[49] and takes aim at the preface of Dominique Schnapper's book, which makes an inappropriate comparison with the roundup of Jews in 1942 at the Paris Vélodrome d'Hiver during the Second World War. Meanwhile, in the "Bookshelf" section of the same periodical, Benjamin Stora defends the same work, emphasizing that at last someone has been talking about the "Republic's forgotten characters;"[50] elsewhere in the volume, the historian Daniel Lefeuvre contributed an article on "Vichy and the Modernization of Algeria"—ten years later, he became one of the leaders of the antirepentance movement in France.[51] A few pages later, Christian Delporte offers a laudatory assessment of the exhibition *Images et colonies* and its catalog; the exhibition is said to have "judiciously filled in some blanks" on the French colonial past—a prototypical example of *deviant* memories for Daniel Lefeuvre.

It was in this context that Daniel Lindenberg contributed an article on "germinating" memory conflicts in French society.[52] In it, he presents a rather complete picture of French memory wars, from the French Revolution to the Dreyfus affair, from the Great War to communism, from the Shoah to Vichy, and from the Algerian War to May 1968. However, he did not foresee the coming conflicts surrounding the issues of slavery and immigration. Referencing a comment by Pierre Vidal-Naquet on the subject of a work by Yosef H. Yerushalmi,[53] he advocated integrating "memory into history," and, concerned about the consequences of such conflicts,[54] he also suggested establishing an immediate limit with respect to the invasion of memories into the present. According to him, we were entering into a new era, one in which open conflicts would redistribute the issues of the present with the past.

For Daniel Lindenberg, forgetting, manipulation, and fragmentary memories are thought to lead to a "war," our relationship to history therefore consisting in "hesitating between forgetting and memory;"[55] the war is a reaction or frustration expressed by those who have not found "their" place in the national narrative. Since the state can only "react" to pressure (he cites the commune and Vendée as examples), a "game of memories" is used to define a kind of middle ground between two expectations: that of an official national memory and that of a specific and fragmentary memory.[56] In fact, each memory-based conflict is thought to be the continuation of the preceding "war," which renews itself through new forms and issues. Dreyfus, the Great War, Vichy, May 1968, and so forth. Each time, he explains, is another attempt at effacement, and each time, the same failure results. Another work was published on these questions, titled "Oublier nos crimes: L'amnésie nationale: une spécificité française?" (Forgetting our Crimes: Is National Amnesia a French Particularity?), in which Dimitri Nicolaïdis brings together thinkers from diverse intellectual backgrounds in an attempt to address the issue set out for them.[57] However, for the most part, they did not venture outside of their own fields of research (the colonies, the camps, cinema, Vendée, textbooks, archives, the French-German relationship, communism, for example); Dimitri Nicolaïdis's foreword—"La nation, les crimes et la mémoire"[58]—and Alain Brossat's and Hélène Dupuy's texts ("A l'heure du consensus" and "Aux origines du mythe," respectively)[59] are the only ones to define a new field of reflection constituted by "memory" as a duty, a place, a subject, and a conflict, selective but also multidimensional, official, or "rebellious." Memory is no longer a topic, at least not only a topic, of state commemoration; it has also become a space of debate, a malleable material that raises questions.[60]

Conflict over memory is certainly not new to French society,[61] beginning with the commune—with the first texts voted in the National Assembly in

March 1879 and July 1880—and continuing up until the case of Algeria and the Gaullist (1962, 1964, 1966, 1968) and socialist (1982) amnesties. Indeed, it has become axiomatic that there is no identity without memory;"[62] that is why most memory conflicts are first and foremost identity conflicts (rarely conflicts on historical fact, with the notable and extreme exception of historical revisionists toward the Shoah), which call into question our notions of the nation, the social bond, and the societal image we wish to project (such as the place of minorities in the collective space). And, although memory is at once immaterial and tangible (monuments, films, commemorations, and so forth), it is above all a mental representation and, as such, the media plays a central role.

More than two decades later, it is in a sense appropriate to wonder if the imaginary dimension has overtaken the discursive dimension. From that perspective, we agree with the idea that there is no spontaneous memory (Pierre Nora), but rather only constructed memories. To be sure, memory is a response to a need, but it is also inscribed in a process of production that functions according to an obvious power relation. Lucine Endelstein and Abdelkader Hamadi have pointed out, for example, that "the way we select national celebrations is a testament to a desire for the past not to undermine our present time."[63] Their conclusions are explicit: "At stake in the duty of remembering is the legitimacy of the present and a preparation for the future: for those reasons, memory is an object of conflict and of manipulation. Indeed, there is no such thing as a unified memory; rather, there are memory-based confrontations that are the result of the plurality of groups composing our societies."[64] That mechanism is the work and strategic issue of the media, which is alone capable of presenting a memory for public debate.

For Dimitri Nicolaïdis, this new "situation," in which the media acts as driving force, has exploded the "traditional narrative," but without (for the moment) offering a new version, thereby yielding in the meantime an "unbound search for truth."[65] In such a framework, we would "resort to memory" and "no longer look at history from an interpretive distance in order to give it meaning," and from that point on, "the past [would] manifest itself within the present, making the historian's bird's-eye-view less natural than before."[66]

The situation is no doubt even more complicated today. Memory has since "crushed" history. How could that not have created "confusion"? For Sylvie Thénault, "excluding historians from the past" makes little sense.[67] To that extent, Dimitri Nicolaïdis' assertion that the effects of memory might create a "fragmented memory" makes perfect sense, in that each group adheres to "its own truth," which in turn would necessarily lead to violent conflict.[68] Meanwhile, the state sets a tone with official commemorations that often prove to be rather conservative. Patrick Garcia recalls several examples: Victor Hugo in

1985, the Capetian millennial and the French Revolution in 1989, Clovis in 1996, and so forth.[69] Such "great moments" (not always capturing the attention of the media), with their missions and committees, have a "memory-ideology"[70] that is relatively static and incapable of attending to new expectations and social demands. The most recent commemorations are revealing: May 10th was established for remembering slavery and its abolition, June 8th was designated for "paying homage to those who died for France in Indochina" (Decree no. 2005-547, 26 May 2005), June 18th for General de Gaulle's radio appeal to the French people to resist the Nazi occupation (Decree no. 2006-313, 10 March 2006), September 25th to pay "homage to the *harkis*" (Decree no. 2003, 31 March 2003), and December 5th "for those who died during the Algerian War and the battles in Morocco and Tunisia" (Decree no. 2003-925, 26 September 2003). The state's memory, which may seem out of sync with the times, is attempting to establish a *memorial line,* in order to prevent chaos.

The disjunction between the official history (an expression of our national specificity and legacies from the past) and new expectations has created conflict. The media have contributed to the process by accelerating and amplifying "crises." There has also been an acceleration in the transition from one crisis to the next, creating the sensation (fifteen years later) that memory wars are ubiquitous. This phenomenon is not new, but it has become more visible. And, read thusly, one has the feeling that "French history has become a succession of internal conflicts, perhaps even a perpetuation, in various forms, of a single civil war."[71]

In that context, recent memory wars seem to have entered the present space and the sphere of debate too early. Ahmed Boubeker has explained that immigration has therefore become imprisoned by a vision of the nation operating in a context in which history is overly preoccupied with the "national" and that does not pay much attention to the "margins," and is therefore incapable of accounting for what he has described as emerging "memories of immigration."[72]

Why a "Memory War"?

More than thirty years after the publication of *Vingtième siècle*'s issue on "Franco-French Wars" and twenty years after Daniel Lindenberg's and Dimitri Nicolaïdis's articles, and with former president Nicolas Sarkozy's statements during the 2007 presidential campaign and his subsequent election in mind, it seems as though we are experiencing an amplified version of what was described back then. Some conflicts have become more difficult to "pacify"[73] (colonization, for instance), which has therefore intensified the context. Daniel Lindenberg sought to take on a veritable "work of memory," underlining "the efforts that remain to be accomplished if we want to get beyond the lies undermining civil peace."[74] In turn, as we saw earlier, Dimitri Nicolaïdis pointed to the work of memory accomplished with respect to Vichy and the Shoah, noting important books and films, and the pioneering role of a new generation of intellectual Jews and particularly their pedagogical struggle. Those memory movements led to well-publicized trials against Touvier, Barbie, and Papon, as well as to lawsuits against negationists, and even solemn words pronounced by President Jacques Chirac."[75]

Can that model serve as an example for the range of conflicts affecting today's society? Daniel Lindenberg noted the "risks" inherent to such an approach, citing the example of "Jewish memory," which could lead to exclusivism and intolerance today, as the republican memory did in the past. His reference to the Puy du Fou—a medieval historical theme park—is also relevant if we consider the power of the media today, and the fact that this theme park welcomes millions of visitors each year thanks to "voluntary" engagement and public subsidies.

Daniel Lindenberg concluded that "memory has now taken on the role of representing the future as an instance of legitimation," and, today we are confronted with a "frenzy of memory," which runs the risk of "emptying the notion of national memory," one of the "cornerstones of the Republican contract."[76] He suggests we adopt a collective memory that can suit and encompass everyone (is that even possible?), striking a balance between the quality and impartiality of what is contained therein. According to him, even the best-intentioned bearers of memory run the risk of providing ammunition to some (he refuses to use the word *communities* or to speak of factionalism) and their "mediocre power strategies."

Daniel Lindenberg's landmark text leaves us at an impasse. To be sure, memory can be used in such a way as to force the state and institutions to break long silences and reconsider voluntary instances of forgetting, but, at the same time, the multiplication of memory claims seems also to jeopardize the "collective memory."[77] Perhaps it is the state's role, as a last resort, to synthesize conflicting memories and build awareness that the "time of silence" is over, signaling the beginning of the "time of forgiveness."[78]

A utopia? Yes, in the sense that the state seems to be cornered into action after a long period of resistance (as in the case of the amnesty laws with respect to Algeria after over forty years). But if instead we look at what has been happening over the past fifteen years, then the answer is no. The state has been "digesting" conflicting memories in more or less subtle ways (for example, on the theme of colonialism in the speech Nicolas Sarkozy delivered in Dakar in 2007,[79] or Jacques Chirac's words on colonization in Paris in 1995 and again in Madagascar in 2005), has maintained memorial policies (Péronne for the

Great War, Caen for the Second World War, Marseille for France Overseas, and the project for a museum of French history at the Invalides), has involved the law (the Taubira law on slavery, the slave trade, and its abolition, and the law of February 2005 on "positive colonization"), and, in some cases, it has anticipated the pillars of a "policy of official memory" (as when the CNHI was installed in the former *Palais des Colonies de la Porte dorée* or in the case of the project for the Official Foundation on the Algerian War).

Even if the word frightens republican France, all of these *communautés* (communities), groups, and collectivities need to be able to recognize their past. Those who express a longing to return to their countries of "origin" are also expressing feelings of exclusion from French society and a need to claim a place in the public space.[80] They have been excluded from history (or they perceive themselves to be), as the state merely represents "history's winners." For Henry Rousso, the phenomenon is a kind of "reappropriation of a past, of a specific history that is considered singular and distinct from general history—for instance, in the case of national history."[81] Françoise Vergès has railed against "reducing these practices and modes of thought to identity claims" that signal a "communitarian approach to the national narrative, as if these experiences [in the case of slavery, for example] only concerned the descendants of slaves; that history, however, is an integral part of the national history."[82]

The danger, therefore, lies in the possibility that such claims remain relegated to the specific groups they represent, never becoming a part of a shared memory. As an example, one might think of the *Indigènes de la République* (the Natives of the Republic), who, basing themselves on the fact of colonial heritage, have built an ethnic memory that has become increasingly racial, or of the Puy du Fou theme park, which turns counterrevolutionary memory into a consumable product that offers "tourists/history buffs" a new framework for reading French history. However, those are exceptions on the chess board that is memory in France. Another danger is that the state begins to instrumentalize these memories.[83] As an explicit precaution, Claude Lanzmann—filmmaker, author of *Shoah*, and editor of the journal *Les Temps modernes*—reacted against the pronouncements of Nicolas Sarkozy when he declared that we must be wary of all "memorial activism that seems, with each upsurge, to rediscover once again what we have already known for a long time"; for him, such memorializing "works to open up secondary paths that lead to forgetting more than they do to memory."[84]

On the one hand, each group has its own form of "suffering," and on the other, there is the sentiment that history is under siege and that national identity is in danger. But let us not forget that the state, as an assembly of territorial collectivities, fashions memory through its policies, its strategies, and its territorial funding. Dialogue is becoming increasingly difficult and the cohabitation between various memories conflictual, including with respect to monuments that are meant to "pacify" groups. For Catherine Brice, for example, "recuperating or abolishing a monument has become an important point of tension in the *memory wars*."[85] And although symbols can be assembled for a ceremony, in the end they tend to become a source of division, with the public becoming more and more sensitive to their potential meaning. In addition, the populace is often unaware of the history of the statues populating our big—and less big—cities. Today, we are less interested in digging up the past than in understanding its effects and continued, evolving impact. It is at this stage that the effects of memory become confused and we become troubled by what Paul Ricœur describes as the "disturbing spectacle of an overabundance of memory in some areas and the overabundance of forgetting in others, which is to say nothing of the influence that commemorations have and the ways in which memory—and forgetting—are abused."[86]

However, even if it might seem paradoxical, this conflict has helped "awaken consciences" and has been a source of "vitality."[87] Still, some reject this "slavery" toward the past (most notably Henry Rousso), and question whether it makes sense to force an entire society to remain so fixated on the past. For others, the issue lies instead in the need to "get beyond memory wars, in which each group has its own truth, and build a shared narrative—that is the historian's true work."[88]

Such a relationship toward the past is a complex and natural process that opposes the state and "relegated memories," the group and the collectivity, the individual and the group, and so forth, and at a time when modes of communication have become such that everyone is capable of organizing his or her own memorial *trajectory*. Time also plays a role in the process. Distance from the past allows for either the resurgence of memory or the institutionalization of forgetting. In some circumstances, wars can die down if there are no fighters; however, new soldiers, either those who have inherited old conflicts from past generations or people from previous generations, can give them renewed life. We have seen that process at work with the "sons and daughters of the deported," and more recently with the "Appel des Indigènes de la République" and the association "Devoirs de mémoires;" the notion of memory can be transgenerational and it can exert new forms of pressure onto the present.

The "militant" fight for recognition for "October 17, 1961," the memory of the 1917 rebellions,[89] and the memory of "heroes" who fought the slave trade demonstrate the multiple ways in which memory seeks present-day outlets of expression and understanding. October 1961 is a cause for second and third generation Maghrebi immigrants, those for whom the march of 1983 did not offer sufficient "national recognition;" they therefore seek recognition for their martyred "fathers." The search for anti–slave trade heroes has become a focal point for "black identity," notably with the 1992 protests against ceremonies commemorating the "discovery" of the Americas, the march of May 23, 1998, and the Taubira law of May 2001 (a process that has been accompanied by growing movements in coastal cities such as Nantes and Bordeaux in response to memory-related projects in their municipalities).[90] Memorializations of the 1917 revolts demonstrate an effort to (re)construct the feeling of national unity that "might have existed" during the Great War by associating *all* the "protagonists" in a "common memory."

These very different examples all show in their own way what is at stake. Here—as in the Dreyfus affair and the army's "mental block"—it is clear that "identity-based groups" are not the only players. The state itself may be a "warmonger" through its erection of walls and its wariness toward potential claims on the past. The law of February 2005 is the most obvious legislative example of that type of strategy; until then, the state had had no part of the CNHI museum, which is to date the most accomplished mobilization of a collective memory on immigration;[91] meanwhile, Guy Môquet's letter and the Bercy speech of April 2007 against May 1968 are surprising political symbols within the political sphere and are reflective of wars that had seemed "pacified."[92] The official tributes for Aimé Césaire and the insertion of the topic of the slave trade into the curriculum (a legal requirement, but one that has been poorly enforced ever since the passage of the Taubira Law in 2001), much like the idea that elementary school students ought to learn about deported Jewish children, shows the extent to which the state can play a central role in issues of memory. Wars die down if there are no fighters, just as wars need rival camps in order to emerge on the center stage of the media and resonate with French society. It can also be a "sign" that one addresses to one's constituents, to one's militants, and to one's electors.

Franco-French wars have started to become increasingly international. The process by which memory has become globalized finds its roots in the intersection of the memory of the Shoah with its co-optation (or *nationalization*, according to some thinkers) by the United States, with the creation of a federal museum of the Holocaust (1995) on European genocide, a somewhat paradoxical engagement with a history many perceived as somewhat "disconnected" from American society.[93]

Wars are becoming increasingly globalized and are beginning to resemble one another more and more. Slavery, Nazism, colonization, the end of dictatorships: they are all considered within a "planetary movement," and the expectations for memorialization are becoming increasingly similar.[94] Public policy, be it in France, Europe, Asia, or the United States, is becoming more and more sensitive to the globalization of memory: "Across the planet, nations are being confronted with concurrent and alternative visions of the past that call into question the traditional domination of national histories."[95]

Beyond what are often overly national or instrumentalized explanations of the past (France might encounter a "weakening" of its "national identity"), and beyond overly ethnic explanations (the rise of "community-based identity"), it is important to note that many groups have begun to "speak out" and "offer historical narratives that tend to reject not only national histories but also an important part of scholarly history."[96] More and more, we are seeing conflicts between "legitimate histories" and the "official history." This new context has resulted in a breakdown of "traditional borders between researchers, politicians, activists, and other players."[97] The risk? That we erase the borders between the past and the present, that we legislate the past, and that "victims" become ubiquitous in the various histories being constructed.

From this perspective, the media have become the sounding board for these debates. They even go so far as to provide a stage for conflict. On the one hand, there is the pressure of public opinion (the famous social demand) and on the other there are the "guardians of knowledge" (the institutions of the past); the media situate themselves between these two poles of history and memory. For instance, a special report in *Le Monde 2* magazine published in 2006, titled "Colonies: Un débat français" (Colonies: A French Debate) suggests we examine the "French malaise" when it comes to the intersection of history and "memories." The report is a sign that times are changing and that the "social demand" is imposing changes and "reactions."

Moreover, beginning in their letter to readers, the editorial staff emphasized the importance of this work for the classroom and for teachers:

> Let us imagine a teacher giving a class on the history of the colonies in a French middle school. Who are her or his students? One is the grandson of a *harki*, another the descendant of a former Algerian colonial. The grandfather of another is an Algerian immigrant living in France, once a militant independentist during the Algerian War. Others come from a West Indian background. Some are the descendants of slaves. Still others of Bretons, Corsicans . . . there are also French youth with Senegalese or Vietnamese backgrounds. How is the educator to broach the question of slavery's history, or those of colonization and decolonization?[98]

The journalist is frank in his choice of words when he describes the present context, this "diverse presence," which has saved the debate from forgetting: "It was with our history teachers in mind that we conceived of this special report on the colonies for *Le Monde 2* . . . in order to take stock of this very French debate."

Six months earlier, from another perspective, *Le Nouvel Observateur* put out a special issue on "La vérité sur la colonisation" (The Truth about Colonization). Their message was clear: it is time to "put an end to partisan caricatures and misleading forms of nostalgia."[99] Here, the project attempted to recast the debate with a focus on the past and issues of time, and it offered a dynamic perspective on how to approach the colonial past. This special report also prepared the reader to look at how the colonial past affects the present, and it allowed researchers to find an echo of the work they had been doing—often with modest means—within the expression of public opinion.

In the media, "conflicts of memory" are becoming visible, with each group choosing its camp. In counterpoint to previous discursive practices, *Le Point* published a special report in May 2008 titled "Quand l'Algérie était française" (When Algeria Was French), and with a subheading, "Le numéro souvenir de la saga pied-noir" (The Souvenir Edition of the Saga of the Pieds-Noirs).[100] Despite the inclusion of an article by Benjamin Stora, the leading authority on Algerian history, and a survey on May 8, 1945, the general tone of the issue was illustrative of an "anachronistic memory" (situating itself somewhere between obvious historic assertions and nostalgia for a lost era). The media therefore revealed the various stakes of an issue within every social stratum of French society, including among historians.

History cannot ignore memory conflicts. It is in some ways reliant on such conflicts, if also perhaps a prisoner to them. Historians should not fear entering the arena and making a place for themselves in the media. True democracies give all stakeholders a voice in an immense forum; they encourage collective and public debate on the past. Is that not a condition of social cohesion, both for the present and the future? The relationship between communication, memory, and history, at a time when the mirage of "national identity" has yet again become an urgent question, is one of the major issues of our time. A global issue, it is media related, and it is also an important question for citizens. Understanding the mechanisms and enduring structures is a precursor to intervening in this complex dynamic. It allows one to be vigilant in preventing memory from becoming co-opted for political ends; it also allows history to exist beyond the purview of the university and that of professional historians.

Pascal Blanchard is a historian and researcher at the Laboratoire Communication et Politique (Paris, France, CNRS), codirector of the ACHAC Research Group, and a documentary filmmaker. He is a specialist on the colonial question in France, contemporary French history and immigration, and author, coauthor, editor, or coeditor of *Human Zoos: Science and Spectacle in the Age of Colonial Empires* (2008), *Human Zoos. The Invention of the Savage* (2011), *Zoos humains et exhibitions coloniales: 150 ans d'inventions de l'autre* (2011), *Colonial Culture in France since the Revolution* (2014), *La France arabo-orientale* (2013), *Les années 30 sont de retour: Petite leçon d'histoire pour comprendre les crises* (2014), *Le Grand Repli* (2015), and *Vers la guerre des identités* (2016).

Isabelle Veyrat-Masson is Research Director at the CNRS and responsible for the Laboratoire Communication et Politique. Her work focuses on media studies and she is coeditor of the journal *Le temps des médias*. Notable publications and coedited volumes include *Quand la télévision explore le temps: L'histoire au petit écran, 1953–2000* (2000), *Télévision et histoire: La confusion des genres: Docudramas, docufictions et fictions du réel* (2008), *Les guerres de mémoires: La France et son histoire* (2008), *Nos histoires parallèles: Entretiens avec Isabelle Veyrat-Masson* (2011), *Médias et élections: La campagne présidentielle de 2007 et sa réception* (2011), and *Histoire de la télévision française de 1935 à nos jours* (2012).

Notes

1. Maurice Halbwachs, *La mémoire collective* (Paris: PUF, 1950) and *Les cadres sociaux de la mémoire* (Paris: PUF, 1952).

2. Pierre Nora, ed., *Les lieux de mémoire* (Paris: Gallimard, 1997). Similarly, it is important to mention Philippe Joutard's pioneering work, *Les canisards* (Paris: Julliard, 1980).

3. Pierre Vidal-Naquet, *Assassins of Memory: Essays on the Denial of the Holocaust*, trans. Jeffrey Mehlman (New York: Columbia University Press, 1992).

4. See for example Henry Rousso, *The Haunting Past: History, Memory, and Justice in Contemporary France*, trans. Ralph Schoolcraft (Philadelphia: University of Pennsylvania Press, 2002).

5. Enzo Traverso, *Le passé, mode d'emploi: Histoire, mémoire, politique* (Paris: La Fabrique Éditions, 2005) and "L'écrit-événement: L'historiographie comme champ de bataille politique," in *Les guerres de mémoires: La France et son histoire*, ed. Pascal Blanchard and Isabelle Veyrat-Masson (Paris: La Découverte, 2008), 220–229.

6. Halbwachs, *La mémoire collective*. See also Jacques Le Goff, *Histoire et mémoire* (Paris: Gallimard, 1988), Marie-Claire Lavabre, "Usages du passé, usages de la mémoire," *Revue française de science politique* 44, no. 3 (June 1994): 480–493, and Paul Ricœur, *La Mémoire, l'histoire, l'oubli* (Paris: Seuil, 2000).

7. See Traverso, *Le Passé, mode d'emploi*, and François Bédarida, *Histoire, critique et responsabilité* (Brussels: IHTP-CNRS/Complexe, 2003).

8. See Patrick H. Hutton, *History as an Art of Memory* (Hanover, NH, and London: University Press of New England, 1993) and Jacques Heers, *L'histoire assassinée: Les pièges de la mémoire* (Paris: Éditions de Paris, 2006).

9. For a concrete example, see Pierre Barral, "L'affaire d'Oradour, affrontement de deux mémoires," in *Mémoire de la Seconde Guerre mondiale: actes du colloque de Metz*, ed. Alfred Wahl (Metz: Centre de Recherche "Histoire et Civilisation de l'Europe Occidentale," 1984), 243–252.

10. Philippe Petit, interviewed by Henry Rousso, *La Hantise du passé* (Paris: Textuel, 1998), 36.

11. Isabelle Veyrat-Masson, *Quand la télévision explore le temps: L'histoire au petit écran (1953–2000)* (Paris: Fayard, 2000).

12. Philippe Petit, *La Hantise du passé.*

13. See Isabelle Veyrat-Masson, "Les guerres de mémoires à la télévision: Du dévoilement à l'accompagnement," in *Les guerres de mémoires*, ed. Blanchard and Veyrat-Masson, 273–286.

14. Pascal Bruckner, *The Tears of the White Man: Compassion as Contempt*, trans. William Beer (New York: Free Press, 1986), and Jean-Noël Jeanneney and Monique Sauvage, eds., *Télévision, nouvelle mémoire: Les magazines de grand reportage de 1959 à 1968* (Paris: Seuil/INA, 1982).

15. Pascal Bruckner, *La Tyrannie de la pénitence: Essai sur le masochisme occidental* (Paris: Grasset, 2006); Paul Aussaresses, *Pour la France: Services spéciaux 1942–1954* (Paris: Éditions du Rocher, 2001), *Services spéciaux, Algérie 1955–1957* (Paris: Perrin, 2001) and *Je n'ai pas tout dit: Ultimes révélations au service de la France* (Paris: Éditions du Rocher, 2008); Pierre Péan, *Une jeunesse française: François Mitterrand 1934–1947* (Paris: Fayard, 1994) and *Noires fureurs, blancs menteurs: Rwanda 1990–1994* (Paris: Fayard/Mille et une Nuits, 2005).

16. Maryline Crivello, "Comment on revit l'histoire: Sur les reconstitutions historiques 1976–2000," *La Pensée du Midi* 3 (Winter 2000): 69–74; Patrick Garcia, *Le Bicentenaire de la Révolution française: Pratiques sociales d'une commémoration* (Paris: CNRS Éditions, 2000); Gérard Namer, *Batailles pour la mémoire: La commémoration en France de 1945 à nos jours* (Paris: Papyrus, 1983). See also Institut d'Histoire du Temps Présent, *La mémoire des Français: Quarante ans de commémorations de la Seconde Guerre mondiale* (Paris: CNRS Éditions, 1986).

17. Jean El Gammal, "La révolution française: Mémoire et controverses," in *Les guerres de mémoires*, ed. Blanchard and Veyrat-Masson, 63–70.

18. Vincent Duclert, "L'affaire Dreyfus: De l'affrontement des mémoires à la reconnaissance de l'histoire," in *Les guerres de mémoires*, ed. Blanchard and Veyrat-Masson, 74.

19. See Veyrat-Masson, "Les guerres de mémoires à la télévision: du dévoilement à l'accompagnement," in *Les guerres de mémoires*, ed. Blanchard and Veyrat-Masson, 273–286.

20. See Dominique Poulot, "Musées et guerres de mémoires: Pédagogie et frustration mémorielle," in *Les guerres de mémoires*, ed. Blanchard and Veyrat-Masson, 230–240.

21. See Traverso, "L'écrit-événement: L'historiographie comme champ de bataille politique," in *Les guerres de mémoires*, ed. Blanchard and Veyrat-Masson.

22. See Louise Merzeau, "Guerres de mémoire *on line*: Un nouvel enjeu stratégique," in *Les guerres de mémoires*, ed. Blanchard and Veyrat-Masson, 287–298; and Gilles Boëtsch, "L'université et la recherche face aux enjeux de mémoire: Le temps des mutations," in *Les guerres de mémoires*, ed. Blanchard and Veyrat-Masson, 187–198.

23. Serge Barcellini, "L'état républicain, acteur de mémoire: Des morts pour la France aux morts à cause de la France," in *Les guerres de mémoires*, ed. Blanchard and Veyrat-Masson, 209–219.

24. See Benoît Falaize and Françoise Lantheaume, "Entre pacification et reconnaissance: Les manuels scolaires et les concurrences des mémoires," in *Les guerres de mémoires*, ed. Blanchard and Veyrat-Masson, 177–186.

25. See for example *Les historiens et le travail de mémoire*, special issue of *Esprit*, 266 (August–September 2000); François Hartog, *Evidence de l'histoire: Ce que voient les historiens* (Paris: Gallimard, 2007); and Jean-Clément Martin, *La guerre civile entre histoire et mémoire* (Nantes: Ouest-France Éditions, 1995).

26. Jean Leduc and Patrick Garcia, *L'enseignement de l'histoire en France de l'Ancien Régime à nos jours* (Paris: Armand Colin, 2003).

27. Marc Ferro, Pascal Blanchard, and Isabelle Veyrat Masson, *Les guerres de mémoires dans le monde* (Paris: CNRS, 2008).

28. See Valérie-Barbara Rosoux, *Les usages de la mémoire dans les relations internationales: Le recours au passé dans la polique étrangère de la France à l'égard de l'Allemagne et de l'Algérie, de 1962 à nos jours* (Brussels: Bruylant, 2001).

29. Bogumil Jewsiewicki and Jocelyn Létourneau, eds., *L'histoire en partage: Usages et mises en discours du passé* (Paris: L'Harmattan, 1996).

30. Jean-Clément Martin and Charles Suaud, *Le Puy du Fou, en Vendée, l'histoire mise en scène* (Paris: L'Harmattan, 1996).

31. Nicolas Offenstadt, "Poilus et fusillés: Les erreurs de Marianne," December 6, 2012, https://blogs.mediapart.fr/edition/usages-et-mesusages-de-lhistoire/article/061212/poilus-et-fusilles-les-erreurs-de-maria.

32. Bernard Pudal, "Le communisme français: Mémoires défaites et mémoires victorieuses depuis 1989," in *Les guerres de mémoires*, ed. Blanchard and Veyrat-Masson, 119.

33. Olivier Wieviorka, "Francisque ou Croix de Lorraine: Les années sombres entre histoire, mémoire et mythologie," in *Les guerres de mémoires*, ed. Blanchard and Veyrat-Masson, 94–106.

34. Paul Schor, "L'instrumentalisation des historiens est inacceptable," *Le Monde*, October 4, 2007.

35. See for example François Dosse, *L'histoire en miettes* (Paris: La Découverte, 1994).

36. Benjamin Stora, "Préface: La France et 'ses' guerres de mémoires," in *Les guerres de mémoires*, ed. Blanchard and Veyrat-Masson, 7–13.

37. Jean-Pierre Azéma, "Cessez de jouer avec les mémoires," *Libération*, May 10, 2006.

38. Gilles Manceron, "Ne jouons pas avec les mémoires!," *Libération*, May 25, 2006.

39. Robert Frank, "La mémoire empoisonnée," in *La France des armées noires*, ed. Jean-Pierre Azéma and François Bédarida (Paris: Seuil, 1993), 544–576.

40. Jean-Michel Chaumont, *La concurrence des victimes: Génocide, identité et reconnaissance* (Paris: La Découverte, 1997).

41. See Merzeau, "Guerres de mémoires *on line*," in *Les guerres de mémoires*, ed. Blanchard and Veyrat-Masson, 287–298.

42. Reinhart Koselleck, *Le Futur passé: Contribution à la sémantique des temps historiques* (Paris: Éditions de l'EHESS, 1990).

43. Traverso, *Le passé, mode d'emploi*, 63.

44. Philippe Artières and Michelle Zancarini-Fournel, "De mai, souviens-toi de ce qu'il te plaît: Mémoire des années 68," in *Les guerres de mémoires*, ed. Blanchard and Veyrat-Masson, 131.

45. Louis Bodin, ed., *Les guerres franco-françaises, Vingtième Siècle: Revue d'histoire* 5, no. 1 (January–March 1985).

46. Benjamin Stora, *La guerre des mémoires: La France face à son passé colonial* (La Tour d'Aigues: Éditions de L'Aube, 2007).

47. Daniel Lindenberg, "Guerres de mémoire en France," *Vingtième siècle: Revue d'histoire* 42, no. 1 (April–June 1994): 77–96.

48. Mohand Hamoumou, *Et ils sont devenus harkis* (Paris: Fayard, 1993).

49. Charles-Robert Ageron, "Le drame des harkis en 1962," *Vingtième siècle: Revue d'histoire* 42, no. 1 (April–June 1994): 6.

50. Benjamin Stora, "Mohand Hamoumou, *Et ils sont devenus harkis*," *Vingtième Siècle: Revue d'histoire*, vol. 42, no. 1 (April-June 1994), 144.

51. Daniel Lefeuvre, *Pour en finir avec la repentance coloniale* (Paris: Flammarion, 2006).

52. Lindenberg, "Guerres de mémoire en France."

53. Yosef Hayim Yerushalmi, *Zakhor* (Paris: La Découverte, 1984).

54. See Emmanuel Terray, "Le grand ménage des mémoires," *Libération*, January 3, in which the author denounces what he sees as a "major house cleaning of our memories."

55. Lindenberg, "Guerres de mémoire en France," 79.

56. For more information on this situation, see Pudal, "Le communisme français: Mémoires défaites et mémoires victorieuses depuis 1989," in *Les guerres de mémoires*, ed. Blanchard and Veyrat-Masson.

57. Dimitri Nicolaïdis, ed., *Oublier nos crimes: L'amnésie nationale: une spécifité française* (Paris: Éditions Autrement, 1994). Contributors included Benjamin Stora, Alain Brossat, Suzanne Citron, François Bédarida, Sonia Combe, Hélène Dupuy, Alfred Grosser, Anne Grynberg, Jean-Martin Clément, Alain Ruscio, and Pierre Vidal-Naquet.

58. Nicolaïdis, "La nation, les crimes et la mémoire," in *Oublier nos crimes*, ed. Nicolaïdis, 4–25.

59. Alain Brossat, "À l'heure du consensus," in *Oublier nos crimes*, ed. Nicolaïdis, 228–240 and Hélène Dupuy, "Aux origines du mythe," in *Oublier nos crimes*, ed. Nicolaïdis, 131–144.

60. See Gérard Namer, *Batailles pour la mémoire* and *Batailles pour la mémoire: La commémoration en France de 1945 à nos jours* (Paris: Papyrus, 1983); Jean Leclant, "Les célébrations nationales: Une institution culturelle," *Le Débat* 3, no. 105 (1999): 185–187.

61. See Nicolaïdis, ed., *Oublier nos crimes*, and Gérard Noiriel, *A quoi sert 'l'identité nationale'* (Marseille: Agone, 2007).

62. See for example Tzvetan Todorov, *Les abus de la mémoire* (Paris: Arléa, 1995).

63. Lucine Endelstein and Abdelkader Hamadi, "Le devoir de mémoire et ses enjeux," in *Mémoires Plurielles, Cinéma et Images: Lieux de Memoire?*, ed. Claudie Le Bissonnais, (Paris: Créaphis, 2007), 7.

64. Ibid., 8.

65. Nicolaïdis, "La nation, les crimes et la mémoire," in *Oublier nos crimes*, ed. Nicolaïdis, 10.

66. Ibid., 11.

67. Sylvie Thénault, Interview with Rosa Moussaoui, "Contre les manipulations de l'histoire," *L'Humanité*, October 5, 2007.

68. Nicolaïdis, "La nation, les crimes et la mémoire," in *Oublier nos crimes*, ed. Nicolaïdis, 11.

69. Garcia, *Le bicentenaire de la révolution française*.

70. Nora, ed., *Les lieux de mémoire*.

71. Nicolaïdis, "La Nation, les crimes et la mémoire," in *Oublier nos crimes*, ed. Nicolaïdis, 12.

72. Ahmed Boubeker, "L'immigration: Enjeux d'histoire et de mémoire à l'aube du xxie siècle," in *Les guerres de mémoires*, ed. Blanchard and Veyrat-Masson, 165–174.

73. Antoine Raybaud, "Deuil sans travail, travail sans deuil: La France a-t-elle une mémoire coloniale?," *Dédale* 5–6 (1997): 87–104.

74. Lindenberg, "Guerres de mémoire en France," 93.

75. See Olivier Wieviorka, "Francisque ou Croix de Lorraine: Les années sombres entre histoire, mémoire et mythologie," in *Les guerres de mémoires*, ed. Blanchard and Veyrat-Masson, 94–106. Jean-François Theullot has taken a very different approach, *De l'inexistence d'un devoir de mémoire* (Paris: Pleins Feux, 2005), much in the same way as Olivier Lalieu, "L'invention du devoir de mémoire," *Vingtième siècle: Revue d'histoire* 69, no. 1 (January–March 2001): 83–94.

76. Lindenberg, "Guerres de mémoire en France," 94.

77. Jean-Claude Métraux, *Deuils collectifs et création sociale* (Paris: La Dispute, 2004).

78. See Académie universelle des cultures, *Pourquoi se souvenir?* (Paris: Grasset, 1999); Sandrine Lefranc, *Politiques du pardon* (Paris: PUF, 2002); and Sandrine Lefranc, ed., *Après le conflit, la réconciliation?* (Paris: Michel Houdiard, 2007).

79. For more on this speech, see Nicolas Bancel and Pascal Blanchard, "La colonisation: Du débat sur la guerre d'Algérie au discours de Dakar," in *Les guerres de mémoires*, ed. Blanchard and

Veyrat-Masson, 137–154; and Makhily Gassama, ed., *L'Afrique répond à Sarkozy: Contre le discours de Dakar* (Paris: Éditions Philippe Rey, 2008).

80. See Esther Benbassa, "À qui sert la guerre des mémoires?," in *Les guerres de mémoires*, ed. Blanchard and Veyrat-Masson, 252–261.

81. Rousso, *La Hantise du passé*, 31.

82. Françoise Vergès, "Esclavage colonial: Quelles mémoires? Quels héritages?," in *Les guerres de mémoires*, ed. Blanchard and Veyrat-Masson, 161.

83. See Gilles Manceron, "La loi: Régulateur ou acteur des guerres de mémoires?," in *Les guerres de mémoires*, ed. Blanchard and Veyrat-Masson, 241–251.

84. Claude Lanzmann, "Le mort saisit le vif," *Le Monde*, February 18, 2008.

85. Catherine Brice, "Monuments: Pacificateurs ou agitateurs de mémoire," in *Les guerres de mémoires*, ed. Blanchard and Veyrat-Masson, 208.

86. Ricœur, *La Mémoire, l'histoire, l'oubli*, 1.

87. Annette Wieviorka, "Le Vél' d'Hiv': Histoire d'une commémoration," *Autrement* 54 (1999): 163.

88. François Gèze, cited by Marc Semo, "La repentance vue par les historiens," *Libération*, December 5, 2007.

89. Nicolas Offenstadt, *Les fusillés de la Grande Guerre et la mémoire collective, 1914–1999* (Paris: Odile Jacob, 2002).

90. See Vergès, "Esclavage colonial: Quelles mémoires? Quels héritages?," in *Les guerres de mémoires*, ed. Blanchard and Veyrat-Masson, 155–164.

91. On the context and emergence of a potential "memory war" regarding the issue of immigration, see Boubeker, "L'immigration: Enjeux d'histoire et de mémoire à l'aube du xxie siècle," in *Les guerres de mémoires*, ed. Blanchard and Veyrat-Masson.

92. See Artières and Zancarini-Fournel, "De mai, souviens-toi de ce qu'il te plaît: Mémoire des années 68," in *Les guerres de mémoires*, ed. Blanchard and Veyrat-Masson, 128–136.

93. See Peter Novick, *L'holocauste dans la vie américaine* (Paris: Gallimard, 2001).

94. Sandrine Lefranc, ed., *Après le conflit, la réconciliation? Actes révisés des journées d'étude organisées par l'institut des sciences sociales du politique* (Paris: Michel Houdiard Editeur, 2007).

95. Rousso, "Vers une mondialisation de la mémoire," *Vingtième siècle: Revue d'histoire* 94 (April–June 2007): 5.

96. Ibid., 4.

97. Ibid.

98. "Colonies. Un débat français," *Le Monde 2*, no. 86 (April–May 2006).

99. Claude Askolovitch, "La vérité sur la colonisation," *Nouvel Observateur*, no. 2144 (December 8–14, 2005): 12–14.

100. "Quand l'Algérie était française: Le numéro souvenir de la saga pied-noir," *Le Point*, no. 1862, May 22, 2008.

1.2. THE RETURN OF THE COLONIAL

7
THE ENEMY WITHIN
THE CONSTRUCTION OF THE "ARAB" IN THE MEDIA

Thomas Deltombe and Mathieu Rigouste

An analysis of print and televised media in France is key to understanding dominant representations of the figure of the "Arab" in France today. The term is used inconsistently, grounded as it is in a series of confused ideas and ambivalent attitudes surrounding a range of often interchangeable symbolic categories that include *immigrant, foreigner, Muslim, Islamist, banlieue youth,* and *terrorist.* In order to grasp the function and functioning of this semantic fog, one must look more carefully at how the "Arab" has been constructed (and reformulated through various discursive practices), beginning in the 1980s.

In order to do this, we have examined a broad range of articles and televised programs dealing with these themes, from the 1970s until the early years of the twenty-first century. Through a comparison of images and categories of language used, we have been able to track a number of variables and constants.[1] This has made it possible to retrace the steps that have culminated in a progressive movement toward an increasingly black and white portrayal of the Arab. The fractures evidenced in the process of opposing "true" and "false" French people, good and bad immigrants, moderate and radical Islam, assimilable and unassimilable groups, and those that are threatening and nonthreatening have become embodied over the past twenty years in stereotypical, recurring characters in the media.

If we dismantle the elements that compose the media's theatrics, in order to probe more deeply into the constant tension that exists between the images and discourse that nurture the production of alterity, we can begin to think the unthinkable, to say what goes left unsaid, and to extract what has heretofore been deeply buried. Our objective will be to show how the images of the "other," as they have been produced within French society, have been recast in such a way as to shape notions of sovereignty and politics.

Essentializing the Muslim Arab

"Will we still be French in thirty years?" *Le Figaro Magazine* asked its readers back in 1985.[2] The cover, which fosters the idea that French identity is under threat, features the bust of Marianne, the ultimate symbol of Frenchness, dressed in what at the time was called a *chador.* The *chador,* representing as it does a blend of religious and cultural stereotypes about Islam, is contrasted with that of the allegorical national symbol of Marianne, playing on the ambivalence between French identity and republican values. The message is rooted in "miscegenation," presented on this occasion as something that goes against nature, but perhaps more importantly implying that the circumstances evoking fear might actually happen.

Looking at media representations in the mid-1980s, one can trace the emergence of the Arab as a threat to French identity and its political regime. The hybrid figure of "Marianne in a *chador*" illustrates the potential of an image to resolve—or seemingly resolve—extremely complex messages through binary thinking. When security-based discourse was applied to issues of identity, clear messages founded on two specific ideas began to emerge, namely, that an enemy has one "nature," which threatens the very foundations of French identity, and then that the enemy must be suppressed if French identity is to be safeguarded.

The conception of an identity under threat in the face of alterity emerged when it became clear that "immigrants," who began to feature prominently in the media in the 1970s, were actually committed to staying in France, that they would inevitably become "French," and that it would therefore become legally impossible to differentiate them from other French people. By the late 1980s, the media had become obsessed with two related questions: Islam, in the aftermath of the first "Islamic headscarf" affair in Creil in 1989, and the *banlieue* housing projects with the "urban riots" in Vaulx-en-Velin in 1990. The twofold theme, in which nonracial language emerges in a logic of identity, soon became the dominant prism through which the media would address the "Arab presence" in France.

"Anti-Islamic arguments have long served as a convenient alibi, cloaking hatred for Arabs and a refusal to welcome Arabs in France in respectability," wrote Jacques Julliard, editorialist for the *Nouvel Observateur,* at the end of the Creil affair.[3] Yet, the *Nouvel Observateur* crusaded against the wearing of the *chador,* a debate which came to a brutal conclusion three months later when the Front National obtained an unprecedented number of votes in regional elections. The Creil affair therefore stands as one of the most obvious examples of this media focus, allowing for the construction of a range of reductive and oversimplified cultural, religious, economic, and social representations of the Arab, yielding the prototype of a menacing ethnic figure while also providing an alibi with which to formulate critiques.

The same observations can be made with respect to the media coverage of the *banlieues*: the territorialization of immigration, the development of a symbolic space for "Muslims" and "delinquents," and the use of the term *ghetto* provide symbolic and unspoken distance with respect to an ethnicized segment of the French population. The construction of the "Arab" therefore served as a response to the media's need for simplification and the production of fear with respect to security.

The Worm in the Fruit

The way in which the First Gulf War appeared in the media (1990–1991), through its portrayal of Arabs threatening France from outside French borders, redefined this issue as an international problem. The question was reformulated as follows: Does the presence of Arabs in France pose the same threat as Arabs abroad? In January 1991, a joint Sofres survey was conducted by France Inter, *L'Express*, and the television program "La marche du siècle," examining French people's opinions related to the different populations "present on French territory," and particularly as related to the conflict in the Middle East. Findings revealed how, with the principle of defense in mind, Arabs had become a homogenized group, with little to no differentiation between internal and external groups. The conclusion speaks for itself: "Domestic security is related to international security."

The findings of this survey were presented during a program on the television station FR3, including a series of background images that strangely resembled the Casbah of Algiers. Numbers flashed on the screen showing the "general opinion," the opinions of "Muslims in general," of "French Muslims," of "non-French Muslims," and of other "Maghrebi Muslims." Despite analyses provided by Olivier Duhamel, the presentation was an unscientific conceptual mess that was summed up clearly by the presenter of "La marche du siècle," Jean-Marie Cavada: "The war has led to a fracture between public opinion and Muslim-Arabs (French or not French): 68 percent of Muslims living in France are against the war, whereas 75 percent of the general population is for it. These two positions are almost diametrically opposed."[4]

Two definitions of French identity seem to coexist. One is broad and legal, and it is often explicitly quoted by journalists; it includes all nationals, regardless of their culture, religion, or the color of their skin. The other is more restrictive and is to be found in media discourse, particularly in its visual grammar that tends to symbolically exclude those who do not belong to the category of "pure French stock"—whom one naturally imagines corresponds to white, predominantly Christian populations who are instinctively faithful to the republican pact of separation of church and state. The opposition between these two definitions of French identity ends up positioning the Arab as simultaneously friend and foe, in other words someone who might very well betray the French or end up a natural accomplice to foreign enemies.

These conclusions come dangerously close to invoking a race war of sorts. The resurgence of a dichotomy between "people of pure French stock" and those who don't comfortably fit into that category was further compounded by two complementary changes that took place in the early 1990s: first, the emergence of a self-critical discourse within the media and the growing valorization of positive figures of "integration." The first change involved the development of techniques and spaces for "self-criticism"—mediators, sections in newspapers devoted to the media, and televised programs—which raised awareness of the "undesirable effects" of media coverage (particularly as they related to questions of identity) while also making it possible for the media to clear its conscience when it came to these issues and questions without actually having to transform its overall structure or, for that matter, the ideological framework underlying that structure's mode of functioning.

The second change, which had far wider implications, sought to reformulate the opposition between those "of pure French stock" and those who were "French through immigration" by contrasting "assimilated immigrants" and "unassimilated immigrants." A number of examples were used to bolster such dichotomies: that of the "educator who struggles against delinquency," of the "enlightened Imam who preaches a moderate Islam," or the "activist speaking out against anti-Semitism in the *banlieues.*" But in reality, these integration models only served to further stigmatize those who were "French through immigration" and who were therefore considered threats to French society, namely the "delinquents," "Islamic extremists," and other "terrorists."

Friend or Foe?

The attacks that occurred in 1995 solidified these two changes. Khaled Kelkal, the presumed coauthor of the attack on the Saint-Michel RER station, was described at once as an "Islamic terrorist born in Mostaganem in Algeria" and a "young delinquent from Vaulx-en-Velin" in France. The media was quick to remind the public not to jump to conclusions based on the assailant's background, despite the blatant generalizations it was itself making. Kelkal embodied a number of social markers: *banlieue* youth, immigrant, Muslim turned extremist, and delinquent turned terrorist. And a number of messages and media techniques catalyzed around him, in an effort to reveal the threat that this hybrid figure posed.

The vast majority of national periodicals shared the same discourse when it came to evoking this character. Kelkal was arrested in the Malval forest outside of Lyon. Two days later, on October 2, 1995, a drawing appeared in the *Parisien* that showed Kelkal leaning against a tree, as a kind of reminder of the "tree that hides the forest." In the background, one sees a character of *his kind*—bearded and fez-clad—hiding behind each tree. Kelkal was held up as tangible proof that all the suspicions people had toward the various groups he was supposed to represent were well founded. The image, even more so than the text, promoted a discourse in which the bodies of "young Maghrebis or Muslims, from the *banlieue* or from abroad" should be viewed as containing the natural potential to convert to radical Islam and terrorism. The image of the forest alone symbolized this hidden and taboo discourse, which the media continued to promote while pretending to avoid such essentialism for the sake of maintaining journalistic integrity.

Kelkal was upheld as proof and as a model. On October 9, 1995, the evening news on France 2 described his trajectory as "classical." He became a reference for those seeking to show how, behind the hybrid bodies belonging to "French Arabs," lurked a greater threat. Any attempt at nuance in the description of this figure was avoided. Instead, a synthesis of ideas about "threatening Arabs" became the order of the day, heralding an overall shift in the media toward security-based thought.

The media's binary thinking underlying this discourse was reconfigured in such a way as to also include a foil for the figures of the absolute enemy (young, Arab, devoted to Islam, and socially outcast): friendly figures. These comprised references to the "successful Arab" or the "assimilated immigrant," notable examples of which included the comedian Djamel Debbouze, the singer Faudel, and the soccer player Zinedine Zidane, mostly taken from the worlds of sports and entertainment. In fact, confining friendly Arab figures to "performance" fueled the idea that the Arab could only be assimilated within the context of entertainment. This particular Arab functioned as the exception that proved the rule, and Arabs outside of entertainment were therefore considered failures.

Upheld as proof of the success of the French assimilation model, these figures allowed for the discussion to focus instead on the unassimilated, those whom society rightfully rebuked for personal failings. Such reasoning served to absolve economic, political, and social structures, redirecting instead the responsibility onto a "nature" that Arabs had to relinquish in order to become assimilable. After the announcement that Zidane would be retiring from the French national team in 2004, *L'Express* stated: "The best soccer player in the world also worked miracles off the field. He was a man who convinced women to love soccer and racists to love Arabs."[5] In a context where successful Arabs can only exist in the world of entertainment, Zidane emerged as an exception, and Djamel Debbouze as some kind of "miracle," making the rest of the Arabs failures! Of course, those that had not been successful were immediately blamed and held responsible for their failure, since there was now evidence that if an Arab just tried hard enough or happened to be brilliant, there was no reason for them not to be loved by racists.

Security-Based Discourse and the Return of the Colonial Imagination

Kelkal and Zidane are not contradictory figures; rather, they are two sides of a binary coin. They are the product of the shifting media discourse toward a security-based mindset. On the one hand, there are Arabs in their "natural," "unassimilable" state, who are considered both past and potential threats. On the other, there are the laudable exceptions. Meanwhile, and this is by no means incidental, this binary coincided with bipartisan convergence over the question of security. The figures of successful Arabs, by exempting economic, social, and political factors, served to cast the blame for discrimination onto the objects of discrimination themselves. Those perceived as victims were thus transformed into both guilty and responsible parties, giving rise to forms of reasoning based on a punitive logic.

The attacks of September 11, 2001, and the French presidential election of April 2002 would further solidify such perceptions. The attacks for which bin Laden claimed responsibility further contributed to the emergence of a global enemy, that of the Muslim, Islamist, terrorist, Arab, and so forth, which had already become pervasive in France following the First Gulf War. When Jean-Marie Le Pen's Front National made it through to the runoff stage in the presidential elections, the national fracture dividing French identity and society into two camps became strikingly conspicuous.

There was further controversy surrounding the wearing of the veil or headscarf in 2003–2004, and this received considerable media attention. Two important ideas defined that period: the supposedly indisputable growth of an international form of Muslim extremism in the French *banlieues,* and the need to distinguish people with "mixed" backgrounds from "true French Republicans" through legal means in order to avoid conflict. These kinds of separations were of course previously associated with the colonies. That twofold conviction began to appear in the media in 1989, but by 2004 embraced a juridical logic (and potentially, even penal logic) as the only solution. In February 2004, a law was voted upon that sought to exclude girls wearing the Islamic headscarf from public schools.

In continuity with that law, Aïssa Dermouche was appointed as a "Muslim *préfet*." In the media, the nomination as a prefect served to establish a positive figure of the "Arab" taking a stand against negative figures, in other words, those who wore "fundamentalist headscarves." The symbolic binary of Kelkal and Zidane was thus displaced onto the legal field, reactivating (unconsciously?) one of the fundamental elements of French colonial domination in Algeria: the promotion of "good Muslims" to positions of responsibility within the administration, in order to better keep the "native masses" in line. Such mimetism in government practices is not surprising, and it is as if the representatives of today's Republic, when confronted with the "immigrant" minority, were still living as yesterday's French colonials in Algeria, finding themselves facing a majority of dominated Muslims.

Regardless, the figure of the Muslim *préfet*, as an embodiment of the state and its assimilation model, was the implicit response to the "Islamic threat." In a form of symmetry, "Dermouche as model of assimilation" symbolized an Islam that had willfully submitted to the Republic, a departure from previous media images in which a veiled Marianne had once symbolized the risk of submission to Islam on the part of the Republic. The promotion of a Muslim woman to the position of *préfet* could thus be seen as the completion of a cycle that sought to couple an essentially security-based political message with the image of the "Arab."

An examination of media representations of the "Arab" in France since the 1980s, therefore, underscores two elements at work in the dominant discourse: the first, which is directly linked to the new international situation, concerns the reshuffling of images in a globalized world, one in which radical Islam is perceived as a major threat; the other, which is clearly reminiscent of a colonial imaginary, reduces the idea of the relationship to the "other" to a set of threats that specifically concern "metropolitan France," and which therefore call for enhanced management solutions that adopt tools and modes of representation inherited from the former empire. These two elements rely on various discursive techniques—stereotyping, denial, homogenization, recourse to "positive" figures and role models, self-criticism, and so forth—a conjunction between a security-based discourse and broader identity concerns. In other words, a process according to which forms of discrimination continue to contribute to the emergence of a material and symbolic fracture that greatly resembles the former "colonial fracture."

Thomas Deltombe is an editor. As a journalist and independent researcher, he has focused on new forms of racism in France. He published *L'islam imaginaire: La construction médiatique de l'islamophobie en France, 1975–2005* (2007), and was coauthor or coeditor of *Au nom du 11 Septembre: Les démocraties à l'épreuve de l'antiterrorisme* (2008) and *Kamerun! Une guerre cachée aux origines de la Françafrique, 1948–1971* (2011).

Mathieu Rigouste is an independent researcher and author of *L'ennemi intérieur: La généalogie coloniale et militaire de l'ordre sécuritaire dans la France contemporaine* (2009), *Les marchands de peur: La bande à Bauer et l'idéologie sécuritaire* (2011), and *La domination policière: Une violence industrielle* (2012).

Notes

1. Thomas Deltombe, *Quelle représentation médiatique sans représentants? Naissance et explosion de l'islam de France au journal télévisé de 20 heures, 1975–1995* (Paris: IEP 2003) and also *L'islam imaginaire: Les musulmans de France à la télévision, 1975–2005* (Paris: La Découverte, 2007); and Mathieu Rigouste, *Les cadres médiatiques, sociaux et mythologiques de l'imaginaire colonial: La représentation de 'l'immigration maghrébine' dans la presse française de 1995 à 2002*, Master's thesis, University Paris 10–Nanterre, 2002.
2. "Serons-nous encore français dans 30 ans?," *Le Figaro Magazine*, October 26, 1985.
3. Jacques Julliard, "Editorial," *Le Nouvel Observateur*, November 23, 1989.
4. Jean-Marie Cavada, *Le syndrome Saddam: La France, ses musulmans et l'Irak*, "La Marche du siècle," FR3, January 30, 1991.
5. Henri Haget, "Nous l'avons tant aimé," *L'Express*, August 16, 2004.

8

ISLAM AND THE REPUBLIC

A LONG, UNEASY HISTORY

Anna Bozzo

THE CENTENNIAL OF the law separating church and state, which was passed in 1905, triggered numerous debates, highlighting not only the fact that this law only partially applied to Islam, but also that the integration of France's second religion into republican society was still far from accomplished. As things stand today, the situation does not seem to be improving: on the contrary, the list of grievances within the Muslim community continues to grow. Indeed, in 1998, the "*Commission Islam et Laïcité*" (Commission on Islam and Secularism), a group composed of Christians, Muslims, Jews, and nonreligious civilians founded in conjunction with the *Ligue de l'enseignement* (Teaching League),[1] met to consider the relationship between Islam and the French model of *laïcité*, and concluded that despite the fact that the law protects Muslim thought and religious expression, "concretely the public expression of that faith poses a problem."[2]

Regrettably, the problems outlined by the commission on that occasion have been exacerbated.[3] For example, the ratification of the law of March 2004 banning the display of ostentatious religious symbols in schools can only be considered a failure of the Republic's ability to manage difference. The conceptualization of this particular law under the auspices of maintaining the separation of church and state, along with the consensus it garnered in the public sphere as a tool with which to defend republican values, instead demonstrated, at various levels, the difficulty within French society to admit that being a French citizen is compatible with the Muslim faith. In short, the Republic is far from having integrated its Muslim population. The fact that everyone insists that "Islam is compatible with the Republic" reveals that, for a significant part of the public, that is simply not the case. It is therefore important to analyze both how the Republic has managed Islam as well as the perception of Islam itself, in particular when it comes to understanding how present-day issues are, in part, related to a colonial legacy.

It Is Difficult to Be Both Muslim and French

Although in principle, Muslims, like practitioners of all other religious faiths, have the right to practice their religion in France, there are, in fact, many social constraints that make the exercise of that freedom difficult. Indeed, although being Muslim does not pose a problem for foreigners in France, things are not quite so simple when it comes to a person actually claiming French citizenship. The French separation of church and state encourages discretion with respect to religion in public spaces. Meanwhile, Muslims are encouraged by their faith to express their religion in a public manner, and for this reason, many Muslims in France express uneasiness. They struggle to understand how the idea of separation of church and state establishes limits that cannot be transgressed, despite the fact that government decisions, as in the matter of the headscarf, for example, are not always evenly applied—or rather, and which is more serious, are considered illegitimate, with lawmakers themselves stating that it is possible to get around them or interpret them differently.

There are several reasons for this uneasiness, all of which contribute to a relationship of mistrust between Islam, as a minority religion, and the Republic. What faith can this religious minority, about which all are aware, have in republican promises of equality for all citizens before the law, when some of society's representatives are quick to judge their religion on negative terms? Some even go so far as to conflate Islam, on the basis of stereotypes promoted by the media, with "fundamentalism" and terrorism. Moreover, this Muslim minority, which wishes to assert its citizenship, tends to attribute a political dimension to the religious, and to experience politics through the prism of religion. It is therefore not surprising that tensions should arise. Not to mention the harmful influence that some media outlets have on collective representations of Muslims—including when Muslims claim their role as citizens—or a broad range of other factors that include the unsatisfactory representation of Islam in school textbooks, the absence of national holidays that take into account Muslim holidays, the low level of safety in places of worship, the bureaucratic obstacles placed on associations wishing to create new ones, or the police management of Islam, which the *Commission Islam et Laïcité* has been denouncing for years.

There is constant suspicion surrounding Muslims, for whom police scrutiny is a daily reality. Such scrutiny marginalizes them and often prevents them from participating in a supposedly free and open political space, as is indicated in the report *Laïcité et l'islam en France*:

> In a security-based framework, believers, and especially practitioners, even those who are not activists, are subjected to discrimination in their administrative affairs. In terms of naturalization, for instance, questions are often asked, such as the applicant's response if asked to choose between Islam and a French identity card. . . . In this context, the influence of anti-Arab racism should not be overlooked. Three levels are at work here: the struggle against terrorism, which affects public order, religious freedom, which the Republic must ensure, and a kind of middle ground in which administrative authorities choose "acceptable" Muslims and those that are not.[4]

The establishment of a *Conseil français du culte musulman* (French Committee for the Muslim Religion, CFCM), in April 2003, was meant to provide Islam in France with a representative body. However, this did not happen without considerable tension and resistance. Although this institutionalization was favorably met in some liberal and secularized circles, it was seen by others, notably in traditionalist circles, as a kind of "clericalization" of French Islam, which went against the Muslim religion. Indeed, it was seen as a resurgence of all-too-memorable colonial practices. Although it was developed to facilitate the rapport between Islam and the Republic, the CFCM seemed rather to complicate matters. For a number of believers, and not simply the most conservative among them, it was perceived as a kind of negotiating tool between institutions and the Republic and the people linked to regimes that descended from France's former colonies—"yes-men" assimilated during the time of colonization who were suspected of wishing to appropriate more illegitimate influence in the name of the community. In reality, the CFCM seems to have operated in such a way as to find itself opposed to the contemporary idea of separation of church and state in France, which did not help facilitate "integration" or the "dissolution" of religious citizens in the Republic.

More recently, a new element has been introduced to the situation that is meant to improve the management of Islam in France: the creation, on March 21, 2005, of a foundation that is supposed to centralize the resources of the Muslim community in order to allow it to receive donations. In theory at least, this measure should guarantee—at long last!—the application of the law separating church and state with respect to Islam, since the guiding principle is that it would provide Muslim associations with the means to manage themselves. Some believe that this is a "double-edged sword," in that it may have an ulterior motive linked to monitoring and surveillance. The feeling is particularly prevalent in some Muslim circles; Tariq Ramadan, for example, a prominent member of the *Commission Islam et Laïcité* since its creation, has been particularly vocal on this issue: "Is the government really applying the 1905 law or is this still a relationship of suspicion and surveillance?"[5] The observation is a relevant one, in the sense that the context in which this new foundation is being established hardly resembles a pivot toward increased trust and independence of French Islam vis-à-vis the Republic.

A Colonial Legacy: Security and Surveillance

At its core, Tariq Ramadan's expression of distrust—along with those of many others—takes us back to the last quarter of the nineteenth century and the first half of the twentieth century. Looking back on the French-Algerian colonial relationship—about which much has already been written, but perhaps not enough—one can see the historical importance of the coupling of suspicion and surveillance in the confrontation between Islam and the Republic in the Algeria of that period. But let us not forget that at the time the Republic was managing a colony in which the minority enjoyed civil and political rights and the majority—"native" Muslims, French "subjects"—did not. Only a small handful of the latter became naturalized. A minority governed this republican system, and in order to do so afforded itself the prerogatives of a legal majority, which led to all sorts of distortions.

The colonial situation created an undeniable rapport of domination with respect to Islam, which was the majority religion of the Algerian population. French colonizers needed to control Islam if they wanted to maintain their position over the long term. And they were so successful in their domination that General Bourmont's famous pact—the one according to which, after the conquest of Algiers in 1830, he swore "on his honor" to allow Muslims to practice their religion, to afford freedom to all residents, their wives, their properties, their industry, and their commerce—was rendered moot.

Nevertheless, things are not so simple. The colonial condition also fostered a tradition of domination—one that recurs throughout the history of the Muslim world—with respect to Islam by the powers in place. As the famous Arab historian Ibn Khaldoun reports in the fourteenth century, since the origins of Islam, all kings exerting power over the Islamic *oumma* had to ensure their authority, in an authoritarian and even despotic manner, if they wanted to maintain power and remain sheltered from criticism from the community of believers—the community being endowed with a right of critique that was almost "sacred," responsible, as such, for putting society on the "right path" whenever the kings failed at their mission. It is therefore characteristic of Islamic communities to present themselves to those who govern, regardless of who they are, and demonstrate their fearsome power of contestation with respect to the governing powers, to the point of delegitimizing them. In history, this often led to efforts on the part of governing powers to reach a consensus with the religious body (*ulamas*), but it also led to repression.

Right or wrong, and with variations depending on the time and place, ever since the conquest of Algeria, France has considered Islam a potential subversive threat from which it must protect itself. In the case of Algeria, this perspective was overdetermined and structured by the military administration, after the parenthetical period that was the Second Republic (1848–1851). Over the course of the Second Empire, the administration's primary preoccupation, when it was not making proclamations about wishing to protect the "natives," was to establish mechanisms that contained and maintained control over the constant threat—perceived or otherwise—posed by Islam. Hence the establishment of a system of control that was more efficient than it was elegant, and that went so far as to grant Muslim religious leaders in Algeria a position within the public administration; it created state *medersas* (Muslim colleges) to train "trustworthy" personnel, and this was well before the Third Republic ever came into existence.

The Disingenuous Application of the Law of 1905 to Algerian Islam

The arrival of the Third Republic in 1870 led to reinforced surveillance in the name of increased security.[6] That was how it was with the law of November 1905 on the separation of church and state, which could not be applied to Algerian Islam, except to undermine the apparatus of control; hence the need to save appearance while finding ways around the law. That was the aim, with all its perverted side effects, of the decree of September 29, 1907, which dealt with the "application" of the law of 1905 with respect to religions in Algeria. It included so many exceptions for each religious group that it lacked substance. Indeed, although priests, pastors, and rabbis continued to receive temporary function-related allowances (which would later become permanent), when it came to Islam, which had not, since the time of conquest, had access to resources that would allow it to manage itself, the scheme was not the same: without altering the situation for the other religious groups, whose dependence was being cultivated, the authorities created fictional—and tightly controlled—cultural associations, which were infiltrated by the police, and it was through those associations that Islam was able to receive administrative financial aid.

That was not a drastic change with respect to the prior Muslim situation, which, being dependent on the colonial state, had already been under its control. In that context, the issue of the *habous's* assets was more symbolic than real. The *habous*—institutes of Muslim law similar to pious foundations whose revenues usually go to funding charities and the upkeep of the place of worship, the imams, and teachers in the Koranic school—were requisitioned and annexed under the domain of the state shortly after the conquest. France was so successful in seizing the religion's assets that it then managed to establish a bureaucratic system over the local Muslim community, with different classes of religious leaders, organized in a kind of clergy. It was then a question of restoring the assets, or what was left of them, as a symbolic gesture and a way of applying the law of 1905 to Islam. But that is not what happened.

After the *habous*'s assets were restored, Algerian Muslims called out for the independence of the Muslim religion, claiming they were exempt from the application of this particular republican law. The law that sought to be applied equally to all had, in fact, returned a kind of independence to the local Muslim community. The paradox is clear: the call for the separation of Algerian Islam from the state became a recurrent theme of the 1930s, 1940s, and 1950s, thanks to the association of *oulemas* (composed of educated religious leaders), which itself actually sought to be apolitical. The assertion of this right was also emphasized in all the platforms and petitions of the national Algerian movement, which ran contrary to the traditional fusion between the Islamic religion and the state (*din wa dawla*). Still, the *oulemas* were insistent, and spoke before the Algerian Assembly (created in 1947), listing all manner of positions and analyses, though all to no avail. To be sure, they were demanding to be separated from the colonial state, but after forty years, those demands had become engrained in people's minds, and led—there is no doubt about it—to the emergence of increasingly secularized mentalities. The shift was as unconscious as it was irreversible. After 1962, this demand was set aside by the leaders of the new independent Algerian state. For ideological reasons, they looked to the past and organized themselves around a state Islam, situating themselves rather paradoxically as the heirs of the colonial state.

Meanwhile, in the former colonial metropole, where French Muslims were predominantly Algerian (three-quarters of the French Muslim population), the need for an authentic separation of the Muslim religion from the state, in the spirit of the 1905 law, had not yet been satisfactorily achieved. It is perhaps, then, time to undertake serious and documented research on the political and legal instruments used by the Third Republic to govern Algeria, particularly as they relate to unapplied republican values; that period has had a lasting impact in France on the relationship between Islam and politics. If we want to understand the roots of today's problems and imagine solutions to the "issue" of Islam in France, we must urgently undertake an honest rewriting—one that avoids ideological distortion for political ends—of the recent history that pertains to the relationship between France and Algeria.

The Republic has a history of deforming the spirit of its own laws in order to fit the "needs of the day," in the present cases, out of a fear of being subverted by a dominated population. It has oscillated between two political extremes: on the one hand, the total assimilation of the population with "Muslim origins," through its adoption of "French civilization" at the expense of tradition; on the other hand, an association that claimed it wished to maintain unassimilable differences—but that, in reality, instituted a pure and simple discrimination against that same population. Hence the strange back-and-forth between the dominated and the dominating, constrained and overseen by a system of suspicion/control that, *mutates mutandis*, still exists today.

Anna Bozzo is a historian who teaches at the University of Roma Tre. She is an associate member of the Groupe Sociétés, Religions, Laïcités, Laboratoire (GSRL) in Paris. Her publications and edited volumes include *Islam e laicità in Algeria* (1992), *Les sociétés civiles dans le monde musulman* (2011), *Polarisations politiques et confessionnelles: La place de l'islam dans les 'transitions' arabes* (2015), and *Vers un nouveaux Moyen Orient? Etats arabes en crises, logiques de division, sociétés civiles* (2016).

Notes

1. The *Ligue de l'enseignement* was established in 1866 with the goal of providing access to public education for everyone.
2. See the report *Laïcité et l'islam en France: Rapport d'étape d'une commission de travail de la Ligue de l'Enseignement*, November 1998, 12.
3. *Commission Islam et Laïcité, 1905–2005: Les enjeux de la laïcité* (Paris: L'Harmattan, 2005).
4. *Laïcité et l'islam en France*, 13.
5. Tariq Ramadan, interview on *France-Soir*, March 25, 2005.
6. Among the numerous examples that could be cited here, it is sufficient to mention the *Code de l'indigénat*, a body of legal texts, decrees, and articles targeting "special native infractions." The code was established in 1874, but was fortified and instituted into law in 1881, and was twice modified—in 1890 and 1914, and it remained in force until the Second World War. See Jean-Claude Vatin, *L'Algérie politique, histoire et société* (Paris: Presses de la FNSP, 1983 [1974]), 133.

9
THE REPUBLIC, COLONIZATION, AND BEYOND . . .

Michel Wieviorka

France was a colonial power well before becoming a republic, and it remained so in the periods separating the five republics that it conceived for itself. Only with the First Republic (1792–1804) can one begin to associate the two terms, *republic* and *colonization*, and that association was not subsequently stable, since the Second Republic was not established until February 25, 1848, ceding its place shortly thereafter to the Second Empire in 1852, which the Third Republic, a zealous promoter of colonial expansion, replaced in 1870. The Third Republic was then replaced by Pétain's France in 1940, to which the Fourth Republic put an end in late 1944. The latter lasted until 1958, when the Fifth Republic was established.

A Paradoxical Association

However, the association of these two categories, *republic* and *colonization*, constitutes an important feature of French history, to the point that it has become appropriate to speak of a "colonial republic" when defining the paradoxical link between the republican idea and the colonial adventure—that "dream" that "nourished generations of colonial administrators, seduced those colonized, and made five generations of French dream."[1] When associated with the Republic, and not simply the nation, the colonial saga was conceived as a civilizing mission; it was, to borrow from Victor Hugo, the march of civilization against barbarism. It is true that the First Republic abolished slavery—but the abolition decree, in 1794, was not applied in the same manner throughout the colonies. The Second Republic made Algeria into a series of departments—but colonials and Muslims received different treatment, and this was ratified in law. It is true that important efforts were made to ensure that a large swath of the colonized population had access to education—but that also contained unrealistic aims of cultural assimilation that did not take into account difference, which colonization dealt with in racist ways.

Because even if the colonial republic considered itself to be a liberating and modernizing presence in its colonies, even if it sought to achieve universalist aims by opening schools and building hospitals and infrastructure, it was always sure to emphasize the inequality between races, to separate the superior races from the inferior. Some, such as Jules Ferry, thought that extensive education would make "inferior races" rise, but never to the point of actually reaching the level of the "white race;" others, such as Paul Bert, sought rather to achieve, over the long term, strict equality. The Republic practiced or tolerated "white" violence, and could itself behave in bloody and even murderous ways, with respect to colonized peoples. Republican values—liberty, equality, fraternity—were applied late and only partially to colonized peoples, who were for the most part denied access to citizenship and excluded from the Republic, which was only theoretically "one and indivisible." The treatment of the colonies by the Republic was hardly republican, including in places where the colonies were considered France—in Algeria, Jews could enter the Republic following the Crémieux decree (1870), but Muslims, who were by far the majority in terms of population, were kept at bay.

Decolonization was also the work of the Republic, a work that was not quite completed, since there remain "smatterings" of the colonial empire, with tensions and violence that resulted from an opposition between desires for sovereignty and independence (I am thinking notably of New Caledonia) and an attachment to republican values, as well as to their associated benefits. Residents of the French West Indies or Réunion often compare their situations to those of the former British Indies or Mauritius, arguing that they are better off in republican France than outside it; at least this way they are included in its economy and have access to its government and public services. And the model that is able to account for these "smatterings" is no longer, on the whole, that of the colonial Republic, with its colonizers and colonized. Residents of the French West Indies or Réunion come from a more complex history, one in which slavery, misery, exploitation, and racism affect not a colonized people but rather groups born of a terrible history (slavery, the slave trade, forced migrations), and they were not, therefore, necessarily colonized, strictly speaking.

Postcolonial France

An increasing number of voices have begun to speak out and criticize postcolonial France in two complementary ways: with respect to its foreign policy, notably toward Africa—France's *pré carré* or neocolonial backyard—and with reference to how France today treats its immigrants and their children, who are in some ways at least the fruit of colonial history.

Here, a particularly important point emerges, one that touches on contemporary politics as well as on how we conceive of the work of historians. Indeed, history is ceasing to be a grand national narrative or ode to France, as it was in the past; it has been according more and more space to victims, to the losers, whose points of view have traditionally been forgotten, downplayed, or minimized. That change is not simply the work of historians themselves. It owes much to the irruption of the figure of the victim into the public space in the 1960s, as well as to the mobilization of various groups who have demanded that their historical experiences be taken into consideration, and to the fact that the social uses of history, itself stimulated by all manner of memories, have entered public debate. Not without difficulty, France has begun to consider its colonial past, as well as to inquire into the ways in which that past has overdetermined its most pressing present-day problems, such as Republican integration and multiculturalism.

Together with the United Kingdom, France is a singular case, since a large portion of its recent immigration comes from its formers colonies, and notably from North Africa. It is therefore natural to consider that France's colonial past not only influenced the Republican past—or at least was part of it—but also that it continues to exert influence over the present. Here it is important to make a distinction between two historic periods in the recent past. The first, which corresponds to what Jean Fourastié dubbed the *Trente Glorieuses* (the thirty-year economic boom that came after the Second World War), a period in which the French economy—and not the Republic in particular—invited workers from the Maghreb to fill what were often unskilled positions in France. Those who had just been colonized by France, during a time when their country was not yet entirely decolonized (the last to be decolonized in the Maghreb was Algeria, with the Evian Accords of 1962), were now becoming immigrant laborers. They were for the most part men and often single; in any case, when they arrived in France, they lived alone. They were socially integrated through their work, but they were not concerned by republican integration. In their minds, they would one day return to their home countries. However, in the mid-1970s, a twofold phenomenon occurred whose structural influence nobody could have anticipated: the end of the classical industrial era, which had been dominated by Taylorism and a massive need for "skilled laborers," and the beginning of a period of unemployment and job insecurity for the worker. The subsequent transformation of that wave of immigration was stunning; those immigrants went from being short-stay guest laborers to long-term populations, particularly since family reunification policies were also adopted at the time, which influenced many to stay in France rather return to their country of origin. The "immigrant laborers" of yesterday, or at least their children, were now being called upon to become French citizens. But the Republic did a poor job of keeping its promises.

The second period is less well known and is made up of more complex and often opaque processes, since it involved illegal or clandestine immigration. Despite high unemployment, immigrants continued to arrive in France from the former colonies, but according to different schemes. They have appeared as undocumented immigrants, homeless and unemployed, and they have contented themselves with working small, under-the-table jobs; ultimately, what they seek from the Republic is basic: the right to stay in France. Two types of debate surrounding the former colonial power recur today in France. The first arises out of the large number of people living in France who are the product of Maghrebi immigration in the 1950s and 1970s; the second is more diffuse, asking important questions without being specifically associated with the history of French colonization and decolonization in the Maghreb.

A Crisis in the Republican Model of Integration

Since the 1970s, France has undergone long-term changes that are often perceived as a generalized crisis. Not only did it practically cease to be a colonial power (with the exception of a few remnant "smatterings" mentioned above), but it underwent a painful exit from the classical industrial era, and thus also from a conflictual structural principle between the labor movement and the masters of the workplace. Against a backdrop of exclusion and social disaffiliation, France was forced to reckon with two distinct but profoundly linked phenomena.

The first was the push from cultural and religious groups seeking recognition in the public space; the second related to the growing difficulties of the Republic's institutions to keep their promises of equality and fraternity. The populations that came out of Maghrebi immigration (but not exclusively these populations) occupied a central place in these two phenomena. More than others, they found themselves to be victims of unemployment and racism, and ghettoized in *banlieues* housing projects that are often disparaged or described in the media as dangerous places, where urban violence and delinquency reign. In such conditions, many found meaning for their experiences in culture and religion.

Some developed artistically (through the body), or valued certain sports or musical forms (hip-hop culture, for example); others turned toward Islam, and sometimes even toward radical Islam.

Mostly though, "French Muslims" are deeply attached to republican values, and wish to find a place for themselves in society. But they are often perceived as a threat to the nation and to its values; that perception comes from a variety of present-day issues (unemployment, which the far-right often characterizes as an immigrant problem) and all sorts of historical memories—from Charles Martel thwarting the Arabs in Poitiers in 732 to decolonization, which took the form of a war in Algeria, by way of the crusades, which were organized to liberate the so-called Holy Land, and, especially, by the more or less mythical memories of the colonial saga and the ideological reconstructions related to what France brought to colonized peoples.

After the first "headscarf" affair in 1989, the dread of Islam, which increased with the growth of global Islamist terrorism, and particularly with the spectacle of the Algerian spiral of terrorism and counterterrorism, became particularly concentrated around public schools. At the time of colonization, the Republic was unconcerned with these kinds of traditions, which were, in fact, fundamentally more cultural than religious. And in the "smattering" leftover from the empire, the headscarf was accepted without debate—to see it, take a short visit to Réunion. But in mainland France today, the headscarf has come to symbolize a challenge to republican values, as well as a mark of male domination.

This has become a real challenge for the Republic: should it combat anything that undermines the idea that in the public space (in schools and elsewhere) all individuals are free and equal in the eyes of the law? Can it do so despite the fact that republican institutions function in unequal ways, be it in the form of racist policing practices or reinforced segregation and discrimination within the schools? And since the issue is cultural, and not simply social, should the Republic accept a certain visibility of Islam in the public space? Should it recognize and tolerate Muslim communities, according to a kind of Americanized scheme?

From that perspective, the idea of the nation, which has been so strongly associated in France with the Republic, has also been undermined, and that becomes clear if we consider all that has been affecting its history and its teaching. The more the memory of colonization is introduced into French society, the more the national narrative becomes unacceptable. History curriculums need to be revisited—and likewise for other disciplines such as literature—to take into account perspectives that arise from populations that, based on their experiences and their historical trajectories, have another vision of the past. In other countries, these issues arise more out of globalization, which encourages transnational movement and the formation of diasporas, than out of a colonial past. But that is not the case in France, where everything is mixed: immigrants from all over the globe (with potentially their own cultures, their own networks, their own histories) and a continuity with colonial history.

Extension of the Field of Debate

The work of some historians, as well as the presence in France of people and groups whose individual and collective histories relate to the colonial past (without their experience being dominated by issues of integration related to the children of Maghrebi immigration from 1940–1970), have recently begun to translate into new debates. On the one hand, the idea that the Republic has refused to consider the colonial dimension of its past and of its present-day issues has been extended to include a large swath of historical experiences. These include, in particular, the slave trade and slavery, which came before the Republic to be sure, but also the reduction of colonized peoples to exoticism (in best cases) and to animality (in the worst), as in the example of "human zoos," about which a team of researchers has shown the place they occupied in entertainment under the Third Republic.[2] And on the other hand, claims for memorials in the public space have been made by groups or individuals seeking recognition for a collective history of victims, leading at times to a good deal of tension, and even to extreme points of view.

The tension stems from the fact that these claims for recognition are interpreted as not only putting into question the greatness of the nation and the universal character of republican values, but also as attempts at imposing a new political culture: by demanding public recognition for historical difference, they are perceived as indistinguishable from the identity claims that undermine the Republic's deepest held beliefs. In that way, they contribute to what many deplore as "American-style" multiculturalism or as the "ethnicization" of collective life, and even to radical vocalizations of republicanism. But they also have the merit of opening up the possibility for useful debates, for instance with respect to "*discrimination positive*" (French style affirmative action)—a notion that was massively rejected in the 1980s and 1990s and is now reappearing in public debate.

Abuses occur when these debates turn toward what Jean-Michel Chaumont has called a "competition among victims,"[3] and when demands for recognition become aggressive and even hateful toward groups other than one's own. That is one source of antisemitism today, with, for instance, absurd accusations that Jews held slaves. But let us conclude on an upbeat note. During the great colonial period, the Republic did not simply speak of liberty, equality, and fraternity. It also faced a decisive question: how to separate reason from faith, passion, and convictions, without relegating faith, passion, or convictions to the shadows of nonsense and barbarism. In other words, it invented the French principle of separation of church and state, and it did so with the law of 1905. Perhaps that principle or that law can provide the tools to facilitate recognition in the current public sphere of the colonial and postcolonial legacy, particularly with respect to Islam. It may in fact already be well equipped to project itself into an open and democratic future.

Michel Wieviorka is Professor of Sociology at the École des Hautes Études en Sciences Sociales (EHESS), and is President of the Fondation Maison des sciences de l'Homme. His research concentrates on social movements, democracy, multiculturalism, but also terrorism, violence, racism, and antisemitism. Notable English-language editions of his publications include *The Arena of Racism* (1995), *The Making of Terrorism* (2004), *The Lure of Anti-Semitism: Hatred of Jews in Present-Day France* (2007), *Violence: A New Approach* (2009), and *Evil* (2012).

Notes

1. Nicolas Bancel, Pascal Blanchard, and Françoise Vergès, *La République coloniale: Essai sur une utopie* (Paris: Albin Michel, 2003), 12.

2. Pascal Blanchard, Nicolas Bancel, Gilles Boëtsch, Éric Deroo, and Sandrine Lemaire, eds., *Zoos humains et exhibitions coloniales: 150 ans d'inventions de l'autre* (Paris: La Découverte, 2011). A major exhibition was also held at the Musée du Quai Branly in Paris in 2011–2012 on the history of "human zoos." See Pascal Blanchard, Gilles Boëtsch, and Nanette Jacominj Snoep, eds., *Human Zoos: The Invention of the Savage* (Paris: Musée du Quai Branly, Arles: Actes Sud, 2011).

3. Jean-Michel Chaumont, *La concurrence des victimes: Génocide, identité, reconnaissance* (Paris: La Découverte, 1997).

10

COLONIAL NATIVES AND INDIGENTS

FROM THE COLONIAL "CIVILIZING MISSION" TO HUMANITARIAN ACTION

Rony Brauman

"Bringing science to ignorant peoples, giving them roads, canals, railroads, cars, the telegraph, the telephone, organizing public health systems, introducing them to human rights: that is a fraternal task. . . . The country that proclaimed human rights, that has made brilliant contributions to science, that has separated education from religion, the country that, among all nations, is the greatest champion of freedom, that country has . . . made it its mission to spread the ideas that made it a great nation to as many places as possible . . . We consider it our duty to instruct, raise, emancipate, enrich, and save peoples who are in need of our collaboration."[1]

Those who currently work in the field of international humanitarian aid should carefully examine the words cited above, which were written in 1931 by the radical Albert Bayet for the Human Rights League's conference on colonization. Although the formulation of Bayet's words may seem outdated, the content—the ideas of social and political modernization—should be given attention by today's aid workers. By the way, in France, the very same conference that saw the condemnation of the "imperialist conception of colonization" also justified it insofar as it contained the "humanitarian" goals described by Albert Bayet.

Altruism and Modernization

The humanist current of colonization viewed itself as a source of benevolence and considered it a duty to intervene in indigenous societies and help them evolve. Such reasoning relied on the assumption that the colonizing society was vastly superior to the peoples in question. Three centuries earlier, when the

Americas were being conquered, Europeans did not act in the name of modernization, but rather in the spirit of Christianization. However, many of the stated aims were similar, with the conquering power insisting "on the good deeds being done by the Spaniards for the savage countries," and we frequently come across the following sort of lists: "the Spanish eliminated barbaric practices such as human sacrifice, cannibalism, polygamy, and homosexuality; and they brought Christianity, European dress, domestic animals, and tools."[2] Bartolomé de Las Casas, a Dominican priest and advocate for Indians who described the disastrous elements of conquest in considerable detail, condemned slavery and the cruel treatment of native peoples, but still defended colonization, which he considered to be the work of religious authorities—and not of soldiers.

At the time, humanitarian aspirations and the colonial project were not considered to have contradictory aims. That can be seen, for example, in the establishment of a modern humanitarian organization such as the Red Cross. In France, the era of colonial imperialism began in the late 1850s, on the eve of the first Geneva Convention (1864), for which Napoleon III's France was the first state signatory and most ardent supporter (the convention almost could have been signed in Paris). The "right to conquest" was not put into question in that convention, no more than was the right to wage war. In fact, the aim of the convention was to set limits to war, not to eliminate it.

Gustave Moynier, the first president of the Red Cross, believed that the organization was "inspired by evangelical morals" and, like most of his contemporaries, saw colonized peoples as foils to civilized nations: "Compassion," he writes, "is foreign to savage tribes, who practice cannibalism. . . . Their language even lacks a vocabulary for it; that is how foreign a concept it is to them. . . . Savage peoples . . . are bellicose, and they give into their brutal instincts without a moment's hesitation. Meanwhile, civilized nations, seeking to humanize them, are forced to admit that not everything they do is appropriate."[3] And in a monthly periodical that he published titled *L'Afrique explorée et civilisée,* he added, "The white race should help the black race . . . and provide it with the tools held by modern civilization so that it can improve its fate in such a way that coheres with the wishes of providence."[4]

No NGO would sign such declarations today. The racist paternalism that motivated them belongs to another time. Indeed, those who belong to international aid organizations today are fierce critics of colonialism. However, looking at the practices of those who consider themselves agents of development, one notices elements of the "civilizing mission" that have survived the end of colonial imperialism. As Jean-Pierre Olivier de Sardan argues, two closely connected categories form the basis of legitimation for many international aid programs: the "altruist paradigm" and the "modernizing paradigm."[5] To varying degrees, depending on the organization in question and the local aspects of the aid market, these two categories structure discourse and practices, be it in the case of the World Bank, the United Nations, or various NGOs. Let it be noted that the aim here is not to put those who work in international aid (the author of this article included) on trial, but rather to examine the discourse and practices of international aid programs with respect to their proximity to colonial forms of representation.

Slow and Advanced Societies

Under the guise of solidarity, development programs, therefore, reinstate hierarchical categories inherited from the colonial past. However laudable their aims, the dynamic of these organizations, once they make use of the opposition "developed vs. underdeveloped" or of other variations of the same type, is almost inevitable. The economic criteria categorizing Least Developed Countries (to borrow the United Nations' jargon), much like the criteria used by anthropologists to describe "backward peoples," belong to the vocabulary of the dominant. One encounters the same types of oppositions in colonial thinking: traditional societies vs. modern societies, community vs. individual, routine vs. innovation, solidarity vs. competition, clientelist relationships vs. bureaucratic relationships.[6]

For decades, thousands of aid programs, particularly as relate to agricultural practices or sanitation campaigns, have been founded on the idea of "community" participation. For instance, in Cambodia—an El Dorado for NGOs since the end of the Cold War—all projects must use the phrase "community participation" in a prominent manner if they want to receive funding. When locals are confronted with that exotic fantasy of a homogenous society based on collaboration and sharing, they express either polite indifference or even flat-out disgust. A report on aid in Cambodia sums up the situation well: "How do villagers react when people from outside arrive in their country and start talking about community development? The foreigners no doubt introduce themselves and explain . . . : 'We want you to cooperate with each other. We want you to work together.' To which the people, sickened and wide-eyed, reply: 'Are you suggesting a return to something resembling the Pol Pot regime?' "[7]

The notion of *community*, a ubiquitous term used by both UN experts and NGO volunteers, is therefore inextricably related to some forms of colonial thought. It acts as a dividing marker between "them" and "us," between slow and advanced societies, forming groups of poor native peoples who get defined by specific risks and needs that happen to coincide with the goals of aid programs. Constructed by and for such programs, the idea of community, by definition, speaks the language of "need." Needs are thought to threaten communities, and it is up to aid organizations to fill the void and rescue them from their own weaknesses.

Health programs provide a good example of that dynamic. The United Nations' specialized organizations, notably UNICEF and the World Health Organization (as well as numerous NGOs), uphold and propagate the deeply held Western belief that most of the diseases in the third world come from poor hygiene. Anglo-Saxon epidemiology (which is dominant in the field today) therefore distinguishes between water-based diseases and water-washed diseases. Dividing water into that which washes and purifies and that which sullies and contaminates, its credo seems to resemble more of a modern catechism than it does a verifiable truth. For evidence of the essentially liturgical dimension of that announcement, consider the epidemiological forecasts formulated by experts every time there is a natural disaster—despite the fact that there is no precedent for such assumptions.[8]

Cleanliness and Redemption

In ordinary times, outside of catastrophic events, "health education" programs mostly focus on promoting the merits of soap, latrines, boiled water, and regular bathing. Such practices are said to prevent 90 percent of contagious diseases. During home visits, the aim is to educate mothers and children to wash their hands, drink boiled water, protect and maintain water sources, eat balanced meals, destroy garbage, and defecate in designated toilet facilities. Doing that, they are promised admittance onto the "road to health." That promise is repeated over and over, establishing a direct causal relationship between poor behavior and sickness, which, according to this implicit dynamic, acts as a kind of punishment.

That misleading and oversimplified assumption serves to justify—in the name of the community's best interests—the intrusion of NGO volunteers into family homes where they have not even been invited. Inquiries into household practices related to water and hygiene, with the aim to reform such practices, has become ubiquitous in the third world since the 1980s, when the number of NGO aid programs began to soar. In the seventeenth century, English Puritans made hygiene into a moral concern. In nineteenth-century France, hygiene became a "pastoral of misery," which sought to transform the mores of the most impoverished in order to eradicate "uncleanliness," which was seen as a "purveyor of vice."[9] Of course today's health educators do not seek to instill good morals, but instead seek to promote a vital good. Nevertheless, one can find here a similar quest for salvation.

The reactions of those targeted by these campaigns do not seem to have had an undermining effect on missionaries. That is probably due to the fact that they are ignored, or rather erased, by questionnaires that only measure "the impact" of a campaign on communities. The study in Cambodia mentioned above shows that few educators, all quick to deplore the weight of tradition, were aware that the only things bridling violent reactions to their intrusive behavior were local rules of politeness and hospitality.[10] Moved by the conviction that they were offering a form of liberating knowledge, they were blinded to the offensive character of the situation they had created by making themselves into educators of the private realm. Yet none of them would have agreed to let outsiders into their homes—to inspect their living quarters, criticize their messy lifestyle, and denounce the poor food they gave their children—without an invitation.

Many would be surprised to learn that they themselves do not meet local standards of cleanliness: entering a home with shoes on is against local Cambodian custom, as is using a tooth pick without covering one's mouth; installing latrines or trash collection sites in front of buildings (as opposed to behind them) is also a clear infringement of social norms prevailing in Cambodia. Those are but a few of the behavioral infractions committed by many Westerners in Cambodia. In all cultures, cleanliness is a question of order, of what is appropriate; it is a form of social decorum, with its own set of rules. As Mary Douglas has argued, "Dirt offends against order"[11]; it is a transgression of limits.

The updated version of Europe's civilizing mission evangelizes hygiene, using a rubric of indistinct terms, with what is clean, healthy, and normal on one side of the spectrum and what is dirty, unhealthy, and pathological on the other. New mentors capable of instilling well-being and progress must lead "underdeveloped" people toward social maturity. Through their teachings, these people will be awakened to the "perils" of fecal matter and will finally be able to act in their own best interests.

Power and Values

To be sure, the role of international aid programs is not limited to disseminating the Good Word. Beyond their in-field operations, NGOs and the United Nations work to produce new regulations in the global political space, and they play a role in public debate. As such, they are the expression of a kind of enriched, participative democracy, at a time when democracy's traditional elective forms seem to be waning (at least in the countries where it was formerly installed). Nevertheless, this new form of legitimacy, with its popular support, is not without consequences. For example, it was used on numerous occasions by the US administration to justify its military offensives after 9/11. At a State Department conference held in October 2001, Colin Powell said: "I am serious about making sure we have the best relationship with the NGOs who are such a force multiplier for us, such an important part of our combat team.... [We are] all committed to the same, singular purpose, to help humankind, to help every man and woman in the world who is in need, who is hungry, who is without hope, to . . . give them the ability to dream about a future that will be brighter."[12]

Although clearly opportunistic, Colin Powell's remarks are undoubtedly sincere. NGOs do not own exclusive rights over the values that they promote. But that is precisely the issue. We no longer think of coalitions working to implement or reinforce rights as promoters of values: rights to health, education, and development, rights of children, women's rights. As Hugo Slim, director of the Institute for Humanitarian Dialogue argues, these values, therefore, translate "their vision of a morally just society," and logically they should lead to the support of a military coalition that would embody them.[13] To be sure, there is an important difference between the intrusion into family homes in the name of health and armed intervention in the name of superior values; however, the two scenarios also stem from a unifying principle: they both operate according to the belief in freeing other peoples who are considered prisoners of tradition or of archaic political systems, as is evidenced by the support for the invasion of Iraq by French supporters of a "humanitarian right to intervene."

Since the outbreak of the "global war on terror," the division between the "civilized" and everybody else has sharpened. That division is primarily a government description that should not be used outside of that context. But in this case, it comes from the dominant power, which has turned a rhetoric of values into a crusading discourse, and that is why it is impossible to ignore. We, along with the peoples included in the colonial empires, are the inheritors of a history in which the discourse of the "civilizing mission" played an essential role. For political, practical, and moral reasons, we should work to free ourselves from it.

Rony Brauman is currently Director of Research at the Foundation Médecins Sans Frontières (MSF) in Paris and Director of the Humanitarian and Conflict Response Institute (HCRI) at the University of Manchester (UK). He is author of several books, essays, and documentary films on humanitarian discourses and practices, primarily focusing on war and natural disaster settings.

Notes

1. Cited by Charles-Robert Ageron, *France coloniale ou parti colonial* (Paris: PUF, 1978), 70.
2. Tzvetan Todorov, *La conquête de l'Amérique: La question de l'autre* (Paris: Seuil, 1982), 181.

3. Cited by Alain Destexhe, *L'Humanitaire impossible ou deux siècles d'ambiguïté* (Paris: Armand Colin, 1993), 34.

4. Ibid., 34.

5. Jean-Pierre Olivier de Sardan, *Anthropologie et développement: Essai en socio-anthropologie du changement social* (Paris: Karthala, 1997), 58.

6. Ibid., 33.

7. Soizick Crochet, "Cet obscur objet du désir," in *Utopies sanitaires*, ed. Rony Brauman (Paris: Le Pommier/Médecins sans frontières, 2002), 62.

8. Claude de Ville de Goyet, "Stop Propagating Disaster Myths," *The Lancet* 26, no. 9231 (August 26, 2000): 762–764.

9. Georges Vigarello, *Le propre et le sale: L'hygiène du corps depuis le Moyen Âge* (Paris: Seuil, 1987), 207.

10. Crochet, "Cet obscur objet du désir," in *Utopies sanitaires*, ed. Brauman.

11. Mary Douglas, *Purity and Danger: An Analysis of Concepts of Pollution and Taboo* (New York: London and Routledge, 2003 [1966]), 2.

12. Colin Powell, "Remarks to the National Foreign Policy Conference for Leaders of Nongovernmental Organizations," October 26, 2001.

13. Interview with Rony Brauman and Hugo Slim, by Pierre Hazan, "Les ONG au cœur de la polémique sur l'humanitaire," *Libération*, December 25, 2004.

11

THE *BANLIEUES* AS A COLONIAL THEATER, OR THE COLONIAL FRACTURE IN DISADVANTAGED NEIGHBORHOODS

Didier Lapeyronnie

> I want money. You want money? You gimme money? Or you no gimme money? Excuse me, I'm just getting back from Réunion!
>
> Marc-Philippe Daubresse, Deputy Minister for housing and cities, at the National Assembly, January 27, 2005.

Over the past twenty years, life in disadvantaged neighborhoods or *banlieues* housing projects has undergone a number of changes. These have included the implementation of protectionist, but isolationist, measures and efforts aimed at restoring "social order" through a process of group segmentation. Communication across gender lines in these neighborhoods has diminished, identities have become increasingly ethnicized, and the importance of religion has been amplified. Today's France is witnessing the creation of ghettos, neighborhoods populated by what are effectively second-class citizens, and who have become increasingly withdrawn into their own communities as a reaction to their lack of integration.

The above-mentioned changes are not simply due to a failure of the "republican model." Nor can they merely be attributed to economic changes, liberal policies, and the "collapse of the working-class job market." Although economic realities do explain unemployment and quality-of-life statistics, they cannot by themselves account for all the "cultural," "ethnic," and "racial" issues that are central to those statistics. The residents of these neighborhoods are not merely poor or marginalized, they are, to borrow Frantz Fanon's, Albert Memmi's, and Vidiadhar Surajprasad Naipaul's use of the word, "colonized." Internalizing the way mainstream society sees them, they are defined by both external and dominant categories. They are "derealized" by the way in which they are treated. The result is a deficit in terms of self-image, a deficit that can be felt at all times and in all conversations. They feel incapable of accessing what is real, and they have the sentiment of not being in control of their lives, bystanders forced to watch their lives slip away before their very eyes, unable to do anything about it. Language betrays residents of the *banlieues*; their own bodies seem "rigged" against them. The social fracture described here is built on the "colonial fracture," which provides the former its meaning and aligns it within a normative order. In this context, immigration appears as a kind of outgrowth of the colonial relationship—and this, long after the era of independence.

To be sure, the *banlieues* are not conquered territory. They are not occupied by an army, and colonials have not come to "exploit" their resources and population in a situation of subordination and dependence that has been justified by racism. Still, discrimination and segregation are real phenomena in these neighborhoods. And many find themselves defined, in the discourse of power, by their ongoing lack of "civilization." They are told to assimilate, but meanwhile society has deprived them of the means of constructing an integrated life. Much of this dynamic recalls the colonial relationship, and for many of those with immigrant backgrounds, it represents a "past that won't pass." Politically speaking, those who live in France's "sensitive neighborhoods" today have no voice. They are economically dependent and socially dominated by a "system" that has institutionalized racism and a colonial dynamic.[1]

An Imposed Image Becomes a Source of Identity

Much like "colonized" peoples, those who reside in disadvantaged neighborhoods feel deprived of a political existence. They see themselves as second-class citizens. Meanwhile, as if to highlight their level of incapacity, all manner of institutions bombard them with "moralizing" encouragements to "take control," to stop being "passive." During a study I undertook from 2002 to 2005 in disadvantaged neighborhoods in Paris and the Angoulême region, I came across the following types of assertions: "They're always trying to teach us a moral lesson, and it seems like they take us for idiots"; "You'd think we were still at school. It's unbelievable; we're not children!"; "They said we were dependent, and that we didn't know how to take charge. They said we were like children!" In the absence of political intervention, life is no longer perceived in terms of people's ability or inability to live according to social norms. Social workers have established "family networks," which have replaced neighborhood associations and activist organizations. Social services designate the inhabitants, who themselves have begun to use the same vocabulary, according to the following "familial categories": "fathers," "moms," "youths." Such categories, centered on reproduction, deny this population social and political validity.

The idea of "changing society" has been erased. Residents are prisoners of a social situation, of racism and discrimination, and their only option for change comes in the form of individual departure. Although many among them are attached to their neighborhood, they are also equally attached to the idea of leaving, since that is the only way they will be able to participate in "normal" society—the dominant society. Leaving is seen as a necessary condition for social integration. So long as an individual remains in the neighborhood, he or she remains a prisoner of the image the dominant society has created for its inhabitants, and he or she fears being put in the same basket as "all the social cases who live here." "It's simple: the only people who live here are social cases, crazy people, and failures. How are we supposed to progress?"

Common perception sees those who inhabit these neighborhoods as "social cases" and also as "Arabs." "I'm Arab," says a young resident of a Parisian housing project. "Right, I'm Arab because I live with Arabs." Other young people who come from immigrant backgrounds say the same thing about their "white" friends who have trouble finding work: "It's because you're like us. You've been living with us for so long that you've become one of us!" At the same time, many residents have lost hope in the ability to leave the neighborhood. Fighting against the system or trying to change their "social destiny" is seen as a waste of time. For many, their life experiences are deprived of meaning or possibility. They are strongly aware of their negative social fate, which is coupled with a collective and individual incapacity to change. Theirs resembles the condition described by Frantz Fanon with respect to colonized peoples: they are torn between an impossible desire to escape "hell" and the suspicion that those who oversee "paradise" are "ferocious watchdogs."[2]

Domination reduces people to general categories and images from which it is almost impossible to escape. Such neocolonial mechanisms are perhaps most present in the relationships between institutional representatives and residents of disadvantaged neighborhoods. Very often, when dialogue is created, "dominant" subjects take pause: Whom are they addressing? Individuals, who can be addressed with the informal *tu*? Or representatives of social groups, who should be addressed using *vous*? Should interlocutors be treated as individuals or generalized entities? A young resident of a Parisian neighborhood, speaking with a politician who has called on him sums up the situation well: "Who are you talking to? One second you address me with *vous* and the next with *tu*? Who are you talking to? To the Arab, to everybody else, or to me?" Individuals are overshadowed by images or stereotypes that dominant society has constructed.

The issue of "qualification" and of image has become an obsession for those who live in these neighborhoods; notably, the descendants of colonial immigrants. For minority social groups, qualification is imposed and experienced as an external constraint. To be "Muslim-Arab" is to be defined by a dominant and negatively connoted vocabulary. It is very difficult to contest or change that definition. This is an example of lived racism, in which categorization is based solely on appearances. Moreover, the identity marker in this case has come to symbolize "bad" people: "It's obvious that they don't like us. When you're walking down the street, you can see that they're wary of us." That everyday experience is reinforced in the political sphere: "Just watch the news. Everything is all mixed up: Arabs, extremists, Muslims, everything! All Muslims are now considered to be extremists. Average French people watching the news think Arabs are terrorists." "When they talk about Arabs, it's always to point out how bad we are."

The individual and the group are, therefore, assigned a negative identity from which they cannot escape. In a group of young adults discussing this experience, one among them shows his arm and pulls at his skin, as if he could tear it off. Speaking to the sociologist present, he says, "Don't you get it? I can never take it off!" "I can't take it off," he repeats when he receives no reply. But to be "Muslim-Arab" is also to be denied that very identity. Making claims based on identity or community attachments is not considered legitimate discourse. Showing one's belonging to a subgroup within French society is not looked upon favorably. When girls were prohibited from wearing the Islamic headscarf in school, it was experienced as a rejection of "Muslims" specifically and "Arabs" more generally. It was seen as a clear message from the state and from French society that signs of Muslim identity would not be tolerated. Individuals therefore find they have been assigned a negative identity, which has been constructed and defined by an external point of view, and which they cannot reclaim according to positive terms. "They call us Arabs and then they criticize us when we call ourselves Arab." Their identities have been constructed for them by the society in which they live, but which remains inaccessible to them. To call themselves "Muslim-Arabs" is a way to reclaim the fate to which they have been condemned, to reclaim their source of humiliation.

This difficulty can be explicitly seen in the reactions to September 11, 2001. The reason probably stems from the ambivalent emotions felt by many "young Muslim-Arabs." On the one hand, the attacks were a source of "pride" that nobody could admit, since it was so shameful, but the fact was that the attacks were considered to be a form of "Muslim" revenge taken against Americans generally and, perhaps more indirectly, against French society which had excluded and humiliated them for so long. "Arabs were actually the ones to do it!" At the same time, 9/11 has also been a negative experience, since it reinforced the stigma against Arabs: "We've been under even more scrutiny since 9/11." Some therefore criticized the terrorists for acting against "Arabs," by making them the indirect victims of their madness. The young people I met had mixed feelings about the event: they were hostile toward the attacks and radical Islam when they spoke with those who were "on their side;" and at times they showed themselves to be "favorable" toward these same attacks, or at least to understanding them, when they were confronted with a society in which the condemnation of terrorism somehow also implicated them.

The importance of the event and its international resonance exacerbated tensions and the prevalence of negative experiences in French public life. When speaking with others, they are always forced to clear themselves of suspicion. They constantly have to confront negative stereotypes about themselves, stereotypes that were constructed by others and through which they do not recognize themselves, but for which they are always called to account. "Tell us that you aren't what we think you are, which we know but can't completely believe!" To escape these kinds of demands, young people with immigrant backgrounds often end up pretending to adhere to stereotypes others have given them even if they do not feel they accurately represent who they are. They play the character and become "Arab" even when they are not. In many cases (such as the Islamic headscarf or Saddam Hussein), then they will often state a position for or against that is precisely the opposite of how they truly feel.

Everything is then interpreted as a way of suppressing "Muslim-Arabs," a way of humiliating them and hemming them into the contradiction. "There was so much media hype around 9/11! It was pure indoctrination. Why didn't we do the same for Iraq? They're appealing to their viewers at our expense. They've been talking about the headscarf for months. Massacres have led to a million deaths in Rwanda, and all we can talk about is 9/11." Some saw the minute of silence held in memory of the American victims as a confirmation of society's condemnation: "Nobody offered to do a minute of silence for the deaths in Algeria or for the five hundred thousand kids who have died over the past ten years in Iraq!" Others, after the 2004 Madrid bombings, flatly refused to observe the minute of silence: "I didn't want to observe the minute of silence. They threatened to throw me out of school. So I ended up doing it. But I didn't want to do it. After all, the people behind the attacks were Moroccans like me."

In Other Words . . .

Often people who say such things refuse to admit it. When speaking with outside interlocutors, they generally try to minimize conflict. Some claim to say "whatever" to those outside their community, treating such interactions as a kind of game. They are not what they say, and they do not say what they think or think what they say. "I did say that, but it was nonsense. It isn't true; I did participate in the minute of silence . . . I don't know why I said I didn't," explains one "Moroccan" young man who claimed the exact opposite the previous week. The written word is considered manipulative and therefore even more unbearable. When reading an interview they had given a journalist, a group of young people from Angoulême cried out: "They tricked us!" However, they did not deny having said the words that appeared in the newspaper.[3]

Although the image appearing in the "mirror" of the newspaper was one they themselves had provided, it was not any more acceptable than the negative image constructed from oversimplifications, racism, and discrimination. Indeed, they may have been even less comfortable with it precisely because it was their own image, one they had constructed, and therefore implied more responsibility. But their feeling of being "tricked" reveals an even deeper reality. The words uttered were not only minimized, they were not allowed to exist as belonging to an individual. They were presented as a form of provocation, a game, the fruit of chance. In the end, they had no meaning for anyone outside of the group, who would be incapable of understanding the meaning or lack of meaning that such words could have for the person uttering them.

Words are often experienced as material obstacles, and not as vectors of communication. They belong to a "decomposed theater," whose unity and integration are provided from the outside, from spectators or viewers, and which the actor not only refuses to accept but also works to thwart or undermine. Words, as Frantz Fanon rightly observed with respect to the colonized, are a kind of external material to the individual.[4] They have weight—notably social weight—which makes them foreign, and even hostile, to individuals, since their meaning is provided by a society that excludes and "racializes."

We can be "tricked" by words because their meaning has weight, and because they belong to society. Whenever they are used, they carry the trace of that hostile exterior. For instance, in the political sphere, the words *equality, republic, citizen,* and *integration* belong to the dominant class. Whereas for some they represent an assertion of identity, for others they are experienced as a command. Their use relates to negative integration, as if their meaning were necessarily directed against some groups. "Words, words, nothing but words.

Blah, blah, blah. All they do is talk all day. I could hear them talking from the time I was in my dad's balls!" To speak is therefore always a bit to speak against oneself.

That is why journalists are often a target for hostility. It is not because they construct a negative image, but because they record words. The act of publishing words is an act against those who uttered them. Words and language are not related to reality; they are not a way of describing experience. Rather, they are an obstacle. They represent the presence of society within the self. They intervene between the self and the self as an image, and as such they end up cutting off the self from one's own reality. In interactions with institutions or with society's representatives, the more individuals speak, the more they find themselves at odds with themselves. They speak with words that they reject and that split them apart.[5] In the end, they can no longer understand themselves.

Words float around as an external reality that intervenes between individuals more than it connects them; words tear everyone apart. And, when they act as detached, objective materials, they can be used to manipulate. Those who are good with words have prestige and are recognized as belonging to the dominant group. Knowing how to manipulate words means knowing how to give them meaning outside of normative society; it means one can literally turn them against society. If language and words are external and hostile, can individuals believe in what they say? The question makes little sense. They believe and don't believe in what they say at the same time. The important thing is not to believe in one's words but to say them. Individuals are never present to their words. They therefore do not feel responsible or committed by what they say.

Residents of disadvantaged neighborhoods, and particularly youths from immigrant backgrounds, are constantly inventing language precisely because they are deprived of language, because the domination to which they are submitted and the absence of political intervention deprive them of language. Their main difficulty is gaining access to reality.[6] Words, like the image that is imposed upon them, deny them access. They live on the "margins" of mainstream society. They are less "dominated" by society than they are ignored by it. Society has constructed them into one of its problems. They have to content themselves with appearances. Their dependence is made up of substitutions and unkept promises (fake work assistance, fake organized pastimes, fake collective apartments, fake income in a fake economy, and so forth), which most often frustrates them, since they only serve to underscore the idea that these populations live at a distance from any kind of "real" social reality. They feel they have to cheat in order to gain access or even hope to gain access to it:

cheating on their resumes, lying over the telephone to get a job or an apartment rental, lying about their identity to get girls.

The Final Stage of "Derealization"

"Derealization" dominates relations between social workers and young men. Young men pretend they want to improve their situations, and social workers pretend they can offer them work or access to better integration. Everyone pretends to believe the other in this asymmetrical relationship. In this way, the *banlieues* resemble the colonies: human relationships are fake. Individuals are divided between their emotions and their expressions, as if they could never be fully present to themselves, to their actions, and to their words, which are "rigged" by the colonial relationship. The brutality of domination together with the importance of assistance "derealizes" a person's existence, relegating her or him to an intermediary universe that has no future and over which the individual has no power. Many turn to "artificial" forms of paradise, dreaming of another society or living in a fantasy world; notably, fantasies of sexual domination.[7]

Domination hollows out a person's life from the inside, leaving only the appearance intact. Everything is focused on form, on skin, since the individual has been turned into a statue and deprived of an internal life. Individuals can only be what the dominant vision of them allows them to be. They can be seen, but the more they are seen the less is actually seen; the more they are visible, the more they are invisible; the more they occupy the field of vision of "others," the less they have a personal reality. It is a way of hollowing people out. And nothing in that process belongs to the individuals themselves—not their appearance (it is attributed to them, but they do not have the right to own it), nor their language (others give meaning to their words). These young people, along with a large portion of those who live in disadvantaged neighborhoods, therefore, construct a kind of counterworld, a parallel society without consistency, one that is dependent and marginal, and one in which they live without living, in which they want to live without wanting to, and which they wish they could leave. It is a ghetto, an empty place. A fake society, or rather a substitute society made up of "fake" individuals. It resembles a theater, with its rituals, its vocabulary, its stage, a theater in which they act more than they exist, and in which they feel as though they are "losing their lives."

Edward W. Said emphasized the extent to which the past only makes sense in light of the present. In order to make use of the past, one must start from the experience of a present that perpetuates that past's attributes and legacy, though perhaps in other forms.[8] Beyond discourse, the colonial is today at the heart of the experience of those who live in immigrant neighborhoods. And it is that experience that makes the urgency of reincorporating memories and history so salient. That is the only way of making sense of this situation and of providing those to whom republican universalism has been denied access to recognition and the ability to build their own integration.

Didier Lapeyronnie is Professor of Sociology at the Sorbonne and a member of the Groupe d'Études des Méthodes de l'Analyse Sociologique de la Sorbonne (GEMASS). He is author of several books focusing on social questions, immigration, urban marginalization, and racism in France over the past twenty years. These include: *Les quartiers d'exil* (1992), *L'individu et les minorités, la France et la Grande-Bretagne face à leurs immigrés* (1994), *Ghetto urbain, violence, pauvreté et ségrégation en France aujourd'hui* (2008), and *Refaire la cité, l'avenir des banlieues* (2013).

Notes

1. See Stokely Carmichael and Charles V. Hamilton, *Le Black Power* (Paris: Payot, 1968).
2. Frantz Fanon, *The Wretched of the Earth*, trans. Richard Philcox (New York: Grove Press, 2004 [1961]), 16.
3. See Philippe Bernard's report, "On nous qualifies sans cesse 'd'Arabes' et on prétend nous empêcher de nous situer par rapport à l'islam," *Le Monde*, July 6, 2004.
4. Frantz Fanon, *Black Skins, White Masks*, trans. Richard Philcox (New York: Grove Press, 2008 [1952]).
5. Albert Memmi, *The Colonizer and the Colonized*, trans. Howard Greenfield (New York: The Orion Press, 1965 [1957]).
6. Patrick Boulte, *Individus en friche* (Paris: Desclée de Brouwer, 1995).
7. Fanon, *Black Skins, White Masks*; and Albert Memmi, *L'homme dominé* (Paris: Payot, 1968).
8. Edward W. Said, *Culture and Imperialism* (New York: Vintage, 1991).

12

THE PITFALLS OF COLONIAL MEMORY

Nicolas Bancel and Pascal Blanchard

SPEAKING ABOUT MEMORY in France is to touch upon a crucial civic value,[1] one that is marked by a bad conscience, commemorations, and even manipulations.[2] A perfect history does not in fact exist,[3] and nor does a perfect memory. If writing history is a process—it can be corrected, recontextualized, reformulated—memory is, at the moment it is articulated, a source of imagination, newfound awareness, and conflict. Its impact—both socially and politically—is immediate and indelible. It leaves its mark on the social imaginary.[4] Memory is therefore an issue that should be considered with much precaution and distance. But is that even possible?

The colonial period perhaps poses even more issues when it comes to the question of memory.[5] Colonial memory in France raises complex questions, and, even more than Vichy, there is a veritable "memory gap" over the past two centuries when it comes to colonization. Three perspectives help shed light on that amnesia. First, analyzing this memory forces us to think more about the relationship between history and memory—in other words, to compare the state of knowledge on an issue (the colonial past) and the forms of socialization that such knowledge uses in its dissemination. Second, because colonial memory has such a tendency to get buried, fragmented, and mythologized, one wonders about the possibility of constructing a colonial memory and the obstacles that stand in the way of such a construction.[6] Finally, historiography itself is the fruit of a process in which scientific advances, intellectual trends, media interests, and academic rivalries converge to determine the form and dynamic of existing knowledge on colonial history. In a sense, French colonial history needs to be "Paxtonized;"[7] it is as if only an external view could provide any clarity to the debate, which has been at a standstill for the past forty years. Yes, France did colonize others!

That context, which elicits all manner of questions when we attempt to describe the state of affairs of colonial memory, provides the outline of a more general movement, which forces us to establish a genealogy of that same memory (or colonial memories), in order to grasp the essential points. Our aim in examining the long-term construction of colonial memory is to understand how this situation, along with changes in the perception of colonization, continues to have repercussions today. How does it resonate in the social body today, and what is its role in current issues related to developing a national memory in France?

What Is Colonial Memory?

Where and in what ways is it apparent? What diffracted clues can be found in French culture that would allow us to evaluate it? Which parts are fantasy, myth, revisions, reinterpretations, or lacunae in the construction of memory?[8] Memory is not history. The case of colonial history is particularly enlightening (and singular) in the sense that accumulated knowledge on colonialism over the past forty years has not played a significant role in the process of socialization and has therefore had a limited impact on the construction of collective knowledge.

However, beyond the work of mourning that is no doubt at play in the refusal to acknowledge this "past that will not pass," there is likely a further difficulty. That difficulty resides in the fact that the work of socializing this memory depends on historians (whose research has been considerably richer over the past few decades or so), on institutions capable of implementing these forms of knowledge, and on various media outlets capable of transmitting the memory of colonization (television reports, radio shows, special issues in periodicals, exhibitions, and so on).[9] For this to occur, the proper conditions for receiving such information within society itself, in all its complexity, would also have to be in place. Historical memory implies a community's roots and imaginary foundations. Such imaginary foundations represent a force of inertia and strength of cohesion that gets constantly renewed by new memory-based information.

Pitfall: "Militancy with Respect to Colonial Memory"

Memory rewrites history, adapts it, molds it to its own possibilities of reception. All historical knowledge is therefore submitted to the work of (re)interpretation, which alone makes new knowledge audible and capable of being incorporated. As a result, the idea of "purifying memory" and making it accessible to historical truth is an empty dream. Utopian, its danger lies in the fact that it prevents concrete access to history. The pitfall of "militancy" with respect to colonial memory would therefore be to misunderstand the ways in which memory gets created and the specific social conditions of reception that make up the condition of the possibility (or impossibility) of constructing a historical memory.

The case of colonial memory (together with that of immigration) is, in that sense, an interesting model. As we have said, over the past forty years, historians have done their work. The archives are open. Associations (antiracist groups, the teachers' league, human rights movements, for example) have fought to have colonial history recognized as a crucial chapter in our collective history (often basing themselves on the most violent aspects of colonization, as in the case of torture in Algeria of FLN militants between 1955 and 1962). Books and articles have been published, sites (often foreign) have been established, but very few televised documentaries on colonization as a whole have been produced (except on Algeria at war). And yet, the failure of these efforts—which are easier to talk about since we ourselves have been the subject of criticism through our various exhibition and conference programs: *Images et colonies, De l'indigène à l'immigré, Miroirs d'empires, L'appel à l'Afrique*—is obvious today. But let us not speak of a lack of sources; as Alain Ruscio has shown, those who wanted to know knew.[10]

Amnesia and Colonial Nostalgia

The situation is such that colonial history remains inaudible and impossible to accept. It is prevented from developing for two crucial reasons. On the one hand, it is a question of time; the "work of mourning" takes at least a generation or two, and it has not really yet begun. Vichy is an interesting example. It took almost fifty years for memories surrounding Vichy to emerge in society and gain in clarity. A landmark book in that process was Robert Paxton's work on Vichy, first published in the United States in 1972 and then translated into French in 1973. It will take time for memories of colonization and colonialism to emerge and be processed. On the other hand, colonial history undermines a number of identity markers that make up the social imaginary. That poses a problem, since it necessitates a (re)establishment and (re)formulation of those identity markers. Simultaneously, it demands a rewriting of history in such a way that would make it possible to incorporate colonial memory into the social imaginary. The construction of memory is dialectical, and history walks away from the exchange unscathed.[11]

Colonial amnesia has given way to mythicization and "colonial nostalgia," which make use of collective forms of representation created during colonization. Thus, the first of these pitfalls linked to a will to create a colonial memory is to legitimize a form of colonial nostalgia, which continues to thrive. Examples of this phenomenon in the 1990s can be seen in the project for a museum of Overseas France and in Jean-Marie Le Pen's frequent declarations expressing a desire to "rehabilitate imperial France through an evocation of French Algeria." However, that kind of nostalgia can also be seen in intellectual and university research fields, in special issues of periodicals, and even in articles by mainstream news sources. The resurgence of colonial nostalgia is not simply, therefore, a scholarly hypothesis; rather, it is the silence around our colonial history that has made it possible. The second pitfall, which parallels the first, has been to ignore the complex dialectics accompanying this past, and to create a space of repentance or commemoration of the "crimes" of the Republic.

A Republican Colonial Ideology?

That being said, we ought to endeavor to better understand what exactly colonial memory undermines in terms of identity markers, and how those markers act as obstacles to the work of memory. The first of these, it seems to us, is the Republic itself, and more specifically the values and ideology on which it is founded. The great expansionist effort, between 1870 and 1912, which established the modern colonial empire, does not correspond to the height of the colonial idea in France. The dissemination of the colonial idea during that inaugural period was the fruit of two concomitant phenomena. First, the organization of private propaganda by the "colonial lobby," and second the promotion of the colonial idea by opportunistic republicans who were in power at the time.

Republicans embraced the colonial idea for several reasons. Notably, they needed to create an ideology that transcended political divisions (the republicans were threatened by the monarchists, the conservative right, and a burgeoning radical left) and social movements (with the establishment of an urban proletariat coming out of the first industrial revolution). To that could be added the army, which was led by an aristocracy rebelling against republican ideas, and the context of cultural disparities between regions, which posed an obstacle to the consolidation of the republican nation-state. The colonial ideal, which was formulated as early as the 1880s as a civilizational utopia (the "civilizing mission") therefore became inscribed in universalist rhetoric preached by the Republic.

"Greater France"

During the construction of the state (and not of the nation), from the inclusion of Languedoc to the annexation of Savoy, and passing by way of Corsica, French space was in a state of constant flux. Meanwhile, a system of values was being developed which the Republic would, or would not, elect to make its own (from Clovis to Saint-Louis, and from Joan of Arc to Napoleon), and which would form the substrata of national identity. The defense of the conquest of souls, hearts, and land should be considered in parallel with the coming colonial expansion and the gestating civilizing mission. The genealogy of the state's colonial discourse—in which the colonial was ably included as an extension of the national and a condition of its power—would continue to develop until the independence era, and with it the rhetoric of spreading the Republic's "enlightenment" to what were perceived as culturally and biologically inferior peoples. For many, under the influence of Ernest Renan's thinking on the community of "living beings in one same territory," France would not be France until it had achieved uniformity among its citizenry (regardless of color) and territory (as in the case of Algeria, which became a French department). France was and would remain a series of conquests (colonial or otherwise); and the notion of empire (including all of the "Roman" symbolism and power implied in the word) became efficient in a "greater France," and which aligned itself with classical schemes of national identity through the concept of assimilation. Colonial territories and various regions were to undergo the same process of absorption into the nation. The important thing was to "become French." "Overseas" colonization was therefore not a departure from the past; in fact, it inscribed itself in a consubstantial continuation of the construction of the French nation, and then, as a kind of legacy, of the Republic.

The republican genesis of the state's colonial ideology leads us to inquire into colonial memory in France. How are we to get to the bottom of colonization and colonial history? The task puts into perspective the foundation of a dominant political ideology, namely republican ideology. And it implicates the Republic (regardless of the political colors in which it is dressed up): first in the conquests themselves; second in the stabilization of the empire through the implementation of a centralized administrative and police network in the colonies; and third in the state's assertive use of colonial propaganda beginning in the late twenties.[12] That is where one must look in order to see one of the primary obstacles to the assimilation of a colonial memory in France today. Confronting colonization is to deconstruct the discursive practices that made it possible, and at the head of that list of practices is colonial-republican discourse itself, and which constitutes one of the most anchored identity and political markers in the collective imagination. Colonial-republican discourse was especially and vigorously promoted in what is today the last republican institution meant to bind the social body: the school system.

Fusion of the Colonial with the National

The second process that makes colonial memory unassimilable was the fusion of the colonial with the national. As we have seen, this process has a lot to do with republicans, since they were quick to promote the colonies as an extension of the national community. The colonies were supposed to reinforce that community and then become part of it. Between 1880 and 1910, the political opposition to colonization was divided between the conservative and monarchist right and the extreme left, which was mostly represented by anarchic-unionism. The groups had diverging motives: the former felt that colonization would lead to diminished French power and that France's interests would be best served by concentrating its resources on reconquering Alsace and Lorraine.[13] For the latter, its stance against colonialism went hand in hand with its traditional fight against the church (missionaries), big investors (companies), and the army (conquerors). But although it condemned the "excesses" of conquest (brutalization of natives, massacres, pacification, forced labor, rape, displacement of populations, torture, violent crack downs, and so on), the extreme left never questioned the rhetoric on the superiority of the European civilization.

Those two forms of anticolonialism would soon lose steam, and they would almost completely disappear after the First World War, to the point that the national right—from the Action Française (in 1920) to Vichy, from Indochina to the OAS—became the most ardent supporter of the colonial idea in the country. The traditional conservative right itself was progressively won over to the idea of colonial greatness, especially since the First World War dashed its old hopes for victory over Germany. For the anarchist and socialist left, colonization became a marginal issue and was measured in terms of the mobilization of the masses and of global revolution. For the communists, it was a major theme until 1932 (under the guidance of Jacques Doriot and especially with the Rif War), despite the lack of interest among militants and voters.

The new political order after the Great War led to consensus on colonialism among the majority of parties. It was also during this period that colonialism became the object of a massive state propaganda campaign. Republicans—despite some quickly abandoned impulses for reform, like the Blum-Viollette project—found themselves on the side of the right in the promotion of the imperial idea as a new national horizon. The fusion of the national and the colonial started to become a conceptual reality. However, the fusion was applicable to land and not to humans. Indeed, the system of discrimination in the colonies (political and legal discrimination, not to mention the appropriation of wealth and the domination of the monetized economy by white colonials) remained intact, since that was the condition upon which the metropole maintained its domination. In the name of the Republic and its ideals, France was therefore producing a national—and therefore exclusionary—identity. This movement, which did not really begin to fracture until repercussions from the Algerian War began to be felt in mainland France (1956–1957), can be understood as an additional difficulty in colonialism being acknowledged.

The Fracture of Forgetting

A fracture—the fracture of forgetting—occurred after the decolonization of Algeria, and the colonies, which were now free from the direct control of the metropole, became indistinguishable from other exotic countries with no ties to the tutelary power. That was no doubt in large part due to the fact that the metropole's twofold discourse on its colonies had now become impossible to sustain. The leitmotiv of colonial propaganda insisted that the colonies "over there" were the same as "here" or at least on the way to becoming so. The palpable desire to be freed of colonial rule by the colonized peoples in those countries made such assertions absurd. We would even posit that colonial propaganda generated a utopian image of the Republic: erasure of class conflict, collective cooperation around the same ideal of progress (economic, social, cultural, civilizational), a metaphor of harmony in a society without conflict, a community that had managed to resolve internal differences, its identity-related issues, and its anxieties in the face of social and technological changes. Colonization, or rather French people's understanding of colonization, acted as a mirror that reflected their own desires, and not only the desire for power or the conceit of chauvinistic pride, but also a desire of who they wished they could be. When the colonial mirror was broken, the colonial utopia collapsed, and with it the hopes and dreams of what the metropole could have been.[14]

From Rupture to Forgetting . . .

Today's deficit of colonial memory can be understood in the context of the "Aussaresses affair," alarmist reactions, and protests against the defense of torture in Algeria. Let us recall that the issue was resolved by historians a long time ago—yes, the army routinely practiced torture in Algeria as early as 1955—and that use of torture was the subject of dissent in 1956 and up until the end of the Algerian War. Hundreds of articles and first-hand reports were published in a variety of periodicals (*Témoignage chrétien*, *Les Temps modernes*, *Esprit*,

L'Express, Le Monde, Le Nouvel Observateur). However, if we only focus our attention on the war (and its crimes), we risk forgetting about the system itself and the various mechanisms that allowed it to operate.[15] In that sense, the duty to remember, in terms of the Algerian War, has unwittingly been transformed into a foreclosure of knowledge. Such stupor in the face of the Algerian War's atrocities is, however, revealing with respect to the state of colonial memory in France in general. It can only be explained through the absence of cultural forms of mediation, which, after independence and up until the present day, could have helped socialize colonial memory. There are many signs of this absence. For instance, the colonial phenomenon is only afforded a very marginal space in textbooks, and the topic is never considered in terms of its cultural and political impact on the metropole. It is precisely that type of perspective—the consequences in the colonies and the creation of a colonial culture in the metropole—that is needed if we wish for students to understand this crucial moment in history. Focusing solely on the two dominant ideologies of the last century (Marxism and fascism), we forget about colonialism (practiced by European countries, the United States, Russia, and Japan) and liberalism, both of which have mostly escaped criticism, particularly by previous generations, and the West's collective work of memory. Today, globalization is the rightful heir of these two ideologies, which continue to shape the twenty-first century.

A crisis surrounding colonial history first emerged in the 1970s, and thirty years later, we are still grappling with it. For Catherine Coquery-Vidrovitch, the crisis of colonial history is connected to the "discipline" and its classical references, as well as to the deep divide between (evolving) Western history and third world (emerging) history.[16] Indeed, the history of colonization (and of colonialism as a system) was born with the independence movements—in a fit of passion—and then quickly dissipated. That does not mean, however, that scholars did not produce work on the topic. On the contrary. But this scholarship was unable to speak to a larger audience and its assertions remained marginalized and ghettoized.

Now that more than a decade has elapsed, it is clear that Catherine Coquery-Vidrovitch's wish to see "colonial history" undergo "decolonization" did not resolve the problem of socializing colonial memory. Indeed, although that history has been decolonized, it has become marginalized between two conflicting trends: an a posteriori legitimation of third-worldist engagement (history and memory are two "legitimate" areas for such debates) and a wholesale rejection of any kind of critique of colonization (under the pretext that colonialism and colonization, especially "French-style" colonization, cannot be mixed). The two trends at work in the memory of French colonialism: the creation and destruction of ideology.

A National Issue?

The memory of colonization has had a direct and major impact on postcolonial history in France. In the early 1980s, the economic crisis, together with the trend toward the long-term settlement of immigrants, the contraction of the republican model of integration, the growth in ultranationalism, and the accompanying rejection of immigration from Africa, in the context of an unacknowledged colonial history, led to the emergence of a twofold image of the "other": that of the "typical foreigner"—who could be assimilated—and the "typical immigrant," which was merely an extension of the colonial image's "typical native." That twofold representation of the "other" supplanted the image of the immigrant guest worker from the 1970s and became an implicit and explicit reference in debates on immigration. Xenophobic discourse became commonplace, which led to immigrants being characterized according to cultural—and sometimes "racial"—differences based on age-old stereotypes. Immigrants were thus not only different from French people, but also from other foreigners. And it was that reified difference that would become the symbol as to why integration was impossible for populations from the former colonial empire. Colonial memory was blocked in order to provide a multiplicity of xenophobic explanations. It was as if immigrants from former colonies were somehow less connected to French history than any other foreigner arriving in France. There is perhaps a third difficulty in the socialization of colonial history in France. The school system has become the only institution enacting integration policies among immigrant populations in this country. That is not an opinion; it is a fact. Since the mid-1950s, the majority of these populations have come from the former colonial empire.[17] They share a common history with France. And that history is also patently neglected in the Republic's curriculum, or only told in such factual terms that it loses all exemplary or systemic value.

The Colonial Imaginary and "Republican Integration"

There are two possible explanations. The first relates to the fact that the "republican" policy of integration, a legacy of the Third Republic's assimilation policies, offers a model in which cultural—and religious—particularities have to be erased in favor of integrating into the universalist republican system (antimulticulturalism).[18] Promoting arguments regarding a history in which the Republic betrayed its values, and addressing the children of the primary victims of that betrayal, are considered threats to society that could result in a contraction of identity and a rejection of the republican model. However, to deny these new generations the ability to understand their own history is to deny them their roots and the genealogy of what they often experience as a double culture. This unacknowledged memory has led to the creation of new forms of sociability and new modes of cultural expression among those who experience French society as a hostile environment. We have denied this memory for too long, and we are reaching the limits of such denial. We have also reached a breaking point in the republican model of integration. The situation in some *banlieues* housing projects is the most obvious and violent expression of that limit.

This naturally leads us to another blind spot, which also comes from the legacy of our unacknowledged colonial past: relationships between identity-based communities. Often they are informed by representations of the colonial "other," which were created over more than a century of colonial history. Let us be clear: discrimination toward immigrant populations has its roots in colonialism.[19] If we want to understand and deconstruct the foundations of that imaginary—and as a consequence, strip it of any vitality—then we have to bring colonial history into the social and public sphere. However, the issue has never been broached according to such terms, and that is precisely because it is difficult to admit that France—like other colonial centers—produced an imaginary based on discrimination within the Republic.

A Gap in Memory

Another sign of a failed colonial memory is the wholesale neglect by museums for the recognition of colonial history. All other former colonial powers have erected sites of "memory" or "recognition" for colonization, or have reimagined their old colonial museums, with the exception of France. The state, although not denying access to information related to this history, and despite the dynamic teams of researchers that exist, provides laughably minuscule sums of funding. Researchers are forced to dig through archives in remote sites scattered around the country. They often rely on private foundations which usually offer richer documentation than what is available in national museums. And there are very few research positions available for those specialized in colonial issues, either at universities or the CNRS research centers.

Researching this issue, one is struck by the gap in memory, which is especially fraught when it comes to policy. Antisemitism has been a persistent issue (Action Française at the time of the Dreyfus affair, leagues during the interwar period, the Vichy Regime, the Front National), although colonial discrimination actually originates in the very heart of the republican system. A country that has a limited number of "scholars," "sites of memory," or "knowledge archives" is not equipped to undertake the long journey of remembering and the process of coming to terms with its colonial history. The vast majority of social actors, traditional political parties, educational structures, and antiracist movements have de facto accepted the marginalization of the colonial issue.

Society would be perfectly capable of functioning in spite of that kind of "self-mutilation," but, as the news confirms, colonization and decolonization continue to have an impact, notably through the stigmatization of certain immigrant groups and their descendants. The ubiquity of that past is unavoidable, and today the Republic—after losing its soul to the colonies—runs the risk of also losing its values. Both in the eyes of its "nationals," but also in the eyes of new arrivals—those who will seek to integrate into the republican system. For the new immigrant generation of colonial descendants, "the promise of integration, which was not kept, led to both direct and micro discriminations... Consequently, we ought to invent new ways of coexisting that do not rely on the ruse of integration."[20] To open the debate on colonial memory is to question the Republic's conceptions of integration and citizenship. It is to question its values. The challenge is great. It is national.

Nicolas Bancel is Professor at the University of Lausanne, Switzerland, and codirector of the ACHAC Research Group. He is author or coeditor of numerous influential books, including *De l'indigène à l'immigré* (1998), *La République coloniale: Essai sur une utopie* (2003), *La République coloniale* (2006), *Human Zoos: Science and Spectacle in the Age of Colonial Empires* (2008), *La France arabo-orientale* (2013), *Colonial Culture in France since the Revolution* (2014), *The Invention of Race* (2014), and *Vers la guerre des identités* (2016).

Pascal Blanchard is a historian and researcher at the Laboratoire Communication et Politique (Paris, France, CNRS), codirector of the ACHAC Research Group, and a documentary filmmaker. He is a specialist on the colonial question in France, contemporary French history and immigration, and author, coauthor, editor, or coeditor of *Human Zoos: Science and Spectacle in the Age of Colonial Empires* (2008), *Human Zoos. The Invention of the Savage* (2011), *Zoos humains et exhibitions coloniales: 150 ans d'inventions de l'autre* (2011), *Colonial Culture in France since the Revolution* (2014), *La France arabo-orientale* (2013), *Les années 30 sont de retour: Petite leçon d'histoire pour comprendre les crises* (2014), *Le Grand Repli* (2015), and *Vers la guerre des identités* (2016).

Notes

1. Pierre Vidal-Naquet, *Les assassins de la mémoire* (Paris: La Découverte, 1987).
2. Jean-Clément Martin and Charles Suaud, "Le Puy du Fou: L'interminable réinvention du passé vendéen," *Actes de la Recherche en sciences sociales* 93 (June 1992): 21–37.
3. Georges Huppert, *L'idée de l'histoire parfaite* (Paris: Flammarion, 1973).

4. Daniel Lindenberg, "Guerres de mémoire en France," *Vingtième siècle: Revue d'histoire* 42, no. 1 (April–June 1994): 77–96.

5. Benjamin Stora, *La gangrène et l'oubli* (Paris: La Découverte, 1991).

6. Lindenberg, "Guerres de mémoire en France."

7. This is in reference to the work by the American Robert Paxton, *Vichy France: Old Guard and New Order, 1940–1944* (New York: Columbia University Press, 1972), *La France de Vichy, 1940–1944*, trans. Claude Bertrand (Paris: Seuil, 1973), which led to a veritable historiographical revolution and opened, once and for all, an old French wound on the Vichy period.

8. See Bernard Lewis, *History: Remembered, Recovered, Invented* (Princeton, NJ: Princeton University Press, 1983).

9. The first on colonization, "Les autres crimes commis au nom de la République," was published in *Marianne* (May 14, 2001). The second, more general in scope, was titled "Polémiques sur l'histoire coloniale," *Manière de voir* 58 (July–August 2001). Finally, "Le temps des colonies," a special issue of *L'histoire* 11 (April 2001).

10. Alain Ruscio, "Y'a bon les colonies," *Autrement* 144 (April 1994): 36–51.

11. With respect to the Shoah, see, for example, the scandal surrounding Norman G. Finkelstein's *L'industrie de l'holocauste* (Paris: La Fabrique éditions, 2001).

12. Nicolas Bancel, Pascal Blanchard, and Laurent Gervereau, eds., *Images et colonies (1880–1962)* (Paris: BDIC-ACHAC, 1993).

13. On this issue see Raoul Girardet, *L'idée coloniale en France* (Paris: La Table Ronde, 1972) and Pascal Blanchard, *Nationalisme et colonialisme*, PhD diss., University of Paris I, 1994.

14. See Alice Conklin, *A Mission to Civilize: The Republican Idea of Empire in France and West Africa, 1895–1930* (Stanford, CA: Stanford University Press, 1997).

15. See Alfred Grosset, *Le crime et la mémoire* (Paris: Flammarion, 1989) and Yves Benot, *Massacres coloniaux: 1944–1950: La IVème République et la mise au pas des colonies françaises* (Paris: La Découverte, 2001).

16. Catherine Coquery-Vidrovitch, "Colonial History and Decolonization: The French Imperial Case," *The European Journal of Development Research: Revue de l'EADI* 3, no. 2 (1991): 28–43.

17. See Gérard Noiriel, *Le creuset français: Histoire de l'immigration—XIXe XXe siècles* (Paris: Seuil, 1988).

18. On this debate, see Pierre-André Taguieff, "La confluence des fatalismes: Emprise globalitaire, dérives identitaires," *Les Temps modernes* 613 (March–May 2001): 131–157; Andrea Semprini, *Le multiculturalisme* (Paris: PUF, 1997); and Fred Constant, *Le multiculturalisme* (Paris: Flammarion, 2000).

19. Pascal Blanchard and Nicolas Bancel, *De l'indigène à l'immigré* (Paris: Gallimard, 1993).

20. Nacira Guénif-Souilamas, "L'intégration, une idée épuisée," *Libération*, July 12, 2001.

13

OVERSEAS FRANCE

A VESTIGE OF THE REPUBLICAN COLONIAL UTOPIA?

Françoise Vergès

Overseas France today is spread across a variety of cultural zones: the Caribbean and the Americas (Martinique, Guadeloupe, Guiana, Saint-Pierre-et-Miquelon), the Pacific (New Caledonia, French Polynesia, Wallis and Futuna), the Indian Ocean (Mayotte, Réunion, and the îles Éparses), and Antarctica. These territories do not all share the same status, history, economy, populations, or even for that matter, the same cultures. The *Départements d'Outre-Mer* (DOM, overseas departments) and *régions d'Outre-Mer* (ROM, overseas regions), known today as the Départements et régions d'outre mer (DROMs), include Martinique, Guadeloupe, Guiana, Réunion, and Mayotte; the *collectivités d'Outre-Mer* (COM, overseas collectivities) are made up of New Caledonia, French Polynesia, Wallis and Futuna, and Saint-Pierre-et-Miquelon; and finally there are the *Terres australes et antarctiques françaises* (TAAF, French Southern and Antarctic Lands). What these territories do share, however, is a colonial past, traces of which are to be found today in fragile economies, weak industry and high rates of unemployment, as well as rampant inequality.[1]

But what is actually known in France and elsewhere of these "overseas" territories? Of their cultures? Of their struggles? What kinds of images, representations, and events do we associate with these places? What are the stereotypes and clichés that accompany such travels? Some clichés have become familiar as a result of military service, teaching positions, from family members working there, or from tourism and vacations, such as tropical landscapes, the jungle, exoticism, populations on welfare, music. . . . But these territories remain outside of the national narrative, major debates, and even the news, except when there is a hurricane or an earthquake. National statistics on education, unemployment, urbanization, health, racism, salaries, and so on, *never* include these overseas territories. Moreover, the very designation "overseas" (*outre-mer*) does little to help make sense of these spaces. Historically, such designations were substituted for the problematic term *colonial*, and that subtle shift has contributed to perpetuating an anachronism on which neither the French public nor the field of research have dwelled.

What Are the Overseas Territories?

When, how, and why did these territories become attached to the French Republic? Why are they still French? Why, when, and how were they forgotten in the national narrative? Among these forgotten spaces, those that experienced the first round of colonization—Guadeloupe, Guiana, Martinique, and Réunion—make up a special case. Relics from the prerevolutionary and pre-republican empire (they were colonized in the seventeenth century)—and therefore predating the colonial empire, which was established in 1830 and which grew under the Third Republic, these territories experienced slavery, the plantation system, indentured labor, forced labor, and later colonialism.[2] Their status as colonies only came to an end in 1946, and their transformation into overseas departments did not signify access to the very thing the people in these territories sought: equality. It was a time during which a significant reconfiguration of the republican space took place. Following the universal condemnation of racism and demand for decolonization after World War II, the French state was forced to reconsider its links to its colonies in a context of the reconstruction of its infrastructure and economy, the creation of the European community, the beginning of the Cold War, and rising US hegemony and nationalist insurrections and revolutions in its colonial empire. In this reconfiguration, the French state decided upon the nondevelopment of the current overseas territories, and thus began to apply two policies: birth control and organized emigration. In the 1960s and 1970s, cultural and political movements were brutally repressed, and murders, censorship, and denial of civil rights were common. By the 1980s and 1990s, leftist and left movements and political parties were protesting against repression in France; with the turn to a neoliberal economy and orthodoxy, overseas territories virtually disappeared from French consciousness. Since then, the French state has oscillated between paternalism (racism's avatar), indifference, negligence, and repression.

The overseas territories are no longer colonies, but neither are they independent territories; they remain subject to positive and negative exceptionalist policies (special laws or exceptions in the law to account for structural lags). The terminology is not without consequences: these spaces do not enter into clear categories, which marginalizes the territories and relegates their populations to clichés (as welfare dependent, closed-in on their own communities). One term, however, seems appropriate: *postcoloniality.*

The postcolony does not strictly refer to a regime of national independence, but rather a situation in which the effects of the colonial regime continue to be felt, and in which new experiences have emerged, such as the decline in local production (sugar, bananas, pineapples), membership in the European zone (and its difficulty competing with European economies due to distance from the mainland, labor costs), globalization (competition with emerging economies), a rise in the number of secondary school and university graduates, the emergence of reparations claims (as a result of the memory of slavery and of colonialism), and assertion of cultural difference. The "coloniality of power" is the perpetuation by the state of policies informed by processes of racialization, techniques of dispossession, and stigmatization.

Processes of Creolization

In colonies where slavery was imposed, creolization was initially propelled by the struggle against inequality—rather than a dynamic of interculturality. Indeed, the groups (of various origins) who founded the overseas populations often came together around issues of equality in order to put an end to the injustices of which they were all victim. That realization, therefore, undermined assertions that suggested cultural difference was a danger to the Republic. These groups were able to build unity precisely through their diversity.

Oppositions between cultural difference and democracy and between religious plurality and the Republic are both opportunistic and ideological. Requests to be recognized as culturally different are automatically viewed as demands from insular communities. Debates opposing rigid "republicans" against essentialist "communitarians" disregard history, with one side arguing for the necessity of universalist abstraction, and the other for atemporal identity. Both points of view, however, mask a politics of exclusion. *Republican entrenchment is a response to identity-based entrenchment.*

This opposition has been covered by the national media and presented in terms of a struggle between "moderns" and "obscurantists." Yet, today, there is no single way of being either modern or European. Beyond these quarrels and avoidance strategies, closer scrutiny of colonialism in all its forms—slavery, forced labor, indentured servitude, discriminatory policies—involves concerted historical work so as to better address a range of complex forms, processes of cross-pollination, and the resulting territories produced by exchanges between the metropole and the colonies. Either we accept that individuals and groups have a singular history, memory, and culture from which to construct a shared narrative, or we demand that all those wishing to become citizens or members of a community erase their singularity. Interactions between singular memories and histories lead to the development of shared narratives, which do not prevent singular memories and histories from surviving. Shared narratives do not erase conflict and responsibility. Rather, they shed light on them, which is not the same as an act of accusation.

Colonial history, in its old form—celebration of the French colonial empire—or in its critical form—which acknowledges dubious aspects of the colonial adventure—has shown little interest in overseas territories. "Neither national, nor completely colonial,"[3] these territories represent an impasse in the colonial and postcolonial narrative and that choice enables us to analyze the presence or absence of overseas territories over the long term. *Inexistence* or *insignificance* is precisely what makes sense, since it reveals the ambiguous status of those territories. The Republic's amnesiac narrative points to a deep ambivalence: the colonies are absent from the historical works that serve as foundational pieces in the idea of the nation and the affirmation of the greatness of French colonization. As I have argued repeatedly over the years, colonization was not simply a political fact. Rather it instituted arbitrary and exceptional measures.

A History That Is a Non-History . . .

The study of this ambivalence provides an opportunity to learn about the reasons for this denegation. Inquiring into the assertions and presuppositions made about these marginalized territories seems useful. In the margins of colonial history, absent from national history, absent from the postcolonial problematic, the overseas territories remain excluded from history, despite being an integral part of the republican space. There are other reasons for this invisibility: lack of heroic narratives, incapacity on the part of the French populace to identify with a moral and political posture of resistance (as in the case of Algeria). The political independence of formerly colonized territories makes it possible to take stock of the colonial situation, since two points of view emerge and confront each other: that of the formerly colonized and that of the former colonizer. But researchers are baffled by the case of postcoloniality.

To think of the presence or absence of the overseas territories is to think of two spaces at the same time: the territory overseas *and* the mainland metropolitan territory. Today, both belong to the same political body (the Republic). However, the establishment of overseas territories preceded the arrival of the Republic. Not only did the Republic inherit these territories from the Revolution, it also claimed that they were an "integral part" of France. The continuity between the Bourbon dream and the republican dream gives these spaces a unique dimension: seen from the colonies, the "metropole" seems like "eternal France" rather than the Republic; and, seen from the metropole, the overseas territories seem to be a manifestation of the ways in which the dream of colonization succeeded—they look like a colonial utopia.

This *ambiguous memory* that is the product of the coexistence of an absence and a presence, is particularly interesting when analyzing expressions of colonial fracture, negated memory, and marginalized history. The relationship between the metropole and colonies has to be considered in terms of multiterritorialization and its configuration in time—prerevolutionary, slave-owning society, colonial, then postcolonial. The point of departure for a rereading of these cross-pollinating histories is the absence of slavery in the national narrative. That absence is a symptom of the difficulties involved in assimilating colonial history, particularly in its oldest manifestations, with the slave trade and slavery. Integrating the figure of the colonized is a difficult task; integrating that of the slave has been nearly impossible.[4]

The Feeling of "Not Enough"

The presence of descendants of slaves and colonized citizens throws another light onto the "racial fracture," since it reveals even more strikingly the resistance and failure to come to terms with colonial racism in French society. In general, it is difficult to account for discrimination in a precise manner in France, but the forms of discrimination faced by those from France's overseas territories are even lesser known.

In the 1960s, the French state created the *Bumidom*[5] to organize what it had planned in the 1940s, namely the massive emigration of young women and men from the overseas departments. As the French were leaving low-level public functions (in hospitals, the postal service, customs), these positions were later filled by Antilleans, particularly in the Ile-de-France area. People from Réunion were scattered throughout the territory. Contrary to popular belief, and as Claude-Valentin Marie's research has shown, when it comes to the Paris area, the difficulties faced by families from the overseas departments are essentially similar to those encountered by immigrants in a more general manner.[6]

The children of immigrants experience discrimination. They are interested in issues of memory and identity politics. In Paris, during the 150th anniversary of the abolition of slavery on May 23, 1998, tens of thousands of West Indian, Guianese, and Réunionese gathered to honor the memory of the slaves and protest the government slogan *Tous nés en 1848* (We Were All Born in 1848), which established the April 27th, 1848 decree abolishing slavery as a kind of foundational myth. The law of May 10, 2001, which classified the slave trade and slavery as crimes against humanity, played a decisive role in that it encouraged symbolic and concrete gestures in the fields of education, research, and culture. However, the feeling remains that "not enough" had been done.

To many, the memory of slavery must become a central issue for French society. But official ceremonies around the memorialization of slavery actually obscure the weight that the colonial and postcolonial situations continue to exert on the present. Abolition, which ought to have decreased slavery's overwhelming effects, was in actuality a partial failure.

The colonial utopia turned the postabolition colonial space into a space of social regeneration, but at the price of denying continued contradictions and inequalities. Republicans wanted to believe that through their will alone, and the application of their principles, they could transform a colony where slavery once held sway into a harmonious society. This was to give principles more power than they could possibly have and to forget that society is not only governed by principles. Elsewhere, I have discussed *paradoxical citizenship* and *colored citizenship* (to be a citizen *and* to be colonized);[7] such citizenship is a symptom of this relationship, which produces inclusion *and* exclusion. Citizenship, equality, and fraternity are concepts that bend to the circumstances; those from the overseas territories can be citizens and colonized, equal but not quite, brothers, but little brothers.

As Aimé Césaire remarked in 1948, the abolition of slavery in 1848 was "at once enormous and insufficient."[8] A moral approach—condemnation—is not enough. Slavery was a social, cultural, and economic system that required complex organization. The current impact of slavery in overseas societies is multidimensional: extremely unequal property ownership, the lingering importance of color, conflictual relationships with manual labor, low levels of diversity in industry, shame and resentment; but there are also Creole languages and cultures and a living oral tradition.

The overseas territories are relics of the monarchic colonial empire. Studying these territories reveals a certain continuity between the monarchy and the Republic. They are proof of the persistence of a European utopia—that of a harmonious colony. It is perhaps in this liminal space that the republican colonial utopia, with the pursuit of an old European dream of a reconciled and conflict-free society, originated. But today, the diversity of overseas territories—spaces where alterity is apparent and which the Republic seems to have trouble recognizing—undermines the vestiges of a colonial utopia.

Françoise Vergès holds the Global South Chair at the Collège d'études mondiales at the Fondation Maison des Sciences de l'Homme and is Consulting Professor at Goldsmiths College, London. She is an international authority on the history of slavery and the slave trade and colonialism, and author of numerous works, including *Abolir l'esclavage: Une utopie coloniale, les ambiguïtés d'une politique humanitaire* (2001), *La mémoire enchaînée: Questions sur l'esclavage* (2006), *La République coloniale: Essai sur une utopie* (2006), *Nègre je suis, Nègre je resterai: Entretiens avec Aimé Césaire* (2007), and *L'homme prédateur, ce que nous enseigne l'esclavage sur notre temps* (2011).

Notes

1. These, and related questions, are explored in Françoise Vergès, *La mémoire enchaînée: Questions sur l'esclavage* (Paris: Albin Michel, 2006).

2. After the abolition of slavery in 1848, colonials in Réunion and the West Indies replaced slaves by "importing" indentured labor (Indians, Chinese, Malays, Madagascans, Mozambicans, among others), who were submitted to living and labor conditions that resembled those of slavery.

3. Myriam Cottias, "Le silence de la nation," *Outre-Mers* 90, nos. 338–339 (2003): 30.

4. See the Comité pour la mémoire de l'esclavage (Committee for the Memory of Slavery) report to the prime minister in April 2005: *Mémoires de la traite négrière, de l'esclavage et de leurs abolitions*, www.comite-memoire-esclavage.fr.

5. *Bureau pour le développement des migrations intéressant les départements d'Outre-Mer* (Bureau for the Development of Migration Related to Overseas Departments): a department created by the state that was tasked with organizing the migration of people from the West Indies, Guiana, and Réunion toward France.

6. Claude-Valentin Marie, "Les populations des DOM-TOM en France métropolitaine," *Espace, populations, sociétés* 4, no. 2 (1986): 197–206.

7. Françoise Vergès, *Abolir l'esclavage: une utopie coloniale: Les ambiguïtés d'une politique humanitaire* (Paris: Albin Michel, 2001).

8. Aimé Césaire, "Discours prononcé à l'occasion de la commémoration du centenaire de l'abolition de l'esclavage," University of the Sorbonne, Paris, April 27, 1948.

PART II

POSTCOLONIAL RUPTURES / 2010

2.1. DEBATING THE COLONIAL LEGACY

14

RETHINKING POLITICS IN THE FRENCH OVERSEAS DEPARTMENTS

Jacky Dahomay

IN 2009, THE four French overseas Départements et régions d'outre mer (Overseas departments and regions, DROMs)—Martinique, Guadeloupe, Guiana, and Réunion—were shaken by protests initiated by various social movements. Guadeloupe was particularly affected. A fifth DROM was added during the same period: Mayotte. The news brought images of the tumult coursing through these small French territories scattered in the Americas and Indian Ocean to audiences in mainland France. How can we begin to explain the fact that conflicts that began in Guadeloupe eventually spread to other overseas departments? What gave rise to them? Does France have a problem with its DOMs? Or perhaps should one examine the problem the other way around. Although the protests were initially informed by a range of social questions linked to the expensive cost of living, rising gas prices, inadequate wages, and so on, they also seemed to exceed purely social considerations in order to gain proximity to what some were calling "societal" questions. But what does that mean exactly? And since these movements were not brought about by political parties, who were themselves surprised by their radical nature, but rather by a variety of civic organizations and unions, the issue of the legal status of the four DROMs in question and their regulatory future emerged as additional factors.

Public opinion in France was for the most part negative: "If the overseas citizens aren't happy, they can have their independence!" Yet, at no moment during these uprisings was the question of independence specifically articulated by leaders of the protesting groups. What, then, were the protesters seeking? It is difficult to say, and that is precisely the problem. If the movements that broke out in France's peripheral departments were not simply social, nor directly political, then the issue must be deeper: it must relate to the very core of identity in the region. What does it mean to be an overseas French citizen? That is the question that has come to light. It is a fundamental, comprehensive issue, one that is also deeply political. I am therefore interested in exploring additionally the question of politics in the French overseas departments. As we shall see, such a task also involves questioning traditional French republican identity.

What Sets the DOMs Apart, Anthropologically and Politically Speaking?

Let us start by setting out the anthropological and political specificities of the French overseas departments. Whereas the French people—that is to say the community of citizens or the French nation—obtained sovereignty in 1789, those living in the overseas departments occupy a peculiar space in the history of the French nation. To be sure, the residents are French citizens, but nationality has never merely been a legal issue. Residents of the overseas departments are of course very attached to their French citizenship, but French nationality is problematic for them. Hence their insistence on identity issues, which have proven extremely difficult to articulate in clear political terms. To untangle these issues, we have to turn to history. Mainland France likely does not share the same history as the overseas departments, nor the same anthropological foundations. Although all French citizens, regardless of origin, have a right to equal participation in the creation of laws and political authority, such legal equality can at times hide strong societal and cultural differences.

The problem resides in knowing the extent to which French republican citizenship, in its universalist aims, is capable of erasing a citizen's affiliation with another culture or history. Is a "pure citizen," an individual that has no cultural or ethnic background, even possible? What might an integration policy founded on republican principles and the notion of peaceful coexistence among a diverse array of cultures resemble? Should a distinction be made between one's political identity and one's cultural identity? History might perhaps shed light on some of these questions. It seems obvious that the social and anthropological foundations of the overseas departments would be different from those of mainland France. Having said this, formal analysis remains crucial, namely more in-depth historical and anthropological research than what is currently available. This is my goal in this chapter.

The most obvious particularity of the overseas departments resides in the fact that they are former colonies that were only recently—a little over a half century ago—made into departments. Why have almost all the other former French colonies (and English colonies, too) gained independence? That is perhaps the fundamental issue that needs to be fleshed out. To do that we would have to review what I call the anthropological foundations of these former colonies in their historical origins; I will focus especially on those in America, since those are the ones I know best.

Initially, the majority of the populations in these former French colonies was essentially made up of African slaves; these were resource colonies rather than colonies to be populated. Slavery in America was based on a threefold form of de-territorialization. The first was physical or geographical; populations were transferred from Africa to America in slave trade ships, which Édouard Glissant aptly dubbed "*transbord*" (transship).[1] The second was social: the form of slavery that was brought to the Americas at the dawn of modernity differed from classical or traditional forms of slavery (many societies have, of course, known slavery). This form of slavery was directly linked to another means of exploiting resources, that of modern capitalism in its first phase of expansion: the mercantilism of the seventeenth century.

There was a transition from societies in which slaves existed to societies that were entirely guided by a mode of capitalist production, what can be called, rigorously speaking, "slave societies." Serfdom, which had already been attempted, did not work, and a wage-earning class had not yet emerged. This was a preindustrial phase, and slaves remained the primary source of labor. The social being of slaves was different from past social situations for laborers, even different from those of the traditional slave in Africa. The third form of de-territorialization was cultural. Africans brought to the colonies on slave ships came from a diverse array of ethnic origins, and they were deprived of all cultural points of reference and frameworks to make sense of their collective existence. This lasted for two centuries. But if the system endured, it was because of a cultural phenomenon known as "Creolization." A kind of anthropological reestablishment took place, one that was completely different from what had occurred in other African or Asian colonies (with the exception of Réunion) conquered by Europe in the second half of the twentieth century. Those other colonies already had an anthropological and political foundation before colonization as well as territorial continuity.

How can we understand the anthropological specificity of the American colonies? On the one hand, the societies in question were not constituted in continuity with the past, as was the case with many communities. At the beginning, there was a kind of *temps zéro* to borrow an expression from Claude Lévi-Strauss with respect to the Americas, almost as if time had remained fixed. Whereas the radical break with the past sought by revolutionaries in mainland France was difficult to bring about (despite the painful episode of the Terror), this succeeded in the colonies, and violence proved foundational.

The state was not born in connection with the dynamics of society. Although, even in the France of the Ancien Régime, the development of the state was riddled with social issues, notably concerning the wars of religion. The absolutist state was therefore a form of autonomy from political authority, and Jacobins were the first republicans to inherit this history of the state and society.

We are far from the idea of a racial historical determinism that would establish a direct link between the present and the past. However, the present has to confront the past at each new historical stage. That is as true for metropolitan France as it is for its overseas departments. Here, it is important to understand, if we seek to make our societies more peaceful, that the past can block the present from effecting changes. Indeed, if slavery's past continues to weigh on us, it is because we have failed to address it—or failed to do so adequately—and that is the case both in the metropole and in the former colonies overseas.

Historically Characterizing the Overseas Departments

One of the first characteristics of the societies installed in the slave-holding colonies of America is located in the fact that, unlike in other communities in which society is formed based on the family, here, society preceded the family. First came the colonials, then, in most cases, they waited for the "disembarkation of girls," to use Saint-John Perse's vocabulary,[2] to choose a wife. For their part, slaves met their companions in slave quarters, but, strictly speaking, the family structure did not come about quite so easily. Male slaves were not real heads of families: they, their children, and their wives all belonged to a master, who was free to use and abuse them as he so pleased. As anthropologists and psychoanalysts have shown, that dynamic shaped male and female roles within the family that help partially explain the current roles of mothers and fathers in West Indian families as well as familial and sexual pathologies and a range of criminality. The problem comes from determining whether such psychological analyses can account for general or political behaviors. There are no doubt correspondences, but it is not within the scope of this chapter to develop a deeper analysis of that point. What is certain, however, is that an analysis of the family structure, such as Emmanuel Todd has done, for example, gives us insight into social behaviors.[3] Such analyses may prove crucial in understanding citizens' relationships to the law in our societies.

A second particularity, that we have already touched upon, is that of the state's role. The state is by nature in a position of exteriority vis-à-vis the society. The colonialist state inherited a political system founded on an original violence, which plays a decisive role in its practices. That does not mean it is not able, at times, to contradict the colonials, who themselves constantly criticized "ministerial despotism." Thus, as paradoxical as it may seem, the only social class capable of gaining autonomy with respect to the state is that of the colonials. The paradox derives from the fact that the state is colonialist and slave-holding—thereby securing its perennial position—yet simultaneously mired in a bureaucratic logic and in legal frameworks proper to the absolutist state. Whereas masters dreamed of total power, without mediation, over the "naked life" of slaves (to borrow a term from Giorgio Agamben),[4] the monarchic power still sought to maintain a legal mediation between the master and the slave—which was one of the functions of the Code Noir. As despicable as the Code Noir was, it nevertheless represented the only limit to the master's power over his slaves.

In 1788, in the colony of Saint-Domingue (where Malouet was governor at the time), slaves filed a complaint against a master for abuse and actually won, which was a scandal among colonials. That might explain why, when the Revolution broke out in 1789, the majority of slaves supported the king, an allegiance that would, of course, shift later. This can be explained by the fact that the majority of slaves came from societies in which multiple forms of royalty existed. Whereas masters harbored dreams of increased autonomy, the middle class, made up of "poor whites" and free colored men, expected social ascension to come from the state. Most of the slaves, who were not even considered human beings at the time, had trouble imagining that a political solution could lead to their emancipation; their only perceived option was escape, but that only rarely occurred.

Finally, the colonialist and slave-based system meant that a civil society could not really exist. Slaves tried to create a society by establishing bonds with slaves in other households, but that took place in the framework of a cultural life that became creolized with respect to Africa and in resistance to oppression, but which does not really constitute a true civil society capable of building a political struggle against the system of domination. Things would progressively change after the French Revolution and the abolition of slavery, but the seeds of a relationship to politics can be found here. The colonialist slave society already featured a number of traits that would later characterize the relationship of the West Indian masses with politics, society, and culture. Those traits would be reconfigured in 1848, with the entry into politics of blacks, but only as a function of that heritage.[5]

The abolition of slavery in 1848 granted citizenship to former male slaves, making them political subjects, but most of the working-class struggles had assimilationist aims, which ran counter to autonomist resistance toward former masters, who themselves looked poorly upon their former slaves' access to equal rights. For the vast majority of the population, autonomist positions could coherently contain a denial of equal rights. The colonialist state was viewed at once as dominating, oppressive, and liberating. The republicans of 1848 requested that slaves forget the past and consider their freedom in terms of an act of generosity on the part of the motherland. A dialectic of assimilation was thus established among the masses along with a repression of the memory of slavery among French republicans. And it is very likely that today's overseas departments, which are societies marked by a history of slavery and colonization, are trapped—much like the politics of the French state—in this unresolved past.

But what gives most pause, beyond the population's "republicanism" which has been so striking to historians, is the extreme insistence on the social question for a period that lasted until 1946. Sensitivity to equal rights, together with social issues in an underdeveloped society does not allow politics to become autonomous with respect to the colonial state within a specific public space. The political life and practice of the elected class are inscribed in such a framework. Political struggles are directly linked to social struggles, or at least they come out of them; this is normal in any society, some might say, except that in these colonies, politics was not a space in which to reflect on one's destiny. That engenders a political class that, on the right and on the left, features a mainly instrumental and management-oriented vision, with clientelist practices and an inability—except in rare cases—to develop projects that are autonomous from the motherland.

All of this explains why, after the Second World War, these old colonies did not choose national independence, even though other colonies in sub-Saharan Africa, North Africa, and Indochina did. After 1946, the social question became even more decisive with demands for social rights (housing, health, education, equal pay). Nevertheless, it would be wrong to describe the attachment of these populations to France solely in terms of these social needs. It is important to remember that mainland politics have been important topics of discussion in these former colonies ever since 1789, a phenomenon which itself is a particularity of French colonialism; and they share a long common history with France. They are, in fact, its oldest colonies, with notably, the two defining moments of the abolition of slavery. Moreover, ever since the Revolution and the Parisian *sans-culottes*, social questions have played a particularly important role in France, something which a number of observers, notably Marx, fastened upon. It therefore makes sense that the French socialism of the era was to have a major impact on the leaders of the West Indian social and political movements of the nineteenth century. Consequently, if politics is indeed defining for the fate of a country, then the fate of these overseas departments merged with that of mainland France.

The year 1946 was not, therefore, the beginning of assimilation, but rather its end. The decade that followed saw the spread of national liberation struggles in Africa and Asia. Meanwhile, an opposite tendency characterized the West Indies. The French state may very well have hesitated with respect to its assimilation policies, what with the decolonization movements unfolding elsewhere, but in 1956, Charles de Gaulle took a trip to the overseas departments and realized how attached the local populations were to France. It was at that time that the state began to reinforce its assimilation policies, despite the appearance of autonomy and independence movements. Although independence movements included social struggles, autonomist strains did not gain traction within the population. The most obvious case was that of the Communist Party in Guadeloupe, which was one of the largest in the overseas departments. Still, there was a parallel rise in identity claims, especially on the cultural level, many of which were expressed in literature, including in the writings of Aimé Césaire. However, Édouard Glissant and other adherents of "Creoleness," had trouble marrying the quest for cultural identity with the concrete development of forms of identity politics. Independence parties therefore never had a large influence over local political life nor in the consciousness of the masses, despite some sensational actions. In Guadeloupe, where that dynamic was at its strongest, powerful social movements were born, notably with the creation of the *Union des travailleurs agricoles* (UTA, Agricultural Workers' Union), the *Union des producteurs de Guadeloupe* (UPG, Guadeloupe Producers' Union), and the *Union générale des travailleurs de Guadeloupe* (UGTG, General Workers' Union of Guadeloupe), but social struggles did not lead to a break with France, even if they did contribute to a renewal of the identity issue.

Attempting to summarize four centuries of history in a few pages, one runs the risk of oversimplification. I am not a historian, nor do I pretend to be one. For me, an overview of that history can be helpful in gaining an understanding of the philosophical and political aspects of these phenomena. The law concerning departmentalization dates back to 1946, and yet the overseas departments are not completely pacified. Current events point to the importance of social struggles, which have reached an unprecedented state, especially in Guadeloupe with the LKP (*Liyannaj kont pwofitasyon,* Stand Up against Exploitation). I have attempted to show how we cannot understand the overseas departments without referencing this history, with which most people in mainland France are not familiar. Let us now attempt to understand the real nature of the political problems affecting these French overseas possessions.

Difficulties of Political Autonomy

A cursory overview of history reveals how a number of elements can be held responsible for the development of political autonomy in the public space in the overseas departments: the history of slavery, the absence of civil society, the extreme importance that social questions have secured, and the prevalence of bureaucratic, clientelist, and assimilationist political practices. Slaves became citizens in 1848, but the colonial context remained long after that date, producing a somewhat unique figure from the vantage point of traditional political philosophy: the colonized citizen (*citoyen colonisé*) or the citizen colonized (*colonisé citoyen*), with Algerians of course having a different status as noncitizen French nationals. Such are the ambiguities and contradictions of French republicanism, repressed in the consciousness of French people in the mainland.

We are witnessing today an upsurge of memory with respect to this past, and that is something deeply troubling to traditional political identity in France. The year 1946 saw the emancipation from a colonial situation and the establishment of equal rights. Once these former colonies were departmentalized, the history of these former colonies could be summed up in terms of the struggle for full access to equal rights. Césaire's political choice in this realm was no doubt popular, since it corresponded to a *desire* on the part of overseas populations, but it was not the fruit of an authentic political *will* that was clearly chosen and debated in civil society. The overseas departments are now confronted with a similar rational and eminently political desire. The issue is essentially one of responsibility. Yet, those living in these overseas departments experience almost schizophrenic or tragic contradictions (conceived as a host of contradictions that cannot be transcended through a straightforward dialectical process), which lead to pathologies in the entire social body. Hence the essential malaise of these societies. A contradiction between social struggles that are deeply integrationist and social struggles led by independentists or autonomists; a contradiction between the will to preserve French citizenship and the fierce need for cultural recognition.

To this, we should add two things. First, the fact that the French state, although having eliminated some colonial practices from the past (notably those of Gaullism), does not understand the overseas departments in economic, social, and political terms. That was flagrantly evident during the Sarkozy presidency (2007–2012) and when Yves Jego was secretary of state for Overseas France (2008–2009). Second, a political class accustomed to managing local institutions and handling negotiations within the framework of centralized power structures and against the backdrop of clientelism, is seemingly incapable of implementing projects susceptible to improving circumstances in these societies. Meanwhile, frozen with fear and confused by contradictions, the electorate time and again have voted to maintain the status quo.

The first contradiction, which opposed social struggles against political consciousness, was expressed during the social conflicts, notably in Guadeloupe, where the LKP provided the most forceful position and offered the greatest hope. These events had an undeniably important international impact and was the context in which the French state decided to organize a commission on the overseas departments. The LKP managed to lead a mass movement based on the two above-mentioned contradictions (social struggles vs. political struggles; identity needs vs. preservation of French citizenship), expressing them with urgency. Yet, from that point of view, the LKP found itself at an impasse in that it was unable to emphasize the societal aspect of a movement that successfully mobilized Guadeloupe's civil society, instead getting bogged down in social demands which had been a constant feature of such struggles since 1848. As such, it failed to capitalize on this opportunity to rethink the political on the basis of civil society, and therefore to seize the moment when it presented itself and make the leap (albeit a daunting one) from the social to the political. How can we explain this failure?

Clearly, transitioning from social struggles to political action is difficult at the best of times, and certainly not something which comes easy to us. The socialist tradition in general, and in France in particular, has confronted such difficulties and continues to do so, despite the crisis of capitalism that we are experiencing today. LKP leaders are militants who found their motivation in the usual forms of Marxist or nationalist ideologies, and proved incapable of moving from social conflict toward a reformulation of political issues in their societies. The main reason for their failure resides in the fact that major political issues are not solely grounded in social struggle, and the essence of politics, contrary to what Marx thought, is not located in the resolution of class conflict.

The political realm is also the space where the question of living harmoniously among a diverse array of groups gets posed, groups that long ago moved beyond categorization as so-called primitive societies. In addition, such difficulties become accentuated depending on specific elements of our society, which I have attempted to describe, notably in the peculiar insistence on the social question, which has tended to invade the political sphere. The second contradiction, which opposed the quest for identity recognition with the desire to maintain French citizenship, needs to be considered beyond the issue of traditional nationalism. Although there are many theories on the nation, the nationalist conception tends to conflate cultural identity and political identity, and produce a very simplified vision of citizenship. For all the above-mentioned reasons, I believe that civil society should provide the foundation upon which we renew the political foundations of the overseas departments.

Toward a Renewed Politics in the Overseas Departments

There are three possible solutions as I see it: first, maintain the departmental status quo; second, grant independence; third, develop a special status within the French Republic. Based on both current events and history, the overseas departments do not want independence. The problem can be summed up in the following question: Is not independence the natural solution, the one chosen by almost all colonized peoples, to resolve their identity problems? Because, surely, is not the rejection of independence also a rejection of sovereignty? Globalization in today's world makes definitive answers to these questions impossible.

In our current historical phase, the two other options seem more realistic. How, then, can we resolve the contradiction that opposes a need for identity recognition and a desire to maintain French citizenship? It is important to acknowledge that this question does not simply concern French citizens overseas. Rather, it inquires into the status of French republican identity itself, notably because of the issues of integration confronting citizens with immigrant backgrounds from former colonies. Despite its universalist aims, which relegates religious, ethnic, and cultural identities to the private sphere, French republicanism is also deeply nationalistic and tends to align the collective political identity with the cultural identity of so-called citizens "of pure French stock."

A good French citizen is thought to be someone who assimilates into the dominant culture. Integration is thus conflated with assimilation, especially since the cultural majority (for historical reasons linked to the colonial past) promotes a negative and disparaging vision of non-European cultures. This helps us understand why overseas citizens have developed over the decades a counterculture that values creole cultures. Has the time come for us to think beyond traditional republican identity and instead emphasize greater communitarianism or factionalist identities? The debate is still raging in France, and particularly in its overseas departments, when it comes to the issue of national identity.

One possible solution to this dilemma is perhaps to distinguish between assimilation and integration, as Jürgen Habermas has done.[6] To do that, we would first need to separate cultural identity from political identity. The former offers an opening toward diversity and particularity in a given political body. As for the latter, identity politics seeks to unify citizens around common values and principles that guide public life. The weight of inheritance, of the clan, and of the family, is paramount to cultural identity, whereas learning, construction, and the rational play essential roles in political identity. The distinction is of course purely one of principle, since articulation is conceivable. However, cultural dialogue within a republican context capable of maintaining such distinctions might prove to be more harmonious. But here again, civil society plays a crucial role, since it is the space where voices are brought together in a framework of ethical discussion. Civil society is always in flux, and it cannot content itself with definitive norms grounded on ahistorical reason. Rather, it is a production site for norms that come out of the interaction of differing worldviews. Beyond this dimension of rationality that belongs to the public sphere, cultural works also communicate in another space—that of a common world that cannot be reduced to the public space. Here, aesthetics compete with rationality. In any case, it would be wrong to believe, as the nationalist ideology has sought to promote, that there exists some kind of linear continuity between politics and culture.

Overseas citizens therefore find themselves confronted, no doubt for the first time in their history (Mayotte is an exception), with the need to choose and make political decisions. Considerations on the nature and conditions for such choices constitute a form of political renewal in these spaces. Neither the state nor elected officials can make such choices by themselves. If, traditionally, social conflict has been the most effective at mobilizing the residents of French overseas departments, then the hour has come to address the political question.

Hence the importance that must be given to civil society. We need to get beyond thinking of history as a source of evil and thinking of identity as a source of suffering. The fact that we still decry the wrongs of the past is evidence that we remain caught in the past; to be truly free, we need to get beyond thinking about identity in terms of victimhood and suffering. A collective praxis would help to transcend all of that. Issues of identity and the question of living together can only be resolved through rational practice, which itself can only take place if civil society is nurtured and developed, something which the LKP started, but was unable to see through to a meaningful conclusion. A major debate needs to take place in civil society with the aim of defining a common mission—not in terms of specific policies, but with respect to new conditions for breathing life into politics and social struggles, since after all, the class struggle is ongoing. Unless civil society is mobilized, then any decision made regarding a change of status or aimed at maintaining the status quo would only serve to perpetuate the current feeling of malaise found in the overseas departments.

Jacky Dahomay is Professeur de chaire supérieure emeritus at the Lycée Général et Technologique de Baimbridge (Académie de la Guadeloupe).

Notes

1. Édouard Glissant, *Caribbean Discourse: Selected essays*, trans. Michael J. Dash (Charlottesville: University of Virginia Press, 1989).
2. Saint-John Perse, *Anabase* (Paris: Gallimard, 1924).
3. Emmanuel Todd, *L'Origine des systèmes familiaux* (Paris: Gallimard, 2011).
4. Giorgio Agamben, *Homo sacer* (Paris: Seuil, 1997).
5. See Jean-Pierre Sainton, *Les nègres en politique: Couleur, identités, et stratégies de couleur en Guadeloupe au tournant du siècle* (Paris: Septentrion Presses Universitaires, 2000).
6. See Jürgen Habermas, *L'intégration républicaine: Essais de théorie politique* (Paris: Fayard, 1998.

15

"RACE," ETHNICIZATION, AND DISCRIMINATION

IS HISTORY REPEATING ITSELF OR IS THIS A POSTCOLONIAL PECULIARITY?

Patrick Simon

IN 1950, THE United Nations Educational, Scientific and Cultural Organization (UNESCO), based in Paris, convened an assembly of eminent scholars to discuss the issue of "race." Following the Universal Declaration of Human Rights (1948), the time had come to develop a strategy aimed at ending racism. The options were *either* to discredit the very concept of race and prohibit the use of the word *or* to preserve its scientific validity (specifically in classifications to describe human populations), but strip it of its hierarchizing value as a means of addressing, and quelling, potential uses for segregation and extermination. Scholars were divided as to which strategy to adopt, and in the end, four versions were successively elaborated, beginning in 1950, and then later in 1951, 1964, and 1967.[1] The prohibition strategy, which was based on a rejection of race's scientific validity and an emphasis on the unity of the human species, ended up winning out at the international level.

There were, however, a few notable exceptions to the rejection of the concept of race that was effected in the 1950s. The European powers continued to subordinate populations based on race in their colonial empires. Of course, that in part changed after 1945, but racial subordination still remained active until independence. The prohibition of the word race from major international texts was, therefore, only relatively meaningful during the period of decolonization, although it did serve as a lever for demands for equality and emancipation by colonized populations. Moreover, the United States and South Africa, to cite but two countries, continued to use race in their explicitly segregationist legal systems—until 1964 in the case of the former and until 1991 for the latter. The subsequent nondiscrimination policies adopted in those countries made use of the concept of race in order to make up for the wrongdoings that such categories themselves helped to engender. Finally, the term "race" is today commonly used in the Anglo-Saxon world, where it is not considered to be racist *per se*.

The prohibition of race is announced in the preamble to France's 1946 Constitution, which reaffirms that "each human being, irrespective of race, religion, or belief, possesses inalienable and sacred rights." That principle is reiterated in Article 2 (then article 1 after its revision) of the 1958 Constitution, which establishes "the equality of citizens before the law, without distinction as to origin, race, or religion." These principles serve as the foundation of a colorblind strategy that has become deeply ingrained in all aspects of French society. In fact, making reference to race in conversation is frowned upon, and it is illegal to use race—either positively or negatively—in legal provisions. That strategy, however, has been undermined by a series of recent changes. The main issue stems less from a return of virulent and explicit forms of racism—although evidence of such displays can be seen in political, media, and social spheres—than from diffuse and veiled forms of ethnic and racial discrimination. Although the phenomenon is not new, it has undergone changes and *displacements* (comparable to those undergone by "spaces of racism")[2] with each successive generation of "postcolonials" since 1945. The social specter of the French population's ethnic and racial diversity has spread. We find ourselves faced with the same dilemma as in the 1950s, but with new parameters.

"Racism without Race"

In the face of "racism without race," which now expresses itself more often but in low-visibility forms of discrimination, the strategy that we have been following since 1945 seems to have reached its limits. Not only does there remain a popular belief in the existence of "race," but the consequences of the prejudices fed by these beliefs have gotten worse, and that is due to at least two reasons. The effective censorship of racist slurs and hate speech succeeded in mitigating explicit forms of racialist ideology, but prejudice continues to inform cognitive schemes, behavior, and actions that, although not conceived as *racist*, are still clearly shaping discrimination. As racial prejudice tends to be formed in the recesses of one's consciousness, those who are activating such prejudices consider themselves to be authentically antiracist.[3]

A new kind of racism has emerged: a racism without ideology or race consciousness, a racism that is incredibly difficult to track or reduce—a colorblind racism. In the late 1960s, international treaties targeting discrimination (such as the convention to eliminate all forms of racial discrimination) sought to respond to such forms of racism. In the 2000s, they gained more authority

(European directives against ethnic and racial discrimination), and showed themselves to be particularly concerned with "the dignity and equality of all human beings" as practical solutions against discrimination.

One of the intractable paradoxes in the fight against discrimination is that it tends to reveal—in the photographic sense of the word—the process of ethnicization and racialization, and at the same time it has the potential to stimulate it through the perpetuation of categories that make reference to ethnic or racial origin. It proves hard to denounce profiling at night clubs, by police, or in housing without speaking of "blacks," "Arabs," "North Africans," "youth from immigrant families," or "visible minorities." To be sure, each term has its own relationship to race and ethnic origin, but the debate on discrimination has inevitably led to the use of a carefully chosen lexicon that was marginalized from public discourse until only recently.[4] The ethnic and the racial terminology has seeped into the public sphere, through victim testimonies in the media, political speeches devoted to discrimination, and research findings on the topic. Even public policies dedicated to the fight against discrimination use a legal definition of the issue—discrimination "due to origin or race"—which in turn defines specific populations.[5] We find ourselves up to our ears in the "racial stuff." *With fear and trembling.*

However, as Etienne Balibar rightly warns us, we should not let ourselves be taken in by the rhetoric based on a "return of race."[6] The *visible* return of race is an optical illusion that originates in our belief that it had disappeared in the first place, but that was only an official construct. As Balibar argues, the disappearance of the idea of race is "pure ideological prejudice" founded on "our illusions and complacency, which made us believe in the incompatibility of democratic and humanist principles with the theory and practice of racism, except in the cases of 'relics' and 'anomalies.'"[7] The fiction pertaining to the reduced level of racialization in France with respect to the United Kingdom or the United States is based on a twofold form of denial. Historically, it is grounded in an arbitrary partitioning between the metropole and the colonial empire, where racialization was more than an affair of representation of the "other" but also a question of legal and administrative status. In France, the legacy of slavery in the United States is heavily criticized, but one often forgets that France was one of the main powers in the triangular trade and that plantation economies were built on slavery on a large scale. Unless we believe that overseas France is not France, we have to admit that slavery played a large role in the racialization of French society. The second form of denial concerns the overlooked fact that for the first time in France's history, racialized populations from the former colonial empire live on the mainland territory, which is by definition a postcolonial situation.[8]

The consequences of the human and symbolic transfer of the colonial legacy into the heart of the metropole is at the center of debates surrounding the postcolonial.[9] "Postcolonial racism" is a particularly thorny issue.[10] Beyond disagreements on the conditions and means of a certain form of colonial continuity after its legal and political dissolution, what is disturbing in the theme of postcolonial racism is that it awakens an old idea of race that was thought to belong to the past. What I will argue here is that "the past is not even past," but rather that history has closets. Marginalizing racist ideologies and delegitimizing racial theories did not prevent the resurgence of colonial imaginaries. Instead, they took on a latent form before being activated when populations that had been ethnicized and racialized in the past arrived in mainland France. To put it simply: attempts to deracialize mindsets and representations were not only incomplete, they were failures, and that was due to the prohibition strategy in the context of colonial aphasia.[11]

My aim is not to delve into a discussion on the specific connections between republican ideology, politics, and colonialism, but rather to place current debates on discrimination and the saliency of race into context. That shall lead us to a discussion of a decisive dimension in this anamnesis: the presence or lack of singularity of postcolonial migrations, specifically in the forms of discrimination suffered by immigrants from the former colonial empire and their descendants as compared to the forms of discrimination experienced by immigrants from other backgrounds.

Postcolonial Migrations and Discrimination

Key to the understanding of the logics of discrimination and its future evolution is to be found in what I shall call the "postcolonial interpretation." The postcolonial interpretation is the meaning given in the analysis to the fact that major migratory waves, beginning in the late 1960s, which concerned for the most part populations from colonized and decolonized territories (with Portuguese and Turkish immigration serving as notable exceptions). Those waves could thus be described as "postcolonial migrations." Are the current difficulties faced by postcolonial migrants, and especially by their descendants, a kind of repetition of the cycle of integration that Germans, Belgians, Poles, Italians, Spanish, and other groups experienced in the first half of the twentieth century? Or do we have to consider that there are radically new conditions, which are connected both to the context and to the origin of the migrants themselves? In terms of the similarities and differences, we often tend to focus on the changes in socioeconomic context, the reduction of the number of low-skilled jobs—where immigrants tend to work—in agriculture and industry and the increase in the service industry and of mass unemployment.

The framework of assimilation through work has drastically changed for laborers and proletarians. The notion of a "cultural distance" has also been invoked to explain "assimilation's failure." With the diversification in migrant's origins, oppositions between European and non-European immigrations, between Catholics and Muslims, have become arguments used to explain why the cycle of integration no longer functions. The economic and social difficulties encountered by immigrants and their descendants are attributed to their being "too different" from the mainstream. In reaction to this commonplace assertion, studies on immigration have instead preferred to highlight the similarities in immigrant experiences, showing that the cultural distance is primarily produced by public discourse and that European and Catholic migrants from the early twentieth century were, like Muslim North African or sub-Saharan Africans today, also perceived as exotic and unassimilable.

Similarly, an examination of political discourse over a century shows overwhelming consistency: the same denigration of foreigners, the same doomsday predictions pertaining to a loss of the national identity, the same fears of mixing and change. As this stream of research claims, migratory waves follow a strikingly standard path: uprootedness, adaptation, racism, inclusion into new social worlds, more or less social mobility, desegregation, and assimilation at the second generation. For them, there is clearly nothing new to be seen in the immigrant experience in the late twentieth century—Algerians are like Italians.

In contrast with this type of study, others point out a series of particularities related to postcolonial migration. The category "postcolonial migration" is based on the common experience of the colony—its political and legal system as well as its mental structures—along with the ongoing postcolonial experience in mainland France, which is marked by ethnic and racial prejudice and experience of discrimination. The high level of inertia with respect to racial stigma can be seen in the fate of "second generation postcolonials." It is important to explain the stunning difference between the rapid invisibility of second generation Poles, Italians, Spanish, and Portuguese, and the high level of social and media visibility experienced by descendants of Algerians, Moroccans, Tunisians, sub-Saharan Africans, and those from the overseas departments. Meanwhile, this latter category is exposed to various forms of discrimination in all aspects of social life, and particularly in the job market.[12] Considering this singular historical experience, I think it would be useful to speak of a structure of inferiorization, expressions of which can be found in colonial systems of management—legal, administrative, and statistical statuses and classifications—and their mainland avatars,[13] their crystallization in a system of representations,[14] which has been prolonged by the repatriation and reclassification of colonial institutions and personnel, along with their discriminatory routines.[15]

Why Algerians Are Not Italians

From the beginning, Algerian immigration was different from other migrant groups. As for other colonial subjects, migration toward the metropole was strongly framed and always seen with wariness. "North African" contingents who participated in the First World War were quickly coerced to repatriate in order to prevent them from spreading throughout the metropole.[16] The integration of those who remained in the mainland during the interwar period was deliberately thwarted by an infralegal categorization created by national and local political actors. Françoise de Barros has, for example, shown how the city of Nanterre sought to cut into unemployment subsidies during periods of economic crisis (notably after 1931) by requesting that "Algerian natives" be repatriated and by appealing for "foreigners"—mainly Italians—to be taken care of directly by the French state.[17]

Migration immediately following the Second World War took place in an even more complex context, which was marked by the steady equalization of the status of the *indigènes* (referred to as Muslims after 1946) and Europeans, against the backdrop of independence wars, tougher policy, and military control over "French Algerian Muslims" living in mainland France. Special institutions were dedicated to them—some of which would later be made available to all immigrants[18]—and their specific type of citizenship,[19] they were not foreigners but not full citizens either—colonial subjects lived under a regime of exceptionalism. This regime would have lasting consequences even after decolonization, since their acquisition of French nationality was linked to special provisions—reintegration, dual *jus soli,* and others.[20]

Finally, the classifications used in the colonial empire, and particularly in Algeria, reflected a citizenship regime operating according to a double standard. Grounded on racial, ethnic, or religious designations, they divided "Europeans" from "natives" in population categories.[21] Such classifications were applied beyond the colonial sphere, and also affected the metropole, where censuses in 1946, 1954, 1962, and 1968 included the category "French Muslims."[22] Listing the evidence that shows how Algerians were treated as second-class citizens and the application of systemic forms of discrimination would go beyond the scope of this chapter. Throughout the 1950s and 1960s—before and after independence—Algerians, "North Africans," or "French Muslims," depending on the designation being employed, were victims of prejudice and marginalized in society; they were discriminated against in the workplace with respect to their colleagues and even other European immigrants who were foreigners. Andrée Michel's excellent monograph on Algerian workers in France, published in 1956, offers an impressive overview of the range of distinctions that made up the "segregated situation" confronting Algerians at work.[23] In general, they were overqualified for their positions, experienced little career progression, and were exposed to difficult and dangerous work. Michel's assertions were further refined by Laure Pitti in her work on professional qualification grids at the car manufacturer Renault in the 1950s and 1960s, wherein she revealed the "vestiges and transformations of a colonial labor model."[24] Such institutionalized discrimination and exclusion explains why, in the case of Algerians, the determining factor of time in migration and integration patterns, which can be seen for other groups, does not hold. Discrimination gets passed down and reinforced from one generation to another, becoming sedimented into social practices. Prejudice with respect to "North Africans," as is also the case for "blacks" and "Asians," has a very different structure than the kind of prejudice applied to European immigrants.

Alain Girard and Jean Stoezel's famous study on the attitudes of the French population towards immigrants, entitled *Français et immigrés* which was conducted in 1951, shows that "North Africans" were second-to-last on a "sympathy" scale, just before Germans.[25] Even when the interviewees "liked" North Africans, they were still against the idea of mixed marriages with North Africans in 70 percent of cases (well ahead of the 45 percent rate against mixed marriages with Germans). The same poll was taken in 1974 (with slightly different formulations), and the results were equally decisive: 55 percent of interviewees had a poor opinion of North Africans, compared to 23 percent for "Black Africans" (of whom there were still very few in France at the time) and less than 15 percent for other groups (Italians, Portuguese, Spanish, Turks, Yugoslavs).[26] Almost twenty-five years after the beginning of Algerian immigration and twelve years after independence, those polled continued to believe, at a rate of 73 percent, that "adaptation" would be difficult if not impossible for North Africans. Even the Portuguese, who had arrived later, were seen as more "adaptable." The issue of "mixing" was still highly contested: 60 percent believed that "North Africans" simply could not mix.

More than forty years and a few generations later, prejudice toward North African populations is still strong, as the CNCDH's annual polls on racism and a number of audit testing initiatives targeted at the job market over the past decade have shown. Categories have changed; we no longer speak of "North Africans," but instead of "Arabs," "blacks," or "Muslims." These categories were forged from the colonial world, the power of which continues to reside in the specific forms of subordination that were practiced and the types of discrimination used against "natives." The stakes of the debates on postcolonial issues and forms of discrimination no longer have to do exclusively with the remnants of colonialism, but with what we must do to *undo race* and the system of domination that is connected to it.

How Can We Become Postracial?

Two controversies emerged from attempts to address anti-discrimination and improving equality, both in response to the question "What to do about race?" In December 2008, President Nicolas Sarkozy, who wanted advice on how to introduce the word "diversity" in the constitution, set up a committee presided over by Simone Veil which delivered an important report. The idea of "authorizing race and ethnicity-based affirmative action policies in the preamble to the constitution, perhaps on a temporary basis," as a way of increasing the effectiveness of equality policies, was rejected.[27] That decision was not of course surprising, and served to reaffirm a colorblind approach. However, the reasoning behind the decision showed increased sensitivity to discrimination, which did not exclude contradictions between the diagnosis and what action needed to be taken.

One argument among those outlined by the committee is particularly reminiscent of the debates on the postcolonial situation. According to the committee, in countries where race and ethnicity-based affirmative action policies had been adopted, they had "resulted from periods of *legal* segregation for the ethnic groups targeted. In other words, affirmative action only makes sense if everyone understands it as a way to catch up for those who have been marginalized by their country's *judicial system*, and who, as a result, occupy a subaltern social position."[28] Such historical motives do not, according to the committee, have an equivalent in France. The argument, which ignores the legal practice of slavery and the existence of racial segregation put in place by the French judicial system in the colonies as well as, to a lesser extent, in mainland France, is troubling.[29] The issue here is not to be found in the committee's recommendation—since it is not so much the wording of the constitution that was being questioned but rather its interpretation—in other words the somewhat mechanical repetition and assertion of French exceptionalism with respect to other multicultural democracies, especially since it is based on historical revisionism and in the name of legal expertise.

The second controversy took place when the Constitutional Council invalidated Article 63 of the Loi du 20 novembre 2007 relative à la maîtrise de l'immigration, à l'intégration et à l'asile (the immigration, integration, and asylum act), also known as the "Hortefeux Law." The reason behind that invalidation was that the article was believed to be "deprived of any connection to the dispositions of the [initial] project of the law."[30] The incriminating article suggested adding a new exception to the interdiction on collecting sensitive information, notably information "directly or indirectly" related to "ethnic or racial origins" that would enable researchers to "conduct studies on levels of diversity, discrimination, and integration."[31] The Constitutional Council added that, "if what is needed to conduct studies on diversity, discrimination, and integration are objective data, the studies themselves cannot be conducted on *objective data* related to ethnic or racial backgrounds without contradicting the principle of the first article of the constitution."[32] According to the council, references to ethnic or racial background in scientific studies, even those that seek to fight discrimination, would go against one of the fundamental principles of the republican model.

In its decision, the Constitutional Council relied on Article 1 of the constitution, which is the same article that Veil's committee was tasked to consider changing: "France shall be an indivisible, secular, democratic, social republic. *It shall ensure the equality of all citizens before the law, without distinction of origin, race, or religion.*" Those famous and ambiguous sentences are a source of philosophical debate and conversations on how to combat ethnic and racial discrimination. In order to guarantee equality, should all distinctions related to origin, race, and religion be suppressed—and not only in the law, but also in all forms of action and observation within French society? Should everybody be expected to be entirely colorblind? Or is it the law, and only the law, that must remain blind to origins and/or race? In other words, does the problem lie in the distinction itself or in the uses of such categories? The Constitutional Council offered an answer to that question: "No distinctions." However, it later tempered its assertion with a "however, maybe in some cases . . ." The status of religion, which is also cited in Article 1, appears to be treated fundamentally differently from that of race. So, either there is a double standard in the implementation of the Constitution, or the phrase is saying something other than what the council has put forth.

Although I am not a legal expert, and therefore in no way qualified to discuss an article of the Constitution, I nevertheless propose an antidiscrimination and postracial rereading of Article 1. If we are to believe in the notion of equality without distinction of race, we should verify first that those who are racialized, for one reason or another, do not experience unequal treatment based on this racialization. That seems to me to be an implicit obligation, and even an imperative, in the "guarantee of equality." The Republic is responsible and accountable for ensuring equality and suppressing all forms of discrimination based on race. In order to do that, and to deracialize social relationships and institutions, it needs to acknowledge race. This enduring paradox echoes a fascinating speech ("A More Perfect Union: Speech on Race") given by Barack Obama in

Philadelphia on March 18, 2008, in which he outlined the racial divide and said: "Race is an issue that I believe this nation cannot afford to ignore right now." Taking race into consideration in order to become postracial: now that is a change in strategy that is going to prove complicated for a colorblind country.

Patrick Simon is Director of Research at the Institut National d'Études Demographiques (INED) and Research Fellow at the Center of European Studies (CEE) at Sciences Po. His work focuses on antidiscrimination policies, ethnic classification and the integration of ethnic minorities in European countries. He coedited a special issue of *Ethnic and Racial Studies* and published *Fear, Anxiety, and National Identity: Immigration and Belonging in North America and Western Europe* (2015).

Notes

1. They can be found in the collective work, *Race, Science, Society* (Paris: UNESCO and New York: Columbia University Press, 1975).
2. See Etienne Balibar and Immanuel Wallerstein, *Race, nation, classe: Les identités ambiguës* (Paris: La Découverte, 1988) and Michel Wieviorka, *L'espace du racisme* (Paris: Seuil, 1991).
3. Linda Hamilton Krieger, *Un problème de catégories: Stéréotypes et lutte contre les discriminations* (Paris: Institut d'Études Politiques de Paris, 2008).
4. Didier Fassin, "Nommer, interpréter: Le sens commun de la question raciale," in *De la question sociale à la question raciale? Représenter la société française*, ed. Didier Fassin and Éric Fassin (Paris: La Découverte, 2006), 19–36.
5. Patrick Simon, "Statistics, French Social Science and Ethnic Relations," *Revue Française de Sociologie* 51 (2010): 159–174.
6. Etienne Balibar, "Le retour de la race," *Mouvements* 50 (June–August 2007): 162–171.
7. Ibid., 163.
8. Marie-Claude Smouts, ed., *La situation postcoloniale: Les postcolonial studies dans le débat français* (Paris: Presses de Sciences Po, 2007).
9. Romain Bertrand, *Mémoires d'empire: La controverse autour du "fait colonial"* (Broissieux: Éditions du croquant, 2006).
10. Saïd Bouamama and Pierre Tevanian, "Peut-on parler d'un racisme postcolonial?," in *Culture postcoloniale 1961–200*, ed. Nicolas Bancel and Pascal Blanchard (Paris: Autrement, Paris, 2005), 243–254.
11. Anne Laure Stoler, "Colonial Aphasia. Race and Disabled Histories in France," *Public Culture* 23, no. 1 (2011): 121–156.
12. Dominique Meurs, Ariane Pailhé, and Patrick Simon, "The Persistence of Intergenerational Inequalities linked to Immigration. Labour Market Outcomes for Immigrants and their Descendants in France," *Population* 61, nos. 5–6 (2006): 645–682.
13. See Laure Blévis, "Les avatars de la cityonneté en Algérie coloniale ou les paradoxes d'une catégorisation," *Droit et Société*, no. 48 (2001/2002): 557–581; Alexis Spire, "Semblables et pourtant différents: La cityonneté paradoxale des 'Français musulmans d'Algérie' en métropole," *Genèses* 4,

no. 53 (2003): 48–68, and Emmanuelle Saada, *Les enfants de la colonie: Les métis de l'Empire français entre sujétion et citoyenneté* (Paris: La Découverte, 2007).

14. See Nicolas Bancel, Pascal Blanchard, Sandrine Lemaire, and Dominic Thomas, eds., *Colonial Culture in France since the Revolution* (Bloomington and Indianapolis: Indiana University Press, 2014).

15. See Todd Shepard, "Une République française 'postcoloniale': La fin de la guerre d'Algérie et la place des enfants des colonies dans la Ve République," *Contretemps* 16 (January 2006): 49–57; and "La colonie rapatriée," *Politix* 76 (2006).

16. Mary Lewis Dewhurst, *The Boundaries of the Republic: Migrant Rights and the Limits of Universalism in France, 1918–1940* (Stanford, CA: Stanford University Press, 2007).

17. Françoise de Barros, "Les municipalités face aux Algériens: Méconnaissances et usages des catégories coloniales en métropole avant et après la Seconde Guerre mondiale," *Genèses* 4, no. 53 (2003): 69–92.

18. Vincent Viet, *La France immigrée: Construction d'une politique 1914–1997* (Paris: Fayard, 1998).

19. Blévis, "Les avatars de la cityonneté en Algérie coloniale ou les paradoxes d'une catégorisation."

20. Patrick Weil, *Qu'est-ce qu'un Français? Histoire de la nationalité francaise de la Révolution à nos jours* (Paris: Grasset, 2002).

21. Kamel Kateb, *Européens, "indigènes" et juifs en Algérie (1830–1962): Représentations et réalités des populations* (Paris: INED, 2001).

22. Patrick Simon, "Nationality and Origins in French Statistics: Ambiguous Categories," *Population: An English Selection* 11 (1999): 193–219.

23. Andrée Michel, *Les travailleurs algériens en France* (Paris: CNRS/Centre d'études sociologiques, 1956).

24. Laure Pitti, "De la différenciation coloniale à la discrimination systémique? La condition d'OS algérien à Renault, de la grille Parodi à la méthode Renault de qualification de travail (1945–1973)," *Revue de l'IRES* 3, no. 46 (2004): 104–105.

25. Alain Girard and Jean Stoezel, *Français et immigrés: L'attitude française, l'adaptation des Italiens et des Polonais* (Paris: PUF, 1953).

26. Alain Girard, Yves Charbit, and Marie-Laurence Lamy, "Attitudes des Français à l'égard de l'immigration étrangère: Nouvelle enquête d'opinion," *Population* 29, no. 6 (1974): 1015–1069.

27. Simone Veil and the Comité de réflexion sur le Préambule de la Constitution, *Redécouvrir le préambule de la Constitution: Report for the French President of the French Republic* (Paris: La Documentation française, 2008), 71.

28. Ibid., 54.

29. On the judicial aspects of "race" in the colonies, see Saada, *Les enfants de la colonie*.

30. Constitutional Council, Decision no. 2007–546 DC of January 25, 2007, http://www.conseil-constitutionnel.fr/conseil-constitutionnel/francais/les-decisions/acces-par-date/decisions-depuis-1959/2007/2007–546-dc/decision-n-2007–546-dc-du-25-janvier-2007.1173.html.

31. "Loi du 20 novembre 2007 relative à la maîtrise de l'immigration, à l'intégration et à l'asile," November 20, 2007, http://www.vie-publique.fr/actualite/panorama/texte-vote/loi-du-20-novembre-2007-relative-maitrise-immigration-integration-asile.html.

32. Constitutional Council, Decision no. 2007–546 DC.

16

FROM THE EMPIRE TO THE REPUBLIC

"FRENCH ISLAM"

Valérie Amiraux

AFTER YEARS OF comparing the different ways in which the European Union's member states treat their Muslim minorities, a kind of convergence has begun to emerge around various hot button issues.[1] The issue that has been the greatest source of disagreement concerns the Islamic headscarf in schools and in the public space in a more general manner.[2] A few additional details can help bring nuance to these situations. What has long set France apart from other European countries is the almost visceral character that these debates have taken over what has now been almost thirty years.[3]

The evolution of French secularism has been riddled with conflict, and this evolution has included a number of important steps or "thresholds."[4] The fact that the issue continues to be a subject of intense debate therefore comes as no surprise. Still, two elements seem to be specific to current debates, and they both pertain to Islam in France. First, the intervention of the state and of public authorities in the process of regulating the private lives of select migrant populations—most notably, Muslims—has become more prevalent.[5] Meanwhile, the conjunction of intentional events and the imperative of equal treatment for all religions under the aegis of the Republic have accelerated the path to establishing a national representative body of the Muslim religion, which, since April 2003, has taken the form of a *Conseil français du culte musulman* (French Council of the Muslim Religion, CFCM).[6] The institutionalization of Muslim representation has also resulted in the creation of a discursive space for Muslims in the public sphere.[7] However, it has not neutralized stigmas and race-based dynamics related to Islam in French society.[8] My aim is, therefore, to explore how this policy of establishing an official space for Islam in the

French public sphere interacts with experiences of discrimination and exclusion reported by Muslims living in France.

My position is that ethnicity, gender and religion as criteria for the identification of individuals sustains/supports their unequal treatment in the public space. They represent "deviances" with respect to republican norms of civic behavior, and they have survived in the French republican context because they were historically naturalized through a narrative that carried over from the colonial empire to the Republic. The challenge is therefore to trace the continuity between the colonial imaginary, its discourse and practices, and today's imaginary, discourses, and practices. To do that, we shall look at the ways in which the authorities have treated Islam, beginning with an analysis of the colonial experience. We shall then proceed with an inquiry into the successive forms of regulation of Islam, and then turn our attention to the Republic's hostility toward some figures who are thought to embody society's difficult interaction with Muslim alterity.

The Empire and the Republic: One History, Multiple Narratives

For Muslims living in France today, public life is an active struggle,[9] whose implicit issues of self-presentation and representation are connected to France's colonial history, which has remained relatively marginalized from the national narrative.[10] The persistence of colonial representations of populations whose countries of origins have long been independent and the echoes of such representations in debates on integration and citizenship have been at the heart of numerous studies that have been produced in the social sciences since the late 1990s,[11] as well as evidenced in political discourse.[12] For some, the postcolonial remains ubiquitous and always takes the form either of political denunciation (as in the case of the movement *Indigènes de la République*) or as an object of mockery.[13] For others, the attention paid to colonial history and its impact on contemporary debates on racism and discrimination are based on the idea that "current forms of social issues are racial because they come from practices and notions that date back to the colonial era."[14] The few researchers who have actually adopted a postcolonial approach in France tend to insist on the Republic's amnesia in their inquiries into the trajectory from native to immigrant. They are often criticized by voices reacting against "easy forms of indignation"[15] and a "reference to the colonial imaginary that suggests . . . forms of recollection that pair guilty self-reflection and redemptive self-criticism."[16] Such criticism is a reaction to what is perceived as an attempt to turn the colonial past into an all-encompassing explanation for society's ills and a tendency toward "patrimonializing the past."

The aim here is not to reduce the complexity of the colonial experience to a matter of the production of difference and categorization. I am not suggesting a linear reading between forms of discrimination, racism, and exclusion that were previously applied to Muslims under the colonial administration and today. Again, the objective is not to establish a causal link between regulations on Islam in Algeria in 1830 and forms of discrimination found in France today. The postcolonial approach rarely focuses on the religious dimension. However, the way in which Muslim issues are framed contribute to suspicion, hint at society's need to control people and places,[17] while also pointing to the subversive nature of Islam and of Muslims and therefore to the potential threat they represent to security and public disorder. To this end, Muslims in France today are to be inscribed in a much longer timeframe, in a historical continuity, one that is strikingly evident in the administrative lexicon.[18]

In her research on naturalization ceremonies, Sarah Mazouz has described the intrinsic contradiction at work in the proceedings. The awkwardness of the public representatives effectively turns the ritual into a veritable qualification test: "At the very moment of integrating—or assimilating—newly naturalized citizens, he [the official in charge] persists in reminding and signifying to them that they are different and illegitimate. . . . I speak of an opposition because the way in which these ceremonies are constructed and the way in which state representatives appropriate legal categories, are also ways of reaffirming the border that separates what is juridical and what lies beyond the legal realm."[19]

Muslim Policies and French Secularism

While the empire was dreamed up in the image of the Republic, the colonial experience proved to be unfaithful to republican ideals.[20] Conquest was made in the name of republican principles—notably, with the project of universal equality—but when it came to religion, colonial practices were marked by ambivalence. The 1905 law separating church and state was therefore at once a rhetorical tool in the civilizing mission and a source of colonial domination. It in fact never actually applied to Muslim cultural organizations: "The *ulemas* pointed out contradictions in this Republic, which was eager to apply the principle of separation of Church and State in the mainland, and to distort it in Algeria whenever issues of controlling the native population came up."[21] Although it was a foundational law in republican France's political culture, secularism was never applied in Algeria, which was a French department until 1947. There was a double standard when it came to French citizens who were Muslim and French citizens from the mainland.

In fact, policies were never the same for Muslims living in territories conquered by the colonial enterprise. Tensions between the republican project and the complex and discriminatory architecture of the colonial bureaucratic machine increased as colonials faced worlds that were more and more different from their own, from Egypt to Morocco. Policies toward Islam were engineered based on the fear that the religion posed a threat to the empire, and they became means of controlling all aspects of social life. After the Arab policies—of which the Algerian conquest is a typical example, with the dual strategy of assimilating new territories to French law and maintaining a separate status for natives[22]—the *consideration policy* (a term used in the late nineteenth century) designated a French practice, in its colonial policy toward natives, that relied on traditional institutions.[23] Muslim policies constituted a kind of "policing of souls,"[24] which made use of scholarly expertise and public bureaucracy in the Muslim territories. "Arab Bureaus," beginning in 1833 in Algeria, and the *Commission interministérielle des affaires musulmanes* (Inter-Ministerial Commission on Muslim Affairs, CIAM),[25] which was created by decree in June 1911, both relied on local points of contact. Coordination with locals was a constant in these bureaucratic regimes. Positions for "Muslim advisers" were even created in 1931. The Republic wanted to show that it was not hostile to Islam.

The obsession with controlling Islam and with aligning it with republican principles was invented long before the Fifth Republic. But in the 1980s and 1990s, which were marked by all manner of tensions, the tendency to institutionalize the representation of Islam was in full force with the establishment of the CFCM.[26] For many of the Muslims consulting with the group established by Jean-Pierre Chevènement (minister of the interior from 1997 until 2000), discussions with the authorities contained traces of colonialism. The notion of illegitimacy with respect to the needs of Islam became clear during the definition of the normative framework of the discussions. The invitation asked Muslim representatives to "sit down at the Republic's table"[27] and were accompanied by the tense signing of a "Declaration of intention relative to the rights and obligations of adherents of the Muslim religion in France," which was later renamed "Legal principles and foundations of the relationship between the authorities and the Muslim religion in France." The advisers on Islam—of which there have been many since 1989—tended to alternate between ideologues ("civilizing the Muslims") and pragmatists (for a "sociological and demographic realism"), explains Vincent Geisser.[28] Some of the representatives chosen for advisory positions, particularly the youngest among them, received the invitation from the Ministry of the Interior as a kind of "colonial . . . paternalist injunction," whereas the older advisers wavered between feelings of incompetence and wariness.[29]

In this dynamic of institutionalization, as was the case in the colonial context, the "*Homo Islamicus*,"[30] who has emerged at the conjunction of public regulations and the needs expressed by Muslim organizations, was a Janus figure. His first face was the product of an institutional understanding of Islam as a religious organization, which had been molded in the bronze of civic virtue and loyalty to the Republic. The second is that of resistance to the normative pressure placed on representatives of Islam when they are seated at the Republic's table. More than the actual altercations between the various organizational representatives, one would do well to notice the paternalism of the political authorities, which has been on the rise since 2002–2003.[31]

Are "Natives" and Muslims Antitheses of Citizens?

The figure of the "other" in the colonial context is represented by two types: that of the "savage" and that of the "native."[32] In the framework offered by these archetypal figures, the "Muslim savage" (the barbarian) is established as the negative of the white man, who is civilized and Catholic.[33] The notions that Arabs are violent by nature, and that they have uncontrollable desires have been mainstays of their portrayal and subsequent stigmatization in French society. As a result, the "Muslim native" was seen as difficult to "educate." Let it be noted as well that Islam is understood more as a culture (albeit a barbarian one) than as a religion. The "Arab boy" (who comes from a North African immigrant background) has recently been portrayed in the media as a troublemaker and a source of danger both within and outside of his community. He is, "a ghost from the colonial past . . . one of the avatars of the native, a Muslim immigrant."[34] At times the figure of that boy was sought out in the colonial era, but today he is the source of contempt. "Arab cruelty," an archetypal pillar of colonial culture, has been renovated around new scenes of confrontation, such as the "gang bangs" that terrified television audiences.[35] The tone is much different from the transnational repertoire, and is mostly dominated by the security paradigm, which equates Islam with terrorist violence.[36]

The stigmatizing here is built around the idea that these people are incapable of controlling their uncivilized nature, "their ineptitude at interiorizing, in their bodies, the rules of civility that govern interactions between men and women, the expression of French exceptionalism."[37] In a very different field—but not without links to the above—Zinedine Zidane's head-butt delivered during the soccer World Cup final in 2006, an act that transgressed public norms and codes of good sportsmanship, constituted for some a sign of his inability to control his private emotions, which they viewed as antithetical to the type of professionalism expected at that level of competition. Yasmin Jiwani underlines the Orientalist, and particularly animalistic, imagery used by the international press to describe and interpret the event, and ultimately to decide that this was a sign of the athlete's failure to integrate.[38] In her work on the

2003–2004 headscarf affair, Nacira Guénif-Souilamas convincingly described the reassuring figures of successful integration, such as the "*beurette*" (young women of North African immigrant background), the "secular Muslim," and their opposing negative figures such as bearded radicals and young girls wearing headscarves.[39] There are also those considered to have been miraculously saved by sports (Zinedine Zidane) or exceptional social success (Rachida Dati, who was named French minister of justice by Nicolas Sarkozy in May 2007). But when these individuals show weakness, it is immediately attributed to their "background" catching up with them. Moreover, they are deemed transgressors of secular morals, even if they do not openly subscribe to Islam. Between the cult of virginity and the propensity to rape, the dangerousness of the native has become the prevalent image, regardless of gender. Indeed, gender equality has in some ways been realized in the realm of ordinary racism, which now not only stigmatizes the male figures (Arab Muslims), but also the female figures (young women in headscarves).

The Islamic headscarf has been a source of stigma for almost thirty years. Debate on the issue in France has gone through several phases, from politically motivated discussions to legal arguments in its favor and against it. The overall consensus in 2003–2004, at the height of the headscarf controversy, was that the headscarf was doubly toxic, for the Republic *and* the girls wearing it. The headscarf was contrasted to the civic mission of school, and it was claimed that it could lead to an "à la carte school," in which authorities other than teachers might offer instruction. For the defenders of secularism and the Republic, the headscarf was seen as a threat to public order and the national symbolic ecosystem. The separation of church and state was the primary motive behind the law of March 2004, which included arguments concerning the protection of veiled girls and the republican values for which the school system remains the primary place of transmission.

In France, the notion of secularism (*laïcité*) acts at once as a principle that regulates differences in the public space and a framework with which to acknowledge the realities of social plurality. Muslims find themselves at the intersection of two contrary injunctions: one requires individual invisibility ("in praise of the invisible immigrant"),[40] and the other encourages acknowledgement of difference through the idea of equal treatment of different religions present in the territory. The expectation of invisibility in the public space is related to the emancipating project of privatizing cultural identities in the name of equality for all. According to such a conception, freedom is contingent on the public space showing no signs of emotional attachment to cultural specificities. Such invisibility is ambiguous. According to Joan Stavo-Debauge, some groups, such as blacks in France, experience the suppression of meaningful markers of identity and the invisibility requirement as a "humiliation, a form of contempt." She continues: "Indeed, to be invisible is to be discounted from the community's—or even a given situation's—full and authorized members. It is also to be excluded from being a full participant, one who is capable of making a contribution that the community may acknowledge or applaud."[41]

The impulse toward acknowledging difference comes from the convergence of Europe around the idea of multiculturalism and the fight against discrimination. This second point is not without ambiguity in the French context, where, with the republican model of integration and conquest, certain attributes are to remain outside of the public space, notably religion. Yet, the "Muslim native tends to become a Muslim client, or the subject of all sorts of solicitude from the public powers, which ends up relegating Muslims to their religious identity, to the detriment of other social identities."[42]

"Rules for Behavior" vs. Diversity

Islam does not have a stable position in France. Its fate is decided by a number of issues (historical, political, legal, social), which all converge around a deficit in trust in the republican system of secularism. As Jürgen Habermas demonstrated in his conversation with Pope Benedict XVI, the secular state is based on a supposition that it is unable to guarantee.[43] The common good relies on more than simply following laws; it implies a costlier commitment in terms of political virtues. And we cannot simply act according to personal interests and constraints if we wish to allow values like solidarity, tolerance, and acknowledgement to flourish. Throughout history, the constant hostility toward various forms of diversity, and even within the context of the private lives of individuals, suggests, with respect to republican discourse and its reflexive hostility toward public expressions, a kind of unspoken nationalism. The deeply modern form of anti-Muslim racism, which is how one can characterize some public European opinions, relies, in the French context, on republican universalism, "a new embodiment of postcolonial imperialism, which makes Islam into an unassimilable 'other' and conflates self-determination of the autonomous subject with the subjectivity of the white European man."[44]

Historically, post-Revolutionary republicanism was established in France around the acknowledgement of the need for making cultural elements, and especially religion, private. The idea was that such a move would foster equal treatment of all citizens in the public space. Some of the fundamental precepts of the secular republican project were freedom of conscience, the reciprocal incompetence of politics and religion, and the equality of religions and convictions in the eyes of the state. Theoretically, the cornerstone of this system (from among all the rules and institutions tasked with implementing its application) resides in neutrality on the part of the public authority. Neutrality is therefore an important indicator of the political reality of secularism and its ability to manage identity-based claims and requests.[45] In practice, the progressive failure of these ideals has become the norm. And tensions surrounding what type of policies to adopt in a multicultural France have contributed to banalizing the idea that secularism is an element of national political culture that is under threat, but one that never ceases to be an ideal horizon toward which we must aim. In other words, secularism, which some are accused of transgressing, remains a foundational idea within the Republic, and it is a conviction that many share, despite the varied interpretations.

Since March 2004, the law against wearing openly religious symbols in public schools turned the issue into a "moral" one, in the sense that it became a "rule of behavior" that could be "punished" if not adhered to, and seemed to ignore the diversity of persuasions that compose a society.[46] In at least one sector of public life, transgressing the rule of secularism is now a punishable offense.[47] Does that really fulfill the initial aims of post-Revolutionary secularism, namely, pacification and reconciliation?

Valérie Amiraux is Professor of Sociology at the University of Montreal where she holds the Canada Research Chair for the Study of Religious Pluralism. Her research interests include the public role of religion in secular contexts (France, Quebec). Recent publications include *Trajectoires de la neutralité* (2014) and *Salomé et les hommes en noir* (2015).

Notes

1. The statistics cited in this chapter are taken from Jonathan Laurence and J. Vaisse, *Integrating Islam: Political and Religious Challenges in Contemporary France* (Washington, DC: Brookings Institution Press, 2006). This chapter is a translation of parts of an article previously published in "De l'empire à la République: à propos de l''islam de France'," *Cahiers de recherche sociologique* 46 (September 2006): 45–60.
2. Valérie Amiraux, "Headscarves in Europe: What is Really the Issue?," in *European Islam: The Challenges for Society and Public Policy*, ed. Samir Amghar, Amel Boubekeur, and Michael Emerson (Brussels: CEPS, 2007), 124–143.
3. The first headscarf affair took place in Creil, outside of Paris, in 1989 (about twenty years before the debate on the "burqa" in France). See Pierre Tevanian, *Le voile médiatique: Un faux débat: "L'affaire du foulard islamique"* (Paris: Raisons d'agir, 2006).
4. Jean Baubérot, *Vers un nouveau pacte laïque?* (Paris: Seuil, 1990) and *Laïcité 1905–2005, entre passion et raison* (Paris: Seuil, 2004).
5. See Betty de Hart, "The Marriage of Convenience in European Immigration Law," *European Journal of Migration and Law* 8, nos. 3–4 (2006): 251–262.

6. Bernard Godard and Sylvie Taussig, *Les musulmans en France: Courants, institutions, communautés: Un état des lieux* (Paris: Robert Laffont, 2006).

7. Valérie Amiraux and Gerdien Jonker, "Introduction: Talking about Visibility: Actors, Politics, Forms of Engagement," in *Politics of Visibility: Young Muslims in European Public Spaces*, ed. Valérie Amiraux and Gerdien Jonker (Bielefeld: Transcript Verlag, 2006), 9–20.

8. Didier Fassin and Éric Fassin, eds., *De la question sociale à la question raciale?: Représenter la société française* (Paris: La Découverte, 2013).

9. See Valérie Amiraux, "Expertises, savoir et politique: La constitution de l'islam comme problème public en France et en Allemagne," in *Les Sciences sociales à l'épreuve de l'action*, ed. Bénédicte Zimmermann (Paris: EHESS, 2004), 209–245.

10. A number of journals have devoted special issues to "state xenophobia," especially in the aftermath of the creation of the Ministry of Immigration, National Identity, Integration, and Co-Development in 2007. See "Xénophobie de gouvernement, nationalisme d'Etat," *Cultures et conflits* 69 (2008); "Institutionnalisation de la xénophobie en France," *Asylon*, no. 4 (2008); "Identités nationales d'Etat," *Journal des anthropologues*, special issue (2007); "Identité(s) nationale(s): Le retour des politiques de l'identité?," *Savoir/Agir*, no. 2 (December 2007); and "Choisir ses immigrés?," *Raisons politiques*, no. 26 (May 2007).

11. See Pascal Blanchard, Nicolas Bancel, and Sandrine Lemaire, eds., *La fracture coloniale: La société française au prisme de l'héritage colonial* (Paris: La Découverte, 2005).

12. Marc Breviglieri, "L'étreinte de l'origine: Attachement, mémoire et nostalgie chez les enfants d'immigrés maghrébins," *Confluences Méditerranée*, no. 39 (2001): 37–47.

13. Joan Stavo-Debauge, "L'invisibilité du tort et le tort de l'invisibilité," EspacesTemps.net, April 19, 2007, http://www.espacestemps.net/articles/invisibilite-du-tort-et-le-tort-de-invisibilite/.

14. Emmanuelle Saada, "Un racisme de l'expansion: Les discriminations raciales au regard des situations coloniales," in *De la question sociale à la question raciale?* ed. Fassin and Fassin, 56.

15. Stavo-Debauge, "L'invisibilité du tort et le tort de l'invisibilité."

16. Isabelle Merle and Emmanuelle Sibeud, "Histoire en marge ou histoire en marche? La colonisation entre repentance et patrimonialisation," paper delivered at the conference "La politique du passé: constructions, usages et mobilisation de l'histoire dans la France des années 1970 à nos jours," September 25–26, 2003, http://chs.univ-paris1.fr/Collo/Merle.pdf.

17. Vincent Geisser and Aziz Zemouri, *Marianne et Allah: Les politiques françaises face à la "question musulmane"* (Paris: La Découverte, 2007), 15–41.

18. Pascal Le Pautremat, *La politique musulmane de la France au XXe siècle: De l'hexagone aux terres d'islam* (Paris: Maisonneuve et Larose, 2003), and Henry Laurens, *Orientales II: La IIIe République et l'islam* (Paris: CNRS Éditions, 2004).

19. Sarah Mazouz, "Une célébration paradoxale: Les cérémonies de remise des décrets de naturalisation," *Genèses* 1, no. 70 (2008): 89.

20. Nicolas Bancel, Pascal Blanchard, and Françoise Vergès, *La République coloniale: Essai sur une utopie* (Paris: Albin Michel, 2003).

21. Raberh Achi, "L'islam authentique appartient à Dieu, 'l'islam algérien' à César: La mobilisation de l'association de oulémas d'Algérie pour la séparation du culte musulman et de l'État (1931–1956)," *Genèses* 4, no. 69 (2007): 65.

22. The *Code de l'indigénat* was established in Algeria in 1881, and later repealed in 1946. Muslim "natives," who were French by nationality but without citizenship, therefore became French Muslims. The ruling of March 1944 dealing with the principle of equal rights and duties between French Muslims and non-Muslims was extremely slow to take effect, and during the Algerian War, legal differences continued to be applied to different categories of French citizens; the law and its uses led to very different practices depending on background. See Alexis Spire, "Semblables et pourtant dif-

férents: La citoyenneté paradoxale des 'Français musulmans d'Algérie' en métropole," *Genèses* 4, no. 53 (2003): 61.

23. In the terms of surrender in 1830, the French authorities committed to respecting local customs, and especially to maintaining a personal status founded on religious law and distinguishing between the different faiths present on Algerian soil. From the date of the Crémieux Decree in October 1870, native Israelites from Algerian departments became French citizens, which left Muslims alone in their status of natives.

24. Claude Liauzu, *L'Europe et l'Afrique méditerranéenne, de Suez (1869) à nos jours* (Paris: Complexe, 1994), 61.

25. Initially placed under the aegis of the Ministry of Foreign Affairs (administrator of Morocco and Tunisia, and of Syria), and the Ministry of the Interior (responsible for Algeria), the CIAM's aim is to further integrate Muslim policy in France.

26. See Malika Zeghal, "La constitution du Conseil français du culte musulman: reconnaissance politique d'un islam français?," *Archives de sciences sociales des religions*, no. 129 (January–March 2005): 97–113, and Rita Hermon-Belot and Sébastien Fath, "La République ne reconnaît aucun culte," *Archives de sciences sociales des religions*, no. 129 (January–March 2005): 7–13.

27. Jean-Pierre Chevènement's expression has been used in an almost liturgical manner by his successors.

28. Geisser and Zemouri, *Marianne et Allah*, 71–99.

29. Ibid., 86–87.

30. Levent Tezcan, "Kultur, Gouvernementalität der Religion und der Integrationsdiskurs," *Soziale Welt* (2007): 51–74.

31. See Franck Frégosi, "Les enjeux liés à la structuration de l'islam en France," in *Musulmans de France et d'Europe*, ed. Rémy Leveau and Khadija Mohsen-Finan (Paris: CNRS Éditions, 2005), 99–114.

32. Nicolas Bancel and Pascal Blanchard, "Civiliser: l'invention de l'indigène," in *Culture coloniale: La France conquise par son Empire, 1871–1931*, ed. Pascal Blanchard and Sandrine Lemaire (Paris: Éditions Autrement, 2002), 149–162.

33. The image of Islam has seen very little change in the European imagination since the Middle Ages. See Norman Daniel, *Islam et Occident* (Paris: Le Cerf, 1993), Jack Goody, *L'islam en Europe: Histoire, échanges, conflits* (Paris: La Découverte, 2004); and Jocelyne Dakhlia, *Islamicités* (Paris: PUF, 2005).

34. Nacira Guénif-Souilamas, "La Française voilée, la beurette, le garçon arabe et le musulman laïc: Les figures assignées du racisme vertueux," in *La République mise à nu par son immigration*, ed. Nacira Guénif-Souilamas (Paris: La Fabrique, 2006), 118.

35. See Laurent Mucchielli, *Le scandale des tournantes* (Paris: La Découverte, 2005).

36. See Thomas Deltombe, *L'islam imaginaire: Les musulmans de France à la television, 1975–2003* (Paris: La Découverte, 2005).

37. Nacira Guénif-Souilamas, "La réduction à son corps de l'indigène de la République," in *La fracture coloniale*, ed. Bancel, Blanchard, and Lemaire, 204.

38. Yasmin Jeewani, "Sport as Civilizing Mission: Zinedine Zidane and the Infamous Headbutt," *Topia, Canadian Journal of Cultural Studies*, no. 19 (2008): 11–33.

39. Guénif-Souilamas, "La Française voilée, la beurette, le garçon arabe et le musulman laïc," 111.

40. Gérard Noiriel, *Immigration, antisémitisme et racisme en France (XIXe-XXe siècle): Discours publics, humiliations privées* (Paris: Fayard, 2007).

41. Stavo-Debauge, "L'invisibilité du tort et le tort de l'invisibilité."

42. Geisser and Zemouri, *Marianne et Allah*, 11.

43. Jürgen Habermas and Joseph Ratzinger, *The Dialectics of Secularization: On Reason and Religion* (San Francisco: Ignatius Press, 2007).

44. Cécile Laborde, "The Culture(s) of the Republic: Nationalism and Multiculturalism in French Republican Thought," *Political Theory* 29, no. 5 (2001): 721.

45. David Koussens, "Le port de signes religieux dans les écoles québécoises et françaises: Acommodements (dé)raisonnables ou interdiction (dé)raisonnée?" *Globe: Revue Internationale d'études québécoises* 11, no. 1 (2008): 115–131.

46. Durkheim suggests that moral facts come after rules, which can be distinguished based on two traits: society intervenes if one deviates from the moral rule; a reaction follows the infraction "with true necessity;" and "the only possible progress comes from what the society does collectively," Emile Durkheim, *De la division du travail social* (Paris: Alcan, 1902) [1893], 16 and 19.

47. "The reality of an obligation is only certain if it manifests itself through some kind of sanction," Durkheim, *De la division du travail social*, 20.

17

IMMIGRATION

FROM *MÉTÈQUES* TO FOREIGNERS

Yvan Gastaut

In April 2014, the conclusions of the annual report published by the National Commission on Human Rights were very clear: according to a poll, 35 percent of the French population is openly racist.[1] Roma and Muslims are particularly targeted by such racism. However, the issue concerns the general behavior of French society in the 2000s and 2010s. As society seemingly becomes more and more open, public opinion and immigration policies have gotten more and more repressive. In that respect, former president Nicolas Sarkozy and current prime minister Manuel Valls share something in common: they both have foreign backgrounds (Hungarian for the former and Spanish for the latter), and they both advocate hard-line immigration policies.

The Progressive Closing Off of Borders

In the 1930s, as is the case today, France had a difficult relationship with alterity. The cause was a period of crisis and collective anxiety, and the result was a violent approach to the "question of immigration" and relations with foreigners, at the level of both the state and that of public opinion.[2] The economic recession played an unquestionable role: as the historian Ralph Schor has demonstrated, the crisis led to a "restrictive management" of immigration by the state, which was reflected in public discourse on migrants.[3] As unemployment rates rise, exclusionary forms of discourse become increasingly common, regardless of the era. It is a classic situation in all Western societies. In the 1930s, as is the case today (and since the mid-1980s, punctuated by Valéry Giscard d'Estaing's 1991 confusion of the words "immigration" and "invasion"), restrictive policies seeking to limit migration into France grew in number and were used as a way to reassure public opinion. Throughout the 1930s, such policies were promoted by right-wing governments and coalitions, as well as radical—and even socialist—groups and parties. That period set the stage for the repressive policies of 1938–1939, and subsequently the racist policies of the Vichy government beginning in the summer of 1940.

However, with the development of mass immigration in the late nineteenth century, France proclaimed itself to be a "country of immigration," which in fact it has become: France leads the rest of Europe in terms of immigration numbers. But it was not until the 1930s, after a first wave of rejection that notably targeted Italian immigrants, and after a decade of debate coming out of the Great War and surrounding the role of foreign and colonial workers, that public officials began establishing real policies on this issue. The state's first reactions to the foreign presence were often contradictory, but such wavering gave way, in 1932, to policies that opposed the arrival of "*métèques*," a pejorative term used to designate refugees (Spanish and Jewish) and colonial workers.

At the end of the nineteenth century, Belgians, Italians, Spanish, Polish, and even Germans and Swiss provided France with a "neighboring" immigration population that was primarily employed in the processing industry, which led to a lot of conflict and even xenophobic crimes, as was the case in Aigues-Mortes with respect to Italians. All of that narrative fits with a "classic" dynamic of fear toward the "other," and a rejection of foreigners.[4] But everything changed with the Great War: for demographic reasons, migration increased and began to include new types of workers, as well as refugees, stateless persons, and victims of territorial restructuring (Armenians, Russians, Greeks, Jews of various nationalities, and so on). During the war, the state had managed the arrival of migrants through the *Service de la main-d'œuvre* (Department of Foreign Labor, but in 1924, a private organization with ties to the employer class, the *Société générale d'immigration* (SGI), was tasked with organizing recruitment, medical and professional selection, transportation, and the distribution of workers to meet corporate demand. The idea was now to emphasize European labor rather than colonial or "Oriental" labor.

The reality was, of course, far more nuanced. Migration reached such peaks following the Great War that when the global crisis began to take effect in 1931, France had a higher rate of foreigners on its territory than the United States by almost 7 percent. Against the backdrop of the great colonial exhibition held in Vincennes in 1931, where France sought to glorify its imperial power, rejection of foreigners was almost immediate. At the same time as the economic crisis seized the country, immigration continued to grow, despite the staggering rise in unemployment. The mainstream media's reaction was at times strikingly xenophobic and violent. Pressure from public opinion, which demanded immediate "protectionist" measure was high, and the center-left radical government (Edouard Herriot's government from June–December 1932), in which Camille Chautemps, a member of the Radical Socialist Party and the minister of interior, proposed reducing immigration through a series of measures that would "close off" France's borders.[5] Parliament voted unanimously (with the exception of the communists, who abstained) for the law of August 10, 1932—the so-called protection of national labor law—which authorized the government to establish caps on foreign workers in companies.[6] Initially, the quota was fixed at 10 percent in private companies and at 5 percent in public companies. France was afraid, and as a result it was changing its immigration policies. All foreigners wishing to remain in France as workers now had to obtain a special ministerial authorization after consulting with the public department of work placement.

The quota system was soon deemed insufficient, and new restrictive measures were adopted (border closings, limitations on papers granted, and work permit renewals), which led to a growth in illegal foreigners (or colonials) on French soil. Then began the era of deportations;[7] access to some professions was also limited.[8] With the decree of February 6, 1935—exactly one year after the Paris riots—a new step was taken: foreigners who could not prove they had been residing on national territory for at least ten years and whose profession was particularly affected by unemployment would be deported. The Popular Front's rise to power put an end to such policies. The situation now resembled that of 1914, which authorized the free circulation of North Africans (from the colonies, for instance), and there was generally more acceptance of European foreigners. But that only lasted as long as the illusions of the Popular Front.

Hard-Line Politics

Upon his nomination in 2007 to the new position of minister of immigration, integration, national identity, and co-development, Brice Hortefeux, following the president's instructions, established an ambitious goal: twenty-five thousand deportations before the end of 2007, a "score" to be improved upon in the future. His detractors accused him of operating based on "number politics."[9] In September 2007, he summoned two dozen prefects who had not yet met deportation objectives so that he could motivate them and underscore their mission.[10] At the same time, he drafted a law on "managing immigration," which was adopted by both chambers on October 23, 2007, and which modified the *Code de l'entrée et du séjour des étrangers et du droit d'asile* (Law on foreign entry and stay, and on asylum rights, CESEDA), and which augmented Sarkozy's 2003 and 2006 laws. Some, like the UMP deputy Thierry Mariani, went so far as to suggest implementing DNA tests in order to verify family relationships for those seeking to enter the territory based on family reunification measures. Brice Hortefeux and Thierry Mariani were unconcerned by the criticism that such measures drew and referenced a poll taken by OpinionWay on October 10 and 11, 2007, showing that more than one in two French people was in favor of introducing DNA tests.

Three years later, during the second semester of 2010, at the same time as presidential discourse became increasingly preoccupied with crime and immigration, a new law "on immigration, integration, and nationality" was being drafted. It was adopted by both chambers on May 11, 2011, though not without a certain amount of wavering and opposition, and it committed the government to more hard-line policies. The "Besson" Law, named after the Socialist Party renegade who replaced Hortefeux at the helm of the Ministry of Immigration, Integration, National Identity, and Co-Development in Sarkozy's administration, implemented even more limits on the rights of some foreigners.

Besson was himself soon succeeded by Claude Guéant, and the tone became even more radicalized with him. A former prefect, appointed general secretary to the presidency in May 2007, Guéant had been Sarkozy's cabinet director when he was minister of the interior, and then he became his campaign director. He understood the rules of the game, and the issue of immigration was familiar to him. It was therefore no surprise when Guéant, considered the right-hand man of the UMP,[11] was appointed in 2011 to head the expanded Ministry of the Interior, the Overseas Departments, the Territorial Collectivities, and Immigration. The aim was to strike at the Front National on its own turf, namely immigration, and to make President Sarkozy's intentions with respect to immigration explicit in the media.[12]

The machine working toward the 2012 presidential elections had been launched, and there was no stopping it. Therefore, Guéant did not hesitate to express himself in terms similar to those used by the Front National, as he did on Europe 1 radio station in 2011: "Uncontrolled immigration has made French people feel as if they are no longer at home."[13] Claude Guéant made a series of more or less targeted verbal faux pas on immigration issues. Then, on April 15, 2011, during an interview on the eight o'clock news on TF1, he announced his intention to reduce legal immigration by two hundred thousand people, saying it would be "the equivalent of a city the size of Rennes;" later, to repeat Sarkozy's trope on "broken down integration," he stated that 24 percent of non-European foreigners currently living in France were unemployed: "That is almost three times the national unemployment rate." However, despite months of gesticulating, the numerous meetings held with political advisor Patrick Buisson, and all manner of media stunts, it proved to be a failure.

During his presidential campaign, François Hollande made a lot of promises. Immigration policy was at the top of his list of things to change. However, after the elections, Manuel Valls, then interior minister in the Ayrault administration, was quick to adopt hard-line policies. In October 2012, he stated that he wanted to bring the number of naturalizations back to previous levels, or to around 110,000 per year, but in January 2013, a directive came into force capping that number at only 30,000 naturalizations per year. In addition, in 2012, almost 37,000 forced deportations were counted, which represented a rise of about 12 percent with respect to 2011. The Roma became the minister's perennial target. Thus, on January 20, 2013, he declared that "Roma should either stay in Romania or return there," and speaking with France Inter, on September 24, 2012, he claimed that Roma were "people with extremely different lifestyles from our own, and they are clearly conflictual." He went on to say that, "I want to help French people against these populations—these populations which are against French people."

On October 9, 2013, at the peak of this toughening of political rhetoric on immigration politics, the "Léonarda Affair" broke out. In fact, following the seizure and subsequent deportation of a fifteen-year old Roma girl during a school outing, Léonarda Dibrani, President Hollande lost credibility, and these immigration policies, compared to the "style of the 1930s" by Jean Ortiz on his blog,[14] continued to unfurl across the French territory. The European deputy Daniel Cohn-Bendit posited that Manuel Valls was racializing the issue, and made an appeal to history: "His discourse is both dangerous and idiotic. Sixty years ago, people talked about Roma and Jews in the same way. In the 1930s, Jews were also deemed unassimilable. They ended up being sent to concentration camps. By expressing himself in this way, Valls is perpetuating extremist thought."[15]

"France for the French!"

The slogan "France for the French," which was used in 1937 by Maurice Thorez and other communists or nationalists of the era, was later reactivated by Jean-Marie Le Pen, and more recently by his daughter Marine Le Pen. It is a testament to the persistence of xenophobia in France. Similarly, after eighty dormant years, exclusionary discourse has reemerged. It is founded on stereotypes that are ingrained in the minds of the French and evidenced in an increasingly visible loathing for foreigners. The discourse shares numerous points of commonality. In *Le Quotidien* in 1930, the Belgian writer Joseph Henri Honoré Boex (also known as J.-H. Rosny the elder), who was also the founder of modern science fiction, argued for "public safety measures" against foreigners whom he claimed were taking over the nice apartments. He also accused immigrants of invading moderate-income housing, which had been put in place by the Loucheur Law of 1928, and which therefore prevented the "good French" from benefiting from it. *L'Ami du Peuple,* a major daily with a run of more than a million copies, published campaigns on this issue, feeding the rumor that the public services of the city of Paris were granting foreigners housing. It was argued that these foreigners (or colonials) were incapable of adapting to basic social principles, of being productive factory workers, or of assimilating into French culture—not to mention the racial danger posed by mixed marriages (with natives), which would lead to the degeneration of the "French race."

In the early 1930s, a generation of "specialists" legitimized that new trend in public policy. A prime and surprising example is that of Georges Mauco, who published his dissertation in 1932 on foreigners in France and their role in the economy.[16] A strong advocate of assimilation, Mauco developed a conception of an "ethnic hierarchy" and defended the principle of superiority of certain groups over others. For him, some "foreigners" were simply unassimilable: Asians, Africans, Arabs, Jews, or "Levantines." He asserted that "these immigrants have customs, views, tastes, passions, and habits that profoundly contradict our civilization," and to conclude, he defined the French thusly: "The moral deficit of some Levantines, Armenians, Greeks, Jews, and other '*métèques*' negotiators and dealers is equally pernicious. The influence of foreigners from an intellectual perspective, although difficult to discern, appears especially to be opposed to reason, to fine thinking, to prudence, and to the meaning of measure, which are so characteristic of the French."[17] Surprisingly, the work was celebrated as "pioneering" in the left-wing press and by demographic specialists. Mauco owed his success to his use of innovative tools that allowed him to make racist assertions through indisputable statistics and studies. His dissertation made his career, and it became an important reference for demographers, often unaware of its contents. Five years later, in a paper on the assimilation of foreigners in France, which was written for the Society of Nations, Mauco spoke for the first time about the "Jewish problem"[18] and suggested relegating "Israelites" to farming and manual labor in rural areas.

But was Mauco a marginal voice? Not at all. The man was a major resource in French public policy in the 1930s and 1940s. He was a respected expert, much like Hugues Lagrange has become today with his theories on "cultural" differences. The ultimate accolade came in January 1938, when, under the leadership of Philippe Serre, the short-lived undersecretary of state tasked with immigration and foreigners, Mauco was included on a presidential advisory board.[19] The board emphasized the idea of invasion by unassimilable and undesirable populations in France. One example of such rhetoric came from the conservative deputy Charles Vallin, the author of an article on immigration, in which he claimed that there was "a growing concern among our compatriots with respect to the foreign invasion."[20] Newspapers also contributed to this rhetoric; for instance, the *Petit Bleu*, which published in 1932 that nothing was "more frightening to consider, when sitting on the terrace of a café on the Grands Boulevards, than the horrible mix of foreign-looking people, with their hook noses, dark hair, and copper or bronze or earth-tone skin."[21] Beyond the common use of the term *métèque*, which represented vicious, wheeling-dealing foreigners who had been thrown out of their own countries only to find in France the ideal refuge, the most shocking form of xenophobia in the French language came from the pen of Louis-Ferdinand Céline in *L'école des cadavres* (The School of Corpses), in which the writer took aim at "Armenian-Croat scum."[22] But he was not the only one, Jean Giraudoux, when speaking of North African workers, explained that they are "primitive and impermeable races whose civilizations, due to their mediocrity and exclusive character, are only able to produce lamentable ideas."[23]

Rejection of the "Other"

Racism has resurfaced in France at the dawn of the twenty-first century. The debate surrounding Christiane Taubira, who was compared, while serving as minister of justice, to a monkey in a photo montage published on the Facebook page of Anne-Sophie Leclère, a Front National candidate in 2013, is a powerful indicator of this racism. But such racism is also evident in all manner of media headlines, offensive comments made on the web, and hostile or even openly racist gatherings. Racist speech abounds.

A number of news stories dominate the press and chronicle the rejection of Maghrebi, West Indian, and "Muslim" immigrants, using a colonial dialectic that was renewed in the 1980s and has since become part of popular culture. Brice Hortefeux, the former minister, even dared to assert on September 5, 2009, at the UMP's summer university that: "So long as there's just one, it's okay, but as soon as there are several, then there are problems." The die is cast. From the results of the first round of voting during the presidential election of 2002 when the Front National made it through to the run-off stage, to the "upheaval" of the European election on May 25, 2014 (marked by the electoral success of the FN), the idea of an ethnic and cultural "fracture" has taken hold.[24] The myth of the "enemy within"[25] has been gaining traction: from the Kelkal affair[26] in September 1995 to the Merah affair in March 2012, the attacks in Brussels in May 2014, or those that occurred in France and Belgium in 2015 and 2016, that figure has reappeared as the embodiment of an internal danger within society.

Doubt has crept in. On February 17, 2011, during the inauguration of the *Salon de l'agriculture* (Agricultural Fair), Nicolas Sarkozy reasserted what he had said during a show on TF1 called *Paroles de Français*: "Yes, multiculturalism is a failure." North Africans, Africans, West Indians, Roma, Arabs, Asians, and Muslims have come to embody one figure. A clear fracture exists between "good" and "bad" "immigrants." The foreign enemy—who is also an intra-European enemy—has been identified as Roma. On the night of July 16–17, 2010, in Saint-Aignan (Loir-et-Cher), twenty-two-year-old Luigi Duquenet, an itinerant traveler (known as *gens du voyage*), was shot dead by police officers at a checkpoint. Afterward, for two days, the little town and its surrounding areas were witness to scenes of violence.[27] On July 28, 2010, President Sarkozy organized a special meeting at the Elysée on "Roma and traveling peoples." During a speech in Grenoble two days later, he announced: "I've asked the Minister of the Interior to put an end to the Roma's unauthorized camp sites . . . Half of those sites will have disappeared throughout France within three months."[28] The Pope, the Catholic church, and the left all criticized the president's policy. Even the American administration expressed its concern. The Romanian president Traian Băsescu condemned the French attitude, and in Sofia, Bulgarian Roma protested in front of the French embassy. The United Nations also criticized France on this point: on August 27, its Committee on the Elimination of Racial Discrimination (CERD) requested that France "guarantee the access of Roma to education, public health and housing, and other temporary facilities, in accordance with the principle of equality."[29] A bit later, Viviane Reding, a politician from Luxembourg, member of the European Parliament and then Vice-President of the European Commission Responsible for Justice, Fundamental Rights and Citizenship, had sharp words regarding what she called "deportations": "This is a situation I had thought Europe would not have to witness again after the Second World War."[30]

The message is clear: France is no longer afraid to show that it has drawn a line, a "fair border," between good and bad immigrants. As a reaction, a march was organized by an association and a collective of residents from a number of Parisian *banlieues* housing projects (Romainville, Les Lilas, Pantin, and Pré-Saint-Gervais) in May 2014 called "*La grande parade des métèques.*" The aim was to remind France, in a time of crisis, of its values of solidarity. Surprisingly, the situation saw little change when the left came to power. Pressure from the Front National and from public opinion has become such that no government would dream of disengaging from the rhetoric. Deportations doubled between 2012 and 2013. The message to the public has been clear: undesirables are being and will be driven out of France. A succession of images reinforced such thinking: those from the Arab Spring, the war in Syria, the beaches in Lampedusa, and the "forced trips" from Melilla and Ceuta.

The Era of Undesirables

Many believed that the era of "undesirables" reached its peak in 1937. It was characterized by the idea that society could no longer accept foreigners who were "unassimilable," "dangerous," or "threatening to the established order." Such foreigners could include any non-French people or the "Empire's subjects." To that end, internment camps for "undesirables" and political refugees appeared to be necessities. Edouard Daladier's government from April 1938 until May 1939 provided especially tough legislation and reached new levels of xenophobia that only the Vichy regime would manage to surpass. On April 14, 1938, after a year during which public opinion was affected by several attacks that involved "foreigners," the minister of the interior, the radical Albert Sarraut, called for swift and decisive action in order to "rid our country of too numerous undesirable elements who circulate and agitate here in complete contempt of [our] laws and regulations, and intervene inadmissably in squabbles or political and social conflicts that concern only ourselves."[31] Supported by the president of the council (Edouard Daladier—also a radical), Albert Sarraut worked toward creating internment camps for non-French people.

In January 1939, the first French camp opened its doors near Mende, in Rieucros, on a mountainous terrain. It was made up of fourteen buildings, which included ten wooden huts, and it was placed under the authority of the Lozère prefect and overseen by the local *gendarmerie*. In November 1939, internment policy went a step further to include French citizens. It was justified by an exceptional law that was a response to the situation linked to the "phony war." In addition to punishing official crimes, prefects were now authorized to punish "potential" crimes in a politics of prevention. In France, the xenophobes had won.

Does the model from the 1930s only arise in times of crisis? Nicolas Sarkozy's proposed strategy was made up of "ever more" restrictive measures and laws on immigration. This legislative frenzy, which first began in 2002 and was subsequently reignited with Brice Hortefeux, Éric Besson, and Claude Guéant (three major figures of Sarkozy's term in office), was echoed throughout the UMP, among centrists, and even within the Socialist Party (as Interior Minister Manuel Valls's policies demonstrated as of 2012), all in the context of growing pressure from the increasingly triumphant Front National. As in the 1930s (1931–1940), one can speak of a continuity in immigration policy, regardless of the political party in power.

Yvan Gastaut is a historian, Professor at the University of Nice Sophia Antipolis, and member of the laboratory Unités de Recherches Migrations et Société (URMIS). He is author of numerous books about immigration in France, including *L'immigration et l'opinion en France sous la Vème République* (2000), *Le métissage par le foot* (2008), *La France arabo-orientale* (2013), and *Les années 30 sont de retour: Petite leçon d'histoire pour comprendre les crises* (2014).

Notes

1. See Elise Vincent, "Les Français sont de moins en moins tolérants," *Le Monde*, April 1, 2014.
2. See Patrick Weil, *La France et ses étrangers: L'aventure d'une politique d'immigration de 1938 à nos jours* (Paris: Calmann-Lévy, 1991) and Ralph Schor, *L'opinion française et les étrangers, 1919–1939* (Paris: Publications de la Sorbonne, 1985).
3. Ralph Schor, *Français et immigrés en temps de crise (1930–1980)* (Paris: L'Harmattan, 2004).
4. A few decades before the 1930s, the state had considered developing ways of better managing migration. In 1887, a census on new arrivals was established; in 1888, foreign residents were now required to register with their local town hall; in 1917, an identity card for foreigners was created; the law of August 11, 1926, prohibited businesses from employing foreigners for professions for which they had not received prior authorization.
5. Jeanne Singer-Kerel, "'Protection' de la main-d'œuvre en temps de crise (Le précédent des années 30)," *Revue européenne de migrations internationales* 5, no. 2 (1989): 7–27.
6. Loi du 10 août 1932 protégeant la main d'œuvre nationale, August 10, 1932, http://travail-emploi.gouv.fr/IMG/pdf/Loi_du_10_aout_1932.pdf.
7. Help was offered to workers who volunteered to return to their countries of origin. Meanwhile, the administration also forced foreigners without jobs to return. In 1935, more than twenty thousand deportations and repatriations were organized, and virtually no one protested these decisions.
8. The Armbruster Law of May 1933 was adopted under the Daladier government (January–October 1933) and the law of June 1934 was adopted under the Doumergue government (February–November 1934).
9. "Des associations critiquent 'la politique du chiffre' du ministre de l'immigration," *Le Monde*, September 12, 2007.
10. Ibid.
11. Christian Duplan and Bernard Pellegrin, *Claude Guéant, l'homme qui murmure à l'oreille de Sarkozy* (Paris: Éditions du Rocher, 2008).
12. "Immigration: Claude Guéant le récidiviste," *L'Express*, November 29, 2011.
13. "'Immigration incontrôlée': Tollé après une phrase de Guéant," *Le Monde*, March 18, 2011. Ironically, Marine Le Pen seized the occasion to applaud Claude Guéant and suggest he could become the "honorary president of the Front National."
14. Jean Ortiz, "J'ai peur de Manuel Valls," January 10, 2014, http://lepcf.fr/J-ai-peur-de-Manuel-Valls.
15. "Roms: Cohn-Bendit déplore que Valls 'racialise la question,'" *L'Obs*, September 28, 2013.
16. Georges Mauco, *Les etrangers en France: Leur rôle dans la vie économique* (Paris: Armand Colin, 1932).
17. Ibid., 558.
18. Georges Mauco, *Mémoire sur l'assimilation des étrangers en France*, Conférence permanente des Hautes études internationales, Paris, June 28–July 3, 1937.

19. Patrick Weil, "Débat sur la nationalité française," in *Dictionnaire historique de la vie politique française au XXe siècle*, ed. Jean-François Sirinelli (Paris: PUF, 1995), 719–721.

20. Charles Vallin, *Le Petit Journal*, November 3, 1938.

21. *Le Petit Bleu*, May 9, 1932.

22. Louis-Ferdinand Céline, *L'école des cadavres* (Paris: Denoël, 1938).

23. Jean Giraudoux, *Les pleins pouvoirs* (Paris: Gallimard, 1939).

24. See Vincent Geisser, *La nouvelle islamophobie* (Paris: La Découverte, 2003) and Nicolas Bancel, Pascal Blanchard, Sandrine Lemaire, eds., *La fracture coloniale: La France au prisme de l'héritage colonial* (Paris: La Découverte, 2005).

25. Mathieu Rigouste, "L'ennemi intérieur, de la guerre coloniale au contrôle sécuritaire," *Cultures & Conflits*, no. 67 (2007): 157–174.

26. See Salim Bachi, *Moi, Khaled Kelkal* (Paris: Grasset, 2012).

27. "Des gens du voyage saccagent une commune du Loir-et-Cher," *Le Figaro*, July 18, 2010.

28. Nicolas Sarkozy, "Discours de Grenoble sur la sécurité et l'immigration," July 30, 2010, http://www.lefigaro.fr/politique/le-scan/2014/03/27/25001-20140327ARTFIG00084-le-discours-de-grenoble-de-nicolas-sarkozy.php.

29. United Nations Committee on the Elimination of Racial Discrimination, *Report of the Committee on the Elimination of Racial Discrimination* (New York: United Nations, 2010), 55. See "L'ONU critique la France sur les Roms," *L'Express*, August 27, 2010.

30. Viviane Reding, "Statement on the latest developments on the Roma situation," September 14, 2010, http://europa.eu/rapid/press-release_SPEECH-10-428_en.htm.

31. Cited in Vicki Caron, *Uneasy Asylum: France and the Jewish Refugee Crisis, 1933–1942* (Stanford, CA: Stanford University Press, 1999), 175.

18

INEQUALITY BETWEEN HUMANS

FROM "RACE WARS" TO "CULTURAL HIERARCHY"

Pascal Blanchard

On May 17, 2013, the novelist Nancy Huston and the biologist Michel Raymond set off a firestorm among scholars and intellectuals by announcing the return of "race." Under the ambiguous title "Sexes et races: Deux réalités" (Sex and Race: Two Realities), they sought to wring the neck of "preconceived ideas," claiming that "the fiction that is currently in fashion suggests that genetic differences between human groups are nil, and that the notion of race is unfounded."[1] That, according to them, is a grave error: "Genetically differentiated human groups do exist," and we would do well to classify and recognize them.[2] For them, we should not be afraid of using the word "race."

The words have been spoken, and not just anywhere: in the columns of *Le Monde* newspaper. The article was cause for scandal and debate, but it now exists; it has been circulating and it is being commented upon. Race is back. Race is a new interpretative grid, and as Nancy Huston and Michel Raymond suggest, helpful for reading social relationships in our mixed societies. The past is new again: in 1927, at the dawn of the 1930s, André Siegfried, a professor at the Collège de France and a prominent scholar in the interwar years, was able to write that by mixing with the "black race," the "superior race itself is risking the loss of part of its dignity."[3] A banality of the era, a triviality today.

Three years before Nancy Huston and Michel Raymond, academic Hugues Lagrange also offered a "cultural" grid for reading the situation of African migrants present in the "*banlieues*" housing projects.[4] His proposal was supported by "left-wing" intellectuals and media outlets, from the periodical *Esprit* to the Seligmann Prize against racism, and by the "right," from *Le Figaro* to *Le Point*. Hugues Lagrange was picking up where Jean-Loup Amselle left off two years earlier when he wrote about "the ethnicization of France" and how race struggles had apparently replaced class struggles.[5] Both were precursors to this new critical reading of the world.

Hugues Lagrange and Jean-Loup Amselle are hardly race fanatics or extremists. In fact, they claim to be "left-leaning," open to "difference," and even "humanists." Jean-Loup Amselle is concerned with decrypting the "identity war" that is at work in new topics of study, and with understanding that those who are reinventing race are in fact multiculturalists. For him, it amounts to a reality (multiculturalism), organized by a (political) will, and motivated by a (structured) ideology, and this "plot" will lead to an identity war. To be sure, the concept of race, if it is to be exhumed, needs to be rehabilitated through the invention of a new descriptive code: the notion of culture.

The Metamorphosis of Racism

Racialization does not come from a "minority plot" or a blindness on the part of advocates for minorities. Some are obsessed with reading society and its fractures in such a way—from the angle of race, ethnicity, cultural differentialism—that diverts the debate, in a manner that recalls the 1930s. Racialists were those who, in "good faith," used to consider racial inequality, without being taxed by racism. They were those who made racial difference a dominant referent. Culture—and the respect of cultures—is today's grid for reading society.

In a late 1990s French comedy, *Taxi* (1998), a Frenchman by the name of Daniel Morales, who is played by an "Arab" actor at the heart of Marseille society, allies himself with the police to save France. The film was a reflection of the era and an exceptional symbol of integration. Fifteen years later, French cinema offers another vision of French society, segmented into "communities" and with a strong notion of race. It was even the topic of a 2014 blockbuster, *Qu'est-ce qu'on a fait au bon dieu*? (*Serial* (*Bad*) *Weddings*), which sold more than ten million tickets at the box office. The film, directed by Philippe de Chauveron, depicts a "very French" family, the Verneuils. Their daughters marry visible "minorities." Each daughter has her own "color": the youngest chooses an "African." The film offers a novel moral: "Everyone is more or less racist, but the virtue of French republicanism and the possibility for everyone to gain access to an upper-class lifestyle allows for family unity, even at the metaphorical, national level."[6]

Race is everywhere in that movie. It is ubiquitous, much like in today's political domain. In 1930, the "film of the year" that opened the new decade, *Le bled* (Jean Renoir) was a colonial saga financed by the government and the *Agence économique des Colonies* in order to commemorate the Centennial of the Conquest of Algeria[7]. Each era has its own way of thinking about relationships of domination. Within the political sphere, one should note, "race" is not an open topic of discussion. On May 16, 2013, the National Assembly adopted a proposal from the Front de Gauche that struck the word *race* from legislation—notably from the Penal Code, the Penal Procedural Code, and the Labor Code, as well as the law of July 29, 1881, on freedom of the press that punished racist discourse. Thus, at the moment when "race" is returning in the collective unconsciousness, scholarly practices, imaginations, and media and political trivialities, it is disappearing from legislation![8] But its return—which is soft and cultural, and banal—goes against reason.

The soft return of race functions without apparent hate and without noise. It relies on the notion of cultural difference—on the respect of cultural difference—in order to better defend all identities and explain that the world is organized around them; the world, it posits, is organized with difference and difference must be protected. Racism has metamorphosed to the point of becoming at times unrecognizable. The community has become the sole referent in this culturalist reading. One is to choose from identities that have been constructed in piecemeal fashion, a "fatal identity" reduced to its simplest form. Others are designated through archetypes and people can understand themselves as being excluded or belonging to a "defeated race;" some even see themselves as "perpetual natives." Many will object that "race no longer exists," but that scientific fact is no longer the majority opinion.

Political elites have popularized the notions of cultural difference, civilizational hierarchy, and community conflicts for more than a decade now. I am thinking specifically of Patrick Buisson and Claude Guéant, among others, especially when the latter stated that "in view of our Republican principles, not all civilizations, practices, or cultures, are equal."[9] Anne Zelensky questioned whether he should have used the notion of culture instead: "The word 'civilization' is inappropriate. I would have preferred he use 'culture,' which is more neutral. A culture is everything that characterizes the practices, customs, and behaviors of a human group. Culture is the spirit of a people. The word has less baggage than civilization, which is a generic term that includes an implicit value judgment."[10] Such assertions are simply thinly veiled precautions for talking about the same thing.

In 1930s France, race—which was conceived differently than in Nazi ideology—formed the basis of a worldview. It was not simply a criterion used to define civilization, it was an essential way of constructing French identity and its relationship to the world. For a number of key thinkers, the future of the West was intimately connected to defending race. A perfect illustration of that idea can be seen in Henri Massis's book *Défense de l'Occident,* which was published in 1927.[11] There, he followed in the footsteps of a "prophet" on the matter, Oswald Spengler. Such thinking was not limited to a single intellectual; one finds the same reflections on the future of the "Western civilization" made by thinkers such as Albert Demangeon with his *Le déclin de l'Europe* in 1920, Maurice Muret in *Le crépuscule des nations blanches,* Lucien Romier in *Explication de notre temps* in 1925, Arnold Decleene in 1936 with *Le règne de la race,* in Henri Decugis's summary of French rights in 1935, *Le destin des races blanches* (with a preface by André Siegfried),[12] and even among nonconformists, as in the case of the *Manifeste* in *Réaction* in 1930.[13] The positive reception of Henri Decugis's book is a fairly good reflection of 1930s thinking. It received a number of flattering reviews, notably in the columns of *L'Emancipation nationale, Le Réveil du peuple, Le Matin, Gringoire, Candide, L'Action française,* and notably in *Je suis partout*—"Henri Decugis tells us about the future of the white races"—with a piece written by Pierre-Antoine Cousteau on June 1, 1937, where he asserts that the title of the book should have been *Le déclin des races blanches.*

In *Le destin des races blanches,* the author, a disciple of Oswald Spengler and Maurice Muret, writes: "The [only possible future for the] African continent, which is for the most part inhabited by extremely backward black populations, is in the disappearance of a number of degenerate black races and the fairly rapid growth of a certain number of native populations."[14] Henri Decugis concludes with this assertion: "In summary, we are witnessing the decline of Europe's prestige throughout the world. Its political influence has waned.... Europe has lost its former uncontested universal primacy."[15] Here, he is repeating an idea put forth by Madison Grant in his book *The Passing of the Great Race.*[16]

The Dusk of the West

Pronouncements on the West's decline can be found in the writings of a number of right-wing columnists and leaders from back then. The historian Jacques Bainville, inspired directly from Maurice Muret's book, asserted in *L'action française,* that recent Asian events showed Westerners that "the web they wove in Europe is being torn apart in Asia with sectarian backwardness."[17] And he concluded that "dusk is becoming a dark night; meanwhile, the rise of peoples of color is like a rising sun."[18] He recalled the work of Alfred T. Mahan, *Le salut de la race blanche* (1906), which featured a preface by Jean Izoulet that presented the West as an "oasis of civilization in a desert of barbarism," and he posited that Europe was now entering "a century of crisis in which the races will wage battle."[19]

Assumptions regarding the West's "superiority" did not go as far as Nazi exterminationism. They were nevertheless a radical point of view that contributed to social problems linked to "native" issues (as was evident in the writings of the minister of the colonies, Albert Sarraut, and those of Georges Hardy, who oversaw the colonial school system until 1932) and questions of immigration (with thinkers such as Georges Mauco and Jean Pluyette who recommended, in the name of racial inequality, not to "favor" immigration from Africa and Asia). These arguments were also expressed in widespread opposition to "conjugal relations" or "mixed marriages" between races, measures designed to protect the great French nation. Albert Demangeon and Charles Maurras posited in *Pages africaines* that these issues represented the greatest danger facing France.[20] According to him, "if we grant citizenship to ten, twenty or thirty thousand natives [as proposed by Blum-Viollette], we won't have any reason to refuse thousands of others . . . The logical extension of such a policy would include all parts of the French empire, and the mainland would then become governed by its multicolored subjects; indeed, they represent 70 to 80 million people to our 40 million," and "French people would disappear."[21]

Such "moderate" (when compared with Germany) racial thinking, which was based on the explicitly stated superiority of the West and the construction of the world (especially the colonies) in terms of "race," became well established in the 1930s. Charles Lambert, a high commissioner for Immigration and Nationalities, was one of the most avid promoters of such thinking and recommended against letting "races mix." The elites of the era were trapped within a single worldview, which always saw other races as "backward." "Arabs" (whom Moscow considered dangerous due to their "religious fanaticism" and "indoctrination") represented an intermediary stage between whites and blacks. They were considered overgrown children. Almost eighty years later, in July 2007, President Nicolas Sarkozy delivered a speech in Dakar (a speech essentially written by Henri Guaino) in which he went so far as to claim that the "tragedy of Africa is that the African has not fully entered into history."[22] In the 1930s, even the most progressive, those with affinities similar to those of the League of Human Rights, people such as Marcel Paon, recommended vigilance with respect to the "race" of workers, suggested that France only accept "families from the European branch."[23]

The generation's expressions of fear marked the end of an era, and even, for some, the end of a world. That, among other reasons, explains the deep hatred for communism, which was seen as coming from the "Orient." It also explained antimodernist and anti-assimilationist discourse, which centered around the idea of an invasion of colonial migrants and the irreversible decline of the

West. Likewise, Jules Romains' epic of the white race, *L'homme blanc*, was published in 1937, illustrating such racial fears:

> I sing for the white man, the first man, the beautiful race;
> undisguised flesh in which blood takes visible steps;
> flesh the day weds . . . the white man,
> such as he comes to us through the ages,
> feels the weight of inescapable fatality. . . .
> A strange worry forces him into ever new conquests,
> in search of new horizons . . .
> The white man is faced with himself,
> and he who believed in his Mission,
> he who thought himself chosen, a leader, a master,
> he must wonder, what has become of his power
> and the message he brought to other men.[24]

Today, it is almost impossible for us to understand the extent to which such a worldview had become a *single norm* in the 1930s, featuring a racial discourse found in the work of scholars and novelists, the fears of journalists, the passions of politicians, and proclamations of decline made by philosophers. In her book *Races, racisme et antiracisme dans les années 1930*, Carole Reynaud-Paligot revealed just how deeply ingrained notions of race had become in the Republic's worldview and within the heart of French society during this period.[25] It was a core belief, one which took hold "despite the contradiction with the Republic's universalist principles," where "scholars, politicians, and colonial bureaucrats shared, to varying degrees, differentialist and inegalitarian views of human kind."[26]

Some of anthropology's most important figures, such as Henri Victor Vallois, who directed the Musée de l'Homme in 1941, helped establish a belief in race and extend the "model" into the postwar years. Vallois authored the first volume of the *Que sais-je?* book series on this very issue, a series which became an important reference point for a generation of researchers.[27] In contrast to their elders or to German researchers and even some American thinkers, these researchers saw the "white races" as equal, but racial difference remained a major factor between the white race and other races. That thought reached the general public in a book published by the Groupe Lyonnais d'Etudes Médicales, Philosophiques, et Biologiques in 1931, *Hérédité et races*, and later in *Les races humaines*, a collective work released in 1936.[28] One of the leading scholars at the time in the field of human sciences, André Siegfried, constantly attributed the characteristics of a given people to their "racial history." And that is only to name a few examples.

Eight decades later (in 2010), when Hugues Lagrange (a researcher at the CNRS and professor at IEP in Paris) published his book *Le déni des cultures* (The Denial of Cultures), many saw in it a return to the 1930s, one that was disguised in scientific methodology. Lagrange responded, in a typical fashion among today's intellectuals, that he was done with being "politically correct." The book received considerable praise on French radio station RTL from Alain Duhamel,[29] who spoke of a "very sensible topic," "a brave book" that "should cause a stir," written by "an esteemed sociologist." Luc Bronner also praised the book in *Le Monde*, Jean Daniel in *Le Nouvel Observateur*, and a special issue of *Le Point* invented pseudopolygamists for the occasion to illustrate his assertions and figures (extrapolated from a handful of disadvantaged neighborhoods and then mapped onto all of France).[30]

Laurent Mucchielli, a researcher at the CNRS reacted to the acclaim, arguing that "Hugues Lagrange makes two generalizations in his work: polygamy is applied to all the families, and his analysis of some of the most disadvantaged neighborhoods in France is then applied to the entire Paris region and even to the rest of France." He also went on to criticize the new media star's reliance on common stereotypes: "Asian youth learn from a young age the importance of learning and concentration, to cite the teachings of Confucius."[31]

Scholarly *Backing*

Hugues Lagrange has without a doubt sought to be honest in his work, and academic integrity is not the issue here. Above all, he has become the spokesperson for a new trend that is shared by both the left and the right, and that is especially popular on the far-right: namely the idea of "cultural difference." His culturalist assertions (explaining individual behavior based on cultural background) serves to provide a "scientific" guarantee for public policies that are being established. In addition, his marketing strategy is perfect: "the brave, left-wing academic, who is almost Green in his political affiliations, who works with underprivileged kids after school, and who thinks it is time to break the silence on a taboo." Another key to his success: the way in which he blends genres in a book that, in the context of a classical sociological study includes very personal analyses and offers simple overall conclusions. The book acts as a kind of guide for "dummies" that can be easily digested by all.

But Hugues Lagrange has not invented anything. French society in 2010 needed its "expert thinker," just as the 1930s had its own. Back then it was Georges Mauco, a geographer (and future member of the PPF), and the author of an influential dissertation in 1932 and successful book called *Les étrangers en France* (based on a study of five thousand immigrant laborers in the Paris region).[32] In his book, Georges Mauco claimed to "prove," through the use of statistics, that "Orientals" and "exotic people" were unassimilable and undesirable. Five years later, he added "Jewish refugees" from Central Europe to that category.

Georges Mauco, who was celebrated by the far-right (*Candide* awarded him with its prize for dissertation of the year), ended up being adopted by the left and the Popular Front! He became a government adviser for the left in 1937, and he served on all commissions dealing with immigration; he was active under Vichy before playing a central role in "anti-exotic" immigration policies in the years between 1945 and 1960, under the Fourth Republic. Later, it was discovered that he had not "really" met any of the "immigrants" in his book; he had simply interviewed factory managers. *Les étrangers en France* paved the way for the laws of August 1932, which restricted entry and residence rights for foreigners in France by stigmatizing undesirables. Today, with fears of cultural invasion and a "great replacement," and with the overuse of Michel Rocard's phrase first pronounced on January 7, 1990, concerning France's inability to take in "all the misery of the world," Hugues Lagrange now has his own ideological role to play.[33] He is the decent man lending authority to processes of exclusion, specific policies, and cultural adaptations.

The difference between the 1930s and today only lies in words, and not in mental processes. In the 1930s, society believed in the existence of a "French race"—as well as an "Italian race" or "German race"—a theory initially developed in 1934 by René Martial, and subsequently republished by Hachette in 1955 with a new title.[34] That model remained unchanged until the 1960s. Today, we think that cultures are different, that Europe is a single unity, and that France is going to lose itself because of "too much mixing," and that we have to protect ourselves from those that oppose our civilization.

As in the 1930s, racism exists, but this time under the euphemistic guise of "cultural difference." Members of the Club de l'Horloge and thinkers of "Indo-European cultures" have impacted minds. It is no longer a right-wing or far-right idea; it has become far more prevalent and runs deeper than it had previously. In this "culturalist" worldview, the "other" is different from society, and in this fearful vision of the world and of ourselves, France is believed to be threatened from the inside. Such thinking gives expression to feelings of revenge—anyone who refuses to admit that those who are not French are irreducibly "other" is considered dangerous and treacherous.

That worldview has been amply promoted by the new "stars" of our era, with people such as Éric Zemmour, a sensationalist polemicist, expounding on whatever backward thinking might capture his audience's attention. He is a kind of brutal version of Hugues Lagrange. On May 23, 2012, speaking on RTL radio, in an effort to criticize François Hollande's minister of justice (Christiane Taubira, a black woman from French Guiana), he gave voice to this ethnic nightmare: "In a few days, Taubira chose her victims and her special cases. In the good camp: women, *banlieue* youth. In the bad camp: white men." The idea now is that one must fight for one's "race" and choose one's "camp." Not long after that statement, others went so far as to compare Christiane Taubira to a monkey.[35]

Decline and culturalism go hand in hand. France is losing itself in the cultural melting pot—as André Siegfried might once have said. In November 2013, Michel Wieviorka pointed out that the revival of racist discourse "means that the old racism is not dead, which is contrary to what was believed in the 1980s and 1990s. There is a general shift in society, which tends toward ethnicization and racialization. France no longer primarily sees itself in terms of social class, but rather in terms of religious and ethnic groups. Whenever a society such as ours becomes so fragmented, it opens itself up to racism."[36]

In April 2014, Christine Lazerges, the president of the *Commission nationale consultative des droits de l'homme* (National Advisory Committee on Human Rights, CNCDH), analyzed the most recent surveys on racist behavior in France, and concluded "that, if one looks at recent history, incidents of racism remain at an elevated level."[37] That is exactly what signals a return to the 1930s—not Nazism, but a general and benign rejection of otherness that is shared by a large portion of society and can be felt in the common culture. Fighting such racism is not obvious. Violence is not yet in the streets as it was in the 1930s. The sickness is within us, in our society, where we have allowed ourselves to accept the worst.

Pascal Blanchard is a historian and researcher at the Laboratoire Communication et Politique (Paris, France, CNRS), codirector of the ACHAC Research Group, and a documentary filmmaker. He is a specialist on the colonial question in France, contemporary French history and immigration, and author, coauthor, editor, or coeditor of *Human Zoos: Science and Spectacle in the Age of Colonial Empires* (2008), *Human Zoos. The Invention of the Savage* (2011), *Zoos humains et exhibitions coloniales: 150 ans d'inventions de l'autre* (2011), *Colonial Culture in France since the Revolution* (2014), *La France arabo-orientale* (2013), *Les années 30 sont de retour: Petite leçon d'histoire pour comprendre les crises* (2014), *Le Grand Repli* (2015), and *Vers la guerre des identités* (2016).

Notes

1. Nancy Huston and Michel Raymond, "Sexes et races: Deux réalités," *Le Monde*, May 17, 2013.
2. Ibid.
3. André Siegfried, *America Comes of Age: A French Analysis*, trans. Henry Harold Hemming and Doris Hemming (New York: Harcourt Brace, 1927), cited in John La Farge, *No Postponement: U.S. Moral Leadership and the Problem of Racial Minorities* (New York: Longmans, Green, 1950), 138.
4. Hugues Lagrange, *Le déni des cultures* (Paris: Seuil, 2013).
5. Jean-Loup Amselle, *L'Occident décroché: Enquêtes sur les postcolonialismes* (Paris: Stock, 2008), *L'ethnicisation de la France* (Paris: Éditions Lignes, 2011) and "La société française piégée par la guerre des identités," *Le Monde*, September 15, 2011.
6. Jacques Mandelbaum, "Comédie: Le bain de jouvence d'une République défaite," *Le Monde*, July 29, 2014.
7. Jacques Cantier, "*Le bled* de Jean Renoir: Une mise en scène de la terre algérienne à l'heure du centenaire de la conquête," *Les Cahiers de la Cinémathèque*, no. 76 (2004): 49–55.
8. Danièle Lochak, "La race: Une catégorie juridique," *Mots/Langage du politique*, no. 33 (1992): 291–303. At the same time, the European Union has upheld the term, as can be seen in Article 10 of the Treaty on the Functioning of the European Union, the European Charter on Fundamental Rights, and the 2000 directive related to equal treatment among persons, which states "without distinction of race or ethnic origin."
9. "Claude Guéant persiste et réaffirme que 'toutes les cultures ne se valent pas,'" *Le Monde*, February 5, 2012.
10. Anne Zelensky, "Le concept d'équivalence des cultures serait-il un avatar de la pensée colonialiste?," *Le Monde*, February 10, 2012.
11. Henri Massis, *Défense de l'Occident* (Paris: Éditions Déterna, 1927).
12. Albert Demangeon, *Le déclin de l'Europe* (Paris: Payot, 1920); Maurice Muret, *Le crépuscule des nations blanches* (Paris: Payot, 1925); Lucien Romier, *Explication de notre temps* (Paris: Grasset, 1925); Arnold Decleene, *Le règne de la race* (Paris: Sorlot, 1936); and Henri Decugis, *Le destin des races blanches* (Paris: Librairie de France, 1935).
13. "Le Manifeste," *Réaction* (April 1930): 1–3.
14. Decugis, *Le Destin des races blanches*, 235.
15. Ibid., 233.
16. Madison Grant, *The Passing of the Great Race* (New York: Scribners, 1916).
17. Jacques Bainville, *L'Angleterre et l'Empire Britannique* (Paris: Plon, 1938), 103.
18. Ibid., 102.
19. Alfred T. Mahan, *Le salut de la race blanche et l'empire des mers*, trans. Jean Izoulet (Paris: Flammarion, 1906), a book that inspired that of Lothrop Stoddard, *Le flot montant des peuples de couleur contre la suprématie mondiale des blancs* (Paris: Payot, 1925).
20. Charles Maurras, *Pages africaines* (Paris: Sorlot, 1940).
21. Ibid.
22. Nicolas Sarkozy, "Discours de Dakar," July 26, 2007, http://www.lemonde.fr/afrique/article/2007/11/09/le-discours-de-dakar_976786_3212.html.
23. Marcel Paon, *L'immigration en France: Conséquences et limitation de l'immigration* (Paris: Payot, 1926), 193.
24. Jules Romains, *L'homme blanc* (Paris: Flammarion, 1937).
25. Carole Reynaud-Paligot, *Races, racisme et antiracisme dans les années 1930* (Paris: PUF, 2007).
26. Ibid., 149.
27. Henri Victor Vallois, *Les races humaines* (Paris: PUF, 1971).

28. Groupe Lyonnais d'Etudes Médicales, Philosophiques, et Biologiques, *Hérédité et races* (Jusivy: Éditions du Cerf, 1931) and Paul Lester and Jacques Millot, eds., *Les races humaines* (Paris: Armand Colin, 1936), Jacques Millot being one of Henri Victor Vallois's successors at the Musée de l'Homme.

29. Alain Duhamel, "Les tabous de l'immigration et de l'insécurité," RTL, September 15, 2010.

30. Luc Bronner, "Il vaut mieux dire les choses, même si elles nous gênent," *Le Monde*, September 13, 2010; Jean Daniel, "Le temps des ruptures," *Le Nouvel Observateur*, October 6, 2010; and the article, "Un mari, trois épouses," written by Jean-Michel Décugis, Christophe Labbé, and Olivia Recasens for a special dossier titled "Tabous et clichés," for *Le Point*, September 30, 2010, turns out to have included a fabricated story about a polygamous marriage. Sociologist Éric Fassin writes, "The article ('Un mari, trois épouses') relies on the testimony of Bintou, the third wife of a Malian from Montfermeil who has become a French citizen. Yet Bintou does not exist," "Polygamie: *Le Point* et la fabrication sociologico-médiatique d'une panique morale," Mediapart, October 4, 2010, https://blogs.mediapart.fr/eric-fassin/blog/041010/polygamie-le-point-et-la-fabrication-sociologico-mediatique-d-une-paniq.

31. See Sabrina Kassa, "L'origine culturelle peut-elle expliquer la délinquance?," November 10, 2010, http://www.regards.fr/acces-payant/archives-web/1 -origine-culturelle-peut-elle,4578; and Laurent Mucchielli, "Déni des cultures ou retour du vieux culturalisme?," October 6, 2010, http://www.laurent-mucchielli.org/index.php?post/2010/10/05/Déni-des-cultures-ou-retour-d-un-culturalisme-désuet. See also Didier Fassin and Éric Fassin, "Misère du culturalisme," *Le Monde*, September 29, 2010.

32. Georges Mauco, *Les étrangers en France: Leur rôle dans la vie économique* (Paris: Armand Collin, 1932).

33. Renaud Camus, *Le grand remplacement* (Neuilly-sur-Seine: Éditions David Reinharc, 2011) and Michel Rocard, "Déclaration de Michel Rocard: Premier ministre, sur l'intégration des immigrés et des Français d'origine étrangère," January 7, 1990, http://discours.vie-publique.fr/notices/903116300.html.

34. René Martial, *Les races humaines par l'image* (Paris: Hachette, 1955).

35. In 2013, Christiane Taubira was compared to a monkey in a photo montage published on the Facebook page of Anne-Sophie Leclère, a Front National candidate in 2013.

36. "Le racisme s'est-il décomplexé en France?," interview with Michel Wieviorka, France TV, November 3, 2013.

37. Christine Lazerges, interview with Sylvain Mouillard, "La gauche doit être visible sur la lutte contre le racisme," *Libération*, April 9, 2014.

2.2. POSTCOLONIAL AND CRITICAL GAZES

19

THE POSTCOLONIAL CHALLENGES OF TEACHING HISTORY

BETWEEN HISTORY AND MEMORY

Benoît Falaize

WHEN FRANCE'S IMPERIAL period came to an end and in light of the trauma of losing Indochina and Algeria, French schools in mainland France continued to teach a very traditional history. The curriculum, which emphasized the glorious feats of France's past, was a legacy from Ernest Lavisse and de Malet and Isaac. A monolithic narrative proudly featured France's Enlightenment thinkers, whose ideas had been spread throughout the world, notably in the colonies. Meanwhile, the French school system was also affected by the *Trente Glorieuses*, the postwar period of economic and social growth in French society.

The shock of decolonization and the end of the *Trente Glorieuses* during the 1970s undermined the theoretical underpinnings of the school system, in terms of both content and form. The baby boom meant that schools were now confronted with unprecedented numbers of students. In peri-urban areas, those numbers also included children from immigrant families. One of the major moments of change in the way history was taught in schools occurred in the 1960s and 1970s, when schools were forced to rethink national history in light of that nation's loss of its empire. Schools were also opening their doors to a large number of students with postcolonial immigrant backgrounds, and at a time of economic crisis, high unemployment, and recession. The first shift in the curriculum related to the postcolonial period—which began in the late 1960s—and involved a deep questioning of important notions such as the nation, the Republic, and France. In the wake of 1968, the 1970s and 1980s saw a new body of literature emerge on pedagogy, which sought to encourage instructors to reconsider how to teach national history.

In the 1950s, Fernand Braudel had already attempted to enlarge the scope of history within the school curriculum. The "Braudel program" imagined history in terms of a discovery of world civilizations over the long term and covered a range of geographic spaces. The "world space" opened up national history. The program was quickly abandoned, but it remained a reference for teachers eager to avoid the "nationalistic and bourgeois" tendencies of the traditional history curriculum, which featured kings and princes, Saint-Louis's oak tree and the Versailles palace, battles against the English, and colonization. Very quickly, thanks to periodicals such as *Cahiers pédagogiques*, in which debates and pedagogical reflections mostly inspired by Suzanne Citron were published, three themes emerged that have today become central issues of pedagogical reflection: colonization, slavery, and the history of immigration.[1] What role does each of these themes play in the French school system? And how do we imagine they will henceforth evolve?

Teaching Slavery, Immigration, and Colonization

Colonization, slavery, and immigration have complex histories. The history of the colonial phenomenon over the long term includes slavery, but it cannot be reduced merely to slavery. Likewise, immigration is related to colonization, although not exclusively. Colonization has always been included in the curriculum (contrary to what is often said) and school textbooks, both at the primary and secondary levels. It was even a key aspect of the history curriculum under the Third Republic, and a sort of ideological matrix for first-year university students from the time of Jules Ferry up until the 1950s/1960s. Colonization was considered an important civic topic for French students. Beginning with Jules Ferry's school system, the colonial project was presented in classes, and students were regularly updated on colonial conquests and the movement of French troops. For instance, Bugeaud and Abdel Kader served as a heroic model. All French students, both those in the mainland[2] and those in the colonies, knew of them.[3] Similarly, the multicolored wall map depicting the various colonies was featured in classrooms until the 1960s.

The Republic flaunted the colonies as an expression of civilization and progress, which can be seen in primary school textbooks up until relatively recently: the mid-1960s.[4] The colonial era represented "France in its greatness," "progress across all manner of fields," as well as France's prestige throughout the world. In essence, the Republic was unthinkable without the colonies. Changes in how the colonial space was represented in school textbooks and curricula also reveal the types of changes that occurred within the world of education, and Françoise Lantheaume has traced the major changes in school textbooks.[5] The first can be seen in what she calls the *dampening* of the issue by textbook authors: colonization was taught at various stages and to different age groups, and in such a way as to relativize the weight of its stakes.[6] Another way of avoiding the issue was to leave out key elements of colonization. For instance, colonial violence, which was celebrated up until the 1960s as a mark of French civilization, was slowly euphemized before being relegated to a cursory explanation and ultimately all but abandoned.

Similarly, colonial racism, which Pierre Vidal-Naquet denounced, was almost never presented in its specificity. Its ideological underpinnings and manifestations were rarely explored. Ultimately, textbooks slowly shifted toward moralizing the colonial conflict: since the 1980s, violence committed by various adversaries has been dismissed. The supposedly reliable and objective critique of colonization (complete with a body of documentary evidence) was based on excesses, notably committed by colonials or members of the FLN. That form of moralization, at times, prevented students from understanding this history in all its complexities. It had the merit, however, of reducing the stakes of the issue and orienting students toward a "natural" consensus on human rights.

One subject that has remained unchanging within the school curriculum—at least in terms of the moral tone of how it is presented—is slavery and the Atlantic slave trade. It is often said that the French school system has never done or said anything about slavery. That opinion is due to a short-term vision.[7] After 1945, and no doubt due to the moral echoes of slavery with Nazi crimes in Europe, the slave trade was included in history textbooks, at both the primary and secondary levels, in chapters devoted to Colbert's mercantilist and colonial policies. Primary school textbooks, for example, broached the topic in the context of commerce under Louis XIV, and in typically colonial style: "Our West Indies were booming, but for that we paid a price: the shame of slavery."[8] The Code Noir and the slave trade were often presented in separate paragraphs; there was also a separate paragraph for Toussaint Louverture, the leader of the Haitian Revolution.[9]

After the 1969 publication of "new programs in secondary education," official documents encouraged teachers to talk about slavery in their classrooms.[10] The role of sugar, which was considerable in the trade of the Ancien Régime, and the role of colonial wealth in the French royalty's commercial interests were used as occasions to present (at times in great detail) the triangular trade, slavery on plantations, and the situation of slaves. Pierre Milza's and Serge Berstein's middle school textbook,[11] which was published in 1970, shows how important this theme could be. It is difficult to say exactly how much it was studied in class, but it seems that Colbert's mercantilist policies (which today have mostly disappeared from curricula and textbooks) were often used as an opportunity to discuss slavery in more or less detail, especially at the primary school level.

The theme was basically withdrawn from the curriculum in the 1980s. That was due to two primary reasons. The first had to do with the fact that a traditional history of France was slowly disappearing. Roland (de Roncev-eaux), Duguesclin, Bayart, and Colbert were no longer considered emblematic figures in national history. The era was more interested in politics and an analysis of the absolute monarchy. Interest in the economy gave way to politics. Bossuet replaced Colbert; the ideologue supplanted the minister. Research into political concepts replaced glorification of loyal and hardworking government officials. Another reason, which is often overlooked, was the form itself of school textbooks. Secondary school textbooks lost half, if not two thirds, of their written content between the 1970s and the 1990s. The part reserved for text grew smaller as the part reserved for documents (images, tables, statistics, and so on) grew bigger.

Allocating roughly two thousand words to a discussion of "colonial growth" in the eighteenth century, as Pierre Milza and Serge Berstein did, and then reducing that to a quarter of that (or less!) is not the same thing. Choices had to be made, and since the map of triangular trade existed as a patrimonial document in educational materials, more recent textbooks elected to include the word *slavery* in the text (leaving out the idea of "trade") with a reference to the illustrative map. The implicit idea behind such a choice was that the teacher knew what slavery was. That stance explained, in part, the weak coverage of the slave trade in school textbooks.

After the Taubira Law was passed in May 2001, which sought to include the Atlantic slave trade in the school curriculum, a report by the Committee for the Memory of Slavery showed the need to observe the educational world with critical distance. To be sure, there is no justification for the "small space that the slave trade and slavery have been given in the curriculum;"[12] nevertheless, the report underlined the extent to which textbook editors and authors were prepared to incorporate changes in research trends, and how for that reason they were often ahead of official legislation. That was particularly true for middle school textbook editors between 1996 and 2006: the significant growth in the number of documents that were included, together with the space granted to the history of slavery, had already occurred over the course of ten years (1995–2005), and without the need for a specific mandate to that effect.[13]

Finally, among the subjects related to the postcolonial, the history of immigration presents in France, as in many European countries, a very special situation.[14] School curricula in France did not take the issue of immigration history into account until the 1970s. Family reunification policies and the increase in youth from immigrant backgrounds led teachers to invent practices that took their students' experiences into account. The family history of students with immigrant backgrounds became an essential tool, particularly at the primary school level, for talking about foreign aspects of recent history, which was strongly tied to postcolonial exile. The development of a formal history of immigration did not occur until the early 2000s, thanks to debates that took place during the creation of the museum of immigration located in Paris at Porte-Dorée—the *Cité nationale de l'histoire de l'immigration* (CNHI). Only very recently have textbooks and curricula (primary school in 2002, and especially the most recent middle school textbooks developed in 2008) begun to include that aspect of how the French nation has been constructed. However, for the most part, the history of immigration remained a veritable "no-go zone" in the educational world (from primary school through higher education), as Gérard Noiriel has often pointed out.[15]

Ongoing Challenges in the Classroom

There are many stumbling blocks related to these issues—from curriculum development to textbook creation to classroom management. In the 2000s, a number of books elicited debate among historians that played out in the media and in intellectual circles.[16] There was also much debate around the so-called Mekachera law.[17] Those discussions led to changes in textbooks and curricula in French schools. The colonial had become a topic of discussion in France much more than it used to be. Textbooks were increasingly keeping up with shifts in research. Still, if one observes what really goes on in the classroom, it becomes clear that the topic of colonization remains a major challenge. The fact that it fueled French nationalism and was constitutive of the Republic poses an ontological difficulty for teachers and textbook makers. How does one speak of the Republic and its values, when these have become a source of derision over the long term? How does one speak of the Sétif and Guelma massacre, especially considering that the French government celebrates Armistice on the same date on which these occurred—May 8, 1945? Likewise, it is difficult to account for figures like de Gaulle in the short time allotted—someone who is presented as a hero in the high school curriculum, but who also authorized such massacres while he was provisional head of state. Another thorny issue: the secret repressive policies with respect to the Algerian FLN (1958–1960).

Moreover, decolonization did not go hand in hand with any kind of newfound consensus, except, perhaps, in the educational world, with a diffuse feeling of guilt. Until the 1960s, the historical narrative in classrooms was a codified and mythologized, but yet coherent, portrait of France and the values it was exporting. These serve to justify colonization and France's role in the world.

The loss of Algeria led to difficulties in the classroom regarding a taboo that had not been resolved on the other side of the Mediterranean or in the Republic itself. As Benjamin Stora has often posited, the war is quietly ongoing.[18]

Teaching the history of the *harkis* is still fraught with tension.[19] There are erroneous interpretations (produced by teachers and students); the scientific knowledge is still under construction;[20] and the situation of the *harkis* during the war, their exile, and their subsequent integration into French society, is extremely difficult to explain for teachers who are interested in evoking what is often an overlooked part of the French-Algerian conflict. Indeed, the *harkis* are considered to be "traitors" in Algeria and "traitors" by the French left; from those nostalgic for French Algeria, they receive ambiguous support. Moreover, at the time of decolonization, the *harkis* were considered illegitimate in terms of immigration and were held for long periods of time in camps.

Teaching these kinds of issues requires tools to help educators respond to student questions and comments. Is it acceptable to speak about every aspect of colonization—from the racist dimension to the colonial imaginary in mainland France? Of course, but how should educators approach these issues when speaking with students who feel discriminated against in French society? Teachers are faced with such issues on a daily basis. Moreover, and this is an important nuance, colonial history has become a topic of classroom discussion in large part due to scholarly research and also because of direct and indirect pressure from the educational community regarding children with "immigrant backgrounds."

Indeed, recent studies on classroom practices pertaining to the history of immigration show that the colonial issue remains a central concern among educators.[21] When colonialism is used to discuss immigration, it is typically done from the perspective of a traumatic memory, rather than from a historical and contextualized perspective. Educators tend to think that students have inherited a colonial past and memory. For that reason, they often construct their lessons in such a way as to define a shared memory of war and of colonization. Questions linked to migration and colonialism (plundering of land, rural exodus, proletarianization, exile, specificity of arrival, status on the mainland) are never—or only very rarely—discussed. Yet such questions form a key element of colonial emigration, which transformed the empire's dispossessed and uprooted *emigrants* into proletarian *immigrants* in the metropole.

Similarly, the construction of the colonial imaginary and its impact on the existence of immigrants on mainland soil are very rarely evoked in the classroom. Rather, the issue of colonial relations and the trauma associated with this history are what get brought up in class, with the justification that educators are responding to student questions—to their identity-based concerns (implicitly attributed to this history). That is why students' families are often discussed in terms of their exile and their settlement into French society. Studying the trajectories of students' families has become a way of accounting for colonial history. In essence, the long-term history of immigration (one that accounts for its multiple geographic—and not simply colonial—perspectives) still remains untold. But the fact that colonization has become the natural framework to which educators refer when teaching immigration demonstrates the ways in which French society conceives of itself in binary terms: "them" and "us," or French natives ("of pure French stock," the majority of educators) and foreigners (the "children from postcolonial immigrant backgrounds").

Finally, the topic of slavery does not escape the effects of how it has been represented elsewhere.[22] The theme of slavery is presented in class in terms of exploitation of blacks by whites, a portrayal that victimizes black populations. In addition, textbooks and classroom curricula are slow to adopt new research. Indeed, the slave trade is treated as a kind of obvious topic. Very rarely do educators delve into the reasons why Europeans went to Africa for their labor needs. The implicit message is that blacks were "naturally" inclined toward slavery. Moreover, the real conditions on plantations and during slavery are often downplayed, which makes it difficult for students to understand the complexities of the slave trade. Similarly, the fact that the Atlantic slave trade is not discussed in the context of other slave trades, such as the sub-Saharan slave trade, lends it an absolute character that no historian would be able to follow. As a recent study shows, slavery is often brought up as a pretext for an annual school project.[23] Moral and educational messages are the ultimate goal of such projects, rather than concerns for historical accuracy. Here again, the civic dimension outweighs the issue of history.

What Could Teaching History Mean in a Postcolonial World?

Inquiring into what history should feature in the postcolonial era means invariably asking questions about the future. It is as if the process of debating pedagogical issues becomes necessary in order to return to the very fundamentals of school: preparing for the future. After confronting issues of memory in the classroom and questions about the entire educational system, we end up returning to the future. No doubt, as the historian Jocelyn Létourneau wrote with respect to issues of memory in Quebec, we also had to "dust off" the past,[24] shed new light on it, and that is essentially what has incited public debate surrounding schools and how to teach history for the past twenty years. And the work is clearly far from done.

An analysis of classroom practices can help us understand the logics informing the work performed by educators—beyond textbooks and beyond the curricula and stated intentions of teachers. Lesson planning, the choice of documents, and the relationship between teachers and their students says a lot about the implicit underpinnings of a reasoned presentation of history. The educational realm has not escaped the debates arising in French society about its history. In fact, it has been a focal point of discussion. "What is to be done about the schools?" Yet, when it comes to these issues, and when the light comes glaring into the room, the school system acts in much the same way as the rest of society's actors. The school system, in its desire to acknowledge the unfortunate aspects of the past, yesterday's faults, and today's painful memories, has no doubt had difficulty escaping a kind of alienation. From the "enchanted future" promised by the traditional narrative of French history (provided, of course, that one followed the virtuous example of the heroes of "our" national history), the school system transitioned to a confrontation with a "disappointing past," in which a form of guilty and repentant memory at times gives way to history as "therapy" for a society that is being assailed by identity claims, issues of memory, and competition between memories, and even competition among victims. The pedagogy of history as a *pharmakon*, as a therapy to heal identity wounds and scars from the past.[25]

After the Shoah and "the duty of memory"—"never again!"—colonization, slavery, and the history of immigration have surged forth in the educational space, with educators wishing to speak of that history and acknowledge the wrongs done to its victims. After some necessary dusting, which makes us cough and forces us to close our eyes as we look for cleaner air, an avenue of discussion has been cleared. In the words of Abdelmalek Sayad on the issue of Algerian history: "Colonial alienation, to which decolonization did not put an end, together with postcolonial alienation have led to a situation in which the history of Algeria is a mutilated history."[26] Alienation is due to the fact that, for a very long time, colonization was primarily discussed in terms of justification or support, or virulent critique in an anticolonial context, but without any further investigation. The education system would do well to rely, whenever possible, on the most recent research. Only rigorous forms of history can provide students and educators with the knowledge necessary to understand without judging.

The project of "disalienating" history starts with a will to historicize all topics related to colonial spaces and to imagining immigration in its postcolonial dimension. The following topic still remains to be broached, since as Achille Mbembe has shown, "the totem which colonized peoples discovered behind the mask of humanism and universalism was not only deaf and blind most of the time, it was also, above all, characterized by the desire for its own death, but insofar as this death was necessarily conveyed through that of others, it was a delegated death."[27] What would a postcolonial pedagogy look like if it allowed for a critique of "the effects of cruelty and blindness produced by a certain conception—I'd call it colonial—of reason, of humanism, and of universalism."[28] The real conditions of colonization and colonial ideology are often underestimated by educators, who instead emphasize more formal and descriptive elements. In addition, increased emphasis on the complexity of the process would show that colonization is not simply a mechanical and arbitrary form of domination that silences natives, imposes violence, and enacts oppression.[29] It would show that the colonized and "natives were not simply passive individuals who endured history and the actions of colonizers; they were not incapable of action or of affecting their futures. All peoples—Native Americans, Indians, Oceanians, Algerians—found a way of exerting their agency within the constraints imposed upon them by their colonizers."[30]

In addition, the diversity of postcolonial and colonial situations, the various ways in which colonizers and natives adapted to the situation suggests a "colonial encounter;" in other words, interactions between colonizers and the colonized went beyond simple oppositions.[31] In terms of knowledge, there is some urgency to address these issues within the school system: research that adds nuance to historical events and periods as well as the ways in which we look at those events and periods needs to be ensured. Teaching in a postcolonial context means refusing to accept oversimplified ideas and lamenting visions (even if they are generous). Only in such conditions will students be able to understand that the history of slavery, colonization, and immigration is not "other" people's history—it is not the history of "foreigners" in France; rather, it is a shared history that extends deep into the past and includes multiple forms of interaction.

When we consider the problems of identity faced by students, it becomes clear that these issues are crucial. Racial and social discrimination present in so-called sensitive neighborhoods (disadvantaged *banlieues* housing projects) underscore the need to deal with these issues of history effectively. The violence occurring in these neighborhoods and even in some schools is all too often attributed, either implicitly or explicitly, to a problem of integration, not to mention the historic dimension of the presence of immigrant families in France, and notably those linked to colonial or postcolonial immigration. The postcolonial situation, it is worth recalling, is not the only aspect of students' identity. Their social and symbolic allegiance are multiple and they cannot be reduced to colonial history.[32]

As the majority of studies on teaching history show, the question of identity is a central concern to educators.[33] In the classroom, the issue of identity is often reduced to student "backgrounds." The school system tends to act "as if everything occurred in a 'pure cultural context,' which is to say in an abstract situation where culture is reified into a transhistorical fact that transcends class difference (for instance, we often speak of immigrants from the Algerian, North African, Spanish, or Portuguese cultures as if they were each a monolithic culture)."[34] In addition to being a construction, identity is also in constant flux. Students in the French school system with postcolonial family backgrounds are mostly French, and they have every right to be included in French society; moreover, they have the right to a future. That is what is primarily at issue in these questions, and it is the precise meaning of Frantz Fanon's words in 1952 in *Black Skin, White Masks* when he wrote "I do not want to sing to the detriment of my present and my future."[35] Understanding the present, in part, involves examining the history of immigration—a history that France has finally begun to acknowledge is a "composed past"[36]—as a long-term phenomenon that includes but is not limited to colonialism.

Meanwhile, the French school system ought to question its own identity-based biases, which often result in making it an undeclared site of communitarianism, that of the majority. The French school system, through the debates on Europe in the curriculum and the definition of "open" or "strict" secularism, often presents itself as an institution that is incapable of questioning its own identity. At times it even resembles an institution that is frozen in an ahistorical position, in which a nostalgia for the Third Republic and its beginnings mask the discomfort of educators who are confronted with an increasingly difficult job.

What does the school system want for the future of history? What common, shared, and unifying narrative should be offered to students who are in search of their own identities? Those are the questions that the school system should urgently answer. With respect to the stakes of memory in historical narratives, Paul Ricœur once spoke of a "fair memory," or an academic history that would be capable of hearing history's memories.[37] Quite clearly, the time has come for a "fair pedagogy" of history, one that would be able to construct a critical history without underestimating the social power of memory at play, one that could be faithful to family and social pasts without rejecting the historical truths established by researchers, one that would be faithful to academic truth. History as it is taught in schools should inscribe itself in a dynamic of memory that does not neglect the painful aspects of history, but that also relies on the work of professional historians. The role of history should be placed at the center of a shared history.

History taught in the postcolonial school system is also crucial to humanity's common future, since the future depends on a common history that delves into all of its diverse facets. Schools share in this responsibility for the future, and should endeavor to construct a narrative that is based on fact more than on affect, on verifiable elements rather than on scattered memories. The aim should be to establish a plural national narrative, one that offers hope and the possibility of achieving coexistence for future generations: "Weaving the threads of history, restoring the continuity of this history, is not simply an intellectual necessity; today, it has become an ethical necessity, in that it has repercussions on the everyday lives of everyone among us and on the ways in which we see ourselves."[38]

Benoît Falaize is Professor at the University of Cergy-Pontoise in the department of teacher education. He is author or coeditor of numerous books focusing on the links between history and memory in schools, slavery, colonization, the Shoah, and immigration history, including *Mémoires et histoire à l'école de la République: Quels enjeux?* (2007), *La France et l'Algérie: Leçons d'histoire: De l'école en situation coloniale à l'enseignement du fait colonial* (2007), *15 séquences. Enseignement moral et civique* (2015), and *Enseigner l'histoire à l'école* (2015).

Notes

1. Suzanne Citron, *Le mythe national: L'histoire de France revisitée* (Paris: Éditions de l'Atelier, Paris, 2008 [1987]).
2. Carine Eizlini, *La colonisation enseignée aux enfants de Jules Ferry à nos jours: Cas des manuels d'histoire du cours élémentaire et moyen*, Master's thesis, University of Paris 5, 2005.
3. Benoît Falaize, "Des hérauts de la colonisation aux héros de la fraternité: L'histoire scolaire dans le *Journal des instituteurs d'Afrique du Nord*," in *La France et l'Algérie, leçons d'histoire*, ed. Frédéric Abecassis et al. (Lyon: ENS Éditions, 2007), 201–215.
4. Eizlini, *La colonisation enseignée aux enfants de Jules Ferry à nos jours.*
5. Françoise Lantheaume, *L'enseignement de l'histoire de la colonisation et de la décolonisation de l'Algérie depuis les années Trente: État-nation, identité nationale, critique et valeurs: Essai de sociologie du curriculum*, PhD diss., EHESS, Paris, 2002.
6. Eighth and ninth grades for junior high, eleventh and twelfth grades for high school, except for those in the scientific track, where the issues of colonization and decolonization are broached in a single unit.
7. See the report by Benoît Falaize, Anne-Catherine Amaloud-Porte, Marguerite Figeac-Monthus, Nathalie François, Anne Hours, Sylvie Lalagüe-Dulac, Sébastien Ledoux, and Carine Pousse-Seoane, eds., *L'enseignement de l'esclavage, des traites et de leurs abolitions dans l'espace scolaire héxagonal*, Institut National de Recherche Pédagogique, June 2010, http://www.cnmhe.fr/IMG/pdf/RAPPORT_ESCLAVAGE_INRP_2011.pdf.
8. Max Grignon, *Des civilisations antiques à la France d'aujourd'hui, fin d'études primaires* (Paris: Sudel, 1950).
9. Blanche Maurel and Jean Equy, *Histoire de France des origines à nos jours* (Paris: J. de Gigord, 1953).
10. "Le XVIIIe siècle: Techniques et découvertes nouvelles, les transformations économiques, l'essor colonial, la traite," *Bulletin officiel de l'éducation nationale*, no. 37, October 2, 1969.

11. Pierre Milza and Serge Berstein, *Histoire* (Paris: Nathan, 1970).

12. Comité pour la mémoire et l'histoire de l'esclavage, *Mémoires de la traite négrière de l'esclavage et de leurs abolitions* (Paris: La Découverte, 2005), 35.

13. See Falaize et al., eds., *L'Enseignement de l'esclavage, des traites et de leurs abolitions*. Since 2011, the middle school program for the eighth grade explicitly includes the slave trade in the topics of study.

14. Benoît Falaize, ed., *Enseigner l'histoire de l'immigration à l'école* (Lyon and Paris: INRP/CNHI, 2008).

15. Gérard Noiriel, *Le creuset français: Histoire de immigration—XIXe XXe siècles* (Paris: Seuil, 1988).

16. Nicolas Bancel, Pascal Blanchard, Gilles Boëtsch, Éric Deroo, and Sandrine Lemaire, eds., *Zoos humains: Au temps des exhibitions humains* (Paris: La Découverte, 2002), Pascal Blanchard, Nicolas Bancel, and Sandrine Lemaire, eds., *La fracture coloniale: La société française au prisme de l'héritage colonial* (Paris: La Découverte, 2005), and Olivier Le Cour Grandmaison, *Coloniser, exterminer: Sur la guerre de l'État colonial* (Paris: Fayard, 2005).

17. As secretary of state charged with war veterans and later as ministerial delegate charged with war veterans, Hamlaoui Mekachera was involved very early on with the "Loi portant reconnaissance de la Nation et contribution nationale en faveur des Français rapatriés" (Law concerning the recognition of the nation and national contribution in favor of repatriated French), known as the Debré 2005-158 Law, February 23, 2005. https://www.legifrance.gouv.fr/affichTexte.do?cidTexte=JORFTEXT000000444898. For critiques of that law, see Claude Liauzu and Gilles Manceron, *La colonisation, la loi, l'histoire* (Paris: Syllepse, 2006).

18. See for example Benjamin Stora, *La gangrène et l'oubli: La mémoire de la guerre d'Algérie* (Paris: La Découverte, 1991), Mohammed Harbi and Benjamin Stora, ed., *La guerre d'Algérie: 1956–2004, la fin de l'amnésie* (Paris: Robert Laffont, 2004), and Benjamin Stora and Alexis Jenni, *Les mémoires dangereuses* (Paris: Albin Michel, 2016).

19. Translator's note: the term *harkis* is generally used to designate Algerians who supported the French presence in Algeria during colonialism, and in France today are known collectively either as *Français musulmans rapatriés* (FMR) or *Français de souche nord africaine* (FSNA).

20. See Fatima Besnaci-Lancou and Abderahman Moumen, *Les harkis* (Paris: Le Cavalier Bleu, 2008); Fatima Besnaci-Lancou and Gilles Manceron, *Les harkis dans la colonisation et ses suites* (Paris: Éditions de L'Atelier, 2007); and Abderahman Moumen, *Entre histoire et mémoire, les rapatriés de l'Algérie: Dictionnaire bibliographique* (Nice: Éditions Gandini, 2003).

21. Falaize, ed., *Enseigner l'histoire de l'immigration à l'école*.

22. Falaize et al., eds., *L'Enseignement de l'esclavage, des traites et de leurs abolitions*.

23. That was the case in the Académie de Nantes in 2007–2008.

24. Jocelyn Létourneau, *A History for the Future: Rewriting Memory and Identity in Quebec*, trans. Phyllis Aronoff and Howard Scott (Montreal and Kingston: McGill-Queen's University Press, 2004).

25. Paul Ricœur, *La mémoire, l'histoire, l'oubli* (Paris: Seuil, 2000), 646–652.

26. Abdelmalek Sayad, *Histoire et recherche identitaire* (Saint-Denis: Éditions Bouchène, 2002), 20–21.

27. Achille Mbembe, "What is Postcolonial Thinking?," *Eurozine*, 2008, 2. http://www.eurozine.com/pdf/2008-01-09-mbembe-en.pdf.

28. Ibid., 1.

29. Dominique Borne and Benoît Falaize, *Religions et colonisation: Afrique-Asie-Océanie-Amériques (XVIe-XXe siècles)* (Paris: Éditions de l'Atelier, 2009).

30. Ibid., 287.

31. Several scholars have begun to do work on those relationships. See for example the special edition "Rencontre(s) coloniale(s)," *Genèses*, no. 43 (June 2001).

32. As Myriam Cottias rightly points out regarding the Taubira law: "This law, as I see it, represents a journey of recognition . . . The aim is simply to recognize that France is diverse, that France was built on such diversity, a diversity of origins and histories, and that that is the source of France's wealth," in "Nos ancêtres les Gaulois . . . La France et l'esclavage aujourd'hui," Myriam Cottias, Crystal Feling, and Seloua Luste Boulbina, *Les Cahiers Sens public* 2, no. 10 (June 2009): 49.

33. Nicole Lautier and Nicole Allieu-Mary, "La didactique de l'histoire," *Revue française de pédagogie*, no. 162 (January–February–March 2008): 95–131; and Nicole Tutiaux-Guillon, "Mémoires et histoire scolaire en France: Quelques interrogations didactiques," *Revue française de pédagogie*, no. 165 (October–November–December 2008): 31–42.

34. Abdelmalek Sayad, *Les usages sociaux de la "culture des immigrés"* (Paris: CIEMI, 1978), 34.

35. Frantz Fanon, *Black Skin, White Masks*, trans. Richard Philcox (New York: Grove Press, 2008), 201.

36. Philippe Dewitte, "La France se conjugue au passé composé," *Hommes & Migrations* 134, no. 1247 (January–February 2004), 1.

37. Ricœur, *La mémoire, l'histoire, l'oubli.*

38. Abdelmalek Sayad, *Les usages sociaux de la "culture des immigrés,"* 21.

20

POSTCOLONIAL STUDIES IN FRENCH ACADEMIA

Catherine Coquery-Vidrovitch

Opponents of postcolonial studies claim that the field's aim is to show the chronological continuity between the colonial and postcolonial periods, asserting, for instance, that, "The mythology of repentance . . . serves to justify a continuum between the colonial period and today."[1] To get a better understanding of postcolonial thought, let us refer to the remarkable synthesis provided by the book *La situation postcoloniale*, published in 2008,[2] which was met with scathing criticism by a team of literary researchers who have a sense of history.[3] The postcolonial is not a period; it is a mode of pluralistic thought that consists in rereading the past and using it in a present that is swollen with a diverse array of legacies. Colonialism plays a role and has left a trace on contemporary society. Those traces are not the same for everyone, and they differ for the formerly colonized, the former colonizers, and even within those two groups. Such legacies are both contradictory and inseparable, as Albert Memmi has convincingly shown since the early 1950s.[4]

Since they first began to emerge, postcolonial ideas have been sidestepped, poorly read, and despised by French intellectuals. *Orientalism*, Edward W. Said's landmark work, was all but ignored in France until a new edition was published in 2005.[5] The works of Congolese thinker Valentin Y. Mudimbe still remains untranslated from English, and therefore largely unknown except by "Africanists."[6] In his work, he deconstructs the "invention of Africa" such as it has been constructed since the sixteenth century by European explorers, travelers, merchants, missionaries, and soldiers. He has studied their descriptions and the forms of prejudice that have become rooted in the minds of many, prejudices which he has eloquently dubbed our "colonial library."

The Origins of Rejection

The first signs of rejection within the French academy with respect to a vision other than the Western vision of the "world of others" can be seen with the publication of critical texts on Africa by Cheikh Anta Diop. To be sure, the trained physician did not always offer convincing arguments for his ideas.[7] But they were nevertheless general reflections based on common sense. Egypt, he recalled, was in Africa. Upper Egypt, near the Nubia of the former Ethiopians (in other words, black Africans), was a place of splendid civilization, whose roots extended northward and southward. It was a global melting pot, where peoples from neighboring areas came to create the civilization that we now know. These people (including some pharaohs) were of all different colors. Back then, racism based on color was not more significant than racism based on culture. People were either civilized or barbarians, and allusions to color were rare in the ancient Mediterranean and eastern world, no doubt because it was made up of such a mix of colors. Mixed parents and the climate meant that most residents had relatively dark skin. Some were surely black, and others surely lighter, and there was an incredible diversity of morphology. One only has to look at the faces depicted in frescoes on tombs.

The aforementioned ideas, which were not exactly scandalous, nevertheless were received as such by Western Egyptologists in the 1950s. The minds of most people were still affected by the legacy of "scientific racism," which was codified in the nineteenth century and which asserted that blacks were inferior to whites in terms of both intelligence and civilization.[8] The episode seems grotesque today. But it seemed perfectly natural in 1974, when a group of academics met in Cairo to evaluate Cheikh Anta Diop's "scandalous" propositions. The final report issued by this learned assembly was a masterpiece of diplomacy that allowed all involved to feel they had won.[9] Professor Leclant, the group leader, and Professor Vercoutter, from the "Mediterranean" camp, agreed that some aspects of Egyptian civilization, in fact, resembled Negro-African cultures. In exchange, it was posited that the Mediterranean role of Egypt was major. That gave way to a compromise: since Egypt was African, it must have been influenced in some way by Africa as well as by other places. That compromise allowed both camps to continue working as they had done before. Thus, some "Afrocentrist" historians came to debatable conclusions on the supposed influence of the hieroglyphic language on the Wolof spoken in Senegal. Meanwhile, some "Northerners" sought to demonstrate that Cleopatra (the last pharaoh), due to her Greek origins, was racist; they also argued that she was as white as her seven generations of Ptolemy ancestors.[10] Interestingly, the first author to associate Cleopatra with a color, the poet William Shakespeare, prudently suggested she was "tawny."

A second shock that anticipated the rejection of the postcolonial was the "Martin Bernal Affair." The Orientalist philologist from Cornell University was interested in cultural and linguistic contamination between Egypt and Ancient Greece. In 1988, he published a book similar to Said's or Mudimbe's essays, in which he asserted that Egyptology (like Orientalism and Africanism) was a "white" science that had been conceived by German scholars in the eighteenth century. This convincing book, which was translated into French, was neglected by national academics, who were shocked that a "nonspecialist" (a specialist neither of Egypt nor of Greece) would dare to speak of Egyptology or Hellenism. Very few among them read more than summaries of the book, which generally provided a very literal reading of the title (*Black Athena*).[11]

In effect, Martin Bernal put forth the hypothesis that the Egyptian civilization could not have developed over the course of millennia on one side of the Mediterranean without, in one way or another, influencing the Mycenaean culture on the other side, and hence participating in the emergence of the "Greek miracle." After all, both the Greeks (during the Trojan War) and the Egyptians likely crossed influences in Asia Minor. Clearly, like Cheikh Anta Diop before him, Martin Bernal had gone too far. His ideas were questionable, notably the idea that ancient Egyptians landed in Crete and occupied Peloponnesia. Still, the idea of cultural diffusion is plausible. French Hellenists were appalled. For them, Martin Bernal was trivializing the "Greek miracle." I asked eminent historian Pierre Vidal-Naquet his opinion on the affair: annoyed, he dismissed the idea, calling it "an American fantasy." Another archeologist I interviewed was more prudent, saying that the idea needed to be developed.

Another example is that of the origin of monotheism. Most historians of religion disagree with the idea that the invention of monotheism dates back to the pharaoh Akhenaton, who sought to replace the Egyptian pantheon with the cult of a single deity: the sun god Ra. The idea here was not to establish causal links between this impulse and the future monotheisms, but rather to get a sense of a trend. It can be disseminated, transformed, and adapted according to different forms via contacts mentioned in the Bible between Egypt and Moses's people. Transcultural currents were at play. It is worth noticing that perhaps the symbol of the cross (via Coptic Christians from the Upper Nile) comes from the "breath of life," which played an important role in the cult of the dead in Egypt. The circle of the god Ra at the top was simply replaced with the upper branch of the cross.

In each of the above examples, we can see an instinctive rejection on the part of French academics to comparative cultural inquiries. The argument is that fields must be studied in depth. The result is that researchers ignore neighboring fields. Where else might one find that rare bird who is familiar with Greece, knows Hebrew letters, and can read hieroglyphs, except in a polyglot like Martin Bernal? In France, there is the comparatist Marcel Detienne, who was originally a Hellenist.[12]

Reasons behind the Reservations

I would tend to attribute the reticence toward postcolonial studies on the part of so many French academics to their insular habits within their specialized fields. For many French academics, who are convinced of their own implicit superiority, ideas from other places—and especially from the anglophone world, whose work, until fairly recently, was rarely read and often looked down upon—are viewed as being less valuable. In the 1970s, I was routinely asked by American academics to give papers on the internationally respected school Les Annales. That obsession ended in the 1980s, but French academics have not taken that change into account. American interest in French theory, such as in the work of Foucault or Derrida, made them smile. It also reassured them in their feelings of superiority, which prevented them from making more of an effort to listen to others. In a way, Pierre Vidal-Naquet's reaction to my questions foreshadowed the disdainful criticism with which postmodern ideas and postcolonial thought in general would be met by French academics. Such criticism can be seen, for instance, in a review of an American book that was published in *L'Homme,* which denounced "the theatric emergence . . . of vulgar postcolonialism"; the American author had dared to critique anthropology and its "heavy colonialist heritage," which "made its production suspicious."[13]

That dismissive attitude has marked the entire academic space in France. Many have opted against reading postcolonial works in English due to language difficulties. That ended with the publication of a collection of "postcolonial" texts translated by the Senegalese historian Mamadou Diouf, who discovered them in the United States.[14] A year prior to that, Mohamed Mbodj, another Senegalese academic working in the United States, called on thinkers, in the conclusion to a collective work that included pieces from Francophone African historians who had until recently been unaware of "postcolonial ideas," to join the debate.[15]

But French thinkers continued to disparage postcolonial studies. From the camp of African studies, two respected scholars made vigorous pronouncements: Jean-François Bayart (and for a while followed by his student Romain Bertrand), claimed they were "useless,"[16] and Jean-Loup Amselle, who was much harsher, went so far as to call them "dangerous."[17] To his credit, Jean-François

Bayart had initiated the idea of a history and politics "from below" (*la politique par le bas*) in Francophone African political history. In other words, he championed a history that told the stories of people from a diversity of social strata, which had previously been neglected. His ideas, which he developed in 1981 in the journal *Politique africaine*, were particularly fruitful for an analysis of the state. For him, postcolonial studies have simply exploited his ideas—although he was not exactly the first historian to examine politics and society "from below." The first issue of *Politique africaine* came out in March 1981, two years after the emergence of subaltern studies.[18] The style was not unusual, but one should not minimize a fundamental fact: the inversion of the angle of approach. It was no longer about observing Africa from a Western perspective, but about trying to understand the "subaltern" point of view. This is a real problem.[19]

Most of the work done prior to postcolonial studies was quite good, and we would do well to think about and familiarize ourselves with it; however, that work was done within a "colonial situation," to use Georges Balandier's expression (his article bearing that title was published in 1951)—in other words, it was done in the context of "decolonization."[20] Today, as a recent work has aptly put it, we are in a "postcolonial situation."[21] We need new tools to dig deeper into understanding the wealth of the Global South. Today, as was the case in the past, we need to innovate; we need to produce new analyses through new theories. Georges Balandier represents a precursor in this regard. He was one of the first to reply to Jean-François Bayart's critiques of postcolonial studies, arguing that "people tend to create their lives, cultures, and meaning based on what they have inherited from the past. There is always a struggle to 'create the present-day' differently."[22]

Jean-Loup Amselle has offered a radical critique that is essentially founded on a misunderstanding; he is only interested in the theoretical weaknesses of postcolonial studies in terms of their adherence to a strict definition of a philosophical thought. His major criticism is that this history from below is made up by international intellectuals, most of whom teach in American universities. They therefore use tools of analysis that are not "specific" to "subalterns." To be sure, Amselle is not wrong in poking fun at those who take these theories to their "logical conclusions" (for instance, the "Afrocentrist" movement). But is that a reason to condemn everything related to "Afrocentrism" (which is not the same thing)? Edward W. Said expressed the inverse idea: an individual in exile taught him that "a full return, or repatriation, is impossible."[23] That can be a source of wealth: the intellectual is able to experience both of his cultures simultaneously, from inside and from outside, which gives him the power to critically examine both cultures and create a synthesis. Located in an "outside place," "against the grain," the intellectual is freed from forms of belonging that are often constraining—ethnicity, nationality, religion.

Not all of the thinkers Said inspired have shared such a viewpoint, and prefer to describe him as being an old-school humanist rather than a "postcolonial" in the American fashion.[24] The historian is pragmatic and more realistic: we know that an observer always has a viewpoint, and that that point of view depends on the place and time in which the observer is situated. It is normal, after centuries of Eurocentrism, that African thinkers are seeking to disengage from the tyranny of intellectual dependence and to "break the ties with the 'Western imperialist center' in order to define an original space of discourse capable of accounting for African modernity."[25] Thinking for oneself does not mean rejecting the thoughts of others (even if some extremists, which I am not trying to defend here, believe so); rather, it means nourishing outside thought with different perspectives. To be sure, nothing is new under the sun, and so what if thinkers coming from the Global South are reappropriating concepts that were first developed by Westerners? All that really matters is that the reappropriation takes place in novel and autonomous ways.

Jean-Loup Amselle's sectarianism is somewhat surprising, especially since he has, remarkably, spent his entire thinking for—"in the place of"—Africans. Why does he deny them that same ability? By doing so, he positions himself as both judge and defendant, and never seems to question his own legitimacy. Judging from the perspective of Western forms of knowledge, which he presumes are universal, and which he claims are the only forms nourished by other cultures (an assertion which is not proven), is to deny the possibility of an "African paradigm in the social sciences."[26]

Searching for Scientific Convergence

The search for an "Afro-centered" (or "Indian-centered," etc.) thought—a thought nourished by an autonomous body of research that was previously neglected or looked down upon—coheres with the cultural patrimony common to all intellectuals from the various continents with ties to the "colonial library." Rather than questioning this legacy, we should instead consider them in light of other "libraries" currently being constructed. Cultural mixing is inextricably linked to the evolution of cultures. In that field, Jean-Loup Amselle was one of the best specialists on African societies.

Here we are confronted with a common trope among our intellectuals: the deep conviction that French universalism is superior. Jean-Loup Amselle's aims are naively national; he seeks to save (French) "Africanism" at the expense of Africans, since "a vision of Africa belonging to Africans [would lead] over time to the disappearance of Africanism."[27] At a time when "Africanism" has come under criticism by French historians of Africa, it is paradoxical to see this outdated concept reemerge as a postulate. Historians from Africa are different: they can only be receptive to the thinking that led to postcolonial studies. Postcolonial studies are a reservoir of fruitful ideas, notably those that underline a clear lack of self-reflection and the need to analyze the superiority complex of whites and their unconscious and brutal rejection of the "other."

The battle over postcolonial studies is gradually being forgottten in France today. Where philosophers develop theories, historians question the efficiency of investigative tools. They challenge the attitude of uncompromising doctrinarians whose ideas get either entirely adopted or rejected. Historical facts are incredibly complex. Unlike the "hard sciences," where mathematical, physical, or astronomical theories support unwavering systems (although discoveries periodically force scientists to abandon, adjust, or invent new theories), theories in the human sciences fluctuate. They express different points of view. Hypotheses are built as solidly as possible, but they have to be adjusted constantly according to ever-evolving social processes.

That is why some arguments border on bad faith. I would like to highlight two such arguments which have recurred all too frequently in recent years. One is to hold it against historians (those with whom one disagrees) when they speak about themselves in the media (which, except for a limited number of star intellectuals, is only a relative occurrence). At the height of disputes over such matters (2004–2005), it more or less became a way of assigning guilt. That type of criticism puts the historian in question on trial for expressing supposedly stupid remarks, since he or she has managed to gain access to the media. Let us be realistic: academics are not angels, and this type of criticism is likely an expression of (unconscious?) professional jealousy. The second "unscientific" criticism, which still appears today, comes from a form of academic snobbery, and that consists in looking down on the work of historians who were not trained in "prestigious universities," since they are merely "high school educators," or because they were not hired by a "prestigious" university. These are the kind of statements made repeatedly by Daniel Lefeuvre, among others. Yet, as in any field, there are mediocre historians working at prestigious universities, and there are good historians working outside of academia. The media has laid down the law: today we often hear the voices of a number of personalities who have not practiced scientific history in years, and whom the media celebrate for other reasons (in France, Max Gallo is one such example). Nevertheless, they should be fought on the grounds of *scientific* argumentation and not through ad hominem attacks.

As a historian, I appreciate postcolonial studies for the "toolbox" that they offer, which includes a number of interesting ideas that are worth exploring.

There is a wide array of postcolonial texts to choose from, in a kind of smorgasbord of ideas and perspectives. As Jacques Pouchepadass, one of the rare French historians who has engaged in close readings of postcolonial texts due to the fact that as a specialist of India he conducted research in English, has remarked that postcolonial studies can be criticized for many things, but they have unquestionably opened up new avenues for thought, even if some of what has been written in their name is stupid.[28] I for one do not mind ignoring all the scribblings of those who feel obligated to write nonsense on these issues. Rejecting postcolonial studies in their entirety is as absurd as holding Marx's writings up to obloquy because, despite his conception of alienation which changed our understanding of the world, he also made mistakes, and because Stalin existed. Or because, as is the case for postcolonial studies, some of his statements were over the top (I am speaking here of written works and not of the political deviations that would occur in the following century).

It is easy to mock ideas from twenty or thirty years ago. It is even at times necessary, since with time, such ideas become outdated or even oppressive. But it is ahistorical to reproach Edward W. Said for constructing the myth of a reified "Western" block from an Asian perspective.[29] The history and biography of Edward W. Said is a kind of multicultural condensed version of an "uncertain identity: a Palestinian educated in Egypt, with an English first name and an American passport."[30] It would be reductive to describe him only in terms of one "evolution" in his thought. Although Edward W. Said posited an acceleration in contact between cultures, he also underscored certain constants: their changing character, which goes hand in hand with the internal plurality of each identity. A generation ago, his postmodern work, which showed how "Orientalism" was a Western construction, shook the anglophone world, which came to understand the extent to which this bias influenced their own work. Similarly, the "Africanist" field was "dismantled" by Valentin Y. Mudimbe, and Egyptology was shaken up by Cheikh Anta Diop and later critiques by Martin Bernal. The same holds true when it comes to the "Westernism" brandished by enemies of the West. That is why Edward W. Said was so completely opposed to the idea of a "clash of civilizations." All of these authors also see themselves as the fruit of a common "library."

French academia, feeling threatened to its very core, has long turned a deaf ear to shifts in thinking. Yet, the postcolonial rebellion represented a major shift, emerging at a time when the only knowledge was Western knowledge. Orientalism—and to an almost equal extent, Africanism—was uncontested and devastating in its impact on thought for almost two centuries. In the same vein, Benedict Anderson had spoken out in the 1980s against the myth of the "community" in ancient African societies, something which the economic anthropologist Claude Meillassoux had already demolished.[31] Such myths had of course been "dreamed up" by Western science to characterize non-Western societies, when in reality these were unequal societies trying to create nations and states.

Immanuel Wallerstein has reminded us of the extent to which Europeans remain implicitly convinced that they are the sole possessors of universal values. According to him, this is a rhetoric of power which has legitimized all sorts of "imperialist" policies and continues to do so. The same rhetorical device was used in the sixteenth century to justify Christian evangelization, in the nineteenth century to glorify the "civilizing mission" of the colonial powers, and in the twentieth century to legitimize political meddling in the name of "human rights." Not that civilization, progress, or human rights do not exist. But such values have been inconsistent throughout time, and vary depending on place and culture. For example, women's rights were not upheld at the time of the French Revolution; Olympe de Gouges was even guillotined. After the 1848 Revolution, "universal" suffrage was extended to all "civilized" men. And the 1945 Universal Declaration of the Rights of Man did not take up the issue of colonialism. Today is the era of human rights. But before requesting others to align themselves with a given philosophical model, we would do well to question its value and limitations. In the past, as well as in the present, the issue is to know up to what point, and in what form, intervention in the affairs of "barbarians" can take place. This is a very difficult question, since we are not, for instance, prepared to accept the mistreatment or stoning of women simply because this is prescribed in Islamic sharia law. Debates surrounding the wearing of the headscarf are indicative of the extent to which these issues are divisive.

At the very least, the universality of the "universal,"[32] because of its link to "cosmopolitanism,"[33] must be addressed critically. That is why the contribution of postcolonial thinkers wishing to make the voices of the Global South heard is so crucial. Whether we like it or not, these transformations in thinking are massive. They force historians of French colonization from this moment on to think of this history as one that is shared with the descendants of former colonial subjects, specifically in France, an intrinsic component of a common patrimony which cannot be reduced exclusively to the French mainland.[34]

Catherine Coquery-Vidrovitch is Professor Emerita of Modern African History at the University of Paris-Diderot. Her publications include *Africa South of the Sahara, Endurance and Change* (1987), *African Women, a Modern History* (1998), *A History of African Cities from the Origins to Colonization* (2005), *Africa and Africans in the 19th Century: A Turbulent History* (2009), and more recently, *Des oubliés du nazisme: Les Allemands noirs dans la première moitié du XXe siècle* (2007), *Enjeux politiques de l'histoire coloniale* (2009), *Petite histoire de l'Afrique de la préhistoire à nos jours* (2011), *Être esclave: Afrique Amériques 16e-19e siècle* (2013), and *Le rapport Brazza: Mission d'enquête du Congo (1905–1907)* (2014).

Notes

1. Daniel Lefeuvre, *Pour en finir avec la repentance coloniale* (Paris: Flammarion, 2006), 199.
2. Marie-Claude Smouts, ed., *La situation postcoloniale: Les postcolonial studies dans le débat français* (Paris: Presses de Sciences Po, 2007).
3. Catherine Coquio, ed., *Retours du colonial? Disculpation et réhabilitation de l'histoire coloniale* (Paris: L'Atalante, 2008).
4. Albert Memmi, *The Colonizer and the Colonized*, trans. Howard Greensfield (London: Earthscan Publications Ltd., 1965 [1957]).
5. Edward W. Said, *Orientalism* (New York: Pantheon, 1978).
6. Valentin Y. Mudimbe, *The Invention of Africa: Gnosis, Philosophy and the Order of Knowledge* (Bloomington: Indiana University Press, 1988) and *The Idea of Africa* (Bloomington: Indiana University Press, 1994).
7. Chiekh Anta Diop, *Nations nègres et culture* (Paris: Présence africaine, 1954).
8. Catherine Coquery-Vidrovitch, "Le postulat de la supériorité blanche et de l'infériorité noire," in *Le Livre noir du colonialisme: XVIe-XXIe siècle*, ed. Marc Ferro (Paris: Robert Laffont, 2004), 646–685.
9. Gamal Moktar, "The Peopling of Ancient Egypt and the Deciphering of Meroitic Script," *General History of Africa*, vol. 2, *Ancient Civilizations of Africa* (Paris and London: Heinemann Educational Books, Ltd., 1981), 58–81.
10. Mary Lefkowitz, *Not Out of Africa: How Afrocentrism Became an Excuse to Teach Myth as History* (New York: Basic Books, 1997).
11. Martin Bernal, *Black Athena: The Afroasiatic Roots of Classical Civilization*, Vol. 1, *The Fabrication of Ancient Greece, 1785–1985* (Brunswick, NJ: Rutgers University Press, 1987).
12. Marcel Detienne, *Comparer l'incomparable* (Paris: Seuil, 2000).
13. Jean-François Baré, "Déconstruire le postmodernisme," *L'Homme* 39, no. 151 (1999): 271.
14. Mamadou Diouf, ed., *L'historiographie indienne en débat: Colonialisme, nationalisme, et sociétés postcoloniales* (Paris: Karthala and Amsterdam: Séphis, 1999).
15. Catherine Coquery-Vidrovitch, Odile Goerg, and Hervé Tenoux, eds., *Des historiens africains en Afrique: Logiques du passé et dynamiques actuelles* (Paris: L'Harmattan, 1998), 351–355.
16. Jean-François Bayart, "La novlangue d'un archipel universitaire," in *La situation postcoloniale*, ed. Smouts, 268–272; and Romain Bertrand, "Faire parler les subalternes ou le mythe du dévoilement," in *La situation postcoloniale*, ed. Smouts, 284.
17. Jean-Loup Amselle, *L'Occident décroché: Enquête sur les postcolonialismes* (Paris: Stock, 2008).
18. Jean-François Bayart, "Le politique par le bas. Questions de méthode," *Politique africaine* 1, no. 1 (January 1981): 53–82.
19. See Gayatri Chakravorty Spivak, "Can the Subaltern Speak?" in *Can the Subaltern Speak?: Reflections on the History of an Idea*, ed. Rosalind C. Morris (New York: Columbia University Press, 2010), 21–78.

20. Georges Balandier, "La situation coloniale," *Cahiers internationaux de sociologie* 11 (1951): 44–79.

21. Smouts, ed., *La situation postcoloniale.*

22. See Georges Balandier and Jean-François Bayart, "Questions de méthodes," in *La situation postcoloniale,* ed. Smouts, 274–275.

23. Edward W. Said, *Reflections on Exile and Other Essays* (Cambridge: Harvard University Press, 2002), xxxv.

24. Tzvetan Todorov, "Edward W. Said, le spectateur exilé," *Le Monde,* May 16, 2008.

25. Amselle, *L'Occident décroché,* 93.

26. Ibid., 65.

27. Ibid., 90.

28. Jacques Pouchepadass, "Le projet critique des *postcolonial studies* entre hier et demain," in *La situation postcoloniale,* ed. Smouts, 173–228.

29. Amselle, *L'Occident décroché,* 16.

30. Said, *Reflections on Exile and Other Essays,* 556–557.

31. Benedict Anderson, *Imagined Communities: Reflections on the Origin and Spread of Nationalism* (London: Verso, 1983) and Claude Meillassoux, "Essai sur l'interprétation du phénomène économique dans les sociétés d'autosubsistance," *Cahiers d'études africaines* 1, no. 4 (1960): 38–67.

32. Immanuel Wallerstein, *European Universalism: The Rhetoric of Power* (New York: The New Press, 2006).

33. Carol Breckenridge et al., *Cosmopolitanism* (Durham, NC: Duke University Press, 2002) and Achille Mbembe and Sarah Nuttall, eds., *Johannesburg: The Elusive Metropolis* (Durham, NC: Duke University Press, 2004).

34. I have developed these ideas further in *Enjeux politiques de l'histoire coloniale* (Marseille: Agone éditeur, 2009). See also Frederick Cooper, "From Imperial Inclusion to Republican Exclusion," in *Frenchness and the African Diaspora,* ed. Charles Tshimanga, Didier Gondola, and Peter Bloom (Bloomington and Indianapolis: Indiana University Press, 2009), 91–119.

21
FROM SLAVERY TO THE POSTCOLONIAL

Patrick Weil

NICOLAS BANCEL: *First of all, could you begin by explaining why you started working on citizenship and nationality?*

PATRICK WEIL: I became interested in these questions while conducting research. After publishing *La France et ses étrangers,* which was based on my doctoral dissertation on immigration policy since 1938, I began to examine the law of November 2, 1945, which has been very important in immigration policy, and which still continues to organize thinking on French policies on these issues.[1] My earlier research had dealt mainly with the period between 1974 and 1986. With this new project, I wanted to reconstruct the decision-making processes related to immigration policy in a context where the world still thought in racial terms. Back then, it was believed that people from different ethnic backgrounds did not share the same capacities for assimilating. The system of selecting immigrants that was adopted by the United States in 1921, which was based on national quotas, was a point of reference.

The final text of the law of November 2, 1945, does not contain any clauses that mention quotas or, for that matter, criteria based on national or ethnic origin. In my efforts to understand and interpret this paradox, I became interested in revisiting the law of October 19, 1945 on *nationality.*[2] So I made a request to consult documents that—for reasons related to the work of the Bureau de la Nationalité at the Ministry of Justice—were still being held in the ministry's onsite archives. I was authorized to view those documents and while I was there, my curiosity led me to look at files being stored nearby. And that was when I came across something that was of tremendous interest to me: documents on nationality policies under Vichy, and especially, a project for a law that would have drastically changed the laws on nationality (the project, which preoccupied high-level officials under Vichy beginning in July 1940 and over the course of more than three years, was eventually rejected by the Nazis).

At the time, I was already thinking about the pertinence of comparing France and Germany, a common practice among my colleagues that was further validated by Rogers Brubaker's book published in 1992.[3] France, it was believed, is governed by the "right of the soil" (*jus soli*) and is a civic nation open to all. Germany, on the other hand, is committed to the idea of "right of blood" (*jus sanguinis*). Yet France was the first to introduce a policy whereby nationality was passed down through filiation (1803), and there was thus clearly a problem in the reasoning.

While I was researching the origin of Prussian law, I discovered that French law had defined Prussian nationality in 1842. Those two discoveries—Vichy and Prussia—led me to write a history of French nationality. It was then that I noticed the dearth of research founded on primary sources. This was primarily due to a lack of documentation. Indeed, the archives of the departments in charge of nationality at the Ministry of Justice were not preserved at the National Archives until 1945—except in rare cases. Still, it was possible to find sources in departmental archives, private foundations, and even abroad. This project on nationality, therefore, began with a question about the veracity of opinions about immigration law (France as the cradle of *jus soli* and Germany as the sanctuary of *jus sanguinis*) and of empirical studies.

N.B.: *How would "Empire citizenship" be granted to those from the colonies, and what could you talk about the ambiguous, or at the very least ambivalent, "French citizenship" granted to Algerians?*

P.W.: My research did not cover all of the colonies. Yerri Urban has written an excellent dissertation on nationality and the colonies.[4] I focused on Algeria since Algeria, unlike most of the other colonies, *was* France. The territory was entirely French from 1848 until 1962. And I have to say that I was shocked by what I learned on nationality in Algeria. Only one chapter in the book *Qu'est-ce qu'un Français?*[5] talks about it, but it led me to reconsider a number of preconceived ideas. When Algeria was incorporated into France in 1848, the Civil Code (as of 1803) stated that all French people enjoyed civil rights. Yet Muslims and Algerian Jews who became French (it was confirmed by the *senatus consultum* on July 14, 1865) did not exactly enjoy civil rights. The official term "French" which was applied to them therefore did not have the same meaning as it did in mainland France. Indeed, it contradicted the Civil Code's definition of what it meant to be "French."

In order to get around that contradiction, the colonial authorities established a distinction between nationality and citizenship. Muslims in Algeria were not full citizens (they were underrepresented and voted in separate electoral colleges), and they also had a different civil status (under the guidance of the Koran) and penal status (the *Code de l'indigénat*). In addition, beginning in 1865, whenever Algerians tried to become fully French, the procedure was called a "naturalization procedure" by the departments in charge of managing it—the process was similar to naturalization procedures for foreigners. They were being "naturalized," meaning they were not French to begin with! There was therefore a contradiction within the regime and the legal discourse. Since the Revolution, French citizens have been defined according to the political and civil rights they enjoy, which represents a break from the Ancien Régime, as Peter Sahlins has shown.[6] They have been defined in negative terms, by the fact that they are not subject to "incapacities" (notably inheritance). The term nationality was invented to signify the full enjoyment of these rights.

A pre-Revolution mechanism was introduced in order to define "colonized Algerians" according to a twofold notion of foreignness that did not emphasize their rights but instead the rights they did not have: in France, they were not considered French, at least not according to the definition laid out in the Civil Code. Outside of the country, they were not foreigners either, since they did not have a foreign nationality. The French "nationality" that was granted to them (the diplomatic protection) was therefore a distorted (*dénaturée*) form of nationality, to use Zouhir Boushaba's words.[7] To resolve this contradiction, the definition of what it meant to be French became an issue of public rights as opposed to private rights: from enjoying civil rights, French citizens would become those with legal connections to the state, be those citizens fully French or French subjects.

The two contradictory definitions both appear in the Law of 1889. In 1921, the Court of Cassation ratified that change in the definition of what it meant to be French, a change that would last until after decolonization.[8] There was resistance toward granting Algerian Muslims full nationality, even though the Algerian territory was itself fully French. That was for reasons of political domination. If they had been given full French citizenship rights, they would have become a majority in some political bodies. And if too many of them had been naturalized, they would have been able to control some of the municipal councils. The 1930s governor Maurice Viollette was very clear that he did not intend to cede any "power" in Algeria to "Muslim natives."

N.B.: *In your work on citizenship and nationality, have you noticed any connections between these principles of colonial law and those that are used toward foreigners today?*

P.W.: The status of Muslims in Algeria was, in many respects, inferior to that of foreigners, but in many others, it was more favorable. Muslims from Algeria, like foreigners arriving in Algeria, had to go through the naturalization process to become French; but the children of foreigners who had been naturalized were (as of 1889) automatically French, whereas the children of Algerian Muslims, who were also born on French territory (in Algeria or in the mainland), still had to go through the naturalization process. In addition, naturalized foreigners could enjoy the same civil rights in France as French people, and they were subject to the same penal laws; they were protected by their government, which was represented in France (and in Algiers) by consuls. Muslims on the other hand were subject to the *Code de l'indigénat,* which was unilaterally applied by France. Theoretically, when Muslims were abroad, they were under the protection of the French consul; but that protection was entirely theoretical, since Muslims were not allowed to leave their villages without prior authorization!

At the same time, Muslims could elect municipal advisers (in a separate electoral college), and they had access to some public sector jobs, which was not the case for foreigners. It was a kind of *sui generis* status, but it was inferior to that of foreigners. "Muslim natives" were for all intents and purposes assigned an ethnic and religious identity, which resulted in a radically different status. One reason cited for this special status was a supposed incompatibility between the Koran and the Civil Code. Issues such as relations in households between men and women, equality between men and women in terms of inheritance, and the status of children were cited. According to such logic, whenever a Muslim converted to Catholicism, obstacles to full nationality should have been lifted. That, however, was not the case. In 1903, for example, the Court of Appeals in Algiers stated that the term *Muslim* "does not strictly apply to religion, but also refers to all people of Muslim background who have not been granted rights, and who therefore must necessarily maintain their Muslim status, regardless of whether or not they belong to the Muslim religion."[9] Conversion did not even grant one access to becoming fully French.

From Slavery to the Postcolonial Situation

N.B.: *Your framework has expanded in order to include slavery, the colonial situation, and the postcolonial situation, as a way of putting these legal and identity issues into perspective.*

P.W.: That is the result and the intersection of my interests as a researcher and of various intellectual experiences. My work on nationality covers two centuries. As we have seen, that history includes various forms of discrimination, both toward those who were colonized and toward, for example, women. In the 1920s, more than two hundred thousand women born in France and living in the country became foreigners because they married a foreigner. If they married an Italian man, they were not allowed to divorce; some who became Chinese were forced to follow their husbands to China, where they discovered they were simply mistresses. Those who were naturalized between 1927 and 1984 were discriminated against. Jews under Vichy experienced discrimination. All of these forms of discrimination were abolished, but they still exist today. Some of these same groups claim to still suffer from exclusion and discrimination, while for others that is no longer the case. It seemed to me that these lingering traces of discrimination—these legacies from a long period of discrimination, which continue to have a symbolic and real impact today—were worth studying.[10]

Moreover, after I realized that in terms of immigration policy, people were being treated differently depending on their nationality—based on a distinction between the law and the state as an actor (the law of 1945 did not make distinctions according to origin, but the state-as-actor did and continues to do so today)—I became interested in how practices that originated under colonization had been reproduced. I also had the chance to follow the work of Laurent Dubois, whom I met at the National Archives—he was a doctoral student back then. We talked about his research topic: the process of the abolition of slavery in Guadeloupe during the French Revolution. We also discussed the revolutionary discoveries he had made about the active role played by slaves, who used ideas from the mainland on human rights to abolish slavery (the first abolition). He was the one to introduce me to this history. At that time, Erik Bleich, had made significant inroads—in addition to having conducted comparative research with the United Kingdom—on the origin of antiracist legislation in France.

Together with Stéphane Dufoix, Fred Constant, and Michel Giraud, we organized three conferences in 2001 (in Guadeloupe, Paris, and at Middlebury College in the United States) on the impact of slavery and colonization on public policies today. Those three comparative conferences led to the publication of a book (in French), *L'esclavage et la colonisation, et après . . .*[11] The book had a huge impact, undoubtedly because it offered the French public a number of high quality articles, notably on the experiences of foreigners.

N.B.: *Could you talk about the relationship between the colonial and the postcolonial?*

P.W.: Discrimination is not necessarily linked to colonization. It also exists independently, both before and in parallel to colonization. We have to be careful not to attribute all forms of contemporary discrimination to colonization. Discrimination encountered by Jews, Russians, and Armenians in France has nothing to do with colonization. For instance, it is clear that in 1945 a large number of political actors were against Algerian immigration, but that no doubt was also the case when it came to both Jews and southern Italians. Systems of hierarchy and classification came to us from the United States; they were not linked to colonization, and therefore constituted an additional form of discrimination. But that does not mean there were no transfers of practices or of specific techniques. Those issues have to be explored; we have to posit hypotheses and then test them.

But of course, it makes sense to include the history of colonization in an overall history of all nations, on the condition, that is, that one reconstitutes the precise role it played and continues to play. In addition, it is heuristically interesting to include this aspect of national history. Sometimes it leads to important conceptual advancements. I am thinking specifically of the work of a colleague at Cornell Law School, Aziz Rana, whose book *The Two Faces of American Freedom* was about to be published by Harvard University Press.[12] The book invited readers to reconsider the origins of the American revolution, showing how "republicanism" was born less from a taxpayer revolt against an authoritarian and hierarchical British kingdom (the usual version promoted by contemporary historiography) than a refusal to extend the British Empire to a "unified" North America that included not only Protestant colonials, but also French Catholics and Native Americans. And, for Aziz Rana, it was that refusal to mix with various forms of alterity that led to revolution and to the creation of a republic of equal brothers from similar backgrounds and a separation from inferior alterities.

That peculiar form of colonial republicanism can be found in colonial Algeria. To put it simply: colonials in Algeria, who were, in their own way, republican and who would have liked to have been independent, lacked the military means to achieve that separation. When Aziz Rana inquired into colonial history, he was also able to rethink the United States' entire past. And he was able to find factual proof to back up his ideas. The work of studying our national history in order to make it more comprehensive is particularly urgent. We still need to test hypotheses, go back to the archives, and corroborate or disprove ideas. It is important to avoid turning this history into a tool for ideological warfare.

N.B.: *From that perspective, how can we understand the "memorial movements" that have appeared these past years in France?*

P.W.: There are two extremes occupying the field: the first group says that it has had enough of requests for recognition by specific groups that wish to impose their stories onto national history (Pierre Nora and René Rémond, for instance); the second group claims that the French government—the French Republic—is racist and that republicanism is discriminatory. In addition, a relatively recent and massive presence of descendants of slaves and colonized people in the mainland has led to the emergence of a debate on these histories and to this clash. In point of contrast, the presence of such populations existed from the inception of the United States of America.

N.B.: *Do you think that there is something about this presence that undermines what some might think of as "national identity"?*

P.W.: First, it is important to distinguish different histories and different groups. The tensions are not the same for descendants of slaves and descendants of those who were colonized. The reason for that difference is simple: the Republic abolished slavery (the First Republic did it in 1794, and the Second Republic in 1848). From the beginnings of the republican regime, it has been possible for slaves and their descendants to identify with the French Republic and its stated principles, which has not been the case in the United States, where slavery took place at the core of republican institutions. The case of colonization is not exactly the same, since the Republic colonized and therefore agreed to put in place a status of inferiority and discrimination in its process of colonization. However, in the metropole, one can also find vigorous opposition to colonization on the part of some republicans—such as Clemenceau. The difference between the colonial regime and the metropole was often palpable for those who were colonized; they did not see the mainland republic in the same way as its colonial version embodied by colonials. And that is part of what makes the situation so complex; indeed, there was always the promise of equality (a very strong principle in the French tradition), but it was never fully established in law until independence. That legacy can be seen in today's France in various legal and political forms. Sometimes these debates lose a sense of that complexity.

N.B.: *I would like to touch on a point of contention: you've just mentioned Clemenceau—who was extremely critical of colonization, but that was before the First World War. After the war, political conflict on colonization became lateral, and a kind of consensus was reached on colonial ownership (beyond the debates on exploitation, legal regimes, and so forth). Within that context, it seems to me that Algeria was the most extreme case of colonial conservatism, since the lobby of Algerian colonials was very well organized in Algeria itself.*

P.W.: They were also very well organized within several political parties in parliament. The First World War was a turning point in the history of the colonization and decolonization of Algeria, because it was at that time that requests for recognition began to include talk of nationality—they had emerged in the early twentieth century, in the years leading up to the war. But they did not come to fruition, despite full participation in the war, and despite efforts made by Clemenceau after the war to bring them into being. Later, Blum-Viollette's project did not go as far as Clemenceau's proposals would have. The year 1919 was a turning point because, with Clemenceau's failure, Algerian reform movements understood that independence was the only solution.

It is often forgotten, but, from the beginning, when France began to expand overseas, with Paris at its center, each time a new territory was conquered, the new territories and populations were granted equal treatment; that created attachment to the French kingdom. For instance, when Corsica was conquered—a difficult feat that resulted in thousands of deaths—Corsicans were granted the same rights as French people. There is therefore an enormous difference between conquest and colonization; conquest resulted in a population becoming French; Algeria was colonized, and Algerians were not given the right to become fully French. Nevertheless, a part of the population long held out hope that it would one day occur.

Correspondences between the Colonial Situation and the Postcolonial Situation

N.B.: *In the optics of the history of immigration, what types of correspondences can we find between colonial history and the postcolonial?*

P.W.: From the perspective of immigration policy, there is an extraordinary contradiction that comes from the fact that French colonials in Algeria (it was thought they would remain there) were granted, through the Evian Accords of 1962, the ability to circulate freely between France and Algeria; meanwhile, newly independent Algerians were granted the same freedom to circulate. But in the months following the Evian Accords, colonials returned to the mainland in droves and the French authorities fought to reduce the favorable status granted to Algerians. From the perspective of nationality rights, beginning in 1962, the children of Algerians born in France had a better status than most foreigners: in most cases, they were considered French citizens at birth, by virtue of a twofold right of birthplace, since they were born in France to a parent born in France (when Algeria was still France). That was despite the fact that the authorities saw them as most "undesirable." From a legal perspective, Algerians and their children had a much more secure status than most other foreigners.

N.B.: *In terms of other waves of immigration from the empire (from the various areas to the "South": Moroccans, Tunisians, sub-Saharan Africans), does it makes sense to talk about legally equivalent immigration policies with respect to foreigners, but social practices that speak to different forms of treatment?*

P.W.: Tunisian and Moroccan immigration was encouraged as a way of slowing down that of Algerians. As Alexis Spire has shown, the "career paper pushers" who granted access to nationality or long-term visas treated applicants differently depending on national background, and these new foreigners were treated less well than their Portuguese or Spanish predecessors.[13] But from the perspective of inducing immigration, successive French governments believed that Moroccans and Tunisians were easier to "keep" than Algerians. That intra-Maghrebi game shows the peculiar place occupied by Algeria in French society. Then, from 1973 until 1993, a double right of birthplace was applied to children born in France to parents born in the former French colonies—even those that, unlike Algeria, were not attached to France. We are therefore dealing with very complicated situations, different legal statuses between nationalities, and, within the same nationality, differences between children depending on their birthdate.

The Republic's principles adorned the pediments of Algeria's city halls under colonization; separation between church and state officially existed. In reality, the regime featured neither liberty, nor equality, nor even secularism. In the mainland, there was always a direct relationship—or a programmatic relationship—between the stated principles and practice. It is therefore understandable that Algerians were confused about the French secular regime. The word came to signify radically opposite legal regimes and practices over the course of just a few years.

N.B.: *As somebody who is familiar with the anglophone academic literature on the subject, you are of course only too aware of the rather vigorous debates taking place within academia on postcolonial studies and subaltern studies.*

P.W.: Laurent Dubois—who does not subscribe to either of those currents—has shown that the abolition of slavery came "from below" during the French Revolution. To be more specific, it came from an interaction: slaves got wind of what was happening in the metropole, and they seized an opportunity to revolt; they revolted in the name of freedom and equality. That insight has fundamentally changed how we do history: the abolition of slavery is now understood within a framework that goes beyond a decree by the Convention. These currents are interesting. They are diverse, and they cannot be defined in the same way across fields—from literature to the human sciences. They also differ depending on the specific region of the world in which they are being developed. Their intellectual program operates as a hypothesis, but when one is a historian, one has to verify the relevance of hypotheses.

I have worked on public policy related to immigration and nationality, and I know that they do not always come into being from on high. I do not think that these currents would have been as revolutionary with respect to research into nationality policies in Algeria, for example, as their names—subaltern studies and so forth—would suggest. That is, in part, due to the fact that "public policies" often leave behind few sources. However, these currents are perspectives that should be included in research hypotheses when a researcher is working on a subject, and one should be able to demonstrate them for each subject.

N.B.: *I do not know if you have followed the debates on these currents in France. They have led to rather heated discussions among historians such as Catherine Coquery-Vidrovitch and Jean-François Bayart, for example. Marie-Claude Smouts has published a book,* La situation postcoloniale, *which elicited viru-*

lent debates on what meaning was to be drawn from the relationship between the colonial and the postcolonial.[14] *Beyond subaltern studies—the idea of doing history "from below" has been generally accepted by historians—postcolonial studies (beginning with Edward W. Said's work on orientalism) offer an updated perspective of how we understand cultural and discursive apparatuses that originate in an imperial imaginary, and more generally in ideas about alterity. The debates have primarily been centered on the risks associated with a postcolonial perspective; some fear that it seeks to explain today's world in terms of an imitation of the colonial situation. Others worry it might establish teleonomic relationships between the two periods. What are your thoughts?*

P.W.: Of course, there is an imperial imaginary in France governing its representations and practices. But slaves from the Caribbean recognized, appropriated, and naturalized ideas of freedom and equality that were not foreign to them. That is what Laurent Dubois has shown.[15] On the issue of the colonial situation being reproduced today: in a sense, that is the message of groups such as the *Indigènes de la République,* which do not claim to be an academic group, but which do nevertheless include a number of academics. In colonial Algeria, discrimination was legal; it was organized and managed by the law. By contrast, discrimination is illegal in France today. And that makes a big difference. It allows, for instance, for the organization of collective protest, and for recourse to the law, something that was not available in colonial Algeria.

Although there are few academics who support these claims, they are actually quite harmful from the perspective of representations and discourse, since they promote the opposite of scientific research. For example, *jus soli* and the Civil Code did not apply to Muslims in colonial Algeria. In contrast, today, it applies to all immigrants of Algerian background. That is not to say that there is no discrimination or difference in treatment (I would be the first to admit that), but we also need to acknowledge inclusiveness in common law and our break with the colonial situation.

N.B.: *Of course, and most people would agree with that.*

P.W.: Well, I wouldn't be so sure. Very few people make that point. And if "most people acknowledge" it, it is simply in passing. But when we do not talk about it, victim-based discourse and thinking tend to prevail. The role of an academic is not to reassure people in their common-sense perceptions. We should be careful not to mix everything together—the center and the periphery, the colonial and the postcolonial. Rather, I would suggest untangling these situations as much as possible in order to distinguish what has been carried over from the colonial period, what has been imported, and what has been abandoned. And those things might differ depending on whether we are discussing the law, public or private actors, or representations.

Let me give an example: in 1993, when I fought against a project that would have forced children born in France to foreign parents to make a formal declaration that they wished to be French, I, like many others, was shocked that a different legal code was being applied to children born to North African or sub-Saharan African parents than the one that was being applied to children of Italian, Polish, and Spanish immigrants. At the time, I did not realize the extent to which this legal framework could be perceived by Muslims from Algeria as a symbolic reproduction of what their ancestors had experienced in Algeria. In other words, like their grandparents before them, they were being forced to prove their nationality! The discursive and practical similarities were striking, even if the legal function was not the same.

That law on nationality acted as a kind of repetition of trauma for descendants of Muslims from Algeria. Similarly, when on November 27, 1967, President Charles de Gaulle described Jews as an "elite people, domineering and sure of themselves," he may very well have symbolically awakened the trauma sustained under Vichy.[16] In the two cases, politics created trouble without realizing it, and that is precisely due to the fact that the history of peripheral groups is . . . peripheral. Other histories are as well. For instance, the history of Alsace and Moselle, which changed nationality five times in sixty years. Such historical traumas are very influential, but they are rarely mentioned. When we forget the history of peripheral groups, we can be haunted by its repercussions for generations.

However, I believe—in reality, I am convinced (much like many American abolitionists such as Charles Sumner were convinced)—that equality under the law is an extremely attractive principle for all humans, regardless of their cultures, religions, or traditions. When discrimination becomes too strong, those submitted to discrimination are forced to "retreat" into their culture. That is the logical outcome when people are not recognized as equals. That is one reason for increased pluralism, which Durkheim called the product of a "division of forced labor" that prevents individuals from "occupying a place suited to their faculties within the social framework."[17]

Demands for acknowledgement of past discrimination do not, therefore, contradict the French Republic and its values. Rather, they are requests to acknowledge the value of equality, which eventually triumphed over subjugation. They are requests for their history to be included in our history, in the general history. To be sure, there may be groups who try to instrumentalize such movements, but that is not the dominant tendency. Politicians, the parliament, and various governments have worked to eliminate conflictual mechanisms and create mechanisms that encourage national unity around our celebrated common values (for instance, who could possibly be against celebrating the abolition of slavery?). It is true that some historians have reacted rather conservatively, which I believe is a reflection of a misinterpretation of French history in this domain, and a debate has developed between historians.

The authors of the text *Liberté pour l'histoire* opposed all memorial laws, put Article 4 of the law of February 2005—which sought to establish that the "positive" aspects of colonization should be taught in school—in the same category as the Gayssot Law, the Taubira Law, and the law on the acknowledgement of the Armenian genocide. In an article published in *Esprit* and also featured in my book *Liberté, egalité, discriminations,* I showed how the Gayssot and Taubira Laws could be inscribed in a series of actions that developed throughout the nineteenth century as a way of overcoming divisions within French society through celebrations and symbols of national unity, and through the abolishment of the causes of division. In 1848, when slavery was definitively abolished, when it was considered a crime against humanity, those who possessed slaves were stripped of their nationality, which was cause for debate among legal experts of the era.

In 1880, July 14th was designated as a holiday to celebrate the Republic, and in 1884, at the end of a century of battles and regime changes, the constitutional laws were amended to specify that the republican form of government could not be changed in the constitution. The issue could not be discussed in parliament, and the royalist opposition was beside itself. However, that prohibition has been upheld and can still be found in the constitution of the Fifth Republic. A century later, when negationists surfaced in public debate, the first political reaction was to create celebrations: the 8th of May was established as a public holiday to remember the victory against Nazism; that was not enough, and the Gayssot Law was therefore established as an instrument to banish negationism.[18]

The Taubira Law of May 10, 2001, classified the slave trade and slavery as crimes against humanity, and celebrated the entry of the descendants of slaves into the national community, something which had not been commemorated previously.[19] That is my interpretation of these laws, and it is by no means limited to my work as a historian. The Taubira Law and the Gayssot Law are both inscribed in a genealogy of extraordinary historical interventions. They are the sign of an evolution in national priorities: in the past, extraordinary political intervention was reserved for uniting French people around the republican regime. Today, it is for the rejection of all forms of discrimination between French people. The Republic's priority today is to ensure that the principle of equality among citizens is upheld.

Nicolas Bancel is Professor at the University of Lausanne, Switzerland, and codirector of the ACHAC Research Group. He is author or coeditor of numerous influential books, including *De l'indigène à l'immigré* (1998), *La République coloniale: Essai sur une utopie* (2003), *La République coloniale* (2006), *Human Zoos: Science and Spectacle in the Age of Colonial Empires* (2008), *La France arabo-orientale* (2013), *Colonial Culture in France since the Revolution* (2014), *The Invention of Race* (2014), and *Vers la guerre des identités* (2016).

Patrick Weil is a senior research fellow at the French National Center for Scientific Research in the University of Paris 1, Panthéon-Sorbonne. Professor Weil's work focuses on comparative immigration, citizenship, and church–state law and policy. His books published in English include *How to Be French: Nationality in the Making since 1789* (2008) and *The Sovereign Citizen: Denaturalization and the Origins of the American Republic* (2013).

Notes

Interview with Patrick Weil by Nicolas Bancel.

1. Patrick Weil, *La France et ses étrangers: L'aventure d'une politique d'immigration de 1893 à nos jours* (Paris: Calmann-Lévy, 1991).
2. Patrick Weil, "Racisme et discrimination dans la politique de l'immigration," *Vingtième Siècle: Revue d'histoire* 47, no.1 (July–September 2005): 77–102.
3. Rogers Brubaker, *Citizenship and Nationhood in France and Germany* (Cambridge, MA: Harvard University Press, 1992) and Patrick Weil, "Immigration, nation et nationalité: Regards comparatifs et croisés," *Revue française de science politique* 44, no. 2 (April 1994): 308–326.
4. Yerri Urban, *Race et nationalité dans le droit colonial français 1865–1946*, PhD diss., University of Bourgogne, 2009.
5. Patrick Weil, *Qu'est-ce qu'un Français? Histoire de la nationalité française depuis la Révolution* (Paris: Grasset, 2002).
6. Peter Sahlins, *Unnaturally French: Foreign Citizens in the Old Regime and After* (Ithaca, NY, and London: Cornell University Press, 2004).
7. Zouhir Boushaba, *Être algérien hier, aujourd'hui et demain* (Algiers: Mimouni, 1992).
8. The right of nationality was not included again in the Civil Code until 1993, at the initiative of Pierre Mazeaud.

9. Court of Appeals, Algiers, November 5, 1903, *Revue algérienne et tunisienne de législation et de jurisprudence* (R.A) 2, no. 25 (1903).

10. Patrick Weil, *Liberté, Egalité, Discriminations: L'identité nationale au regard de l'histoire* (Paris: Grasset: 2008).

11. Patrick Weil and Stéphane Dufoix, eds., *L'esclavage, la colonisation, et après . . . : France, États-Unis, Grande-Bretagne* (Paris: PUF, 2005).

12. Aziz Rana, *The Two Faces of American Freedom* (Cambridge, MA: Harvard University Press, 2010).

13. Alexis Spire, *Etrangers à la carte: L'administration de l'immigration en France (1945–1975)* (Paris: Grasset, 2005).

14. Marie-Claude Smouts, ed., *La situation postcoloniale: Les postcolonial studies dans le débat français* (Paris: Presses de Sciences Po, 2007).

15. Laurent Dubois, *Les esclaves de la République* (Paris: Calmann-Lévy, 1998).

16. Charles de Gaulle, "Conférence de presse de Charles De Gaulle, extrait relatif à Israël," November 27, 1967, http://www.voltairenet.org/article176398.html.

17. Emile Durkheim, *De la division du travail social* (Paris: PUF, 2007), 370.

18. The law of July 13, 1990, also known as the "Gayssot Law," makes it an offense in France to question the existence or magnitude of crimes against humanity as defined in the London Charter of 1945 on the basis of which Nazi leaders were convicted by the International Military Tribunal at Nuremberg in 1945–1946. Negation or denial of extermination camps, gas chambers, crematoriums, and the extermination of Jews were the specific targets of this law.

19. Loi no. 2001-434 du 31 mai 2001 tendant à la connaissance de la traite et de l'esclavage en tant que crime contre l'humanité decreed that "the French Republic recognized that the trans-Atlantic slave trade—along with the slave trade perpetrated since the fifteenth century in the Americas, the Caribbean, the Indian Ocean, and Europe against the African, Amerindian, Madagascan, and Indian populations—constitute crimes against humanity," *Journal Officiel*, no. 119 (May 23, 2001): 8175. Article 2 of the law adds that "School curricula and research programs in history and human sciences shall afford the slave trade and slavery the space they deserve," and finally it established (Article 4) an annual commemoration in metropolitan France "to ensure that the memory of these crimes lives forever in future generations." The date was set at May 10th, the date on which the law was unanimously adopted by the senate.

22

THE GREAT STRIP SHOW

FEMINISM, NATIONALISM, AND THE BURQA IN FRANCE

Elsa Dorlin

In a speech delivered on June 22, 2009, at the Chateau de Versailles in a joint session of parliament, the first time a French president had addressed that body in over one hundred years, Nicolas Sarkozy made the following pronouncement: "The burqa is not welcome on French soil." Seizing the opportunity to capitalize on yet another "headscarf affair," this declaration was made in spite of the fact that a parliamentary fact-gathering mission initiated by André Gérin (Communist Party) was already underway in response to an obscure report released by the French internal security police (the sous-direction de l'information générale, SDIG) claiming that "367 women currently wear the full-face veil in France."[1]

That summer, debates roared and protagonists were quick to pick their sides on the battlefield: Islam, secularism, the Republic, women's rights, terrorism. However, the target—the burqa—posed a problem that was even more salient than in previous "affairs": concealment. André Gérin described them as "itinerant ghosts," and women who veiled part or all of their faces quickly became—in the space of just a few months—monstrous figures. They were now considered the antithesis of a new norm of social existence based on openness and visibility.

In a sense, it is strange that we should be concerned about not being able to identify these women, since their choice of clothing actually makes them more visible in the public space and clearly states their religious affiliation and obedience. Does the issue then come from the difficulty of being able to interpret the social, moral, or political identity of others? Nobody really seems concerned about the social personality of a given French citizen or resident within the French territory. Historically, the social personality of individuals has always expressed itself through "masks,"[2] or more or less freely expressed social markers. Yet, if one reads the different positions adopted in favor of a law that would ban the burqa, it becomes clear that the problem, in fact, comes from a kind of "anthropological" identification of individuals rather than an acknowledgement of their social personality and political identity; that "anthropological" identification, acting as a *biometric,* corresponds to the final stage of Bertillon-style practices.[3]

The system of constantly submitting individuals to various forms of identification—and for which today's police techniques are only one extreme expression[4]—goes hand in hand with a form of social existence that functions almost exclusively according to what could be called a "mandate to be transparent." We are required to show ourselves as we *are,* so that society can recognize us, which amounts to an ethnic and nationalist means of identification. A limitless promotion of individuals, in all their idiosyncrasies, with an emphasis on our singular characters, our intrinsic qualities, our proper resources, and our essential value is thus combined with a normative requirement: in order to be acknowledged, respected, and valued, we have to embody a "type."[5] In other words, the aim is to resemble as much as possible a predetermined national prototype, and to define oneself in relation with competing prototypes.[6]

In the process of prototyping individuals, the Christian religion and its supposed values act as a marker of Europeanness for the French.[7] Discourse on French identity is not new, but what is relatively novel is today's *mythologization* surrounding it. We are essentially witnessing a coming out on the part of the dominant: debates on violence in social relations and on how to achieve legal equality among citizens have been replaced by the talk of respecting the *French mask.*

While the criminalization of the headscarf and policies related to the headscarf constitute extreme cases targeted at specific groups, they also impose a kind of generalized "strip show" on all of us—"Show yourself!" The unveiling of women who wear burqas is not, in that sense, a case of special treatment. Prohibiting the burqa in the name of fighting security issues is a way of imposing nationalized, typically French, gender norms on *all* women. Our society's incessant demands that we be authentic—what could be called a mandate to *out* our private characters—is not about establishing an authentic relationship between individuals or an acknowledgement of alterity. Rather, they result in two effects. On the one hand, they force individuals to reduce themselves to types and boil themselves down to a given identity. That identity is a fiction, which functions as a smoke screen with respect to a reduction of individuals to anthropometric measures, making all forms of social and political self-determination problematic.[8] On the other hand, they normalize the incessant exhibition of individuals, tracking down all efforts to escape the procedures of identification, to the point of brandishing France and national security as higher interests. The "full-face veil" is therefore no longer simply a provocative expression with respect to principles of secularism. It has become a source of concern, a subversive practice that undermines the process of reducing individuals to a "social" identity. It represents an "unmasked" identity, a "personless identity," to cite Giorgio Agamben.[9] The laws against the veil are therefore similar to other measures such as the *Loi interdisant la dissimulation du visage dans l'espace public* (Law prohibiting concealment of the face in public spaces), the so-called "anti-hood" law, which banned the wearing of face-covering headgear, including masks, helmets, balaclava, niqābs and other veils; they can also be compared to attempts at prohibiting practices related to "transvestitism."[10]

The efficiency of "total security" relies on the use of criteria of discrimination that allow authorities to identify individuals, starting with criteria of class, "sex," and "race." *Who is hiding behind that veil*? A victim or a terrorist? A French woman or a "foreigner"? A man or a woman? To wear the "full-face veil" is to be identified as an enemy of French identity, and, more problematic still, it is to undermine the mechanisms established for identifying *Frenchness*. In an age when the baguette and the beret have begun to fizzle out, it is as though we have asked that allegorical national symbol that is Marianne to shorten her skirt.

Act I: Freedom—The Skirt, a New National Mythology

The intellectual Elisabeth Badinter has often been invited to speak on this issue, and as a result, she has become an important voice for uninitiated lawmakers.[11] In parliament on September 9, 2009, she spoke of the urgency of passing legislation on the "burqa."[12] Her argument was organized around three main points: "liberty, equality, and fraternity."[13] According to her, wearing the burqa in public raised another thorny issue—the freedom to wear a skirt. Her argument was simple: letting women clothe themselves from head to toe amounted to a backlash against modern values of freedom—for women to be in various states of *undress*.

She went on to refer to a controversial film by Jean-Louis Lilienfeld, *Skirt Day* (2009). For her, this was an issue of individual freedom in terms of clothing; it was important to guarantee women the right to wear a skirt where and whenever they wished—and especially in *banlieues* neighborhoods and housing projects—considering that wearing skirts had become increasingly difficult for women of "pure French stock." If one takes Elisabeth Badinter's argument to its logical conclusion, female nudity such as it has been codified in advertising[14] would be the ultimate sign of female freedom—the standard of a society that has rid itself of heterosexism. Moreover, skirts would not be a social marker or a "mask" imposed by social codes in a given society. Rather, they would become "natural markers" of the female sex in the West.

There has been a kind of slippage from a legal issue concerning individual liberty to dress however we see fit (within the confines of what is legally permissible) to "ethnic" considerations, which enforce a double moral standard through gender norms, between women who are *overdressed*, and women who are *underdressed*. Whether we are talking about extreme Salafist rules with respect to modesty or rules that make up French gallantry, we are essentially dealing with a social and historically determined relationship to power.[15] In both cases, we are talking about *policing gender*. Behind the redefinition of "modesty rules" (aspects of all societies in which gender, as well as class- and color-based, antagonisms exist), there is a racialist determination as to what constitutes *real women*.

Let us return to the issue of the full-face veil. For many in the French feminist movement, the veil is a symbol of patriarchal oppression of Muslim women, and of those women's victimhood. However, there has been an insidious slippage toward a negative definition of women's liberation; an ahistorical and nationalist definition of feminism itself. Indeed, if the women in question removed their veils, if they took off that piece of clothing that stigmatizes them and makes them into telegenic icons of domination, then they would pass for being liberated.[16] The discussion does not touch on possibilities of true liberation and sexual equality in France, but speaks rather to the national symbolism of veiled women. Concretely, this is a form of culturalizing and ethnicizing of a power relationship.

In *Les filles voilées parlent* (Young Veiled Girls Speak), the words of Jihene and Fatima are eye-opening.[17] They report on negotiations with a nurse and a high school principal in 2004, which persuaded them to find a colorful head covering (not white or dark colored, both of which were deemed "too Iranian")—a scarf that was not too "Middle Eastern" looking—(they looked for novel ways to tie it, to wear a bandana or a "Latin-American" style scarf), and let a few wisps of hair show. Under those conditions, the process of removing the veil—or the skirt itself—can easily be disassociated from a complex history—one in which individuals were subjected to social, gendered, and national dress code mandates—to become a symbol or, more precisely, a sign of female liberation. A crucial moment in the creation of a truly reinvigorated "national mythology," the removal of the veil transformed women's liberation and sexual equality into an affair of native costumes. Regardless of its ambiguity, the skirt now has a totally new significance, which is to support the myth of French sexual equality and participate in erasing heterosexist and racist violence.[18]

The conclusions are startling: all women with bare heads and who wear skirts are liberated women, and all liberated women are French or assimilated women.

In addition, in the post-9/11 context, attention is now centered on sectarian or "Salafist" forms of extremist Islam. Only women wearing the full-face veil are under fire. A tension lies beneath two forms of justification with respect to the law prohibiting the burqa in France: either the women wearing the burqa must be protected from the abusive men who force them into wearing it, or the other women—the real women—must be protected from those who wear the full-face veil. If we face the terms of the issue, the burqa, it is claimed, relates to the fight against sectarianism. But if that were truly the case, then why is so much attention being paid to the full-face veil? We are forgetting that dress codes—distinctive markers whereby individuals show their belonging to a given social group—do not simply concern women. The snarling figure of the "Taliban terrorist"—a bearded man in a turban wearing traditional Pakistani dress (the *khamiss* or tunics such as *djellabas* and *gandouras*)—would in a sense be a better penal target than the burqa.[19] If women are being forced to wear burqas by "their" men, then it should be those men who are subject to a law. We could prohibit beards or even ban men from wearing dresses. If women in burqas and men in *djellabas* are suspected of actively proselytizing—and indoctrinating children—then we should impose strict dress codes based on gender: girls would have to wear skirts, and boys, pants. One can imagine the news reports: "A new case of a young man wearing a dress in Seine-Saint-Denis," with the image of a young boy in a *djellaba,* forbidden from going to school.

Act II: Equality—A Man's World

That methodological fiction has the merit of shedding light on an untenable contradiction, to which a number of "pro-law" feminist currents should draw their attention. The fact that the veil affairs deal only with women—who are believed to be victims of sexism—rather than with men is simply incomprehensible. If wearing the veil is a sexist practice, would it not make more sense to go after those guilty of infringing on the liberty of others?

Consider this example: a woman is forced by her husband to remain inside her home (her husband controls or limits her freedom of movement and prohibits her from going outside). What does the law do in such cases? It condemns the perpetrator of a violent act—illegally confining his wife. But it would never occur to anyone to force that woman to spend her days and her nights outside. Moreover, let us say that it is necessary to adopt laws related to the wearing of veils in order to guarantee women's freedom and sexual equality; then we should condemn those who are guilty of breaking that constitutional principle; we should not legally force women to remove their veils (who, if they were forced to wear the veil in the first place, would then be forced to remove it by the law). That argument throws suspicion on feminist arguments with respect to the wearing of veils. Rather than working to fight against sexism, a certain form of feminist discourse seems to have agreed to become the spearhead of a new nationalism.[20]

Indeed, at least since the presidential elections of 2007, political parties have appropriated a certain feminist rhetoric, suddenly overcome with concern for the condition of women in France and in the world. Although on both sides of the political aisle the condition of women captivated candidates, the campaign was particularly influenced by statements made by Nicolas Sarkozy: "Those who seek to subjugate their wives, those who wish to practice polygamy, female genital cutting, or forced marriages, those who wish to impose the laws of older brothers onto their sisters, those who do not want their wives to dress as they wish [do not belong in France]."[21] In this example, the antagonism between "them" and "us" is targeted at *men*; and that antagonism is established in the name of women. The difference between "them" and "us" therefore lies in the treatment of "one's" women; the "us" designates a group of "French men." Women, who are victims of "these" forms of violence (female genital cutting, forced marriages, polygamy, the law of elder brothers, the veil, and so forth) are therefore systematically considered to be *foreigners*. In that way, they are denied French citizenship (because they symbolize absolute heteronomy) and they are excluded from French nationality, even though some of them are in fact French. *Nationality is no longer defined in terms of* jus soli, *but instead in reference to an imagined sexual community.*[22]

It is now clear how the issue of the condition of women has become the armed wing of European migratory policies.[23] The choice of which forms of violence were mentioned in Sarkozy's words was not innocent. Notably, he made no mention of violence "originating" in France. Violence experienced by women is thus divided into two categories: what is borne by "their" women and what is borne by "our" women, with special attention paid to a continuum of heterosexist violence (physical, sexual, psychological). In addition, the specificity of the vulnerability of "their" women is emphasized. Those women are threatened in the private space. Meanwhile, "our" women are essentially vulnerable in the public space, in the sense that the public space is where they are most threatened by "others."[24] As if by magic, "French women" now only have to face exogenous violence based on sex; they are only threatened by "non-white" or "non-Christian" attackers. To fight violence against women is then an issue of fighting illegal immigration or about issues of "integrating" populations from the Global South in general, and Muslims in particular. Therein lies the state of politics against sexism in France; and only when we are confronted with terrible events like the murder (involuntary manslaughter) in 2003 of the actress Marie Trintignant at the hands of her boyfriend do we recall that violence against women affects all social classes, religions, and ages.[25]

Because we have a tendency to culturalize or racialize heterosexist violence, it has become a tool for managing immigration policies and/or social policies. Furthermore, the state claims to protect women who are victims of "those" men by integrating them into the national community.[26] As a candidate, Nicolas Sarkozy stated the following during a meeting in Bercy on April 29, 2007: "I want France to offer protection to all women who are victims of violence throughout the world by giving them the possibility of becoming French."[27] The suggestion was a major topic of discussion—what about women who were already "French" and victims of violence? What about, for example, women who wear skirts, white women, middle-class women, or Catholic women? Is the state prepared to rescind citizenship from "white" men from the middle class and of Catholic background if those men abuse their wives? Clearly not—those men are exonerated from such crimes. According to the logic at work, "true Frenchmen" cannot, by definition, be violent toward women, since "sexual equality" is part of the very definition of the French identity. The "Frenchman," who is supported in his efforts by feminists,[28] therefore works to save "foreign" victims; he is a kind of republican knight for "their" women.[29]

Act III. Fraternity: From Victimization to Coming Face to Face with the "New Enemy Within"

One could conclude that such considerations originate in a form of affirmative action toward "these" women. But an important contradiction has emerged. A few years ago, the issue of the veil was posed as an issue of consent. If women were forced to wear it—be it through legal means or peer pressure—it was not a freely chosen act but rather a form of discrimination related to personal freedom. In 1989, 1994, and 2004, those who defended various laws prohibiting overt religious symbols in schools argued that if women—even just one woman—were forced to wear the veil, then the state should get involved. Yet consent has never been discussed in a very rigorous manner, with the exception of debates on prostitution. It is as if the issue of the material conditions in which women's choices are made only applied to Muslim women, descendants of postcolonial immigration, and immigrant women. Which implies that all other women have voluntarily submitted themselves to a form of social organization that is far from having eradicated heterosexism.

In parallel to such discussions on consent, some have argued that women having freely chosen to wear a veil represent a threat to secularism, since their choice must necessarily be the result of coercive proselytism. In 2009, the issue of consent was not a core aspect of the debates; rather, the issue was now the women themselves who wore burqas. During her interview before the parliamentary fact-finding commission, Elisabeth Badinter posited the following:

> The full-face veil symbolizes an absolute refusal to enter into contact with the other, or more specifically a refusal of reciprocity. Women wearing the full-face veil can see me, but I am denied access to seeing them. Beyond the violence symbolized by that lack of reciprocity, I cannot help but see a kind of pathological contradiction. On the one hand, they refuse to show their faces under the pretext that they do not want to be the object of impure gazes—between you and me it is strange to assume that all men who see you want to rape you . . . [laughter]. On the other hand, they are participating in a form of ultimate self-exhibitionism, since everyone's attention is drawn to this unidentified object. Is it a woman? Is it a man? Is this person ugly, or a mysterious beauty? . . . In short: these women become objects of fantasy. They are observed without being seen; and they observe others but hide behind a veil. They are essentially enjoying a three-fold form of perverse satisfaction: power over others due to the lack of reciprocity, exhibitionism, voyeurism . . . I think these women are very sick—I'm not kidding when I say this—and I do not think that we should have to adjust ourselves to such pathology.[30]

The women Elisabeth Badinter describes are neither objects nor subjects; in her eyes, they are literally abject. Women who wear the full-face veil have gone from being victims to deviants and twisted perverts. And that is how they have been recast, from objects of violence to violent subjects.[31] In order to arrive at such a conclusion—that the women in question are "very sick"—Elisabeth Badinter has implicitly referenced a philosophical history that, from Erasmus to Levinas, and passing by Rousseau, has put the face at the center of reflections on life in "society."[32]

In her critique of women who wear the veil, Elisabeth Badinter refers to principles that have been in place since at least the sixteenth century: those having to do with civility, understood as a collection of rules on how to live, both as a euphemism for violent social standards and as a number of strategies for appearing in society, strategies that transform the face and the body into a more or less faithful mirror of one's qualities, as well as of one's psychological, moral, economic, and political resources.[33] In that sense, Elisabeth Badinter speaks of the full-face veil as a kind of "civil self-mutilation": a practice whereby a person purposefully excludes herself from the social game. In this case, women wearing burqas or *niqabs* are akin to recluse nuns; they are like hermits taking refuge within the core of society itself. That may very well be the case. However, unlike nuns, "such women [women wearing full-face veils] are often married and even mothers, and they impose themselves on the public space, although they do so in such a way as to hide their identities, their bodies, and they have taken care to erase all signs of humanity."[34] A surprising argument, which echoes the previous remarks. In the end, if a person is wearing a veil, who is to say that that person is really a woman—or even a "human?"[35]

Behind the paranoid emphasis, that argument is based on an idea of essential "sexual difference;"[36] moreover, it turns aesthetics ("Is this person ugly, or a mysterious beauty?"), sexual availability, and heterosexual reproduction into crucial criteria for "liberated" femininity. In other words, all women wishing to participate in civic life must correspond to a stereotype of womanhood, a veritable caricature of a feminine ideal. The promotion of French-style gender norms is an assertion of civilizational superiority.[37] Thus, women wearing the full-face veil have made themselves unintelligible, both civically and humanly speaking.

Figures of incivility par excellence: rioters in 2005, hooded protesters, veiled women, transvestites, and queers.[38] They are also vulnerable to such assessments of criminality, since they are literally dehumanized; they are purely and simply excluded from a national community that has claimed itself to be "humankind." The law has intervened in some such cases: when civility does not provide enough constraints, the law steps in. Criminalizing "incivilities" (all practices that go against procedures of identification) is akin to a new "civilizing mission," which not only affects "others" but also all members of the national community. If one considers the logics of this mythology with respect to the history of nationalist ideologies, it becomes clear that the veiled woman constitutes a new mythological object circulating in the French public space and, at the same time, she represents an old symbol.[39] Historically, an advantage of the "headscarf affair" has been that it deals with an article of clothing, a "reversible marker."[40] The focus on the headscarf presented a threefold advantage: an affirmation of an ultraconservative idea of "sexual difference," which is not founded on an idea of nature but on a mythology (that of the French or European civilization and its "Christian roots"); it dissociates feminism and the fight against heterosexism from historical and political movements and turns them into a political tool for "Fortress Europe;" and in the final instance erects a supremacist politics on the dying embers of universalism. All those who agree to remove their veils and masks are promised an opportunity to be *civilized*, and only then can they expect to be *assimilated* into the new nation.

Epilogue. Levinas vs. Kipling: An Imaginary and Improbable Duel

We will continue to hear about the "face" and basic rules of civility for a long time. What about the "bare face," France's new way of proudly asserting its values? After the national and international health authorities distributed masks to fight an epidemic of influenza A,[41] those who are currently fighting tooth and nail for antitransvestite measures will have trouble defending their cause. For philosophical and ethical reasons, I would like to take a short detour to speak about the work of Emmanuel Levinas, which Elisabeth Badinter has recently motivated me to reread. For Levinas, recognition of the "other" as an alter ego takes place through a reflection on the face. The face of the "other" is a focal point of intersubjectivity. The "other" is at once radically foreign and entirely familiar to me. He is fundamentally vulnerable and fundamentally sacred. "The way in which the other presents himself, exceeding *the idea of the other in me,* we here name face. This *mode* does not consist in figuring as a theme under my gaze, in spreading itself forth as a set of qualities forming an image. The face of the Other at each moment destroys and overflows the plastic image it leaves me."[42] When Levinas speaks of the face, he never insists on the bareness of that part of the human body. For him, the face is an expressive presence (a silhouette, a gesture, an exchange of looks) that goes beyond exhibition. The face is not an ensemble of anatomical traits that present an object for objectivizing scrutiny. The face is not a picture taken in a photo booth or by a surveillance camera.

In Levinas's ethics, between myself and others, the recognition of alterity is never reduced to a comparison. In other words, it is not a simple question of identification. Recognizing the "other" as my alter ego does not correspond to recognizing in that person what I know of myself; rather, it is to let myself be invaded by the "other's" absolute foreignness. Vision alone cannot create a community bond between the "same" and the "other." It is the expressiveness of the "other's" face that enables such a bond; the fact that I enter into a relationship with the "other," via language, and that her speech, which is by definition unanticipated, is always incommensurable (it exceeds, overflows, surprises, and makes all knowledge and discourse on the "other" a failure). Elisabeth Badinter speaks of the right to see without being seen that women in burqas grant themselves; but the issue was never one of the "other's" expressiveness, be it in the form of her presence, her gaze, or her speech. Thus, the symbolic violence of which Elisabeth Badinter feels herself a victim (what she judges to be a refusal of intersubjective reciprocity) is in fact a modern version of Kipling's poem, "The White Man's Burden:" the lament of a white woman who has to sustain "the hate of [the woman she must guard]."[43]

Elsa Dorlin is Professor of Political and Social Philosophy in the Department of Political Science at the University of Paris 8 Vincennes/Saint-Denis. She is author of several books, including *La matrice de la race: Généalogie sexuelle et coloniale de la nation française* (2006), *Sexe, genre et sexualité* (2008), and *Se défendre: Une philosophie de la violence* (2016), the editor of *Black feminism: Anthologie du féminisme africain américain 1975–2000* (2007) and *Sexe, race, classe: Pour une épistémologie de la domination* (2009), and editor of *Comment s'en sortir?*, a journal focusing on feminist, queer and postcolonial studies.

Notes

1. See Willy Le Devin, "Moins de 400 femmes porteraient le voile intégral en France," *Libération*, July 30, 2009.

2. Originally, the word *person* comes from the "mask" worn by an actor.

3. Alphonse Bertillon (1853–1914) was a French criminologist who helped invent criminal anthropometry. He was particularly interested in physical anthropology, the identification and classification of "savage races" (1888), and the identification of recidivist criminals (1893/1898) through their finger prints.

4. When I speak of a "national mythology," I am by no means deemphasizing security policies. Debates on police checks and "racial profiling" speak to this tension: the "security complex"—methods of anthropometric and biometric identification, video surveillance, tracing techniques, commercial profiling, and servers devoted to "tribal" sociability—makes use of criteria of discrimination (gender, sexuality, religion, background, skin color, for instance). On that point, a reading of Giorgio Agamben's work is interesting, especially *Nudités* (Paris: Rivages, 2009).

5. See Michel Foucault's work on "human capital" in *Naissance de la biopolitique: Cours au collège de France (1978–1979)* (Paris: EHESS/Gallimard, 2004).

6. See Minister of the Interior Brice Hortefeux's "stolen" statements from September 10, 2009. A female social worker, speaking about an activist named Amine: "He's Catholic—he eats pork and he drinks beer."

7. Elsewhere, I have called the phenomenon "génotechnie" a term developed after studying production techniques of the national people in the eighteenth century. See Elsa Dorlin, *La matrice de la race: Généalogie sexuelle et coloniale de la nation française* (Paris: La Découverte, 2006).

8. Judith Butler's work on the "disciplinary production of gender" and more generally on the personal identity of individuals is interesting: "The displacement of a political and discursive origin of gender onto a psychological 'core' precludes an analysis of the political constitution of the gendered subject and its fabricated notions about the ineffable interiority of its sex or of its true identity," *Gender Trouble: Feminism and the Subversion of Identity* (New York: Routledge, 1990), 136.

9. "Where [that personless identity] forces an individual into a purely biological and asocial identity, it allows that person to wear any and all masks on the Internet and take on second and third lives, although none of them can ever really, properly speaking, belong to him or her," Agamben, *Nudités*, 92.

10. On September 29, 2009, member of parliament Christian Vanneste submitted a proposal for a law aiming to prohibit all clothing or accessories that would mask the identity of a person. See "Proposition de loi visant à interdire l'ensemble des vêtements ou accessoires permettant de masquer l'identité d'une personne," http://www.assemblee-nationale.fr/13/propositions/pion1942.asp.

11. It is worth noting that the French intellectual Elisabeth Badinter (born 1944) is also a businesswoman, the heiress to the fortune of her father, Marcel Bleustein-Blanchet, the founder of the Plubicis public relations company. She has benefited from extensive media coverage for what has been described as a particular brand of "Republican feminism," for her defense of French "laïcité," and for her support of laws and regulations against the wearing of the veil in France.

12. The term evokes Afghan women who are victims of violence under the Taliban.

13. See "Interdire le voile intégral au nom de la dignité de la personne," *Libération*, Setember 9, 2009.

14. See Mona Chollet, *Rêves de droite: Défaire l'imaginaire sarkozyste* (Paris: Zones, 2008).

15. See Duncan Kennedy, *Sexy Dressing: Violences sexuelles et érotisation de la domination* (Paris: Flammarion, 2008), which discusses gendered dress codes based on a study of sexy clothing and the figure of the "slut."

16. Hence the embarrassment of the veil's critics when they were faced with Shirin Ebadi, who was awarded the Nobel Peace Prize in 2003, and who has declared herself to be against the law prohibiting the veil (adopted in France in 2004). Hence the preference for spokespeople like Chahdortt Djavann and Ayaan Hirsi Ali.

17. Ismahane Chouder, Malika Latrèche, and Pierre Tevanian, *Les filles voilées parlent* (Paris: La Fabrique, 2008).

18. Roland Barthes, *Mythologies* (Paris: Seuil, 2007) [1957].

19. A few days after the 9/11 attacks, Fox News broadcast a pedagogical piece to explain how to distinguish between a practicing Muslim and a practicing Sikh (notably by showing differences in how they tie their turbans), with the aim of reducing mistakes in the event of lynchings.

20. The argument stating that the burqa is a sign of female submission should be a topic of debate among feminists (see Lila Abu Lughod, "The Muslim Woman: The Power of Images and the Danger of Pity," *Eurozine*, September 1, 2006, http://www.eurozine.com/articles/2006-09-01-abulughod-en.html).

21. Statement by Nicolas Sarkozy at a UMP meeting in Toulon on February 7, 2007.

22. See Benedict Anderson, *Imagined Communities: Reflections on the Origin and Spread of Nationalism* (London: Verso, 1983).

23. See Éric Fassin's work, and especially "La démocratie sexuelle et le conflit des civilisations," *Multitudes*, no. 26 (December 2006): 123–131.

24. Nacira Guénif-Souilamas and Éric Macé, *Les féministes et le garçon arabe* (Paris: Éditions de l'Aube, 2004).

25. One only has to refer to the National Survey on violence against women in France (ENVEFF), *Les violences envers les femmes: Une enquête nationale* (Paris: La Documentation française, 2003).

26. If that were the case, the French state could start by eliminating bilateral conventions with a number of other governments and authorize on "its" territory the application of "foreign" legal codes. Some aspects of the Algerian "family code" related to individual status and marriage, for example, are applied in France, legitimizing sexist discrimination. Many feminist organizations, in Algeria and in France, have been fighting these conventions for years.

27. Nicolas Sarkozy, "Discours à Bercy," April 29, 2007, http://sites.univ-provence.fr/veronis/Discours2007/transcript.php?n=Sarkozy&p=2007-04-29.

28. See Chandra Talpade Mohanty, "Under Western Eyes: Feminist Scholarship and Colonial Discourses," in *Feminism Without Borders: Decolonizing Theory, Practicing Solidarity* (Durham: Duke University Press, 2003), 17–42 and Gayatri Chakravorty Spivak, "Can the Subaltern Speak?," in *Can the Subaltern Speak?: Reflections on the History of an Idea*, ed. Rosalind C. Morris (New York: Columbia University Press, 2010), 21–78.

29. Those women find themselves in a "contradictory" situation, in which they are pulled between "emancipation/betrayal" and "submission/loyalty." See Nacira Guénif-Souilamas, *Les beurettes*

(Paris: Hachette, 2003); and Christelle Hamel, "La sexualité entre sexisme et racisme: Les descendantes de migrant-e-s du Maghreb et la virginité," *Nouvelles Questions Féministes* 25, no. 1 (2006): 41–58.

30. See "Mission d'information sur la pratique du port du voile intégral sur le territoire national," September 9, 2009, http://www.assemblee-nationale.fr/13/dossiers/voile_integral.asp.

31. For her, they are even violent toward men, whom these women are thought to consider as violent rapists.

32. Be it on proper behavior in society in Erasmus's "On Civility in Children," in Rousseau's discussion of "sincerity," or in human society defined as an ethical community in Emmanuel Levinas' *Totality and Infinity: An Essay on Exteriority*, trans. Alphonso Lingis (Pittsburgh: Duquesne University Press, 1969).

33. Jean-Jacques Courtine and Claudine Haroche, in their description of the progressive civilization of modern man's mores, write: "Individuation through expression is a form of socializing individuals that relies on mimicry, observation, mannerisms, attitudes, posture turned outward, and which come from the deepest part of the subject. It is a process of obeying codes, constraints, and social conventions and demonstrating at the same time the singular ineffability of an internal life," in *Histoire du visage: Exprimer et taire ses émotions (XVI*[e]*-début XIX*[e] *siècle)* (Paris: Éditions Payot & Rivages, 2007), 282.

34. "Mission d'information sur la pratique du port du voile intégral sur le territoire national."

35. Ibid.

36. The position is surprising considering that Elisabeth Badinter was scathingly critical of feminists who advocated for the law on parity based on that same argument (the division of the human species into two sexes).

37. See Dorlin, *La matrice de la race.*

38. What about "folles" (a queen or effeminate gay man), butch women, drag queens, drag kings, and trans people? Are we prepared to penalize the use of makeup, packing, hormones, surgeries? Elsa Dorlin, *Sexe, genre et sexualités* (Paris: PUF, 2008).

39. See Frantz Fanon, *Sociologie de la révolution* (Paris: Maspero, 1982).

40. Collette Guillaumin, *Sexe, race et pratique du pouvoir: L'idée de nature* (Paris: Côté-femmes, 1992).

41. I am taking the liberty of borrowing from a remark made to me by the French writer and editor Hugues Jallon.

42. Levinas, *Totality and Infinity*, 50–51.

43. "Take up the White Man's burden/And reap his old reward:/The blame of those ye better/The hate of those ye guard," Rudyard Kipling, "The White Man's Burden," *McClure's Magazine* 12, no. 4 (1899): 291.

23

FROM THE RED PERIL TO THE GREEN PERIL

THE NEW ENEMY WITHIN

Renaud Dély

THE ENEMY—RED IN the past, today green—is at our door. Ready to overcome us. On the verge of subverting our society and of perverting our way of life—of subjugating our civilization. In the 1930s, the enemy sought to "Sovietize" France, to take power, to impose Soviets, and to destroy our colonial empire; in the early twenty-first century, the enemy intends to "Islamize" our country, destroy our "national identity," wage international jihad, destroy Israel. Every decade has its color. Every era has its "enemy within." In the 2010s, as in the 1930s, France continues to perceive of itself as being under siege. Worse still, it believes that the enemy is already here, within itself. That it has been infiltrated by the enemy; the enemy was born on its territory—it is even "French." French Communists took their orders from Moscow! French Muslims are followers of "Salafism 2.0;" they have been brainwashed over the internet or in obscure mosques which seek to upend society and "impose their religious dogma," much like the reds from the past wanted to wrench enterprises from the hands of their bosses and order from the bourgeoisie.

New Fellow Travelers

The enemy is within us. It is conquering us. Communism seduced the troubled youth of the ruling classes; it subverted the future generation; it even infiltrated the École normale supérieure from which Paul Nizan graduated and went on to write in his novel *La conspiration* of a generation torn between the sharp truth of communism and the decline of the world. Islam is said to convert French youth from the *banlieues* housing projects—those worrisome neighborhoods where halal and Ramadan are the norm, and where *pains au chocolat* are torn from innocent mouths during the month of fasting, according to the right-wing politician Jean-François Copé.

During the presidential election of 2012, a debate broke out on the issue of halal meat, which was said to have invaded all of Paris's and France's abattoirs. The Algerian anthropologist and philosopher Malek Chebel has commented ironically on these debates, explaining how "France is terrified of becoming Muslim when it eats." The enemy is creeping in. It is devouring us and changing our very nature—our identity. From within the still healthy body of our society, it relies on allies and partners, who minimize the evil, conceal the truth, and refuse the real. They were known as the "fifth column" or as "useful idiots" during the communist era; today they are referred to as "dhimmis" or "Islamo-journalists." Anyone could be a potential partner. During the era of the Front Populaire, the right-wing satirist Sennep described Herriot being swallowed by Blum and Blum by Cachin thusly: "Radicals are always swallowed by socialists; socialists are always swallowed by communists."[1] Martine Aubry, mayor of Lille and former first secretary of the Socialist Party, has been accused of collaborating with Islamists because her husband defended girls who choose to wear headscarves. Such are the fantasies of the people.

Such fears work particularly well if they include something real. Violent communism existed in the 1930s, when Stalin purged the Red Army and asserted his power in the Moscow Trials. In his *Retour d'URSS*, André Gide was frank about what the totalitarian USSR inspired in terms of revulsion in free minds.[2] Maurice Thorez, the leader of the French Communist Party, effectively took his orders from Moscow, and the Union des gauches, in 1935, owed as much to Stalin as it did to the masses. Similarly, radical Islam and modern jihadism are a real danger, which is not just the concern of professional worrywarts. Terrorists born here (Mohamed Merah and Mehdi Nemmouche, for example) are proof of a potentially dangerous reality. Social fractures and communitarian discourse are threatening; so is the rise of religious radicalism. But what characterizes the invention of the "enemy within" is the fantastical and generalizing transformation of a political phenomenon. The extrapolation of normal reactions within the social body—neighborhood riots in today's landscape, factory occupations in the 1930s—to a vast foreign plot.

The enemy within: to turn a young Muslim girl wearing a headscarf into a potential al-Qaeda recruit; or a dancing proletarian in a factory into a lead representative of the Comintern. The ideology of "the enemy within" often goes hand in hand with concerns with social decline: communists or Muslims are strong when the West is in decline, or so think those who lament the present day and express nostalgia for a mythologized past. The transmutation is what interests me here—the mechanism that leads to the construction of an enemy figure that makes sense to public opinion, gives meaning to our diplomacy, and serves to justify our armed interventions, and, of course, the fight against terrorism.[3]

The peril was red eighty years ago; today it is green. As a means of protecting itself, the national community has to exclude the enemy from society. A communist could not be considered to be a true patriot: that was the 1930s assessment. A Muslim cannot be considered to be truly French: that is the consensus today. Such rhetoric is constant throughout history, as if France needed an enemy in order to construct and reinforce its own identity. In the 1930s the enemy came from the East; now, the enemy comes from the South. The simple presence and existence of this figure engenders hateful reactions and a violent discourse of rejection. A generalizing and totalitarian logorrhea.

The anticommunism of the past, much like today's anti-Islamism, was not nuanced in its efforts to expel foreign bodies. The issue is not one of effective nationality. Communists and Muslims are considered foreign agents, regardless of whether or not they are officially French. Worse still, French communists took their orders from Moscow; today French people from the *banlieues* go to Afghanistan or Syria to learn jihad. Facts are facts, but to generalize them is a form of stereotyping. The two forms of discourse operate in the same way. They start by profiling an adversary, who is a threat by essence, due to his or her presumed allegiance to a foreign body that is hostile to our national interests. The adversary is governed by distant institutions whose sole aim is to impose their ideological yolk upon us. In the past, it was Moscow and the Comintern; today it is Mecca, al-Qaeda, and the emirate of Qatar. During the interwar years, it was common to read such statements as "Moscow orders: the communists obey" or that the leadership of the French Communist Party was a structure that "aimed to promote all the resolutions taken in Moscow" (*Le Figaro*, January 22, 1923). For many French people of that era, the French Communist Party was an instrument of the Soviet Union, and in order to protect French liberties, it was imperative to fight the imperialist appetites of this foreign state. As such, communists were considered "Soviet disciples and servants of Moscow" (*Le Journal des Débats*, May 20, 1925), and *Le Petit Parisien* joked on June 1, 1925: "Beware of the unruly militant! . . . The eye of Moscow is watching him! . . . and the eye of Moscow is terrifying when it wanders."

Anti-France

Beginning in the 1920s, virulent anticommunists demonized the Bolshevik Revolution, which red agents claimed to be importing. The director of the newspaper *La Liberté*, Camille Aymard, had the following despairing words to say: "To the Bourgeoisie of France: do you know what's in store for you? Do you know what a revolution is? The masses are the same everywhere. Revolution is always the same, in all countries, in all eras; it leads to the same types of torture and atrocities."[4] At the same time, Henri de Kérillis and his propaganda agency published all manner of posters denouncing the "reds," the "anti-French radicals," the "cartel that reports to Moscow," and "Abd el-Kriminel," who killed French troops in Morocco (in a poster where Jacques Doriot, then head of the French Communist Party, is handing a knife to the Riffian leader so that he can stab the shadow of the Marianne—symbol of the Republic).

The French Communist Party was accused of trying to import the Bolshevik Revolution into France. It was also suspected of Germanophilia, especially since the Soviet Union and Germany established official ties in 1939 (the German-Soviet Pact). For L'Action française, the French Communist Party represented the driving force behind a strange coalition of anti-French groups, whose sole aim was to dissolve the country's identity and disrupt national cohesion. In 1936, Jacques Doriot, the "treacherous communist" par excellence, expressed visceral anticommunist sentiments,[5] which coincided with the core platform of his Parti Populaire Français (PPF). His book/pamphlet was titled *La France ne sera pas un pays d'esclaves*.[6] In the introduction, Jacques Doriot posed a serious question to indicate the enemy: "Is he your master?" He also shared "what you should know about Joseph Stalin," portraying him as the demiurge of an international plot, in which the French Communist Party was merely a cog—a zealous pawn interested in tearing down France's flag: "There are some exceptions from the past and in the present, but on the whole French Communists are simply passive implementers of policies that have been determined by the Russian leaders of The Communist International. Those policies are strictly linked to Soviet interests. The Soviets are the driving force behind global Communism. . . . In addition, French Communism cannot be judged according to the same criteria as other national, free, and democratic parties. It has to be evaluated as a function of the Soviet Union's interests."[7]

The anticommunism of the 1930s demonized the party's ideology as antinational, brandishing the French flag against the red flag, and banishing all sympathizers of Maurice Thorez's party—regardless of their level of involvement or activism. Such logics of exclusion applied to all communists and adhered to the era's ubiquitous anticommunist propaganda.[8] They were all suspicious, all dangerous, all guilty! They were considered "subhuman" and "barbarians," ill-adapted for full citizenship, which led to the internment of members of the Communist Party after the German-Soviet Pact of August 1939. Little attention was paid to the fact that many of these sympathizers and militants unhesitatingly enlisted to fight Nazi Germany in both the fall of 1939 and in

June of 1940. Jacques Doriot went on to claim: "Stalin's slaves—or French Communists—play a miserable role against their own country and against French workers, in the name of one-way Internationalism. They may disguise themselves as patriots; they may wave the French flag; they may sing the French national anthem; they are and will always be the dangerous instruments of a foreign nationalist country."[9]

Communists in 1934—who were suspected of being in a subversive alliance with socialists and radicals—like Muslims today—who protest in support of Palestinians—were accused of being "bad French." Suspicions regarding communists were rampant and ubiquitous. They infused all of society. Anticommunism during the 1930s was a massive trend, which took hold of elites and the working class alike. It functioned as fuel for those on the right, for parts of government represented in parliament, and for the muscled leagues pounding the pavement—a cement that united all these various trends. But it was a minimal program—a common denominator for a number of concurring forces. Such discourse was attractive to both the top echelons and bottom segments of French society. Islamophobia (or anti-Muslim discourse) now plays exactly the same role in French public debate. Communism is no longer perceived as a threat; Muslims have replaced communists in the pantheon of our horrors, as Thomas Deltombe shows in his work on the coverage of Islam in the media.[10] That shift first began to take form with the Marche pour l'égalité et contre le racisme (an antiracist march described in the media as the "Marche des beurs") in 1983, later becoming established in 1986 with the attacks on French territory. At the top of our list of nightmares, this new danger became a source of worry for "real French" people and threatened to pollute our sacred and pure "national identity."

The "Foreign" Threat

From the time of the Shah's overthrow in Iran (1979) until the Arab Spring (2011), "foreign" Muslims have become an inspiration for multiple types of regimes. Some, as in Tunisia, are moving toward democracy; others, for instance, in Iran and Saudi Arabia, have become even more confined within dictatorships. The simple presence of several million North Africans, Middle Easterners, and Africans—be they atheists, Muslims, believers, or otherwise—is thought, by the most ardent Islamophobes to have placed France in a dangerous situation vis-à-vis a "foreign threat." From that perspective, it is believed that the army, the police, and urban policymakers have to keep an eye on "sensitive neighborhoods" (*banlieues* housing projects) and contain radical "homes." Here again, everyone is suspicious, everyone is dangerous, everyone is guilty! As Mathieu

Rigouste explains, "a political and military thought that is both governmental and private," has begun to emerge, "according to which a transnational threat is activating a social and ethnic fifth column hidden within the Muslim population . . . With the disappearance of the Soviet enemy, the immigrant body has begun to appear as the enemy within . . . The first Iraq war, followed by the 1995 attacks in France also served as arguments to support fears of a potential postcolonial civil war."[11] Rejected wholesale, these populations "who look Muslim" (to use Nicolas Sarkozy's dreadful expression) feed a fear of the Muslim as the absolute enemy,[12] an invader who seeks to subjugate "true" French people. For those who fear them, these enemies have to be fought in a veritable counterrevolutionary war. As was the case in the 1930s, this kind of thinking is typical of right-wing and extremist parties (as can be seen in the repeated diatribes of the Front National's leader, Marine Le Pen), but is certainly not uncommon on the left either.

Every international crisis and every terrorist attack becomes an opportunity to stir up anti-Muslim sentiment and renew the idea that all Muslims in France are complicit in the violent acts committed by a handful of extremists. "How many Mohamed Merahs are arriving every day in France on boats and planes filled with migrants?" asked Marine Le Pen on March 25, 2012, forgetting that the man behind the massacres in Montauban and Toulouse was a Frenchman born in France. On the same day, during a presidential campaign meeting in Nantes, she added: "The problem is not about one madman; what happened is the beginning of a green invasion in our country."

The designs of the far-right are clear. When it comes to the traditional right though, the situation is more complex in terms of the ways in which it is playing on the "fears" of its electorate. For example, references are made to a range of other concerns, such as the left's concern regarding secularism. For in the construction of today's enemy within, progressives have also entered the ring. Indeed, elected officials from the left have suggested prohibiting nursery staff from wearing Muslim headscarves. Socialist minister of the interior, Manuel Valls, expressed interest in a proposal from an advisory board on integration (another left-wing creation) that would prohibit women from wearing headscarves at universities. The motivations and interpretations between political perspectives may not be quite the same, and the outright rejection evidenced on the far-right is not the same as the left's preoccupation with secularism. However, in the end, a consensus has been established around the idea of the "problematic Muslim." From preserving secularism in the name of positive values—notably, equality between men and women—we run the risk of developing too rigid an idea of identity. A confused continuum has begun to emerge, in spite of the various actors. Elisabeth Badinter, who could never be suspected of supporting the Front National, nevertheless has said that "Only Marine Le Pen is defending secularism."[13] She, along with other progressive intellectuals, has been actively involved in a fight against the Muslim headscarf since 1989. Borders are porous from both ends of the spectrum.

Beyond the left's linguistic precautions and mindsets ("French Muslims are France," declared the very secular Manuel Valls in July 25, 2014, at the Evry-Coucouronnes Mosque), the intolerant, meanwhile, have been taking advantage of the turmoil. They accuse all immigrant populations living in France of seeking to colonize France and impose their cultures, their way of life, and their religion—which is embodied by the terrifying symbol of sharia law. For many, "French Muslims" today are supporters of al-Qaeda, either active or dormant militants, but all potential allies of each other. They constitute an "enemy within"[14] that is already in place and that is seen as being especially dangerous since it lives among "ally" populations and hides away in disadvantaged neighborhoods, an underground movement that has its own territory within France and operates cells within its borders.

The virulence of anticommunism in the 1920s and 1930s was so widespread and diverse in nature that it would be impossible to make an exhaustive comparison here. As Jean-Jacques Becker and Serge Berstein write, "Almost 90 percent of the French electorate rejected Bolshevism in 1919, from the extreme left to the extreme right."[15] After the Tours Congress, the Russian Revolution, the hatred toward "Bolshevism," and the fear of Moscow had permeated almost all of French society. After the colonial wars in Syria, Lebanon, and Morocco, and with the Rif War and Indochina in 1930, the sentiment that international communism was France's enemy had become widespread. Every campaign by the French Communist Party was perceived as an "anti-French threat," resembling the reactions to the Rif War.

Only with changes in Moscow in June 1934 and a strategy of alliance with the Rassemblement Populaire (socialists and radicals) did such ambient discourse begin to soften. Nevertheless, things took a violent turn to the right, which criticized the left's alliance with "France's enemies." With the 1936 strikes and the outbreak of the Spanish Civil War, anticommunist discourse became the central theme in the right-wing press and in poster and leaflet campaigns. In 1938, anticommunism was perceived as "proof" of patriotism. Not being anticommunist was the same as being a bad French citizen. For many, the Berlin-Moscow pact was proof that the fight against the "reds" was justified, providing an interpretation of the world that led to the support of Vichy. The fracture was such that some militants and elected officials within the French Communist Party quit the party. *L'Humanité* newspaper was banned in August 1939, followed by the party itself in September.

Anxious Visions

Whereas "reds" are no longer an important target in today's France, "greens" (Muslims) have come to occupy a similar space. Common themes in the dynamics of rejection include an obsession with being invaded, a fear of "Islamization"—an expansionism paired with a will to dominate that recalls the evil ambitions of yesteryear's totalitarian ideologies (communism and Nazism). Indeed, if anticommunism was a "French civil war" that lasted more than twenty years (1917–1939) before undergoing a period of change with the postwar independence and various social movements (1945–1968), the struggle against Islam in France has been engaged in a similar dynamic for just as long (1983–2001). The struggle was further extended in 2001 with multipolar conflicts within France and abroad. The 2005 riots in disadvantaged *banlieues* neighborhoods were presented by a number of politicians as a "revolt" that was engineered by Muslims.

The leader of the far-right Progress Party in Norway, Carl Hagen, declared in a conference in Bergen in 2005: "Muslims, like Hitler, have long been clear in their intentions. Their long-term goal is to Islamize the world. . . . They have now reached Europe." They are already here, and tomorrow, they will be everywhere. In an effort to stoke anxieties, the far-right (in practically all European countries) has been enumerating apocalyptic prophecies that predict a dark future shaped by ethnic clashes and civil war. Islamophobia has grown as a result of such fears and a perceived need for self-defense. The fear of "Islamization" is grounded in two supposedly indisputable facts: the proportion of Muslims living in France is thought to be growing at astronomical rates (polygamy and high birth rates are often mentioned) and the idea that Muslims seek to undermine "us"; those two ideas have been used to justify the military rhetoric and allusions to a state of war.

By pretending to defend secularism, Islamophobes have managed to convince activists—some of them on the left—to join their cause. Such is the case, for example, of the duo who founded the *Riposte Laïque*—Pierre Cassen and Christine Tasin—and who are also co-organizers of the "Apéro Géant: saucisson et pinard" (a happy hour gathering of wine and deli meat cold cuts whose ingredients include pork) and the "Assises contre l'islamisation de notre pays" (Conference against the Islamization of our Country). During the presidential campaign of 2012, they published a fictional political novel in which one can find a summary of the fantasies that feed anxieties about Muslims in France. The book recounts what would happen in the case of a left-wing victory. Entitled *La faute du bobo Jocelyn*, it tells the story of Jocelyn Lefranc, the son of left-leaning middle-class teachers from Paris (the wealthy sixteenth arrondissement), who marries a socialist activist.[16] After supporting President Francis Laslande (François Hollande) and his prime minister Marie Bory (Martine Aubry), he ends up joining the Resistance when he learns that the left-wing government's agenda (immigration, affirmative action, European Union, globalization, etc.) includes affording power to "verlamistes" (*greenlamists*), who preach a "totalitarian religion that seeks to conquer France."[17]

The narrative is filled with a lexicon from the Second World War. The authors rewrite history, using great figures from France's past to fight the Muslim enemy. Anyone who does not join their fight is called a "collaborator." Notable figures from the Resistance are evoked as well as "the Franks," who "relinquished their barbarian mores in order to assimilate into Gallo-Roman culture." Joan of Arc is featured as having "kicked the occupiers out of France." Other featured figures and events include the sans-culottes, the Parisian populace of the barricades during the July Revolution of 1830, the 1848 Revolution, "Marianne and her Phrygian bonnet," Montaigne, Rabelais, Voltaire, and even the "Manouchian group, who despite being foreign, were shot for defending freedom and France." The book is shameless in its manipulative use of history.

Similarly, the Resistance flag was used by the group Génération Identitaire on October 20, 2012. They occupied the construction site of the future Mosque of Poitiers, climbing on its roof and shouting, "Charles Martel! Charles Martel!" (Frankish statesmen and military leader from 718 to 741), "Identity is ours; we fought to take it back, and we will fight to defend it!" They then unfurled a banner: "732: Génération Identitaire." Such crude symbols are presumed to stage a heroic gesture and in turn politicize it in the face of this new space devoted to Muslims in Poitiers. For this handful of enlightened souls, "resisting" the Muslim "invasion" in Poitiers in 2012, as had been the case previously in 732, was therefore aimed at preventing Muslims from spreading to the North and conquering all of France's territory. The leader of Bloc Identitaire, Fabrice Robert, had these words to say in the follow-up to the demonstration at the Poitiers Mosque: "This initiative highlights the advance of Islamization, and the entire political class is ready to collaborate."[18] The same group has organized similar demonstrations since 2010: they occupied a fast-food Halal Quick in Villeurbanne (Rhône) and have organized several "saucisson-pinard" cocktail hours in disadvantaged neighborhoods. Like-minded groups (the Résistance Républicaine, the Riposte Laïque, etc.) joined them in a demonstration that included a thousand participants on March 9, 2014, in the streets of Paris. The participants, which included writer Renaud Camus, yelled, "This is Our Home!" and called for a referendum to ban immigration, citing the example of a Swiss vote limiting "massive immigration." Ah, the famous "Swiss model."

Raphaël Liogier has delineated the historical evolution in the ways in which France has perceived Islam since the nineteenth century—fascination, demeaning, fear, paranoia.[19] Things began to change dramatically in the late 1970s with the oil crisis and the arrival to power of the Ayatollah Khomeini in Iran. Destabilized, the Middle East was now seen as dangerous, and Muslims began to be perceived as a threat. Meanwhile, the 1970s was also the period during which North African immigrants began to settle in France, notably thanks to a new policy known as "family reunification." Gilles Kepel has explicitly linked the conflict in the Middle East with France: "The worst-case scenario would be that it would allow jihadists returning from Syria or Iraq . . . to carry out anti-Jewish attacks under the pretext of avenging victims in Gaza."[20] The idea is that the enemy within (born in our disadvantaged neighborhoods) would become indoctrinated by extremists (from Algeria or the Middle East), financed by Qatar or other foreigners, and would then go "there" for jihad, before coming back "here" to launch the holy war.

Arab one day, Arab forever; all Muslims (converts or those with religious backgrounds, by choice or by designation) are potential Kelkal-Merah-Nemmouches. The situation, Gilles Kepel goes on to say, "has changed due to poverty and the marginalization of a large portion of the immigrant youth . . . and Salafism in disadvantaged neighborhoods has tremendous appeal as a marker of territory since its core values contradict those of French society."[21] For Kepel, the mechanism that will lead to a "civil war" has been activated. We are living in the prelude to global jihad, and all the actors are in place: there is a repressive state, a "community" bonded through exclusion, misery, and discrimination. Everything is in place. And to conclude: "If we do not attend to this issue [in its totality] we will be giving free rein to those who use identity politics to their own ends, people like Soral and Dieudonné."[22]

An Undigested Past

A review of the past several decades reveals how this anti-Islam sentiment developed. In 1989, the Rushdie affair (following the publication of his controversial novel *The Satanic Verses*) and the first debates on the presence of the headscarf in schools (in a middle school in Creil) gave a second wind to fears of Islam—henceforth present in the highest political, police, and military spheres in France—which then spread in a chaotic manner throughout the country.[23] The fall of the Berlin Wall and the disappearance of communist regimes in Eastern Europe led to a new dualism in the 1990s, with respect to the Southern "Muslim" world (but also including Afghanistan), which was still poorly defined, but which became the only alternative to the "Western world"—the supposed bearer of progress and enlightenment values. The end of history did not take place with the fall of the Berlin Wall. Rather, a clash of civilizations—between China, the Muslim world, and the West—was now under way.

The so-called "Black Decade" that resulted from an extremist insurgency in Algeria from 1992 on stoked latent anxieties regarding the history of France (the Algerian War and its aftermath), the Gulf Wars, and several waves of terrorism. Furthermore, it embodied a fear of the "other" that was now transformed into an organic rejection of a portion of the nation's "citizens." French citizens of Algerian descent were, like yesterday's communists, French by right, but "anti-French" in practice. The divide is deep, and that is due in large part to an undigested colonial history (as illustrated by the February 2005 law on "positive colonization"), a hardening of political discourse (establishment of the *Indigènes de la République* in 2005), and an unprecedented urban crisis (with the "revolts" in the *banlieues* housing projects in October and November 2005), which made headlines throughout the world for weeks. The danger is now green; it wears a headscarf; it prays in the streets; it seeks to erect minarets.

However, it was 9/11 that opened a new phase in anti-Muslim sentiment. Raphaël Liogier explains that after that, both in the media and in political circles, security became the primary preoccupation, an obsession even, that has translated into broader debates on European identity itself.[24] With this in mind, the media has aggravated this collective anxiety; weeklies and television channels continue to publish a dizzying array of the following types of headlines: "Should we be afraid of Islam?," "Worry-free Islam," and "Is Islam Compatible with the Republic?" The media machine is in full swing; the Front National is surfing the wave; politicians find themselves in a game of one-upmanship.

Marine Le Pen has been reaping the benefits of this climate of hate. She makes free use of a vocabulary inherited from the dark years of the war, as in her descriptions of the Muslim presence in France in a speech delivered in Lyon on December 10, 2010: "Fifteen years ago, there was the headscarf, and we've been seeing more and more of them. Then, there was the burqa, and we've been seeing more and more of them, too. And then, there were prayers in public spaces . . . Now, there are ten or fifteen places where a number of people come to lay claim." Driving her point home, she went on to argue that "More and more zones find themselves under the yoke of religious laws that have replaced the laws of the Republic. Yes, this is an occupation. Yes, we are being illegally occupied."[25]

Although hatred toward Islam and Muslims has reached unprecedented levels, fantasies of invasion by means of immigration are not in themselves new. More than four decades after its initial publication, the recent rerelease of Jean Raspail's book *Le Camp des Saints* and its subsequent rise to the top of bestseller lists is a reminder of that.[26] The book, which first came out in 1973, described the dramatic consequences of a massive wave of immigration on Western civilization. Originating from the Ganges Delta, a million miserable immigrants arrive on the French Riviera and flood a France whose authorities prove incapable of containing them. The new arrivals are described as a teeming mass of hungry rats set upon destroying everything that makes up French culture and identity.[27] Terrified, the "white French" flee the "putrid masses" that have pillaged the hospitals, schools, and supermarkets, and raped some "white women." A small cohort of valiant "whites" have dared to stand up to the invader, but their efforts are in vain.

When it was first published, the book was applauded by a number of very right-wing authors such as Jean Cau, Louis Pauwels, and Michel Déon.[28] But it was in 2011, on the occasion of the publication of a new edition, that the book really showed itself to resonate with an era, which has seen a tremendous growth in xenophobia and fears of immigrant invasion. Sales skyrocketed: more than twenty thousand copies were sold in less than three months, making it a bestseller. Clearly, Renaud Camus did not invent anything new when he published his manifesto titled *Non au changement de peuple et de civilisation* on September 11, 2013, writing that "The Great Substitution is the biggest shock that our nation has ever experienced over the course of its history. If the change in people and civilization, which is already well underway, reaches its final stage, history will no longer belong to it or to us."[29] The idea of the "grand remplacement" (what we call a "great substitution") has gained traction within contemporary discourse, and it is used by the most active agents of Islamophobia, from *Figaro* journalist Ivan Rioufol ("For the past forty years, the right and the left have passively sat back and watched as other peoples have flooded our borders. In some areas, our country has become completely unrecognizable. It makes sense to talk about a great substitution")[30] to polemicist Éric Zemmour, and including the periodicals *Valeurs Actuelles* and *Causeur*.[31]

Over the past fifteen or so years, successive debates on the "Christian roots" of Europe, the European Union's aborted Common Constitution, and efforts to maintain "national identity" have aggravated what Raphaël Liogier has called "the narcissistic wound of the European world, which is particularly salient for France, with its myth of its own exceptionality and universality."[32] For him, "Islamization has become the morbid enactment of the extinction of European culture . . . which feeds a new form of populism that is neither left nor right-wing."[33] Rome fell due to barbarian invasions. If we are not careful, the West will follow suit! Nothing has changed since the time of the Crusades—except, that is, thirteen centuries of shared presence on French soil.[34]

The collective imagination views Muslims today as warmongers and foreign bodies within the nation. That is exactly the role that was played by communists in the 1930s. Back then, the majority opinion was convinced: communists sought to provoke international conflict as a way of exerting their ideological designs, and they had to be stopped. Throughout the interwar period, radical minister Albert Sarraut's slogan, "Communism is the enemy" (declared during a speech in 1927), became a rallying cry for political elites. The height of such anticommunist sentiment occurred in the fall of 1938, with the crisis of the Munich Accords. It was believed that "Communism is war," and that French communists were Moscow agents whose aim was to force France into a bloody war to the detriment of its national interests. In the 1930s, such thinking led a large number of French elites to conclude: "Better Hitler than Blum." During the Spanish Civil War, the recruitment of French youth by the Comintern was viewed as additional proof that the scourge had reached the core of the French nation and its youth. Some anticommunists even went so far as to enroll in the Legion of French Volunteers for the Wehrmacht in order to fight Bolshevism. On June 22, 1942, in celebration of the first anniversary of the entry of the German and Russian army, Pierre Laval gave a speech on the radio (Vichy) in which he famously summed up the devastating effects of the collective obsession with anticommunism: "I hope for Germany's victory because without it, tomorrow Bolshevism will be everywhere."

When we make Muslims into the absolute enemy of "French identity," and when we cast some French people and foreigners living in France in the role of "enemies within," we rally the French populace around a common cause. The fear of the "other"—I am by no means ignoring the real risks of terrorism and the brainwashing of some youths—serves to authorize security-based policies, all manner of political choices, and a myriad of diplomatic strategies. But Islamophobia—or hatred of Muslims—has created a new form of blindness, which resembles that of the 1930s. It deforms analyses regarding changes that have taken place in French society over the past two decades, and it has served to drive a growing portion of the populace straight into the arms of the far-right. A dangerous refrain can be heard today across social milieus and throughout the country. The refrain goes: "I hope for Marine Le Pen's victory, because without it, Islamization will be everywhere." Our obsession with fantasies of invasion—be they green or red—sully our own blue-white-red values.

Renaud Dély is a journalist and former deputy editorial managing director at the newspaper *Libération*, deputy editorial managing director at *Marianne*, and managing director-editor at *L'Obs*. Recent publications include *Les années trente sont de retour. Petite leçon d'histoire pour comprendre les crises* (2015), *La* *droite brune: UMP-FN, les secrets d'une liaison fatale* (2012), and *Frères ennemis: L'hyperviolence en politique* (2015).

Notes

1. See Dominique Lejeune, *La peur du "rouge" en France: Des partageux aux gauchistes* (Paris: Éditions Belin, 2003), 166.
2. André Gide, *Return from the USSR*, trans. Dorothy Bussy (New York: Alfred A. Knopf, 1936).
3. Mitchell D. Silber and Arvind Bhatt published a report entitled *Radicalization in the West: The Homegrown Threat* (New York: NYPD Intelligence Division, 2007), which Alain Bauer translated into French (*La radicalisation en Occident: La menace intérieure*, 2008), and circulated widely among a number of government ministers, from Nicolas Sarkozy to Manuel Valls. On this point, see David Revault d'Allones and Laurent Borredon, *Valls, à l'intérieur* (Paris: Robert Laffont, 2014).
4. Camille Aymard, *Bolchevisme ou Fascisme? Français, il faut choisir!* (Paris: Flammarion, 1925).
5. Jean-Jacques Becker and Serge Berstein, *Histoire de l'anticommunisme en France 1917–1940* (Paris: Orban, 1987).
6. Jacques Doriot, *La France ne sera pas un pays d'esclaves* (Paris: Les Œuvres françaises, 1936), 157.
7. Ibid., 21.
8. Philippe Buton and Laurent Gervereau, *Le couteau entre les dents: Soixante-dix ans d'affiches communistes et anticommunistes (1917–1987)* (Paris: Le Chêne, 1989).
9. Doriot, *La France ne sera pas un pays d'esclaves*, 111.
10. Thomas Deltombe, *L'islam imaginaire: La construction médiatique de l'islamophobie en France (1975–2005)* (Paris: La Découverte, 2005).
11. Mathieu Rigouste, "L'ennemi intérieur, de la guerre coloniale au contrôle sécuritaire," *Cultures & Conflits*, no. 67 (Autumn 2007): 168. See also Mathieu Rigouste, *L'ennemi intérieur, la généalogie coloniale et militaire de l'ordre sécuritaire dans la France contemporaine* (Paris: La Découverte, 2009).
12. Mathieu Rigouste explains that the highest military authorities have largely accepted the idea of the "enemy within" (and the antirevolutionary struggle), a concept that has been prevalent for the past twenty-five years and that has been a structuring element of the national defense's overall strategy.
13. "Pourquoi Elisabeth Badinter a provoqué un clash à l'Observatoire de la Laïcité," *Metronews*, January 12, 2016.
14. Rigouste, "L'ennemi intérieur, de la guerre coloniale au contrôle sécuritaire."
15. Jean-Jacques Becker and Serge Berstein, "L'anticommunisme en France," *Vingtième Siècle: Revue d'histoire*, no. 15 (July–September 1987): 18.
16. Pierre Cassen and Christine Tasin, *La faute du bobo Jocelyn* (Éditions Riposte Laïque, 2011).
17. At the end of the book, Jocelyn Lefranc, who has decided to participate in the "Reconquista," has committed to fighting the invaders. The writers state: "As is always the case, there were cynical collaborators who didn't have any principles, last-minute resistance fighters (who only joined the cause when it became clear it was on the side of the winners), and authentic heroes, who would give their lives for their country and their children's future."
18. See "Les identitaires et la mosquée de Poitiers . . . dans les coulisses de l'opération," *Minute*, October 23, 2012.
19. Raphaël Liogier, *Le mythe de l'islamisation: Essai sur une obsession collective* (Paris, Seuil, 2012), 33. See also Deltombe, *L'islam imaginaire*.

20. Interview with Gilles Kepel, "Kepel: La France est en panne d'un discours fédérateur," by Alexandra Schwarzbrot, *Libération*, July 20, 2014.

21. Ibid.

22. Ibid.

23. During the 1990s, several researchers focused on the issue of "domestic" and border control, notably at the *Institut des hautes études de défense nationale* (IHEDN, Institute of National Defense), referencing reports (Retex) on interventions in Baghdad, Srebrenica, Abidjan, and even Clichy-sur-Bois (2005). Emphasis was on the urgent need to galvanize around the struggle against the enemies within and control international migrants and hotbeds of terrorism throughout the world.

24. Liogier, *Le mythe de l'islamisation*, 42–43.

25. See, for example, "Marine Le Pen compare les 'prières de rue' des musulmans à une 'occupation,'" *Le Monde*, December 11, 2010.

26. Jean Raspail, *Le Camp des Saints* (Paris: Éditions Robert Laffont, 2011).

27. The book's themes can be traced back to the novel by Captain Danrit (Émile Driant), *L'invasion noire: La mobilation africaine* (Paris: Flammarion, 1895), which tells the story of an invasion of France by hordes of Africans led by Muslim Arabs.

28. The book has had many lives. It made comebacks throughout the 1980s and 1990s, related to events connected to immigration. Samuel Huntington even called it a "luminous" book in his famous book *The Clash of Civilizations and the Remaking of World Order* (New York: Simon & Schuster, 1996).

29. Renaud Camus, "*Non au changement de peuple et de civilisation*," September 11, 2013, http://www.bvoltaire.fr/renaudcamus/non-au-changement-de-peuple-et-de-civilisation,35190.

30. Ivan Rioufol, "Bloc-notes: La libanisation de Marseille, première alerte," *Le Figaro*, September 13, 2013.

31. See for example Éric Zemmour, *La mélancolie française* (Paris: Fayard, 2010) and *Le suicide français: Ces quarante années qui ont défait la France* (Paris: Albin Michel, 2014).

32. Raphaël Liogier, "L'islamisation est un mythe," *Le Monde*, March 28, 2013.

33. Ibid.

34. Pascal Blanchard, Naïma Yahi, Yvan Gastaut, and Nicolas Bancel, eds., *La France arabo-orientale: Treize siècles de présences du Maghreb, de la Turquie, d'Égypte, du Moyen-Orient et du Proche-Orient* (Paris: La Découverte, 2014).

PART III

APARTHEID AND THE WAR OF IDENTITIES IN FRANCE / 2015

3.1. THE END OF THE "FRENCH MODEL"?

24

FROM THE DAKAR SPEECH TO THE TAUBIRA AFFAIR

Ariane Chebel d'Appollonia

General Recommendation No. 35, which was adopted by the United Nations Committee on the Elimination of Racial Discrimination (CERD) in 2013, introduced the notion of "racist hate speech" in order to improve prevention and aid in the fight against various forms of discrimination.[1] Indeed, CERD mentions "racism" only in the context of "racist doctrines and practices" in direct relationship to Article 4 pertaining to the condemnation of the dissemination of ideas based on racial superiority.[2] The committee's position was that the traditional definition of racism only allowed for sanctions with respect to the dissemination of ideas founded on a belief in a racial hierarchy, as well as to incitement to hatred based on an explicit reference to race. Judging that "racist hate speech can take many forms and that it is not confined to explicitly racial remarks," it included all discursive practices promoting discrimination toward members of a racial or ethnic group for reasons of "race," color, ancestry, or national background—including expressions of mockery or libel.

In its definition of "hate speech," the committee also included expressions of discrimination via electronic media, as well as nonverbal expressions such as symbols and images. It also deemed "expressions of racism" from public authorities and institutions to be of "particular concern," notably on the part of high officials and political personalities. The notion of racist hate speech does not have, however, a directly applicable legal value. Much like Article 4 of the CERD (to which France has been a signatory since 1971), states have to adapt it into their respective legislation. France equipped itself with a robust antiracist arsenal (including the law of 1972, which made inciting hatred a crime, various amendments to the penal code, and the Gayssot Law of 1990). A number of measures have been adopted since 2013 in reaction to the propositions listed in Recommendation No. 35, notably a National Action Plan Against Racism and Anti-Semitism (PNACRA), the implementation of which was entrusted to the Inter-Ministerial Delegation in the Fight Against Racism and Anti-Semitism (DILCRA).

After the attacks of January 2015, President François Hollande made the fight against racism and antisemitism a national cause. During a presentation on France in April 2015, the French representative at the United Nations applauded the "voluntary policy and commitment toward the fight against racism and all forms of discrimination," underscoring in particular the "prevention and education measures against racial hatred."[3] However, the United Nations' committee was more critical. Several members expressed concern over the treatment of the Roma and the reception of migrants, refugees, and asylum seekers. The main objection, summarized by the General Rapporteur in his introduction, was that "the principle of equality is not entirely reflected in the reality, and there are some gaps," which he attributed to "intolerance and racism." The Rapporteur spoke harshly about a "kind of banalization of hate speech" in France, due in part to the absence of incrimination specific to hate crime.

French law does not use the Anglo-Saxon notion of hate crime; instead, the racist or xenophobic character of an offense is considered an "aggravating circumstance."[4] Furthermore, France has refrained from adopting Article 4 of the CERD, maintaining the right not to adopt antiracist legislation that would be incompatible with freedoms of opinion and expression. The UN committee therefore asked: "Considering Recommendation 35, and in light of the fact that some political parties and media outlets continue to disseminate xenophobic, intolerant, and racist speech, what does the government propose to do?"[5]

From Ordinary Racism to Everyday Hatred

The National Consultative Commission on Human Rights (CNCDH) can legitimately highlight the government's efforts to fight against and prevent racism, particularly in the context of a national action plan (2012–2014, renewed with increased funding for 2015–2017). An array of ministries have been mobilized, including that of education, in order to promote the prevention of racism in schools and to organize "moral and civic lessons" in the framework of reforming the "Republic's school system." In addition, convictions for crimes linked to racism and discrimination have risen since 2003, with the rate of penal response reaching 82 percent in 2012.[6]

Nevertheless, the increasing banalization of hate speech extends far beyond the current legislation in force. It is only the latest step in a trend that encompasses the entire political class and whose origins can be found in the use of differentialist racism by members of the "new right" (*Groupement de recherche et d'études pour la civilisation européenne,* Research and Study Group for European Civilization, GRECE, and the *Club de l'Horloge*)[7] starting in the 1980s.[8] The "right to be different," an idea supported by the left during the golden age of SOS Racisme, has been critiqued by the nationalist right according to the following tripartite logic: (1) there is no such thing as inequality, rather there are "objective differences" between ethnic groups, which allow for a pseudovalorization of diversity while masking a phobia of miscegenation and mixing; (2) affirming the right to difference authorizes preferences for some groups over others, and the mutual respect of differences between groups allows for the creation of ethnic and cultural barriers in order to preserve the purity of each group; (3) cultural preferentialism justifies a discourse of exclusion, which replaces racial inequality with a so-called cultural hierarchy; in reality, however, it relies on implicit biological assumptions with respect to ethnic and cultural differences.[9]

The Front National made differentialist racism a mainstream issue by linking a kind of objective assertion ("different races exist, different ethnicities exist, different cultures exist") with a preferential hierarchy ("hierarchies, preferences, and affinities are only natural. I am French, so I prefer French people").[10] Beginning in the 1990s, a significant portion of conservatives aligned themselves with ideas of national identity and national preference—an important consequence of which was the cleaning up (what they have described as a process of *dédiabolisation,* in other words de-demonization) of the far-right's image. As prejudice has become more commonplace, differentialist racism has become ordinary. In 1996, according to a CNCDH poll, the majority of the French population believed that xenophobia was an acceptable "opinion" in the name of freedom of expression and should not be sanctioned. Fifty-three percent of those polled agreed that it was acceptable, during a political campaign, to say that blacks and North Africans were "inferior races," and in response to the question as to whether such "opinions" should be allowed in the press, 48 percent agreed.[11] Since then, the targets of ordinary racism have multiplied: immigrants, Muslim immigrants, French Muslims, Roma, refugees, and asylum seekers. In the introduction to its 2014 report, the CNCDH noted, "Expressions of racism have become increasingly commonplace against the backdrop of cyber anonymity, a shock culture, debates on what defines humor, and a general distrust of antiracism, which is seen in terms of censorship. Such banalization can be seen at all levels of society—among citizens and elected officials, and in the media—and is worrisome at international levels; one wonders about the image that France is giving of itself abroad."[12]

Identity-Based Coloring

Prejudice has become so commonplace that racism is now freely expressed. It is justified as a "freedom of speech" issue that enables us to revisit subjects such as colonization, the existence of "biological races," and the Holocaust. Semantic gymnastics are no longer needed for expressions of differentialist racism: those who don't like blacks have only to say that they prefer whites; those who don't like immigrants can simply evoke "antiwhite racism."

In the context of debates on decolonization, there has been a progressive trend toward memory-based arguments. The idea of the "positive effects" of decolonization marked a first step in purging guilt for colonialism from national history. For instance, the Law of February 23, 2005 attempted to include a eulogy on positive colonization, stipulating the following in Article 4: "In particular, school curricula acknowledge the positive role of France's presence overseas, notably in North Africa, and grant to those from these territories who fought for France's army the place in history they deserve."[13] The strategy of *antirepentance,* to refer to the term used by a group of historians,[14] was followed by a series of controversies, notably on the presentation of colonialism in school curricula and on the notion of "chosen or selected immigration" such as it was defined by the law of July 24, 2006 on immigration and integration.

Nicolas Sarkozy's July 26, 2007, speech in Dakar is a perfect illustration of the identity-based coloring implied in such rereadings of the past. On the one hand, the negative aspects of colonization are balanced out by references to the "good will" on the part of colonials, who "believed they were fulfilling a civilizing mission; they were men who believed they were doing something good." Such assertions are used to reject ideas of repentance: "I'm not here to speak to you about repentance . . . It doesn't make sense to ask today's generations to atone for a crime perpetrated by past generations. No one would ask a son to atone for the crimes of his father."[15] The past cannot be erased, but the troubled postcolonial conscience can be whitewashed.

On the other hand, "Africa bears some of the responsibility for its own misfortune," since "colonization is not responsible for all of today's difficulties in Africa."[16] Rhetorical retaliation transfers France's bad conscience onto Africa: to be sure, Africans are victims, but they are mostly victims of their own actions—they are too invested in "the nostalgia of a paradise lost." All the evils in Africa, for which "colonization is not responsible" (civil wars, genocides, dictatorships, fanaticism, corruption, pollution), can be explained through an ahistoric reading of African history (euphemism for civilization): "The tragedy of Africa is that the African has not fully entered into history."[17] The speech was the source of heated controversy, in France, in Africa, and even at the United

Nations, which, in 2007, through the intermediary of its special Rapporteur on racism, accused the French president of legitimizing racism under the guise of defending national identity. French and African intellectuals spoke out against what they called "a denial of history" grounded in racist prejudice.[18]

Inversely, the strategy of nonrepentance has been celebrated by partisans of the colonial "golden legend" in a context of electoral one-upmanship. Such controversies have fed a "memory war," taken up by a number of networks in defense of the memory of the Organization of the Secret Army (OAS); they have been opposed by memorial collectives equating the colonial past with present-day racism. In this sense, the demands of the *Indigènes de la République*[19] reveal the extent to which "this comparison between the colonial past and present-day politics relies on a historical and sociological conflation that is established through an assertion: that there is an equivalence, which signals a fundamental republican fault, between the past's colonized peoples and today's forms of 'discrimination' toward 'immigrants.'"[20]

These two readings share a point in common: they both provide a Manichean reconstruction of various identities that relies on essentialist constructions. The white man should not have to apologize for being white, particularly when it is a question of fighting "anti-French" sentiment embodied by ethnic and religious minorities who—like colonized peoples—should be held responsible for their own inadequacies. The black man should continue to fight against the colonial ideology in which republican ideology is grounded and which constitutes an implicit system of reference used by public authorities to discriminate against minorities. The most troubling result of this identity and memory war is the return of a biological notion of race in political and media discourse.

For example, the Party of the Indigènes de la République (PIR) combats racism by exposing the "colonial continuum" at work in the "white political field," and by contrasting "working-class whites" with immigrant working-class populations, and by criticizing the "antiracist solidarity of whites"—all in the name of a "social race struggle."[21] A similar form of semantic ambivalence can be found in the opposite camp of those who defend "whiteness" and protect against "anti-French racism." That is the context in which one must consider Islam's attacks against France's (and Europe's) "new colonization." Muslims have become the "new 'other' in Europe," the enemy within, the antiwhite entity par excellence.[22]

The Effects of the Taubira Affair

In today's context of identity-based tensions, the banalization of hate speech is founded on three mechanisms aimed at rejecting "otherness." The first includes the "whitewashing" of individual and collective identities, a phenomenon that transcends the opposition between "whites" and "nonwhites;" it excludes all those who do not fit the criteria of "whiteness," regardless of skin color. The second is a return to antiblack racist tropes, as was demonstrated in 2013 with the attacks on then minister of justice Christiane Taubira, who was compared to a "monkey" by an FN candidate on Facebook and then later in the weekly far-right publication *Minute*. The third form of rejecting "otherness" is the result of a competition for victimhood between identity-based groups who justify their hate speech through an aggressive validation of their minority status. Dieudonné is a good illustration of such "racialized racism" when he claims to ally himself with victims of colonialism (Arabs and blacks) to the detriment of Jews, and in the name of "anti-imperialist solidarity."

The justice system has sanctioned Dieudonné on numerous occasions for assertions contesting crimes against humanity that amount to racial defamation, and that incite racial hatred. The attacks against Christiane Taubira, including the ones launched by *Minute*, gave rise to emotional debate. Of all forms of hate speech, hate speech grounded in biological racism is the least accepted in France. A number of organizations protested the attacks, with prominent public figures publishing an op-ed titled "We are all French monkeys." *Minute* was fined ten thousand euros in October 2014 for racial libel, a judgment that was upheld in September 2015. Christiane Taubira celebrated the penal response, highlighting the idea that, in consideration of France's "indelible greatness," the attacks of which she was a victim were not simply "an event from which we should draw lessons." To that end, it is important to mention two dark areas in the struggle against everyday racial prejudice. On the one hand, legislation has made the distinction between infractions for hate speech and freedom of expression an uneasy one. Public officials waiver between sanctioning hate speech (notably through the transfer of hate speech from the framework of the 1881 law into the general penal code) and preserving freedom of speech. The CNCDH's objections to the use of penal law against youth who refused to state "Je suis Charlie" after the January 2015 attacks showed it is difficult to strike the right balance.

On the other hand, the increase in racist assertions by political figures (against the Roma, Muslims, refugees, for example) has worked to make hate speech commonplace in French society. Such banalization has a price: according to the CNCDH, the tolerance index has dived twelve points since 2009, and the level of explicit racism is on the rise. This dynamic, which has been confirmed by opinion polls, indicates that France has entered an area of political uncertainty.

Ariane Chebel d'Appollonia is Professor at the School of Public Affairs and Administration (SPAA) and the Division for Global Affairs (DGA) at Rutgers, State University of New Jersey. She is also Senior Researcher affiliated to the Center for Political Research, Sciences Po Paris (CEVIPOF). Her recent publications include *Les frontières du racisme* (2011), *Frontiers of Fears: Immigration and Insecurity in the United States and Europe* (2012), and *Migrant Mobilization and Securitization in the US and Europe: How Does It Feel to Be a Threat?* (2015).

Notes

1. United Nations Committee on the Elimination of Racial Discrimination, General recommendation No. 35, GE.13–47139, CERD/C/GC/35, September 26, 2013, http://tbinternet.ohchr.org/_layouts/treatybodyexternal/Download.aspx?symbolno=CERD%2fC%2fGC%2f35&Lang=en.
2. International Convention on the Elimination of Racial Discrimination, December 21, 1965, www.ohchr.org/FR/ProfessionalInterest/Pages/CERD.aspx.
3. Examination of France by the Committee on the Elimination of Racial Discrimination, April 29, 2015, http://www.ohchr.org/FR/NewsEvents/Pages/DisplayNews.aspx?NewsID=15904&LangID=F.
4. The Law of February 3, 2003 (Lellouche Law) made racist, xenophobic, and antisemitic motives into aggravating circumstances and misdemeanors for some crimes. The Law of March 9, 2004 (Perben II) extended aggravating circumstances related to racist motives to new infractions such as threats, theft, and extortion.
5. Examination of France by the Committee on the Elimination of Racial Discrimination.
6. CNCDH, *Rapport racisme, xénophobie, antisémitisme 2013* (Paris: La Documentation française, 2014).
7. Translator's note: The Club de l'Horloge (The Clock Club) is a French conservative association, established in 1974.
8. Pierre-André Taguieff, "L'identité nationale saisie par les logiques de racisation: Aspects, figures et problèmes du racisme différentialiste," *Mots* 12, no. 12 (March 1986): 91–128.
9. Ariane Chebel d'Appollonia, *Les frontières du racisme: Identités, ethnicité, citoyenneté* (Paris: Presses de Sciences Po, 2011).
10. Jean-Marie Le Pen, *Les Français d'abord* (Paris: Carrère/Lafon, 1984).
11. CNCDH, *Rapport racisme, xénophobie, antisémitisme 1997* (Paris: La Documentation française, 1996).
12. CNCDH, *Rapport racisme, xénophobie, antisémitisme 2013.*
13. "Loi portant reconnaissance de la Nation et contribution nationale en faveur des Français rapatriés" (Law concerning the recognition of the nation and national contribution in favor of repatriated French), known as the Debré 2005-158 Law, February 23, 2005, https://www.legifrance.gouv.fr/affichTexte.do?cidTexte=JORFTEXT000000444898. Article 4, requesting that teachers and textbooks "acknowledge and recognize in particular the positive role of the French presence abroad" was subsequently abrogated.
14. Catherine Coquery-Vidrovitch, Gilles Manceron, and Benjamin Stora, "La mémoire partisane du president," *Libération*, August 21, 2007.

15. Nicolas Sarkozy, "Discours de Dakar," July 26, 2007, http://www.lemonde.fr/afrique/article/2007/11/09/le-discours-de-dakar_976786_3212.html.

16. Ibid.

17. Ibid.

18. Makhily Gassama, ed., *L'Afrique répond à Sarkozy: Contre le discours de Dakar* (Paris: Philippe Rey, 2008); and Jean-Pierre Chrétien, ed., *L'Afrique de Sarkozy: Un déni d'histoire* (Paris: Karthala, 2008).

19. *Indigènes de la République*, January 2005, http://indigenes-republique.fr/le-p-i-r/appel-des-indigenes-de-la-republique.

20. Romain Bertrand, "La mise en cause(s) du fait colonial," *Politique africaine*, no. 102 (June 2006): 28–49.

21. Malik Tahar-Chaouh, "Quelques observations sur un reportage de Politis à propos de l'anniversaire des dix ans du PIR," June 5, 2015, http://indigenes-republique.fr/quelques-observations-sur-un-reportage-de-politis-a-propos-de-lanniversaire-des-dix-ans-du-pir.

22. Ariane Chebel d'Appollonia, "Plus blanc que blanc: Réflexion sur le monochrome populiste en Europe," in *De quelle couleur sont les Blancs? Des petits Blancs des colonies au racisme anti-Blancs*, ed. Sylvie Laurent and Thierry Leclère (Paris: La Découverte, 2013), 232–239.

25

COULD ISLAMOPHOBIA BE THE START OF A NEW IDENTITY-BASED BOND IN FRANCE?

Rachid Benzine

ARE THE MAJORITY of French people afraid of Islam? A number of opinion polls over the past decade would appear to suggest as much, just as the rise in popularity of the Front National (a populist party that has fed on the fear of foreigners since its creation in 1972) during recent regional elections also seems to confirm (27 percent of votes in December 2015). However, the French are not necessarily more mistrustful of Muslims than are the Italians, Polish, Spanish, Dutch, Germans, or the British. The French context must be understood in historical terms that are not merely attributable to a colonial past, but also very much contained in the particular relationship of the Republic with religion.

Over the past forty years, due in large part to labor-based immigration, major Western European countries—with France chief among them—have seen the makeup of their populations shift. France today includes between five and six million people with a family connection to Islam (roughly 7 and 8 percent of its population), most of which are from the former French colonial empire, essentially from North Africa, West Africa, and the Middle East (Syria and Lebanon). The North African and Muslim portion of the population, which was discrete at first, has become increasingly visible over the years as a result of its growing size and also because settlement in the French nation has coincided with the revivalism of Islam on the global stage. Moreover, the Muslim portion of the population in France is now mostly made up of French citizens, and it has become increasingly vocal in calling for a proper place in society.

Muslim immigrants of the 1950s to 1980s lived in the shadows, afraid of causing a disturbance. New generations of French Muslims on the other hand want to be recognized. That shift has shaken up society and its institutions; it has modified the human landscape of a number of disadvantaged *banlieues* housing projects in France; and it has led to new topics of reflection that are at times painful.[1] One thing is certain: France is having trouble accepting and defining its ties with Muslims.

Resistance?

In reaction to this new dimension of its identity, it is common to hear that France is a "Judeo-Christian" country, and that that characteristic is shared with most other European countries. It is worth noting, however, that before the Holocaust, France and other European countries did not define themselves as "Judeo"-Christian, but simply as "Christian" (either Catholic or Protestant). And although the Bible shaped Europe for many centuries, Europe is also the fruit of classical Greek and Latin culture, as well as other old cultures (Celtic, Germanic, Iberian, and so on). It also owes more to Islam than it admits (all that Arabs brought to Europe between the ninth and thirteenth centuries, and that led to the Renaissance).

Nevertheless, it is true that Europe—especially Western Europe (Central Europe has a different history due to its proximity to the Ottoman Empire and the experience of being dominated by it until the beginning of the twentieth century)—was built on a distinction from and a rejection of the Muslim world (the Reconquista and the Crusades). At the time of the Crusades (1095–1291) and the Reconquista (between the ninth and the fifteenth centuries), the figure of the Muslim was constructed, in the dominant culture and in the minds of the people, as a threatening, enemy figure; that image has left a trace on the collective and individual perception of Islam by the French and by the Europeans.

However, the perception of Muslims as a threat ebbed in the nineteenth and early twentieth centuries, when the Muslim world in general found itself dominated by the European world, a situation that was due to the colonial conquests and the collapse of the Ottoman Empire (1918), has been replaced by another conception of Muslims, now seen as inferior and contemptible. In the past, they were a people to "civilize," instrumentalize, and dominate.[2] In today's France, Islamophobia has three main sources: the strong memory of the Algerian War, international current events, and the difficult economic and social situation, particularly in the disadvantaged *banlieues* neighborhoods. To that we should also add the accelerated de-Christianization of France, the weakening of republican values as a reference point, and new forms of radical Islam around the world as well as in France, which have been spurred by the oil states of the Arabian peninsula (especially Saudi Arabia and Qatar).

The Algerian War (1954–1962) was a people's revolution fought in the name of the right to self-rule; but it was not fought in the name of a Muslim people against a colonial power with different philosophical and religious affiliations. Nevertheless, in the minds of many French people, this conflict became associated with "Muslim violence." The colonial power described residents of Algeria not as citizens, with the same rights as those living in the mainland, but rather as "Muslim subjects." The war was thus portrayed as a revolt by the subjects of the "French departments in Algeria." The war was as violent as the hundred years of colonial rule, with hundreds of thousands of North African deaths. European deaths were much fewer in number (approximately twenty-five thousand soldiers were killed, and about four thousand Europeans from Algeria). But in France the focus has tended to be on the violence committed by those who revolted. That is due to the "*pied-noir* exodus," which saw a million Europeans forced out of Algeria (including the native Jewish population, since it was granted French nationality in 1870, unlike native Muslims). In addition, almost three million civilians were conscripted into the army during the Algerian War.

Although significantly fewer in number than reprisals by the French army, beheadings and attacks in the streets of Algiers (and in France) left an indelible mark on collective French memory.[3] A million *pieds-noirs* were repatriated to France, but they did not exactly receive a warm welcome (in addition, many of these French from Algeria had Spanish, Italian, and Maltese backgrounds). As a result, they have tended to focus on their pain and nostalgia. Despite being somewhat cut off from society, the *pieds-noirs* and their worldview have had a much larger impact on French society than one might imagine. In particular, the *pied-noir* community acted as an incubator for the Front National, as shown by the various successes of the party within its communities.[4]

Ghosts of the Algerian War

Current events, in which the return of Islam onto the global political scene (notably beginning with the Islamic Revolution in Iran) has received considerable attention since the 1980s, and has awakened ghosts from the Algerian War among a large portion of the French public. First, there were the attacks that occurred in France in the mid-1980s, which were related to the war between Iraq and Iran, and France's commitment to backing the state of Israel. Then there were the attacks in France by the Groupe Islamique Armé (Armed Islamic Group, GIA) in the 1990s, which were related to the new "dark years" experienced by Algeria. Algeria had become a target of armed Islamic extremism, a multifaceted phenomenon that included the legacy of the Muslim Brotherhood (that of the Islamic Salvation Front) and the Salafist resurgence of war in

Afghanistan (marked by the return to Algeria of soldiers from the war against the Soviets in Afghanistan).

After a seventeen-year "lull" (the years between the Khaled Kelkal attacks and others in 1995 and the crimes of Mohamed Merah in Toulouse and in Montauban in 2012), attacks related to international events have become an ongoing threat for French society, potentially occurring at any moment, and with everyone a possible target. The horrors committed in the Middle East and elsewhere by self-proclaimed "jihadist" organizations (al-Qaeda, Boko Haram, Daesh) have now reached Europe, becoming a European obsession. France has been more affected than other European countries, and that is due to its involvement in several wars abroad (Libya, Mali, Syria); but it is also due to its large Muslim population. A radical shift has occurred: a portion of France's "Muslim" youth, with backgrounds from the former colonial empire, although still small in number (and one hopes that it will remain so), subscribe to Daesh's conspiracy theories and have become an armed branch of the al-Baghdadi caliphate from within the country.[5]

In such a context, the majority of French Muslims live in fear of being targets of retaliation; they have doubts regarding their future in the French nation; and they have proven unable to develop a convincing discourse capable of reassuring society. When French people are asked to describe what is the main threat to their security, terrorist attacks are high on the list, and the association between terrorism and Islam is often quickly evoked, even if the majority of respondents emphasize the importance of not conflating "Muslims" with "terrorists." Forty years of massive unemployment (a million jobseekers in 1976 versus four million in 2016!) have strained the fabric of French society, creating inequality between residents and fostering delinquency and crime, decreased voter turnout in disadvantaged neighborhoods, increased far-right votes (a third of voters), and led to insular communities organized around ultraconservative forms of Islam.

Among those most affected by the economic crisis are families with recent immigrant backgrounds (over the past few decades), who find themselves on the bottom of the social ladder. The deterioration in the quality of life in *banlieues* neighborhoods is often associated with North African and African youth, who are predominantly Muslim, mostly out of work (while the average unemployment rate in France is 10 percent, it can reach 30 to 50 percent in *banlieues* neighborhoods), who engage in a parallel illegal economy, whose public behavior flies in the face of social harmony, and who flaunt their religious affiliation in public.[6] The *banlieues,* together with their residents, who often have ties to the former colonial empire (that is how they are seen and consider themselves, including "third-generation" immigrants), are viewed by the rest of the

French populace as dangerous places. And even if many "*Français de souche*" or people of "pure French stock"—a category that has emerged in recent years to speak of those who are not "people of color"—also live in such neighborhoods (all told, five million people live in these suburban zones), the overwhelming image of them is one where "immigrants" from Africa and their descendants live. The media, political discourse, and the minds of many French people are dominated by the threat these *banlieues* represent with respect to social harmony and in terms of international terrorism. As a result, a dichotomy has begun to assert itself within the French populace, between "us, non-Muslims" and "them, Muslims," which is mirrored by the dichotomy "us, Muslims" and "them, non-Muslims."

France is undoubtedly still traumatized by the loss of its colonial empire (which also put an end to its illusions of being a great power) and by the wake of the Algerian War; it has proven unable to adequately integrate the children of its postcolonial immigrants into society through work; over the past forty years, France (whether under socialist or liberal right governance) has failed to weave the Muslim portion of its population into the social fabric of the nation and into its national narrative—to the point that the majority of Muslims feel that they are "second-class citizens," "natives of the Republic,"[7] and "illegitimate French" citizens.

Since the vast majority of French Muslims comes from North African or sub-Saharan African backgrounds (sometimes Turkish as well, but to a lesser degree), the perception of belonging to Islam is automatically associated, in the minds of most people, with a foreign ethnic or national background. Thus, the *question musulmane* (the "Muslim question")[8] is also an ethnic issue, or, as it would be called in other countries (notably in the Anglo-Saxon world), a "racial issue."

A "Shifting" Society

The shift in French society, which includes a history of immigration and poorly managed integration (especially bad since French society refuses to accept that it is a society of immigrants, despite being so since the nineteenth century), is occurring not only in a context of economic crisis and a change in the labor market—with the end of the exponential growth of the period between 1950 and 1970—but also within the framework of massive de-Christianization and the decreasing influence of republican culture and its values of equality and fraternity.

Between 1980 and 2015, the proportion of Catholics in France fell almost thirty points, with half of French people now claiming they "have no religion." The drop in Christian affiliation has gone hand in hand with decreased attachment (except in brief moments, as was the case after the attacks in January and November 2015 in Paris) to the Republic's great values and symbols. Indeed, French society has, for the most part, become a society of individuals who behave more as consumers than as citizens, and who measure their value based on their purchasing power. Displays of Islam in the national space have therefore been interpreted as a rise in power of a "strong" religion capable of replacing Christianity, which has been in retreat. The fear is that Islam will spread throughout French society, which itself no longer has a common set of identity markers or ethnic references.

People are afraid of Islam for reasons that go beyond painful memories and the murderous monsters that have emerged within France. Indeed, Islam contains the threat of a return to religion in a society that, for more than two centuries, has been in the process of freeing itself from religious powers and limiting their influence over government. Whereas Western Europe has experienced a decreasing rate of Christianity over the past sixty years, France began that process much earlier, with the 1789 Revolution, which was waged in large part against the Catholic Church—a pillar of the monarchy. France is also a country where the memory of the Wars of Religion between Catholics and Protestants (that raged throughout Europe in the sixteenth century) is still strong; the fear of seeing the resurgence of such violence is very real.

The first major debates surrounding Islam in France appeared in 1989, when the first Muslim headscarves appeared in schools. The reaction within public opinion—beginning with teachers—was, for the most part, to vigorously contest a return of "religion" to public education. For many (and this is a radical difference between today's Western European societies and the United States), religion is a threat to individual liberties, freedom of thought, the ability to lead our lives according to our own values, and more generally, since religion tends to undermine social unity, it is seen as a threat to social harmony.

Moreover, the fact that Islam in Europe may be the result of trends toward new forms of Islamization, which are being orchestrated by Saudi Arabia's Wahhabism and Qatar's Sunnism (similar to the Muslim Brotherhood), does not put French society at ease. It seems to many that Muslim French citizens are seeking to reintroduce references to God and their commitment to his commandments into society. In addition, many precepts embodied by militant Islam contradict habits acquired by Western European societies over the past several decades, and even centuries—strict divisions between genders in public spaces, limitations of sexual freedom (from this point of view, Western Europe, and France in particular, is much more liberal than the United States), dietary restrictions, and so on. Militant Islam is thus seen as an instrument of warfare against social evolutions that, one should not forget, were generally developed in opposition to the Catholic Church (the latest such evolution being same-sex marriage). Together, all of these accumulated fears toward Islam, which is seen in terms of its growth and aspirations of conquest, characterize French society as a whole. They are shared by large portions of the working class, by large swaths of the middle class, and by both sides of the political spectrum.

In a France that, since the 1980s (with the arrival of the left to power), has had trouble defining its present-day identity and the reasons and values of "social harmony," the fear of Islam could very well offer a new form of bonding. When we have trouble defining who we are, the most natural reaction is to decide "who we are not." In the context of today's crises, the "we are not Muslim" may seem like an easy solution to our identity issues. However, it comes with some dangerous risks. Almost 10 percent of the French population has (to varying degrees) some ties to Islam. If we are to imagine a peaceful future society, we will have to work "with Muslims" and not "against" them.

Rachid Benzine is a specialist on Islam, affiliated with the Institut d'Etudes Politiques (Aix-en-Provence), and author of numerous works including *Les nouveaux penseurs de l'islam* (2004), *Le Coran expliqué aux jeunes* (2013), and *La République, l'Église et l'islam: Une révolution française* (2016).

Notes

1. American political journalist Christopher Caldwell conducted an in-depth study (*Reflections on the Revolution in Europe: Immigration, Islam, and the West* [New York: Doubleday, 2009]) on the upheavals brought about as a result of Islam taking root in France. His conclusions are debatable, but they have the merit of putting a finger on realities that are rarely studied with such calm, nonpartisan thinking in France. See also Jonathan Laurence and Justin Vaïsse, *Intégrer l'islam: La France et ses musulmans, enjeux et réussites* (Paris: Éditions Odile Jacob, 2007).

2. See the important collaborative book edited by French-Algerian scholar Mohammed Arkoun, *Histoire de l'islam et des musulmans en France du Moyen Âge à nos jours* (Paris: Albin Michel, 2006). See also Sadek Sellam, *La France et ses musulmans: Un siècle de politique musulmane (1895–2005)* (Paris: Fayard, 2006).

3. Todd Shepard published a very relevant book on the repercussions of the Algerian War and the independence of Algeria on French identity, the functioning of its institutions, and on social peace: *The Invention of Decolonization: The Algerian War and the Remaking of France* (Ithaca, NY: Cornell University Press, 2008).

4. See Jean-Yves Camus and Nicolas Lebourg, *Les droites extrêmes en Europe* (Paris: Seuil, 2015).

5. See the surveys conducted over more than thirty years by Gilles Kepel, *Les banlieues de l'islam: Naissance d'une religion en France* (Paris: Seuil, 1987) and more recently, Gilles Kepel and Antoine Jardin, *Terreur dans l'Hexagone: Genèse du djihad français* (Paris: Gallimard, 2015).

6. Gilles Kepel, *Quatre-vingt-treize* (Paris: Gallimard, 2012). An updated and very detailed portrait of Islam in France such as it appears in Seine-Saint-Denis, French department number 93 located in the Île-de-France near Paris, and commonly referred to as the "93."

7. The "*Indigènes de la République*" (Natives of the Republic) is the name used by a political movement that appeared in France in 2005 and that speaks out against the "neocolonial culture" of French society, particularly as regards the political establishment, and in its relationship with generations related to the former colonial empire that represent today an important part of the population.

8. This was in fact the title chosen by a retired police officer and former adviser to numerous French ministers of the interior for what is a rather dense book, yet one that nevertheless offers a wealth of information on the complex reality of Islam in France: Bernard Godard, *La question musulmane en France* (Paris: Fayard, 2015).

26

THE BLACK QUESTION AND THE *EXHIBIT B* CONTROVERSY

Alain Mabanckou and Dominic Thomas

When it comes to the question of colonialism in France, more often than not, the tendency is to conjure a range of "philanthropic" or "humanist" measures. This is somehow deemed necessary in the process of extracting populations residing is far-flung places out of the heart of darkness, and thereby justifying overseas colonial expansion. As a consequence, there has been no real debate on these and related questions, even though formerly colonized peoples and their descendants continue to be the object of racial prejudice and subjected to humiliation. Nevertheless, efforts have been made to alleviate tensions and to encourage the authorities to recognize how the legacy of colonialism continues to impact contemporary society.

Among these initiatives is the controversial *Exhibit B* performance (2010–2014), events that share important points of commonality with other important contemporary cultural, political, and social debates on the question of "Black France" and "Human Zoos." As it so happens, the artistic installations of South African Brett Bailey featured real black actors playing the roles of "savages," thereby effectively reenacting scenes once staged at exhibitions during the colonial era at which their forefathers had been exhibited as a way of entertaining white audiences.

Exhibiting the Black "Savage" Yesterday and Today

Let us not forget, as the *Dictionnaire de l'Académie française* reminds us, that to "exhibit" is first and foremost to "represent or to show something with the aim of producing a certain effect." In fact, if one reads a little further, one discovers that the definition is in fact pejorative, implying "complacency" and "impudence."

In other words, the very process of exhibiting at one time was aimed specifically at staging the "savage."

These exhibitions have, in recent years, been extensively studied and findings widely disseminated, most notably at the Quai Branly Museum in Paris that held an important exhibition, "The Invention of the Savage," during 2011 and 2012 and that attracted over three hundred thousand visitors.[1] However, the phenomenon of the human exhibition can itself be inscribed in a much longer history that dates back to the end of the fifteenth and beginning of the sixteenth centuries and that were very common all the way up until the twentieth century. Children, women, and men from Africa, the Americas, Asia, and Oceania were displayed in Europe in museums, freak shows, zoos, universal exhibitions, fairs, and at the circus. These exhibitions functioned simultaneously as tools of propaganda and as great sources of entertainment, shaping perceptions of the "other" while also having a significant impact on racialist thinking at the time and also today in terms of how humans are divided, differentiated, classified, and hierarchized.[2] But they also served to bolster the myth of the "savage" (in the United States and in Europe, but also further afield in Japan), including concepts of "race" and segregationist practices. They may seem shocking today but at the time they were considered "normal," opportunities to familiarize oneself with colonized peoples that needed to be rescued from backward conditions and barbarism. Rarely was it enough for the "savage" to just be different, he or she was expected to play the roles whites expected and had ascribed to them.

Exhibit B was thus a show that had pedagogical objectives, but that was also designed with the aim of provoking audiences, since Brett Bailey's show, staged as it was in twenty-first century France (among other locations), included twelve scenes with living black characters. Brett Bailey has been a relentless advocate for his project, although no doubt was somewhat surprised by the polemical reaction it triggered in France. When *Exhibit B* was staged at the Avignon Festival in 2013, Brett Bailey sought to clarify his position, explaining that the "work in question focuses on 'human zoos,' a phenomenon that was widespread during the colonial era and that attracted tens of millions of European and American visitors at the time, and that have been forgotten about today. My research made it possible for me to better understand the hidden aims of these exhibitions, and how they were used to propagate racial stereotypes and legitimize colonialism and therefore various atrocities perpetrated by colonizers."[3] As he went on to argue, "*Exhibit B* critiques the 'human zoos' and ethnographic displays that showed Africans as objects of scientific curiosity through the 19th and early 20th centuries. Translated here into twelve tableaux, each features motionless performers placed in settings drawn from real life. Collectively they confront colonial atrocities committed in Africa, European notions of racial supremacy and the plight of immigrants today."[4]

The indignation felt by some and the decision to cancel the South African artist's "show" demonstrates how difficult it is today in France to talk about "race." As Fatima El-Tayeb recently argued in a book on racial identity in Europe, "it seems that instead of reconceptualizing Europe in order to include minorities, the unification process creates a narrative that not only continues to exclude racialized minorities but also defines them as the very essence of non-Europeanness in terms that link migration to supposedly invincible differences of race, culture, and religion."[5]

A Very French Debate?

Brett Bailey later ran into problems at the Barbican Center in London in 2014 where the show was also canceled. The sociologist Kehinde Andrews, in a conversation with the artist Stella Odunlami, published in the *Guardian* newspaper on September 27, 2014, condemned the exhibition and leveled accusations of racism. According to him, "such objectification was at the heart of the human zoos, and recreating this re-exoticizes and reproduces the original racism."[6]

Across the channel in France, Olivier Barlet, the editor of the journal *Africultures*, shared Andrews's assessment, stating that "claims for equality cannot be made simply by displaying the inventory of all the injustices incurred by victims."[7] Film critic and regular contributor to *Africultures*, Claire Diao, asked: "Is this polemic not perhaps an opportunity for France's black community, that has no rights—from a legal point of view—to define itself in those terms, to seek a space in the media from which to voice its concerns on the subject of widespread discrimination that is experienced on a daily basis, and on the rise?"[8]

The artist's approach to the history of racism and its legacies in contemporary society have been described as "shocking," "humiliating," and even "racist." However, Brett Bailey's goal is to challenge us to interrogate the boundaries of history, to look at ourselves in the mirror, to see whether our ancestors were "exhibited" or the "exhibitors." In other words, to what degree can we reconstitute the most humiliating chapters in the history of a subjugated people that were put on display in zoological gardens? Might the cinema or the theater, or even certain literary forms such as the novel, the short story, or a fable have been more appropriate artistic means of reconstituting this history than the "direct" work of an artist who decided to have actors "pose," actors, one should not forget, who had auditioned to play these roles?

Given that Brett Bailey is a white South African, born in 1967 and who therefore grew up under the apartheid system, and whose previous work includes the installation *Terminal: Blood Diamonds* as a way of drawing attention to racial inequalities, one might be inclined to reproach him for shedding "the tears of the white man," that feeling of self-hatred and guilt that drives some to seek redemption through repentance for the sins of their white forefathers.[9] But it would be intellectually dishonest to reduce the artist's work to a settling of accounts or a simple search for redemption.

One might be able to reproach the artist for his courage and originality, the privilege of artistic expression, no matter which form it takes. To this end, we share Éric Fassin's consideration of the complex way in which art can be misunderstood, in other words between "intentionality" and "effect": "How can a work of art, anti-racist in its intentions, be deemed racist in its effects [and] how does one begin to represent the dehumanization of the persecutors without at the same time repeating what they did to their victims? "[10]

Brett Bailey would like us to return to our history books, something that is all the more complicated in France where there is tremendous reluctance, resistance even, to examining colonial history. Often, one finds the persistence of notions of "grandeur" alongside pride for the "civilizing mission" over, as the Martinican poet Aimé Césaire wrote, "those who have invented neither powder nor compass, those who could harness neither steam nor electricity."[11] This complacency has been an obstacle to a concerted reckoning with the nation's colonial past and, in particular, its legacy on the postcolonial subject's unconscious, marked by a "neurosis" which, as Frantz Fanon reminded us in 1952, means that "scientific objectivity had to be ruled out, since the alienated and the neurotic were my brother, my sister, and my father."[12]

How does one begin the process of moving on, of starting afresh, when some members of the French population, notably those that are today described as belonging to a "Black France," believe their ancestors were not only humiliated but that these humiliations are ignored in history textbooks?[13] Let us not forget that the figure of the "savage" that black populations in France today just happen to be the descendants of, was born and had been fabricated *in* and *by* the West as a way to illustrate the opposition between civilized peoples and those who had presumably remained in the heart of darkness.

The reluctance therefore, in France, to look into the mirror is related to the absence of an "objective" or "scholarly" discourse on the methods that shaped colonial propaganda. This has slowed down the process of integrating these citizens into a nation in which "Black France" played a crucial role in "building" the France of today and who are still waiting for the contributions of their great-grandparents to be included in history textbooks. Pascal Blanchard continues to remind us, and with the kind of irony he is known for, that France has more museums than any other country—including several museums dedicated to the history of the "sabot" (a traditional wooden shoe found in Brittany, among other places), and yet not a single one devoted to its colonial history! Only too aware of the need for curricular materials in this underrepresented area, his position serves to counter those critiques formulated against Brett Bailey's exhibition: "More dialogue is needed with audiences and those who are critical of the exhibition so that this past can be deconstructed. The duty of memory should not be boycotted, but rather transmitted. . . . Not enough attention has been paid to this history and it remains relatively unknown, few people know what happened here, in this country of ours."[14] The greatest challenge then is to find a way to tell this history, to recount it, to identify the legacy of that past in today's society and to recognize that there is no such thing as a French nation without these "others" who have traveled through history initially as "savages," then as "natives," and then later as "*tirailleurs* infantrymen" in the wars in Europe. *Exhibit B* stands therefore as an important reminder as to the role of memory, while also pointing to the West's ingratitude for these "others" who were once treated little better than cattle at a time when the imperative was to bolster the French empire.

Those French associations that described the exhibition as "racist" failed to grasp the artist's intentions that were specifically aimed at fighting against racial prejudice and criticizing the long history of human exhibitions and zoos in which black people had been put on display by white people. In other words, the former were put on display precisely *because they were black*, "strange," "savage," and not because they had particular skills or artistic qualities that might otherwise have justified attendance at the spectacle. For Brett Bailey, the motivation comes from wanting to make sure that the dust of forgetting does not end up covering over memory; "the preferable option is to take the opportunity presented by the installation and the controversy it has generated, as a starting point for a discussion on the representation of racism and the under-representation of those who are racialized [*racisés*]."[15] One might very well argue that had France done a better job of devoting a space in which colonial history could be explored, *Exhibit B* would most likely not have been the source of so much disagreement.[16] This exhibition and installation force us to rethink the place and status of black people in French society, at a time when offensive comments and declarations made by politicians have become all too common, seemingly unaware of some of the darkest chapters in French history. In fact, we find ourselves in an era in which there has been a resurgence of racialized discourse and in which discriminatory statements are everyday occurrences.

The Resurgence of Racialized Discourse

On January 20, 2015, French prime minister Manuel Valls underscored the existence in France of a "territorial, social, and ethnic apartheid," of forms of discrimination associated with family names, gender inequalities, and in terms of our focus in this chapter, with those pertaining to "skin color." The political right adopted a diametrically opposed response, insisting on the crucial importance of identity and constitutional principles. On February 5, 2012, during the presidential campaign, then minister of the interior Claude Guéant, whose UMP party were concerned with inroads being made by the Front National, declared that "in view of our republican principles, not all civilizations, practices, or cultures, are equal." A year later, the minister of justice, Christiane Taubira, who is a black woman from Guiana, was compared to a monkey by Anne-Sophie Leclère, a Front National candidate at the upcoming local elections. And then, on September 27, 2015, the former government minister and member of the European Parliament, Nadine Morano, announced on the television program "On n'est pas couché" on *France 2* that France was a "Judeo-Christian country" of "white race."

Needless to say, taken together, these statements are both insulting and contemptuous toward the figure of the "other," while also revealing the extent to which racial taxonomies and conceptions of race elaborated several centuries ago and that made the degrading classification of people possible, are very much alive and well.[17] When it comes to discussing the question of a "Black France," critics are quick to point out that France has adopted a colorblind approach to such questions, from which we find the tenuous relationship between cultural, political, and social visibility, and constitutional principles organized around the invisibility of citizens and the centrality of republican ideals and values. Having said this, these have by no means precluded the existence of discrimination based on origins and yet again, one finds oneself having to remind people that this so-called "Black France" is the story of a diasporic presence in metropolitan France coming from all four corners of the world and over several centuries.[18]

In fact, the word *nègre* was used in the eighteenth century to refer to populations of African descent, as for example in the *Encyclopédie ou dictionnaire raisonné des sciences, des arts et des métiers* in which one could find under the entry *nègre* from 1765 that "not only the color, but also the facial traits distinguish them from other men: large and flat noses, thick lips, and wool instead of hair. They appear to constitute a new species of mankind." As Achille Mbembe has shown, "Those we once referred to as Blacks were later to appear as people who, precisely because of their ontological difference had represented a caricature of the principle of exteriority (opposition to the principle of inclusion). It was therefore extremely difficult to imagine that they were in fact just like us, that we could be similar."[19]

The French "Legacy" and "Heritage"

The term *apartheid* is, of course, a loaded one, most commonly used to describe the *racial segregation* imposed by the National Party in South Africa after 1948, and a range of juridical documents such as the Prohibition of Mixed Marriages Act (1949) that prohibited marriage between whites and members of other "races" or the Populations Registration Act (1950) that categorized people according to racial characteristics and their rights. We could also mention the Immorality Amendment Act (1950) that prohibited sexual relations between whites and nonwhites and the Group Areas Act that divided up land according to racial criteria. In a broader sense then, the term *apartheid* can be applied to the context of both British and French empires or, for that matter, to forms of racial segregation practices in the United States that would only officially come to an end in the 1960s. Achille Mbembe confirms these observations: "A key element of French colonial humanism consisted in acknowledging in the features of peoples who had been conquered by France the multiple faces of humanity. . . . The colonial enterprise itself had been a relatively multiracial project. . . . Minorities were progressively hidden away, placed in the dark and covered with a veil of prudery that obfuscated their visibility in the nation's political and public life."[20] The French case may not be the result of a "legal" apartheid, but what we have before us is a situational apartheid that has been handed down as a "legacy" or "heritage." This postcolonial racism which France does not want to hear about serves to elucidate the present situation and lends credence to Manuel Valls' declaration."[21]

"We Are No Longer from Over There . . . Henceforth, We Are from Here"

The integration of this "other" remains one of the greatest challenges confronting France, all the more so given that this "other" is connected to the French territory over a much longer history and in terms of an increasing presence and visibility, including as a representative of the nation itself both within France and also at an international level. Having said this, for those French people who are "from elsewhere" or descendants of parents from the African continent, this process of identification has not always been straightforward. In 2012, in the preface to *La France noire*, Alain Mabanckou (one of the authors of this chapter), wrote that "today, it is nothing short of outright heresy to say out loud that one is no longer from *over there* but rather *from here*. Severing the umbilical cord is the first step toward a new life. But just how many Blacks of

France have broken this Gordian knot? We desperately want to be admitted on a territory while at the same time clinging in our unconscious—and even in our consciousness—to a substitute territory, a mythic territory that in reality we know nothing about and that in any case is not waiting for us."[22]

In his book *La condition noire,* Pap Ndiaye described a kind of "minority politics" that made it possible to "concentrate on the ways in which specific groups, minorities, are discriminated against, in other words subject to a different treatment because of illegitimate criteria . . . a group of people sharing, *nolens volens,* the social experience of being generally considered Black."[23] When segregation officially ended in the United States, several measures were taken to eliminate a range of linguistic terms susceptible to perpetuate discrimination. The word *negro,* for example, associated as it was with color, was deemed pejorative and humiliating and replaced with *African American,* a reference deemed closer to the origins of the individuals concerned and who claimed roots in that heritage. In France, "the word *nègre* was to be avoided because of its contemptuous nature and strong colonial connotation."[24] Interestingly enough, recourse was initially made to the term as a way of claiming one's origins, indeed in order to create a particular aesthetic that would reach its apogee in the Negritude movement. As early as 1927, the Comité de défense de la race nègre published an article in the newspaper *La Voix des Nègres* stating that "It is our Negro race that we wish to set on the path of complete liberation from the yoke of slavery it has endured. It is our unfettered right and our duty to enforce the respect due to our race, and to insist upon its having equal status with all the world's other races, and we call ourselves Negroes!"[25]

And so what might well define what it is to be black today? Éric Fassin offers a fruitful lead:

> What defines Black people is less their origin than the manner in which they are treated (as foreigners) because of their appearance . . . Racialization not only affects those who are racialized [*racisés*]; in a society in which everyone is defined in racial terms, through no fault of their own (or not, as the case may be), well even White people become . . . Whites . . . And this is reason for concern today since are we not at risk of a gulf opening up between a "White" antiracism and a "non-White" antiracism? This is what was so worrisome in the controversy surrounding *Exhibit B* . . . Namely a tension between two opposing ways of approaching antiracism that appear to be getting racialized.[26]

The controversy that Brett Bailey's exhibition triggered, in addition to sparking further debate on the question of "race" in France—and therefore also a consideration of "Black France"—provided an indication as to the crucial importance of attending to those "memory gaps" in national history. The former "grandeur" of the French empire should not justify forgetting humiliation and suffering which, if they remain unacknowledged as such, might very well gradually provide the contours of a group identity for those who will never otherwise find a way to identify with republican values, perceived as prescribed by a "Judeo-Christian" society of "white race," to use the nauseous terms which, thus far at least, have yet to fill certain right-wingers with indignation.

Another glaring example of French paternalism came with the launch by the government in November 2009 of the "Grand Debate on National Identity," a political event that coincided with the award of the prestigious Goncourt literary prize to Marie NDiaye (the daughter of a white French woman and black Senegalese father) for her novel *Trois femmes puissantes* (*Three Strong Women*),[27] a writer who had been critical of President Nicolas Sarkozy's immigration policies and had opted to leave France and go and live in Berlin.[28] Learning of the comments she had made in an interview, Éric Raoult, an elected UMP deputy and mayor of Raincy, declared: "We awarded her the Goncourt Prize . . . France has given her the Goncourt Prize."[29] The question remains as to what exactly remains lurking behind this "we" and this "France." This is where the main identity challenges and issues of the day confronting France, and the main tensions surrounding the "black question," are to be found.

Alain Mabanckou is a Franco-Congolese author and Professor of French and Francophone Studies at UCLA. His novels include *Blue White Red* (1998), *African Psycho* (2003), *Broken Glass* (2005), *Memoirs of a Porcupine* (2006), *Black Bazaar* (2009), *Tomorrow I'll Be Twenty* (2010), and *The Lights of Pointe-Noire* (2013). He is the recipient of numerous literary prizes, such as the *Grand Prix Littéraire de l'Afrique noire*, *Prix Renaudot*, *Prix Georges Brassens*, and the *Grand Prix de Littérature Henri Gal* from the Académie Française for his life's work.

Dominic Thomas is Madeleine L. Letessier Professor and Chair of the Department of French and Francophone Studies at UCLA. Elected to the Academy of Europe in 2015, his books include *Black France: Colonialism, Immigration, and Transnationalism* (2007) and *Africa and France: Postcolonial Cultures, Migration, and Racism* (2013), and he is coauthor, editor, or coeditor of *Museums in Postcolonial Europe* (2010), *A Companion to Comparative Literature* (2011), *La France noire* (2011), *Colonial Culture in France since the Revolution* (2014), *The Invention of Race* (2014), *Francophone Afropean Literatures* (2014), and *Vers la guerre des identités* (2016).

Notes

1. See Pascal Blanchard, Gilles Boëtsch and Nanette Jacomijn Snoep, *Human Zoos: The Invention of the Savage* (Paris and Arles: Actes Sud/Musée du quai Branly, 2011), Pascal Blanchard, Nicolas Bancel, Gilles Boëtsch, Éric Deroo, and Sandrine Lemaire, eds., *Human Zoos: Sciences and Spectacle in the Age of Empire* (Liverpool: Liverpool University Press, 2008), and Pascal Blanchard, Nicolas Bancel, Gilles Boëtsch, Éric Deroo, and Sandrine Lemaire, eds., *Zoos humains et exhibitions coloniales: 150 ans d'invention de l'autre* (Paris: La Découverte, 2011).

2. See Nicolas Bancel, Thomas David, and Dominic Thomas, eds., *The Invention of Race: Scientific and Popular Representations* (New York: Routledge, 2014).

3. Jean-François Perrier, "Entretien avec Brett Bailey," Avignon Festival, 2013.

4. Ibid.

5. Fatima El-Tayeb, *European Others: Queering Ethnicity in Postnational Europe* (Minneapolis: University of Minnesota Press, 2011).

6. Stella Odunlami and Kehinde Andrews, "Is Art Installation Exhibit B Racist?," *The Guardian*, September 27, 2014.

7. Olivier Barlet, "*Exhibit B*: Un spectacle à critiquer," *Africultures*, December 3, 2014, www.africultures.com/php/index.php?nav=article&no=12593.

8. Claire Diao, "*Exhibit B*: Bien plus qu'une polémique," *Africultures*, November 26, 2014, www.africultures.com/php/index.php?nav=article&no=12563.

9. Pascal Bruckner, *The Tears of the White Man: Compassion as Contempt*, trans. William R. Beer (New York: The Free Press, 1986).

10. Éric Fassin, "L'art doit tenir compte de la sensibilité des victimes du colonialisme," *Le Monde*, November 28, 2014.

11. Aimé Césaire, *Notebook of a Return to the Native Land*, in *Aimé Césaire: The Collected Poetry*, trans. Clayton Eshleman and Annette Smith (Berkeley and Los Angeles: University of California Press, 1983 [1939]), 67.

12. Frantz Fanon, *Black Skin, White Masks*, trans. Richard Philcox (New York: Grove Press, 2008 [1952]), 200.

13. See for example Dominic Thomas, *Black France: Colonialism, Immigration, and Transnationalism* (Bloomington and Indianapolis: Indiana University Press, 2007).

14. Pascal Blanchard, "*Exhibit B:* Ce spectacle n'est pas raciste, c'est l'inverse," *L'Obs*, November 29, 2014.

15. Fassin, "L'art doit tenir compte de la sensibilité des victimes du colonialisme."

16. For the most recent contribution to this debate, see Pascal Blanchard and Nicolas Bancel, "Pour un musée des colonisations et de l'esclavage!," *Le Monde*, May 15, 2016.

17. See Sonya Faure, interview with Pascal Blanchard, "Insultes envers Taubira: 'C'est un racisme pur et dur, un racisme de peau,'" *Libération*, October 29, 2013.

18. See and Pascal Blanchard et al., *La France noire: Trois siècles de présences* (Paris: La Découverte, 2011).

19. Achille Mbembe, "Le noir n'existe pas plus que le blanc," *Africultures*, nos. 92–93 (February 2013): 11.

20. Achille Mbembe, "Provincializing France," trans. Janet Roitman, *Public Culture* 23, no.1 (2011): 89.

21. Nicolas Bancel, Pascal Blanchard, and Dominic Thomas, "Postcolonial France: From the Colonial Fracture to Ethnic Apartheid (2005–2015)," *Occasion* 9 (2015), http://arcade.stanford.edu/sites/default/files/article_pdfs/Occasion_v09_bancel-Blanchard-Thomas_01Pass_final.pdf.

22. Alain Mabanckou, "Préface," in *La France noire*, ed. Blanchard et al., 7 [6–7] See also the documentary by Isabelle Boni-Claverie, *Trop noire pour être française?* (Quark/Arte France, 2015).

23. Pap Ndiaye, *La condition noire: Essai sur une minorité française* (Paris: Calmann-Levy, 2008), 368 and 21–24.

24. Sylvie Chalaye, "'Noir,' 'nègre,' 'homme de couleur' . . . ces mots réducteurs," *Africultures*, nos. 92–93 (February 2013).

25. Comité de défense de la race nègre, "'Le mot Nègre,'" *La Voix des Nègres*, no. 1 (January 1927). See Christopher L. Miller, *Nationalists and Nomads: Essays on Francophone African Literature* (Chicago: University of Chicago Press, 1998).

26. Éric Fassin, Interview with Caroline Trouillet, "Les pouvoirs publics sont responsables d'une racialisation de la société qu'ils prétendent pourtant combattre," *Afriscope*, no. 42, September 23, 2015, www.africultures.com/php/?nav=article&no=13222.

27. Marie NDiaye, *Trois femmes puissantes* (Paris: Gallimard, 2009); *Three Strong Women*, trans. John Fletcher (New York: Vintage, 2012).

28. See Nelly Kaprièlian, "Marie Ndiaye aux prises avec le Monde," *les inrockuptibles*, no. 726 (November 18–24, 2009): 32.

29. See Dominic Thomas, "The 'Marie NDiaye Affair,' or the Coming of a Postcolonial *Évoluée*," in *Africa and France: Postcolonial Cultures, Migration and Racism* (Bloomington and Indianapolis: Indiana University Press, 2013), 139–155.

27

CULTURAL ORIENTALIZATION OR POLITICAL OCCIDENTALISM?

Nicolas Lebourg

THE FRONT NATIONAL, which reached new heights in popularity in the first round of regional elections in December 2015, has developed a strategy, since 2010, around exposing Islamization, which it claims is inherent to multicultural society. Meanwhile, Islamophobia cannot be limited to members of the Front National, and it has certainly not replaced antisemitism. Unburdened from ideological partisanship, antisemitism has become a product of cultural consumption. The move to the political right in thinking about such questions has created a fragmented image of a French society in need of an authoritarian response. It has revitalized the fear of otherness in a variety of forms. Such thinking, like the appeal of the idea that French people are being "replaced" by North African Muslims, shows that the notion of racism based on biology has not disappeared. Cultural racism has not replaced biological racism. The fear of others is based on a play between the ethnic and the cultural. Indeed, under the Vichy regime, the Jewish "race" was defined by the cultural practices of one's forbears.

Antisemitism and racism based on biology are both factors of social marginalization. The "replacement" myth (also invoked as a "substitution" or in terms of "supplantation") mentioned above is a testament to that (much like the idea of Eurabia), but it did not gain widespread acceptance until it was dissociated from the notion of a "Jewish plot." The issue is not, however, to decide which poses the greatest threat, antisemitism or Islamophobia. Rather, I am interested in better understanding the fears introduced by the idea that France is somehow being wiped out by Middle Eastern influences, which some social actors perceive as being Judeo-Israeli and others as Arab-Muslim. Some see themselves as victims of a massive import of Middle Eastern conflicts; they believe they are victims of competition with Eastern economies.

Tension against Islam

Although the first occurrence of "Islamophobia" dates back to 1910 (quickly following the invention of the term "xenophobia" in 1901), the issue of Islamophobia is hardly a colonial one. Nationalist figures such as Charles Maurras and Édouard Drumont praised Islam and Arabs in the late nineteenth century—even if the former began to worry about Islam with the construction of the Great Mosque, inaugurated in 1926, and the first migratory influx from North Africa in the early 1920s—while Maurice Bardèche, one of the most influential adherents of French fascism, praised the virility—seen as Roman—of the Koran.

In Algeria, between 1900 and 1945, colonials and their descendants developed a derogatory lexical field for natives (*bicots, bougnoules, gris,* and so on; the terms are still used in racist discourse, with the addition of *muzz* in 2001) that dealt more in ethnic prejudices than it did in Islamophobia. Indeed, the reference to religion was preferred to avoid referencing ethnicity. The colonial administration referred to Algerians as "French Muslims" or "French from Muslim backgrounds." Before gaining success in elections, the Front National made use of such designations to avoid relying on "Arabs," for fear of being accused of racism.[1] Today, Marine Le Pen takes every available opportunity to pay tribute to the *harkis.*[2] Such a strategy allows her to claim that she is not Islamophobic, and to assert that she does not conceive of nationality in terms of ethnic criteria. Having said this, at the Front National's 2015 summer university held in Marseille, Stéphane Ravier, a senator and mayor who embraces an ethnic conception of the nation, gave the welcome speech in which he decried the issue of "replacement." Moreover, the arrival of the *harkis* was perceived by some members on the left, speaking from an anti-imperialist perspective,[3] as an ethnic and religious invasion which contributed to making this population one of the key points of argumentation for the Front National in relation to the memory of French Algeria.

The relationship between French nationalism and Islam will not evolve based on endogenous factors. The issue of Algeria and the end of the colonial wars (during which communism was still the designated enemy) were further aggravated by the impact of the Iranian Revolution in 1979 and the dialectical game between the electoral far-right and small groups from the radical right. Jules Monnerot, a specialist of global "communist subversion" and subsequent Front National member, began to alter his discourse on the Muslim-Arab world in the 1980s. An external threat, an internal subversion: anticommunist denunciation schemes were applied to Iran, Islam, and immigrants.[4]

The Iranian issue seems to have shifted and undermined ideological positions. A portion of the far left, notably within the Trotskyist Fourth International, likely misinterpreted the meaning of the Iranian Revolution according to the principle of "marching separately and striking together." On the secular left, the first marker came on February 11, 1982, when Prime Minister Pierre Mauroy referred in *Le Monde* newspaper to a strike by immigrant laborers as the actions of "Islamist agitators," comparable to "ayatollahs." In short, a portion of the left, being confronted with political responsibilities and the ambition to implement economic changes, sought to delegitimize immigrant laborers through its traditional identity markers (for example, secularism, human rights, equality). Another of the left's historical identity markers was affected in 1989, with the debates surrounding the headscarf in schools.

However, at the time, the media and politicians did not speak of the *hijab*, but rather used the Iranian term *chador*, which further accentuated the divide and created confusion. The obsession with Iran was an important element, as evidenced fifteen years later when a cohort of left-wing intellectuals (in particular, Caroline Fourest and Pierre-André Taguieff) rejected the use of the term *Islamophobia* on the erroneous basis that the term had originated in Iranian propaganda developed in 1979. The popularity of the idea underscores the extent to which Iran was viewed as "evil," and that such a view even went so far as to put into question the idea of secularism within the French left. Meanwhile, radicals found a new social outlet with the electoral successes of the Front National.

Members of the Nouvelle Droite (the new right) worked on framing the party. In 1989, a month after the fall of the Berlin Wall, Bruno Mégret, neo–right winger and number two of the Front National, launched an ideological periodical called *Identité*. The opposition between partisans of "identity," from the Front National to Islamism, and partisans of the "new world order" was thus established. The ethnic component of this discourse thus either refused to address the religious dimension or incorporated in positive terms the Islamism in the "identity wake-up call" it announced. Islamophobia initially emerged in French and European radical circles and among social elites with the breakup for the former Yugoslavia (1991–1995). For the most part, far-right parties took their cues from Serbian propaganda, viewing the conflicts in the Balkans as essentially the result of an "American plot" to create (thanks to Islam) an area of turbulence in Europe in order to prevent the European Union from progressing.

The idea that the United States was manipulating Islamism against Europe was echoed in some French academic and military circles. Bruno Mégret split from the Front National in January 1999. Faced with justifying his new party's autonomy and differentiating it from the Front National for the European elections of 1999, he used Islamophobic themes related to the war in Kosovo for his own political agenda, before reaching out to French Jews after 9/11.[5] The rapid acceptance of the idea of a "clash of civilizations," which opposes liberal Western democracies to an Islamism conceived as a unique phenomenon descended from fascism, contributed to a reshuffling of cards within the political imaginary. On the left, the elections of 2002 saw Pierre-André Taguieff publish a pamphlet promoting the candidacy of Jean-Pierre Chevènement, presenting him as a man capable of harmonizing a nation that had been torn apart by identity politics—in other words, according to him, by a tendency toward a Muslim leftist Judeophobia.[6]

Such a notion is symptomatic of an anti-Islam radicalization among the middle and upper classes, whose social and cultural capital has slowed down a polarization toward the far-right. Still, for the upper social and professional categories, the secular and Islamophobic arguments included in Marine Le Pen's discourse after 2011 play a conciliatory role, making it easier to establish links between ethnic and nationalist ideas and the values of their milieu. In 2012, 35 percent of upper socioeconomic classes considered Islam to be a threat; and at a rate higher than that of employees and workers, they associated Islam with a "rejection of Western values" (25 percent versus 23 percent) and "submission" (21 percent versus 18 percent).[7]

The radical left, confronted with the issue of "antisemitism among youth with immigrant backgrounds," has denied it entirely, while the nationalist left has questioned whether its commitment to secularism would lead to a break with its antiracism. The French left has been divided on this issue. On the one hand, a liberal and Atlanticist tendency has emerged that seeks to fight antisemitism and anti-Zionism, which it attributes to people linked to the Muslim-Arab worlds. They reject the word *Islamophobia* so as not to have to assume the side effects of such discourse, which tends toward Nazifying the Muslim-Arab worlds. On the other hand, there is an antiliberal tendency that is concerned about the fate of Palestinians. It advocates a strong state in terms of social assistance but a weak one in terms of society. It has few qualms Nazifying Israel, rejecting the idea that such a discourse constitutes a strong vector of antisemitism.

Radical Anti-Zionism and Antisemitism

In consideration of the flood of protest calling on French voters to defend the Republic against the "threat" of Jean-Marie Le Pen in the runoff election in the 2002 presidential elections, Marine Le Pen's advisors have worked toward "dedemonizing" (what they call a process of *dédiabolisation*) the party: antisemitic expressions have been muted, radical anti-Zionist opinions silenced, radical party members and militant Catholic nationalists have either been removed or made to fall in line with a "more refined" and "less religious" Front National, which has chosen to orient itself more toward social politics, with a focus on referendum proposals in order to counter accusations of fascism.[8]

Anti-Zionism had been a core position within the party and among its leaders since the mid-1970s, and Marine Le Pen was committed to breaking with this tradition. She wanted to be welcomed in Israel, and Louis Aliot made a trip there in 2011. Rather than indicators that the Front National has now become pro-Israel, such shifts are strategies designed to combat accusations of antisemitism and allow the party to better align itself with the right of the conservative party, in which economic liberalism goes hand in hand with supporting Israel. The process has had its fair share of hiccups. In 2006, the Front National announced the inclusion of Alain Soral into its ranks, with the writer claiming during a press conference that "Marx would have voted FN." With the help of former Groupe union et défense (Union and Defense Group, GUD) member Philippe Péninque, Alain Soral created the organization Égalité & Réconciliation in order to explore ethnic and religious segments of the population, as well as to recruit Front National leaders with "diverse" backgrounds, which was a strategy aimed at neutralizing accusations of racism.[9]

It may seem surprising that the Front National actively sought out ethnic diversity and a "left-wing" marker of anti-Zionism to incorporate into the party. However, one has to remember that the year before (2005) saw the creation of the *Indigènes de la République*. The group enjoyed support from a portion of the radical left (notably within the Nouveau Parti anticapitaliste, NPA) in the name of "intersectionality" and "convergence" of struggles. However, the Party of the Indigènes de la République (PIR, established in 2010, five years after the *Appel des Indigènes de la République*) rejected that principle in the name of autonomy for natives and their rejection of universalism. According to the party's spokesperson Houria Bouteldja, a "decolonial project cannot be thought from individualities but only from oppressed cultures and identities. The PIR recognizes a communitarian organization if it stands up for a racially oppressed community."[10] Her anti-Zionism was accompanied by a denunciation of the "state's philo-Semitism," advocating at the same time not mixing with whites and, at the very least, in cases of interethnic marriage, the conversion of whites to Islam.

With the exception of the last element, such arguments correspond well with the positions advocated by the European Liberation Front in the 1990s, which was an umbrella for Europe's neo-right-wing and nationalist-revolutionary structures. Soral's project coheres well with a moment of oscillation on the margins. In this context, one could also cite the success on the left of the conspiracy theory works of Annie Lacroix-Riz.[11] Alain Soral slammed the door on the Front National in 2009 after being denied a spot at the top of the party's list during the European elections. Instead, he concentrated his efforts on his successful organization, developing a cultural battle whose effects are today palpable. His positions are hardly novel—for example, his reading of Zionism as what propelled denationalization in the West is in line with what the nationalist-revolutionary and former number two of the Front National, François Duprat, had previously argued. However, he formulated the question differently, with the support of the French comedian Dieudonné, who made the notion of a competition between the memories of slavery and the extermination of Jews in Europe widespread, such as it has been developed in the Black American movement since the 1970s.

Alain Soral has played the devil's advocate, to the point of representing himself as a "national-socialist," even if his absence of racialism makes it difficult to compare him to a Nazi. His books are sold in the tens of thousands. His videos, and those of Dieudonné, are viewed by millions. Antisemitism has been removed from the political sphere and now appears on the cultural market. Yet, there is a temptation to tend toward partisanship. Soral and Dieudonné have gotten along with Shiites from the Centre Zahra (close to the Iranian regime, the Syrians, and Hezbollah) and their anti-Zionist party, putting anti-Zionism on the ticket during the European elections in 2009 (1.3 percent of the vote in Île-de-France, the only district where they were present). After that, Égalité & Réconciliation considered becoming a political party. They eventually rejected the idea, but not without having excluded the disciples of François Duprat who hoped to turn it into a nationalist-revolutionary party. In the end, deciding that the Front National had betrayed them with what they considered to be a pro-Israeli stance, the duo created the Réconciliation Nationale party in late 2014.[12] Nevertheless, the offer encountered a few difficulties, perhaps due to the generalization of the monetization of available products. Traffic to Égalité & Réconciliation's website fell between January and October 2015, and it did not pick up again until the attacks of November 13, 2015. Moreover, interest on the web is not simply French. On November 26, 2015, 31 percent of Alain Soral's 32,492 Facebook fans were not from "France" (according to the network).

In terms of militant structures, in 2011, Marine Le Pen made a show of excluding leaders who belonged to the Œuvre Française (considered an extreme right-wing neofascist and antisemitic organization), which gave rise to the idea that perhaps she represented a new Front National. Yvan Benedetti, who has been open about being "anti-Zionist, antisemitic, and anti-Jewish" was emphasized in particular. After the ban on the Œuvre Française in 2013, Yvan Benedetti and Alexandre Gabriac ran a campaign during the municipal elections of 2014 in Vénissieux, during which they encouraged their voters to "make a *quenelle* at the polls" (a provocative gesture considered an expression of antisemitism).[13] They managed to obtain 11.49 percent of the vote. Local chapters of the former Œuvre Française also established organizations (named after their respective territories and designated with the adjective "nationalist"), all of which joined the Parti Nationaliste (PNF) in late 2015.[14]

The issue of the reaction to the banalization of antisemitism is intertwined with the issue of the increasing popularity of the ideas of a "clash of civilizations." They both explain the reactions on the part of French Jews and the changes in the Front National over the last decade. The Jewish Defense League is a self-defense group founded in 2000, a year during which antisemitic violence rose by six times, and overall violence by four. Marine Le Pen defended herself when the idea that she might be banned (as are her equivalents in Israel and the United States) arose.

Following the attacks of 2012, emigration toward Israel rose sharply, according to the Jewish Agency for Israel (1,917 departures in 2012, 7,231 in 2014). The percentage of Jewish voters casting ballots for the Front National rose from 4.5 percent in 2007 to 13.5 percent in 2012, a sign of accelerated normalization, since that rise is almost triple that of the general electorate (from 10.4 percent to 17.9 percent). Islamophobia is a propelling force that amplifies the perception (rampant since 2009) that France is becoming increasingly fragmented into hostile communities,[15] which has led to new alliances and political frontiers.

A World View

Opinion polls show the extent to which a trend toward authoritarianism has emerged. In 2015, 85 percent of those polled believed that "we need a real leader in France to reestablish order;" 52 percent that the death penalty should be reinstated; 62 percent that "there is too much dependency on welfare;" and 40 percent would accept an "authoritarian regime, to the point of weakening democratic checks and balances within government." Such a trend toward authoritarian politics can be explained by the perception of a lack of social integration, notably due to its multicultural dimension, as two recent polls suggest: 70 percent of those polled believed that France "was better before;" 54 percent that Islam is not compatible with "the values of French society;" and 74 percent that "secularism is in danger."[16]

Critiques of multiculturalism are accompanied by demands for authoritarianism. That demand is growing, since the correspondence between domestic and foreign enemies is a key element in generating fear. The development of a proto-state by Daesh, domestic terrorism, and the refugee crisis are factual elements that help structure a fearful view of society. Having experienced many attacks over the years, anxiety about terrorism in French society is at a high (around 50 percent of those polled between the fall of the Berlin Wall and the attacks of March 2012, with a spike to 64 percent in October 2001). The dismantling of jihadist networks demonstrated the extent to which the phenomenon was no longer simply foreign, but also included French people from all over France, which made fears hegemonic (93 percent of those polled were worried after the attacks of January 2015). All the elements are therefore in place for an "identity war" in France.

According to the Ministry of the Interior, there were 570 French people in Daesh's caliphate in late November 2015. Those individuals have repudiated their place of national origin. Fears regarding Islamism are well founded. However, the fact that for 34 percent of those polled, Islam's image has been damaged following the attacks of January 2015, is irrational. The context has also framed reactions to the migrants crisis. An opinion poll in October 2015 showed that out of seven European countries, France was the most hostile to the idea of opening its borders to refugees.[17]

When it comes to migration issues, the death penalty, ongoing debates on the Roma, or Marine Le Pen's ambiguous comments on the use of torture, biopolitical measures have been invoked to which the Front National alone has proven able to respond.[18] Whereas the proposition of "national preference" implicitly targets African and North African foreigners, "intelligent protectionism" (a Front National issue since 2011) is presented as a response to competition from Asia. Both cases are efforts to de-Orientalize the social space. Populist debates tend to make similar arguments, as for example those of Robert Ménard (a radical right mayor) against the proliferation of kebab eateries. For him, globalization is a form of Orientalization and authoritarianism offers a return to full sovereignty (cultural, political, and economic). Such thinking is to be inscribed in a much wider framework. According to political scientist Gaël Brustier, after the oil crisis of 1973, the West's self-image became one of anxiety and decline. Hence the myth of an East and of an Islam that is at once imperialist and barbarian in contrast with an "Occidentalism," a true "ideology of crisis" structured around the idea of decline.[19]

Over the past forty years and on both sides of the Atlantic, there has been a shift to the right. It includes a dismantling of the social state and a decline in ideas of egalitarian humanism, factors linked to an ethnicization of social issues. The result has been a growth of the penal state. This process includes demands for authoritarianism, which is a reaction to change and the atomization of society in a globalized economic world—in which the West is no longer the center.

In the nineteenth century, the first wave of globalization saw the success of racist theories and practices. The second wave of globalization, due to its postmodernist cultural impact, has led to a social demand for authoritarianism, which is especially accentuated in a centralized cultural territory such as France. The atomization of social structures makes it seem as though French society has become divided into identity-based groups. That has contributed to the dissemination of a social fiction according to which Muslim-Arab populations are believed to represent a unified social, cultural, and religious body. That has reified the image of an "us," composed of diverse individuals, against a "them," which is believed to be a cohesive whole. The mechanism accounting for the wave of fear with respect to otherness comes from changes in the relationships between the state, society, and the market, presented as a defense of "a way of life." For Islamophobes, the socioeconomic fragmentation of the welfare state is attributed to multiculturalism and blamed on the presence of Muslim-Arab populations. For antisemites, geopolitical transnationalization is seen as an effect of Zionism. Meanwhile, the Front National has managed to appeal to a wide spectrum of the population, presenting itself as the solution to what it has defined as Orientalization.

Such thinking undoubtedly has a political future. Not only does the West now understand that it is not alone in the world, but the capacity of radical Islamism to strike at the heart of any state and to contest the legitimacy of democracy has placed Europe in a geostrategic crisis. In France, that has translated into a demand for national unity and authority. The Front National's protectionism is an Orientalism from within; in other words, it is a tangible political translation of Occidentalism. That is also why, if it stands to benefit from the social unrest that is the product of antisemitism as a cultural good, a societal diagnosis corroborated by any sign of intercommunitarian conflict, it no longer recognizes itself in the wake of past anti-Jewish positions, finding itself now on a new eschatological horizon.

Nicolas Lebourg is a historian of far-right movements. He is a nonresident research fellow at the Institute for European, Russian and Eurasian Studies at George Washington University, an affiliated scholar at the Centre d'Études Politiques de l'Europe Latine (CNRS-Université de Montpellier), and a member of the Observatoire des radicalités politiques at the Fondation Jean Jaurès (Paris). He is author of numerous books, most recently of *Les droites extrêmes en Europe* (2015) and *Dans l'ombre des Le Pen: Une histoire des numéros 2 du FN* (2015).

Notes

1. Emmanuel Sivan, "Colonialism and Popular Culture in Algeria," *Journal of Contemporary History* 14, no. 1 (January 1979): 21–53; Jean-Paul Honoré, "La 'hiérarchie des sentiments,' description et mise en scène du Français et de l'immigré dans le discours du Front national," *Mots* 12, no. 1 (March 1986): 129–157.

2. Translator's note: the term *harkis* is generally used to designate Algerians who supported the French presence in Algeria during colonialism, and in France today are known collectively either as *Français musulmans rapatriés* (FMR) or *Français de souche nord africaine* (FSNA).

3. Nicolas Lebourg and Abderahmen Moumen, *Rivesaltes, le camp de la France, 1939 à jours* (Perpignan: Trabucaire, 2015).

4. Romain Ducoulombier, "Penser et combattre: Jules Monnerot face à la subversion des 'sociétés ouvertes,'" in *Subversion, anti-subversion, contre-subversion*, ed. François Cochet and Olivier Dard (Paris: Éditions Riveneuve, 2010), 45–61.

5. Nicolas Lebourg and Joseph Beauregard, *Dans l'ombre des Le Pen: Une histoire des numéros 2 du FN* (Paris: Nouveau Monde, 2012).

6. Pierre-André Taguieff, *La nouvelle judéophobie* (Paris: Mille et une nuits, 2002).

7. Institut français d'opinion publique (IFOP), "L'image de l'islam en France" (2012).

8. Radical anti-Zionism is a position that denies Israel the right to exist as a state, and deliberately conflates Jews and Zionists, considering all Jews as representatives and agents of the Israeli state.

9. Caroline Monnot and Abel Mestre, *Le système Le Pen: Enquête sur les réseaux du Front national* (Paris: Denoël, 2011).

10. Paul Guillibert, Caroline Izambert, and Sophie Wahnich, "Revendiquer un monde décolonial: Entretien avec Houria Bouteldja," *Vacarme*, no. 71 (Spring 2015): 67.

11. See Jean-Yves Camus and Nicolas Lebourg, *Les droites extrêmes en Europe* (Paris: Seuil, 2015).

12. Meanwhile, the Islamophobic organization Riposte laïque (on the left, but having garnered support from the far-right, and sometimes acting with the Bloc Identitaire) vigorously denounced the Front National's pro-Arab-Muslim betrayal.

13. Dieudonné has been famously provocative with this gesture, which he created and which is often seen as an expression of antisemitism. It consists in pointing the right arm downwards while extending the left hand toward the opposing shoulder and moving it in such a way as to simulate "fisting." It is a gesture Dieudonné addresses to "political Judaism," to use an expression from the Œuvre Française. On September 9, 2013, the LICRA (International League Against Racism and Anti-Semitism) addressed an open letter to then minister of defense Jean-Yves Le Drian comparing the "quenelle" to an "inverted Nazi salute."

14. The PNF was established in 1983 by the former Waffen SS Pierre Bousquet and Jean Castrillo, who turned their backs on the Front National. They believed that Jean-Marie Le Pen had become a puppet for Israel after the assassination of François Duprat in 1978. The PNF was inactive for many years, but the organization never completely dissolved. The rallying of the leadership of the former Œuvre Française was not considered to be legally problematic, in terms of resuscitating a dissolved party (a practice that could be compared to the way in which, after it was dissolved by the state in 1968, the Mouvement Occident was reformed through the work of a dozen small groups that, in 1969, announced the birth of a united movement, Ordre Nouveau).

15. Jérôme Fourquet and Alain Mergier, *Janvier 2015: Le catalyseur* (Paris: Fondation Jean Jaurès, 2015).

16. Institut français d'opinion publique (IFOP), "L'attirance des Français pour un gouvernement technocratique ou autoritaire" (2015); and Brice Teinturier and Stéphane Zumsteeg, "Fractures françaises" (Paris: IPSOS-Sopra, 2015).

17. "L'image des musulmans et de l'islam auprès des Français" (Paris: Odoxa, 2015); Institut français d'opinion publique (IFOP); "Les Européens face à la crise des migrants" (2015); Fourquet and Mergier, *Janvier 2015: Le catalyseur*; and Mattei Dogan, "Le nationalisme en Europe: Déclin à l'Ouest, résurgence à l'Est," in *Nations et frontières dans la nouvelle Europe: L'impact croisé*, ed. Éric Philippart (Brussels: Éditions Complexe, 1993), 141–174.

18. Michel Foucault showed that the extension of the state was related to its "biopolitical" function, namely the management of bodies, a public power that establishes itself on a biologically normative territory with respect to the population that it governs.

19. Gaël Brustier, *La guerre culturelle aura bien lieu... L'occidentalisme ou l'idéologie de la crise* (Paris: Mille et une nuits, 2013).

28

FACES OF THE FRONT NATIONAL (1972–2015)

Sylvain Crépon

AFTER FORTY YEARS at the head of the Front National, Jean-Marie Le Pen (finally) passed the baton on January 11, 2011. The eighty-three-year-old leader, who had participated in just about every shift on the French far-right since the 1950s, entrusted his party to his youngest daughter, Marine. Beyond the fact the she bore her father's name (not irrelevant in a party where the leader had always embodied its very essence), Marine received massive support during an internal primary—67.65 percent—an unprecedented level of support in the FN, in a race which had pitted her against Bruno Gollnisch.

Whereas Bruno Gollnisch's orthodox nationalism very closely resembled that of Jean-Marie Le Pen (who did not hesitate, for instance, to question the work of historians on the Holocaust),[1] during the internal campaign, Marine Le Pen was able to play the card of modernity and renewal. In order to do that, she made a show of highlighting the differences between her father and herself, notably with respect to antisemitism and the memory of the Second World War.[2] Barely a month after she was elected to the head of the Front National, she further emphasized such differences in an interview with the magazine *Le Point*, stating that she believed the Holocaust was "the height of barbarism."[3] This statement clearly established her politics in opposition to the antisemitic and even negationist aspects of her father's public beliefs. For his part, he never hesitated to say that the extermination of Jews was simply a "detail" in history, and that inequality between "races" was a given, and even that the repression exerted by the Gestapo during German occupation was not "all that inhuman."

Turning her back on what could be called Jean-Marie Le Pen's provocations, the new leader of the Front National has since multiplied her statements regarding a shift within her party toward more democratic politics, blending liberal values with republican principles and denouncing persecution suffered by women, Jews, homosexuals, and even whites in some *banlieues* housing projects, which she claims are dominated by conservative and reactionary Islamism.[4] That is how she has been able to claim that she supports secular ideas, which according to her are the only thing that can effectively combat identity politics and community insularism in French society, and especially the danger of Islamism itself.

Many observers in France, notably journalists, have commented that the Front National is not the same as it was under its founding leader, and that Marine Le Pen has been working to tame its more nationalist and extreme elements. In the wake of the December 2015 regional elections, which saw the Front National receive six then seven million votes during the first and second rounds (which forced the socialist left to withdraw from two regions and prevented the right from declaring an unchallegend victory, provoking a potential political reshuffle just eighteen months from the presidential elections), it is precisely that supposed shift that I wish to investigate here. In fact, after attentively studying identity issues such as they have been conceived by the Front National since its inception, my position is that Marine Le Pen has simply adapted the nationalist reasoning proper to the far-right to contemporary political issues.

From a Small Party to Electoral Emergence (1972–1990)

At the end of the Second World War, nationalism in France was mostly neglected by the public, which was traumatized by the discovery of concentration camps. Most figures of the far-right were associated with the collaborationist regime of Vichy. Opposition to decolonization, which emerged in the 1950s, nevertheless allowed it to temporarily restructure itself around the Poujadist Movement, but that was short-lived.

Once Algerian independence was ratified, public opinion rejected imperialist nationalism, overwhelmingly voting "yes" to the 1961 referendum on Algerian independence (72.25 percent in the mainland, and 69.09 percent in Algeria). The nationalist outliers of the electorate, which could have turned toward Poujade's antifiscalist populism, were then drawn toward General de Gaulle's patriotism, which embodied a conservative and republican France, and which held its own in the community of nations by standing up to the United States.[5] The far-right's political development was therefore extremely tenuous in the 1960s. Nationalist lawyer Jean-Louis Tixier-Vignancour, formerly a member of the Croix-de-feu de La Rocque and the Parti Populaire Français (PPF) of Doriot in the 1930s and 1940s, received just 5 percent of the vote in the presidential elections of 1965. After that interlude, the far-right movement had a small, mostly student-based following. In addition, multiple street scuffles with left-wing groups gave it a poor reputation and led to the dismantling of its most extreme factions.

Under the aegis of the Ordre Nouveau, a neofascist group, the Front National emerged in October 1972—a decade after the end of the Algerian War—in the context of structural and ideological desolation within the far-right. The founders' aim was to create a classical partisan structure that would give them electoral legitimacy and allow them to disseminate their ideas.[6] They entrusted the presidency to Jean-Marie Le Pen, then considered a relatively moderate figure. His experience in parliament under Poujade (1950s), as Tixier-Vignancour's campaign manager in 1965, and as a soldier during the colonial conflicts (Indochina and Algeria) lent him a certain prestige in nationalist and military circles.

It being the Cold War, the Front National was first and foremost anticommunist. As a nationalist party, it was against immigration, especially immigration from the Maghreb, underscoring the *racial* dangers for the host country. It also intimated the loss of France's empire and the long Algerian conflict. In terms of immigration issues, a turning point occurred in 1978. The party's main idea man, François Duprat, sought a way to compete with the French Communist Party in its ability to mobilize the working class. His solution to the problem was to use *racial* rather than *social* ideas. With that aim in mind, he coined the following slogan: "A million unemployed persons equals a million too many immigrants."

France was in an economic crisis, with high rates of unemployment. The slogan was meant to place immigration at the center of political debate and position the Front National at the forefront of the political stage. Surprisingly, Jean-Marie Le Pen was not initially enthusiastic about the slogan, but he ended up ceding under François Duprat's persuasive insistence and the success it encountered within nationalist circles.[7] François Duprat was convinced early on that the right would eventually be forced to include the Front National's identity politics within its platform, which would benefit the Front National, since voters tend to prefer the original to the copy. Moreover, the Front National's rivalry with the French Communist Party would give the former increased visiblity during major elections between 1978 and 1981.

When the Front National achieved electoral success in the European elections of 1984 and the legislative elections of 1986, that slogan encapsulated the party's mentality. Indeed, the Front National had consistently called for the deportation of immigrants as a means of curbing unemployment, abuses of social aid, and violence, which it attributed to the presence of foreigners and of their descendents. The leader of the Front National did not distinguish between immigrants and their descendents, even though the latter category were French. Moreover, the party's platform included a proposal to reform citizenship laws that would replace *jus soli* with *jus sanguinis*. Such a change suggested an ethnic view of nationality and a rejection of ideas of assimilation.

During that period, Jean-Marie Le Pen made numerous scandalous statements. On December 13, 1987, during the television program *Le Grand Jury* RTL-*Le Monde*, he claimed that concentration camps were "a mere detail in the history of the Second World War." That would be the first in a long series of such assertions.[8] The most recent instance of the "detail affair"[9] led to his suspension and ultimate expulsion from what had become his daughter's party.[10] Such crafted and tested statements were also part of a planned strategy. In addition to generating media attention, this strategy made it possible for him to neutralize all those within his party who sought to ally with the right-wing administration, and ultimately left them with little choice but to rally behind him.[11]

The "Differentialist" Turning Point of the 1990s

As Iraqi troops invaded Kuwait in August 1990, Jean-Marie Le Pen, going against the French and Western political class, spoke out against the allied intervention that was being prepared to free the small oil state. At the same time, he voiced his unwavering support for Saddam Hussein, whom he considered an emblematic counterforce to the new international order established by the United States. In order to back up his words, he traveled to Iraq to meet its dictator. Thirteen years later, when George W. Bush made the decision to invade Iraq, Jean-Marie Le Pen once again opposed British-American intervention. This time, the political class was for the most part opposed to intervention as well, but Le Pen's arguments did not fail to surprise. With his party continuing to speak out against the dangers posed by an Arab and Muslim population on French soil, Le Pen praised Arab and Middle Eastern dictatorships, underscoring the stability that they provided and even applauding the cultures and civilizations in which they existed.[12] In order to justify his stance against the invasion, he made himself into a spokesperson for differentialism: "If we wish for our Christian civilization to be respected, we have to respect other people's right to live as they please in their country."[13]

One event illustrates this change of mind: the fall of the Berlin Wall, which was accompanied by the collapse of Soviet communism. Although the Front National had aligned itself with the West during the Cold War—hence its support of the American nuclear umbrella, South American dictatorships, and South African apartheid—the demise of the Soviet empire meant it no longer had to take a side in what was now an outmoded conflict. The Front National was therefore in search of a new ideological paradigm, one that would allow it to adapt its nationalist platform to the geopolitical issues emerging in the early 1990s. Inspired by the intellectual production of the Nouvelle Droite, and more precisely of the *Groupe de recherche et d'étude pour la civilisation européenne* (Research and Study Group for European Civilization, GRECE), the Front National began to transform itself.

The GRECE was established in 1968 by nationalist intellectuals who sought to adapt the antiegalitarian foundations of the far-right to the context following decolonization. Although they were associated for a moment with racialist, and even racist, theories, they oriented themselves more and more toward a new identity-based model inspired by anthropological concerns. Relying on the work of structuralist anthropologist Claude Lévi-Strauss, they conceptualized a form of "cultural differentialism" that was much more closely aligned with political issues linked to the defense of cultural minorities emerging in France in the 1970s. The biological concept of "race" was progressively abandoned in favor of anthropological and cultural conceptions. The idea of a hierarchy between people was eventually replaced by the need to respect difference. As a result, the adherents of GRECE opposed miscegenation—and therefore immigration—but in the name of preserving cultural identities.[14] For political reasons, they quickly distanced themselves from both capitalism and communism. Both systems, each in its own way, were considered to be avatars of Christian universalist thinking. Through their denial of cultural and religious diversity, Christian ethics were seen as seeds of totalitarianism. The GRECE adhered to a kind of neopaganism as an attempt to realign itself with the original religious foundations of Europe.

Alain de Benoist, a key intellectual figure in the GRECE, denounced the individualism of human rights, which he saw as an infringement on the rights of peoples. He promoted an essentialist paradigm that understood individuals in terms of their cultural background.[15] Such thinking led adherents to this intellectual movement to openly criticize France's colonial past. Let us not forget that these were the same people who fought against the process of decolonization. Now they criticized the republican regime and its universalist values of "ethnocide" with respect to colonized peoples.[16] According to the same reasoning, they rejected the nation-state, becoming vocal supporters of regional autonomy, which they considered a better way of repecting the multiple identities that make up most nations. Geopolitically speaking, they argued for a multipolar world and took up the construction of Europe as a cause. For them, the commonality among European peoples should not undermine their local diversity.

The GRECE and the Front National shared only marginal connections up until the late 1980s. Their respective positions on capitalism and religion made alliances impossible.[17] However, with the collapse of the Soviet Union, the GRECE became an important source of inspiration for the Front National. It drew selectively on the GRECE's ideological framework, using it to adapt its nationalist foundations to the geopolitical shifts of the 1990s. Although it had seen the United States as France's and Europe's natural ally in the context of the Cold War, the Front National now considered the United States to be a threat to a multipolar world, be it through the "imperialist wars" waged in the Middle East, its unfailing support of Israel, or its reliance on a "globalist" process whose mercantile paradigm threatened national economies and cultures. In the context of the invasion of Iraq, Jean-Marie Le Pen sharply criticized the United States, saying it "wanted to enlist the Muslim masses . . . under Mammon and the high priest of the dollar."[18] The Front National opposed the invasion of Iraq and any bellicose actions against the Baathists in the Middle East (from Iran and nationalist Serbia in the 1990s) as a result of its adoption of that differentialist paradigm. Using a semantics that suggested immigration was a threat for autochthonous and allochthonous populations (defined as the primary victims of immigration), and careful to avoid assertions that could be censured by antiracist legislation, the Front National used differentialist ideas to position itself in opposition to the migratory process.

Politically speaking, although the party still attracted a growing number of working-class voters, it began to emphasize social benefits as part of its platform. For instance, it included the following type of slogan on its printed propaganda: "The Front National Cares About Social Issues!" It also reappropriated a slogan from the Parti Populaire Français, which had been the French Communist Party's major opponent in the 1930s, as a way of denying France's sharp social and political divisions: "Neither right-wing, nor left-wing, we are French." The Front National became divided between those oriented toward social issues and differentialism (such as Samuel Maréchal, president of the Front National youth and then son-in-law of Jean-Marie Le Pen) and those like Bruno Mégret, who argued for a more traditional right-wing platform, which he considered to be essential to developing an alliance—and thereby gaining access to the party in power—with the right-wing administration in place at the time.

After 2002: The Integration of the Republican Paradigm

April 21, 2002, has often been considered the electoral height of the Front National, the date on which the party came in second in the first round in the general election. However, after the initial euphoria of the first round of voting, many Front National leaders saw that day as an electoral slap in the face. In the second round runoff elections, voters overhelmingly rallied against them, and members of the Front National had to come to terms with the fact that their leader would never become president of the Republic—a supposition that had perhaps been a bit presumptious. That crushing defeat—unheard of under the Fifth Republic (Jean-Marie Le Pen scraped together just 18 percent of votes during the second round)—led Marine Le Pen to develop a team called Générations Le Pen, which was tasked with modernizing the party.

The team scoured sociological voting data, which showed that a strong majority of voters believed the Front National represented a threat to democracy (75 percent in March 1997), a finding which was corroborated by a majority of its own electorate three years earlier (53 percent in 1994).[19] Faced with that fact, Générations Le Pen implemented a new strategy, which would become that of Marine Le Pen herself when she became president of the Front National in 2011: de-demonization (*dédiabolisation*) and normalization. Cognizant of the fact that the republican paradigm remains unshakable in today's France—no party could hope to gain access to power if it opposed republican values—Générations Le Pen understood that it had to make its party republican leaning, while still maintaining its specificity, namely its radicality.[20] Marine Le Pen therefore relied on former supporters of Bruno Mégret (people like Nicolas Bay and Steeve Briois) who had come back into the fold of the party in order to implement the normalization strategy of her father's former rival from the 1990s, while avoiding allying herself directly with the moderate right.

Marine Le Pen was named Jean-Marie Le Pen's campaign manager for the 2007 presidential elections. During that time, she worked to craft Front National rhetoric around republican values, relying on personalities such as Philippe Péninque (from the GUD) and Alain Soral.[21] That is the context in which one should understand Jean-Marie Le Pen's 2006 call upon youth with immigrant background, his famous speech in Valmy, and the poster featuring a young, Maghrebi-looking woman with her thumbs pointed downward, denouncing the failure of previous administrations' integration and secularism policies: "Nationality, assimilation, social ladder, secularism: right/left, they're all broken!"

Such republican semantics abound in Marine Le Pen's discourse, be it during her campaign to lead the party or, once she was actually elected as its head. Rejecting the principle of integration, which she claimed had led to the rise of insular communities within France and, by extension, to radical Islam, she preferred to focus on assimilation, a model whereby immigrants give up their customs in favor of French culture. Her aim, she asserted, was to return to a society reminiscent of the Republic's golden age, when France was easily able to assimilate European immigrants.[22] Although Marine Le Pen and her entourage asserted that nationality had nothing to do with race or religion, they also claimed that some populations living on French soil promoted cultural and religious values that were incompatible with republican values, a fact that, according to them, made any proccess of acculturation, integration, or even assimilation impossible.

Despite the republican veneer, one could notice a persistent "mixophobic" differentialism.[23] Marine Le Pen and her entourage submitted that liberal, democratic, and republican values—secularism, male/female equality, religious tolerance—could only flourish in a cultural framework linked to Christianity, a religion that, unlike Islam, made the distinction between the human world and God's world, a prelude to the flourishing of secularization and democratic values that accompanied it. In her autobiography, Marine Le Pen posited that "our Republican values come from Christian culture."[24]

Front National leaders now regularly describe Muslims in France as being inflexible with respect to sexual permissiveness and other principles of European democracies. Areas with large immigrant populations, notably from the Maghreb and sub-Saharan Africa, are described as potentially dangerous for women, homosexuals, Jews, and even whites. The rhetoric of "security hedonism,"[25] which the Front National borrowed from European populist groups like the Dutch PVV (Geert Wilders) and the Swiss UDC (Oscar Freysinger), and whose xenophobic reasoning is built from a societal framework that grew out of the left wing, has paid off at the ballots.[26] Since its creation in 1972 by former Vichyists, partisans of French Algeria, and revolutionary nationalists, the Front National has therefore proven adept at adapting to cultural and political changes within French society. It has promoted Maurras-style antisemitism, imperialist nationalism, and colonial nostalgia, xenophobia built on racism and socioeconomic or ethnic differentialism. Today, the Front National has shifted its rhetoric toward republican semantics, and it claims to promote secularism and assimilation.

In a context where racist and xenophobic prejudices are less and less appealing to citizens (despite the recent outbreak), as the annual report by the National Commission on Human Rights has shown, and in which republican values are unanimously agreed upon in France, Marine Le Pen's Front National has been able to adapt nationalist ideas to ethical changes by proposing a political offering that makes her "mixophobic" logics audible. Meanwhile, it offers a partisan translation of prejudices that, if more present in people's minds today than in the past, did not have political outlets. Identity issues, which were politically marginalized during the *Trente Glorieuses* period of economic growth until the early 1970s, have become unavoidable in the field of French politics. The risk now was once prophesized by François Duprat, namely that voters always prefer the original to the copy.

Sylvain Crépon is a sociologist, Maître de conférences in Political Science at the University of Tours. A specialist on nationalist movements and religious symbols in Europe, recent publications and edited volumes include *Les sciences sociales au prisme de l'extrême droite* (2008), *Enquête au cœur du Front national* (2012), and *Les faux semblants du Front national: Sociologie d'un parti politique* (2015).

Notes

1. On October 11, 2004, Jean-Marie Le Pen declared in response to the publication of the Rousso report on negationism at the university Lyon 3: "I am not questioning the existence of concentration camps; rather, I am questioning the number of deaths, which historians could debate. As for the existence of gas chambers, it is up to historians to weigh in," *Libération*, October 12, 2004.

2. Christiane Chombeau, *Le Pen: Fille & père* (Paris: Panama, 2007).

3. Saïd Mahrane, Interview with Marine Le Pen, "Les camps ont été le summum de la barbarie," *Le Point*, February 3, 2011.

4. On December 10, 2010, in Lyon, at the half way point in the internal campaign for the presidency of the FN, Marine Le Pen declared: "I have been hearing more and more testimony on the fact that in some neighborhoods it is not good to be a woman, homosexual, Jewish, or even French or White."

5. Jean-Pierre Rioux, "Des clandestins aux activistes (1945–1965)," in *Histoire de l'extrême droite en France*, ed. Michel Winock (Paris: Seuil, 1993), 215–241.

6. Alexandre Dézé, *Le Front national: À la conquête du pouvoir?* (Paris: Armand Colin, 2012).

7. Nicolas Lebourg, *Le monde vu de la plus extrême droite: Du fascisme au nationalisme révolutionnaire* (Perpignan: Presses Universitaires de Perpignan, 2010).

8. On September 2, 1988, during his party's summer session, Jean-Marie Le Pen attacked the minister of public service Michel Durafour (Michel Rocard's administration) with the following play on words: "Dura*four* crematorium" (*four* is the French word for oven). On August 2, 1996, during his party's summer session in La Grande Motte, he said: "Yes, I believe in racial inequality. Of course I do. All of history proves it." Then, in the weekly magazine *Rivarol*, on January 7, 2005, he stated that "the German occupation was not particularly inhuman" and even that the Gestapo helped prevent civil massacres.

9. During the political television show hosted by Jean-Jacques Bourdin on BFM-TV on April 2, 2015, Jean-Marie Le Pen asserted that what he had said in 1987 "corresponds to his beliefs."

10. "Jean-Marie Le Pen exclu du Front national," *lemonde.fr*, August 20, 2015.

11. Dézé, *Le Front national: À la conquête du pouvoir?*

12. During a speech organized by the group SOS Enfants d'Iraq (founded and run by his wife Jany) on February 2, 2003, Jean-Marie Le Pen praised Iraq, calling it a nation with a "history that goes back more than 8,000 years, and that was the birthplace of civilization," the country of "Sumerians, who invented writing, that of the Assyrians, whose empire reached the Mediterranean, and that of the Chaldeans, with Nebuchadnezzar, who turned Babylon into the most beautiful city in the world."

13. Jean-Marie Le Pen, "Vive l'Irak!," *National Hebdo* 976 (April 3–9, 2003).

14. See the lexicological work of Pierre-André Taguieff on GRECE discourse: *Sur la Nouvelle Droite: Jalons d'une analyse critique* (Paris: Descartes & Cie, 1994).

15. Sylvain Crépon, "Du racisme biologique au différentialisme culturel: Les sources anthropologiques du GRECE," in *Les Sciences sociales au prisme de l'extrême droite: Enjeux et usages d'une récupération idéologique*, ed. Sylvain Crépon and Sébastien Mosbah-Natanson (Paris: L'Harmattan, 2008), 159–189.

16. Sylvain Crépon, "Une littérature post-coloniale d'extrême droite? Réflexion sur un 'braconnage' intellectual," in *Postcolonial studies, modes d'emploi*, ed. Collectif Write Back (Lyon: Presses universitaires de Lyon, 2013), 137–149.

17. This impossibility can also be explained by the fact that the Front National was supported by Bernard Antony's fundamentalist Catholics, who exerted influence over the party in the 1980s.

18. Le Pen, "Vive l'Irak!"

19. SOFRES interview, cited by Pascal Perrineau, *Le Symptôme Le Pen* (Paris: Fayard, 1997).

20. Dézé, *Le Front national: À la conquête du pouvoir?*

21. Abel Mestre and Caroline Monnot, "Les réseaux du Front national," in *Les faux-semblants du Front national: Sociologie d'un parti politique*, ed. Sylvain Crépon, Alexandre Dézé, and Nonna Mayer (Paris: Presses de Science Po, 2015), 51–76.

22. The work of Patrick Weil has shown that this republican golden age is mostly a myth. Before the Second World War, many descendants of immigrants (Italians and Poles) were members of communitarian organizations, continued to speak their parents' language, and were even educated in schools where class was conducted in that language, a situation that is not found in France today (Patrick Weil, *La République et sa diversité: Immigration, intégration, discrimination* [Paris: Seuil, 2005]).

23. Taguieff, *Sur la Nouvelle Droite.*

24. Marine Le Pen, *À contre flots* (Paris: Grancher, 2006).

25. Gaël Brustier and Jean-Philippe Huelin, *Voyage au bout de la droite: Des paniques morales à la contestation droitière* (Paris: Mille et une nuits, 2011).

26. Hans-Georg Betz, *La droite populiste en Europe: Extrême et démocrate?* (Paris: Autrement, 2004).

29
INFILTRATION OF LIQUID POPULISM

Raphaël Liogier

For 67% of those interviewed, "More is being done for immigrants than for the French."
IFOP Survey, October 2013

THE OVERUSED NOTION of "populism" should not be conflated with the term bandied about by politicians who say what they think voters want to hear. Nor is populism related to popular preoccupations, those of artisans, fishermen, workers, hunters, farmers, engineers, doctors, the rich, or the poor. In the enthusiasm surrounding populism, concrete categories within the population—professions, at times contradictory interests, class distinctions—tend to be elided over in favor of a fiction of an all-encompassing, omnipresent, and omniscient people, who are believed to have a single soul and unified identity. Populists can be either Marxist, like Stalin, or from the German Reich, like Hitler. In both cases, the populist identifies himself with an abstraction of the People. In one case, he abandons the socialist critique based on concrete class relations. In the other, he relinquishes distinctions between nobles and commoners, which are proper to any aristocratic regime.

The populist attitude is therefore unique. It can be described as the attempt to express oneself in the name of the people as a whole, generally in emphatic terms and with a hint of mysticism. The mystic claims to be directly connected to the absolute, which is represented by the name of God in the case of the Christian, Jewish, and Muslim religions. Expression takes place in ecstatic terms in order to relate to experience, and the basis for power is located solely in the intuitive connection to the absolute. For unbelievers, such posturing lends the mystic a kind of grandiloquence that appears surrealistic and even ridiculous. For believers, it is an irrefutable demonstration of truth. Populists function in more or less the same way, with the difference being that their prophecies and convictions do not come from God but rather from the people.

Since populists speak for the people as a whole, they can bypass the democratic system, its institutions, parliament, and the justice system, which they claim are corrupt. They do not have to have a well-defined platform. Instead, theirs is to defend the people against an imminent threat, an attack that strikes at their very essence. The populism of 1930s Germany claimed to be defending the people from an attack on their racial essence, their biological purity. In today's Europe, populists tend to refer more to threats to Europe's cultural essence and national identities, which they claim are threatened by the euro, immigration, and Islam. Such an attack against Europe's identity, and the French people in particular, is claimed to be waged by foreign elites and upper-middle-class multiculturalists—politicians, journalists, intellectuals, business people. Those elites are believed to favor ethnic minorities, immigrants, foreigners, Muslims, homosexuals, and other enemies of the people. Unlike the populism of the 1930s, which was ideologically very structured, today's populism is insidious and diffuse. It plays on murky notions about culture, values, and identity. It is a kind of *liquid populism,* which eats away at democratic institutions rather than violently overturning them.

The Feeling of Being Under Siege

Europe is the place on earth where globalization is most frequently criticized. According to the Eurobarometer, 62 percent of residents polled in the European Union believe that globalization does not contribute positively to its citizens.[1] And according to a survey conducted by OpinionWay in May–June 2012,[2] 60 percent of French people polled stated that globalization was a danger, and even a threat to French businesses and the social model. Globalization has practically become synonymous with the idea of an external threat. According to a study by the *Centre d'étude de la vie politique française* (Research Center on French Political Life, CEVIPOF), the percentage of voters expressing a need for protection against globalization went from 30 percent in 2009 to 46 percent in 2012.[3] A rise of 16 percent over the course of just three years is simply astounding.

Europe is also the place in the world where popular rejection of immigration is the most widespread. In France, whereas in 2007, according to an Institut français d'opinion publique (IFOP) poll,[4] 49 percent responded that immigration was an opportunity for France, six years later, in October 2013, in a poll by the same institution and following the same methodology, that number had dropped to 24 percent.[5] Meanwhile, in April 2006, again according to IFOP, 62 percent of those polled asserted that they wished to shift from "endured immigration" to "selected immigration;"[6] seven years later, that number had grown to 86 percent, according to a poll taken under the same conditions.[7] French people also believe that they are being put at a disadvantage with respect to immigrants, whom they see as pampered. Indeed, in the same poll, 67 percent of respondents claimed: "More is being done for immigrants than for the French." According to IFOP, that number was only 40 percent in 2006. More is being done for the "other" than for "us." The "system," invisible but omnipresent, is believed to be made up of elites who are betraying the people in favor of ethnic and cultural minorities.

Such a shift in opinion, which amounts to differentialism ("us" versus "them"), cannot solely be attributed to the economic crisis and the dramatic growth in unemployment. If that were the case, the Swiss Confederation would not have voted 50.3 percent in favor of a referendum on limiting immigration, including immigration from the European Union (February 9, 2014). The initiative was introduced by the Swiss People's Party, a far-right nationalist party that is also known for its law against minarets.[8] If it enters into force, the new law will severely limit the flow of migration and will allow for selective immigration, which goes against the treaty regarding the free circulation of persons signed with the European Union. If such a protectionist measure were in the objective best interests of the country, it would be understandable. But that is far from the case. Most economists agree that the Swiss economy's health (3.5 percent unemployment rate and 2 percent growth) is due in large part to immigration from the European Union. It is also worth noting that business leaders, who tend to be pragmatic, were unanimously and vocally opposed to restrictions on immigration.

Something else, beyond economics, is therefore at work: Europe's perceived need to defend itself from foreign intrusion. Marine Le Pen is an enthusiastic example of this trend seen in the Swiss people's victory against the oligarchy—or the multiculturalist elite. The Front National aims to introduce the same referendum in France as a way of curbing the elite's immigrationist dogma. It highlights the idea that 70 percent of French people supposedly believe there are too many foreigners in France.[9] Moreover, its economic platform—although spruced up with subtle rhetoric—is haunted by a war with the foreign. A striking example can be seen in its proposed policies on customs duties, which would institute quotas on products manufactured abroad. Such a measure, which would be catastrophic in terms of the chain of economic consequences it would unleash (with immediate reactions from countries that import French goods), can only be justified by identity-based reasoning.

When questioned regarding the turn from national liberalism, one bordering on general deregulation (the discourse of Jean-Marie Le Pen), to policies leading to state insularism and nationalization as a means of preventing foreign capital from competing with national industry, Marine Le Pen has argued that conditions have changed. In the 1980s, communism was still the threat. Today, liberalism has dissolved our borders.[10] In other words, in the 1980s, the enemy (communists) was precise and distant. Today, enemies are everywhere; they are embodied by the open borders themselves, and therefore, by immigration.

To summarize recent findings, such as those published by the Organization for Economic Cooperation and Development (OECD) in the *International Migration Outlook* 2013 report, immigrants are considered to be supremely coddled, receiving social benefits denied to natives, who have been neglected. Yet the total sum of social benefits paid per household (all benefits included: social aid, unemployment benefits, family support, and support for housing) to immigrant populations amounts to, on average, 8,735 euros per year, as compared to 10,129 euros per year for natives.[11] Some might say that the figure cited above is too generous. Angela Merkel would not let such sums fall into the pockets of immigrants. However, if one performs the same calculations for Germany, one finds that immigrant households receive on average 11,209 euros per year, compared to an average of 8,840 euros per year for natives.[12] Studies show that GDP (gross domestic product) actually goes up in the short term in proportion to the number of immigrants. Moreover, when immigrants have skills, as in the case of Switzerland, the relationship between government expenditures on social benefits for them and tax revenue very clearly shows a benefit to the host country. Inversely, when immigrants have few skills, the relationship between tax revenue and social expenditures may result in a slight deficit, as is the case in France (-0.52 percent , but that is a smaller number than in Germany: -1.13 percent).[13]

What is the real issue here? Debates have not been centered around an evaluation of the concrete costs and benefits, or the advantages and disadvantages of immigration. No precise arguments, backed up by figures, have been developed or put forth. The only argument with any traction is the following accusation: that government authorities are not in sync with the "real," with the common sense of the people. In any case, no argument could convince those who feel the "real," and there are many, or who believe the war being waged is not happening. The collective feeling of being duped by foreign forces is too strong and too persistent. It bolsters populist discourse, which has become increasingly prevalent in both France and Europe. And it is due to that populism—which is now affecting not just extremist parties but also reputable members of government, respected journalists, and well-known personalities—that we have gone from segregative thinking to fears of intrusion from the "other."

Symbolic Hodgepodge

Liquid populism is not suddenly going to disrupt our institutions and transform our society into a totalitarian prison overnight. However, we are at risk of slipping toward a liquid totalitarianism, which could eat away at public freedoms and lead to laws that go against our constitutions. Differences between the right and the left, pragmatism, and conflicts of interest appear to dissolve into the collective fear of the "other"—of ethnic, religious, sexual, and other types of minorities who are believed to be taking advantage of the true people and their values.

Consider the protests against the "marriage equality" law. Civitas fundamentalist Catholics found themselves side by side with members of the Groupe union défense (GUD) making the Nazi salute. There was also Frigide Barjot (an obvious pun on the famous French actress Brigitte Bardot), a self-proclaimed progressive, who repeated slogans from the Front de Gauche, "We won't give up anything," and protesters wearing revolutionary symbols like the Phrygian cap, a clenched fist, or hands drawn in such a way as to recall SOS Racisme's slogan "*Touche pas à mon pote*" (Leave my buddy alone). Rigid adherents of the Union des organisations islamiques de France (Union of Islamic Organizations of France, UOIF) holding the hand of former minister Christine Boutin, leader of the Parti Chrétien Démocrate. Self-proclaimed anticapitalist groups, antiliberals, anti-Europeans (against the *diktat* in Brussels). And in the midst of these disparate groups were members of the organization Avenir de la Culture, who represent Catholics against homosexual marriage, marching with supporters of the comedian Dieudonné. The former sought to denounce a plot by the homosexual lobby surrounding the French president; for the comedian, gay marriage was supposedly a Zionist plot.

The coming together of progressives, Marxists, revolutionists, and members of the far-right was surprising, to say the least. The mix of religious traditionalists who tend not to see eye to eye—orthodox Muslims and Catholics. Strange also to see anti-Zionists in support of Palestine rubbing shoulders with members of the reactionary bourgeoisie, who tend to see Palestinians as thugs and Israelis as the Middle East's dispensers of justice. It is not clear how "marriage equality" and the Palestinian cause relate. Nor is it apparent how a law authorizing same-sex parenthood might be at the service of neoliberalism and multinational companies. According to the website Boulevard Voltaire, the answer is simple: the management of otherness leads to new outlets and possibilities. A social movement needs a target, an aim, an ideological coherence, which is not the case here.

There is a second reason it cannot be considered a true social movement. Protesters were not fighting against social or economic inequality. They did not seek to obtain a right that had been denied them. Nor was their aim to protect a right that could have been lost. The law on "marriage equality" did not grant those who benefited from it—homosexuals—a right to impose anything on anyone. The law did not impose anything, nor did it remove rights from those who refused to engage in this type of marriage. In short: it did not change the daily lives of any of those who protested against it. Massive protests, which were strikingly dissimilar from the March for Equality and against Racism (known as the *Marche des Beurs*) that took place in the fall of 1983 or the Movement Defending Freedom of Schools from the spring of 1984—which were undeniable social movements, raising clear issues and with specific aims. There were also protests to prevent rights and advantages from being taken away, as in the case of the École Libre movement which sought to block the Loi Savary in its attempt at folding private and public primary and secondary education into one system, integrating what were primarily Catholic private schools into public education.

Protests against marriage equality—known in France as the *Manif pour Tous* or Movement for All—cohere neither with a project to extend rights to individuals nor with an effort to defend previously acquired benefits. That is clear in the use of the word *tous* (all). The idea of the law behind "marriage for all" clearly relates to extending rights to individuals who did not have them in the first place. Whether one agrees with it or not, it involves a process of universalization. The law's aim is to grant marriage rights, and the accompanying tax incentives (for example), to all members of the population, regardless of sex. Meanwhile, the "all" of the *Manif pour Tous* refers to all the people, who demand (as in all forms of populism) restrictions on individual rights. Protesters are de facto believed to represent the people as a whole. For instance, during debates on the law that took place during spring 2013, Nicolas Sarkozy's former adviser Henri Guaino, believing that he represented the truth of the people, railed at his colleagues in parliament, insisting that they let the people speak: the People "want to speak, they demand it, they require it!"

Beyond Ideological Oppositions

But just who are these "People" demanding to speak? Beyond economic classifications, conflicts of interest, and differences between the right and the left, the people here are all those who feel frustrated and who attribute their suffering to the "system." Regardless of how they define the system (it varies from person to person and from group to group), that is how men and women who typically do not agree on issues find themselves united in a cause—not out of common ideas, but out of frustration.

Populist discourse therefore bases itself on emotions. In the case of today's liquid populism, it is targeted at an indeterminate evil that must be fought. The words used to speak of that evil are vague because their real subject is this fundamental sense of frustration. The new Front National of the 2000s is the first party in France to have established itself in this populist atmosphere. Its platform is particularly telling. It would be unrecognizable to those accustomed to the nationalist and liberal discourse—which was, above all, antisocialist and anti-Marxist—of the Front National's old guard in the 1980s. Today's Front National speaks of flagship French industries, the redistribution of wealth to help the poor, social justice, and to fighting liberalism and globalization; although it continues to champion Joan of Arc and "our" Catholic roots, it also vocally supports secularism.

Populism is intrinsically defensive, adapting to external events and conditions that can always, depending on the circumstances, become threats. The feeling of being at war predominates. A war against the "other," and against all adverse circumstances that can be attributed to that "other." Since it is founded on notions of decay, populism always conjures scenes in which the people—betrayed and downtrodden heroes—are the losers. The "other" is always presented as being strong, with allies throughout the world. That results in the strange effect of the majority feeling as if it were the minority. The "other's" weaknesses—for instance, in terms of numbers—are always considered to be illusions. "We" are the victims, and even if "they" appear weak, "they" are stronger. That is why "we" have to be aggressive, although "we" would never consider ourselves to be the aggressors. Populism is always located beyond ideological oppositions. That is because it is a response to a general threat. It is therefore always both nationalist (it protects the people of a nation, against the rest of the world) and socialist (it also protects the true poor, who have been neglected); it is both traditionalist (it protects the endangered values of the people) and progressive (it protects a future that should restore its due grandeur).

Defense and Illustration of *Natural Culture*

To view the people as a perfect whole is to differentiate them from concrete populations that are in conflict with them. Populism's all-encompassing vision of the people is a way of dividing society and staging antagonistic relationships between good and evil—between the real country and the legal country (to use Charles Maurras's language), between the pure and the impure, between the true people and the false. In the 1930s, such antagonisms, which went beyond differences between the right and the left, between conservatives and progressives, were crystallized around the idea of race. The true people belonged to a pure race, and the false were members of an impure race attempting to insinuate itself into our home. Today's noble people also transcend traditional topics of difference. They represent at once progressive workers and Christian conservatives; the main criterion for membership is to be a true French-European. However, what is perceived to be under threat today is not race but rather culture. Here, culture is understood as its values, lifestyle, and tastes. "Culture" can include anything. That is why contemporary populism is so fluid; that is why it does not represent a specific ideology. Rather, it adapts according to the fluctuations of what is known as "public opinion."

Today's liquid populism is not ideological; it is *opinionological.* It projects a black-and-white vision of public life, opposing the true people against those threatening their values. But the definition of the true people is constantly changing, depending on who is being presented as a threat. The parade of those deemed enemies of "our" culture is dizzying: the Roma, immigrants in general, foreigners, *banlieue* youth, homosexuals. Officially speaking, populism never attacks people or their freedoms; it does not direct itself at "races." Gay marriage protesters were not attacking homosexuality or homosexuals, *who have the right to live as they please*; rather, they were *protecting* themselves from a form of filiation that might infiltrate all of society. In other words, they believed they were protecting the true culture, what did not go against nature. It resulted in a kind of oxymoron: they were protecting *natural culture.*

Still, as fluctuating as it may be, the notion of cultural defense needs an anchor. Muslims fill that role. Although the Roma often serve as substitute Muslims. Even if Muslims can at times be allies, for instance, in "our" struggle against homosexuals, transsexuals, and other values linked to "gender theory," they remain a fundamental enemy to "our" culture. Marine Le Pen, uncontested leader of this new populism, has tended to avoid the topic, though without repudiating or ignoring protests against marriage equality, because she has understood that Muslims necessarily embody a cultural antithesis (Western, Republican, Christian).

The Dualization of Public Life

As I have shown elsewhere,[14] signs of Islam are immediately associated with a frightful image of Islamization—with the *denaturation* of "our" culture. Myriad factors have contributed to making Islam into the antithesis of Western culture, modernity, Europe—in short, "us." The history of colonization and decolonization lurks in the background. Immigrant populations, the majority of which come from the mostly Muslim former colonies, have progressively become European citizens, and many fear a "reverse colonization."[15] And since a large number of ethnic and cultural minorities in Europe—Turks in Germany, Pakistanis in the United Kingdom, North Africans in France—also happen to be Muslim, many believe in a kind of Muslim plot that goes beyond their concrete ethnic differences. Meanwhile, there is the terrorism that associates itself with Islam, because it is identified as an enemy of the West.

Muslims represent the two-headed Janus off of which today's liquid populism feeds. On one side, they are Christian Europe's multisecular enemy; they are the Saracens who "reached Poitiers" (recall October 20, 2012, when Bloc Identitaire occupied a mosque being constructed in Poitiers, symbolically resisting Muslim invaders) or the Ottomans who once threatened the city of Vienna (during recent elections, the leader of Austria's Freedom Party was depicted on posters as a Teutonic knight fighting against Ottoman invaders!).[16] On the other side, Muslims are considered enemies of modern values, democracy, the separation of powers, human rights, sexual freedom, and freedom of expression. The two-faced representation of Muslims makes it possible to engage reactionaries who are concerned about the decline in traditional values as well as progressives who seek to protect modern values. The Roma are at times substituted for Muslims, and that raises no issues of coherence, since the notion that "our" culture is in danger is all-encompassing.

A constant problem for many is not the specific enemy, but rather those multiculturalist traitors who have pledged their allegiance to Islamization out of naïveté, leftism, vice, weakness, foolishness, or simply delusion; such traitors also take the form of "laxists" who insist on "banning prohibitions," and who leave the door open to anarchy, unmanageable hybridity, unbridled lifestyles like homosexuality, transsexuality, and bisexuality, which are believed to pose a threat to the sanctity of family. Synonyms for multiculturalists include: post–sixty-eighters, hippies, bobos, "elites." Public life is becoming increasingly *dualized*, with necessary opposites like Valls/Dieudonné. Each casts the other as plotting against a fragile and monolithic culture. Democratic institutions are perhaps not being undermined by racist ideologies—as was the case in the 1930s, but public freedoms and human rights are becoming increasingly secondary, especially since 2015 and the attacks. The "need" for security has become paramount. And that need has been built around the notion of an identity war—a war of civilizations. Biological racism has been discredited. In its stead, a liquid, protean racism has emerged. It finds its justification in the name of protecting European national identities, which are believed to be under attack by hordes of ethnic and cultural minorities.

Raphaël Liogier is University Professor at Sciences Po (Aix-en-Provence) and at the Collège international de philosophie (Paris). Recent books include *Le mythe de l'islamisation: Essai sur une obsession collective* (2012), *Ce populisme qui vient* (2013), *Le mythe de l'islamisation* (2012, 2016), and *La guerre des civilisations n'aura pas lieu: Coexistence et violence au XXI*[e] *siècle* (2016).

Notes

1. "L'opinion publique dans l'Union européenne," *Eurobaromètre standard*, no. 73, November 2010.
2. Cited by Pascal Perrineau, *La France au front* (Paris: Fayard, 2014).
3. "La montée de la demande de protection par rapport à la globalisation," *Baromètre de la confiance politique*, CEVIPOF, December 2012.
4. Institut français d'opinion publique (IFOP), February 2007.
5. Institut français d'opinion publique (IFOP), October 2013.
6. Institut français d'opinion publique (IFOP), April 2006.
7. Institut français d'opinion publique (IFOP), October 2013.
8. The party was once simply conservative. Since the mid-2000s it has become "extremely" far-right, a bit like the French UMP, with its tendency toward the so-called strong right.
9. Statement made by Marine Le Pen on the radio program *Matins de France Culture*, February 13, 2014.
10. Le Pen, *Matins de France Culture*.
11. Organization for Economic Cooperation and Development (OECD), *International Migration Outlook 2013* (Paris: OECD Publishing, 2013).
12. Ibid.
13. Ibid.
14. Raphaël Liogier, *Le mythe de l'islamisation: Essai sur une obsession collective* (Paris: Seuil, 2016).
15. As Éric Zemmour argues in his books or on his weekly television show *Z&N* on Paris Première, notably on December 9, 2015.
16. Liogier, *Le mythe de l'islamisation*.

3.2. THE REJECTION OF THE OTHER, IDENTITY RADICALIZATION, AND THE COLONIAL UNCONSCIOUS

30
NANORACISM AND THE FORCE OF EMPTINESS

Achille Mbembe

AT FIRST GLANCE, our era appears to have discovered its truth. Liberated from its inhibitions, it can now bare itself, naked. It can let its masks fall and shed its costumes. The era of repression (supposing there ever really was one) has given way to an era of disinhibition—but at what price, for whom, and how long will it last? Indeed, in the salty marshes of this nascent century, there is nothing left to hide. All taboos have been lifted; all interdictions banished. Everything is today transparent, and thus also fully accomplished. The water tank is almost full and night is falling. We will soon learn if the outcomes are spectacular or not. In the meantime, racism—in France, Europe, and the rest of the world—shall remain in our midst for the foreseeable future. That is not only the case in mass culture, but also—and it is important not to forget this—among those in high society.

In the past, amusement was found in games, circuses, intrigues, rumors, and secrets. Europe has become a boring ice floe, and entertainment is now found in nanoracism—a form of patched-together narcotherapy. Nanoracism is a covert but yet pungent gas. Numbing, it engenders paralysis, particularly in this era when all elasticity has been lost and everything seems to have suddenly contracted. Contraction and paralysis: that is what we should be talking about, along with the cramps, spasms, and narrow-mindedness. Nanoracism has left its mark. Today, very few question what is normal and what is not. And since there is very little linking us to others, the only field of shared joy is that of racism. Premeditated, planned, and organized joy. Racism is accessible to all—the well-off, the not-so-well-off, the down-and-out. Racism has become a means for expressing both frustration and perversion.

The Strange Need to Stigmatize and Besmirch

"Nanoracism": addictive prejudices that get expressed in everyday, seemingly harmless gestures, looks, laughter, words, jokes, allusions, insinuations, lapses, and innuendo. Yet it should be stated also that such apparently harmless communicative acts are also mean-spirited and targeted; they are also malicious. They come from a strange desire to stigmatize others, to inflict harm, to humiliate and besmirch those we do not consider to be one of us. Clearly, in this era when all we care about are ourselves, nobody wants to hear about others (capitalized or uncapitalized, it doesn't matter). Let them stay in their own countries. When they insist on living with us, in our home, they appear filthy and despicable. Today's nanoracism is a sewage racism, a sooty racism, of swine wallowing in filth.

It turns us into thick-skinned and malevolent soldiers. It relegates most of those we take for *undesirables* to intolerable conditions. We inflict incalculable wounds on them, stripping them of all rights and dishonoring them to the point that they have no option but self-deportation. A "great departure" from a place that could never be theirs. And, since we are on the topic of racist wounds, let it be pointed out that such lesions inflicted on human beings represent a painful and indelible blow that attacks both the material body and intangible aspects of the self (dignity, self-esteem, and so forth). Those scars are especially powerful in part because they are invisible.

And, since we are on the topic of lesions and blows, let it be pointed out that there are thousands of people exposed to racist injuries in Europe every day. They are constantly under threat of racist attacks by individuals, institutions, voices, and public and private authorities. They are constantly being asked to justify why they are here, asked to state how long they plan on staying, where they come from, where they are going, and of course when they will be leaving. These authorities and voices shock, irritate, and offend. And in many instances, they violate people. Indeed, they attack people where they are most vulnerable, intruding on what is most private.

And, since we are on the topic of lesions and blows, let it be pointed out that nanoracism is not the privilege of "poor white people"—those subalterns who are tormented by resentment, who deeply hate their own condition, and whose ultimate nightmare would be to wake up one day as a black or Arab person. No, as was the case in the colonies, nanoracism is proper to the target's own country.

On the Mechanics of Racism

Nanoracism is an obvious complement to hydraulic racism—that of micro- and macro-, legal, bureaucratic, and institutional mechanisms. Hydraulic racism is the government machine that shuffles and multiplies undocumented and illegal persons and militarizes borders. It is the impetus behind the surveillance of buses, air terminals, metros, and streets. It is the ideology behind *unveiling* Muslim women, increasing the number of detention centers and transit camps, investing in deportation techniques, discriminating in broad daylight despite claims of neutrality, impartiality, secularism, and republicanism. Meanwhile, the government insists on invoking, in an example of glaring hypocrisy, notions of "human and citizen rights." Nanoracism is a culture of racism. It is commonplace, banal. It has managed to seep into society's pores and veins, at a time of generalized lobotomy and mass hypnotism. The great, visceral fear is that of Saturnalia, when today's *jinns*—negroes, Arabs, Muslims—exchange places with their masters and plunge the nation into predation, chaos, and darkness.

What is the definition of "nanoracism"? Shameless dealings in words and deeds, symbols, and language. A series of repeated, mimetic blows, ever more brutal. Secularism and its inverted mirror, fundamentalism. Cynicism reigns. All names have lost their first names. There are no more names to name the scandal. There is no language to speak of this vile thing. The center cannot hold. There is mucus in the nostrils, viscous and purulent, although the need to sneeze has passed. The call of common sense, of the good old Republic. The call of yellow-bellied humanism. The call of decaying feminism. None of it moves anyone anymore. As a result, we have to forget all of that, all these ossified mythologies. We have to move on to something else. But what?

Despite the horrors of the slave trade and colonialism's skeletons, of fascism, Nazism, the Holocaust, and other genocides and massacres, European nations, whose intestines are swollen with all kinds of gas, continue to mobilize racism in the service of all sorts of stories, each more preposterous and more murderous than the last—stories about foreigners, intruders that have to be expelled, enemies that have to be eradicated, terrorists that have to be exploded from a distance; stories about blood, slit throats, soil, the nation and traditions, identity, pseudocivilizations, national security; all manner of stories concocted and told ad infinitum.

There is a fear that these stories, having fomented misery and chaos from afar (far from the gaze of their citizens), may lead to reprisals and acts of vengeance, according to the logics of an eye for an eye. As a way of protecting themselves from vengeful impulses, they rely on racism, which was first forged in the era of slavery and the colonies as a kind of curved blade, a poisonous attribute of a tattered nationalism. Indeed, nationalism has been weakened by the trends of denationalizing decision-making centers and offshore wealth, of hemming in real powers and raising levels of debt.

An Obscene Right to Foolishness and Violence

If racism has become insidious, it is also because it coheres with the instinctual mechanisms and economic subjectivity of our time. It has not simply become a product of consumption like so many other goods, objects, and merchandise. In these obscene times, it is the resource without which, to use Guy Debord's words, the "society of the spectacle" could not exist.[1] In many cases, it has become an extravagance. We treat ourselves to it, not because it is a rare commodity, but in response to a generalized tendency toward neoliberalism's bawdiness. Forget general protests. Today, brutality, sensuality, and hysterical antipathy prevail. Fun and games are the order of the day. How can I show that I am satisfied in myself and fully exercising my right to folly, my right to ridicule those weaker than me? This lucre-obsessed era is a mix of lewdness, brutality, and sensuality. It favors a process of assimilating racism through the "society of spectacle," thinkers who are "media darlings," and contemporary modes of consumption.

We engage and contribute to racism without realizing it. Then we act surprised when others point out our behavior or bring us back into line. Racism feeds our need for amusement and provides an escape from the ambient ennui and monotony of modern life. We pretend that our words and deeds are meaningless. We are offended when values from another order deny us the right to laugh, of the right to a form of humor that is never directed at ourselves (self-mockery) or at those in power (satire). It is always directed at the weakest among us—the right to laugh at the expense of the people we seek to stigmatize. A carefree and joyous nanoracism thanks to which we take pleasure in being ignorant and uphold our right to foolishness and violence. That is our current situation.

That is the spirit of our times. And we should be concerned that the shift is already underway. That it may be too late. That the Great Withdrawal is already here. And that, in the end, the dream of a decent society is now just that—nothing but a dream. We should be concerned about the violent return of an era where racism is no longer contained to the "shameful parts" of society, those that we try to hide. We will dress ourselves in valiant and ribald racism and, because of it, a quiet rebellion against society will become increasingly vehement.

The issue of belonging remains unsolved. Who is from here and who is not? What do those terms, here and there, even mean? Who must be kept at bay, why, and how? We are here for all manner of reasons, and most of them are known to us. Once again we have to insist on one of those reasons. France, real or official, will never be as before—monochrome. There will never again be—

if indeed there ever was—a single way to be French. From now on, France will be branded with the plural, and there is absolutely nothing we can do to reverse this trend.

Achille Mbembe is a philosopher and political scientist, and is Research Professor at the WITS Institute for Social and Economic Research (WISER) at the University of Witwatersrand in South Africa. His books include *Les jeunes et l'ordre politique en Afrique noire* (1985), *La naissance du maquis dans le Sud-Cameroun, 1920–1960: Histoire des usages de la raison en colonie* (1996), *On the Postcolony* (2001), *Sortir de la grande nuit: Essai sur l'Afrique décolonisée* (2010), *Critique de la raison nègre* (2013), and *Politiques de l'inimitié* (2016).

Notes

1. Guy Debord, *The Society of the Spectacle*, trans. Donald Nicholson-Smith (New York: Zone Books, 1994 [1967]).

31

ANTIRACISM

A FAILED FIGHT OR THE END OF AN ERA?

Emmanuel Debono

THE PERCEIVED RESURGENCE of different forms of racism, and the question of the failure of the antiracism movement, has been a recurrent topic in the media. In October 2013, OpinionWay published a poll showing that 70 percent of those interviewed considered antiracism organizations ineffective; meanwhile, 74 percent of interviewees were unfamiliar with such organizations, and 86 percent expressed a lack of interest.[1]

As with all great causes, antiracism includes at least three aspects: individual, collective, and institutional. At a time when antiracism movements are under attack, often being reduced to their most militant forms, it seems important to preface this chapter with the observation that the failure of some collective movements should not necessarily undermine the legitimacy of a cause. Moreover, it is important to acknowledge the difficulties inherent in harmonizing the three above-mentioned aspects, especially since antiracism movements also involve moral imperatives, political interests, and multiple subjectivities.

Government initiatives targeting racism have always elicited criticism, both from opponents of the cause and from those who make up the antiracism sphere, which has become fractured over the past several years. The situation may seem paradoxical: antiracism has never garnered as much interest and media attention; yet, at the same time, the cause no longer manages to mobilize the kind of support that it had in the past. Rallies and marches have given way to academic and think tank conferences, which are attended by a much more restricted crowd. What does antiracism activism look like in France today? With the Front National receiving more votes than ever before, does it make sense to speak of "failure"? Or is this instead a redistribution of cards in a deeply disrupted national and international climate?

The Failure in Questions

To question antiracism activism is necessarily to ask about its track record. Have antiracism organizations failed?[2] Do they still serve the causes they claim to serve?[3] In today's climate, where racist speech has become more commonplace, they have been asked to account for themselves and explain how they are useful. To speak of failure in a struggle such as antiracism is, in itself, to admit that the phenomenon under attack has not been eradicated. Worse: that it has been renewed, that it is reemerging and metamorphosing. Today's resurgence of racism undermines the belief that education, coupled with legal consequences, was the solution. To speak of failure is also to presume that eliminating this complex and shifting issue was ever possible. We know, however, how difficult it is to change mentalities, be they collective, individual, or structural. Finally, it is also to blame those who have been fighting for this cause—be they members of antiracism organizations or state institutions—for the failure of the fight, despite the plurality of explanatory factors.

The following considerations invite us to put the weight of antiracism activism into perspective and to acknowledge the elements over which it does not have direct control: globalization, the economic crisis, geopolitical tensions and conflicts, migratory flows, and so forth. That is not to call such activism powerless. Indeed, its involvement in society and public policy has had an impact on democratic life. Traditionally, antiracism organizations have acted as watchdogs. They monitor racist speech and actions in society. The adoption of a more or less adequate antiracism legal framework has helped discredit racist behavior. In that sense, lobbying from antiracism organizations has played an undeniable role in helping shift opinion and in making racism more unacceptable. However, it has not completely erased displays of racial hatred.

The legal framework established to fight racism cannot be viewed as a complete failure. It has succeeded in changing individual and collective behavior. As a counterpoint, organizations have been accused of policing thought and torpedoing public debate. For instance, they are criticized of undermining debates surrounding immigration. Organizations, which have given themselves the mission of tracking racism and establishing an antiracist norm, are seen as censoring. They are called "virtue leagues," and they are often critiqued for political correctness and self-righteousness.[4] The twentieth century saw antiracism become increasingly institutionalized. Initially limited to a handful of specialized leagues, such as the Ligue des droits de l'homme (Human

Rights League, LDH)[5] and the Ligue internationale contre l'antisémitisme (International League against Anti-Semitism, LICA),[6] over time it became ubiquitous throughout society, particularly at the level of government. The socioeconomic status of activists (lawyers, politicians, elected officials, etc.) favored its spread through such milieus. Events of the Second World War—with the exterminations being perceived as a demonstration of the destructive power of hate speech—also played a role.

It is also important to note the important influence of European and international institutions and, in particular, UNESCO (beginning in the 1950s). Antiracism represented a set of values and principles, which were incorporated into the Fifth Republic's constitution. Those values and principles were subsequently translated into codes of conduct and voluntarist policies (notably within the national education system). Many, liberals included, considered such inclusions to be too ideological, suffocating, and liberticidal. In itself, that type of criticism cannot be considered a "failure" of antiracism activism. Rather, these inclusions are an example of activists achieving what they had set out to do. What would constitute a failure would rather be a set of actions ill adapted to racism such as it exists in French society. That would, in part, explain the divisions within the antiracism "movement" or "loose conglomeration." The antiracism landscape is fragmented. As such, it can appear to be in decay. But if one takes a long-term view, one can see a process of continual rebuilding.

Fragmented Antiracism Landscape

Antiracism activism has always encountered criticism, some forms pointing to contradictions[7] and others dismissing its ends and means on grounds of principle.[8] Detractors have always criticized its moral weight, political influence, methods, and limits. For instance: when the LICA became the Ligue internationale contre le racisme et l'antisémitisme (International League against Racism and Anti-Semitism, LICRA) in 1979, it was accused of threatening freedom of expression, advocating for Jewish interests (identity politics today), and working to dismantle the nation.

Such criticism was voiced in the postwar years, when the creation of new antiracism structures, such as the Movement contre le racisme, l'antisémitisme et pour la paix (Movement against Racism, Anti-Semitism, and for Peace), later becoming the Movement contre le racisme et pour l'amitié entre les peuples (Movement against Racism and for Friendship Among People, MRAP) in 1977 or the Comité d'action de défense démocratique (Action Committee in Defense of Democracy), in 1960, exposed ideological fractures surrounding communism, which prevented antiracism groups from marching under the same banner. Dissent was also expressed in the 1970s, when a new generation of organizations defending immigrants (such as the Movement des travailleurs arabes [Movement of Arab Laborers], MTA) and those who rallied around the periodical *Sans Frontière* expressed a desire to dispense with advocates and fight for their own rights.[9]

In 1983, the Marche pour l'égalité et contre le racisme (March for Equality and against Racism), inappropriately dubbed the *Marche des Beurs*, led to the creation of the movement of SOS Racisme the following year.[10] The organization was accused of turning the struggle against racism into a media spectacle. It was also criticized for maintaining a paternalistic view of Arabs (*Beurs*). Enthusiasm for diversity led to relativistic thinking, which put French society's republican framework into question, particularly with respect to the issue of Islam's place in the public domain. The left was accused of abandoning the proletariat in favor of immigrants and foreigners (advocacy for "undocumented" persons), leaving the former to seek out representation with its historic ally, the Front National.[11]

The process by which antiracism activism became fractured had always existed in some form at the organizational level. Such divisions reflected openness toward social and political debates. They also denoted democratic functioning. Organizations are places for people to express themselves, often in contradictory manners. Through dialogue, they establish mission statements and action plans. All organizations, at some point in their history, experience heated debate, divisions, and schisms. The expression of diverse opinions has led the movement to think about antiracism in its plurality. It is not a church. It does not rely on doctrine, nor does it promote a single idea. But that does not mean that activists are sheltered from being dogmatic. Its discourse changes with time, in reaction to events and the changing sociological milieus of the different organizations. Attacks that view the antiracism movement in frozen and monolithic terms are not credible. The complex and chaotic history of the movement are proof of that. Some attacks are simply thinly veiled excuses to fight the general philosophy and moral stance of antiracism.

Over time, institutionalization has made antiracism ubiquitous in society. Pressured by the increasing electoral popularity of the Front National, the political sphere has become preoccupied with antiracist ideas, translating them into political measures. The creation of government entities like the Haute Autorité de lutte contre les discriminations et pour l'égalité (High Authority for the Fight Against Discrimination and for Equality, HALDE), in 2004, the Défenseurs des droits (Defender of Rights) in 2008 with its first mandate in 2011, or the Délégation interministérielle à la lutte contre le racisme et l'antisémitisme (Inter-Ministerial Delegation for the Fight against Racism and Anti-Semitism, DILCRA), in 2012,[12] can be viewed as the accomplishment of a process that began in the early twenty-first century. Those entities represent an effort to implement government initiatives geared toward fighting racism. They have also been subject to criticism, which has tended to focus on the state's use of authoritarian language and its preoccupation with its own agenda. Some see such initiatives as a way for the state to wash its hands of real issues (discrimination, segregation, "invisibility" of those with immigrant backgrounds). They accuse the state of using the antiracism "cause" for its own ends. Such criticism grew in the early 2000s, particularly after the urban riots of November 2005, which led to the creation of new organizations seeking to listen directly, without intermediaries, to victims of racism and discrimination (notably in disadvantaged neighborhoods).

The End of a Model of Antiracism?

The fractured landscape of antiracism activism can be explained by both structural and economic causes. Its current dynamic may even appear to signal the change of an era. Rather than a "failure" of antiracism, are we not instead witnessing the limits of one model of antiracism? The answer is multifaceted. From a certain point of view, antiracist organizations of the past (LDH, LICRA, MRAP, SOS Racisme) formed a "common front" in November 2013, in response to racist insults directed at then minister of justice, Christiane Taubira.

Despite diverging interpretations of the situation and political positions, those organizations were forced to agree, in a more or less flexible form of universalism, on an antiracist republican discourse that took into account all victims of racism. Despite some disagreements (for example, concerning the opportunity to dissociate the antiracism movement from the fight against antisemitism), they offered an overarching interpretation of the situation and cooperated with public authorities (financing, conferences, partnerships). Today, there seem to be two competing paradigms for understanding the issue of racism. The first can be described as a traditional approach. It tends to locate the cause of racism in ignorance and social poverty, viewing prejudice as a fuel for hate speech and actions. Those who adhere to this paradigm consider racism in terms of its interindividual and intergroup forms. Solutions proposed include education and the implementation of antiracist legislation, with an emphasis on the following concepts: the value of otherness, tolerance, human rights, fraternity, the values of the Republic, solidarity, diversity, social harmony, the duty to remember, democracy, vigilance, antifascism, and so forth. Unable to grasp the full reality of discrimination, this moralizing approach has been attacked by a new generation of activists, who are quick to point out its limitations.

The second form of criticism is based on a sociological reading of relationships of domination, which are perceived to act within society, particularly with respect to racial tensions. References are made to oppressed minorities, the dominant and the dominated, white privilege, racialization, and invisibility. *Coloniality* has been designated as key to reading these social phenomena. The continued existence of colonial and neocolonial mentalities is viewed as the reason why a portion of the French population (with backgrounds tied to the former colonies) has been kept in an inferior position, and why it has been denied access to true and full citizenship. That form of antiracist thinking derives its inspiration from black struggles for emancipation in the United States, transferring aspects from that context, with little attention to nuance, onto the French situation.[13] It is also applied to other minority struggles, and it has adopted the idea of "intersectionality," which was introduced in the early 1990s by American feminist Kimberlé Crenshaw.[14] Intersectionality is the assertion that different forms of domination exist for different people, and that they cannot be understood jointly. It is also worth noting the pro-Palestinian sentiment expressed by these organizations; that explains why some of them, such as the Parti des Indigènes de la République (PIR), present radical anti-Zionist tendencies. Antisemitism, which has been bracketed from these movements' agendas, is relegated and even relativized. "Minority" activism blames the state and the "system." It also finds inspiration in black movements against segregation in the United States, notably that of the Black Panthers. It denounces "institutional racism," which it also calls "state racism" and "systemic racism." The authorities and political culture are deemed the primary sources of discrimination.

However, the break with so-called mainstream antiracism movements is not all-encompassing. Dialogue does exist between old guard organizations and the new generation. The latter offer nuance to the former's approach, acting in productive ways that blend their struggle against prejudice with the need for reparations (for slavery and colonization). One example is the Conseil représentatif des associations noires (Representative Council of Black Organizations, CRAN). Others, like the PIR and the Brigade anti-négrophobie (Anti-Negrophobia Brigade, BAN), deny "white" organizations the ability to act and express themselves in the name of victims.

The *Exhibit B* affair in late 2014—after memorials for the thirtieth anniversary of the *Marche des Beurs* by some organizations tied to North African immigration—clarified the need to reappropriate struggles co-opted by white antiracism movements. Such activists favored an identity-based and selective approach to antiracism that assigned victimhood identities to individuals and groups who did not fundamentally perceive themselves as such.

Points of Friction

The emergence of new trends, which are still held by a minority but which also impact public debate, is a testament to the lacunae in traditional antiracist thinking. Divisions abound, both in terms of diagnoses and goals. I will offer some examples here, reminding readers that antiracism traditionally faces two types of obstacles: how to qualify the phenomena under question, and finding the proper tools to evaluate their true social impact.

The issue of "Islamophobia" occupies an important place in current debates, most prominently in the context of new activist structures. It has engendered deep divisions in the field of antiracism, between those who seek to make it a focus of current protests against racism and those who do not believe that criticism of the Muslim religion should be included in conversations about racism. Another layer in that heated debate resides in the fact that the rejection of "Islamophobia" as a form of racism has led some people to ignore the reality of racism against Arabs and Maghrebis. Inversely, community-based organizations such as the Collectif contre l'islamophobie en France (Collective against Islamophobia in France, CCIF) emphasize the porousness of culture and religion as a means of acknowledging the right to difference in the public space. Given the climate, where frequent slippage has become harmful to republican and democratic values, it is important to actively reexamine the definition of secularism. That would help guarantee freedom of religion and ward off extremism of all stripes.

More generally, the right to difference has become a divisive subject. Antiracism actors do not agree on the shape and limits of such a right. The struggle against racism and antisemitism has always included internal tension, particularly in its aim to draw attention to singular entities within the national culture. The limits of such tolerance were stretched in the 1970s, which was a decade that celebrated multiculturalism and interculturality. In the end, differentialism became accepted and advocated thanks to trends in identity politics. Critics were thus able to suggest that the antiracism movement undermined national cohesion through its emphasis on expressions of individual identity over common values. Debates have become particularly heated today because of pressures created by globalization, a weakening of republican values, militant identity politics, and have in turn bolstered ethnocentrism. In today's chaotic climate, which some observers attribute to "cultural insecurity,"[15] antiracists defend diverging causes, some emphasizing the importance of the republican state, others questioning what they perceive as that state's inherent racism. The Republic has therefore been accused of privileging some communities and embracing "philo-Semitism."

The republican regime's vision of the assimilationist ideal changed under integration pressures in the postwar years. In the past, antiracism movements advocated integration measures. That is no longer the case for all groups within the antiracism nebula. Some universalist organizations emphasize integration as an aim, while others see the term as normative and condescending. For some, a democratic society should protect diversity, which is often described as a strength. Integration, which is expected of foreign populations, could also, through a perversion of thought, be a constituting element of the French population, due to autonomy maintained with regard to the national culture. Debates surrounding national identity under the Nicolas Sarkozy administration (2007–2012) added to the confusion over immigration and diversity within the French populace. Elites have shown themselves to be inept at thinking alterity. Multicultural society has been upheld as a foil, despite its historical and sociological reality. Tensions surrounding the subject, together with unbridled stigmatizing speech, sometimes at the highest levels of government, have contributed to accentuating some social and cultural fractures.

The issue of "antiwhite racism" reveals divergent understandings of paradigms about racism. The reality of the phenomenon is rejected by those who consider that racism can only occur in relationships of domination. So-called racialized populations, which are defined as being dominated, are believed incapable of being at the origin of racist acts—or at least at the extreme margins—since they are not in a position to exercise discriminatory actions. Some observers base their ideas on a restricted reading of racism, ignoring interindividual relationships. Due to their systematic rejection of the possibility of "racism by victims," their reality is incomplete. On the other hand, the LICRA was the plaintiff in a case in which a man had been physically attacked in the Paris metro and called a "white bastard" or "whitey" (2010). It is also worth noting that the MRAP underwent an internal crisis for having appropriated, for its own purposes and fleetingly, the notion of "antiwhite racism."[16]

A debate like the one dealing with antiwhite racism shows different interpretations of racism. One focuses on discrimination and structures. The other attempts to expose all forms of racism, regardless of their source. SOS Racisme has been conducting real-world operations to test levels of racism since 1996. Such operations are viewed as a waste of time by activists like the collective Stop le Contrôle au Faciès! (End Racial Profiling), which seeks to expose discrimination by authorities. Exposing systematic racism generally goes hand in hand with an anticapitalist discourse that draws inspiration from the far left. Rather than the end of an era, it seems more appropriate to speak of a shift in the history of antiracism. Old forms of activism have seen a drop in adherents, and new organizations have been working to renew political action in this domain. Radical discourse and media operations have nevertheless restricted their audience.

The difficulties in establishing unified action can be seen in the scattered forms of political engagement described above. The climate in France today is one of crisis, and French society is deeply divided. A new generation of activists is unlikely to replace older versions, especially if one considers the antiestablishment weight of new organizations. Detractors or defenders of antiracism may one day free themselves of reductive thinking, dismissive practices, and invective speech. But they will not be able to free themselves completely of a dense activist heritage. A fundamental fight is taking place today regarding the Republic's values, especially that of secularism. The antiracism movement, where ideals of social harmony clash with identity politics and a universalism that can exclude others, may not be an appropriate venue for that fight to take place. If the antiracism movement needs renovation, it would be imprudent—and even irresponsible—to eradicate, through impoverished criticism, its existence. It is difficult to imagine that a democratic society can thrive without it. Perhaps it can be reimagined as a demand for universality, beyond the abuses of imperial and ethnocentric universalism.

Emmanuel Debono is a historian, Research Director at the Institut français in Paris, Chargé d'études at the École normale supérieure in Lyon, and the representative in France of the USC Shoah Foundation. Recent publications include a special edition of the journal *Archives juives* on *Années trente: L'emprise sociale de l'antisémitisme en France* (2010) and the book *Aux origines de l'antiracisme: La LICA, 1927–1940* (2012).

Notes

1. The poll was commissioned by the Ligue internationale contre le racisme et l'antisémitisme (LICRA) and conducted by OpinionWay (October 2013), with a sample of 1,003 French people.
2. Broadcast of *Service public* from May 13, 2014 on France Inter.
3. Broadcast of *Du grain à moudre* from November 18, 2014 on France Culture.
4. See Richard Millet, *De l'antiracisme comme terreur littéraire* (Paris: Pierre-Guillaume de Roux, 2012).
5. Emmanuel Naquet, *Pour l'humanité: La Ligue des droits de l'homme, de l'affaire Dreyfus à la défaite de 1940* (Rennes: Presses universitaires de Rennes, 2014).
6. Emmanuel Debono, *Aux origines de l'antiracisme: La LICA (1927–1940)* (Paris: CNRS Éditions, 2012).
7. Pierre-André Taguieff, *La force du préjugé: Essai sur le racisme et ses doubles* (Paris: La Découverte, 1988), *Face au racisme* (Paris: Seuil, 1991), and *Les fins de l'antiracisme* (Paris: Michalon, 1995).

8. See Henry de Lesquen, ed., *Penser l'antiracisme* (Paris: Godefroy de Bouillon, 1999).

9. Daniel A. Gordon, *Immigrants and Intellectuals: May 68 and the Rise of Anti-Racism in France* (London: The Merlin Press Ltd., 2012).

10. Philippe Juhem, "SOS-Racisme, histoire d'une mobilisation 'apolitique': Contribution à une analyse des transformations des représentations politiques après 1981," PhD diss., University of Nanterre, 1998.

11. See the critique of "immigrationism" in Paul Yonnet, *Voyage au centre du malaise français: L'antiracisme et le roman national* (Paris: Gallimard, 1993).

12. The interministerial delegation was placed under the authority of the prime minister in November 2014.

13. See, for example, the "March for Dignity and against Racism," organized by the Marche des Femmes pour la Dignité (Mafed), which took place in Paris on October 31, 2015.

14. Kimberlé Crenshaw, "Mapping the Margins: Intersectionality, Identity Politics, and Violence against Women of Color," *Stanford Law Review* 6, no. 43 (July 1991): 1241–1299.

15. Laurent Bouvet, *L'insécurité culturelle* (Paris: Fayard, 2015).

16. Sylvie Laurent and Thierry Leclère, eds., *De quelle couleur sont les Blancs? Des petits Blancs des colonies au racisme anti-Blancs* (Paris: La Découverte, 2013). The book includes both academic and activist contributions.

32

CLOSING BORDERS AGAINST FEAR

EUROPE'S RESPONSE TO THE 2015 "MIGRANTS CRISIS"

Claire Rodier

In October 2015, Frontex, the European Agency for the Management of Operational Cooperation at the External Borders of the Member States of the European Union, announced that 710,000 migrants had illegally crossed onto European soil during the first nine months of the year. This represented a sharp rise, given that it had announced in early June 2015 having recorded approximately 100,000 illegal crossings since the month of January, compared with 40,000 over the same period in 2014. These numbers fed a climate of panic that had emerged a few months earlier in Europe following two devastating shipwrecks off the Sicilian coast which had resulted in the deaths of almost fifteen hundred people. Meanwhile, media images depicted hordes of exiles landing on Greek and Italian shorelines and crossing the Balkans. Those images represented what has been described as an unprecedented "migratory crisis."

When questioned as to calculation methods used to produce such figures, Frontex acknowledged that they represented the number of illegal border crossings into Europe—not the actual number of people who had illegally entered Europe. They explained that "Irregular border crossings may be attempted by the same person several times in different locations at the external border. This means that a large number of the people who were counted when they arrived in Greece were again counted when entering the EU for the second time through Hungary or Croatia."[1] The nuance is an important one. Indeed, the numbers provided do not account for the proportion of migrants recorded several times. Nor do they indicate the means by which people were recorded. The reliability of these numbers is an issue, since border teams hired by Frontex—which are made up of civil servants from concerned member states—may have an interest in inflating the number of "illegals" setting foot on their soil. Waving the red flag of migratory invasion may be a means of pressuring European partners regarding the very real issue of hosting migrants. It could even be used as an instrument of political blackmail.

Indeed, in March 2015, the Greek minister of defense threatened the Eurogroup with "flooding Europe with migrants" if Europe abandoned Greece in the crisis. Migrant data has also been used to create fear among Europeans with respect to foreigners. The Hungarian prime minister Viktor Orban did as much when, seeking to justify the construction of a wall with Serbia and Romania, he spoke of the arrival of a "hundred million [migrants], coming from the Middle East and Africa."[2] Although presented in a smooth fashion, the French Interior Minister's discourse does not differ in substance from Viktor's Orban populist and racist stands. During a visit to Calais on September 21, 2015,[3] he referenced the Frontex figures ("710,000 immigrants entered the EU in the first nine months of 2015"), emphasizing that as many migrants had arrived "in nine months as had arrived between 2009 and 2015."[4] He failed to mention the nuances Frontex had added regarding those figures.

The Real Victims of the European Migrants Crisis

Regardless of whether or not the number of migrants arriving in Europe in 2015 has been overstated, the high number of migrants does indicate a crisis. But the European Union, despite what official communications may have us believe, is not the party that is primarily affected. The crisis first and foremost affects the hundreds of thousands of people who have been forced to flee their countries due to war, mistreatment, and living conditions that threaten their survival. Moreover, it places them in a situation where they have no other choice but to arrive in host countries illegally. A striking number of those migrating, being forced to do so by illegal means, risk their lives (more than five thousand people died trying to reach Europe between January 2014 and December 2015, totaling more than thirty thousand since the late 1990s)—to the point that the International Organization for Migration (IOM) has deemed Europe "the most dangerous destination in the world for undocumented migration." The crisis also affects so-called initial host countries, which are located near sources of exodus.

The example of Syria is eye-opening: in October 2012, the United Nations High Commission for Refugees (UNHCR), noticing that most refugees fleeing Syria (344,000 at the time) were arriving in neighboring countries (Iraq, Jordan, Lebanon, and Turkey), recommended that countries in the European Union "ensure access [to their] territory and access to asylum procedures," and that they "offer mutual support between member states." The appeal was in vain. A million people fled the country in 2013, three million in 2014, four million in 2015. Of those millions, only a few tens of thousands were able to reach Europe, with the additional peril of losing their lives. In fact, most member states in the European Union have denied visas to Syrians, forcing them to attempt to cross the Mediterranean in dangerous conditions, the result of which has been repeated shipwrecks, as headlined in the news.

The European Union ignored urgent requests from the United Nations to provide financial support to international aid programs working to help initial host countries. Meanwhile, they bolstered surveillance measures at their borders. Over the four years during which the crisis began to unfold at their doorstep, European governments, in the name of combatting illegal immigration, chose to turn their backs on refugees and ignore the impact of migrant arrivals in host countries like Lebanon (where Syrians now represent a quarter of the population) and Turkey (which counted two million refugees in late 2015).

Europe's posture of avoidance when it comes to exiles seeking protection is an extension of a global inequality. Eighty percent of the world's 60 million victims of forced migration live in developing countries. Of the 16.7 million refugees accounted for by the UNHCR, fewer than 20 percent are in industrialized countries. The "block" that includes Europe, the United States, Australia, and Canada only hosts 15 percent. By comparison, there are 25 percent in sub-Saharan Africa. The European Union's twenty-eight member states host just 1.7 million, which is the same number as in Pakistan alone. Since 2013, the continuous arrival of vessels carrying tens of thousands of *boat people* to the southern coasts of the European Union has been striking, but it cannot be termed invasion. Since May 2015, European leaders have held dozens of meetings on how to manage the migrants who have already arrived on their soil, acknowledging that Greece and Italy cannot continue to bear the responsibility alone.

The European Commission has orchestrated a gang of hypocrites. To wit: the British home secretary suggested migrants crossing the Mediterranean be sent back; or those supporting an equitable distribution of refugees within the European Union, one based on variables like GDP (Gross Domestic Product), unemployment rates, and the number of refugees already being hosted (as suggested by France). In reality, discussions on refugee "quotas" have shown that European Union member states, with a few rare exceptions, are mostly preoccupied with receiving as few migrants already present on European soil as possible. Furthermore, they reluctantly accept taking in refugees now on the premise that they will not have to let in additional migrants later.

From Quotas to Relocation

Since May 2015, those two concerns—limiting the number of migrants to take in, and avoiding additional migrants—have constituted the cornerstone of Europe's policy toward the "migrants crisis." The policy has been organized according to a number of elements. In September 2015, after several months of negotiations and stalling, the president of the European Commission announced the conclusions of the agreement made by European member states to distribute a portion of the refugees that had already arrived in the southern parts of the Union.

The term *quota* was replaced by *relocation* to designate taking on a portion of asylum seekers—mostly Syrians and Eritreans already present in Italy and Greece. That amounted to 160,000 people, a negligible number with respect to the scale of the Syrian exodus, at a time when almost 6,000 refugees were arriving each day on the Greek coasts.[5] It represented a dramatic difference between what was being offered and what was needed, not only in terms of the actual flow of migration at Europe's borders, but also in terms of time line. Despite the urgency of this situation, member states gave themselves two years to reach their goal, which in any case they are not likely to meet. A number of obstacles stand in their way. Relocation relies on the cooperation of individual "host" states, some of which were reluctant to sign the agreement in the first place and have since backed out of commitments. For instance, after the November 2015 attacks in Paris, Poland, which was "assigned" 7,000 people, stated that it could no longer uphold its end of the agreement, of which it had always been critical.

Sweden has traditionally been open to migration, and it also initiated the new program in late October 2015 when it received nineteen Eritreans selected in Italy. Nevertheless, Sweden announced a month later that it was no longer in a position to appropriately host refugees. As a result, it requested that some of its refugees be relocated in other countries in the European Union. The program does not take into account migrant requests as to where they ought to be relocated. Yet those arriving in Europe often have plans to live near family or members of their community, which would provide them with better opportunities for integration. Relocations, given the authoritarian form it has taken in the European Union and the reluctance of member states to host migrants, seems like an arduous task.

An example can be seen in the difficulties encountered by Italy in late 2015, when it tried to persuade migrants eligible for relocation (notably Eritrean refugees) to transfer toward countries where they did not want to go. A progress report, written by the European Commission in June 2016, shows the difficulties of implementing the program. To date, around 2,000 people, of the 160,000 initially targeted, have been relocated. The situation surrounding such relocations is increasingly tense, which does not bode well.

Hotspots for Sorting Migrants

Complementing the "host" element of the program implemented to manage the migrants crisis, a sorting mechanism has been established in the two countries where there is supposedly the largest number of asylum seekers to be relocated, Italy and Greece. Known as the "hotspot approach," this is an attempt to reassure European Union member states reluctant to welcoming asylum seekers chosen through the relocation process. Essentially, it manages the arrival of the *boat people* on the Greek islands and in southern Italy, sorting out people eligible for asylum status from "economic migrants," who are to be sent back to their countries of origin.

For a number of reasons, it is risky business, first, in terms of the distinction it seeks to establish. The complex situations that force people to flee their home countries make differences between "migrants" and "refugees" unclear. Those situations often include a complex combination of social, political, and economic factors. Any logic aimed at definitively sorting out these distinctions is therefore arbitrary. Then there are the means through which the mechanism has been implemented. The "hotspot approach" presupposes an ability to clearly identify those arriving—as a means of determining to which category they belong. It implies the use of coercion and reduced rights at Europe's southern borders.

In the name of protecting people, new types of camps have been created. Although run by European civil servants from Frontex or the European Asylum Support Office (EASO), they are not refugee camps (in theory, characterized by humanitarian care provided for by international law); nor are they holding centers, the standards for which are framed by European law. Located as they are near to sites of migrant arrival, the "hotspot" camps symbolize the "inner circle" of border delocalization; they have been a defining element in Europe's immigration and asylum policy since the early 2000s. The elimination of border control within the Schengen space also coincided with increased surveillance on its external borders, as a way of preventing undesirables from penetrating "Fortress Europe." Fifteen years later, Schengen is wavering and there has been talk and growing support for reintroducing European border checkpoints, and fences and walls have already been erected and are beginning to hinder the freedom of circulation established in the late 1990s. But despite all that, increased security around Europe, to which today's hotspots contribute, goes unquestioned.

Outsourcing Migration Management

Another element of the European Union's program to manage the "migrants' crisis" is to establish an "outer circle" of delocalization. Generally speaking, it consists in sending refugees back to their countries of origin or to countries through which migrants transit. In the name of "sharing the burden," and as a way of making neighboring countries responsible for managing migratory flow, European Union member states have long used economic partnerships and cooperation as a way of encouraging countries of emigration to maintain their populations and prevent them from coming to Europe. To that end, numerous agreements have been reached in North African and sub-Saharan African countries since the early 2000s. As a result, Morocco, Mauritania, and Senegal are today allies in the European Union's struggle against undocumented immigration. In France, "immigration control" and "development initiatives in countries of origin" were a key focus of the Ministry of Immigration, Integration, National Identity, and Co-Development during Nicolas Sarkozy's presidency. The outsourcing of the "management of migratory flow" is often very harmful to migrants and asylum seekers. In 2004 and 2005, more than a dozen people died trying to scale the walls erected around the Spanish enclaves of Ceuta and Melilla, which are under the surveillance of the Moroccan police and military.

Outsourcing migration management has remained a fundamental part of the program agreed upon by European Union member states throughout 2015, since, alongside a number of mechanisms already in place designed to manage those refugees already present on European soil, the goal has been to dissuade others from attempting to make the trip. As an extension of a European-African dialogue begun in late 2014, which put the twenty-eight member states in direct relationships with a dozen African countries, efforts were also made in East Africa. There was talk of "developing cooperation at bilateral and regional levels between countries of origin, transit and destination to tackle irregular migration and criminal networks, through concrete measures on a voluntary basis such as initiatives in the area of information-sharing, focused training and capacity building, technical assistance and the exchange of best practices." There was also talk of helping participating countries implement and manage reception centers and provide access to asylum processes "in line with international law."[6]

The presence of authoritarian regimes, major "suppliers" of refugees, among the partners involved (Eritrea, Ethiopia, Sudan) should not come as a surprise. In March 2015, the European commissioner overseeing the initiative stated: "We can't be naïve. The fact that we are cooperating with dictatorial regimes does not mean that we are legitimizing them. But we have to cooperate in order to fight contraband and human trafficking."[7] Reacting to dramatic migration episodes, the European Commission made a proposal two months later to manage migrants prior to their arrival on European shores, in order to spare them the dangers associated with crossing the Mediterranean. To that end, it announced the opening of a "multi-functional pilot center" in Niger—a kind of Sahelian hotspot—where those interested in migrating could get information on the reality of the process, local protection, and options for voluntary return for undocumented persons. The project was outlined during a European-African summit held in Malta in November 2015. During that summit, European states, asserting that they wished "to attack the deep causes of migration, work toward peace, stability, and economic development," attempted (not without meeting some resistance) to trade public development aid—a fiduciary fund of 1.8 billion euros was earmarked to fight poverty—for greater cooperation with African partners, thereby furthering their objective of curbing the flow of migrants.

Negotiations with Turkey during fall 2015 were dominated by the same goal, and the European Union was successful in reaching an agreement with Turkey, which was host to the largest number of exiled Syrians, on a "common plan of action" to manage the refugee crisis. Turkey, like East Africa, had become an important step on migration routes toward Europe. In exchange for three billion euros, Turkey was expected to open welcome centers for asylum seekers. The scheme was devised to prevent refugees from crossing Europe's borders. Then, in early December 2015, while discussions were still under way, Turkish authorities stopped thirteen hundred people (including Syrians, Afghans, Iraqis, and Iranians) preparing to cross the Aegean Sea for the Greek islands. Was that a goodwill gesture directed at the European Union? During the negotiations, French president François Hollande could not have summed up Europe's cynical dialectic any better: "We urgently need to ensure that non-EU countries hosting refugees—I am thinking of Turkey, Jordan, and Lebanon—receive help, because otherwise we all know what will happen: departures toward European coasts, with the kinds of catastrophic events I want to avoid." Europe's primary response to the plight of refugees therefore consists in drawing a quarantine line around itself and keeping them at bay.

Claire Rodier is a lawyer and the cofounder of the Euro-African network Migreurop. She works for the Groupe d'information et de soutien des immigrés (GISTI) and her research focuses on European immigration and asylum policy.

She has written several books and contributed to numerous works on these questions, including *Immigration: Fantasmes et réalités* (2008), *L'atlas des migrants en Europe* (2012), *Xénophobie business: À quoi servent les contrôles migratoires?* (2012), and *Migrants & réfugiés: Réponse aux indécis, aux inquiets et aux réticents* (2016).

Notes

1. Nando Sigona, "Seeing Double? How the EU Miscounts Migrants Arriving at Its Borders," *theconversation.com*, October 21, 2015.
2. Viktor Orban, "Interview with Viktor Orban," by Stéphane Kovacs, *Le Figaro*, September 15, 2015.
3. During this particular visit to the north of France, Bernard Cazeneuve announced increased security measures in ports and at the tunnel under the channel aimed at preventing migrants from crossing to the United Kingdom.
4. "710,000 Migrants Entered EU in First Nine Months of 2015," Report from the Frontex Agency, October 13, 2015, http://frontex.europa.eu/news/710–000-migrants-entered-eu-in-first-nine-months-of-2015-NUiBkk.
5. At the same time, the United Nations High Commissioner for Human Rights estimated that the European Union had the means "to offer asylum, for a certain number of years, to a million refugees coming from conflict zones in Syria and elsewhere."
6. Declaration of the Ministerial Conference of the Khartoum Process (EU-Horn of Africa Migration Route Initiative), Rome, November 28, 2014.
7. Cited by the Agence France Presse, March 14, 2015.

33

TOWARD A REAL HISTORY OF FRENCH COLONIALISM

Alain Ruscio

WHEN THE INK on the bottom of the French-Algerian Evian Accords, signed on March 18, 1962, dried, officializing the end of paternalistic colonialism,[1] a new era might very well have gotten underway, both at the level of international relations and for both French and Algerian societies. One might have thought that the *Colonial Party's* old forms of justification—and even self-aggrandizement—would slowly give way to a thoughtful appraisal of France's presence overseas.[2] A new era *might* very well have begun, one could have thought. But in the history of human societies, there is always a gap between what is possible and what is real. In the case of colonialism, that gap turned out to be a chasm. The nostalgic tunes from the empire and for *Greater France*—which never really disappeared—have become a symphony concert. With clear distinctions between one ideological family and another, one could argue that a *Parti néocolonial* has now been established, or, to be more precise, a *néo-Parti colonial.*

How can one be anything but stunned by the words of politicians and intellectuals who persist in justifying colonization through references to the length of roads built, the number of students educated, and narratives of fraternal relations between colonizers and *natives*? Stunned by a discourse—yes, the very same—that historians continue to dig up in the archives, find in news articles from the past, in written pleas in defense of colonization from 1885 (Jules Ferry to the House) to 1931 (Paul Reynaud at the Colonial Exhibition in Vincennes) to 1956 (Guy Mollet on television). In such a context, calling this offensive *reactionary* should not be seen as controversial. To be *reactionary*, in the political lexicon, means to encourage a return to values from the past.

February 23, 2005, saw the passage of a peculiar law, which was not an isolated episode if we consider that Chirac subsequently gave up on the infamous Article 4, which underscored the *positive aspects of colonization,* since the remainder of the law remained in force. And the left, which had held the majority in the assembly since 2011, never for a second dreamed of repealing it. Colonialism is in the process of being rehabilitated. The clan of those I shall call the *rehabilitators,* for lack of a better term, is on the offensive. Its members come from a wide array of backgrounds—ranging from former combatants of the decolonization wars to bitter intellectuals who regret their political commitments back in 1968. At their core, these *nostalgerians*[3] of all stripes today wage their offensive on all levels, from establishing monuments honoring the Organization of the Secret Army (OAS) assassins to spouting pseudohistorical claptrap on the internet.

Politicians have also taken up the cause. There is Nicolas Sarkozy and his "African man" who has yet to "enter History," Claude Guéant and his hierarchy of civilizations, Nadine Morano and her "white race," hundreds of local officials who continue to court former members of the OAS, intellectuals, such as the pathetic Éric Zemmour, now the most read author in France,[4] the recent appointee to the Académie Française, Alain Finkielkraut, who should have known better when he contrasted those of "pure French stock" with "youth with African and North African backgrounds."[5] According to him, there is no such thing as racism in France, that is, except racism on the part of those with non-French backgrounds: "Hating France has become de rigueur among a large swath of the new French population. You would have to be living under a rock to believe that militant Francophobia is actually a response to racism."[6] Jean Ferrat, alluding to his home department of Ariège and to the ardent patriot Paul Déroulède (1846–1914), once jokingly called himself the "Déroulède de l'Ariège." Today, we have our very own "Déroulède du quai de Conti" (the site of the Académie). How could one not be enraged to see the *wound on the bull's forehead,* pierced with Mauriac's spear, reborn from its ashes, and trotting through the arena? Historians are not—and cannot be—passive spectators of this rehabilitation. It is up to us to bring some order to these ideas about the past.

Some Ideas on Colonialism

More than sixty years ago now, Aimé Césaire offered a definition of colonization in his *Discourse on Colonialism*: "Bridgehead in a campaign to civilize barbarism from which there may emerge at any moment the negation of civilization pure and simple."[7] That is a definition that all hypocrites weeping over the death of the great man should have reread. Aimé Césaire's demonstration remains just as powerful and relevant today: colonization's fundamental offense was to have interrupted the historical processes of peoples who had asked for nothing, in the name of values that were not their own. Colonialism was a presence imposed onto entire peoples who rejected it, a "bridgehead to civilize barbarism," designed to "break the hold of other civilizations," and which, though no doubt less technologically evolved, nevertheless possessed infinite potential. All the rest is a consequence. One consequence: the negation of national existence—affirmed or gestating—of these countries. Another consequence: the negation of civilizations and cultures. Yet another consequence: the negation of the very humanity of the people who lived in these places. Neither patriots, nor civilized people, nor even men.

How did these people, who were conquered, repudiated, and despised, react? They resisted. And the response to that response was naturally further repression. Hence the violence that always, to varying degrees, went hand in hand with the system. One of the most damning texts in the history of ideas, as pertains to colonialism, was not written by a military brute, nor by a basic racist. It was written by a brave man, a republican, a rationalist, an editor for the socialist periodical *L'Humanité* (pre-1914), the man behind the 1920s notion of "pre-logical mentality," namely Lucien Lévy-Bruhl, who wrote the following in 1922:

> Generally speaking, primitive societies tend to be hostile to everything that comes from the outside . . . Change, even if it is clearly a form of progress, has to be forced onto them. If they are free to choose to welcome them or reject them, their choice is not a mystery . . . Relationships that seem natural and inoffensive between human societies might now expose the group to ill-defined and dubious dangers . . . Hence, the signs of dread and distrust among primitives which the whites races often interpret as expressing hostility, resulting in bloodshed, reprisals, and sometimes even the extermination of a group.[8]

Yes, you read it correctly: *extermination*. Yet another word that has cropped up in recent debates.[9] Not as a result of cold calculation or in the name of an ideology negating the right of natives to exist, but rather as a consequence of radical incomprehension of the causes behind their resistance. A classic colonial chain: conquest-revolt-repression.

Extreme Repression, but against What Advances?

The "smoke-outs" during the conquest of Algeria, the bloody marches in Tonkin, the use of aircraft against civilian populations beginning in 1914 (in Morocco). More details? Napalm in Vietnam beginning in 1951 (before the Americans!), then on Algerian soil . . . mere profits and losses? Poulo-Condore, Haiphong, Rif, Sétif, the Algiers Casbah, Madagascar, Bizerte, Cameroon, Ouvéa. Forgotten places? The torture of poor *native* bodies under tropical skies by French hands, using electricity several decades before Jacques Massu would, for example in Algeria's police stations or in the buildings of the police headquarters in Saigon. Incidental phenomena? And the guillotine, used here and there, casting a bloody shadow on France's tricolored flag. Slander? Let us reread Victor Hugo, denouncing "civilization, which arrived in Algiers in the form of a guillotine."[10] The first person guillotined in the history of colonized Algeria was named Abdelkader ben Zelouf ben Dahman. He was executed in Bab-el-Oued on February 16, 1843. The last was named Mostefa Oïs. His head fell on August 12, 1959. One hundred and sixteen years of superior civilization.

These radical forms of violence were accompanied by instances of everyday violence. They can be found in hurtful vocabulary—does one need to be reminded of derogatory appelations like *bicots, bougnoules, négros, nha-qués?*—or the constant use of the informal *tu* throughout tropical countries; of the slaps and corrective kicks administered to clumsy houseboys, or the whippings doled out to *lazy* coolies. These quotidian blows to self-esteem played a significant role in the revolts against colonialism as well as in the large waves of repression. Humiliation, swallowed rage, these were key elements in the life of the colonized. "Here," writes Monseignor Duval in a pamphlet addressed to the priests of the Algiers Diocese, "is what a North African worker living in Paris confided to me last April: 'What is most unbearable to us is not hunger, it is the fact of being an object of scorn.'"[11] In 1939, the journalist Andrée Viollis asked a Tunisian nationalist if he really believed that his country had once been a paradise. His response to her: "We don't mourn for paradise, we mourn for the loss of our country." The journalist persisted in this line of questioning, asking: "If the French left, would you be better off?" Her interlocutor offered this image in reply: "Our people would prefer the baton of a Spahi, a man of our race, to the order of a French military policeman."[12] This is of course a long way from the soaring lyricism of the decolonization era. But that small phrase says more about the process than any textbook does.

Those attempting to justify the course of history point to roads, hospitals, schools, and so forth. To this end, stories are conjured about teachers devoted to their work and living like peasants, doctors unconcerned by financial gain dispensing care and medicine (Pierre Fresnay portraying Albert Schweitzer in the black and white movies of our childhood!), nuns treating lepers, Yersin,[13] who discovered the bacillus responsible for the plague, living out his last days among the peasants of Annam, and Brazza visiting African villages ("Touch this flag, and you will be free men!"), Pavie journeying to *win over the hearts* of Laotians. A certain form of anticolonialism no doubt attempted to negate all of that. None of it was human, scientific, or convincing.

Yes, *France* did build roads and railroads, but if one considers colonization from the point of view of the colonized, as opposed to that of the colonizer, things look rather different. The capital and the technicians were French. So were the profits. But what about the labor? Who suffered, who (too often) died during the interminable construction periods? Let us not forget that forced labor was the institutionalized norm until 1945. What positive aspects of colonization could possibly ever erase the horrific slaughter that took place during the construction of the railroad system, as in the case of the famous Congo–Ocean line? Albert Londres, André Gide, and Georges Simenon, all gave shocking reports, citing estimates (never refuted) that make one's head spin. Indeed, most historians agree on the figure of twenty thousand deaths for the Congo–Ocean railway construction project alone.[14] After all that, didn't the *natives* have the right to lay claim to the infrastructure, for which they had paid so dearly with their sweat and blood?

Yes, *France* did build infrastructure that was far more modern than what existed previously in the conquered countries, but the *natives* were the ones who bore the cost, before, it is true, France made investments (after the Second World War) as a response to the generalized risk of revolt in the colonies that were no longer cost effective. Will those who subscribe to the *positive effects of colonization* dare to scrutinize the balance sheets from colonial Indochina where also, in some years, over half of the revenue was accounted for by proceeds from the state-owned industries of salt, opium, and alcohol? What that means concretely is that colonial authorities forced each province, each district, and each village to buy salt (one is reminded of the medieval salt tax), drugs, alcohol, and rice wine from the state or its distributors!

Yes, the admirable devotion on the part of colonial doctors, pasteurian researchers, and nuns often did reduce disease, but the *overall* picture is far from being inspiring. In Tunisia, seven hospitals were built during the seventy years that colonization lasted. By 1956, there was one hospital or clinic bed for every ten thousand inhabitants, a ratio one hundred times smaller than in the mainland. At the same time in Algeria, there was still only one doctor per 5,250 people (in France, one for every thousand). And 70 percent of generalists were located in Algiers and in large cities, where the European population mostly lived. In rural areas, the proportion went down to one doctor per fourteen thousand residents. In 1946, in all of French West Africa, there were eight hospitals; in French Equatorial Africa, there were six. One simply cannot ignore the discrepancy between the propaganda—photographs of gleaming hospitals in the weekly editions of *L'Illustration*—and the reality, in other words, the practical impossibility for the vast majority of colonized people to gain access to basic care.

Yes, hundreds of thousands of children and adolescents received an education, but millions of others remained illiterate. During the heyday of colonialism, in the 1930s, there were exactly 21,439 school establishments spread throughout the empire. Despite the fact that there were an estimated 25 million children of school age. In French West Africa, for instance, which was immense, 528 schools accommodated 70,176 students out of an eligible population of 3 million children; in Indochina, 582,478 were matriculated, for an eligible population of 8 to 9 million. Because of these statistics, illiteracy was a massive issue. As for Algeria, which had the status of a *French department*, 92.4 percent of Muslim youth between the ages of ten and fourteen were illiterate as late as 1948 (to be fair, a large effort was made between 1954 and 1962, but that was quite late!). And Algeria is certainly not an isolated case. Throughout the empire, the proportion of illiterate persons neared, and even surpassed, 80 percent. I look forward to hearing from those who wish to contradict me on these points.

Let's not be naive: the system built infrastructure (or rather, as we have just seen, had it built) because it *needed* it. It provided health care to *natives* because it needed the labor. It educated some natives because it needed local and subaltern administrators. Albert Sarraut, a politician, wrote candidly in 1923 about these issues in *La mise en valeur des colonies françaises*.[15] There was indeed a certain level of *mise en valeur*, of development. But for whose *benefit*? All systems seek to be profitable, and there is nothing fundamentally wrong with that. Nothing, that is, so long as these economic calculations aren't dressed up as philanthropy seventy years later!

What "Progress"?

Yes, *France* improved the lives of a number of *natives*. It is important to remain clear-headed about such issues, and to avoid being seduced by either colonial propaganda or militant anticolonialism, both of which tended to elide over inconvenient facts. Similarly, it is likely that some colonized people lived better lives during the French presence than they had done before. After all, that's not much to expect after a century, give or take a few years depending on the colony, of presence. Workers and peasants in the mainland also lived better in 1960 than they did back in 1830.

A portion of the *native* population was even able to profit substantially (economic collaborators) or minimally (demanding servant positions, odd jobs, small businesses), from its relationship with whites. Another portion, who held industrial or rural wage jobs, was able to reach a degree of stability in their lifestyle, however modest. But the real drama, the real scandal of colonialism becomes patent if we compare the *average revenue* (taking all necessary precautions when applying this notion) of Europeans to that of colonized people. Every study conducted on the subject has revealed glaring disparities between the *conquerors* and those *conquered*. They were literally worlds apart. The former held management positions in the production process, and the latter slaved away. The former lived in extremely comfortable neighborhoods, and the latter lived in dark streets reserved for *natives* or in shantytowns on the outskirts of the cities. The former knew that their children would receive an education, even if only to the level of a basic school certificate; the latter for the most part sent their children out to look for work at the age of eight or ten, or to beg in the streets.

Vast pockets of misery existed and continue to exist throughout these countries. One only has to cast a cursory glance at the accounts of first-hand witnesses, who were not on principle opposed to colonialism, but were reminded of the dirt-eating peasants in the French countryside under Louis XIV: Roland Dorgelès writing about Indochina,[16] Lucien Febvre on Morocco,[17] Albert Londres on sub-Saharan Africa,[18] Albert Camus on Kabylia.[19] The ethnologist Germaine Tillion coined the word *clochardisation* (a term that combines vagrancy and homelessness, and that was used to describe the movement of rural populations to urban centers) as a way of characterizing the plight of the Algerian populace.[20] The concept could very well be applied to all of the former empire.

I am not saying, however, that *all* French people overseas were colonial brutes, racists, and exploiters. If only out of respect for the memory of Ismaÿl Urbain, Étienne Dinet, Isabelle Eberhardt, Jules Boissière, Paul Monet, Maurice Leenhardt, Jean Sénac, André Malraux, Albert Camus, André Mandouze, Fernand Iveton, Maurice Audin, and others—tens of thousands no doubt—who remain anonymous but who doubtless extended a hand to the "other," at times defended him, and even shared in her struggle. But let us not forget that they were *always* the minority, and that they were often treated by their fellow citizens as, in the best cases, naive (they scornfully were called *indigénophiles* [nativophiles]), and in the worst cases, traitors. In the colonial world, French people who did not adhere to the racial hierarchy were considered to be rebelling against their social milieu. Colonialism, of course, had its humanists—or, more precisely, there were humanists within the system—but it was essentially, terribly, an antihumanist practice.

The balance sheet? One has already been provided by those who are most concerned: the colonized. The narrative of the conquests, then the different phases of the history of colonialism, show that the people who were colonized, crushed by the superior mechanical force of Europe, never relinquished their independence, despite, at times, the appearances of *French peace*. Later, when the mainland appeared vulnerable to all in the aftermath of the Second World War, the storm came and swept away the edifice. The best judges, flouting statistics, ignoring the impassioned speeches, had made up their minds. They condemned colonialism in the name of superior values, national independence, the desire to choose together, as compatriots, what organizational form their own societies would take. As Ernest Renan had declared in 1882, "The wish of nations is, all in all, the sole legitimate criterion, the one to which one must always return."[21]

Alain Ruscio is a historian and independent researcher who has published extensively on colonial Indochina and decolonization. His numerous works include *La guerre française d'Indochine (1945–1954)* (1992), *Le credo de l'homme blanc: Regards coloniaux français, XIXe—XXe siècles* (1996), *Amours coloniales: Aventures et fantasmes exotiques, de Claire de Duras à Georges Simenon* (1996), *Que la France était belle au temps des colonies: Anthologie de chansons coloniales et exotiques françaises* (2001), *Y'a bon les colonies?: La France sarkozyste face à l'histoire coloniale, à l'identité nationale et à l'immigration* (2011), and *Nostalgérie: L'interminable histoire de l'OAS* (2015).

Notes

1. *Colonialisme à la papa* (Daddy-style colonialism) is a reference to General de Gaulle's famous statement on April 28, 1959: "Daddy's Algeria is dead, and if we don't understand that, we'll die with it," cited in *L'écho d'Alger* on April 29, and widely reprinted by mainland newspapers on April 30.
2. This article is an updated version of a number of previous texts published by the author.
3. Alain Ruscio, *Nostalgérie: L'interminable histoire de l'OAS* (Paris: La Découverte, 2015).
4. A campaign was launched with the support of the far-right newspaper *Valeurs actuelles* (no. 4113, September 24, 2015), encouraging Éric Zemmour to run for office.
5. Alain Finkielkraut, "J'assume," *Le Monde*, November 27, 2005.
6. "Finkielkraut-Badiou: Le face-à-face," by Aude Lancelin, *Le Nouvel Observateur*, December 17, 2009.
7. Aimé Césaire, *Discourse on Colonialism*, trans. Joan Pinkham (New York: Monthly Review Press, 2000), 40. The first publication of *Discours sur le colonialisme* dates back to 1950 and not to 1955 as most of Césaire's biographers claim. The book was first published in the form of a small volume by an editor close to the French Communist Party (Éditions Réclame). See Alain Ruscio, "Césaire et le communisme, les communistes et Césaire: Une longue histoire," in *Aimé Césaire à l'œuvre*, ed. Marc Cheymol and Philippe Ollé-Laprune (Paris: Item/Éditions des Archives contemporaines, 2010), 193–202.
8. Lucien Lévy-Bruhl, *La mentalité primitive* (Paris: Librairie Félix Alcan, 1922), http://classiques.uqac.ca/classiques/levy_bruhl/mentalite_primitive/mentalite_primitive_2.pdf, 114.
9. Olivier Le Cour Grandmaison, *Coloniser, exterminer: Sur la guerre et l'état colonial* (Paris: Fayard, 2005).

10. Victor Hugo, "Notes, 20 octobre 1842," in *Choses vues: Souvenirs, journaux, cahiers* (Paris: Gallimard, 1972).

11. Léon-Étienne Duval, *Au nom de la vérité: Algérie (1954–1962)* (Paris: Éditions Cana, 1982), 22.

12. Andrée Viollis, *Notre Tunisie* (Paris: Gallimard, 1939), 36.

13. In Ho Chi Minh, Vietnam preserved a Rue Yersin, despite the fact that all names of admirals, generals, and colonial administrators were removed a long time ago.

14. Catherine Coquery-Vidrovitch, *Le Congo au temps des grandes Compagnies concessionnaires (1898–1930)* (Paris/La Haye: Mouton & Co., 1972).

15. Albert Sarraut, *La mise en valeur des colonies françaises* (Paris: Payot, 1923).

16. Roland Dorgelès, *Sur la route Mandarine* (Paris: Albin Michel, 1929).

17. Lucien Febvre, *Les annales*, September 30, 1936.

18. Albert Londres, *Terre d'ébène: La traite des Noirs* (Paris: Albin Michel, 1929).

19. Albert Camus, "Misère de la Kabylie," *Alger républicain*, June 5–15, 1939, in *Actuelles*, vol. 3, *Chroniques algériennes (1939–1958)* (Paris: Gallimard, 1958).

20. Germaine Tillon, *L'Algérie en 1957* (Paris: Les Éditions de Minuit, 1957); ibid., *Algeria: the Realities*, trans. Ronald Matthews (New York: Knopf, 1958).

21. Ernest Renan, "What Is a Nation?," trans. Martin Thom, in *Nation and Narration*, ed. Homi Bhabha (New York: Routledge, 1990), 20.

34

IS A COLONIAL HISTORY MUSEUM POLITICALLY IMPOSSIBLE?

Nicolas Bancel and Pascal Blanchard

After three decades of silence (1960–1990) and amnesty/amnesia, we have now entered a time of confrontation—set off by debates surrounding the Algerian War in the 1990s—memory wars at the highest levels of politics—from the law on "positive colonization" in 2005 to the memorial laws of 2011—and from the "chaos of individual grief"[1] toward claims articulated by every *community* for recognition. The colonial past has become *political*. On the one hand, there is the left, which has never been able to confront this history or even imagine a scholarly approach to it. On the other, there is the right, which has turned it into a fight against "repentance"—as exemplified by Nicolas Sarkozy's speech in Toulon in February 2007 and the one he gave in Rouen a few weeks later—and into a way to garner electoral support.[2] Then there is also of course the far-right, which has made colonial nostalgia into a facet of its political identity. The far-right has also used the colonial period to establish a relationship between the past's conflicts (French Algeria) and the rejection of postcolonial immigrants today (the new electoral slogan of the Front National is, after all, "This is our home"). Such propaganda is especially paradoxical since the colonial period was founded on the idea of expanding France into "their home."

The collective refusal to acknowledge colonial history since the time of independence (as Alain Ruscio argued in the previous chapter), the inability to transmit an inclusive history over the course of three decades, the absence of any kind of collective memory (as opposed, for instance, to the efforts to understand such histories in Belgium, the Netherlands, Germany, and the United Kingdom), have led groups to seek out their "own" memory through nostalgia and demands for recognition. De facto, the French state has always played a central role in commemorations and in the public appropriation of history, the latter being conceived, beginning with the Third Republic, as the basis of a national memory that guarantees national unity. As concerns the imperial past, the rule in force appears to be the status quo and "kindly nostalgia."[3] Dealing with such a heavy legacy is not simple, especially considering that the potential for conflict is very high, a phenomenon in large part due to the fact that authorities have made it into an issue of identity. Meanwhile, successive administrations have left the question of memory up to activists.

As Benjamin Stora points out, "With the arrival of Jacques Chirac to power in 1995, those nostalgic for French Algeria were awakened from their slumber. President Chirac closed the case on Vichy with his famous speech of July 16, 1995, in which he acknowledged the role of the French state in the deportation of Jews. But he did not open the case on Algeria. A new memory-based war began, with the far-right instrumentalizing the suffering and nostalgia of the Pieds-Noirs and such ideology leeching bit by bit into the UMP."[4] The entry of Vichy into the pantheon of memory resulted in the reawakening of conflictual memories surrounding colonialism. As such, the "Chirac period" was marked by strong nostalgia for the colonial period, which, in 2002, led to the construction of the Mémorial national de la guerre d'Algérie et des combats du Maroc et de la Tunisie on the Quai Branly, just steps away from the new Quai Branly Museum of *arts premiers* ("primitive" or "indigenous" arts) that was inaugurated in 2006.[5] President Chirac asserted, on the occasion, that: "The soldiers from North Africa [held], like their elders in 1914 and 1940, a place in the memory of our country." The memorial (the idea for which came from the socialist Lionel Jospin) was instrumentalized by Jacques Chirac and the right as a way of washing their hands of colonization's military past.[6]

Jacques Chirac (who was himself an officer in the Algerian War, beginning in 1956, and was deeply affected by that experience) was convinced that paying tribute to those who died would create consensus around the issue, even if it did not address colonization in its totality.[7] During his first mandate (in 1996 to be precise, one year after his speech on Vichy), a memorial to "veterans of North Africa" was discreetly erected in the Buttes-Chaumont park, but nevertheless sent a strong political message.[8] That is why the second memorial effort was seen as a real opportunity to make a clear statement to his supporters, by leaving a long-term mark that would definitively establish a national memorial.

When Jacques Chirac inaugurated "his" Quai Branly Museum project on June 20, 2006, he stated in his official speech, without a trace of irony, that "France wished to pay homage to peoples to whom, throughout the ages, history has all too often done violence. Peoples injured and exterminated by the greed and brutality of conquerors. Peoples humiliated and scorned, denied even their own history. Peoples still now often marginalized, weakened, endangered by the inexorable advance of modernity." Not once in that speech did he broach the topic of France's role in what he described as a "tumultuous history" or for that matter of the colonial past. Nevertheless, the "colonial issue" slowly began to emerge in the public debates that followed and surround the various exhibits on offer. However, given the relative public appeal of this ode to the "primitive arts" of Africa, Asia, Oceania, and the Americas, one has to wonder about the degree to which museum-goers walk away conscious of the fact that the majority of the peoples on earth actually have a history, or with any kind of understanding that our common history has been strongly colored by "colonial culture."[9]

The 2005–2006 Turning Point

The height of the conflicts surrounding colonial memory can be situated in 2005–2006, when intellectual, scholarly, media, and cinematographic productions crashed onto the scene. However, that turning point did not lead to a collective public appropriation of colonial history. On the contrary, the stakes of memory were once again politicized around identity issues, debates on immigration, "repentance" (instrumentalized by neoreactionary intellectuals like Pascal Bruckner and Éric Zemmour), and the rejection of a "dangerous" history for the Republic (Pierre Nora and Daniel Lefeuvre). The increase in memory-based claims linked to the colonial past was, without a doubt, a catalyst in the process of ending "colonial aphasia." However, the ensuing debates also made it impossible to establish a pacified form of memory. As a counterreaction to a "reevaluation" of imperial nostalgia, projects seeking to "rehabilitate" colonial history and French activities in the colonies were developed around organizations of repatriated persons and *harkis*, represented throughout the territory by a number of officials from the Front National, the UMP, and even the socialist left in southeastern France. At the same time, the development of memory-based claims, which seek acknowledgment of colonial violence and of its legacy, still mostly come from postcolonial minorities in the diaspora—after having spearheaded antiracist militants or participated in the ultra-left third-worldist movement of the 1970s—as can be seen in the emergence of the movement *Indigènes de la République*.

The case of colonial memory is unique. The processes of assimilation, incorporation, and public appropriation that were prevalent under Vichy, during the Resistance, and evident in deportation mechanisms cannot be found when it comes to the colonial past. It has simply not been "officially" included in the national narrative. Indeed, throughout the decades preceding 2005–2006, monuments and museum projects that dealt with the colonial past were characterized by a nostalgic memory (pro-French Algeria and pro-OAS), and they took place in a very limited geographical area: the south of France (from Nice to Marseille, from Toulon to Montpellier, from Aix-en-Provence to Béziers). The Socialist Party and the far left abandoned the issue to the ideologues on the right and far-right, with figures such as Patrick Buisson being one of the most persuasive among them, and to the most radical militants represented by community-based associations.

As Alain Ruscio has underscored, extreme political views have, for decades, been devoted to "holding almost all representatives of other political entities up to public obloquy; they select the few scholars who, at least in part, agree with their ideas, and then assert that the others are simply leftist ideologues. They parade, petition, feast, and congratulate themselves, and cry 'anti-French' when political adversaries contradict them."[10] He has also noted that since "the 2000s, monuments to French Algeria have been erected in dozens of French cities, with assassins . . . being celebrated, street signs honoring former heads of the OAS (Edmond Jouhaud, Raoul Salan) have been inaugurated, museums have been opened, ceremonies have been hosted. In late 2013, there were some seventy such memory sites."[11] For the activists supporting these initiatives, peppering the territory with a vast memorial network is a way of not losing the "memorial war of Algeria" and of simultaneously turning postcolonial immigrants into the *fellaghas* of our time.[12]

Conquering the Public Space

The oldest monument dates back to 1965 and is located in Aix-en-Provence, a city that regularly pays homage to French Algeria. During a ceremony in 2007, Mayor Maryse Joissains-Masini (today in the Républicains party) criticized "junk historians" promoting "repentance" and "anti-French sentiment." The speech was in keeping with the "local tradition" started four decades earlier. One is also reminded of a memorial erected in Nice by an organization of repatriated French settlers with the help of the mayor Jacques Médecin in 1973 (future member of the 1976 Chirac government), which paid tribute to Roger Degueldre, former head of Delta commandoes of the OAS who was shot to death in 1962. "Pierre Nora, who had just spent several years with the Pied-Noir community," writes Alain Ruscio, "perfectly sums up the state of mind of these extremists: 'They have set themselves up against evolution; they have blocked history.' "[13] Using the monument and its symbolic impact, they essentially sought to establish a nostalgic view of the colonial past, their aim clearly being to contribute to the nation's official position.

Another threshold was crossed in 1980 in the city of Toulon, once again in southeastern France, when government officials appeared alongside local leaders during the inauguration of another monument.[14] Although this "official" inauguration also elicited protest within parliament and the administration, it nevertheless constituted a turning point. The monument in question measures six feet in height and eighteen feet in width, symbolizing a slain parachutist, his epaulettes torn from his shoulders, and with the inscription "Pour une parole donnée" (in reference to the promise to "keep Algeria French"). Although this monument was destroyed on June 8, 1980, the inauguration ceremony still went ahead on June 14, 1980, in the presence of two thousand people, on the occasion of the 150th anniversary of the French troops landing in Algeria (1830). In addition to militants, activists, and General Edmond Jouhaud (honorary president of the Front National for repatriated French), the secretary of state in charge of repatriated French, Jacques Dominati, was in attendance,[15] a presence that was far more than symbolic, lending, as it did, official recognition to the event. A prefect, Jean-Claude Gaudin (future mayor of Marseille), and right-wing elected officials such as François Léotard alongside the deputy-mayor of Toulon, together placed flowers on the monument. The coming together of the far-right and the republican right on this issue, therefore, marked a turning point—merely a year before the arrival of the left in power and a few months before the electoral emergence of the Front National—which led to the joint development of increasingly large-scale heritage projects.

Monuments representing colonial nostalgia were erected throughout the 1980s and 1990s. And the trend picked up steam in the 2000s, in the hands of a new generation. In Théoule-sur-mer, in 2002, those nostalgic for France's empire erected a thirty-foot-high replica of Notre-Dame-d'Afrique, which bears the following inscription: "For all those who died defending French Algeria." It has since become a site for pilgrimages by those nostalgic for French Algeria. Then Perpignan emerged as one of the new commemoration sites for the imperial past. In the same movement, the city of Toulon again paid tribute to colonial nostalgia when it named a junction after a symbol of French Algeria: Raoul Salan. In 2003, Hubert Falco (now in the Républicains party), mayor of Toulon, made a subtle change to the name, "Colonel Salan–Libération de Toulon–August 1944," but then went on to authorize a ceremony in 2006 paying tribute to the "Algiers Expedition" of 1830.

Barely a year later, on February 7, 2007, at the height of his presidential campaign, candidate Nicolas Sarkozy delivered his famous speech glorifying the colonial enterprise in the city of Toulon that had now come to "symbolize" imperial nostalgia. In this speech, he spoke of the "work of civilizing" overseas territories. Few observers understood the symbolism of this speech being given in that place—with the exception, that is, of "repatriated" militants and members of the Front National, who saw it as acknowledgement of their fight and faith in "France's colonial work" forty-five years after the independence movements.[16] The speech was a deliberate appeal to nostalgic sentiments for the empire and strategically given in a place where the Front National had achieved significant support. Indeed, Jean-Marie Le Chevallier (mayor of Toulon between 1995 and 1999), had been elected to the National Assembly in 1995 as the region's deputy.

Stelae, Monuments, and Museums . . .

After fifteen years of struggling against their opponents (1988–2003), of fights against "repentant historians," of vain attempts to oppose changes to school textbooks,[17] the trend of nostalgia still remains strong.[18] Activism in the realm of memory in southern France—and represented in the north by the member of parliament Christian Vanneste (the Républicains party)[19]—now has support from several elected officials and from the national memorial network. Notable examples include the mayor of Marignane (in the Bouches-du-Rhône region of Provence), Daniel Simonpiéri, who, in 2005, granted a pristine parcel in his town's new cemetery to the Association de défense des intérêts moraux et matériels des anciens détenus et exilés politiques de l'Algérie française (Association for the Defense of the Moral and Material Interests of Former Detainees and Political Exiles of French Algeria, ADIMAD) and erected a monument paying tribute to the OAS, on which the following inscription can be read: "To those who were executed and who died fighting for French Algeria." Marignane is but the latest in a series of commemorations symbolizing nostalgia for the colonial era that are strongly marked by battles linked to Algeria.[20]

In 2003, a stela was placed in the Béziers cemetery, bearing the following inscription: "To the memory of our civilians and soldiers who died overseas." Two years later, a new stela was erected in Marignane in the Saint-Lambert cemetery (it would later be removed after considerable protest). As Alain Ruscio rightly notes, "Doing away with the strength of this fringe group's convictions, erasing the impact of their ideas, and extinguishing their ability to polarize this issue would be impossible."[21] It was in this "favorable" context that the idea of a national memorial conferring political and scholarly legitimacy to nostalgia for colonization emerged. For its supporters, such a monument could only be established in southern France, a region marked by colonial nostalgia. The idea was restated in July 2003 in the presence of Perpignan's mayor Jean-

Paul Alduy (UDI party), on the foundations of an old project. A stela was thus inaugurated under the aegis of former OAS members in Perpignan (such as Philippe Castille),[22] a city now considered "the capital for those nostalgic for French Algeria," followed shortly thereafter in 2012 by the dedication of a wall for French people who died in Algeria and a resource center devoted to French of Algeria.[23] The environment has become especially inviting for the Front National, which launched a spirited campaign in the Pyrénées-Orientales in support of its candidate, no less than Louis Aliot, the vice president of the party, who went on to garner an important percentage of the vote in the second round of the 2015 regional elections.[24]

Meanwhile, similar debates were taking place in Marseille around a plan to build a Mémorial de la France d'outre-mer (Memorial for France Overseas), a proposal made by the local right and Jean-Claude Gaudin, and an equivalent project specifically devoted to Algeria in Montpellier (actively supported this time by the regional left, led by Georges Frêche). An impressive local network was established around this time: Nice, Toulon, Aix-en-Provence, Montpellier, Marseille, Nîmes, Béziers, Théoule-sur-mer, Marignane. The obvious strategy was to occupy a memorial space on colonialism that had been left empty at the national level. It sought to establish an "official" site, a museum, ideally in Marseille (former capital during empire)—or else in Montpellier—as a means of asserting a definitive and unequivocal reading of the imperial past.

Times have certainly changed. A new generation of postrepatriated militants is now in command, and it has sealed an alliance with the former Gaullist enemies. New projects endeavor to appear less militant or specifically geared toward "repatriated" populations. Instead, their architects aim to suggest that these places are somehow sanctioned by the state and that it is part of a larger process of normalizing museum culture around which there exists some kind of consensus. The "anti-OAS taboo" appears to have been lifted. This has given way to a "positive" rereading of this past, including on the left, and even among the active inheritors of Gaullism. These new ideological allies now find themselves in agreement around identity-based issues and the question of immigration. For political scientist Bertrand Badie, "imperial memory" is not a mere "psychological trait" but rather a whole way of being, doing, and thinking in international relations.[25] The 2005 law regarding the teaching of the "positive" aspects of the colonial past (voted by parliament in February of that year) was a sign that those nostalgic for the colonial past had won, thereby also eliciting increased energy for the Marseille museum project, especially given that candidate Nicolas Sarkozy had explicitly committed himself to it.

Regaining "Greater France"

By focusing on this museum project, we can better understand just how such memory-based thinking functions in France. In Montpellier, in parallel with Marseille, with the Museum of the History of France in Algeria (1830–1962), a second pillar in this colonial nostalgia was put in place. The project was initially entrusted to a historian of colonial Algeria, Daniel Lefeuvre (one of the spokespeople in the fight against "repentance"). He eventually resigned from the scientific advisory board in the wake of heated debates surrounding the project's priority objective which was to glorify the work performed by the French in Algeria.

Initially launched by Georges Frêche, the project was then put on hold for a while until it was resuscitated by the new socialist mayor of Montpellier, Hélène Mandroux, in 2008. Under her direction, both the project itself and the members of the scientific advisory board were more open, historiographically speaking. But the election of Philippe Saurel (DVG, left-wing politician with no party affiliation) in 2014 marked the end of the project, which the candidate had promised to eliminate due to the numerous polemics surrounding its creation. Yet Montpellier was only the second locale for a "great project" targeted primarily at Marseille,[26] a project that came to be known as the Mémorial national de la France d'outre-mer (National Memorial of France Overseas, MoM). This project deserves further attention. Indeed, it remains the most symbolically important of all such memorials, because it included the participation of the state, involved a large French city, and one of the leaders in the UMP at the time.

This major project was supposed to be the concrete symbol of a "national" consensus around the memory of the colonial past and was to include the whole spectrum of colonization, not just Algeria. In addition, a handful of academics supported it, including Daniel Lefeuvre and Marc Michel,[27] working with Jean-Pierre Rioux—a researcher at the Institut d'histoire du présent (IHTP), inspector general of the national education system, close ally of the centrist Modem party, columnist at *Le Monde* newspaper, and radio commentator on *France Culture*[28]—and the historian Jean-Jacques Jordi. Despite the project's official character, it was the subject of considerable opposition—on the part of historians and organizations based in Marseille—oppositions that, in all likelihood, contributed to the project eventually being abandoned.

Let us go back a few years earlier in order to understand its genesis. Movements of repatriated persons first led the project in the early 1980s, when socialist mayor Gaston Defferre (in 1983), at the time the minister of the interior, decided to support it and allocated thirty million francs to establish this "site of memory." After several studies were commissioned, the memorial was gradually forgotten about. Then, in March 1996, Guy Forzy, interministerial delegate in charge of repatriated persons, in the wake of the return of the right to power, decided to reactivate the project by establishing a partnership around the idea of a Mémorial de la France d'outre-mer in the Fort Saint-Jean in Marseille, with a budget of almost one hundred million francs.

After a second period of political hesitation, Jean-Claude Gaudin, mayor of Marseille and one of the right's leaders, decided to support the memorial in 2000 by allocating funds from the city's budget. His aim was to appeal to organizations of repatriated persons, whose vote was perceived as strategic in Marseille. Two years later, with the return of the right to government, Jean-Claude Gaudin obtained financial backing from a number of ministries. On August 4, 2003, Prime Minister Jean-Pierre Raffarin, announced that the state would henceforth officially support the project and contribute financially. The political climate at that time favored colonial memorials, and six months earlier, Philippe Douste-Blazy had gathered a large number of signatures from deputies endorsing the recognition of France's colonial work.[29]

This support from the state had an immediate impact on the scope of the Marseille project, expanding from approximately thirty thousand to just over forty thousand square feet, and now with a provisional budget of eleven million euros. The memorial was slated for opening in 2007 on Boulevard Rabatau. Everyone on the right supported it, the Front National seemed appeased, whereas the left in Marseille, only too aware of the importance of the "*pied-noir* vote" and conscious of the importance of immigration in the region, remained silent. At the same time, in Marseille, the memorial's team coordinated its efforts to marginalize the other museum project that was underway and that threatened to overshadow it, namely the future Musée des civilisations de l'Europe et de la Méditérranée (The Museum of European and Mediterranean Civilizations, MuCEM). The two projects in the Phocaean capital were now in competition.

For those backing it, the National Memorial of France Overseas was primarily meant to retrace the history and sustain the memory of people who lived in the French colonies in the nineteenth and twentieth centuries. The aim was to pay *tribute* to their "civilizing" actions; it was not conceived as a site for *learning*. Upon the request of organizations for the repatriated, who were well represented on the scientific advisory board, Algeria was defined as the "central point of the memorial." It is worth mentioning that in the first draft of the governmental text developed by Michèle Alliot-Marie in 2003 (following Philippe Douste-Blazy's lobbying of members of parliament), which culminated in the Law of February 2005 (spearheaded by the deputies Christian

Kerk, Michèle Tabarot,[30] and Christian Vanneste),[31] the memorial project was clearly linked to the law on "positive colonization." Every indication was that things were on track.

The shift in positions within the republican right, beginning in 1995 with Jacques Chirac's speech in Toulon and continuing with the Douste-Blazy/Alliot-Marie draft bill and its passage into law on February 23, 2005, had been significant and explains the emergence of this project. This shift allowed for an old claim that had never been satisfied to finally be recognized, but with several benefits, not only at the level of politics in terms of the mobilization of repatriated voters,[32] but also because "colonial pride" had now become an acceptable argument for the republican right in its competition with Le Pen's right. "Colonial pride" was even a desirable trait for some on the right, notably in southeastern France, while also providing a point of distinction with respect to "leftist" discourse which had tended to be critical of the colonial past.[33]

However, the project was too obviously nostalgic, particularly given the passionate debates surrounding the Law of February 2005 that ultimately forced Jacques Chirac to repeal Article 4 that pertained to the mandate that "school programs highlight the positive aspects of the French overseas presence, notably in North Africa." Reactions were strong because the colonial past was being rediscovered during these key years, and most historians refused to support such a clearly nostalgic project.[34] A conference was even organized to denounce the project,[35] and a "call for vigilance" was emitted regarding the project's one-sided presentation of history, questioning its overall historiographical seriousness. Nevertheless, Nicolas Sarkozy committed, in a letter to various concerned organizations during his 2007 campaign, that he would rescue the project and promised that the Marseille memorial would open with his support in 2009. But by this point it was already too late and the project had become too politically risky at the national level, and the new president instead became involved in a new project which was considered less incendiary—but that ended up being equally divisive, namely, the Maison de l'Histoire de France, which was placed under the same leadership as the project in Marseille, that of Jean-Pierre Rioux.

Nicolas Offenstadt, like many observers, was dead right when he noted that this new project bracketed the colonial issue, just like the highly questionable report that had preceded it had done: "Delivered in 2008 by Hervé Lemoine, in charge of heritage conservation . . . From the opening lines, the text is alarming. The primary concern of the future museum was taken straight out of the work of Max Gallo and his formulations touting 'France's soul.' "[36] The project of the Maison de l'Histoire de France—which, due to the controversy it elicited, never came to fruition—in the same way as the memorial projects in Marseille, Montpellier, Montredon-Labessonnié,[37] and Perpignan betrayed a deep-seated desire to give value to the French colonial presence, particularly in North Africa, and especially in Algeria. That desire is indicative of the general orientation of memorial policies on the issue up until 2012. Yet, even though they ultimately all failed (the Marseille project was definitively abandoned in 2011), the fact remains that for more than two decades (1995–2015), these projects neutralized any possibility of seeing a real museum project on colonization emerge.

Bracketed Critical Memory

Beginning in 2012, and after the failure in Marseille was "digested," a new power relationship came into being with the aim of refuting yet again all efforts geared toward "repentance," something which the socialists now back in office were supposedly promoting. Minister of Justice Christiane Taubira became the symbol of this new trend, as did Najat Vallaud-Belkacem when she became minister of national education, higher education, and research. Battles over memorials now took on a new character, precluding any possible advances in the realms of the colonial past and slavery. New stelae and memorials were planned and installed in an attempt to regain ideological territory. The underlying idea became clear: following the failure of Nicolas Sarkozy's mandate, the abandonment of the Marseille and Montpellier projects, and the effective placing on hold of the 2005 law, the time had come to build upon the renewal symbolized by the Front National and Marine Le Pen, the newly elected officials in the south of France, and the still active plethora of nostalgic militants, and wait out the "Hollande" presidency in the hope of reigniting the torch after the general election in 2017.

The political foundations of the struggle to "legitimate" a museum (or its equivalent) valorizing the colonial past have been established through a variety of factors: the international context, the ubiquitous nature of neoreactionary discourse, the crisis of the *banlieues*, victories by the Front National in the municipal elections in towns like Béziers and Fréjus, but also in a mayoral district in Marseille, along with the strong showing during the December 2015 regional elections. Critical counterexamples to these monuments and to the discourse in "defense of France's colonial œuvre" exist, but on a much smaller scale. Over the past several years (including during François Hollande's mandate), one can speak of a status quo, unambiguously founded upon a fear that this colonial past could very well become a political instrument for "community-based" identity politics and for those youth with postcolonial immigrant backgrounds who have inherited their elders' "humiliation."

In terms of these ethnic minority youth, the search for a hero in the antislavery and anticolonial struggle has also led to the development, in France, of memorial demands by communitarian associations. Such a dynamic emerged with the 1992 protests against commemorations of the discovery of America, the May 23, 1998, silent march held in Paris to honor the memory of the millions of victims of slavery, or the Taubira Law of May 2001 that recognized the Atlantic slave trade and slavery as a crime against humanity, processes that were accompanied by an emerging awareness in some coastal cities, such as Bordeaux and Nantes, of their historical role in the trade, and that foreshadowed a range of memory-based projects in their respective municipalities.

What Remains Feasible?

For the most part, these nostalgic museum projects were conceived as a way of responding to the desires of repatriated French people on the far-right and the most vocal nostalgics of the colonial era, and thwarting the neutrality of the state whose primary concern should be to neutralize social conflict. At the same time, they have managed to polarize the debate over the past quarter century in such a way that the construction of a site of shared knowledge,[38] one stripped of ideology,[39] has been impossible. The consequence of this has been to frustrate concerned "inheritors" from all sides of France's colonial history.

In contrast, the history and memory of slavery have found a significant place in the museums and memorials, as exemplified by the Mémorial de l'abolition de l'esclavage (Memorial for the Abolition of Slavery), which was inaugurated in Nantes in 2012, and the ACTe memorial established in Pointe-à-Pitre in Guadeloupe in 2015. It has been an evolving process, one which originated with the Taubira Law in 2001. In contrast, the history and the memory of colonialism have yet to benefit from the same kind of official recognition. This difference can be partially explained in terms of the length of time since the occurrence of the events—barely fifty years since the end of colonialism versus one hundred and fifty years since the end of slavery—and of course because of the political sensitivity of the issue. Colonial memories still remain confined to the private sphere. They are expressed in whispers, "from below," both among defendants of the "positive aspects of colonization"—who dominate local commemorative and memorial spaces—praising the "civilizing mission" and the "sacrifices" made by colonials and soldiers, as they are among those who call for the "crimes of colonization" to be recognized, albeit only represented by a minority which, although active, receive almost no local political support.

Memories of colonization are still heavily charged, and they continue to play out an opposition between colonialists and anticolonialists. The memories of the Algerian War are demonstrative of a clear epistemological front that seems to oppose irreconcilable differences.[40] They have been stoked by neoreactionaries and declinists who see the loss of the empire as one of the explanations for the current crisis. Above all, they have provided the basis for the electoral and ideological discourse of the Front National and of the far-right of the Républicains party (formerly the UMP), who consider the memorial issue to be a political issue. This was evident in Nicolas Sarkozy's opposition to President François Hollande's choice of the date of March 19 to commemorate the cease fire in the war with Algeria and honor victims of this conflict (March 19, 1962), a date which some continue to see as a symbol of the French defeat.[41]

On the opposite end of the spectrum, memories are manipulated by radical "anticolonialists" of all stripes, from Dieudonné to other agitators on the web. They are also found in statements made by jihadists who emphasize the "humiliation" of the past to inspire and recruit a youth desperate for an identity and who find themselves living in the countries of "former colonizers."[42] Such memories do indeed go hand in hand with very real social forces. That is what makes the work of public appropriation of the past at a national level so difficult. To make matters more complicated, the museum world is not actively seeking to establish such a space, a space which the Musée du Quai Branly has ended up occupying by default, symbolically—if imperfectly. The situation in France is today both extraordinary and marginal, and when it comes to former colonial powers, it is one of the few that has proven incapable of developing museographic tools devoted to processing this key moment in world history.[43]

The question that remains is whether a museum devoted to colonial history is feasible given the current political climate—a museum that would be irreproachable from a scholarly perspective, include all forms of historiographic sensibilities in France in a genuinely comparative framework, emphasize debate as the primary mode of engagement, shed light on the complexities of the colonial phenomenon without shying away from any awkward questions, the intrinsic violence, ambivalences, or long-term consequences. For Benjamin Stora, "ideally such a museum would neither be a 'museum of natives' nor a 'museum of French communities,' for any project should avoid reducing history to a single dimension. The privileging of any one community over another [must] be avoided in such places."[44] It will be difficult to achieve such a "desire," since no major political movement today stands behind such a cause. Yet, a site for knowledge and learning of this kind is sorely needed at this moment of crisis and in light of the current identity angst affecting the country, offering a potential path out of the identity wars and *dangerous* memories gripping our current era.[45]

Nicolas Bancel is Professor at the University of Lausanne, Switzerland, and codirector of the ACHAC Research Group. He is author or coeditor of numerous influential books, including *De l'indigène à l'immigré* (1998), *La République coloniale: Essai sur une utopie* (2003), *La République coloniale* (2006), *Human Zoos: Science and Spectacle in the Age of Colonial Empires* (2008), *La France arabo-orientale* (2013), *Colonial Culture in France since the Revolution* (2014), *The Invention of Race* (2014), and *Vers la guerre des identités* (2016).

Pascal Blanchard is a historian and researcher at the Laboratoire Communication et Politique (Paris, France, CNRS), codirector of the ACHAC Research Group, and a documentary filmmaker. He is a specialist on the colonial question in France, contemporary French history and immigration, and author, coauthor, editor, or coeditor of *Human Zoos: Science and Spectacle in the Age of Colonial Empires* (2008), *Human Zoos. The Invention of the Savage* (2011), *Zoos humains et exhibitions coloniales: 150 ans d'inventions de l'autre* (2011), *Colonial Culture in France since the Revolution* (2014), *La France arabo-orientale* (2013), *Les années 30 sont de retour: Petite leçon d'histoire pour comprendre les crises* (2014), *Le Grand Repli* (2015), and *Vers la guerre des identités* (2016).

Notes

1. Catherine Coquio, *Le mal de vérité ou l'utopie de la mémoire* (Paris: Armand Colin, 2015).

2. In Toulon, Nicolas Sarkozy took the opportunity to declare the following: "The European dream needs the Mediterranean dream. . . . a dream which was Bonaparte's dream in Egypt, Napoleon III's dream in Algeria, Lyautey's in Morocco," concluding thusly: "This dream was not so much a dream of conquest but of civilization." And then in Rouen, three weeks later, he reasserted his desire to "honor France" by denouncing "repentance, which is a despicable posture on which I ask you to turn your backs," recalls Marc Olivier Baruch, "Éloge de la repentance," *Le Monde*, May 12, 2007.

3. Nicolas Bancel, Pascal Blanchard, and Françoise Vergès, *La République coloniale* (Paris: Hachette Littératures, 2006).

4. Rosa Moussaoui, Interview with Benjamin Stora: "Le récit colonial n'a été pris en charge ni par les partis politiques, ni par l'école," *L'Humanité*, July 26, 2006. See also Benjamin Stora, *La guerre des mémoires: La France face à son passé colonial: Entretiens avec Thierry Leclère* (La Tour-d'Aigues: Éditions de l'Aube, 2007).

5. Having decided to place the "national memorial" for French soldiers who died in North Africa just steps from the future Quai Branly Museum, Jacques Chirac declared, as a way of muting the effects of this monument: "Our Republic must fully assume its duty to remember." Three months later, during a trip to Algeria and following a speech by the French ambassador, he also evoked the conflict and this "still painful" past.

6. The monument to the dead is highly symbolic. It contains three columns and the three colors of the nation, and it features lighted panels showing the names of 22,959 French and *harkis* who died for France.

7. Jacques Chirac and Jean-Louis Barré, *Chaque pas doit être un but: Mémoires* (Paris: Nil, 2009).

8. Olivier Le Cour Grandmaison, "Le colonialisme a la peau dure," *Libération*, March 30, 2005. The author recalls that on this occasion, and during the speech, Jacques Chirac set the political tone in this realm: "It is important to recall the importance and the depth of the work that France did there; France is proud of that work." The term *work* is key, and one finds it again in Article 1 of the Law of February 2005, which was voted into law one month later.

9. Nicolas Bancel, Pascal Blanchard, Sandrine Lemaire, and Dominic Thomas, eds., *Colonial Culture in France since the Revolution* (Bloomington and Indiana: Indiana University Press, 2014).

10. Alain Ruscio, *Nostalgérie: L'interminable histoire de l'OAS* (Paris: La Découverte, 2015), 10.

11. Ibid., 10.

12. The *Fellagha* were armed anti-colonial militants and partisans of Algerian independence.

13. Ruscio, *Nostalgérie*, 8.

14. Hélène Chaubin, "Le Sud, terre d'élection de l'activisme? L'OAS-Métro dans l'Hérault," in *La France en guerre (1954–1962): Expériences métropolitaines de la guerre d'indépendance algérienne*, ed. Raphaëlle Branche and Sylvie Thenault (Paris: Autrement, 2008), 299–308.

15. Jacques Dominati chose two active partisans of French Algeria to be his cabinet heads: Jean-Marie Le Chevallier (future Front National mayor of Toulon) and Gérard Longuet (former member of the *ultra-droite* and future minister of defense). After his visit to Toulon, there was a heated session at the National Assembly. Pierre Messmer, speaking on behalf of the "Gaullist right," spoke of a "scandal" and "provocation;" the left criticized the government's role.

16. Emmanuelle Comtat, *Les pieds-noirs et la politique quarante ans après le retour* (Paris: Presses de Sciences Po, 2009).

17. The fight over school textbooks is ongoing. In 2015, for instance, philosopher Luc Ferry said, in relation to the pedagogic reform project, "[It is] scandalous to present Europe and European civilization solely through the prism of the slave trade and colonization" (cited by Séverin Graveleau, "Les programmes d'histoire réveillent la guerre scolaire," *Le Monde*, May 2, 2015). Pierre Nora made the following radical assessment in an interview with Vincent Tremolet de Villers published in *Le Figaro* on May 25, 2015, "La France vit le passage d'un modèle de nation à un autre": "Inversely, a globalized history is needed in this era of globalization. However, more often than not, it hides the fact that it is a history written solely from the point of view of victims. It is pure moralization, since it reads the past through the prism of our present-day moral criteria. Such moralizing can be seen in the lexicon used in the history program for early high schoolers, 'a world dominated by Europe: colonial empires, commercial exchanges, and slave trades.' Domination, condemnable, replaced expansion, of which domination is but one of the effects."

18. In addition to stelae and monuments, there are also several plaques on various religious monuments: the Sacré-Cœur of Antibes or the church of Saint-Nicolas du Chardonnet, which pays tribute to those who "died" in March and July 1962. See Sébastien Jahan and Alain Ruscio, eds., *Histoire de la colonisation: Réhabilitations, falsifications et instrumentalisations* (Paris: Les Indes savantes, 2007).

19. See "Christian Vanneste ou la droite extrême du bon sens," available on the Toulon *Ligue des droits de l'homme's* website (www.ldh-toulon.net). The text recalls the talk given by Christian Vanneste at the Club de l'Horloge on November 20, 2005, in which he justifies colonization.

20. In Théoule (Alpes-Maritimes) in 2002, a stela was installed with the following inscription: "To all our fellow citizens who died defending French Algeria."

21. Ruscio, *Nostalgérie*, 9.

22. The new bronze stela inaugurated in Perpignan was called the "stela for those who were executed." It represents a man connected to a crumbling pole, and it bears the text, "Land of Algeria" and the names of former activists of French Algeria. On this issue, see Roger Hillel, *La triade nostalgérique: Stèle, mur, musée de Perpignan* (Céret: Alter Ego Éditions, 2015).

23. The Cercle Algérianiste fought for this issue, whose president, Suzy Simon-Nicaise (UMP), is also deputy mayor in Perpignan.

24. In Languedoc-Roussillon, voters have been seduced by the Front National. Louis Aliot received 40.43 percent of the vote, ahead of the Socialist Party, which received 40.12 percent. Even without the merger of the greater region, the Front National would have won Languedoc-Roussillon.

25. Bertrand Badie, *Le temps des humiliés: Pathologie des relations internationales* (Paris: Odile Jacob, 2014).

26. A third space was to be devoted to the Algerian War and to the "events" of decolonization in Morocco and Tunisia, in Montredon-Labessonnié in the Tarn (which already features a memorial dedicated to French civilian and military deaths during the Algerian War and the battles in Tunisia and Morocco), a project led by academic Jean-Charles Jauffret. However, the memorial lacks political support and has been stalled for the past ten years (the first stone was placed by socialist Jean-Pierre Masseret in June 2001).

27. Marc Michel is author of a book with a rather telling title: *Essai sur la colonisation positive: Affrontements et accommodements en Afrique noire (1830–1930)* (Paris: Perrin, 2009). Together with Daniel Lefeuvre (a tribute to his memory was recently organized on Radio Courtoisie), he was one of the main organizers behind the website *Études coloniales*, an active supporter of these different projects, and increasingly committed to a neoreactionary position.

28. Many recent works underscore this historian's shift toward a "conservative" reading of history and anxieties in the face of memory conflicts: Jean-Pierre Rioux, *Vive l'histoire de France!* (Paris: Odile Jacob, 2015), *De Gaulle et l'Algérie* (Paris: De Vive voix, 2010), *La France perd la mémoire* (Paris: Perrin, 2006)—three very different works from his earlier and first pioneering work, *La Guerre d'Algérie et les Français* (Paris: Fayard, 1990). Concretely, he is committed to historical conservatism, corresponding perfectly with the position of the scientific commissioner for the future Marseille memorial. Aligned with those nostalgic for colonialism, but not for the same reasons (in the name of the danger of letting colonial memory escape), he has the perfect profile to depoliticize the project.

29. Another aspect of governmental policies toward memorials was evident in the government's decision to transform, at the same time and under the leadership of Jacques Toubon, the Palais des Colonies of the Porte Dorée into a National Museum on the History of Immigration (CNHI), which opened in 2007. It was a way of "neutralizing" the colonial issue in that site of memory, where the International Colonial Exhibition took place in 1931.

30. Whose father, Robert Tabarot, was one of the leaders of the OAS in Oran.

31. Sandrine Lemaire, "Une loi qui vient de loin," *Le Monde diplomatique*, January 2006, 28.

32. Éric Savarese, *Algérie, la guerre des mémoires* (Paris: Non lieu, 2007).

33. Benjamin Stora, Interview with Marie Poinsot, "La guerre des mémoires," *Hommes & migrations*, no. 1268–1269 (July–October 2007): 208–216.

34. Daniel Hémery, "À propos du 'Mémorial de l'œuvre française outre-mer,'" Open Letter, *Outre-mers: Revue d'histoire* 88, no. 330 (2001): 309–310.

35. A conference was held in Marseille on the project on October 21, 2006: "A propos du Mémorial de l'outre-mer ou Historial du colonialisme?"

36. Nicolas Offenstadt, "'L'Âme de la France' au musée . . . ," April 22, 2008, https://blogs.mediapart.fr/edition/usages-et-mesusages-de-1 -histoire/article/220408/1 -ame-de-la-france-au-musee. See also his *L'histoire bling bling: Le retour du roman national* (Paris: Éditions Stock, 2009).

37. To which could be associated the memorial wall in Perpignan, which was inaugurated by the mayor Alain Marleix in 2007, and which pays tribute to the soldiers and *harkis* killed by the FLN.

38. Pascal Blanchard, "Le Musée des colonisations: un grand projet présidentiel?," *Libération*, June 3, 2013; Pascal Blanchard, Françoise Vergès, Nicolas Bancel, and Marc Cheb Sun, "Manifeste

pour un musée des histoires coloniales," *Libération*, May 8, 2012; Pascal Blanchard, "Un musée pour la France coloniale," *Libération*, June 17–18, 2000.

39. See our most recent contribution to this debate: Pascal Blanchard and Nicolas Bancel, "Pour un musée des colonisations et de l'esclavage!," *Le Monde*, May 15, 2016.

40. Benjamin Stora, *Le transfert d'une mémoire: De l'Algérie française au racisme anti-arabe* (Paris: La Découverte, 1999).

41. See Nicolas Sarkozy, "Choisir la date du 19 mars, c'est entretenir la guerre des mémoire," *Le Figaro*, March 18, 2016; and Olivier Faye, Alexandre Lemarié and David Revault D'Allonnes, "La guerre d'Algérie enfièvre le débat politique: La commémoration du 19 mars 1962 par M. Hollande suscite l'indignation de la droite et de l'extrême droite," *Le Monde*, March 20–21, 2016.

42. See David Thompson, *Les Français djihadistes* (Paris: Les Arênes, 2014).

43. See Dominic Thomas, ed., *Museums in Postcolonial Europe* (London and New York: Routledge, 2010); and Iain Chambers, Alessandra De Angelis, Celeste Ianniciello, Mariangela Orabona, and Michaela Quadraro, eds., *The Postcolonial Museum: The Arts of Memory and the Pressures of History* (Farnham, UK and Burlington, VT: Ashgate, 2014).

44. Benjamin Stora, "Il faudrait qu'un consensus national se fasse sur la reconnaissance de la souffrance des autres," April, 2007, http://ldh-toulon.net/Benjamin-Stora-il-faudrait-qu-un.html. See Stora, *La guerre des mémoires*.

45. Benjamin Stora and Alexis Jenni, *Les mémoires dangereuses* (Paris: Albin Michel, 2016).

35

AFTER *CHARLIE*

A NEW ERA OR UNFINISHED BUSINESS?

Alec G. Hargreaves

On February 5, 2016, Socialist prime minister Manuel Valls told the French National Assembly: "We have entered a new world. We are now in a new era."[1] Warning that the jihadist attacks perpetrated in France in January and November 2015 signaled the advent of an unprecedented wave of threats to the nation to which no early end could be foreseen, Valls urged the adoption of constitutional revisions designed to give the state sweeping emergency powers and the right to strip terrorists of French citizenship. It is true that France has never before faced attacks on this scale from French citizens who, acting in conjunction with Middle East–based groups in the name of a totalitarian vision of Islam, are intent on committing mass murder and are willing to lose their own lives in the process. Yet it should not be imagined that this new turn of events is unconnected with France's past. On the contrary, there is abundant evidence to show that the current crisis is deeply imbricated in the legacy of French colonialism and, in particular, in the long-standing failure of political elites on both the left and the right to protect postcolonial immigrant minorities, referred to in everyday discourse as "Arabs, "blacks" and "Muslims," from prejudices and injustices that have bred deep-seated resentment among victims of social exclusion. Few politicians have been willing to acknowledge this failure, which has been largely elided in public debate since the attacks of 2015. This elision is symptomatic of the decades of neglect and marginalization that have driven France into the present impasse, where small but growing numbers of hate-filled young people have given up any hope of social reform and turned instead to Islamist movements bent on the destruction of the society into which they were born. This has made it easy to portray them as aberrations visited upon the nation under the influence of sinister Middle Eastern forces. But we must not allow talk of a "new era" of violent extremism linked with ideologies conceived in distant places to deflect attention from the domestic policy shortcomings that underlie recent events. This is not simply or even primarily a matter of apportioning blame for past mistakes. It is equally if not more important to understand what lies behind the present crisis if wise counsels are to prevail in shaping the nation's future.

Denial

In the *Charlie-Hebdo* and Hyper-Casher killings of January 2015, carried out by two young Frenchmen of Algerian origin and a third of Malian descent, most of the seventeen victims were satirical cartoonists and journalists targeted as "blasphemers" against Islam, police officers assigned to protect them, and Jews held to be tools of Zionism. In the wake of these attacks, political debate was dominated by two main themes: the need to ensure the security of the French population against similar attacks in the future, and the perceived need to step up educational efforts on the value of *laïcité* (France's state-defined system of secularism limiting the role of religion in the public sphere) as a model of tolerance and mutual respect, thereby dissuading other young people tempted to engage in or support jihadist actions. On this reading, the source of the religious fanaticism proclaimed by the killers and of the sympathy they appeared to enjoy in certain quarters lay in an inadequate understanding of the principles of the French Republic, especially among French youths of Muslim heritage. This ignored the fact that young people from Muslim and other immigrant families originating in former colonies, most of whom have grown up in disadvantaged *banlieues* in outlying areas of French cities, have been through the same educational system and share to a very large extent the same secularly based social aspirations as their majority ethnic peers,[2] but have frequently found their paths blocked by stigmatization and discrimination, leading many to conclude that the promises of equality proclaimed by the Republic are a sham.[3]

In the massacres of November 13, 2015, most of the 130 slain were young middle-class people enjoying an evening out in cafés, restaurants, and at the Bataclan theater in the eleventh arrondissement of Paris, emblematic of a socially successful lifestyle beyond the reach of the marginalized populations from among whose ranks most of the killers came. Raised predominantly in low-income households by parents with little or no formal education, children of postcolonial immigrants, primarily of Muslim heritage, generally enter the labor market with lower levels of certified skills than job applicants from majority ethnic backgrounds, and even when equally qualified, they face extremely high levels of discrimination, to the point where many come to believe that they have no real chance of getting a decent-paying job, supporting a family, and participating on an equal footing in mainstream society. Hence the attraction of entering alternative, radicalized groups that, under the spell of well-resourced Middle Eastern organizations promising divinely sanctioned earthly empowerment and a blissful afterlife, offer a strong, self-valorizing sense of community and vengeance against a society from which they feel excluded. The fact that the perpetrators of the November 13 attacks—most of whom came from disadvantaged North African immigrant backgrounds in France and neighboring Belgium—blew themselves up with explosive vests attests to how little they felt they had to lose in life.[4] The government response to these horrific acts focused overwhelmingly on security concerns and punitive measures, with air strikes against the self-styled Islamic State in Syria and Iraq, in whose name the November attacks and January's Hyper-Casher killings were carried out, the declaration of a state of emergency within France, and proposals for constitutional changes, including powers to strip terrorist killers of French citizenship, all of which suggested that the causes of the crisis lay in fundamentally foreign forces that had to be obliterated in distant lands and expelled where they had infiltrated into the body of the nation. Few politicians were prepared to discuss the possibility that it might also be necessary to address injustices within French society that may have contributed to the hatred shown by the killers and to widespread distrust of the authorities among other young people from similar backgrounds.

A fleeting exception to this came in brief remarks made by Valls a few weeks after the January attacks, when he said that these events could not be understood without taking into account "urban marginalization and ghettoes, which I described in 2005 as a kind of territorial, social and ethnic apartheid that has established itself in our country, with social deprivation compounded by daily experiences of discrimination when people don't have the right name or the right color of skin."[5] Unlike in South Africa, where, prior to 1989, apartheid was institutionalized as a policy of state-led segregation and discrimination, a policy of this nature has never been pursued under republican governance in metropolitan France. But discriminatory policies based on ethnic divisions were built into the bedrock of the French overseas empire, which the Republic vigorously expanded and defended, and if apartheid is understood as a de facto situation (as distinct from an avowed policy goal) in which ethnic groups live to a large extent separately from each other, it is clearly pertinent to relations between postcolonial minorities in the *banlieues* and the rest of French society today.

In the face of these divisions, Valls called for a "policy of population management"[6] so as to reduce ghetto-like crowding of minority ethnic groups by spreading more evenly across the nation's urban areas the social housing in which these low-income minorities are concentrated. Legislation designed to achieve this had been introduced by the left in 2000, but relatively affluent town and city councils controlled by the right often flouted it, preferring to pay financial penalties rather than accept their designated share of social housing. Because of this, postcolonial immigrant minorities have remained concentrated in less prosperous areas. The largest of these are in the *département* of Seine-Saint-Denis, forming the *banlieues* of northeastern Paris. Other such areas are found in other outlying areas of the capital, including towns such as Grigny and neighboring Evry, where Valls was *député-maire* until his appointment as interior minister in 2012. In 2009, Valls was heard lamenting during a TV documentary that parts of Evry did not have enough "whites,"[7] implicitly suggesting that the "colored" population was too large. In the measures he announced as prime minister in March 2015, to address the social and ethnic divisions to which he had referred in the wake of the January attacks, Valls focused on forcing localities run by recalcitrant center-right mayors to increase their share of social housing. The effect of this would be to reduce the presence of racialized minorities in areas where they are at present concentrated. Yet moving those minorities—widely perceived as unwelcome burdens on the majority ethnic population—from one locality to another would do nothing to protect them from discrimination in access to employment and other social goods, a matter on which Valls proposed little of any substance.[8] A month later, further evidence of the low priority accorded to the protection of postcolonial minorities from unfair treatment came in remarks made by a senior civil servant, Gilles Clavreul, when interviewed by *Libération* journalist Alice Géraud concerning his work as délégué interministériel à la lutte contre le racisme et l'antisémitisme (coordinator for government policy against racism and antisemitism). In the following extract from her account of the interview, Géraud begins by quoting Clavreul as saying:

> "All forms of racism are reprehensible, but anti-Arab and anti-Black racism don't have the same roots as anti-Semitic violence. We have to be clear about the particular nature of anti-Semitism." He [Gilles Clavreul] elaborates on "the hatred of Jews that unites the far right and Islamists" and which "resurfaces every time a society is in trouble." But he is more circumspect regarding Islamophobia, a term that he refuses to employ. He distrusts the splitting of antiracism between different pressure groups such as those against Islamophobia and negrophobia, which he clearly considers to be *communautariste* [sectarian]. "They are engaged in a discourse of victimhood through which to gain recognition for specific groups by accusing France of every crime under the sun: slavery, colonization, . . ."[9]

Granted that it is a matter of historical record that France engaged overseas in policies of slavery (under the monarchy) and colonization (under the

Republic as under other regimes) characterized by systemic abuses of human rights, why should it be illegitimate to criticize this? In France today, hatred of Muslims is as real as hatred of Jews. Why, then, refuse to speak of Islamophobia while insisting on the need to speak out against antisemitism? In the remarks by Clavreul reported by *Libération* there is no clear answer to these questions. What is unequivocally clear is that in the eyes of a senior French official responsible for public policy against racism and antisemitism, the fight against antisemitism is unequivocally important and valid whereas groups campaigning against anti-black racism, anti-Arab racism and/or Islamophobia are held to be engaged in an illegitimate process of *communautarisme* (ethnic sectarianism) through the manipulation of victimhood.

It is hard not to hear here echoes of an ethnic hierarchy inherited from the colonial period, when French citizenship was granted *en masse* to European settlers and Algerian Jews but withheld from most Muslims, by far the majority of Algeria's colonized population, who were subjected to a legal code known as the *indigénat* that institutionalized the denial of rights to them. A comparable system of legalized discrimination has never been practiced by the French Republic in metropolitan France. The antisemitic policies pursued by the Vichy régime left an enduring sense of national shame as a result of which postwar governments have maintained a high level of vigilance against any manifestation of antisemitism. But there has been no comparable degree of state mobilization against anti-Arab, anti-black or Islamophobic behavior in France. Slurs against Arabs, blacks and Muslims have been commonplace in political discourse, and laws formally prohibiting racial and ethnic discrimination have been very poorly enforced. As a result, discrimination against postcolonial minorities in access to jobs, housing and other social goods has been widely practiced with virtual impunity,[10] relegating its victims to the status of second-class citizens. There is, in this respect, a very real sense in which it may be said that France has not yet fully decolonized.

Shortly after Clavreul's remarks I was invited by the BBC World Service to participate in an hour-long radio debate in Paris focusing on the question "Is France's model of integration broken?" A center-right Union pour un mouvement populaire (UMP)[11] *député* was invited to speak first. After singing the praises of French "integration" policy, which he said was exemplified by the principle of *laïcité,* he refused to listen to the concerns of minority ethnic panelists, interrupting them angrily, and he shook his head dismissively when, in highlighting the discrimination suffered by ethnic minorities, I cited research data showing that French job applicants from Maghrebi backgrounds with the same qualifications as "white" applicants with more typically French names were five times less likely to be given the chance of an interview.[12] With only about twenty minutes of the debate gone, he stormed out of the room after some of those present insisted, against his protestations, on their right to call themselves black. The debate continued in his absence. The completed recording was advertised on the BBC's website for broadcast on the World Service two days later. A few hours before the appointed time, all references to the program disappeared from the advertised schedule and the debate was replaced by alternative programming. I learned later that the broadcast had been canceled after the speaker from the UMP complained to the BBC that the program lacked balance. To the extent that there was any basis to that claim, it arose not from any failure on the part of the BBC to seek inclusion of a broad range of opinions but from the refusal of politicians across a large part of the political spectrum to properly engage with the issues at stake. Representatives of all the main parties who had been invited to participate in the program had declined to do so, with the sole exception of the UMP *député* who walked out when confronted with the concerns of minority ethnic speakers and evidence of racial and ethnic discrimination. Continuing a long-established tradition among French politicians concerning these issues, he preferred to break the thermometer rather than read the temperature.

Valls turned in a similar direction in the wake of the November 13 attacks. Casting aside his earlier acknowledgement of the significance of discrimination, he reacted angrily when Economy Minister Emmanuel Macron broke ranks with the rest of the government by venturing to suggest that the nation's political elites were partly to blame for what had happened. While attributing primary responsibility for the attacks to "human madness and the manipulative totalitarianism of certain people," Macron said that by allowing discrimination to go unchecked, politicians had provided fertile ground for the resentment out of which jihadist extremism had grown.[13] In support of his remarks, Macron cited the results of a recent study showing that, with equal qualifications, a man with a Muslim name in France has four times fewer chances of getting a job interview than an applicant with a Catholic name.[14] Addressing the French Senate a few days later, Valls snapped back: "I've had enough of people constantly trying to provide cultural or sociological excuses or explanations for the events that have taken place."[15] As professional associations representing French sociologists pointed out, it was unreasonable to suggest that explaining an event amounted to excusing or justifying it. No less importantly, they observed that just as the explanations provided by geologists and biologists concerning earthquakes and cancer facilitate greater protection against these dangers, so in the social sphere "properly researched explanations are essential as a basis for action, be it political, economic or military."[16] By the same token, in refusing to properly consider contributory causes, Valls and others were simultaneously obfuscating understanding of the present crisis and weakening the chances of finding workable solutions to it.

Unfinished Business

Such refusals to confront unpalatable truths reflect long-standing blockages in attitudes towards France's former colonial empire and the immigrant minorities originating there.[17] Many on the right have harbored an enduring sense of grievance over the loss of empire and a deep-seated unwillingness to accept as equals in present-day France citizens descended from populations formerly colonized overseas. Since its foundation in 1972, the far-right Front National, led by Algerian War veteran Jean-Marie Le Pen and, more recently, by his daughter Marine Le Pen, has advocated the reform of French nationality laws so as to exclude from citizenship populations whose loyalty to the nation is regarded as suspect. In response to the electoral breakthrough of the FN in 1983, the center-right parties led by Jacques Chirac made similar proposals for restricting access to citizenship, and a watered-down version was enacted in 1993 under the premiership of Edouard Balladur. This was removed from the statute book in 1997 following the return to power of the left, whose leaders have generally opposed exclusionary citizenship laws. But in a striking volte-face, following the jihadist attacks of November 2015, Socialist president François Hollande announced his support for calls from the right to strip French terrorists of citizenship. While opposition to this was voiced by significant figures on the left including Justice Minister Christiane Taubira (who resigned over the issue), and a parliamentary stalemate eventually forced Hollande to drop the proposal, his shift was symptomatic of the contagious nature of exclusionary tendencies which, during the past forty years, have contaminated political thinking in France.

Today's vision of an "enemy within" feeds not only on the murderous deeds of small numbers of young fanatics but also on memories of the Algerian war of independence, when Algerian migrant workers in France were the largest single source of funding for the Front de Libération Nationale (FLN).[18] Many Algerians, like migrant workers from other (ex-)colonies who took up jobs in France during the *Trente Glorieuses*, intended to return in due course to their country of origin, where their families generally remained, but the lack of economic opportunities militated against this. Instead, they began to bring their families to France, where after independence, growing numbers of children were born to (post)colonial migrants, most of whom came from predominantly Muslim regions in North and West Africa.[19] The outlook and aspirations of this new generation and of those born to it, in turn, have been very different from those of their migrant forebears. In contrast with their parents and grandparents, to whom education was generally denied under the colonial system, the new generations born and raised in France have been through the public education system and generally share far more extensively in the cultural norms dominant there than in the home countries of their ancestors. As natives and citizens of France, the vast majority want to make successful futures there, but they have often been treated with suspicion, casting doubt on their loyalty to France. With the passage of time, the patterns of social exclusion resulting from this have bred among some of those concerned the very enmity projected onto them by their deprecators.

An early scare story surrounding these new generations concerned the question of military service. Because children born in France to Algerian immigrants after independence in 1962 were automatically citizens of both countries, young men of Algerian origin in France reaching adulthood from the late 1970s onwards found themselves called up to perform military service in both countries. To spare young men with dual citizenship from being conscripted twice over, France and Algeria signed an agreement in 1983 that allowed those concerned to choose which country to serve in. This prompted suspicions that young Frenchmen of Algerian descent might pledge military allegiance *en masse* to a state that had been founded in insurrection against France. These suspicions appeared to gain credibility through headline statistics released in 1987 showing that 90 percent of recorded choices were in favor of Algeria. But a more thorough examination of the data showed that fewer than 20 percent of Franco-Algerian binationals were opting for Algeria; the vast majority were not bothering to formally register a choice and were reporting, as a matter of course, for duty in their native country, France.[20]

Far from plotting subversion, the earliest and largest political movements organized by young members of postcolonial minority groups were inspired by the values proclaimed by the French Republic, above all that of equality before the law. The first major political demonstration organized by second-generation Maghrebis, the 1983 March for Equality and against Racism, was modeled on the nonviolent civil rights movement that had been led in the United States by Martin Luther King Jr. on behalf of African Americans. In contrast with wars of decolonization, in which the central demand was political independence from an occupying power, the civil rights movement pressed peacefully for the recognition of equal rights within the polity into which African Americans were born, and the 1983 marchers in France did the same on behalf of those born there of North African immigrants. Despite kind words from the socialist government of the day, little was done in practice to curb discrimination, which by the end of the 1990s, helped to push unemployment among young Franco-Algerians to close to 50 percent, far higher than among their majority ethnic peers.[21]

The long-standing failure of governments of both the left and right to ensure equality of opportunity for all French citizens, irrespective of racial or ethnic differences, has fed numerous forms of disruptive behavior towards figures regarded as representatives of an unjust and discriminatory social system. With the passage of time and the deepening of resentment and despair, behavior of this kind has become increasingly violent and extremist. Since the late 1970s, there have been countless confrontations in the *banlieues* between youngsters of immigrant origin and the police, by whom dozens of unarmed young men have been shot dead, sometimes at the wheel of stolen cars and in other cases while held in police custody. In a recurrent pattern, exemplified in Mathieu Kassovitz's 1995 movie *La haine* (Hate), police killings of this nature have sparked renewed rioting in the *banlieues,* where police stations and other official buildings have been attacked with stones and in some cases Molotov cocktails. Disturbances of this kind reached their paroxysm in 2005, when the electrocution of two teenagers while attempting to avoid a police identity check sparked the most serious civil disturbances seen in France in almost half a century. In order to impose a curfew, recourse was made by the authorities to a law promulgated in 1955 during the war in Algeria. The sense of injustice at the heart of those events was compounded when, in May 2015, two police officers charged in connection with the 2005 riots were acquitted. Their acquittal by the criminal justice system of the charge brought against them—nonassistance to persons in danger—may be read as a cruelly ironic synecdoche for the systemic injustices suffered for decades by the minority ethnic groups concentrated in the *banlieues.*

In 1992, a German sociologist interviewed Khaled Kelkal, a young man of Algerian immigrant descent who had grown up in Vaulx-en-Velin, one of the most disadvantaged of the *banlieues* that line the eastern edge of Lyon. Discussing the riots that had recently scarred Vaulx-en-Velin, Kelkal remarked:

> These were all guys who couldn't get jobs saying: "Stop! Think about us! You're leading an easy life downtown, but come and take a look at life out here in the *banlieues,* see the poverty and drugs here." You've got kids now who are only fourteen or fifteen years old stealing big cars to cause trouble for the rest of society, especially the police. They can't take any more.... These kids want jobs. Why aren't they given jobs so they can get on with their lives? It's only after there are riots that people start to understand.[22]

After suffering racism and falling behind at high school, Kelkal had drifted into acts of petty criminality for which he was sentenced to prison, where he became radicalized under the influence of a Muslim cellmate. Treated as an outsider in French society, he told his interviewer that he found in Islam a sense of community and inner peace, calming violent impulses against a social system from which he felt excluded. Three years later, Kelkal was recruited by Islamist militants engaged in a civil war in Algeria and died in a shootout with the police after becoming the prime suspect in the first jihadist attacks committed in France involving young men of postcolonial immigrant descent.

Kelkal's observation that the discontent of those suffering in the *banlieues* seemed to draw significant attention only when disorders broke out was illustrated immediately after his death, when Chirac, who had recently been elected president, visited Vaulx-en-Velin to learn more about the situation. Chirac declared himself to be "stunned" when writer and sociologist Azouz Begag, a native of Lyon of Algerian immigrant descent, described the high levels of discrimination experienced by young Arabs and blacks.[23] But it was not until ten years later that, pressed to comply with European Union directives, Chirac inaugurated a publicly funded body charged with combating discrimination, the Haute Autorité de lutte contre les discriminations et pour l'égalité (HALDE). With limited powers that made it one of the weakest such bodies in Europe, the HALDE drew fierce criticism from antiracist movements, who denounced it as a smokescreen complying "at a purely minimal level with European requirements . . . a mere public relations exercise designed to conceal the lack of political commitment to taking the radical measures required to combat discrimination."[24]

Interviewed when the HALDE was inaugurated in June 2005, its director, Louis Schweitzer, made it clear that racial and ethnic discrimination ranked low on his priority list. "We will prioritize the most widespread forms of discrimination, those suffered by women, the sick, the handicapped and the elderly," said Schweitzer. "These are the cases that come up most often. Minorities aren't the only people suffering discrimination. We have to fight against all forms of abuse."[25] As the HALDE had not yet begun to operate, it is difficult to see how Schweitzer could know in advance that cases of discrimination affecting those he refers to as "minorities," meaning those defined by "race" and ethnicity, were less numerous than those concerning other groups such as the elderly and the sick. In point of fact, throughout the five years of the HALDE's existence prior to its dissolution in 2011, complaints of ethnic and racial discrimination were to far outnumber those concerning gender, age, and any other criterion. But it was clear from the outset that the fight against racial and ethnic discrimination was to be accorded a low priority.

In the face of these long-standing patterns of marginalization, some have been tempted to turn in extremist directions. Thus in the fall of 2000, the beginning of the second Intifada in occupied Palestinian territories was followed by a sharp rise in recorded cases of antisemitism in France, which, for most of the subsequent decade, outnumbered offenses against Arabs and blacks, who until then had been the main victims of racist violence.[26] The upsurge in antisemitism was attributed by the Interior Ministry to disaffected youths in the *banlieues,* who saw in the Palestinians fellow victims of social injustice, whose struggle against Israeli occupation now appeared to be prompting the scapegoating of Jews in France, perceived as part of a privileged ruling class.[27] Simultaneously, small numbers were joining the ranks of jihadist networks acting in the name of puritanical Salafist strains of Islamic ideology engaged in distant theaters of war that sometimes spilled over into terrorist actions targeting France, first seen in the case of Kelkal and other young men from the *banlieues* recruited by Algerian Islamists in 1995. The United States–led interventions launched in Afghanistan in 2001 and in Iraq in 2003 attracted scores of French recruits to engage there and in nearby countries in support of groups linked to al-Qaeda, which had masterminded the 9/11 attacks on the United States. With the aid of social networks and other forms of internet-borne communications, the pace quickened after the outbreak of the civil war in Syria in 2011. In 2012 a twenty-three-year-old Franco-Algerian, Mohamed Merah, gunned down three Jewish schoolchildren and one of their teachers in his native Toulouse; a few days earlier he had slain three French soldiers of North African descent, who in his eyes were betraying Islam by serving with French forces fighting against the Taliban in Afghanistan.[28] Three years later almost 150 were killed in the massacres carried out in and around Paris in January and November 2015. By the beginning of 2016, jihadist networks based in Syria and neighboring Iraq, principally the offshoot of al-Qaeda calling itself the Islamic State and the caliphate proclaimed under its aegis, had attracted over two thousand recruits from France, more than from any country in Europe.[29]

While there is, of course, no monocausal explanation for a phenomenon such as jihadism, in which multiple factors—social, political, ethnic, psychological—are undoubtedly involved, a number of features nevertheless stand out. The most senior positions in the jihadist networks that in the past twenty years have struck targets in the United States, France, and other western countries are Middle Eastern men, often professionally skilled, who are equally committed to destroying the regimes that rule their home countries, men that resent being excluded from power and have directed mass killings that cumulatively exceed those inflicted in the West. These jihadist elites—who, while peddling grandiose religious rhetoric, often build their power base by engaging in mafia-style activities—have been supported by tens of thousands of foot soldiers, recruited mainly from among the disaffected lower social echelons of formerly colonized regions in and around the Middle East, together with relatively small but growing numbers from among Europe's postcolonial immigrant minorities. These disempowered social strata are in many ways today's "damnés de la terre" (wretched of the earth)—postcolonial equivalents of the nineteenth century proletarians evoked in the opening lines of the "Internationale"[30] and of the twentieth-century colonized masses chronicled by Frantz Fanon[31]—who now see themselves as victims, on the one hand, of systemic discrimination within European societies rooted in ethnic hierarchies inherited from the colonial period, and on the other, of exploitation by corrupt, authoritarian postindependence regimes that have failed to deliver the social justice promised by national liberation movements.[32]

The resentment aroused by the self-serving and often nepotistic regimes that have ruled the Middle East and neighboring regions in the decades since decolonization is a clear sign that present-day jihadism cannot be explained purely and simply as a consequence of colonial empires that ended half a century ago. Another such sign lies in the fact that within Europe, some of those joining jihadist movements are converts to Islam from "white," middle class backgrounds, with no personal experience of racial or ethnic discrimination. Converts of this kind, who are more liable to be motivated by adolescent identity crises than by social deprivation, account for most of the radicalized French youths reported by family members to the Centre de prévention contre les dérives sectaires liées à l'islam (CPDSI), an organization set up with government support to help prevent recruitment into jihadist networks. Such cases are, however, not typical of the majority of French jihadists. A widely cited report produced by the CPDSI[33] has often been misunderstood to mean that the upsurge in jihadism has little do with ethnic discrimination or social injustice. In reality, the vast majority of French jihadists—who are underrepresented among the persons reported to the CPDSI—come from disadvantaged postcolonial immigrant backgrounds. Almost 80 percent of French jihadists present in Syria in the fall of 2014 were young people from Muslim immigrant families,[34] who account for around 10 percent of their age group among the national population of France. All of the French jihadists involved in the January and November 2015 massacres carried out in and around Paris came from backgrounds of this type. Young men from low-income Muslim families are also heavily overrepresented among France's prison population.[35] Few of the families from which these men come are well versed in Islamic scriptures; for most, Islam is more a matter of ancestral tradition than of politics. The turn to crime and, in some cases, to jihadism has arisen not from exposure to Islam per se but in response to social exclusion which has fueled the conviction among young people stigmatized as Arabs, blacks, and Muslims that conventional avenues of earning a living, supporting a family, and participating more widely in French society are blocked.

As Farhad Khosrokhavar has observed, among those tempted to engage in criminal activities such as theft and drug dealing, this may seem "the only means open to them in practice to help their family realize the middle class consumer society dream, but often at a high price in the form of a prison sentence and the vicious circle of re-offending followed by further prison terms."[36] For some, the dead end of imprisonment has, in turn, been the site of a process of radicalization through which a jihadist "becomes 'someone.' He is no longer worthless but worthy in the eyes of God, and those who reject him are 'godless' and 'heretical,' damned to be massacred without the slightest moral scruple. He thus burns all his bridges with those who might help him climb out of marginalization and delinquency by working hard to overcome the daunting obstacles placed in his way so as to join the middle classes by regular means."[37]

If today's jihadists have decided to burn their bridges with French society, it is precisely because, unlike the marchers of the 1980s and those who took part in the civil disturbances of 2005, pressing the Republic to honor its promises of equality, they believe those promises to be empty and see no hope of overcoming the discriminatory practices that bar their way with impunity. Instead, as Olivier Roy has remarked, they seek to turn the tables through extreme acts of violence designed to produce "a world where losers suddenly become winners, be it only for the length of a terrorist attack."[38] In drawing attention away from the broad mass of the nation's postcolonial minorities, who continue to seek social advancement through peaceful means, the jihadists play into the hands of those who have long claimed that Muslim minorities originating in former colonial territories are fundamentally hostile to the values of the Republic and have no rightful place in France. The alternative community into which the extremists have entered, posited as a divinely sanctioned global project destined to destroy secular nations such as France in the name of a totalitarian vision of Islam, bears little resemblance to the national liberation movements that pressed for an end to the colonial era. In the Manichean vision of the jihadists, all those who run or profit from the prevailing social order—be it in the West, in formerly colonized regions, or in any other part of the planet—instead of submitting to their supposedly divinely ordained dictates, are destined to be annihilated. In Middle Eastern and neighboring countries, social injustices that have festered under postcolonial regimes lacking in popular legitimacy have led disaffected elements to throw in their lot with jihadist movements. At the same time, beneath the surface of the new era proclaimed from one side by the jihadists and from the other by those who, like

Valls, seek to defeat them, there lies in France—Europe's largest supplier of jihadist recruits—an impasse that is in large measure grounded in injustices steeped in the unfinished business of the colonial past.

Alec G. Hargreaves is Emeritus Professor of Transcultural French Studies at Florida State University, where he directed the Winthrop-King Institute for Contemporary French and Francophone Studies. A specialist on postcolonial minorities in France, he has authored and edited numerous works including *Immigration and Identity in Beur Fiction: Voices from the North African Immigrant Community in France* (2nd edition, 1997), *Memory, Empire and Postcolonialism* (2005), *Multi-Ethnic France: Immigration, Politics, Culture and Society* (2007), and *Transnational French Studies: Postcolonialism and* Littérature-monde (2010).

Notes

1. Manuel Valls, "Discours du Premier ministre—Examen du projet de loi de révision constitutionnelle à l'Assemblée nationale," February 13, 2016, http://www.assemblee-nationale.fr/14/cri/2015–2016/20160122.asp#P719606. All translations are by the author.

2. Michèle Tribalat, *De l'immigration à l'assimilation: Enquête sur les populations d'origine étrangère en France* (Paris: La Découverte, 1996); Sylvain Brouard and Vincent Tiberj, *Français comme les autres? Enquête sur les citoyens d'origine maghrébine, africaine et turque* (Paris: FNSP, 2005); Cris Beauchemin, Christelle Hamel and Patrick Simon, eds, *Trajectoires et origines: Enquête sur la diversité des populations en France* (Paris: INED, 2015).

3. Alec G. Hargreaves, "Empty Promises? Public Policy Against Racial and Ethnic Discrimination in France," in *French Politics, Culture and Society* 33, no. 3 (Winter 2015): 95–116.

4. Among the nine men known to have participated directly in the November 13 attacks in downtown Paris and outside the national sports stadium in Saint-Denis, seven came from North African immigrant families in France and Belgium; two others, who at the time of writing have yet to be firmly identified, appear to have entered Europe a month earlier carrying false Syrian passports. Seven of the nine blew themselves up during the attacks; the two others died during a subsequent shootout with the police when one of them detonated his explosive vest. Several other men from similar minority ethnic backgrounds who appear not to have participated directly in the killings were involved in organizing the attacks and providing logistical support.

5. "Manuel Valls évoque un 'apartheid territorial, social, ethnique' en France," *Le Monde*, January 20, 2015.

6. "Manuel Valls annonce la tenue d'un comité interministériel consacré à la lutte contre les inégalités, au combat pour l'égalité dans les quartiers, début mars," Ministère de la Ville, January 22, 2015, http://www.ville.gouv.fr/?manuel-valls-annonce-la-tenue-d-un.

7. Documentary broadcast by Direct 8, June 16, 2009, http://www.ina.fr/video/3933266001036.

8. Lilian Alemagna and Laure Bretton, "Après 'l'apartheid,' les demi-mesures," *Libération*, March 5, 2015.

9. Alice Géraud, "Gilles Clavreul, la valse antiraciste," *Libération*, April 16, 2015.

10. Despite abundant evidence demonstrating the widespread nature of racial and ethnic discrimination, those engaging in this practice are seldom prosecuted and fewer still are convicted. For instance, between 2008 and 2012, successful prosecutions for racial and ethnic discrimination in the labor market—the field most frequently cited by victims of discrimination—averaged only two or three a year: Justice Ministry data cited in annual reports of the Commission nationale consultative des droits de l'homme, *La Lutte contre le racisme et la xénophobie*, 2010–2014 (Paris: La Documentation française, 2011–2015).

11. The party has since change its name to Les Républicains.

12. Jean-François Amadieu, *Enquête "Testing" sur CV* (Adia/Paris I-Observatoire des discriminations, 2004), http://www.observatoiredesdiscriminations.fr/images/stories/presentation_du_testing_mai2004.pdf.

13. Emmanuel Macron, "Discours d'Emmanuel Macron: Conclusion de la 5ème Université des Gracques," November 23, 2015, http://lesgracques.fr/discours-demmanuel-macron-conclusion-de-la-5eme-universite-des-gracques/.

14. Marie-Anne Valfort, *Discriminations religieuses à l'embauche: Une réalité* (Paris: Institut Montaigne, 2015). The close similarity between these findings and those of the 2004 study conducted by Jean-François Amadieu, cited earlier, is one of many indicators of the lack of progress in combatting discrimination.

15. Remarks made by Manuel Valls in the French Senate, November 26, 2016, http://www.senat.fr/seances/s201511/s20151126/s20151126005.html.

16. Frédéric Lebaron, Fanny Jedlicki and Laurent Willemez, "La sociologie, ce n'est pas la culture de l'excuse!," *Le Monde*, December 14, 2015. For a further elaboration on the distinction between explaining and excusing jihadist violence, see Pierre Joxe, "Quand l'histoire coloniale pèse tellement sur le présent, il vaut mieux la connaître," Bondy Blog, posted March 21, 2016, http://bondyblog.liberation.fr/201603210001/pierre-joxe-quand-lhistoire-coloniale-pese-tellement-sur-le-present-il-vaut-mieux-la-connaitre/.

17. Benjamin Stora, *La gangrène et l'oubli: La mémoire de la guerre d'Algérie* (Paris: La Découverte, 1991); Pascal Blanchard, Nicolas Bancel, and Sandrine Lemaire, eds., *La fracture coloniale: La société française au prisme de l'héritage colonial* (Paris: La Découverte, 2005).

18. Mathieu Rigouste, *L'ennemi intérieur: La généalogie coloniale et militaire de l'ordre sécuritaire dans la France contemporaine* (Paris: La Découverte, 2009).

19. Smaller numbers of non-Muslim (post)colonial migrants have come from regions such as the Caribbean and Indochina.

20. *Être Français aujourd'hui et demain: Rapport de la Commission de la nationalité*, vol. 2 (Paris: Union générale d'éditions, 1988), 260.

21. Michèle Tribalat, "Une estimation des populations d'origine étrangère en France en 1999," *Population* 59, no. 1 (2004): 75.

22. "Moi, Khaled Kelkal," interview conducted by Dietmar Loch in 1992, *Le Monde*, October 7, 1995.

23. Dominique Le Guilledoux, "'Votre histoire de boîte de nuit, ça me sidère'!," *Le Monde*, October 14, 1995.

24. Collectif pour une autorité indépendante universelle de lutte contre les discriminations, "Projet de loi HALDE: Une autorité pour rien?," October 4, 2004, www.gisti.org.

25. "'Lutter contre tous les abus,'" interview with Louis Schweitzer by Cécilia Gabizon, *Le Figaro*, June 23, 2005.

26. See the French Interior Ministry data for 1993–2010 in Commission nationale consultative des droits de l'homme, *La Lutte contre le racisme, l'antisémitisme et la xénophobie: Année 2010* (Paris: La Documentation française, 2011), 98.

27. Commission nationale consultative des droits de l'homme, *La Lutte contre le racisme, l'antisémitisme et la xénophobie: Année 2002* (Paris: La Documentation française, 2003), 84.

28. While all three of the soldiers were of North African origin and two came from Muslim families, the third was a Catholic.

29. "Discours de Manuel Valls, Premier Ministre," February 5, 2016, http://www.gouvernement.fr/sites/default/files/document/document/2016/02/20160205_discours_de_manuel_valls_premier_ministre_-_examen_du_projet_de_loi_de_revision_constitutionnelle.pdf.

30. First sung in 1871 during the Paris Commune, this anthem of the left calls upon the "damnés de la terre" (wretched of the earth) to rise up against their capitalist oppressors.

31. Frantz Fanon, *Les damnés de la terre* (Paris: Maspéro, 1961).

32. For a contrary view, attributing jihadism to "the autonomous power of religion," see interview with Jean Birnbaum, "Les djihadistes ne sont pas les damnés de la terre," Causer.fr, February 16, 2016.

33. Dounia Bouzar, Christophe Capenne, and Sulayman Valsan, *La métamorphose opérée chez le jeune par les nouveaux discours terroristes: Recherche-action sur la mutation du processus d'endoctrinement et d'embrigadement dans l'islam radical*, Centre de prévention contre les dérives sectaires liées à l'islam, November 2014, http://www.bouzar-expertises.fr/images/docs/METAMORPHOSE.pdf. The document is based on 160 cases of "radicalization" reported by family members (usually parents) to the CPDSI. Radicalization, defined by the CPDSI and the French Interior Ministry as the adoption of "a position that draws upon religious precepts presented as Muslim in order to lead a young person to self-exclusion and to sever all ties with 'all those who are not like him' " (6), is a relatively broad category, and by no means all of those concerned are jihadists, i.e., persons committed to the use of violence in pursuit of Islamist goals. By early 2016, when over eight thousand reports of radicalization had been received by the authorities, the Interior Ministry put the number of French recruits involved in jihadist networks at just over two thousand, among whom a thousand had traveled to the war zones in Syria and Iraq: Samuel Laurent, "Que disent les chiffres sur la radicalisation en France?," *Le Monde*, February 3, 2016.

34. French Interior Ministry data cited in Cécile Chambraud, "Les nouveaux visages du jihad français," *Le Monde*, November 18, 2014. By contrast, 80 percent of the cases of radicalization on which the CPDSI report was based concerned young people from atheist families, with the remaining 20 percent originating among families adhering to a range of religious faiths including Catholicism and Islam. Some 84 percent of the young people in the CPDSI sample were from middle or upper class backgrounds, and half had parents engaged in teaching and related educational professions: *La métamorphose opérée chez le jeune par les nouveaux discours terroristes*, 7–9. These profiles were quite unrepresentative of most French jihadists.

35. Farhad Khosrokhavar, *L'islam dans les prisons* (Paris: Balland, 2004); Didier Fassin, *L'ombre du monde: Une anthropologie de la condition carcérale* (Paris: Seuil, 2015).

36. Farhad Khosrokhavar, "Approche sociologique: Anatomie de la radicalisation," in *Le jihadisme: Le comprendre pour mieux le combattre*, David Bénichou, Farhad Khosrokhavar, and Philippe Migaux (Paris: Plon, 2015), 287.

37. Khosrokhavar, "Approche sociologique: Anatomie de la radicalisation," 287.

38. Interview with Olivier Roy conducted by Haoues Seniguer, "Comment l'islam est devenu la nouvelle idéologie des damnés de la planète," *Atlantico*, July 4, 2015.

BIBLIOGRAPHY

Académie universelle des cultures. *Pourquoi se souvenir?* Paris: Grasset, 1999.

Achi, Raberh. "L'islam athentique appartient à Dieu, 'l'islam algérien' à César: La mobilisation de l'association de oulémas d'Algérie pour la séparation du culte musulman et de l'Etat (1931–1956)." *Genèses*, 4, no. 69 (2007): 49–69.

Agamben, Giorgio. *Homo sacer.* Paris: Seuil, 1997.

———. *Nudités.* Paris: Rivages, 2009.

Ageron, Charles-Robert. *France coloniale ou parti colonial.* Paris: PUF, 1978.

———."Le drame des harkis en 1962." *Vingtième siècle: Revue d'histoire* 42, no. 1 (April–June 1994): 3–6.

Ageron, Charles-Robert, and Marc Michel, eds. *L'ère des décolonisations.* Paris: Karthala, 1995.

Ageron, Charles-Robert, Jacques Thobie, Gilbert Meynier, and Catherine Coquery-Vidrovitch. *Histoire de la France coloniale, de 1914 à 1990.* Paris: Armand Colin, 1990.

Agier, Michel. *Gérer les indésirables: Des camps de réfugiés au gouvernement humanitaire.* Paris: Flammarion, 2008.

Aïssaoui, Boualem. *Images et visages du cinema algérien.* Algiers: Ministère de la culture et du tourisme—Office national pour le commerce et l'industrie cinématographique, 1984.

Alduy, Cécile, and Stéphane Wahnich. *Marine Le Pen prise aux mots: Décryptage du nouveau discours frontiste.* Paris: Seuil, 2015.

Alemagna, Lilian, and Laure Bretton. "Après 'l'apartheid,' les demi-mesures." *Libération*, March 5, 2015.

Allen, Theodore W. *The Invention of the White Race.* New York: Verso Books, 2012.

d'Allones, David Revault, and Laurent Borredon. *Valls, à l'intérieur.* Paris: Robert Laffont, 2014.

Amadieu, Jean-François. *Enquête "Testing" sur CV.* Adia/Paris I-Observatoire des discriminations, 2004. http://www.observatoiredesdiscriminations.fr/images/stories/presentation_du_testing_mai2004.pdf.

Amara, Noureddine, Joel Beinin, Houda Ben Hamouda, Benoît Challand, Jocelyne Dakhlia, Sonia Dayan-Herzbrun, Muriam Haleh Davis, Giulia Fabbiano, Darcie Fontaine,

David Theo Goldberg, Ghassan Hage, Laleh Khalili, Tristan Leperlier, Nadia Marzouki, Pascal Ménoret, Stéphanie Pouessel, Elizabeth Shakman Hurd, Thomas Serres, and Seif Soudani. "Nuit de Cologne: 'Kamel Daoud recycle les clichés orientalistes les plus éculés.'" *Le Monde*, February 11, 2016.

Amellal, Karim, Khalid El Bahji, Jean-Eric Boulin, Faïza Guène, Dembo Goumane, Habiba Mahany, Samir Ouazen, Mabrouk Rachedi, Mohamed Razane, and Thomté Ryam. *Qui fait la France? Chroniques d'une société annoncée*. Paris: Stock, 2007.

Amghar, Samir. "Les salafistes français: Une nouvelle aristocratie religieuse." *Maghreb-Machrek*, no. 185 (Spring 2005): 13–32.

Amiraux, Valérie. "Expertises, savoir et politique: La constitution de l'islam comme problème public en France et en Allemagne." In *Les sciences sociales à l'épreuve de l'action*, edited by Bénédicte Zimmermann, 209–245. Paris: EHESS, 2004.

———. "Headscarves in Europe: What Is Really the Issue?" In *European Islam: The Challenges for Society and Public Policy*, edited by Samir Amghar, Amel Boubekeur, and Michael Emerson, 124–143. Brussels: CEPS, 2007.

Amiraux, Valérie, and Gerdien Jonker. "Introduction: Talking about Visibility: Actors, Politics, Forms of Engagement." In *Politics of Visibility: Young Muslims European Public Spaces*, edited by Valérie Amiraux and Gerdien Jonker, 9–20. Bielefeld: Transcript Verlag, 2006.

Amselle, Jean-Loup. "La société française piégée par la guerre des identités." *Le Monde*, September 15, 2011.

———. *L'ethnicisation de la France*. Paris: Éditions Lignes, 2011.

———. *L'Occident décroché: Enquête sur les postcolonialismes*. Paris: Stock, 2008.

Amselle, Jean-Loup, and Elikia M'Bokolo. *Au cœur de l'ethnie: Ethnies, tribalisme et état en Afrique*. Paris: La Découverte, 1985.

Anderson, Benedict. *Imagined Communities: Reflections on the Origin and Spread of Nationalism*. London: Verso, 1983.

Arkoun, Mohammed. *Histoire de l'islam et des musulmans en France du Moyen Âge à nos jours*. Paris: Albin Michel, 2006.

Artières, Philippe, and Michelle Zancarini-Fournel. "De mai, souviens-toi de ce qu'il te plaît: Mémoire des années 68." In *Les guerres de mémoires: La France et son histoire*, edited by Pascal Blanchard and Isabelle Veyrat-Masson, 128–136. Paris: La Découverte, 2008.

Askolovitch, Claude. "La vérité sur la colonisation." *Nouvel Observateur*, no. 2144 (December 8–14, 2005): 12–14.

———. *Nos mal-aimés: Ces musulmans dont la France ne veut pas*. Paris: Grasset, 2013.

Aussaresses, Paul. *Je n'ai pas tout dit: Ultimes révélations au service de la France*. Paris: Éditions du Rocher, 2008.

———. *Pour la France: Services spéciaux 1942–1954*. Paris: Éditions du Rocher, 2001.

———. *Services spéciaux, Algérie 1955–1957: Mon témoignage sur la torture*. Paris: Perrin, 2001.

Aymard, Camille. *Bolchevisme ou Fascisme? Français, il faut choisir!* Paris: Flammarion, 1925.

Azéma, Jean-Pierre. "Cessez de jouer avec les mémoires." *Libération*, May 10, 2006.

Bachi, Salim. *Moi, Khaled Kelkal*. Paris: Grasset, 2012.

Badie, Bertrand. *Le temps des humiliés: Pathologie des relations internationales*. Paris: Odile Jacob, 2014.

Bailey, Brett. "Entretien avec Brett Bailey." By Jean-François Perrier. Avignon Festival, 2013.

Bainville, Jacques. *L'Angleterre et l'Empire Britannique*. Paris: Plon, 1938.

Balandier, Georges. "La situation coloniale." *Cahiers internationaux de sociologie* 11 (1951): 44–79.

Balandier, Georges, and Jean-François Bayart. "Questions de méthodes." In *La situation postcoloniale: Les postcolonial studies dans le débat français*, edited by Marie-Claude Smout, 267–276. Paris: Presses de Sciences Po, 2007.

Balibar, Etienne. "Le retour de la race." *Mouvements*, no. 50 (March–April 2007): 162–171.

Balibar, Etienne, and Immanuel Wallerstein. *Race, nation, classe: Les identités ambiguës*. Paris: La Découverte, 1988.

Bancel, Nicolas, and Pascal Blanchard, "Civiliser: L'invention de l'indigène." In *Culture coloniale: La France conquise par son Empire, 1871–1931*, edited by Pascal Blanchard and Sandrine Lemaire, 149–162. Paris: Éditions Autrement, 2002.

———. "La colonisation: Du débat sur la guerre d'Algérie au discours de Dakar." In *Les guerres de mémoires: La France et son histoire*, edited by Pascal Blanchard and Isabelle Veyrat-Masson, 137–154. Paris: La Découverte, 2008.

———. "La fondation du républicanisme colonial: Retour sur une généalogie politique." *Mouvements* 2, no. 38 (March–April 2005): 26–36.

Bancel, Nicolas, Pascal Blanchard, Gilles Boëtsch, Éric Deroo, and Sandrine Lemaire, eds. *Zoos humains: Au temps des exhibitions humains*. Paris: La Découverte, 2002.

Bancel, Nicolas, Pascal Blanchard, and Ahmed Boubeker. *Le grand repli*. Paris: La Découverte, 2015.

Bancel, Nicolas, Pascal Blanchard, and Francis Delabarre. *Images d'Empire, 1930–1960: Trente ans de photographies officielles sur l'Afrique française*. Paris: La Martinière/La Documentation française, Paris, 1996.

Bancel, Nicolas, Pascal Blanchard, Laurent Gervereau, eds. *Images et colonies (1880–1962)*. Paris: BDIC-ACHAC, 1993.

Bancel, Nicolas, Pascal Blanchard, Sandrine Lemaire, and Dominic Thomas, eds. *Colonial Culture in France since the Revolution*. Bloomington and Indianapolis: Indiana University Press, 2014.

Bancel, Nicolas, Pascal Blanchard, and Dominic Thomas. "Postcolonial France: From the Colonial Fracture to Ethnic Apartheid (2005–2015)." *Occasion* 9 (2015). http://arcade.stanford.edu/sites/default/files/article_pdfs/Occasion_v09_bancel-Blanchard-Thomas_01Pass_final.pdf.

Bancel, Nicolas, Pascal Blanchard, and Françoise Vergès. *La colonisation française*. Toulouse: Milan, 2007.

———. *La République coloniale: Essai sur une utopie*. Paris: Albin Michel, 2003.

———. *La République coloniale*. Paris: Hachette Littératures, 2006.

Bancel, Nicolas, Thomas David, and Dominic Thomas. *The Invention of Race: Scientific and Popular Representations*. New York: Routledge, 2014.

Barcellini, Serge. "L'état républicain, acteur de mémoire: Des morts pour la France aux morts à cause de la France." In *Les guerres de mémoires: La France et son histoire*, edited by Pascal Blanchard and Isabelle Veyrat-Masson, 209–219. Paris: La Découverte, 2008.

Baré, Jean-François. "Déconstruire le postmodernisme." *L'Homme* 39, no. 151 (1999): 267–276.

Barlet, Olivier. "*Exhibit B*: Un spectacle à critiquer." *Africultures*, December 3, 2014. www.africultures.com/php/index.php?nav=article&no=12593.

Barr, James. *A Line in the Sand: Britain, France and the Struggle That Shaped the Middle East*. New York: Simon & Schuster, 2011.

Barral, Pierre. "L'affaire d'Oradour, affrontement de deux mémoires." In *Mémoire de la Seconde Guerre mondiale: Actes du colloque de Metz*, edited by Alfred Wahl, 243–252. Metz: Centre de Recherche "Histoire et Civilisation de l'Europe Occidentale," 1984.

de Barros, Françoise. "Des Français musulmans d'Algérie aux 'immigrés': L'importation de classifications coloniales dans les politiques du logement en France (1950–1970)." *Actes de la recherche en sciences sociales*, no. 159 (2005): 27–45.

———. "Les municipalités face aux Algériens: Méconnaissances et usages des catégories coloniales en métropole avant et après la Seconde Guerre mondiale." *Genèses* 4, no. 53 (2003): 69–92.

Barthes, Roland. *Mythologies*. Paris: Seuil, 2007 [1957].

Baruch, Marc Olivier. "Éloge de la repentance." *Le Monde*, May 12, 2007.

Bass, Loretta. "What Motivates European Youth to Join ISIS." *Syria Comment*, November 20, 2014.

Baubérot, Jean. *Laïcité 1905–2005: Entre passion et raison*. Paris: Seuil, 2004.

———. *La Laïcité falsifiée*. Paris: La Découverte, 2014.

———. *Vers un nouveau pacte laïque?* Paris: Seuil, 1990.

Baverez, Nicolas. *La France qui tombe: Un constat clinique du déclin français*. Paris: Perrin, 2003.

Bayart, Jean-François. "La novlangue d'un archipel universitaire." In *La situation postcoloniale: Les postcolonial studies dans le débat français*, edited by Marie-Claude Smout, 268–272. Paris: Presses de Sciences Po, 2007.

———. "Le politique par le bas. Questions de méthode." *Politique africaine* 1, no. 1 (January 1981): 53–82.

Beauchemin, Cris, Christelle Hamel, and Patrick Simon, eds. *Trajectoires et origines: Enquête sur la diversité des populations en France*. Paris: INED, 2015.

Beaud, Stéphane, and Michel Pialoux. *Violences urbaines, violence sociale: Genèse des nouvelles classes dangereuses*. Paris: Fayard, 2003.

Beaugé, Florence. "Comment *Le Monde* a relancé le débat sur la torture en Algérie." *Le Monde*, March 17, 2012.

Becker, Jean-Jacques, and Serge Berstein. *Histoire de l'anticommunisme en France 1917–1940*. Paris: Orban, 1987.

———. "L'anticommunisme en France." *Vingtième Siècle: Revue d'histoire*, no. 15 (July–September 1987): 17–28.

Becquet, Valérie, and Chantal De Linares, eds. *Quand les jeunes s'engagent: Entre expérimentations et constructions identitaires*. Paris: L'Harmattan, 2006.

Bédarida, François. *Histoire, critique et responsabilité*. Brussels: IHTP-CNRS/Complexe, 2003.

Benali, Adelkader. *Le cinéma colonial*. Paris: Le Cerf, 1999.

Benbassa, Esther. "À qui sert la guerre des mémoires?" In *Les guerres de mémoires: La France et son histoire*, edited by Pascal Blanchard and Isabelle Veyrat-Masson, 252–261. Paris: La Découverte, 2008.

Benot, Yves. *Les lumières, l'esclavage, la colonisation*. Paris: La Découverte, 2005.

———. *Massacres coloniaux. 1944–1950: La IVème République et la mise au pas des colonies françaises*. Paris: La Découverte, 2001.

Bernabé, Jean, Patrick Chamoiseau, and Raphaël Confiant. *Éloge de la créolité/In Praise of Creoleness*. Translated by Mohamed B. Taleb-Khyar. Paris: Gallimard, 1991.

Bernal, Martin. *Black Athena: The Afroasiatic Roots of Classical Civilization*. Vol. 1: *The Fabrication of Ancient Greece, 1785–1985*. Brunswick, NJ: Rutgers University Press, 1987.

Bernard, Philippe. "Banlieues: la provocation coloniale." *Le Monde*, November 18, 2005.

———. "Des 'enfants de colonisés' revendiquent leur histoire." *Le Monde*, February 21, 2005.

———. "On nous qualifies sans cesse 'd'Arabes' et on prétend nous empêcher de nous situer par rapport à l'islam." *Le Monde*, July 6, 2004.

Bertrand, Romain. "Faire parler les subalternes ou le mythe du dévoilement." In *La situation postcoloniale: Les postcolonial studies dans le débat français*, edited by Marie-Claude Smout, 276–289. Paris: Presses de Sciences Po, 2007.

———. "La mise en cause(s) du fait colonial." *Politique africaine*, no. 102 (June 2006): 28–49.

———. *Mémoires d'empire: La controverse autour du "fait colonial."* Broissieux: Éditions du croquant, 2006.

Besnaci-Lancou, Fatima, and Gilles Manceron. *Les harkis dans la colonisation et ses suites*. Paris: Éditions de L'Atelier, 2007.

Besnaci-Lancou, Fatima, and Abderahman Moumen. *Les harkis*. Paris: Le Cavalier Bleu, 2008.

Betz, Hans-Georg. *La droite populiste en Europe: Extrême et démocrate?* Paris: Autrement, 2004.

Birnbaum, Jean. "Les djihadistes ne sont pas les damnés de la terre." Causer.fr, February 16, 2016.

Blanchard, Pascal. "*Exhibit B*: Ce spectacle n'est pas raciste, c'est l'inverse." *L'Obs*, November 29, 2014.

———. "Insultes envers Taubira: 'C'est un racisme pur et dur, un racisme de peau.'" Interview with Pascal Blanchard. By Sonya Faure. *Libération*, October 29, 2013.

———. "Le Musée des colonisations: Un grand projet présidentiel?" *Libération*, June 3, 2013.

———. *Nationalisme et colonialisme*. PhD diss., University of Paris 1, 1994.

———. "Un musée pour la France coloniale." *Libération*, June 17–18, 2000.

Blanchard, Pascal, and Nicolas Bancel, eds. *Culture postcoloniale*. Paris: Éditions Autrement, 2006.

———. *De l'indigène à l'immigré*. Paris: Gallimard, 1993.

———. "Pour un musée des colonisations et de l'esclavage!" *Le Monde*, May 15, 2016.

Blanchard, Pascal, Nicolas Bancel, Gilles Boëtsch, Éric Deroo, and Sandrine Lemaire, eds. *Zoos humains et exhibitions coloniales: 150 ans d'inventions de l'autre*. Paris: La Découverte, 2011.

Blanchard, Pascal, Nicolas Bancel, Gilles Boëtsch, Éric Deroo, Sandrine Lemaire, and Charles Forsdick, eds. *Human Zoos: Sciences and Spectacle in the Age of Empire*. Liverpool, UK: Liverpool University Press, 2008.

Blanchard, Pascal, Nicolas Bancel, and Sandrine Lemaire. "Introduction: La fracture coloniale: une crise française." In *La fracture coloniale: La société française au prisme de l'héritage colonial*, edited by Pascal Blanchard, Nicolas Bancel, and Sandrine Lemaire, 9–30. Paris: La Découverte, 2005.

———, eds. *La fracture coloniale: La société française au prisme de l'héritage colonial*. Paris: La Découverte, 2005.

Blanchard, Pascal, Gilles Boëtsch, and Nanette Jacomijn Snoep, eds. *Human Zoos: The Invention of the Savage*. Paris and Arles: Actes Sud/Musée du quai Branly, 2011.

Blanchard, Pascal, Sylvie Chalaye, Éric Deroo, Dominic Thomas, and Mahamet Timéra, eds. *La France noire: Trois siècles de présences des Afriques, des Caraïbes, de l'Océan Indien et d'Océanie*. Paris: La Découverte, 2011.

Blanchard, Pascal, and Armelle Chatelier, eds. *Images et colonies*. Paris: Syros, 1993.

Blanchard, Pascal, Marc Ferro, and Isabelle Veyrat-Masson, eds. *Les guerres de mémoire dans le monde*, *Hermès*, no. 52 (October 2008).

Blanchard, Pascal, and Sandrine Lemaire, eds. *Culture coloniale*. Paris: Éditions Autrement, 2003.

Blanchard, Pascal, Françoise Vergès, Nicolas Bancel, and Marc Cheb Sun. "Manifeste pour un musée des histoires coloniales." *Libération*, May 8, 2012.

Blanchard, Pascal, and Isabelle Veyrat-Masson, eds. *Culture impériale*. Paris: Éditions Autrement, 2004.

———. *Les guerres de mémoires: La France et son histoire*. Paris: La Découverte, 2008.

Blanchard, Pascal, Naïma Yahi, Yvan Gastaut, and Nicolas Bancel, eds. *La France arabo-orientale: Treize siècles de présences du Maghreb, de la Turquie, d'Égypte, du Moyen-Orient et du Proche-Orient*. Paris: La Découverte, 2014.

Blévis, Laure. "Les avatars de la cityonneté en Algérie coloniale ou les paradoxes d'une catégorisation." *Droit et Société*, no. 48 (2001/2002): 557–581.

Bodin, Louis, ed. *Les guerres franco-françaises: Vingtième Siècle: Revue d'histoire* 5, no. 1 (January–March 1985).

Boëtsch, Gilles. "L'université et la recherche face aux enjeux de mémoire: Le temps des mutations." In *Les guerres de mémoires: La France et son histoire*, edited by Pascal Blanchard and Isabelle Veyrat-Masson, 187–198. Paris: La Découverte, 2008.

Boisbouvier, Christophe. *Hollande l'Africain*. Paris: La Découverte, 2015.

Boni-Claverie, Isabelle. *Trop noire pour être française?* Quark/Arte France, 2015.

Borne, Dominique, and Benoît Falaize. *Religions et colonisation: Afrique-Asie-Océanie-Amériques (XVIe–XXe siècles)*. Paris: Éditions de l'Atelier, 2009.

Bouamama, Saïd, and Pierre Tevanian. "Peut-on parler d'un racisme postcolonial?" In *Culture postcoloniale 1961–2006*, edited by Nicolas Bancel and Pascal Blanchard, 243–254. Paris: Autrement, Paris, 2005.

Boubeker, Ahmed. *Les mondes de l'ethnicité: La communauté d'expérience des héritiers de l'immigration maghrébine*. Paris: Balland, 2003.

———. "L'immigration: Enjeux d'histoire et de mémoire à l'aube du xxie siècle." In *Les guerres de mémoires: La France et son histoire*, edited by Pascal Blanchard and Isabelle Veyrat-Masson, 165–174. Paris: La Découverte, 2008.

Boucheron, Patrick. *Ce que peut l'histoire*. Paris: Fayard, 2016.

Boulte, Patrick. *Individus en friche*. Paris: Desclée de Brouwer, 1995.

Boushaba, Zouhir. *Être algérien hier, aujourd'hui et demain*. Algiers: Mimouni, 1992.

Bouvet, Laurent. *Le sens du peuple: La gauche, la démocratie, le populisme*. Paris: Gallimard, 2012.

———. *L'insécurité culturelle*. Paris: Fayard, 2015.

Bouzar, Dounia, Christophe Capenne, and Sulayman Valsan. *La métamorphose opérée chez le jeune par les nouveaux discours terroristes: Recherche-action sur la mutation du processus d'endoctrinement et d'embrigadement dans l'islam radical*. Centre de prévention contre les dérives sectaires liées à l'islam, November 2014. http://www.bouzar-expertises.fr/images/docs/METAMORPHOSE.pdf.

Braconnier, Céline, and Nonna Mayer, eds. *Les inaudibles: Sociologie politique des précaires*. Paris: Presses de Sciences Po, 2015.

Branche, Raphaëlle. *La torture et l'armée pendant la guerre d'Algérie*. Paris: Gallimard, 2001.

Branche, Raphaëlle, and Sylvie Thenault, eds. *La France en guerre (1954–1962): Expériences métropolitaines de la guerre d'indépendance algérienne*. Paris: Autrement, 2008.

Bras, Hervé. *Le sol et le sang.* La Tour-d'Aigues: Éditions de l'Aube, 1994.

Brauman, Rony, and Hugo Slim. "Les ONG au cœur de la polémique sur l'humanitaire." Interview with Rony Brauman and Hugo Slim. By Pierre Hazan. *Libération*, December 25, 2004.

Breckenridge, Carol A., Sheldon Pollock, Homi K. Bhabha, and Dipest Chakrabarty, eds. *Cosmopolitanism.* Durham, NC: Duke University Press, 2002.

Breviglieri, Marc. "L'étreinte de l'origine: Attachement, mémoire et nostalgie chez les enfants d'immigrés maghrébins." *Confluences Méditerranée*, no. 39 (2001): 37–47.

Brice, Catherine. "Monuments: Pacificateurs ou agitateurs de mémoire." In *Les guerres de mémoires: La France et son histoire*, edited by Pascal Blanchard and Isabelle Veyrat-Masson, 199–208. Paris: La Découverte, 2008.

Bronner, Luc. "Il vaut mieux dire les choses, même si elles nous gênent." *Le Monde*, September 13, 2010.

Brossat, Alain. "À l'heure du consensus." In Dimitri Nicolaïdis, ed., *Oublier nos crimes: L'amnésie nationale: une spécifité française.* Paris: Éditions Autrement, 1994, 228–240.

Brouard, Sylvain, and Vincent Tiberj. *Français comme les autres? Enquête sur les citoyens d'origine maghrébine, africaine et turque.* Paris: Presses de Sciences Po, 2005.

Brubaker, Rogers. *Citizenship and Nationhood in France and Germany.* Cambridge, MA: Harvard University Press, 1992.

Bruckner, Bruckner. *La tyrannie de la pénitence: Essai sur le masochisme occidental.* Paris: Grasset, 2006.

———. *The Tears of the White Man: Compassion as Contempt.* Translated by William R. Beer. New York: The Free Press, 1986.

Brustier, Gaël. *La guerre culturelle aura bien lieu . . . L'occidentalisme ou l'idéologie de la crise.* Paris: Fayard, 2013.

Brustier, Gaël, and Jean-Philippe Huelin. *Voyage au bout de la droite: Des paniques morales à la contestation droitière.* Paris: Mille et une nuits, 2011.

Buisson, Patrick, and Pascal Gauchon. *OAS: Histoire de la résistance française en Algérie.* Bièvres: Éditions Jeune Pied-Noir, 1981.

Bui Trong, Lucienne. *Les racines de la violence: De l'émeute au communautarisme.* Paris: L. Audibert, 2003.

Butler, Judith. *Gender Trouble: Feminism and the Subversion of Identity.* New York: Routledge, 1990.

Buton, Philippe, and Laurent Gervereau. *Le couteau entre les dents: Soixante-dix ans d'affiches communistes et anticommunistes (1917–1987).* Paris: Le Chêne, 1989.

Caldwell, Christopher. *Reflections on the Revolution in Europe: Immigration, Islam, and the West.* New York: Doubleday, 2009.

Camus, Albert. "Misère de la Kabylie." *Alger républicain*, June 5–15, 1939. In *Actuelles*, vol. 3, *Chroniques algériennes (1939–1958).* Paris: Gallimard, 1958.

Camus, Jean-Yves, and Nicolas Lebourg. *Les droites extrêmes en Europe.* Paris: Seuil, 2015.

Camus, Renaud. *Le grand remplacement.* Neuilly-sur-Seine: Éditions David Reinharc, 2011.

———. "Non au changement de peuple et de civilisation." September 11, 2013. http://www.bvoltaire.fr/renaudcamus/non-au-changement-de-peuple-et-de-civilisation,35190.

Cantier, Jacques. "*Le bled* de Jean Renoir: Une mise en scène de la terre algérienne à l'heure du centenaire de la conquête." *Les Cahiers de la Cinémathèque*, no. 76 (2004): 49–55.

Carmichael, Stokely, and Charles V. Hamilton. *Le black power.* Paris: Payot, 1968.

Caron, Vicki. *Uneasy Asylum: France and the Jewish Refugee Crisis, 1933–1942*. Stanford, CA: Stanford University Press, 1999.

Cassen, Pierre, and Christine Tasin. *La faute du bobo Jocelyn*. Éditions Riposte Laïque, 2011.

Cavada, Jean-Marie. *Le syndrome Saddam: La France, ses musulmans et l'Irak*. "La Marche du siècle," FR3, January 30, 1991.

Céline, Louis-Ferdinand. *L'école des cadavres*. Paris, Denoël, 1938.

Césaire, Aimé. *Discourse on Colonialism*. Translated by Joan Pinkham. New York: Monthly Review Press, 2000 [1950].

———. *Notebook of a Return to the Native Land*. In *Aimé Césaire: The Collected Poetry*. Translated by Clayton Eshleman and Annette Smith. Berkeley and Los Angeles: University of California Press, 1983 [1939], 32–86.

Chalaye, Sylvie. "'Noir', 'nègre', 'homme de couleur . . . ces mots réducteurs." *Africultures*, nos. 92–93 (February 2013).

Chambers, Iain, Alessandra De Angelis, Celeste Ianniciello, Mariangela Orabona, and Michaela Quadraro, eds. *The Postcolonial Museum: The Arts of Memory and the Pressures of History*. Farnham, UK and Burlington, VT: Ashgate, 2014.

Chambraud, Cécile. "Les nouveaux visages du jihad français." *Le Monde*, November 18, 2014.

Charle, Christophe. *Les élites de la République, 1880–1900*. Paris: Fayard, Paris, 1987.

Chaubin, Hélène. "Le Sud, terre d'élection de l'activisme? L'OAS-Métro dans l'Hérault." In *La France en guerre (1954–1962): Expériences métropolitaines de la guerre d'indépendance algérienne*, edited by Raphaëlle Branche, and Sylvie Thenault, 299–308. Paris: Autrement, 2008.

Chaumont, Jean-Michel. *La concurrence des victimes: Génocide, identité et reconnaissance*. Paris: La Découverte, 1997.

Chebel d'Appollonia, Ariane. *Les frontières du racisme: Identités, ethnicité, citoyenneté*. Paris: Presses de Sciences Po, 2011.

———. *L'extrême droite en France: De Maurras à Le Pen*. Paris: PUF, 1987.

———. "Plus blanc que blanc: Réflexion sur le monochrome populiste en Europe." In *De quelle couleur sont les Blancs? Des petits Blancs des colonies au racisme anti-Blancs*, edited by Sylvie Laurent and Thierry Leclère, 232–239. Paris: La Découverte, 2013.

Chirac, Jacques, and Jean-Louis Barré. *Chaque pas doit être un but: Mémoires*. Paris: Nil, 2009.

"Choisir ses immigrés?" *Raisons politiques*, no. 26 (May 2007).

Chollet, Mona. *Rêves de droite: Défaire l'imaginaire sarkozyste*. Paris: Zones, 2008.

Chombeau, Christiane. *Le Pen: Fille & père*. Paris: Panama, 2007.

Chouder, Ismahane, Malika Latrèche, and Pierre Tevanian. *Les filles voilées parlent*. Paris: La Fabrique, 2008.

Chrétien, Jean-Pierre, ed. *L'Afrique de Sarkozy: Un déni d'histoire*. Paris: Karthala, 2008.

Citron, Suzanne. *Le mythe national: L'histoire de France en questions*. Paris: Les Éditions ouvrières, 1987.

———. *Le mythe national: L'histoire de France revisitée*. Paris: Éditions de l'Atelier, 2008 [1987].

"Claude Guéant persiste et réaffirme que 'toutes les cultures ne se valent pas.'" *Le Monde*, February 5, 2012.

Cloarec, Vincent, and Henry Laurens. *Le Moyen-Orient au 20e siècle*. Paris: Armand Colin, 2003.

CNCDH. *Rapport racisme, xénophobie, antisémitisme 1997*. Paris: La Documentation française, 1996.

———. *Rapport racisme, xénophobie, antisémitisme 2013*. Paris: La Documentation française, 2014.

Colas, Dominique. *Race et racisme, de Platon à Derrida: Anthologie critique*. Paris: Plon, 2004.

Collectif pour une autorité indépendante universelle de lutte contre les discriminations. "Projet de loi HALDE: Une autorité pour rien?" October 4, 2004. www.gisti.org.

"Colonies. Un débat français." *Le Monde 2*, no. 86 (April–May 2006).

Comité de défense de la race nègre. "'Le mot Nègre.'" *La Voix des Nègres*, no. 1 (January 1927).

Comité pour la mémoire et l'histoire de l'esclavage. *Mémoires de la traite négrière, de l'esclavage et de leurs abolitions*. Paris: La Découverte, 2005.

Commission Islam et Laïcité, 1905–2005: Les enjeux de la laïcité. Paris: L'Harmattan, Paris, 2005.

Commission nationale consultative des droits de l'homme. *La Lutte contre le racisme, l'antisémitisme et la xénophobie: Année 2002*. Paris: La documentation française, 2003.

———. *La Lutte contre le racisme, l'antisémitisme et la xénophobie: Année 2010*. Paris: La Documentation française, 2011.

———. *La lutte contre le racisme et la xénophobie*, 2010–2014. Paris: La Documentation française, 2011–2015.

Comtat, Emmanuelle. *Les pieds-noirs et la politique quarante ans après le retour*. Paris: Presses de Sciences Po, 2009.

Conklin, Alice. *A Mission to Civilize: The Republican Idea of Empire in France and West Africa, 1895–1930*. Stanford, CA: Stanford University Press, 1997.

Constant, Fred. *Le multiculturalisme*. Paris: Flammarion, 2000.

Constitutional Council. Decision no. 2007-546 DC. January 25, 2007. http://www.conseil-constitutionnel.fr/conseil-constitutionnel/francais/les-decisions/acces-par-date/decisions-depuis-1959/2007/2007-546-dc/decision-n-2007-546-dc-du-25-janvier-2007.1173.html.

Cooper, Frederick. "From Imperial Inclusion to Republican Exclusion." In *Frenchness and the African Diaspora*, edited by Charles Tshimanga, Didier Gondola, and Peter Bloom, 91–119. Bloomington and Indianapolis: Indiana University Press, 2009.

Coquery-Vidrovitch, Catherine. "Colonial History and Decolonization: The French Imperial Case." *The European Journal of Development Research: Revue de l'EADI* 3, no. 2 (1991): 28–43.

———. *Enjeux politiques de l'histoire coloniale*. Marseille: Agone éditeur, 2009.

———. *Le Congo au temps des grandes compagnies concessionnaires (1898–1930)*. Paris/La Haye: Mouton & Co., 1972.

———. "Le postulat de la supériorité blanche et de l'infériorité noire." In *Le livre noir du colonialisme: XVIe–XXIe siècle*, edited by Marc Ferro, 646–685. Paris: Robert Laffont, 2004.

———. "Réflexions comparées sur l'historiographie africaniste de langue française et anglaise." *Politique africaine*, no. 66 (June 1997): 91–100.

Coquery-Vidrovitch, Catherine, Odile Goerg, and Hervé Tenoux, eds. *Des historiens africains en Afrique: Logiques du passé et dynamiques actuelles*. Paris: L'Harmattan, 1998, 351–355.

Coquery-Vidrovitch, Catherine, Gilles Manceron, and Benjamin Stora. "La mémoire partisane du president." *Libération*, August 21, 2007.

Coquio, Catherine. *Le mal de vérité ou l'utopie de la mémoire*. Paris: Armand Colin, 2015.

———, ed. *Retours du colonial?: Disculpation et réhabilitations de l'histoire colonial*. Paris: L'Atalante, 2008.

Costa-Lacoux, Jacqueline. "L'ethnicisation du lien social dans les banlieues françaises." *Revue européenne des migrations internationales* 17, no. 2 (2001): 123–138.

Cottias, Myriam. "Le silence de la nation." *Outre-Mers* 90, nos. 338–339 (2003): 21–45.

Cottias, Myriam, Crystal Feling, and Seloua Luste Boulbina, "Nos ancêtres les Gaulois . . . La France et l'esclavage aujourd'hui." *Les Cahiers Sens public* 2, no. 10 (June 2009): 45–56.

Courtine, Jean-Jacques, and Claudine Haroche. *Histoire du visage: Exprimer et taire ses émotions (XVIe–début XIXe siècle)*. Paris: Éditions Payot & Rivages, 2007.

Court of Appeals, Algiers, November 5, 1903. *Revue algérienne et tunisienne de législation et de jurisprudence* (R.A.) 2, no. 25 (1903).

Crenshaw, Kimberlé. "Mapping the Margins: Intersectionality, Identity Politics, and Violence against Women of Color." *Stanford Law Review* 6, no. 43 (July 1991): 1241–1299.

Crépon, Sylvain. "Du racisme biologique au différentialisme culturel: Les sources anthropologiques du GRECE." In *Les Sciences sociales au prisme de l'extrême droite: Enjeux et usages d'une récupération idéologique*, edited by Sylvain Crépon and Sébastien Mosbah-Natanson, 159–189. Paris: L'Harmattan, 2008.

———. "Une littérature post-coloniale d'extrême droite? Réflexion sur un 'braconnage' intellectual." In *Postcolonial studies, modes d'emploi*, edited by Collectif Write Back, 137–149. Lyon: Presses universitaires de Lyon, 2013.

Crivello, Maryline. "Comment on revit l'histoire: Sur les reconstitutions historiques 1976–2000." *La Pensée du Midi*, no. 3 (Winter 2000): 69–74.

Crochet, Soizick. "Cet obscur objet du désir." In *Utopies sanitaires*, edited by Rony Brauman, 45–77. Paris: Le Pommier/Médecins sans frontières, 2002.

Daeninckx, Didier. *L'école des colonies*. Paris: Hoëbeke, 2015.

Dakhlia, Jocelyne. *Islamicités*. Paris: PUF, 2005.

———. "'S'enfermer dans l'idée d'un choc des cultures,' c'est la vraie défaite du débat." *Le Monde*, March 1, 2016.

Daniel, Jean. "Le temps des ruptures." *Le Nouvel Observateur*, October 6, 2010.

Daniel, Norman. *Islam et Occident*. Paris: Le Cerf, 1993.

Daoud, Kamel. "Cologne, lieu de fantasmes." *Le Monde*, January 31, 2016.

———. *Meurseault, contre-enquête*. Arles: Actes Sud, 2014.

——— *The Meurseault Investigation*. Translated by John Cullen. New York: The Other Press, 2015.

Debono, Emmanuel. *Aux origines de l'antiracisme: La LICA (1927–1940)*. Paris: CNRS Éditions, 2012.

———. "Un nouvel antiracisme s'affirme par l'exclusion du Blanc." *Le Monde*, November 12, 2015.

Debord, Guy. *The Society of the Spectacle*. Translated by Donald Nicholson-Smith. New York: Zone Books, 1994 [1967].

Decleene, Arnold. *Le règne de la race*. Paris: Sorlot, 1936.

Decugis, Henri. *Le destin des races blanches*. Paris: Librairie de France, 1935.

Décugis, Jean-Michel, Christophe Labbé, and Olivia Recasens. "Un mari, trois épouses." In "Tabous et clichés," *Le Point*, September 30, 2010.

Deltombe, Thomas. *L'islam imaginaire: La construction médiatique de l'islamophobie en France, 1975–2005*. Paris: La Découverte, 2005.

———. *Quelle représentation médiatique sans représentants?: Naissance et explosion de l'islam de France au journal télévisé de 20 heures, 1975–1995*. Paris: IEP, 2003.

Deltombe, Thomas, Manuel Domergue, and Jacob Tatsitsa. *Kamerun!: Une guerre cachée aux origines de la Françafrique (1948–1971)*. Paris: La Découverte, 2011.

Dély, Renaud, Pascal Blanchard, Claude Askolovitch, and Yvan Gastaut. *Les années 30 sont de retours: Petites leçon d'histoire pour comprendre les crises du présent*. Paris: Flammarion, 2014.

Demangeon, Albert. *Le déclin de l'Europe*. Paris: Payot, 1920.

Depaule, Jean-Charles, ed. *Les mots de la stigmatisation urbaine*. Paris: Unesco/Maison des sciences de l'homme, 2010.

Deroo, Éric, and Sandrine Lemaire. *L'illusion coloniale*. Paris: Tallandier, 2006.

"Des associations critiquent 'la politique du chiffre' du ministre de l'immigration." *Le Monde*, September 12, 2007.

"Des gens du voyage saccagent une commune du Loir-et-Cher." *Le Figaro*, July 18, 2010.

Destexhe, Alain. *L'humanitaire impossible ou deux siècles d'ambiguïté*. Paris: Armand Colin, 1993.

Detienne, Marcel. *Comparer l'incomparable*. Paris: Seuil, 2000.

Dewhurst, Mary Lewis. *The Boundaries of the Republic: Migrant Rights and the Limits of Universalism in France, 1918–1940*. Stanford, CA: Stanford University Press, 2007.

Dewitte, Philippe. "La France se conjugue au passé composé." *Hommes & Migrations* 134, no. 1247 (January–February 2004): 1.

Dézé, Alexandre. *Le Front national: À la conquête du pouvoir?* Paris: Armand Colin, 2012.

Diao, Claire. "*Exhibit B*: Bien plus qu'une polémique." *Africultures*, November 26, 2014.www.africultures.com/php/index.php?nav=article&no=12563.

Diop, Cheikh Anta. *Nations nègres et culture*. Paris: Présence africaine, 1954.

Diouf, Mamadou, ed. *L'historiographie indienne en débat: Colonialisme, nationalisme, et sociétés postcoloniales*. Paris: Karthala and Amsterdam: Séphis, 1999.

Dogan, Mattei. "Le nationalisme en Europe: Déclin à l'Ouest, résurgence à l'Est." In *Nations et frontières dans la nouvelle Europe: L'impact croisé*, edited by Éric Philippart, 141–174. Brussels: Éditions Complexe, 1993.

Dorgelès, Roland. *Sur la route Mandarine*. Paris: Albin Michel, 1929.

Doriot, Jacques. *La France ne sera pas un pays d'esclaves*. Paris: Les Œuvres françaises, 1936.

Dorlin, Elsa. *La matrice de la race: Généalogie sexuelle et coloniale de la nation française*. Paris: La Découverte, 2006.

———. *Sexe, genre et sexualités*. Paris: PUF, 2008.

Dosse, François. *L'histoire en miettes*. Paris: La Découverte, 1994.

Douglas, Mary. *Purity and Danger: An Analysis of Concepts of Pollution and Taboo*. New York: Routledge, 2003 [1966].

Driant, Émile (Captain Danrit). *L'invasion noire: La mobilation africaine*. Paris: Flammarion, 1895.

Dubois, Laurent. *Les esclaves de la République*. Paris: Calmann-Lévy, 1998.

Duclert, Vincent. "L'affaire Dreyfus: De l'affrontement des mémoires à la reconnaissance de l'histoire." In *Les guerres de mémoires: La France et son histoire*, edited by Pascal Blanchard and Isabelle Veyrat-Masson, 71–82. Paris: La Découverte, 2008.

Ducoulombier, Romain. "Penser et combattre: Jules Monnerot face à la subversion des 'sociétés ouvertes.'" In *Subversion, anti-subversion, contre-subversion*, edited by François Cochet and Olivier Dard, 45–61. Paris: Éditions Riveneuve, 2010.

Duhamel, Alain. "Les tabous de l'immigration et de l'insécurité." RTL, September 15, 2010.

———. "Marine Le Pen, retour aux années 30." *Libération*, March 31, 2011.

Dulucq, Sophie, and Colette Zytnicki, eds. *Décoloniser l'histoire?: De l''histoire coloniale' aux histoires nationales en Amérique latine et en Afrique (XIXe–XXe siècle)*. Paris: SHOM, 2003.

Dumont, Louis. *Essai sur l'individualisme: Une perspective anthropologique sur l'idéologie moderne*. Paris: Seuil, 1983.

Dupin, Éric. *L'hystérie identitaire*. Paris: Le Cherche-Midi, 2004.

Duplan, Christian, and Bernard Pellegrin. *Claude Guéant, l'homme qui murmure à l'oreille de Sarkozy*. Paris: Éditions du Rocher, 2008.

Dupuy, Hélène. "Aux origines du mythe." In *Oublier nos crimes: L'amnésie nationale: Une spécifité française*, edited by Dimitri Nicolaïdis, 131–144. Paris: Éditions Autrement, 1994.

Durand, Pascal, and Sarah Sindaco, eds. *Le discours "néo-réactionnaire": Transgressions conservatrices*. Paris: CNRS Éditions, 2015.

Durkheim, Emile. *De la division du travail social*. Paris: Alcan, 1902 [1893].

Duval, Léon-Étienne. *Au nom de la vérité: Algérie (1954–1962)*. Paris: Éditions Cana, 1982.

Eizlini, Carine. *La colonisation enseignée aux enfants de Jules Ferry à nos jours: Cas des manuels d'histoire du cours élémentaire et moyen*. Master's thesis, University of Paris 5, 2005.

El Gammal, Jean. "La révolution française: mémoire et controverses." In *Les guerres de mémoires: La France et son histoire*, edited by Pascal Blanchard and Isabelle Veyrat-Masson, 63–70. Paris: La Découverte, 2008.

El-Tayeb, Fatima. *European Others: Queering Ethnicity in Postnational Europe*. Minneapolis: University of Minnesota Press, 2011.

Endelstein, Lucine, and Abdelkader Hamadi. "Le devoir de mémoire et ses enjeux." In *Mémoires plurielles, cinéma et images: Lieux de memoire?*, edited by Claudie Le Bissonnais, 6–9. Paris: Créaphis, 2007.

Être Français aujourd'hui et demain: Rapport de la Commission de la nationalité, vol. 2. Paris: Union générale d'éditions, 1988.

Examination of France by the Committee on the Elimination of Racial Discrimination. April 29, 2015. http://www.ohchr.org/FR/NewsEvents/Pages/DisplayNews.aspx?NewsID=15904&LangID=F.

Falaize, Benoît, ed. "Des hérauts de la colonisation aux héros de la fraternité: L'histoire scolaire dans le *Journal des instituteurs d'Afrique du Nord*." In *La France et l'Algérie, leçons d'histoire*, edited by Frédéric Abécassis, Gilles Boyer, Benoît Falaize, Gilbert Meynier, and Michelle Zancarini-Furnet, 201–215. Lyon: ENS Éditions, 2007.

———. *Enseigner l'histoire de l'immigration à l'école*. Lyon and Paris: INRP/CNHI, 2008.

Falaize, Benoît, and Françoise Lantheaume. "Entre pacification et reconnaissance: Les manuels scolaires et les concurrences des mémoires." In *Les guerres de mémoires: La France et son histoire*, edited by Pascal Blanchard and Isabelle Veyrat-Masson, 177–186. Paris: La Découverte, 2008.

Falaize, Benoît, Anne-Catherine Amaloud-Porte, Marguerite Figeac-Monthus, Nathalie François, Anne Hours, Sylvie Lalagüe-Dulac, Sébastien Ledoux, and Carine Pousse-Seoane, eds. *L'enseignement de l'esclavage, des traites et de leurs abolitions dans l'espace scolaire hexagonal*, Institut National de Recherche Pédagogique, June 2010. http://www.cnmhe.fr/IMG/pdf/RAPPORT_ESCLAVAGE_INRP_2011.pdf.

Fanon, Frantz. *Black Skin, White Masks*. Translated by Richard Philcox. New York: Grove Press, 2008 [1952].

———. *Les damnés de la terre*. Paris: Maspéro, 1961.

———. *Sociologie de la révolution*. Paris: Maspero, 1982.

——— *The Wretched of the Earth*. Translated by Richard Philcox. New York: Grove Press, 2004 [1961].

Fassin, Didier. "La souffrance du monde: Considérations anthropologiques sur les politiques contemporaines de la compassion." *L'Évolution psychiatrique* 67, no. 4 (October–December 2002): 676–689.

———. *L'ombre du monde: Une anthropologie de la condition carcérale*. Paris: Seuil, 2015.

———. "Nommer, interpréter: Le sens commun de la question raciale." In *De la question sociale à la question raciale?: Représenter la société française*, edited by Didier Fassin and Éric Fassin, 19–36. Paris: La Découverte, 2006.

Fassin, Didier, and Éric Fassin, eds. *De la question sociale à la question raciale?: Représenter la société française*. Paris: La Découverte, 2006.

———. "Misère du culturalisme." *Le Monde*, September 29, 2010.

Fassin, Éric. *Démocratie précaire: Chroniques de la déraison d'état*. Paris: La Découverte, Paris, 2012.

———."L'antiracisme en voit de toutes les couleurs." *L'Humanité*, January 8, 2016.

———. "L'art doit tenir compte de la sensibilité des victimes du colonialisme." *Le Monde*, November 28, 2014.

———. "La conscience du préfet et l'inconscient du ministre." *Regards*, October 1, 2009.

———. "La démocratie sexuelle et le conflit des civilisations." *Multitudes*, no. 26 (December 2006): 123–131.

———. "Laïcité négative: Une islamophobie sans voile." *Médiapart*, April 10, 2011.

———. "Les pouvoirs publics sont responsables d'une racialisation de la société qu'ils prétendent pourtant combattre." Interview with Éric Fassin. By Caroline Trouillet. *Afriscope*, no. 42, September 23, 2015.

———. *L'inversion de la question homosexuelle*. Paris: Amsterdam, 2005.

———. "Polygamie: *Le Point* et la fabrication sociologico-médiatique d'une panique morale." *Médiapart*, October 4, 2010. https://blogs.mediapart.fr/eric-fassin/blog/041010/polygamie-le-point-et-la-fabrication-sociologico-mediatique-d-une-paniq.

Faye, Olivier, Alexandre Lemarié, and David Revault D'Allonnes. "La guerre d'Algérie enfièvre le débat politique: La commémoration du 19 mars 1962 par M. Hollande suscite l'indignation de la droite et de l'extrême droite." *Le Monde*, March 20–21, 2016.

Febvre, Lucien. *Les annales*, September 30, 1936.

Ferro, Marc, ed. *Le livre noir du colonialisme: XVIe–XXIe siècle: De l'extermination à la repentance*. Paris: Hachette, 2004.

Ferro, Marc, Pascal Blanchard, and Isabelle Veyrat Masson. *Les guerres de mémoires dans le monde*. Paris: CNRS, 2008.

Fidès, Laurent. *Face au discours intimidant: Essai sur le formatage des esprits à l'ère du mondialisme*. Paris: Éditions du Toucan, 2014.

Finchelstein, Gilles. *Piège d'identité. Réflexions (inquiètes) sur la gauche, la droite et la démocratie*. Paris: Fayard, 2016.

———. "Quant le clivage gauche-droite s'efface, c'est l'identité qui s'impose." *Le Monde*, January 30, 2016.

Finkelstein, Norman G. *L'industrie de l'holocauste*. Paris: La Fabrique éditions, 2001.

Finkielkraut, Alain. "J'assume." *Le Monde*, November 27, 2005.

———. *La défaite de la pensée*. Paris: Gallimard, 1987.

———. *La seule exactitude*. Paris: Stock, Paris, 2015.

"Finkielkraut-Badiou: Le face-à-face: Interview Debate between Alain Badiou and Alain Finkielkraut." By Aude Lancelin. *Le Nouvel Observateur*, December 17, 2009.

Foucault, Michel. *Naissance de la biopolitique: Cours au collège de France (1978–1979)*. Paris: EHESS/Gallimard, 2004.

Fourquet, Jérôme, and Alain Mergier. *Janvier 2015: Le catalyseur*. Paris: Fondation Jean Jaurès, 2015.

France coloniale, deux siècles d'histoire. Special issue of *Histoire et Patrimoine* (2005).

Frank, Robert. "La mémoire empoisonnée." In *La France des armées noires*, edited by Jean-Pierre Azéma and François Bédarida, 544–576. Paris: Seuil, 1993.

Frégosi, Franck. "Les enjeux liés à la structuration de l'islam en France." In *Musulmans de France et d'Europe*, edited by Rémy Leveau and Khadija Mohsen-Finan, 99–114. Paris: CNRS Éditions, 2005.

de Gantes, Gilles. "De l'histoire coloniale à l'étude des aires culturelles: La disparition d'une spécialité du champ universitaire français." *Outre-Mers, Revue d'histoire* 90, nos. 388–89 (2003): 7–20.

Garcia, Patrick. Interview with Blandine Le Cain. "L'hommage aux Invalides 'élève les victimes au même rang que des héros militaires.'" *Le Figaro*, November 26, 2015.

———. *Le Bicentenaire de la Révolution française: Pratiques sociales d'une commémoration* Paris: CNRS Éditions, 2000.

Garin, Christine. "Un regard critique sur la société française." *Le Monde*, January 30, 2002.

Gassama, Makhily, ed. *L'Afrique répond à Sarkozy: Contre le discours de Dakar*. Paris: Philippe Rey, 2008.

de Gaulle, Charles. Conférence de presse de Charles De Gaulle, extrait relatif à Israël." November 27, 1967. http://www.voltairenet.org/article176398.html.

———*Mémoires de guerre*. Vol. 1: *L'appel*. Paris: Plon, 1954.

Geisser, Vincent. *La nouvelle islamophobie*. Paris: La Découverte, 2003.

Geisser, Vincent, and Aziz Zemouri. *Marianne et Allah: Les politiques françaises face à la "question musulmane,"* 15–41. Paris: La Découverte, 2007.

Géraud, Alice. "Gilles Clavreul, la valse antiraciste." *Libération*, April 16, 2015.

———. "Pour beaucoup, l'islamophobie est devenu un racisme acceptable." *Libération*, September 21, 2013.

Gervereau, Lauent, Pierre Milza, and Émile Temine, eds. *Toute la France: Histoire de l'immigration en France au xxe siècle*. Paris: Somogy, 1998.

Gide, André. *Return from the USSR*. Translated by Dorothy Bussy. New York: Alfred A. Knopf, 1936.

Gilroy, Paul. *Postcolonial Melancholia*. New York: Columbia University Press, 2005.

———. *There Ain't No Black in the Union Jack: The Cultural Politics of Race and Nation*. Chicago: The University of Chicago Press, 1987.

Girard, Alain, Yves Charbit, and Marie-Laurence Lamy. "Attitudes des Français à l'égard de l'immigration étrangère: Nouvelle enquête d'opinion." *Population* 29, no. 6 (1974): 1015–1069.

Girard, Alain, and Jean Stoezel. *Français et immigrés: L'attitude française, l'adaptation des Italiens et des Polonais*. Paris: PUF, 1953.

Girardet, Raoul. *L'idée coloniale en France: De 1871 à 1962*. Paris: La Table Ronde, 1972.

———. *Mythes et mythologies politiques*. Paris: Seuil, 1986.

Giraudoux, Jean. *Les pleins pouvoirs*. Paris: Gallimard, 1939.

Giudice, Fausto. *Arabicides: Une chronique française (1970–1991)*. Paris: La Découverte, 1992.

Glissant, Édouard. *Caribbean Discourse: Selected Essays*. Translated by J. Michael Dash. Charlottesville: University of Virginia Press, 1989.

Godard, Bernard. *La question musulmane en France*. Paris: Fayard, 2015.

Godard, Bernard, and Sylvie Taussig. *Les musulmans en France. Courants, institutions, communautés: Un état des lieux*. Paris: Robert Laffont, 2006.

Godet, Aurélie. *Le Tea Party? Portrait d'une Amérique désorientée*. Paris: Éditions Vendémiaire, 2012.

Gondola, Didier. "La crise de la formation en histoire africaine en France vue par les étudiants africains." *Politique africaine* 65 (1997): 132–139.

Goody, Jack. *L'islam en Europe: Histoire, échanges, conflits*. Paris: La Découverte, 2004.

Gordon, Daniel A. *Immigrants and Intellectuals: May 68 and the Rise of Anti-Racism in France*. London: The Merlin Press Ltd., 2012.

Grant, Madison. *The Passing of the Great Race*. New York: Scribners, 1916.

Graveleau, Séverin. "Les programmes d'histoire réveillent la guerre scolaire." *Le Monde*, May 2, 2015.

Grignon, Max. *Des civilisations antiques à la France d'aujourd'hui, fin d'études primaires*. Paris: Sudel, 1950.

Grosset, Alfred. *Le crime et la mémoire*. Paris: Flammarion, 1989.

Groupe Lyonnais d'Etudes Médicales, Philosophiques, et Biologiques. *Hérédité et races*. Jusivy: Éditions du Cerf, 1931.

Guénif-Souilamas, Nacira. "La Française voilée, la beurette, le garçon arabe et le musulman laïc: Les figures assignées du racisme vertueux." In *La République mise à nu par son immigration*, edited by Nacira Guénif-Souilamas, 109–132. Paris: La Fabrique, 2006.

———. "La réduction à son corps de l'indigène de la République." In *La fracture coloniale: La société française au prisme de l'héritage colonial*, edited by Nicolas Bancel, Pascal Blanchard, and Sandrine Lemaire, 199–209. Paris: La Découverte, 2005.

———. *La République mise à nu par son immigration*. Paris: La Fabrique, 2006.

———. *Les beurettes*. Paris: Hachette, 2003.

———. "L'intégration, une idée épuisée." *Libération*, July 12, 2001.

Guénif-Souilamas, Nacira, and Éric Macé. *Les féministes et le garçon arabe*. Paris: Éditions de l'Aube, 2004.

Guillaumin, Colette. *Sexe, race et pratique du pouvoir: L'idée de nature*. Paris: Côté-femmes, 1992.

Guillibert, Paul, Caroline Izambert, and Sophie Wahnich. "Revendiquer un monde décolonial: Entretien avec Houria Bouteldja." *Vacarme*, no. 71 (Spring 2015): 44–69.

Habermas, Jürgen. *L'intégration républicaine: Essais de théorie politique*. Paris: Fayard, 1998.

Habermas, Jürgen, and Joseph Ratzinger. *The Dialectics of Secularization: On Reason and Religion*. San Francisco, CA: Ignatius Press, 2007.

Haget, Henri. "Nous l'avons tant aimé." *L'Express*, August 16, 2004.

Hajjat, Abdellali. *Immigration postcoloniale et mémoire*. Paris: L'Harmattan, 2005.

———. *Les frontières de l'identité nationale: L'injonction à l'assimilation en France métropolitaine et coloniale*. Paris: La Découverte, 2012.

Halbwachs, Maurice. *La mémoire collective*. Paris: PUF, 1950.
———. *Les cadres sociaux de la mémoire*. Paris: PUF, 1952.
Hamel, Christelle. "La sexualité entre sexisme et racisme: Les descendantes de migrant-e-s du Maghreb et la virginité." *Nouvelles Questions Féminists* 25, no. 1 (2006): 41–58.
Hamoumou, Mohand. *Et ils sont devenus harkis*. Paris: Fayard, 1993.
Harbi, Mohammed, and Benjamin Stora, ed. *La guerre d'Algérie: 1956–2004: La fin de l'amnésie*. Paris: Robert Laffont, 2004.
Hargreaves, Alec G. "Empty Promises? Public Policy against Racial and Ethnic Discrimination in France." *French Politics, Culture and Society* 33, no. 3 (2015): 95–113.
———. "French Muslims and the Middle East." *Contemporary French Civilization* 40, no. 2 (2015): 235–254.
de Hart, Betty. "The Marriage of Convenience in European Immigration Law." *European Journal of Migration and Law* 8, nos. 3–4 (2006): 251–262.
Hartog, François. *Evidence de l'histoire: Ce que voient les historiens*. Paris: Gallimard, 2007.
Heers, Jacques. *L'histoire assassinée: Les pièges de la mémoire*. Paris: Éditions de Paris, 2006.
Hellal, Abderrezak. *Image d'une révolution: La révolution algérienne dans les textes français durant la période du conflit*. Algiers: OPU, 1988.
Hémery, Daniel. "À propos du 'Mémorial de l'œuvre française outre-mer'." Open letter. *Outre-mers: Revue d'histoire* 88, no. 330 (2001): 309–310.
Hermon-Belot, Rita, and Sébastien Fath. "La République ne reconnaît aucun culte." *Archives de sciences sociales des religions*, no. 129 (January–March 2005): 7–13.
Hillel, Roger. *La triade nostalgérique: Stèle, mur, musée de Perpignan*. Céret: Alter Ego Éditions, 2015.
Hollande, François. *Changer de destin*. Paris: Robert Laffont, 2012.
Honoré, Jean-Paul. "La 'hiérarchie des sentiments,' description et mise en scène du Français et de l'immigré dans le discours du Front national." *Mots* 12, no. 1 (March 1986): 129–157.
Houellebecq, Michel. *Soumission*. Paris: Flammarion, 2015.
———. *Submission*. Translated by Lori Stein. New York: Farrar, Straus and Giroux, 2015.
Hugo, Victor. "Notes, 20 octobre 1842." In *Choses vues: Souvenirs, journaux, cahiers*. Paris: Gallimard, 1972.
Huntington, Samuel. *The Clash of Civilizations and the Remaking of World Order*. New York: Simon & Schuster, 1996.
Huppert, Georges. *L'idée de l'histoire parfaite*. Paris: Flammarion, 1973.
Hussey, Andrew. *The French Intifada: The Long War Between France and Its Arabs*. London: Faber and Faber, 2014.
Huston, Nancy, and Michel Raymond. "Sexes et races: Deux réalités." *Le Monde*, May 17, 2013.
Hutton, Patrick H. *History as an Art of Memory*. Hanover, NH, and London: University Press of New England, 1993.
"Identité(s) nationale(s): Le retour des politiques de l'identité?" *Savoir/Agir*, no. 2 (December 2007).
"Identités nationales d'Etat." *Journal des anthropologues* (2007).
"Immigration: Claude Guéant le récidiviste." *L'Express*, November 29, 2011.
"'Immigration incontrôlée': Tollé après une phrase de Guéant." *Le Monde*, March 18, 2011.
Indigènes de la République. "Nous sommes les indigènes de la République!: Appel pour les assises de l'anticolonialisme postcolonial." January 11, 2005. http://indigenes-republique.fr/le-p-i-r/appel-des-indigenes-de-la-republique/.

Institut d'Histoire du Temps Présent. *La mémoire des Français: Quarante ans de commémorations de la Seconde Guerre mondiale.* Paris: CNRS Éditions, 1986.

Institut français d'opinion publique (IFOP). "L'attirance des Français pour un gouvernement technocratique ou autoritaire" (2015).

———. "Les Européens face à la crise des migrants" (2015).

———. "L'image de l'islam en France" (2012).

"Institutionnalisation de la xénophobie en France." *Asylon,* no. 4 (2008).

"Interdire le voile intégral au nom de la dignité de la personne." *Libération,* September 9, 2009.

International Convention on the Elimination of Racial Discrimination. December 21, 1965. www.ohchr.org/FR/ProfessionalInterest/Pages/CERD.aspx.

Jacob, Antoine. "L'Europe du Nord gagnée par le populisme de droite." *Politique internationale* 127 (March–April 2010): 221–238.

Jahan, Sébastien, and Alain Ruscio, eds. *Histoire de la colonisation: Réhabilitations, falsifications et instrumentalisations.* Paris: Les Indes savantes, 2007.

Jaurès, Jean. Lecture at the Alliance Française, 1884.

"Jean-Marie Le Pen exclu du Front national." *lemonde.fr,* August 20, 2015.

Jeanneney, Jean-Noël, and Monique Sauvage, eds. *Télévision, nouvelle mémoire: Les magazines de grand reportage de 1959 à 1968.* Paris: Seuil/INA, 1982.

Jenni, Alexis. *L'art français de la guerre.* Paris: Gallimard, 2011.

Jenni, Alexis, and Benjamin Stora. *Les mémoires dangereuses: De l'Algérie coloniale à la France d'aujourd'hui suivi.* Paris: Albin Michel, 2016.

Jewsiewicki, Bogumil, and Jocelyn Létourneau, eds. *L'histoire en partage: Usages et mises en discours du passé.* Paris: L'Harmattan, 1996.

Jiwani, Yasmin. "Sport as Civilizing Mission: Zinedine Zidane and the Infamous Head-Butt." *Topia, Canadian Journal of Cultural Studies* 19 (2008): 11–33.

Joutard, Philippe. *Les canisards.* Paris: Julliard, 1980.

Joxe, Pierre. *À propos de la France: Itinéraires 1* (interviews with Michel Sarrazin). Paris: Flammarion, 1998.

———. "Quand l'histoire coloniale pèse tellement sur le présent, il vaut mieux la connaître." Bondy Blog. March 21, 2016. http://bondyblog.liberation.fr/201603210001/pierre-joxe-quand-lhistoire-coloniale-pese-tellement-sur-le-present-il-vaut-mieux-la-connaitre/.

Judaken, Jonathan. *Jean-Paul Sartre and the Jewish Question.* Lincoln and London: University of Nebraska Press, 2006.

Juhem, Philippe. "SOS-Racisme, histoire d'une mobilisation 'apolitique': Contribution à une analyse des transformations des représentations politiques après 1981." PhD diss. University of Nanterre, 1998.

Julliard, Jacques. "Editorial," *Le Nouvel Observateur,* November 23, 1989.

Kaprièlian, Nelly. "Marie Ndiaye aux prises avec le Monde." *les inrockuptibles* 726 (November 18–24, 2009): 28–33.

Kassa, Sabrina. "L'origine culturelle peut-elle expliquer la délinquance?" http://www.regards.fr/acces-payant/archives-web/l-origine-culturelle-peut-elle,4578, November 10, 2010.

Kateb, Kamel. *Européens: "Indigènes" et juifs en Algérie (1830–1962): Représentations et réalités des populations.* Paris: INED, 2001.

Kelkal, Khaled. "Moi, Khaled Kelkal." Interview by Dietmar Loch. *Le Monde,* October 7, 1995.

Kennedy, Duncan. *Sexy dressing: Violences sexuelles et érotisation de la domination.* Paris: Flammarion, 2008.

Kepel, Gilles. "Gilles Kepel: 'Le logiciel du djihadisme a changé.'" Interview with Gilles Kepel. By Christophe Ayad. *Le Monde*, December 26–28, 2015.

———. "Kepel: La France est en panne d'un discours fédérateur." Interview with Gilles Kepel. By Alexandra Schwartzbrot. *Libération*, July 20, 2014.

———. *Les banlieues de l'islam: Naissance d'une religion en France*. Paris: Seuil, 1987.

———. *Quatre-vingt-treize*. Paris: Gallimard, 2012.

Kepel, Gilles, and Antoine Jardin. *Terreur dans l'Hexagone: Genèse du djihad français*. Paris: Gallimard, 2015.

Khebizi, Samir. "Moi, Samir, binational." *Libération*, December 24, 2015.

Khosrokhavar, Farhad. "Approche sociologique: Anatomie de la radicalisation." In *Le jihadisme: Le comprendre pour mieux le combattre*, by David Bénichou, Farhad Khosrokhavar, and Philippe Migaux, 265–323. Paris: Plon, 2015.

———. *L'islam dans les prisons*. Paris: Balland, 2004.

Kipling, Rudyard. "The White Man's Burden." *McClure's Magazine* 12, no. 4 (1899): 290–291.

Koselleck, Reinhart. *Le futur passé: Contribution à la sémantique des temps historiques*. Paris: Éditions de l'EHESS, 1990.

Koussens, David. "Le port de signes religieux dans les écoles québécoises et françaises: Acommodements (dé)raisonnables ou interdiction (dé)raisonnée?" *Globe: Revue Internationale d'études québécoises* 11, no. 1 (2008): 115–131.

Krieger, Linda Hamilton. *Un problème de categories: Stéréotypes et lutte contre les discriminations*. Paris: Institut d'Études Politiques de Paris, 2008.

Kritzman, Lawrence. "Identity Crises: France, Culture and the Idea of the Nation." *Substance* 24, nos. 1–2 (1995): 5–20.

Kundnani, Arun. *The Muslims Are Coming! Islamophobia, Extremism, and the Domestic War on Terror*. New York: Verso, 2014.

Laborde, Cécile. "The Culture(s) of the Republic. Nationalism and Multiculturalism in French Republican Thought." *Political Theory* 29, no. 5 (2001): 716–735.

"La colonie rapatriée." *Politix* 76 (2006).

La colonisation en procès: L'Histoire, no. 302 (2005).

La Farge, John. *No Postponement: U.S. Moral Leadership and the Problem of Racial Minorities*. New York: Longmans, Green, 1950.

Lagrange, Hugues. *Le déni des cultures*. Paris: Seuil, 2013.

Lahire, Bernard. "Comprendre le monde tel qu'il est, ce n'est pas 'excuser' les individus qui le composent." Interview with Bernard Lahire. By Julie Clarini. *Le Monde*, January 8, 2016.

———. *Pour la sociologie: Et pour en finir avec une prétendue "culture de l'excuse."* Paris: La Découverte, 2016.

Laïcité et l'islam en France: Rapport d'étape d'une commission de travail de la Ligue de l'enseignement, November 1998.

Lalieu, Olivier. "L'invention du 'devoir de mémoire.'" *Vingtième Siècle: Revue d'histoire* 69, no. 1 (January–March 2001): 83–94.

"La montée de la demande de protection par rapport à la globalisation." *Baromètre de la confiance politique*, CEVIPOF, December 2012.

Lantheaume, Françoise. *L'enseignement de l'histoire de la colonisation et de la décolonisation de l'Algérie depuis les années Trente: État-nation, identité nationale, critique et valeurs: Essai de sociologie du curriculum*. PhD diss., EHESS, Paris, 2002.

Lanzmann, Claude. "Le mort saisit le vif." *Le Monde*, February 18, 2008.

"La politique en Afrique noire: Le haut et le bas." *Politique africaine* 1, no. 1 (1981).

La question postcoloniale. Hérodote, no. 121 (2006).

Laroui, Fouad. *De l'islamisme: Une réfutation personnelle du totalitarisme religieux*. Paris: Robert Laffont, 2015.

Laufer, Laurie, and Laurence Rochefort, eds. *Qu'est-ce que le genre?* Paris: Petite Bibliothèque Payot, 2014.

Laurence, Jonathan, and Justin Vaisse. *Integrating Islam: Political and Religious Challenges in Contemporary France*. Washington, DC: Brookings Institution Press, 2006.

———. *Intégrer l'islam: La France et ses musulmans, enjeux et réussites*. Paris: Éditions Odile Jacob, 2007.

Laurens, Henry. *Orientales II. La IIIe République et l'islam*. Paris: CNRS Éditions, 2004.

Laurent, Samuel. "Que disent les chiffres sur la radicalisation en France?" *Le Monde*, February 3, 2016.

Laurent, Sylvie, and Thierry Leclère, eds. *De quelle couleur sont les Blancs? Des petits Blancs des colonies au racisme anti-Blancs*. Paris: La Découverte, 2013.

Lautier, Nicole, and Nicole Allieu-Mary. "La didactique de l'histoire." *Revue française de pédagogie*, no. 162 (January–February–March 2008): 95–131.

Lavabre, Marie-Claire. "Usages du passé, usages de la mémoire." *Revue française de science politique* 44, no. 3 (June 1994): 480–493.

La vérité sur la colonisation. Nouvel Observateur, December 8–14, 2005.

Lazerges, Christine. Interview with Sylvain Mouillard. "La gauche doit être visible sur la lutte contre le racisme." *Libération*, April 9, 2014.

Lebaron, Frédéric, Fanny Jedlicki, and Laurent Willemez. "La sociologie, ce n'est pas la culture de l'excuse!" *Le Monde*, December 14, 2015.

Le Bars, Thierry, and Claude Liauzu. "Et l'histoire de la présence française outre-mer?" *L'Humanité*, March 10, 2005.

Lebourg, Nicolas. *Le monde vu de la plus extrême droite: Du fascisme au nationalisme révolutionnaire*. Perpignan: Presses Universitaires de Perpignan, 2010.

Lebourg, Nicolas, and Joseph Beauregard. *Dans l'ombre des Le Pen: Une histoire des numéros 2 du FN*. Paris: Nouveau Monde, 2012.

Lebourg, Nicolas, and Abderahmen Moumen. *Rivesaltes, le camp de la France, 1939 à jours*. Perpignan: Trabucaire, 2015.

Le Bris, Michel, and Jean Rouaud, eds. *Je est un autre: Pour une identité-monde*. Paris: Gallimard, 2010.

Leclant, Jean. "Les célébrations nationales: Une institution culturelle." *Le Débat* 3, no. 105 (1999): 185–187.

Le Cour Grandmaison, Olivier. *Coloniser, exterminer: Sur la guerre de l'état colonial*. Paris: Fayard, 2005.

———. "Le colonialisme a la peau dure." *Libération*, March 30, 2005.

Le Devin, Willy. "Moins de 400 femmes porteraient le voile intégral en France." *Libération*, July 30, 2009.

Leduc, Jean, and Patrick Garcia. *L'enseignement de l'histoire en France de l'Ancien Régime à nos jours*. Paris: Armand Colin, 2003.

Lefeuvre, Daniel. *Pour en finir avec la repentance coloniale*. Paris: Flammarion, 2006.

Lefkowitz, Mary. *Not Out of Africa: How Afrocentrism Became an Excuse to Teach Myth as History*. New York: Basic Books, 1997.

Lefranc, Sandrine, ed. *Après le conflit, la réconciliation?: Actes révisés des journées d'étude organisées par l'institut des sciences sociales du politique.* Paris: Michel Houdiard Éditeur, 2007.

———. *Politiques du pardon.* Paris: PUF, 2002.

Le Goazious, Véronique, and Laurent Mucchielli. *Quand les banlieues brûlent... Retour sur les émeutes de novembre 2005.* Paris: La Découverte, 2006.

Le Goff, Jacques. *Histoire et mémoire.* Paris: Gallimard, 1988.

Le Guilledoux, Dominique. "'Votre histoire de boîte de nuit, ça me sidère!'" *Le Monde,* October 14, 1995.

Lejeune, Dominique. *La peur du "rouge" en France: Des partageux aux gauchistes.* Paris: Éditions Belin, 2003.

Lemaire, Sandrine. "Une loi qui vient de loin." *Le Monde diplomatique,* January 2006, 28.

"Le Manifeste." *Réaction* (April 1930): 1–3.

Le Pautremat, Pascal. *La politique musulmane de la France au XXe siècle: De l'hexagone aux terres d'Islam.* Paris: Maisonneuve et Larose, 2003.

Le Pen, Jean-Marie. *Les Français d'abord.* Paris: Carrère/Lafon, 1984.

———. "Vive l'Irak!" *National Hebdo* 976 (April 3–9, 2003).

Le Pen, Marine. *À contre flots.* Paris: Grancher, 2006.

———. "Les camps ont été le summum de la barbarie." Interview with Marine Le Pen. By Saïd Mahrane. *Le Point,* February 3, 2011.

Le Petit Bleu. May 9, 1932.

Le racisme devant la science. Paris: UNESCO/Gallimard, 1973.

"Le racisme s'est-il décomplexé en France?" Interview with Michel Wieviorka, France TV, November 3, 2013.

"Les autres crimes commis au nom de la République." *Marianne* (May 14, 2001).

Les historiens et le travail de mémoire, special issue of *Esprit* 266 (August–September 2000).

de Lesquen, Henry, ed. *Penser l'antiracisme.* Paris: Godefroy de Bouillon, 1999.

Lester, Paul, and Jacques Millot, eds. *Les races humaines.* Paris: Armand Colin, 1936.

Les violences envers les femmes: Une enquête nationale. Paris: La Documentation française, 2003.

"Le temps des colonies." *L'Histoire* 11 (April 2001).

Létourneau, Jocelyn. *A History for the Future: Rewriting Memory and Identity in Quebec.* Translated by Phyllis Aronoff and Howard Scott. Montreal, QC, and Kingston, ON: McGill-Queen's University Press, 2004.

Le trou de mémoire. Special issue of *Hommes et Libertés,* no. 131 (2005).

Levinas, Emmanuel. *Totality and Infinity: An Essay on Exteriority.* Translated by Alphonso Lingis. Pittsburgh, PA: Duquesne University Press, 1969.

Lévy-Bruhl, Lucien. *La mentalité primitive.* Paris: Librairie Félix Alcan, 1922. http://classiques.uqac.ca/classiques/levy_bruhl/mentalite_primitive/mentalite_primitive_2.pdf.

Lewis, Bernard. *History: Remembered, Recovered, Invented.* Princeton, NJ: Princeton University Press, 1983.

"Le XVIIIe siècle: Techniques et découvertes nouvelles, les transformations économiques, l'essor colonial, la traite." *Bulletin officiel de l'éducation nationale,* no. 37, October 2, 1969.

Lia, Brynjar. *Architect of Global Jihad: The Life of Al-Qaida Strategist Abu Mus'ab al-Suri.* New York: Columbia University Press, 2008.

Liauzu, Claude, ed. *Colonisation: Droit d'inventaire.* Paris: Armand Colin, 2004.

———. *Dictionnaire de la colonisation française.* Paris: Larousse, 2007.

———. *L'Europe et l'Afrique méditerranéenne, de Suez (1869) à nos jours*. Paris: Complexe, 1994.

Liauzu, Claude, and Gilles Manceron, eds. *La colonisation, la loi et l'histoire*. Paris: Syllepse, 2006.

"L'image des musulmans et de l'islam auprès des Français." Paris: Odoxa, 2015.

Lindenberg, Daniel. "Guerres de mémoire en France." *Vingtième siècle: Revue d'histoire* 42, no. 1 (April–June 1994): 77–96.

———. *Le Rappel à l'ordre: Enquête sur de nouveaux réactionnaires*. Paris: Seuil, 2002.

Liogier, Raphaël. *Ce populisme qui vient*. Paris: Textuel, 2013.

———. "Il n'y a pas de guerre des civilisations car il n'y a qu'une seule civilisation." *Libération*, January 10, 2016.

———. *La Guerre des civilisations n'aura pas lieu: Coexistence et violence au XXI*[e] *siècle*. Paris: CNRS Éditions, 2016.

———. *Le mythe de l'islamisation: Essai sur une obsession collective*. Paris, Seuil, 2012.

———. "L'islamisation est un mythe." *Le Monde*, March 28, 2013.

Lochak, Danièle. "La race: Une catégorie juridique." *Mots/Langage du politique*, no. 33 (1992), 291–303.

"Loi Debré 2005-158, February 23, 2005." https://www.legifrance.gouv.fr/affichTexte.do?cidTexte=JORFTEXT000000444898.

"Loi du 10 août 1932 protégeant la main d'œuvre nationale." August 10, 1932. http://travail-emploi.gouv.fr/IMG/pdf/Loi_du_10_aout_1932.pdf.

"Loi du 20 novembre 2007 relative à la maîtrise de l'immigration, à l'intégration et à l'asile." November 20, 2007. http://www.vie-publique.fr/actualite/panorama/texte-vote/loi-du-20-novembre-2007-relative-maitrise-immigration-integration-asile.html.

"Loi portant reconnaissance de la Nation et contribution nationale en faveur des Français rapatriés" (Law concerning the recognition of the nation and national contribution in favor of repatriated French), Debré 2005-158 Law. February 23, 2005. https://www.legifrance.gouv.fr/affichTexte.do?cidTexte=JORFTEXT000000444898.

Londres, Albert. *Terre d'ébène: La traite des Noirs*. Paris: Albin Michel, 1929.

"L'ONU critique la France sur les Roms." *L'Express*, August 27, 2010.

"L'opinion publique dans l'Union européenne." *Eurobaromètre standard*, no. 73, November 2010.

Lughod, Lila Abu. "The Muslim Woman: The Power of Images and the Danger of Pity." *Eurozine*, September 1, 2006. http://www.eurozine.com/articles/2006-09-01-abulughod-en.html.

Luizard, Jean-Pierre. *Le piège Daech: L'état islamique ou le retour de l'histoire*. Paris: La Découverte, 2015.

Mabanckou, Alain. *Le sanglot de l'homme noir*. Paris: Fayard, 2012.

———. "Préface." In *La France noire: Trois siècles de présences*, by Pascal Blanchard et al., 6–7. Paris: La Découverte, 2011.

Mabilon-Monfils, Béatrice, and Geneviève Zoïa. *La laïcité au risque de l'autre*. La Tour-d'Aigues: Éditions de l'Aube, 2014.

Macron, Emmanuel. "Discours d'Emmanuel Macron: Conclusion de la 5ème Université des Gracques." November 23, 2015. http://lesgracques.fr/discours-demmanuel-macron-conclusion-de-la-5eme-universite-des-gracques/.

Mahan, Alfred T. *Le salut de la race blanche et l'empire des mers*. Translated by Jean Izoulet. Paris: Flammarion, 1906.

Makarian, Christian. "Alain Finkielkraut: 'La France se désintègre.'" *L'Express*, October 7, 2010.

Manceron, Gilles. "La loi: Régulateur ou acteur des guerres de mémoires?" In *Les guerres de mémoires: La France et son histoire*, edited by Pascal Blanchard and Isabelle Veyrat-Masson, 241–251. Paris: La Découverte, 2008.

———. *Marianne et les colonies: Une introduction à l'histoire coloniale de la France*. Paris: La Découverte, 2005.

———. "Ne jouons pas avec les mémoires!" *Libération*, May 25, 2006.

Mandelbaum, Jacques. "Comédie: Le bain de jouvence d'une République défaite." *Le Monde*, July 29, 2014.

"Manifeste par le collectif *Qui fait la France*." *Les inrockuptibles*, no. 614 (September 4, 2007): 18.

"Manuel Valls annonce la tenue d'un comité interministériel consacré à la lutte contre les inégalités, au combat pour l'égalité dans les quartiers, début mars." Ministère de la Ville, January 22, 2015. http://www.ville.gouv.fr/?manuel-valls-annonce-la-tenue-d-un.

"Manuel Valls évoque un 'apartheid territorial, social, ethnique' en France." *Le Monde*, January 20, 2015.

Marie, Claude-Valentin. "Les populations des DOM-TOM en France métropolitaine." *Espace, populations, sociétés* 4, no. 2 (1986): 197–206.

Martial, René. *Les races humaines par l'image*. Paris: Hachette, 1955.

Martin, Jean-Clément. *La guerre civile entre histoire et mémoire*. Nantes: Ouest-France Éditions, 1995.

Martin, Jean-Clément, and Charles Suaud. "Le Puy du Fou: L'interminable réinvention du passé vendéen." *Actes de la Recherche en sciences sociales* 93 (June 1992): 21–37.

———. *Le Puy du Fou, en Vendée, l'histoire mise en scène*. Paris: L'Harmattan, 1996.

Maspero, François. *L'honneur de Saint-Arnaud*. Paris: Plon, 1993.

Massis, Henri. *Défense de l'Occident*. Paris: Éditions Déterna, 1927.

Mauco, Georges. *Les étrangers en France: Leur rôle dans la vie économique*. Paris: Armand Colin, 1932.

———. "*Mémoire sur l'assimilation des étrangers en France*." Paper presented at the Conférence permanente des Hautes études internationales, Paris, June 28–July 3, 1937.

Maurel, Blanche, and Jean Equy. *Histoire de France des origines à nos jours*. Paris: J. de Gigord, 1953.

Maurin, Éric. *Le ghetto français: Enquête sur le séparatisme social*. Paris: Seuil, 2005.

Maurras, Charles. *Pages africaines*. Paris: Sorlot, 1940.

Mazouz, Sarah. "Une célébration paradoxale: Les cérémonies de remise des décrets de naturalisation." *Genèses* 1, no. 70 (2008): 88–105.

Mbembe, Achille. "Le noir n'existe pas plus que le blanc." *Africultures*, nos. 92–93, February 2013.

———. "L'intarissable puits aux fantasmes." In *L'Afrique de Sarkozy: Un déni d'histoire*, by Jean-Pierre Chrétien, Jean-François Bayart, and Achille Mbembe, 91–132. Paris: Karthala, 2008.

———. "Provincializing France." Translated by Janet Roitman. *Public Culture* 23, no.1 (2011): 85–119.

———. *Sortir de la grande nuit: Essai sur l'Afrique décolonisée*. Paris: La Découverte, 2010.

———. "What is Postcolonial Thinking?" *Eurozine*, 2008, 1–13. http://www.eurozine.com/pdf/2008-01-09-mbembe-en.pdf.

Mbembe, Achille, and Sarah Nuttall, eds. *Johannesburg: The Elusive Metropolis*. Durham, NC: Duke University Press, 2004.

Meillassoux, Claude. "Essai sur l'interprétation du phénomène économique dans les sociétés d'autosubsistance." *Cahiers d'études africaines* 1, no. 4 (1960): 38–67.

Memmi, Albert. *The Colonizer and the Colonized*. Translated by Howard Greenfield. New York: The Orion Press, 1965 [1957].

———. *L'homme dominé*. Paris: Payot, 1968.

Merle, Isabelle, and Emmanuelle Sibeud. "Histoire en marge ou histoire en marche?: La colonisation entre repentance et patrimonialisation." Paper delivered at the conference "La politique du passé: Constructions, usages et mobilisation de l'histoire dans la France des années 1970 à nos jours," September 25–26, 2003. http://chs.univ-paris1.fr/Collo/Merle.pdf.

Merzeau, Louise. "Guerres de mémoire *on line*: Un nouvel enjeu stratégique." In *Les guerres de mémoires: La France et son histoire*, edited by Pascal Blanchard and Isabelle Veyrat-Masson, 287–298. Paris: La Découverte, 2008.

Mestre, Abel, and Caroline Monnot. "Les réseaux du Front national." In *Les faux-semblants du Front national: Sociologie d'un parti politique*, edited by Sylvain Crépon, Alexandre Dézé, and Nonna Mayer, 51–76. Paris: Presses de Science Po, 2015.

Métraux, Jean-Claude. *Deuils collectifs et création sociale*. Paris: La Dispute, 2004.

Meurs, Dominique, Ariane Pailhé, and Patrick Simon. "Persistance des inégalités entre générations liées à l'immigration: L'accès à l'emploi des immgrés et de leurs descendants en France." *Population* 61, no. 5 (2006): 763–802.

Meyer, Jean, Jean Tarrade, Annie Rey-Goldzeiguer, and Jacques Thobie. *Histoire de la France coloniale, des origines à 1914*. Paris: Armand Colin, 1990.

Michel, Andrée. *Les travailleurs algériens en France*. Paris: CNRS/Centre d'études sociologiques, 1956.

Michel, Marc. *Essai sur la colonisation positive: Affrontements et accommodements en Afrique noire (1830–1930)*. Paris: Perrin, 2009.

Miller, Christopher L. *Nationalists and Nomads: Essays on Francophone African Literature*. Chicago: University of Chicago Press, 1998.

Millet, Richard. *De l'antiracisme comme terreur littéraire*. Paris: Pierre-Guillaume de Roux, 2012.

Milza, Pierre, and Serge Berstein. *Histoire*. Paris: Nathan, 1970.

"Mission d'information sur la pratique du port du voile intégral sur le territoire national." September 9, 2009. http://www.assemblee-nationale.fr/13/dossiers/voile_integral.asp.

Mohammed, Marwan, and Abdellali Hajjat. *Islamophobie: Comment les élites françaises fabriquent le "problème musulman."* Paris: La Découverte, 2013.

Mohanty, Chandra Talpade. "Under Western Eyes: Feminist Scholarship and Colonial Discourses." In *Feminism Without Borders: Decolonizing Theory, Practicing Solidarity*, 17–42. Durham, NC: Duke University Press, 2003.

Moktar, Gamal. "Le peuplement de l'Egypte ancienne et le déchiffrement de l'écriture méroïtique." *Histoire générale de l'Afrique*. Vol 2, *Afrique ancienne*. Paris: UNESCO, 1980, 795–819.

Monnot, Caroline, and Abel Mestre. *Le système Le Pen: Enquête sur les réseaux du Front national*. Paris: Denoël, 2011.

Mosse, George L. *Toward the Final Solution: A History of European Racism*. New York: Howard Fertig, 1997.

Moumen, Abderahman. *Entre histoire et mémoire, les rapatriés de l'Algérie: Dictionnaire bibliographique*. Nice: Éditions Gandini, 2003.

Mouralis, Bernard. *République et colonies: Entre histoire et mémoire, la République française et l'Afrique*. Paris: Présence africaine, 1999.

Mucchielli, Laurent. "Déni des cultures ou retour du vieux culturalisme?" October 6, 2010. http://www.laurent-mucchielli.org/index.php?post/2010/10/05/Déni-des-cultures-ou-retour-d-un-culturalisme-désuet.

———. *Le scandale des "tournantes."* Paris: La Découverte, 2005.

Mudimbe, Valentin Y. *The Idea of Africa*. Bloomington: Indiana University Press, 1994.

———. *The Invention of Africa: Gnosis, Philosophy and the Order of Knowledge*. Bloomington: Indiana University Press, 1988.

Muret, Maurice. *Le crépuscule des nations blanches*. Paris: Payot, 1925.

Namer, Gérard. *Batailles pour la mémoire: La commémoration en France de 1945 à nos jours*. Paris: Papyrus, 1983.

Naquet, Emmanuel. *Pour l'humanité: La ligue des droits de l'homme, de l'affaire Dreyfus à la défaite de 1940*. Rennes: Presses universitaires de Rennes, 2014.

Nay, Catherine. "Panique à bord." *Valeurs actuelles*, March 16, 2015.

NDiaye, Marie. *Three Strong Women*. Translated by John Fletcher. New York: Vintage, 2012.

———. *Trois femmes puissantes*. Paris: Gallimard, 2009.

Ndiaye, Pap. *La condition noire: Essai sur une minorité française*. Paris: Calmann-Lévy, 2008.

Nicolaïdis, Dimitri, ed. "La nation, les crimes et la mémoire." In *Oublier nos crimes: L'amnésie nationale: Une spécificité française*, edited by Dimitri Nicolaïdis, 4–25. Paris: Éditions Autrement, 1994.

———. *Oublier nos crimes: L'amnésie nationale: Une spécificité française*. Paris: Éditions Autrement, 1994.

Nicolet, Claude. *L'idée républicaine en France (1789–1924)*. Paris: Gallimard, 1982.

Noiriel, Gérard. *A quoi sert 'l'identité nationale.'* Marseille: Agone éditeur, 2007.

———. *Immigration, antisémitisme et racisme en France (XIXe–XXe siècle): Discours publics, humiliations privées*. Paris: Fayard, 2007.

———. *Le creuset français: Histoire de immigration—XIXe–XXe siècles*. Paris: Seuil, 1988.

———. *Qu'est-ce que l'histoire contemporaine?* Paris: Hachette, 2001.

Nora, Pierre. "La France vit le passage d'un modèle de nation à un autre." Interview with Pierre Nora. By Vincent Tremolet de Villers. *Le Figaro*, May 25, 2015.

———. "La question coloniale: Une histoire politisée." *Le Monde*, October 15, 2011.

———, ed. *Les lieux de mémoire*. Paris: Gallimard, 1997.

Nordman, Charlotte, ed. *Le foulard islamique en questions*. Paris: Amsterdam, 2004.

Novick, Peter. *L'Holocauste dans la vie américaine*. Paris: Gallimard, 2001.

Odunlami, Stella, and Kehinde Andrews. "Is Art Installation Exhibit B Racist?" *The Guardian*, September 27, 2014.

Offenstadt, Nicolas. "'L'Âme de la France' au musée . . ." April 22, 2008. https://blogs.mediapart.fr/edition/usages-et-mesusages-de-l-histoire/article/220408/l-ame-de-la-france-au-musee.

———. *Les fusillés de la Grande Guerre et la mémoire collective, 1914–1999*. Paris: Odile Jacob, 2002.

———. *L'histoire bling bling: Le retour du roman national*. Paris: Éditions Stock, 2009.

———. "Poilus et fusillés: Les erreurs de Marianne." December 6, 2012. https://blogs.mediapart.fr/edition/usages-et-mesusages-de-lhistoire/article/061212/poilus-et-fusilles-les-erreurs-de-maria.

Orban, Viktor. "Interview with Viktor Orban." By Stéphane Kovacs. *Le Figaro*, September 15, 2015.

Organization for Economic Cooperation and Development (OECD). *International Migration Outlook 2013*. Paris: OECD Publishing, 2013.

Ortiz, Jean. "J'ai peur de Manuel Valls." January 10, 2014. http://lepcf.fr/J-ai-peur-de-Manuel-Valls.

Ory, Pascal. *Ce que dit Charlie: Treize leçons d'histoire*. Paris: Gallimard, 2016.

Paon, Marcel. *L'immigration en France: Conséquences et limitation de l'immigration*. Paris: Payot, 1926.

Patricot, Aymeric. *Les petits blancs: Un voyage dans la France d'en bas*. Paris: Plein Jour, 2013.

Paxton, Robert. *La France de Vichy, 1940–1944*. Translated by Claude Bertrand. Paris: Seuil, 1973.

———. *Vichy France: Old Guard and New Order, 1940–1944*. New York: Columbia University Press, 1972.

Péan, Pierre. *Noires fureurs, blancs menteurs: Rwanda 1990–1994*. Paris: Fayard/Mille et une Nuits, 2005.

———. *Une jeunesse française: François Mitterrand 1934–1947*. Paris: Fayard, 1994.

Perrineau, Pascal. *La France au front*. Paris: Fayard, 2014.

———. *Le symptôme Le Pen*. Paris: Fayard, 1997.

Perse, Saint-John. *Anabase*. Paris: Gallimard, 1924.

Pitti, Laure. "De la différenciation coloniale à la discrimination systémique?: La condition d'OS algérien à Renault, de la grille Parodi à la méthode Renault de qualification de travail (1945–1973)." *Revue de l'IRES* 3, no. 46 (2004): 69–107.

Plenel, Edwy. *Pour les musulmans*. Paris: La Découverte, 2015.

"Polémiques sur l'histoire coloniale." *Manière de voir* 58 (July–August 2001).

Pouchepadass, Jacques. "Le projet critique des *postcolonial studies* entre hier et demain." In *La situation postcoloniale: Les postcolonial studies dans le débat français*, edited by Marie-Claude Smout, 173–228. Paris: Presses de Sciences Po, 2007.

Poulot, Dominique. "Musées et guerres de mémoires: Pédagogie et frustration mémorielle." In *Les guerres de mémoires: La France et son histoire*, edited by Pascal Blanchard and Isabelle Veyrat-Masson, 230–240. Paris: La Découverte, 2008.

"Pourquoi Elisabeth Badinter a provoqué un clash à l'Observatoire de la Laïcité." *Metronews*, January 12, 2016.

Powell, Colin. "Remarks to the National Foreign Policy Conference for Leaders of Nongovernmental Organizations," October 26, 2001.

Prochasson, Christophe. *Les années électriques, 1880–1910*. Paris: La Découverte, 1991.

Pudal, Bernard. "Le communisme français: Mémoires défaites et mémoires victorieuses depuis 1989." In *Les guerres de mémoires: La France et son histoire*, edited by Pascal Blanchard and Isabelle Veyrat-Masson, 117–127. Paris: La Découverte, 2008.

"Quand l'Algérie était française: Le numéro souvenir de la saga pied-noir." *Le Point*, no. 1862, May 22, 2008.

Ramadan, Tariq. Interview on *France-Soir*, March 25, 2005.

Rana, Aziz. *The Two Faces of American Freedom*. Cambridge, MA: Harvard University Press, 2010.

Raspail, Jean. *Le Camp des Saints*. Paris: Éditions Robert Laffont, 2011.

Raybaud, Antoine. "Deuil sans travail, travail sans deuil: La France a-t-elle une mémoire coloniale?" *Dédale* 5–6 (1997): 87–104.

Reding, Viviane. "Statement on the Latest Developments on the Roma Situation," September 14, 2010. http://europa.eu/rapid/press-release_SPEECH-10-428_en.htm.

Renan, Ernest. "What is a Nation?" Translated by Martin Thom. In *Nation and Narration*, edited by Homi Bhabha, 8–22. New York: Routledge, 1990.

"Rencontre(s) coloniale(s)." Special issue of *Genèses*, no. 43 (June 2001).

Rennes, Juliette. "L'argument de la décadence dans les pamphlets d'extrême droite des années 1930." *Mots* 58, no. 1 (March 1999): 152–164.

Repenser le passé colonial. Special issue of *Nouveaux Regards* 30 (July–September 2005).

Reynaud-Paligot, Carole. *Races, racisme et antiracisme dans les années 1930*. Paris: PUF, 2007.

Richard, Jean-Luc. *Partir ou rester?: Destinées des jeunes issus de l'immigration*. Paris: PUF, 2004.

Ricœur, Paul. *La mémoire, l'histoire, l'oubli*. Paris: Seuil, 2000.

Rigouste, Mathieu. "L'ennemi intérieur, de la guerre coloniale au contrôle sécuritaire." *Cultures & Conflits*, no. 67 (2007): 157–174.

———. *L'ennemi intérieur, la généalogie coloniale et militaire de l'ordre sécuritaire dans la France contemporaine*. Paris: La Découverte, 2009.

———. *Les cadres médiatiques, sociaux et mythologiques de l'imaginaire colonial: La représentation de 'l'immigration maghrébine' dans la presse française de 1995 à 2002*, Master's thesis, University Paris 10, Nanterre, 2002.

Rioufol, Ivan. "Bloc-notes: La libanisation de Marseille, première alerte." *Le Figaro*, September 13, 2013.

Rioux, Jean-Pierre, ed. *De Gaulle et l'Algérie*. Paris: De Vive voix, 2010.

———. "Des clandestins aux activistes (1945–1965)." In *Histoire de l'extrême droite en France*, edited by Michel Winock, 215–241. Paris: Seuil, 1993.

———. *Dictionnaire de la France coloniale*. Paris: Flammarion, 2007.

———. *La France perd la mémoire*. Paris: Perrin, 2006.

———. *La Guerre d'Algérie et les Français*. Paris: Fayard, 1990.

———. *Vive l'histoire de France!* Paris: Odile Jacob, 2015.

Rivet, Daniel. "Le fait colonial en nous: Histoire d'un éloignement." *Vingtième siècle* 33 (January–March 1992): 127–138.

Robinson, Charles. *Fabrication de la guerre civile*. Paris: Seuil, 2016.

Rocard, Michel. "Déclaration de M. Michel Rocard: Premier ministre, sur l'intégration des immigrés et des Français d'origine étrangère." January 7, 1990. http://discours.vie-publique.fr/notices/903116300.html.

Rodier, Claire. *Xénophobie Business: À quoi servent les contrôles migratoires?* Paris: La Découverte, 2012.

Romains, Jules. *L'homme blanc*. Paris: Flammarion, 1937.

Roman, Joël. "Pour un multiculturalisme tempéré." *Hommes & migrations* 1197 (April 1996): 18–22.

Romier, Lucien. *Explication de notre temps*. Paris: Grasset, 1925.

"Roms: Cohn-Bendit déplore que Valls 'racialise la question.'" *L'Obs*, September 28, 2013.

Rosoux, Valérie-Barbara. *Les usages de la mémoire dans les relations internationales: Le recours au passé dans la politique étrangère de la France à l'égard de l'Allemagne et de l'Algérie, de 1962 à nos jours*. Brussels: Bruylant, 2001.

Rousso Henry. *The Haunting Past: History, Memory, and Justice in Contemporary France*. Translated by Ralph Schoolcraft. Philadelphia: University of Pennsylvania Press, 2002.

———. *La Hantise du passé*. Paris: Textuel, 1998.

———. "Vers une mondialisation de la mémoire." *Vingtième siècle: Revue d'histoire* 94 (April–June 2007): 3–10.

Roy, Olivier. "Comment l'islam est devenu la nouvelle idéologie des damnés de la planète." Interview with Olivier Roy. By Haoues Seniguer. *Atlantico*, July 4, 2015.

———. *L'échec de l'islam politique*. Paris: Seuil, 2015.

———. "Le djihadisme est une révolte générationnelle et nihiliste." *Médiapart*, December 2, 2015.

Ruscio, Alain. "Césaire et le communisme, les communistes et Césaire: Une longue histoire." In *Aimé Césaire à l'œuvre*, edited by Marc Cheymol and Philippe Ollé-Laprune, 193–202. Paris: Item/Éditions des Archives contemporaines, 2010.

———. *Nostalgérie: L'interminable histoire de l'OAS*. Paris: La Découverte, 2015.

———. "Y'a bon les colonies." *Autrement* 144 (April 1994): 36–51.

Rushdie, Salman. *East, West*. London: Jonathan Cape, 1994.

Saada, Emmanuelle. *Les enfants de la colonie: Les métis de l'Empire français entre sujétion et citoyenneté*. Paris: La Découverte, 2007.

———. "Une nationalité par degré: Civilité et citoyenneté en situation coloniale." In *L'esclavage, la colonisation et après... France, États-Unis, Grande-Bretagne*, edited by Patrick Weil and Stéphane Dufoix, 193–226. Paris: PUF, 2005.

———. "Un racisme de l'expansion: Les discriminations raciales au regard des situations coloniales." In *De la question sociale à la question raciale?: Représenter la société française*, edited by Didier Fassin and Éric Fassin, 55–71. Paris: La Découverte, 2006.

Sahlins, Peter. *Unnaturally French: Foreign Citizens in the Old Regime and After*. Ithaca, NY, and London: Cornell University Press, 2004.

Said, Edward W. *Culture and Imperialism*. New York: Vintage, 1991.

———. *Orientalism*. New York: Pantheon, 1978.

———. *Reflections on Exile and Other Essays*. Cambridge, MA: Harvard University Press, 2002.

Sainton, Jean-Pierre. *Les nègres en politique: Couleur, identités, et stratégies de couleur en Guadeloupe au tournant du siècle*. Paris: Septentrion Presses Universitaires, 2000.

de Sardan, Jean-Pierre Olivier. *Anthropologie et développement: Essai en socio-anthropologie du changement social*. Paris: Karthala, 1997.

Sarkozy, Nicolas. "Choisir la date du 19 mars, c'est entretenir la guerre des mémoires." *Le Figaro*, March 18, 2016.

———. "Discours à Bercy," April 29, 2007. http://sites.univ-provence.fr/veronis/Discours2007/transcript.php?n=Sarkozy&p=2007-04-29.

———. "Discours de Dakar," July 26, 2007. http://www.lemonde.fr/afrique/article/2007/11/09/le-discours-de-dakar_976786_3212.html.

———. "Discours de Grenoble sur la sécurité et l'immigration," July 30, 2010. http://www.lefigaro.fr/politique/le-scan/2014/03/27/25001-20140327ARTFIG00084-le-discours-de-grenoble-de-nicolas-sarkozy.php.

———. "Discours sur la nation," March 9, 2007. http://sites.univ-provence.fr/veronis/Discours2007/transcript.php?n=Sarkozy&p=2007-03-09.

Sarraut, Albert. *La mise en valeur des colonies françaises*. Paris: Payot, 1923.

Sarrazin, Thilo. *Deutschland schafft sich ab: Wie wir unser Land aufs Spiel setzen*. Munich: DeutscheVerlags-Anstalt, 2010.

Sartre, Jean-Paul. *Anti-Semite and Jew: An Exploration of the Etiology of Hate.* Translated by George J. Becker. New York: Schocken, 1948 [1946].

———. "*Black Orpheus.*" Translated by Samuel W. Allen. Paris: Présence africaine, 1976 [1948].

Saux, Jean-Louis. "Les Français d'outre-mer se plaignent de discriminations en métropole." *Le Monde*, December 11, 2004.

Savarese, Éric. *Algérie, la guerre des mémoires.* Paris: Non lieu, 2007.

Sayad, Abdelmalek. *Histoire et recherche identitaire.* Saint-Denis: Éditions Bouchène, 2002.

———. *La double absence: Des illusions de l'émigré aux souffrances de l'immigré.* Paris: Seuil, 1999.

———. "Les enfants illégitimes (Part I)." *Actes de la recherche en sciences sociales* 25, no. 1 (1979): 61–81.

———. "Les enfants illégitimes (Part II)." *Actes de la recherche en sciences sociales* 26, no. 1 (1979): 117–132.

———. *Les usages sociaux de la "culture des immigrés."* Paris: CIEMI, 1978.

Schor, Paul. "L'instrumentalisation des historiens est inacceptable." *Le Monde*, October 4, 2007.

Schor, Ralph. *Français et immigrés en temps de crise (1930–1980).* Paris: L'Harmattan, 2004.

———. *L'opinion française et les étrangers, 1919–1939.* Paris: Publications de la Sorbonne, 1985.

Schweitzer, Louis. Interview with Cécilia Gabizon. "'Lutter contre tous les abus.'" *Le Figaro*, June 23, 2005, 9.

Sellam, Sadek. *La France et ses musulmans: Un siècle de politique musulmane (1895–2005).* Paris: Fayard, 2006.

Semo, Marc. "La repentance vue par les historiens." *Libération*, December 5, 2007.

Semprini, Andrea. *Le multiculturalisme.* Paris: PUF, 1997.

"Serons-nous encore français dans 30 ans?" *Le Figaro*, October 26, 1985.

"710,000 Migrants Entered EU in First Nine Months of 2015." Report from the Frontex Agency, October 13, 2015. http://frontex.europa.eu/news/710-000-migrants-entered-eu-in-first-nine-months-of-2015-NUiBkk.

Sharpley-Whiting, Tracy Denean, ed. *The Speech: Race and Barack Obama's* A More Perfect Union. New York and London: Bloomsbury, 2009.

Shepard, Todd. *The Invention of Decolonization: The Algerian War and the Remaking of France.* Ithaca, NY: Cornell University Press, 2008.

———. "Une République française 'postcoloniale': La fin de la guerre d'Algérie et la place des enfants des colonies dans la Ve République." *Contretemps* 16 (January 2006): 49–57.

Siegfried, André. *America Comes of Age: A French Analysis.* Translated by Henry Harold Hemming and Doris Hemming. New York: Harcourt Brace, 1927.

Sigona, Nando. "Seeing Double? How the EU Miscounts Migrants Arriving at Its Borders." *theconversation.com*, October 21, 2015.

Silber, Mitchell D., and Arvind Bhatt. *Radicalization in the West: The Homegrown Threat.* New York: NYPD Intelligence Division, 2007.

Simon, Patrick. "La population française a pris conscience qu'elle vit dans une société multiculturelle." Interview with Patrick Simon. By Marilyne Baumard. *Le Monde*, January 8, 2016.

———. "Les revirements de la politique d'immigration." *Cahiers français* 369 (2012): 86–91.

———. "Les statistiques, les sciences sociales françaises et les rapports sociaux ethniques et de 'race.'" *Revue française de sociologie* 49, no. 1 (2008): 153–162.

———. "Nationalité et origine dans la statistique française: Les catégories ambiguës." *Population* 53, no. 3 (1998): 541–567.

Simon, Patrick, and Vincent Tiberj. *Sécularisation ou regain religieux: La religiosité des immigrés et de leurs descendants*. INED, *Document de travail*, no. 196 (July 2013).

Simon, Patrick, and Sylvia Zappi. "La politique républicaine de l'identité." *Mouvements* 2, no. 38 (March–April 2005): 5–7.

Singer-Kerel, Jeanne. "'Protection' de la main-d'œuvre en temps de crise (Le précédent des années 30)." *Revue européenne de migrations internationales* 5, no. 2 (1989): 7–27.

Sivan, Emmanuel. "Colonialism and Popular Culture in Algeria." *Journal of Contemporary History* 14, no. 1 (January 1979): 21–53.

Smouts, Marie-Claude, ed. *La situation postcoloniale: Les postcolonial studies dans le débat français*. Paris: Presses de Sciences Po, 2007.

Spire, Alexis. *Etrangers à la carte: L'administration de l'immigration en France (1945–1975)*. Paris: Grasset, 2005.

———. "Semblables et pourtant différents: La citoyenneté paradoxale des 'Français musulmans d'Algérie' en metropole." *Genèses* 4, no. 53 (2003): 48–68.

Spivak, Gayatri Chakravorty. "Can the Subaltern Speak?" In *Can the Subaltern Speak? Reflections on the History of an Idea*, edited by Rosalind C. Morris, 21–78. New York: Columbia University Press, 2010.

Stavo-Debauge, Joan. "L'invisibilité du tort et le tort de l'invisibilité," EspacesTemps.net. April 19, 2007. http://www.espacestemps.net/articles/invisibilite-du-tort-et-le-tort-de-invisibilite/.

Stoddard, Lothrop. *Le flot montant des peoples de couleur contre la suprématie mondiale des blancs*. Paris: Payot, 1925.

Stora, Benjamin. "Guerre d'Algérie: 1999–2003, les accélérations de la mémoire." *Hommes & Migrations* 1244 (July–August 2003): 83–95.

———. "Il faudrait qu'un consensus national se fasse sur la reconnaissance de la souffrance des autres." April 2007. http://ldh-toulon.net/Benjamin-Stora-il-faudrait-qu-un.html.

———. "La décolonisation des imaginaires n'est pas une question achevée." Interview by Jérôme Skalski. *L'Humanité*, January 8, 2016.

———. *La dernière génération d'octobre*. Paris: Stock, 2003.

———. *La gangrène et l'oubli: La mémoire de la guerre d'Algérie*. Paris: La Découverte, 1991.

———. "La guerre des mémoires." Interview by Marie Poinsot. *Hommes & migrations*, no. 1268–1269 (July–October 2007): 208–216.

———. *La guerre des mémoires: La France face à son passé colonial: Entretiens avec Thierry Leclère*. La Tour-d'Aigues: Éditions de l'Aube, 2007.

———. "Le récit colonial n'a été pris en charge ni par les partis politiques, ni par l'école." Interview by Rosa Moussaoui. *L'Humanité*, July 26, 2006.

———. *Le transfert d'une mémoire: De 'l'Algérie française' au racisme anti-arabe*. Paris: La Découverte, 1999.

———. "Mohand Hamoumou, *Et ils sont devenus harkis*." *Vingtième siècle: Revue d'histoire* 42, no. 1 (April–June 1994): 143–144.

———. "Préface: La France et 'ses' guerres de mémoires." In *Les guerres de mémoires: La France et son histoire*, edited by Pascal Blanchard and Isabelle Veyrat-Masson, 7–13. Paris: La Découverte, 2008.

Stora, Benjamin, and Alexis Jenni. *Les mémoires dangereuses*. Paris: Albin Michel, 2016.

de Suremain, Marie-Albane. "L'histoire coloniale dans le *Bulletin du Comité d'études historiques et scientifiques de l'A.O.F.-IFAN*, 1916–1960." In *Décoloniser l'histoire? De l''histoire coloniale' aux histoires nationales en Amérique latine et en Afrique (XIXe–XXe siècle)*, edited by Sophie Dulucq and Colette Zytnicki, 39–57. Paris: SHOM, 2003.

al-Suri, Abu Musab. *The Global Islamic Resistance Call*. 2004. https://archive.org/details/TheGlobalIslamicResistanceCall.

Taguieff, Pierre-André, ed. *Face au racisme*. Paris: Seuil, 1991.

———. "La confluence des fatalismes: Emprise globalitaire, dérives identitaires." *Les Temps modernes* 613 (March–May 2001): 131–157.

———. *La force du préjug: Essai sur le racisme et ses doubles*. Paris: La Découverte, 1988.

———. *La nouvelle judéophobie*. Paris: Mille et une nuits, 2002.

———. *Le retour du populisme: Un défi pour les démocraties européennes*. Paris: Encyclopaedia Universalis, 2004.

———. *Les fins de l'antiracisme*. Paris: Michalon, 1995.

———. "L'identité nationale saisie par les logiques de racisation: Aspects, figures et problèmes du racisme différentialiste." *Mots* 12, no. 12 (March 1986): 91–128.

———. *Sur la Nouvelle Droite: Jalons d'une analyse critique*. Paris: Descartes & Cie, 1994.

———. *Une France antijuive? Regards sur la nouvelle configuration judéophobe*. Paris: CNRS Éditions, 2015.

Tahar-Chaouh, Malik. "Quelques observations sur un reportage de Politis à propos de l'anniversaire des dix ans du PIR." June 5, 2015. http://indigenes-republique.fr/quelques-observations-sur-un-reportage-de-politis-a-propos-de-lanniversaire-des-dix-ans-du-pir.

Taraud, Christelle. *La prostitution coloniale*. Paris: Payot, 2003.

Teinturier, Brice, and Stéphane Zumsteeg. *Fractures françaises*. Paris: Ipsos/Sopra, 2015.

Terray, Emmanuel. "Le grand ménage des mémoires." *Libération*, January 3.

Tevanian, Pierre. *La République du mépris: Les métamorphoses du racisme dans la France des années Sarkozy*. Paris: La Découverte, Paris, 2007.

———. *Le voile médiatique: Un faux débat: "L'affaire du foulard islamique."* Paris: Raisons d'agir, 2006.

Tezcan, Levent. "Kultur, Gouvernementalität der Religion und der Integrationsdiskurs." *Soziale Welt* (2007): 51–74.

Thénault, Sylvie. "Contre les manipulations de l'histoire." Interview by Rosa Moussaoui. *L'Humanité*, October 5, 2007.

———. *Histoire de la guerre d'indépendance algérienne*. Paris: Flammarion, 2005.

———. *Une drôle de justice: Les magistrats dans la guerre d'Algérie*. Paris: La Découverte, 2001.

Theullot, Jean-François. *De l'inexistence d'un devoir de mémoire*. Paris: Pleins Feux, 2005.

Thomas, Dominic. *Africa and France: Postcolonial Cultures, Migration, and Racism*. Bloomington and Indianapolis: Indiana University Press, 2013.

———. *Black France: Colonialism, Immigration, and Transnationalism*. Bloomington and Indianapolis: Indiana University Press, 2007.

———. "Fortress Europe: Identity, Race and Surveillance." *International Journal of Francophone Studies* 17, nos. 3–4 (2014): 445–468.

———. "The 'Marie NDiaye Affair', or the Coming of a Postcolonial *Évoluée*." In *Africa and France: Postcolonial Cultures, Migration, and Racism*, 139–155. Bloomington and Indianapolis: Indiana University Press, 2013.

———, ed. *Museums in Postcolonial Europe*. London and New York: Routledge, 2010.

Thompson, David. *Les Français djihadistes*. Paris: Les Arênes, 2014.

Thoraval, Yves. *Les écrans du croissant fertile*. Paris: Séguier, 2003.

Thuram, Lilian, François Durpaire, Pascal Blanchard, Rokhaya Diallo, and Marc Cheb Sun. *Appel pour une France multiculturelle et postraciale?* Paris: Respect, 2010.

Tillon, Germaine. *Algeria: The Realities*. Translated by Ronald Matthews. New York: Knopf, 1958.

———. *L'Algérie en 1957*. Paris: Les Éditions de Minuit, 1957.

Todd, Emmanuel. *L'Origine des systèmes familiaux*. Paris: Gallimard, 2011.

Todorov, Tzvetan. "Edward Said, le spectateur exilé." *Le Monde*, May 16, 2008.

———. *La conquête de l'Amérique: La question de l'autre*. Paris: Seuil, 1982.

———. *Les abus de la mémoire*. Paris: Arléa, 1995.

Traverso, Enzo. "L'écrit-événement: L'historiographie comme champ de bataille politique." In *Les guerres de mémoires: La France et son histoire*, edited by Pascal Blanchard and Isabelle Veyrat-Masson, 220–229. Paris: La Découverte, 2008.

———. *Le passé, mode d'emploi: Histoire, mémoire, politique*. Paris: La Fabrique Éditions, 2005.

Tribalat, Michèle. *De l'immigration à l'assimilation: Enquête sur les populations d'origine étrangère en France*. Paris: La Découverte, 1996.

———. "Une estimation des populations d'origine étrangère en France en 1999." *Population* 59, no. 1 (2004): 51–82.

Tutiaux-Guillon, Nicole. "Mémoires et histoire scolaire en France: Quelques interrogations didactiques." *Revue française de pédagogie*, no. 165 (October–November–December 2008): 31–42.

United Nations Committee on the Elimination of Racial Discrimination. General recommendation No. 35, GE.13-47139, CERD/C/GC/35. September 26, 2013. http://tbinternet.ohchr.org/_layouts/treatybodyexternal/Download.aspx?symbolno=CERD%2fC%2fGC%2f35&Lang=en.

———. *Report of the Committee on the Elimination of Racial Discrimination*. New York: United Nations, 2010.

Urban, Yerri. *Race et nationalité dans le droit colonial français 1865–1946*. PhD diss., University of Bourgogne, 2009.

Vaisse, Justin. *Intégrer l'islam: La France et ses musulmans, enjeux et réussites*. Paris: Éditions Odile Jacob, 2007.

Valfort, Marie-Anne. *Discriminations religieuses à l'embauche: Une réalité*. Paris: Institut Montaigne, 2015.

Vallin, Charles. *Le Petit Journal*, November 3, 1938.

Vallois, Henri Victor. *Les races humaines*. Paris: PUF, 1971.

Valls, Manuel. "Discours du Premier ministre—Examen du projet de loi de révision constitutionnelle à l'Assemblée nationale." February 5, 2016. http://www.assemblee-nationale.fr/14/cri/2015-2016/20160122.asp#P719606.

Vanneste, Christian. "Proposition de loi visant à interdire l'ensemble des vêtements ou accessoires permettant de masquer l'identité d'une personne" (prohibit all clothing or accessories that would mask the identity of a person), September 29, 2009. http://www.assemblee-nationale.fr/13/propositions/pion1942.asp.

Vatin, Jean-Claude. *L'Algérie politique, histoire et société*. Paris: Presses de la FNSP, 1983 [1974].

Veil, Simone, and the Comité de réflexion sur le Préambule de la Constitution. *Redécouvrir le préambule de la Constitution. Report for the President of the French Republic.* Paris: La Documentation française, 2008.

Vergès, Françoise. "Esclavage colonial: Quelles mémoires? Quels héritages?" In *Les guerres de mémoires: La France et son histoire,* edited by Pascal Blanchard and Isabelle Veyrat-Masson, 155–164. Paris: La Découverte, 2008.

———. *La mémoire enchaînée: Questions sur l'esclavage.* Paris: Albin Michel, 2006.

Vervaecke, Philippe, ed. *À droite de la droite: Droites radicales en France et en Grande-Bretagne au xxe siècle.* Villeneuve-d'Ascq: Presses universitaires du Septentrion, 2012.

Veyrat-Masson, Isabelle. "Les guerres de mémoires à la télévision: Du dévoilement à l'accompagnement." In *Les guerres de mémoires: La France et son histoire,* edited by Pascal Blanchard and Isabelle Veyrat-Masson, 273–286. Paris: La Découverte, 2008.

———. *Quand la télévision explore le temps: L'histoire au petit écran (1953–2000).* Paris: Fayard, 2000.

Vidal-Naquet, Pierre. *Assassins of Memory: Essays on the Denial of the Holocaust.* Translated by Jeffrey Mehlman. New York: Columbia University Press, 1992.

———. *Les assassins de la mémoire.* Paris: La Découverte, 1987.

Vidas, Dominique, and Karim Bourtel. *Le mal-être arabe: Enfants de la colonisation.* Marseille: Agone éditeur, 2005.

Vieillard-Baron, Hervé. *Les banlieues françaises ou le ghetto impossible.* La Tour-d'Aigues: Éditions de l'Aube, 1994.

Viet, Vincent. *La France immigrée: Construction d'une politique 1914–1997.* Paris: Fayard, 1998.

Vigarello, Georges. *Le propre et le sale: L'hygiène du corps depuis le Moyen Âge.* Paris: Seuil, 1987.

Vincent, Elise. "Les Français sont de moins en moins tolérants." *Le Monde,* April 1, 2014.

Viollis, Andrée. *Notre Tunisie.* Paris: Gallimard, 1939.

Wacquant, Loïc. *Urban Outcasts: A Comparative Sociology of Advanced Marginality.* Cambridge, UK and New Malden, MA: Polity Press, 2008.

Wallerstein, Immanuel. *L'universalisme européen: De la colonisation au droit d'ingérence.* Paris: Demopolis, 2008.

Weber, Eugen. *La France des années 30: Tourments et perplexités.* Paris: Fayard, 1996.

Weil, Patrick. "Débat sur la nationalité française." In *Dictionnaire historique de la vie politique française au XXe siècle,* edited by Jean-François Sirinelli, 719–721. Paris: PUF, 1995.

———. "Immigration, nation et nationalité: Regards comparatifs et croisés." *Revue française de science politique* 44, no. 2 (April 1994): 308–326.

———. *La France et ses étrangers: L'aventure d'une politique d'immigration de 1938 à nos jours.* Paris: Calmann-Lévy, 1991.

———. *La République et sa diversité: Immigration, intégration, discrimination.* Paris: Seuil, 2005.

———. *Liberté, egalité, discriminations: L'identité nationale au regard de l'histoire.* Paris: Grasset, 2008.

———. *Qu'est-ce qu'un Français? Histoire de la nationalité francaise depuis la Révolution.* Paris: Grasset, 2002.

———. "Racisme et discrimination dans la politique de l'immigration." *Vingtième Siècle: Revue d'histoire* 47, no.1 (July–September 2005): 77–102.

Weil, Patrick, and Stéphane Dufoix, eds. *L'esclavage, la colonisation, et après . . . : France, États-Unis, Grande-Bretagne.* Paris: PUF, 2005.

Wesseling, Henk. "Overseas History." In *New Perspectives on Historical Writing*, edited by Peter Burke, 67–92. Cambridge: Polity Press, 1991.

Wieviorka, Annette. "Le Vél' d'Hiv': Histoire d'une commémoration." *Autrement* 54 (1999): 161–165.

Wieviorka, Michel. *Le Front national entre extrémisme, populisme et démocratie*. Paris: Maison des sciences de l'homme, 2013.

———. *L'espace du racisme*. Paris: Seuil, 1991.

———. "Nicolas Sarkozy, sur les pentes de l'idéologie." *L'Obs*, February 2, 2012.

Wieviorka, Olivier. "Francisque ou Croix de Lorraine: les années sombres entre histoire, mémoire et mythologie." In *Les guerres de mémoires: La France et son histoire*, edited by Pascal Blanchard and Isabelle Veyrat-Masson, 94–106. Paris: La Découverte, 2008.

"Xénophobie de gouvernement, nationalisme d'Etat." Special issue of *Cultures & Conflits* 69 (2008).

Yerushalmi, Yosef Hayim. *Zakhor*. Paris: La Découverte, 1984.

Yonnet, Paul. *Voyage au centre du malaise français: L'antiracisme et le roman national*. Paris: Gallimard, 1993.

Zeghal, Malika. "La constitution du Conseil français du culte musulman: Reconnaissance politique d'un islam français?" *Archives de sciences sociales des religions*, no. 129 (January–March 2005): 97–113.

Zelensky, Anne. "Le concept d'équivalence des cultures serait-il un avatar de la pensée colonialiste?" *Le Monde*, February 10, 2012.

Zemmour, Éric. *La mélancolie française*. Paris: Fayard, 2010.

———. *Le suicide français: Ces quarante années qui ont défait la France*. Paris: Albin Michel, 2014.

Zytnicki, Colette. "'La maison, les écuries': L'émergence de l'histoire coloniale en France (des années 1800 aux années 1930)." In *Décoloniser l'histoire?: De l''histoire coloniale' aux histoires nationales en Amérique latine et en Afrique (XIXe–XXe siècle)*, edited by Sophie Dulucq and Colette Zytnicki, 9–23. Paris: SHOM, 2003.

INDEX

abolition of slavery, 130, 169–70, 179–80, 261, 266, 269, 406
academia, 62–67, 95, 249–54
ACTe memorial, 406
activism: antiracist, 368–72, 373, 375–76; memorial, 92, 103, 263, 369–270, 400
affirmative action, 15, 135, 194, 278
Afghanistan, 314, 422
Africa: migration management, 383–84; Sarkozy speech on, 306–307. *See also specific countries*
African Americans, 326, 419
Africanism, 251–52, 253
Africultures, 321
Afrocentrism, 250
Agamben, Giorgio, 179, 274, 282n9
Agence économique des Colonies, 221
Ageron, Charles-Robert, 98
aid programs, international, 138–42
Aix-en-Provence, memorials in, 398
al-Baghdadi caliphate, 314
Alduy, Cécile, 27
Alduy, Jean-Paul, 400–401
Algeria: Algerian War (*see* Algerian War); colonialism, 70, 126–29, 130–31, 200–201, 206–7nn22–23, 267–68, 331, 388–92; extremist insurgency in, 295; French citizenship and, 52n4; independence and decolonization, 132, 264, 342; migrants from, 57–58, 59, 192–93, 238, 265–66; Muslims in colonial, 259–62; nationality and, 258–61
Algerian War: about, 9, 313; as cause of Islamophobia, 312–13; commemoration of, 396, 398–402, 408nn5–6, 409n12, 409n18, 409n20, 410n26; education and, 80–81, 82–83, 238, 240; ghosts of, 313–14; memory, 20, 21, 53–58, 59, 60n5, 96, 159–60, 407
Aliot, Louis, 334, 401, 410n24
Alliot-Marie, Michèle, 403–404
al-Qaeda, 5, 21, 26, 291, 314, 422
Alsace, 44, 46, 52n8, 158, 268
altruism, 138–39
Amadieu, Jean-François, 426n14
American revolution, 262–63
"A million unemployed persons equal a million too many immigrants," 343
amnesty laws, 54, 102
"A More Perfect Union: Speech on Race" (Obama), 29, 195–96
Amselle, Jean-Loup, 220–21, 249, 250, 251
Anderson, Benedict, 253
Andrews, Kehinde, 321
anthropological foundation of Overseas France, 176–77
anticolonialism, 49, 158, 389, 406–7
anticommunism, 285–86, 287–89, 291, 296–97, 331

antiracism, 14, 326, 368–76; about, 368; criticism of and fractures in, 370–72, 374–76; failure question of, 369–70; law and policy on, 303–304, 371, 421; Marche pour l'égalité et contre le racisme, 289, 356, 371, 373, 419; models, 372–73

antirepentance movement, 90, 98, 306–307, 395, 408n2

Anti-Semite and Jew (Sartre), 24

antisemitism, 24, 330–31, 338, 339n13, 374; antiracism and, 370, 371, 372, 373; Clavreul on, 415–16; colonial memory and, 162; Dreyfus Affair, 26, 93; Front National and, 333–36, 341–42; Islam and, 333; law and policy, 304, 309n4, 369–70, 371; rise in, 93, 135, 422; as a source for Muslim discontent, 7

antiwhite racism, 306, 375

anti-Zionism, 333–36, 339n8, 355, 373

Antony, Bernard, 350n17

apartheid, 2–3, 4, 12, 15, 324–25, 414

"Apéro Géant," 292

Arab Bureaus, 201

Arabs: *banlieues* stigmatization, 146, 147; representations of, 115–21, 193, 202–203, 224

Arab Spring, 5

Armenians, 214, 215, 262, 269

Artières, Philippe, 97–98

artistic expression, 322

assimilation: colonial memory and, 157–58, 161–62, 397; embodied, 74; enemy within and, 118, 119–20, 121; failure of, 145, 191; Front National and, 344, 347–48; incapability of, 204, 213, 214–15, 217, 227, 257; Overseas France and, 179–80, 181, 184; politics, 129; veils and burqas and, 276, 280. *See also* integration

Assises contre l'islamisation de notre pays (Conference against the Islamization of our Country), 292

Association de défense des intérêts moraux et matériels des anciens détenus et exilés politiques de l'Algérie française (Association for the Defense of the Moral and Material Interests of Former Detainees and Political Exiles of French Algeria, ADIMAD), 400

Association des Anciens Amateurs de Récits de Guerres et d'Holocaustes (Association of Former Enthusiasts of War and Holocaust Stories), 92

atomization of society, 337–38

Attenborough, Richard, 55

Aubry, Martine, 286

Aussaresses, Paul, 21, 159

Austria, 28, 359

Autan-Lara, Claude, 56

authoritarianism, 330, 336, 337–38

autonomy of Overseas France, political, 181–85

Avenir de la Culture, 355

Aymard, Camille, 287–88

Azéma, Jean-Pierre, 96

Badie, Bertrand, 401

Badinter, Elisabeth, 274, 279–80, 281, 283n11, 284nn31–32, 284n36, 290–91

Bailey, Brett, 319, 320–23

Bainville, Jacques, 223

Balandier, Georges, 250

Balibar, Etienne, 189

Balkans conflicts, 332

Balladur, Edouard, 418

Bancel, Nicolas, 4, 8

banlieues neighborhoods: colonial fracture in, 145–52; current state of, 314–15, 414–15; enemy within and, 285–86, 289–90, 298n12; Front National and, 9, 342, 349n4; media and, 117, 120, 133; recent changes in, 5–6, 19, 32n25, 144–45; unrest in, 5, 11–12, 116, 292, 295, 372, 420–21

Barbican Center, 321

Barcellini, Serge, 94

Bardèche, Maurice, 331

Barjot, Frigide, 355

Barlet, Olivier, 321

de Barros, Françoise, 192

Bâsescu, Traian, 216

Bataclan theater attack, 1–2, 413–14, 417, 425n4

Bay, Nicolas, 347

Bayart, Jean-François, 236, 249–50

Bayet, Albert, 137

BBC World Service debate, 416–17

Becker, Jean-Jacques, 38n146, 291

Begag, Azouz, 421

ben Dahman, Abdelkader ben Zelouf, 389

Benedetti, Yvan, 335–36
Benedict XVI, Pope, 204
de Benoist, Alain, 345
Bercy speech of Nicolas Sarkozy, 105, 278
Berlin Wall, fall of, 294–95, 344
Bernabé, Jean, 7
Bernal, Martin, 248, 253
Bernard, Philippe, 82
Berstein, Serge, 38n146, 235, 236, 291
Bert, Paul, 131
Bertillon, Alphonse, 273, 282n3
Bertrand, Romain, 249
Besson, Éric, 212, 217
Béziers, 8, 33n41, 398, 400, 405
BFM-TV, 349n9
Bhatt, Arvind, 298n3
Bibliothèque Historique de la Ville de Paris, 92–93
bin Laden, Osama, 5, 120
biological notion of race, 306, 307, 308, 330, 345, 359
biopolitics, 337, 340n18
birthplace, right of, 265–66, 268
Black Athena (Bernal), 248
Black Decade, 295
Black France, 322, 324, 326–27
Black Panthers, 373
Black question, 319–27; *apartheid* and, 324–25; *Exhibit B* controversy and, 319–23; identity and, 325–27
Black Skins, White Masks (Fanon), 242
Blanchard, Pascal, 4, 8, 322–23
Bleich, Erik, 261–62
Bleustein-Blanchet, Marcel, 283n11
Bloc Identitaire, 293, 339n12, 359
Blum-Violette project, 158, 224, 264
body, reducing natives to, 70–76
Boex, Joseph Henri Honoré, 213–14
Bolshevik Revolution, 287–88
Bolshevism, 291, 297
Bonaparte, Napoleon, 52n5
border control, 211, 299n23, 380, 382
border crossings, illegal, 378–79, 384
Boubeker, Ahmed, 8, 66, 101
Boucheron, Patrick, 1
Boulevard Voltaire website, 355
Bourdin, Jean-Jacques, 349n9
Boushaba, Zouhir, 259
Bousquet, Pierre, 339n14
Boussole (Énard), 10
Bouteldja, Houria, 334
Boutin, Christine, 355
Bouvet, Laurent, 8
Boxer Rebellion, 55
Braudel, Fernand, 65, 234
Braudel program, 234
Brice, Catherine, 104
Brigade anti-négrophobie (Anti-Negrophobia Brigade, BAN), 373
Brossat, Alain, 99
Brubaker, Rogers, 258
Bruckner, Pascal, 8, 9–10, 92, 397
Brustier, Gaël, 337
Buisson, Patrick, 19, 21, 212, 222, 398
Bumidom, 169, 171n5
burqas, 272–76, 278–80, 281, 283nn11–12, 283n16
Butler, Judith, 282n8
Buttes-Chaumont park memorial, 396

Cahiers pédagogiques, 234
Caldwell, Christopher, 317n1
Cambodia, 139, 141
Camus, Albert, 392
Camus, Renaud, 10, 33n39, 293, 296
Candide, 223, 227
capitalism, 177
Carolingian Europe, 44
Carpita, Paul, 56
Carrère d'Encausse, Hélène, 96
Cassen, Pierre, 292–93, 298n17
Castrillo, Jean, 339n14
categorization, 14, 139, 146–47, 191–92, 193, 206–7nn22–23, 325
Catholics, 191, 216, 315, 316, 317, 350n17, 355
Cau, Jean, 296
Causeur, 296
Cavada, Jean-Marie, 117
Cazeneuve, Bernard, 385n3
Céline, Louis-Ferdinand, 215
Centre de prévention contre les dérives sectaires liées à l'islam (CPDSI), 423, 427nn33–34
Centre d'étude de la vie politique française (Research Center on French Political Life, CEVIPOF), 352

Centre Zahra, 335
"Ce que peut l'histoire" (Boucheron), 1
Cercle Algérianiste, 410n23
Césaire, Aimé, 89, 105, 170, 181, 182, 322, 387–88, 393n7
CFCM *(Conseil français du culte musulman),* 125, 198, 201–202, 207n27
chadors, 116–17, 332
Chamoiseau, Patrick, 7
Changer de destin (Hollande), 22
Charlie-Hebdo attacks, 2, 10, 413, 423
Chaumont, Jean-Michel, 135
Chautemps, Camille, 211
de Chaufferons, Philippe, 221
Chebel, Malek, 286
Chevènement, Jean-Pierre, 201, 207n27, 333
Chirac, Jacques: antidiscrimination and, 421; colonial memory and, 102, 396–97, 408n5; election of, 21; positive colonialism and, 387, 404, 409n8
Christianity, 254, 273, 296, 312, 315–16, 345, 348
Christianization, 16, 138, 315
cinema, 54–57, 92, 221, 274, 420. *See also specific films*
Cité nationale de l'histoire de l'immigration (National Museum on the History of Immigration, CNHI), 96, 103, 105, 237, 410n29
citizen colonized, 182
citizenship: binationals, 6; in the colonies, 52n4, 72, 258–60, 416; Front National and, 344; immigrants and, 76, 124, 192, 199, 200, 265, 418; Muslims and, 124, 206–7nn22–23; Overseas France and, 170, 176, 179, 182–83, 184; terrorists and, 412, 414; women and, 277. *See also* nationality
Citron, Suzanne, 234
Civil Code, 258–59, 260–61, 267, 270n8
civilization process, 72
civilizing mission: colonial memory and, 156–57, 322, 406; in curriculum, 80, 81, 83; government of bodies and, 70–72; humanitarianism and, 137–39; modern, 139–42, 280; Republic and, 47–49, 50, 130; separation of church and state and, 200
civil rights movement, 419
civil rights of Algerians, 258–59
clash of civilizations, 17–18, 86, 253, 295, 333, 336
classification of citizenship, 192, 206–7nn22–23
Clavreul, Gilles, 415–16
cleanliness, 140–41
Clemenceau, Georges, 22, 264
Cleopatra, 247–48
Club de l'Horloge, 227, 305, 309n7, 409n19
CNCDH *(Commission nationale consultative des droits de l'homme),* 193, 228, 304, 305, 308, 348, 426n10
CNRS (Centre National de la Recherche Scientifique), 31n16, 162, 226
Code de l'entrée et du séjour des étrangers et du droit d'asile (Law on foreign entry and stay, and on asylum rights, CESEDA), 211
Code de l'indigénat, 50, 83, 129n6, 201, 206n22, 259, 260
Code Noir, 179, 235
coexistence, peaceful, 8, 24, 243
Cohn-Bendit, Daniel, 213
Collectif contre l'islamophobie en France (Collective against Islamophobia in France, CCIF), 374
collective memory, 19, 85, 102, 105, 395
collectivités d'Outre-Mer (overseas collectivities, COM), 165
Collège de France, 64, 68n7
"Cologne, lieu de fantasmes" (Daoud), 17
Cologne sexual assaults, 16–17
colonial consensus, 46, 48, 158–59
colonial fracture. *See* Republic and the colonial fracture
colonial imaginaries, 161–62, 190, 199, 238
colonialism: in Algeria, 70, 126–29, 130–31, 200–201, 206–7nn22–23, 267–68, 331, 390; civilizing mission of (*see* civilizing mission); consensus on, 46, 48, 158–59; consequences of, 388; defined, 387–88; education on (*see* education); government of bodies and, 70–72; humanism and, 49, 137, 240–41, 319, 325, 392; humanitarianism and, 137–38, 139, 142; justification of, 386, 389; memory and (*see* memory, colonial); opposition to, 49, 158, 389, 406–407; politics of, 395–97; postcolonial studies and, 246; racism and, 373; recognition of (*see* commemorations,

memorials, monuments, and museums); repetition of Islam relations from, 125–26, 199–201, 202; repression and, 388–93; Republic and (*see* Republic and the colonial fracture); study on, 61–65, 68n7; terrorism connection to, 412–14, 418, 423, 424–25
Colonialisme à la papa, 393n1
coloniality of power, 167
colonial lobby, 63–65, 156
colonial memory. *See* memory, colonial
colonial nostalgia, 7, 85, 156, 348, 395–96, 399–400, 402. *See also* commemorations, memorials, monuments, and museums
colonial pride, 404
colonial studies, 61–65, 68n7. *See also* postcolonial studies
colonial utopia, 48, 156, 159, 169, 170
"Colonies: Un débat français," 106
colonization and republic term association, 130
colonized citizen versus citizen colonized, 182
colored citizenship, 170
Comité d'action de défense démocratique, 370
Comité de défense de la race nègre, 326
commemorations, memorials, monuments, and museums: for Algerian War, 396, 398–402, 408nn5–6, 409n12, 409n18, 409n20, 410n26; colonialism and, 398–405, 410n29, 410n35; education and, 85; expectations of, 95–96, 135; Invalides, 2; laws on, 96–97, 269–70, 271nn18–19; memory and, 90, 91, 92, 94, 100–105, 162, 170, 271n19; politics and, 387, 396–97. *See also* museums; *specific commemorations, memorials, monuments, and museums*
Commission for Racial Equality (UK), 15
Commission interministérielle des affaires musulmanes (Inter-Ministerial Commission on Muslim Affairs, CIAM), 201, 207n25
Commission Islam et Laïcité (Commission on Islam and Secularism), 123, 124
Commission nationale consultative des droits de l'homme (National Consultative Committee on Human Rights, CNCDH), 193, 228, 304, 305, 308, 348, 426n10
Committee for the Memory of Slavery, 236
Committee on the Elimination of Racial Discrimination (CERD), 216, 303–304
communism, 14, 25, 224, 285–89, 291–92, 297, 331, 344
Communist Party: French, 286, 287, 288–89, 291, 297, 343, 346; in Guadeloupe, 181
communitarianism, 58–59, 103, 184, 242, 286, 334, 406
community participation, 139–40
comparative culture studies, 247–49
Comptian positivism, 46
concentration camps, 213, 342, 344, 349n1
Confiant, Raphaël, 7
Congo-Ocean line, 390
conquests of Third Republic, 44–47
conquest versus colonization, 264
Conseil français du culte musulman (French Committee for the Muslim Religion, CFCM), 125, 198, 201–202, 207n27
Conseil représentatif des associations noires (Representative Council of Black Organizations, CRAN), 373
consent, 278–79
consideration policy, 201
Constant, Fred, 262
Constitutional Council, 194–95
constitution of France, 12, 15, 188, 194–95, 269, 370, 412, 414
construction in the colonies, 390
contact between natives and Europeans, 71, 72
converts to Islam, 423
convictions for discrimination crimes, 304, 426n10
Copé, Jean-François, 286
Coquery-Vidrovitch, Catherine, 62, 160, 266
Corsica, 44, 157, 264
Cottias, Myriam, 245n32
Courtine, Jean-Jacques, 284n33
Court of Cassation, 259
Courtois, Gérard, 6
Cousteau, Pierre-Antoine, 223
CPDSI (Centre de prévention contre les dérives sectaires liées à l'islam), 423, 427nn33–34
Creil affair, 116–17, 205n3, 294
Crémieux Decree, 52n4, 131, 207n23
Crenshaw, Kimberlé, 373

creolization, 167, 177, 179
crimes against humanity, 169–70, 269–70, 271nn18–19, 308, 406
crisis context, current, 6–8
cross, symbol of, 248
Crusades, the, 36n101, 45, 134, 312
cultural areas studies, 65
cultural distance, 191
culture: discrimination and, 268; education and, 87, 241–42; mixing of, 251; of Overseas France, 179, 184; race and, 221, 222–23, 227, 228; threat to European, 296, 312, 358–59
customs duties, 353

Daesh, 2, 5, 7, 26, 314, 336–37, 414, 422
Dahmani, Ahmed, 5
Dakhlia, Jocelyne, 17
Daladier, Edouard, 217
Daniel, Jean, 226
Daoud, Kamel, 17
Dati, Rachida, 203
Daubresse, Marc-Philippe, 144
Days of Glory, 92
death penalty, 336, 337
Debbouze, Djamel, 119, 120
Debord, Guy, 366
Decaux, Alain, 92
de-Christianization of France, 312, 315–16
decline of France question, 8–11
decolonization: in cinema, 55; education and, 80, 233, 237; GRECE and, 345; immigration and, 7, 238; memory and, 7, 306; Republic and, 69–70, 131, 166. *See also* Algerian War
Decree on Pardons of February 6, 1935, 211
Decugis, Henri, 223
dédiabolisation of Front National, 13, 305, 333, 347
Défense de l'Occident (Massis), 222–23
Défenseurs des droits (Defenders of Rights), 371
defensive identity, 8, 11, 24
Defferre, Gaston, 402–403
Degueldre, Roger, 398
De la colonisation chez les peuples modernes (Leroy-Beaulieu), 48
Delafosse, Maurice, 49
Delavignette, Robert, 49
Délégation interministérielle à la lutte contre le racisme et l'antisémitisme (Inter-Ministerial Delegation for the Fight against Racism and Anti-Semitism, DILCRA), 304, 371–72, 377n12
Delporte, Christian, 98
Deltombe, Thomas, 289
Demaison, André, 49
Demangeon, Albert, 223, 224
Déon, Michel, 296
Départements d'Outre-Mer (DOM), 165. *See also* Overseas France
Départements et régions d'outre mer (DROMs), 165, 175. *See also* Overseas France
deportations, 14, 211, 213, 216–17, 218nn7–8, 343
derealization, 151–52
Dermouche, Aïssa, 121
Déroulède, Paul, 387
descendants of colonized peoples: as eternal natives, 72–73; government of bodies and, 70–76; integration and, 84; school curriculum and, 83, 84–85. *See also* immigrants and children of
"Des Parisiens sous l'occupation" (Zucca), 93
de-territorialization, 177
Detienne, Marcel, 249
Deutschland schafft sich ab (Sarrazin), 11
Diao, Claire, 321
Dibrani, Léonarda, 213
Dictionnaire de l'Académie française, 319–20
Dieudonné, 294, 308, 335, 339n13, 355, 359
differentialism, 344, 345, 346, 348, 353, 374
differentialist racism, 305–306
Diop, Cheikh Anta, 247, 253
Diouf, Mamadou, 249
disalienating history, 240
Discourse on Colonialism (Césaire), 387–88, 393n7
discrimination, 169, 261; apartheid and, 324, 414; colonial, 159, 262; elimination efforts, 194–95, 375; government of bodies and, 70, 72–73; HALDE and, 421; immigrants and, 169–70; media and, 120–21; new parameters of, 188–90; positive, 49; Republic and, 46, 47, 162, 163; today, 13, 15, 145, 416–17, 419–21, 426n10, 426n14
discrimination positive, 135

disease, 140, 390
dispossession, 70, 72, 74, 167
diversity, 167, 170, 194–95, 204–5, 245n32, 375
Djavann, Chahdortt, 283n16
DNA tests, 211–12
Dominati, Jacques, 399, 409n15
domination, 409n17; antiracism movement and, 373, 375; *banlieues* and, 146, 150, 151; colonialism and, 50, 126, 159
Dorgelès, Roland, 392
Doriot, Jacques, 14, 158, 288, 289, 342
Dossiers de l'écran, 92
double right of birthplace, 265–66, 268
Douglas, Mary, 141
Douste-Blazy, Philippe, 403–4
dress, 274–76, 283n19
Dreyfus Affair, 26, 93, 99
Driant, Émile, 299n27
Droit d'inventaire, 92, 97
Drucker, Marie, 92
Drumont, Édouard, 331
Dubois, Laurent, 261, 266, 267
Duclert, Vincent, 93
Dufoix, Stéphane, 262
Duhamel, Alain, 226
Duhamel, Olivier, 117
Dulucq, Sophie, 62
Duprat, François, 335, 339n14, 343, 348
Dupuy, Hélène, 99
Duquenet, Luigi, 216
Durafour, Michel, 349n8
Durkheim, Emile, 208nn46–47, 268
Duval, Jules, 48
Duval, Léon Étienne, 389

Ebadi, Shrin, 283n16
Ecole Libre movement, 356
economy, 209–11, 314, 353–54
education, 78–87, 233–43; antiracism in, 304; classroom challenges, 237–43; in the colonies, 131, 391; gaps in colonial and immigration history, 84–87, 160; history of teaching colonization, slavery, and immigration, 78–79, 87, 233–37, 243n6, 244n13; of immigrants and their children, 419; pedagogy, 233–34, 235, 239–43; positive colonization and, 306; religion and, 134, 316; schism of national and colonial history, 80–82, 83; textbooks (*see* textbooks); traumatic event focus of, 82–84, 238
Égalité & Réconciliation, 334–35
Egyptology, 247–48, 253
elections, European, 215, 332–33, 335, 343
elections, French: 1965, 342; 2002, 21, 120, 215, 333–34, 346–47; 2007, 5, 347; 2012, 212–13, 286, 324; 2014, 335–36; 2015, 6, 342, 401, 405
El Gammal, Jean, 93
Elias, Norbert, 72
el-Kriminel, Abd, 288
El-Tayeb, Fatima, 321
Énard, Mathias, 10
Encyclopédie ou dictionnaire raisonné des sciences, des arts et des métiers, 324
Endelstein, Lucine, 100
enemy within: Communism as, 285–86, 287–89, 291, 296–97; Islam as, 285, 286–87, 289–91, 292–97, 299n23; today's vision of, 418
equality, 15; gender, 74, 203, 275, 276–78; HALDE, 371, 421; marriage, 355–56, 358; Overseas France and, 166, 167, 170, 176, 180, 182; race and, 187–88, 194–95, 221, 305; Republic and, 24, 43, 45, 46, 47, 51, 131
Eritrea, 383–84
Eritrean migrants, 381
eroticization, 71–72, 73, 75
Esprit, 159, 220, 269
Ethiopia, 383–84
ethnic factionalism, 16, 58–59
ethnicization, 13, 117, 189–90, 228, 275, 337. *See also* racialization
Études coloniales, 410n27
Eurobarometer, 352
European Asylum Support Office (EASO), 382
European Commission, 380–82, 383–84
European Liberation Front, 334
European rejection of Islam, 312
European Union, 229n8, 353, 378–84, 385n5, 421. *See also* European Commission
Evian Accords, 132, 265, 386
Evry, 415
exceptionalism, French, 192, 194, 202
Exhibit B, 319, 320–23, 326–27, 373
exhibitions, 54, 84, 92–93, 98, 155, 319–20, 323
Explication de notre temps (Romier), 223
extermination, 388

faces, 281
factionalism, ethnic, 16, 58–59
Falaize, Benoît, 94
Falco, Hubert, 399
family networks, 146
family reunification policies, 133, 211–12, 236–37, 294
family structure, 178
Fanon, Frantz, 7, 145, 146, 149, 242, 322, 423
Fassin, Éric, 14, 17, 230n30, 322, 326
Faudel, 119
Febvre, Lucien, 392
Fédération républicaine, 14
fellaghas, 398, 409n12
feminism, 275, 276–78, 280, 283n11, 283n20, 283n26
Ferrat, Jean, 387
Ferro, Marc, 94
Ferry, Jules, 20, 22, 46, 48, 131, 234
Ferry, Luc, 409–10n17
fifth column, 286, 290
Fifth Republic, 130, 269, 370
Fifty-Five Days at Peking (Ray), 55
Fillon, François, 20, 96
films. *See* cinema
Finkielkraut, Alain, 8, 10, 34n52, 387
First Gulf War, 117
First Republic, 46, 130, 263
First World War, 158, 192, 264
FLN (Front de Libération Nationale), 155, 235, 237, 410n37, 418
forced labor, 166, 268, 390
foreigners: citizenship and naturalization of, 6, 14, 124, 259–61, 265; fear of, 6, 210, 311; immigrant differences from, 161, 192; as immigrants, 72, 87, 192, 210–11, 213–15, 217, 218n4, 218n7; unemployment and, 212; women as, 277
forgetting, 96, 97, 99, 102, 103–104, 159–60
Forzy, Guy, 403
Foucault, Michel, 62, 340n18
Fourastié, Jean, 132–33
Fourest, Caroline, 332
Fourth Republic, 82, 130, 227
Fox News, 283n19
FR3, 117
fractures: colonial, 2–3, 145–52, 159 (*see also* Republic and the colonial fracture); cultural, 215–16; in history education, 78–79, 86–87; racial, 169; social, 14, 23–24, 27, 145
Fractures françaises study, 9, 33n46
fragmentary memory, 96, 99, 100
Français de souche nord africaine (FSNA), 60n4
Français et immigrés study, 193
Français musulmans rapatriés (FMR), 60n4
France 2, 119, 324
"France for the French," 213
France Inter radio, 2, 117, 213
Frêche, Georges, 401, 402
freedom of speech, 306, 308
Freedom Party (Austria), 11, 359
French, being, 18–19, 259
French Algeria. *See* Algeria
French Communist Party, 286, 287, 288–89, 291, 297, 343, 346
French Equatorial Africa, 390
French identity: colonialism and, 44, 45, 49–50, 80; definitions, 117–18; memory and, 103, 107, 157; Overseas France and, 184; race and, 222, 305, 307; sexual equality and, 278; threat to, 2, 11, 13, 103, 116, 191, 273–74, 289, 297
French model, 45–46
French Muslims: about, 128, 134, 192, 206n22; current struggles of, 311–15, 316, 317n1; as the enemy within, 285–87, 289–91, 297–98, 299n23; population of, 311–12; populism and, 358–59; public opinion polls on, 311, 333, 336–37; radical, 115–21, 134, 286, 312, 313–14, 338; Republic and, 123–28, 200–202, 204, 206–7nn22–23, 207n25; sharia law, 254, 291. *See also* Islam
French Overseas. *See* Overseas France
"French race," 71, 214, 227
French Revolution, 93, 261, 266
French socialism, 180
French West Africa, 390, 391
French West Indies, 131
Fresnay, Pierre, 389
Front de Gauche, 222, 355
Front de la liberté agreement, 14
Front de Libération Nationale (FLN), 155, 235, 237, 410n37, 418
Frontex, 378–79, 382
Front National de la Jeunesse (National Front of the Youth, FNJ), 14

Front National party, 6, 35n71, 341–48; antiracism and, 371; antisemitism and, 333–34, 335, 336; commemorations and memorials and, 399, 400, 401, 403, 405, 407; decline of France and, 9–10; economic platform of, 353–54; elections and, 116–17, 120, 215, 346–47; emergence and rise of, 2, 24, 311, 324, 332–33, 338, 343–44; French Algeria and, 313, 331; GRECE and, 345–46, 350n17; immigration and, 212, 216, 353–54; intelligent protectionism and, 337; Islamization and, 295, 330; nationality and, 418; opposition to, 339n12, 339n14; populism and, 357; slogan of, 9, 14, 395; transformation and de-demonization of, 333–34, 335, 341–42, 344–46

Front Populaire, 14, 286

Fuchs, Alain, 31n16

fundamentalism, 26, 124

Gabriac, Alexandre, 335–36

Gallo, Max, 10, 92, 252, 404

Gambetta, Léon, 48

Gandhi (Attenborough), 55

Garcia, Patrick, 2, 100–101

Gaudin, Jean-Claude, 399, 401, 403

de Gaulle, Charles, 8, 58, 181, 237, 268, 342, 393n1

Gaullism, 182, 401

Geisser, Vincent, 201

gender: equality, 203; identity and, 282n8; norms, 75–76, 273–74, 275–76, 280, 282n8, 283n15; policing, 275; separatism, 71, 73–74

generalization, 286–87

General Recommendation No. 35, U.N., 303–304

Génération Identitaire, 293

Générations Le Pen, 347

Géraud, Alice, 415

Gérin, André, 272

Germany: enemy within and, 288; identity and, 11; immigration and, 190, 210, 354; nationality policy of, 258; populism in, 351, 352; sexual assaults in, 16–17; in WWII, 288

Gide, André, 286, 390

Gilroy, Paul, 19

Girard, Alain, 193

Girardet, Raoul, 62

Giraud, Michel, 262

Giraudoux, Jean, 215

Giscard d'Estaing, Valéry, 209

Glissant, Édouard, 7, 177, 181

Global Islamic Resistance Call, The (al-Suri), 5, 32n21

globalization, 8, 11, 135, 337–38, 352, 409n17; of memory, 91, 94–95, 105–6, 107, 135, 160

Godard, Jean-Luc, 56

golden age of Republic, 347, 350n22

Gollnisch, Bruno, 341

Goncourt Prize, 10, 327

Gondola, Didier, 66

"government of bodies," 70–72

"Grand Debate on National Identity," 327

grandeur of France, 8, 322

grand remplacement, 8–9, 296

Grant, Madison, 223

great departure, 8–9

Greater France, 45, 49, 157, 386

great substitution, 8–9, 296

Greece, 248, 378–79, 380, 381, 382

Greek miracle, 248

Grigny, 415

Gringoire, 223

Griotteray, Alain, 10

gross domestic product (GDP), 354, 380

Group Areas Act (South Africa), 325

Groupe Islamique Armé (GIA), 313

Groupe Lyonnais d'Etudes Médicales, Philosophiques, et Biologiques, 225

Groupement de recherche et d'études pour la civilisation européenne (Research and Study Group for European Civilization, GRECE), 305, 345–46

Groupe union et défense (GUD), 334, 355

Guadeloupe, 165, 166, 175, 181, 183, 406

Guaino, Henri, 224, 356

Guardian, The, 321

Guéant, Claude, 18, 212, 217, 222, 324, 387

Guénif-Souilamas, Nacira, 66, 203

Guiana, 165, 166, 175

guillotine deaths, 254, 389

Gulf Wars, 117, 295

Habermas, Jürgen, 184, 204

habous, 127–28

Hagen, Carl, 292

halal meat, 285–86

Halbwachs, Maurice, 89
Hamadi, Abdelkader, 100
Hamoumou, Mohand, 98
Hardy, Georges, 49, 224
harkis, 53, 60n4; Front National and, 331; history and, 82, 98, 238; memorials to, 408n6, 410n37; memory and, 57, 58, 101, 397
Haroche, Claudine, 284n33
hate crimes, 304, 309n4
hate speech, 188, 303–304, 307–308, 370, 372
Haute Autorité de lutte contre les discriminations et pour l'égalité (HALDE), 371, 421
headscarves, Islamic: gender norms and, 273; media focus on, 116–17, 120–21; natives and, 71; public space banning of, 28, 121, 134, 147, 198, 205n3, 290, 294; separation of church and state and, 134, 316; stigma of, 75, 203; as a symbol, 280
healthcare in the colonies, 390–91
health education programs, 140
Hérédité et races (Groupe Lyonnais d'Etudes Médicales, Philosophiques, et Biologiques), 225
Herriot, Edouard, 211, 286
hierarchies: aid programs and, 139; differentialist racism and, 305; ethnic and racial, 81, 131, 187, 214, 225, 303, 416; for immigration, 262; patriarchal, 70–72
Hirsi Ali, Ayaan, 283n16
Histoire du visage (Courtine and Haroche), 284n33
historians, role of, 62–63, 95–96
history marginalization, colonial and postcolonial, 61–67, 68n7
Hollande, François: antiracism and, 304; colonial past and, 20, 405, 407; immigration and, 213, 384; memory and, 22; Paris attacks, 1–2, 418
Holocaust and Front National, 341, 344, 349n1
Holocauste, 92
"Homo Islamicus," 201–2
homosexual marriage, 355–56, 358
Hortefeux, Brice, 96, 211–12, 215, 217
hospitals, 390
Hossein, Robert, 92
hotspot approach to migrant relocation, 382, 384
Houellebecq, Michel, 10
Hugo, Victor, 130, 389
human exhibitions, 84, 135, 136n2, 319–23
humanism, 49, 137, 240–41, 319, 325, 337, 392
humanitarianism, 137–42
human rights, 47–48, 137, 187, 254, 345, 359
Human Rights League, 137
human sciences, 65, 252
Hungary, 378–79
Huntington, Samuel, 299n28
Hussein, Saddam, 344
Huston, Nancy, 220
hydraulic racism, 364–65
hygiene, 140–41
Hyper-Casher attacks, 413, 414, 423

Identité, 332
identity, 6–8; in *banlieues,* 145–48, 149; burqa and, 272–74, 282nn3–4, 282n10, 283n20; cultural, 181, 183–85; defensive, 8, 11, 24; education and, 241–42; French (*see* French identity); of jihadists, 26; memory and, 95–96, 100, 103, 106, 107, 157; national (*see* French identity); Overseas France and, 176, 181, 183–85; political, 182–83, 184–85; politics of, 16–19, 43–44, 169, 181, 343, 374, 405; racism and, 306–308; religious, 25, 204, 260; transnational, 28; wars, 3, 29, 221, 337
identity-based coloring, 306–307
illiteracy, 391
Images et colonies, 98, 155
immigrants and children of: Algerian, 192–93, 238; current state of, 7, 412–13, 418–19, 426n19; European, 192–93, 209, 210; as laborers, 132–33, 311, 332; North African, 193, 265; social benefits for, 354. *See also* immigration
immigration: 1930s discourse on, 213–15; Algerian, 57–58, 59, 192–93, 265–66; *Bumidom,* 169, 171n5; discrimination and, 190–93; education and, 84–85, 86–87, 234, 236–37, 238, 241–42; in Europe, 353; French history of, 209–11, 218n4, 218nn7–8; Front National and, 6, 343–44, 346, 347–48, 350n22; GRECE and, 345; identity and, 27–28; illegal or clandestine, 133, 211, 277–78; invasion fantasies, 295–96; law on,

194–95, 257, 306; media and, 116–17, 118; memory and, 101, 105, 161; migrant crisis, 336–37, 378–84, 385n3, 385n5; moves to ban, 293; polls on, 9, 33n46, 193, 212, 337, 351, 352–53; post WWII, 132–33, 192; sexual violence and, 16–17, 277–78. *See also* immigration policy
immigration policy, 17–19, 209–13, 217, 218n4, 218nn7–8, 227; Hortefeux Law, 194–95; population management, 414–15; Weil on, 257, 258, 261, 262, 265–66
Immorality Amendment Act (South Africa), 325
indentured labor, 166, 171n2
independence question for Overseas France, 175–76, 180–81, 184
Indigènes de la République (Natives of the Republic), 70; about, 78, 199, 267, 318n7; memory and, 82, 103, 104, 397; PIR, 307, 334, 373; positions of, 307
indigenization, 69, 76
individuals: in *banlieues,* 146–47, 149–51; identification and, 273–75, 282nn8–9
Indochina, 56, 180, 390, 391
Indochine, 92
Institut des hautes études de défense nationale (Institute of National Defense, IHEDN), 299n23
Institute on Immigration and Integration, 96
Institut Français d'opinion publique (IFOP) studies, 84, 351, 352–53
institutionalization: of antiracism, 369–72, 377n15; of colonial history, 62, 65–66; of Islamic representation, 125, 198, 201–202
institutional racism, 27, 145, 373, 414
Institut national d'études démographiques (National Institute for Demographic Studies, INED) study, 15, 33n46
integration, 16–17; antiracism movement and, 375; *banlieues* and, 149–50, 151, 152; discrimination and, 24; education and, 84–85, 241; Front National and, 347–48; interwar and postwar, 192–93, 350n22; law on, 306; media and, 118; Overseas France and, 184; Republican model of, 133–35, 161–62, 163, 204; study on, 84. *See also* assimilation
intelligent protectionism, 337
Inter-Ministerial Delegation in the Fight Against Racism and Anti-Semitism (DILCRA), 304, 371–72, 377n12
"Internationale," 423, 427n30
internationalism, 50
International League Against Racism and Anti-Semitism (LICRA), 339n13, 370
International Migration Outlook report, 354
International Organization for Migration (IOM), 379
internet, 92, 94
internment, 217, 288
interracial marriage: Front National and, 334; as a norm deviation, 73–74; polls on, 193; prohibition of, 52n5, 325; as a threat to French culture, 214, 224
intersectionality, 334, 373
Invalides, 1–2, 94
Invention of Africa, The (Mudimbe), 246
Invention of Decolonization, The (Shepard), 317n3
"Invention of the Savage" exhibit, 320
invisibility in public space, 203–204
Ipsos study, 9
Iran, 289, 294, 313, 331–32
Iranian Revolution, 313, 331–32
Iraq, 290, 313, 344, 346, 349n12, 414, 422, 427n33
ISIS, 2, 5, 7, 26, 314, 336–37, 414, 422
Islam: aggression against, 28; Algerian War and, 313–14; as the enemy within, 285, 286–87, 289–91, 292–97, 299n23; European history of, 312; faith practice in France, 124, 134; fear of (*see* Islamophobia); growing tension against, 331–33; image of, 202, 207n33; Islamization, 292, 293, 296, 297, 316, 330, 358–59; jihad (*see* jihad); media and, 115–21; police management of, 124–25; as a political issue, 5–6, 25–26. *See also* French Muslims
Islamic State, 2, 5, 7, 26, 314, 336–37, 414, 422
Islamophobia, 289, 297, 311, 336; history and sources of, 292–96, 312–13, 316–17, 330–33; racism and, 374, 415–16
Israel, 285, 313, 333, 334, 336, 339n8, 339n14
Israelites, 207n23, 214

Italian immigrants, 86–87, 191, 193, 210, 262, 350n22
Italy, 22, 28, 378, 380, 381–82
Izoulet, Jean, 223

Jallon, Hugues, 284n41
Jammot, Armand, 92
Jauffret, Jean-Charles, 410n26
Jaurès, Jean, 48
Jego, Yves, 182
Jenni, Laurent, 10
Je suis partout, 223
Jewish Agency for Israel, 336
Jewish Defense League, 336
Jews: Algerian, 131, 258–59, 313, 416; citizenship and, 52n4; French, 333, 336, 422; Front National and, 336, 341, 348, 349n4; as immigrants, 210, 213, 214, 227, 336; memory and, 102; under Vichy regime, 261, 262, 268, 330, 396; Zionism and, 339n8. *See also* antisemitism
jihad, 5, 24, 25–26; attacks of, 1–2, 337, 413–14, 417, 423, 425n4 (*see also specific attacks*); causes and growth of, 407, 417, 422–25, 427n33; threat and fear of, 286, 294, 314, 337, 412
Jiwani, Yasmin, 202
Joissains-Masini, Maryse, 398
Jordi, Jean-Jacques, 402
Jospin, Lionel, 396
Jouhaud, Edmond, 398, 399
journalists, 150
Joxe, Pierre, 23
Judeo-Christian society, 312, 324, 327
judicial system and race, 194
Julien, Charles-André, 64
Julliard, Jacques, 116
jus sanguinis, 258, 344
jus soli, 192, 258, 267, 277, 344

Kaddour, Hédi, 10
Kassovitz, Mathieu, 420
Kelkal, Khaled, 118–19, 120, 121, 420–21
Kepel, Gilles, 5, 294
de Kérillis, Henri, 288
Kerk, Christian, 403–404
Khaldoun, Ibn, 126
Khosrokhavar, Farhad, 424
Kipling, Rudyard, 281
Koran, 259, 260, 331
Kuwait, 344

labor, 133, 171n2, 177, 210–11, 390, 426n10
labor-based immigration, 311
La condition noire (Ndiaye), 326
La conspiration (Nizan), 285
Lacroix-Riz, Annie, 334
L'Action française, 223, 288
La faute du bobo Jocelyn (Cassen and Tasin), 292–93, 298n17
La fracture coloniale, 3, 31n8
La France ne sera pas un pays d'esclaves (Doriot), 288
La France noire preface (Mabanckou), 325–26
L'Afrique explorée et civilisée, 138
La gangrène et l'oubli (Stora), 53
La grande parade des métèques, 216
Lagrange, Hugues, 214, 220–21, 226, 227
La haine (Kassovitz), 420
Lahire, Bernard, 4
laïcité. *See* secularism
Laïcité et l'islam en France report, 125
La Liberté, 287–88
"La marche du siècle," 117
Lambert, Charles, 224
L'Ami du Peuple, 214
La mise en valeur des colonies françaises (Sarraut), 391
Languedoc-Roussillon, 410n24
Lantheaume, Françoise, 94, 234–35
Lanzmann, Claude, 103
La réforme intelectuelle de la France (Renan), 48
La République coloniale (Vergès), 49
la Roque, François de, 14
L'art français de la guerre (Jenni), 10, 34n51
Las Casas, Bartolomé de, 138
La situation postcoloniale (Smouts), 246, 266–67
La Tyrannie de la pénitence (Bruckner), 92
Laval, Pierre, 297
La Voix des Nègres, 326
Lazerges, Christine, 228
Lebanon, 7, 25, 379, 380, 384
Le bled (Renoir), 221
Le Camp des Saints (Raspail), 295–96, 299nn27–28

Le Chevallier, Jean-Marie, 400, 409n15
L'echo d'Alger, 393n1
Leclère, Anne-Sophie, 23, 215, 230n35, 324
L'école des cadavres (Céline), 215
Le crépuscule des nations blanches (Muret), 223
Le déclin de l'Europe (Demangeon), 223
Le déni des cultures (Lagrange), 226
Le destin des races blanches (Decugis), 223
Lefeuvre, Daniel, 10, 98, 252, 397, 402, 410n27
Le Figaro, 6, 33n39, 97, 220, 287, 297, 409n17
Le Figaro Magazine, 116
"Legal principles and foundations of the relationship between the authorities and the Muslim religion in France," 201
Legion of French Volunteers, 297
Le Grand Jury RTL-Le Monde, 344
Le Grand Repli (Bancel, Blanchard, and Boubeker), 8, 12
Le Journal des Débats, 287
Lemaire, Sandrine, 4
L'Emancipation nationale, 223
Le Matin, 223
Lemoine, Hervé, 404
Le Monde, 3–4, 15, 17, 220, 226, 332
Le Monde 2, 106
Le Nouvel Observateur, 107, 116, 226
Léonarda Affair, 213
Léotard, François, 399
Le Pen, Jean-Marie, 213; about, 341, 343; elections and, 21, 333, 347; Holocaust and, 344, 349n1, 349nn8–9; Iraq and, 344, 346, 349n12; Israel and, 339n14; memory and, 156; United States and, 346
Le Pen, Marine, 213, 291, 297, 336; anti-Islam speech of, 295, 333; elections and, 341, 347; Guéant and, 218n13; *harkis* and, 331; immigration and, 21–22, 290, 353–54; Iraq and, 344, 349n12; memory and, 405; as new leader of Front National, 341–42, 349n4; party modernization and de-demonizaton, 333–34, 335, 347–48; populism and, 358; torture and, 337
Le Petit Parisien, 287
Le Point, 107, 226, 230n30, 341
Le Quotidien, 213–14
Le règne de la race (Decleene), 223
Le Réveil du peuple, 223
Leroy-Beaulieu, Paul, 48
Le salut de la race blanche (Mahan), 223
Les âmes grises, 92
Les Annales school, 249
L'esclavage et la colonisation, et après (Weil and Dufoix), 262
Les colonies et la politique de la France (Duval), 48
Les étrangers en France (Mauco), 226–27
Les filles voilées parlent (Chouder, Latrèche, and Tevanian), 275
Les guerres de mémoires dans le monde (Ferro), 94
Les Prépondérants (Kaddour), 10
Les races humaines, 225
Les rendez-vous des quais, 56
Le suicide français (Zemmour), 9
Létourneau, Jocelyn, 239
Lévy-Bruhl, Lucien, 388
Levinas, Emmanuel, 281, 284n32
Lévi-Strauss, Claude, 177, 345
L'Express, 117, 120
L'Homme, 249
L'homme blanc (Romains), 225
L'Humanité, 291, 388
liberalism, 160, 353–54
Libération, 97, 415, 416
Liberté, égalité, discriminations (Weil), 269
Liberté pour l'histoire, 269
L'idée coloniale en France (Girardet), 62
Ligue de l'enseignement (Teaching League), 123, 129n1
Ligue des droits de l'homme (Human Rights League, LDH), 369–70, 372
Ligue internationale contre l'antisémitisme (International League Against Anti-Semitism, LICA), 370
Ligue internationale contre le racisme et l'antisémitisme (International League against Racism and Anti-Semitism, LICRA), 339, 370, 372, 375, 376n1
Lilienfeld, Jean-Louis, 274
L'illustration, 71, 390
Lindenberg, Daniel, 98, 99, 101–102
L'invasion noire (Driant), 299n27
Liogier, Raphaël, 18, 294, 295, 296
liquid populism, 352, 355, 357, 358, 359
Little Soldier, The (Godard), 56
LKP *(Liyannaj kont pwofitasyon)*, 181, 183, 185

lobby, colonial, 63–65, 156
Loi du 29 juillet 1881 sur la liberté de la presse, 222
Loi du 26 juin 1889 sur la nationalité française, 259
Loi du 9 décembre 1905 concernant la séparation des églises et de l'état, 127–28, 136, 200
Loi du 13 juillet 1928 établissant un programme de constructions d'habitations à bon marché et de logements, en vue de remédier à la crise de l'habitation (Loi Loucheur), 214
Loi du 10 août 1932 protégeant la main d'œuvre nationale, 211
Loi du 21 avril 1933 réservant l'exercice de la médecine en France aux citoyens français (Loi Armbruster), 218n8
Loi du 13 juillet 1990 tendant à réprimer tout acte raciste, antisémite ou xénophobe (Loi Gayssot), 269–70, 271n18, 304
Loi du 21 mai 2001 tendant à la reconnaissance de la traite de l'esclavage en tant que crime contre l'humanité (Loi Taubira), 103, 105, 236, 245n32, 269–270, 271n19, 406
Loi du 3 février 2003 visant à aggraver les peines punissant les infractions à caractère raciste, antisémite ou xénophobe (Loi Lellouche), 309n4
Loi du 15 mars 2004 encadrant, en application du principe de laïcité, le port de signes ou de tenues manifestant une appartenance religieuse dans les écoles, collèges et lycées publics, 123, 203, 205
Loi du 23 février 2005 portant sur la reconnaissance de la Nation et contribution nationale en faveur des Français rapatriés (Loi Debré), 4, 244n17, 269, 295, 409n8; education and, 78–79, 80, 309n13; memory and, 103, 105, 403–404
Loi du 24 juillet 2006 relative à l'immigration et à l'intégration, 306
Loi du 20 novembre 2007 relative à la maîtrise de l'immigration, à l'intégration et à l'asile (Loi Horteufeux), 194–95
Loi du 11 octobre 2010 interdisant la dissimulation du visage dans l'espace public, 274
Loi du 16 juin 2011 relative à l'immigration, à l'intégration et à la nationalité (Loi Besson), 212
Loi Mekachera, *See Loi du 23 février 2005 portant sur la reconnaissance de la Nation et contribution nationale en faveur des Français rapatriés,* 4, 20, 32, 78–79, 237, 244n17, 309n13
Loin (Téchiné), 56
Londres, Albert, 390, 392
Longuet, Gérard, 409n15
L'ordonnance du 19 Octobre 1945 sur la nationalité, 257, 261
Lorraine, 44, 46, 52n8, 158
Louverture, Toussaint, 235

Mabanckou, Alain, 21, 68n7, 325–26
Macron, Emmanuel, 417
Madrid bombings, 148
Maghrebis, 10, 17, 59, 119; demonstrations by, 419; discrimination of, 73, 416; immigration of, 7, 133–34; memory and, 104–105
Mahan, Alfred T., 223
Maison de l'Histoire de France, 404–405
Manceron, Gilles, 96
Mandroux, Hélène, 402
Manifeste, 223
Manif pour Tous (Movement for All), 356
manipulation and memory, 97, 99, 100, 150, 153
Marche des Beurs, 289, 356, 371, 373, 419
Marche pour l'égalité et contre le racisme (March for Equality against Racism), 289, 356, 371, 373, 419
Maréchal, Samuel, 346
Mariani, Thierry, 211–12
Marianne symbol, 116, 121, 274, 288
Marie, Claude-Valentin, 169
Marignane, 400, 401
Marleix, Alain, 410n37
marriage equality, 355–56, 358
Marseille museums and memorials, 401–405
Martial, René, 227
Martin Bernal Affair, 248
Martinique, 165, 166, 175
masks, 273, 274, 282n2, 282n9
Maspero, François, 57
Masseret, Jean-Pierre, 410n26
Massis, Henri, 222–23
Mauco, Georges, 214, 224, 226–27
Mauritania, 383
Mauroy, Pierre, 332

Maurras, Charles, 8, 224, 331, 357
Mayotte, 165, 175, 185
Mazouz, Sarah, 200
Mbembe, Achille, 15, 240, 324–25
Mbodj, Mohamed, 249
Médecin, Jacques, 398
medersas, 127
media: "Arab" representations in, 115–21, 124; historians in, 252; integration issues and, 85; Islam and, 289, 295; memory and, 90, 91–94, 96–97, 100–101, 102, 106–107, 155, 164n9; Muslims in, 25; racism in, 215, 368
Mediapart, 95
Mégret, Bruno, 332–33, 346, 347
Meillassoux, Claude, 254
Mekachera, Hamlaoui, 244n17
Memmi, Albert, 145, 246
memorial activism, 103, 263, 269–70, 400
Mémorial de l'abolition de l'esclavage (Memorial for the Abolition of Slavery), 406
memorial laws, 96–97, 269–70, 271nn18–19
Mémorial national de la France d'Outre-mer (National Memorial of France Overseas, MoM) project, 20, 401, 402–405, 410–11n28
Mémorial national de la guerre d'Algérie et des combats du Maroc et de la Tunisie, 396, 408nn5–6
memorials. *See* commemorations, memorials, monuments, and museums
memory, colonial, 53–59, 153–63; affect on national narrative, 134; Algerian War and, 53–54, 57–58, 60n5, 313; amnesia of, 69, 84–86, 153, 156, 159–60, 169, 199; background and overview of, 153–54; cinema and, 54–57; current state of, 102, 406–407; decolonization and, 306; education and, 238, 239–40, 242; fusion of colonial with national and, 158–59; gaps in, 162–63; generational change of, 58–59; ideology and, 156–58, 160; knowledge availability and, 154–55; Overseas France and, 180; politics and, 395–96; socialization of, 153, 154, 160, 161; turning point in, 397–98; wars of (*see* memory wars). *See also* commemorations, memorials, monuments, and museums
memory wars, 89–107; background and overview, 89–91, 93–96, 107; exposure and discourse on, 98–102; globalization of, 91, 105–6, 107; history and, 89–91, 94, 97–98, 100–101, 106, 107; identity and, 307; media and, 90, 91–94, 96–97, 100–101, 102, 106–107; state and, 102–105
Ménard, Robert, 8, 33n41, 337
Merah, Mohamed, 32n25, 286, 422, 427n28
mercantilism, 177, 235–36
Merkel, Angela, 354
Messmer, Pierre, 409
métèques, 8, 210, 215
Meursault, contre-enquête (Daoud), 17
Michel, Andreé, 192–93
Michel, Marc, 402, 410n27
migrant crisis, 336–37, 378–84, 385n3, 385n5
military service, 419
Milza, Pierre, 235, 236
Ministry of Foreign Affairs, 207n25
Ministry of Immigration, Integration, National Identity, and Co-Development, 212, 383
Ministry of Interior, the Overseas Departments, the Territorial Collectivities, and Immigration, 212
Ministry of Justice, 257–58
Ministry of the Interior, 201, 207n25, 337, 422, 427n33
Minute, 23, 308
minutes of silence, 148–49
Mitterrand, François, 20
mixed marriage. *See* interracial marriage
mixing of race, 10, 13, 71, 220, 224, 247, 305. *See also* interracial marriage
modernization, 137–39
Monnerot, Jules, 331
monotheism, 248
Montpellier, memorial in, 401, 402
monuments. *See* commemorations, memorials, monuments, and museums
Môquet, Guy, 105
Morales, Daniel, 221
morality, 205, 208n46
moralization in education, 235, 409n17
Morano, Nadine, 324, 387
Morocco, 383, 388
Moselle, 44, 268
Mosque of Poitiers, 293
Moutet, Marius, 49

Mouvement des travailleurs arabes (Arab Workers Movement, MTA), 26, 371
Mouvement Occident, 339n14
Movement contre le racisme, l'antisémitisme, et pour la paix (Movement against Racism, Anti-Semitism, and for Peace), 370
Movement contre le racisme et pour l'amitié entre les peuples (Movement Against Racism and for Friendship Among People, MRAP), 370, 372, 375
Movement Defending Freedom of Schools, 356
Movement des travailleurs arabes (MTA), 371
Moynier, Gustave, 138
Mucchielli, Laurent, 226
Mudimbe, Valentin Y., 246, 253
multiculturalism, 135, 204, 216, 221, 336, 338, 359, 374–75
Munich Accords, 297
Muret, Maurice, 223
Muriel (Renais), 56
Musée de l'Homme, 225
Musée des civilisations de l'Europe et de la Méditerranée (Museum of European and Mediterranean Civilizations, MuCEM), 403, 410n35
Musée du quai Branly, 320, 396–97, 407, 408n5
Museum of the History of France in Algeria, 402
museums, 323; CNHI, 96, 103, 105, 237, 410n29; memory and, 92, 94, 96, 162, 398; projects for, 401–405, 406–407, 410n35. *See also* commemorations, memorials, monuments, and museums; *specific museums*
Muslim, term of, 260–61
Muslim advisers, 201–2
Muslim-Arabs, 117, 147–48, 338
Muslim Brotherhood, 313–14
Muslim policies of the Republic, 200–201, 206–7nn22–23, 207n25
Muslim *préfet*, 121
Muslim question, 315, 318n8
Muslims, French. *See* French Muslims; Islam
Muslims in colonial Algeria, 259–62
Naipaul, Vidiadhar Surajprasad, 145
nanoracism, 363–67
Napoleon, 52n5
Napoleon III, 44, 138
National Action Plan Against Racism and Anti-Semitism (PNACRA), 304
National Assembly, 3, 99–100, 222
National Consultative Commission on Human Rights (CNCDH), 193, 228, 304, 305, 308, 348
nationalism, French, 237, 277, 331, 342, 348, 365
nationality, 192; Front National and, 331, 344, 418; overseas departments and, 176; policy on, 206n22, 257–61, 264–66, 268, 269, 270n8, 418; sexuality and, 277. *See also* citizenship
National Museum for the History of Immigration (CNHI), 96, 103, 105, 237, 410n29
National Party (South Africa), 12, 325
national preference, 13, 18, 305, 337
natives: in cinema, 55, 57; citizenship and, 52n4, 192, 201, 206n22, 224; civilizing, 46, 47–49, 50; in curriculum, 81, 241; humanitarian aid and, 137–42; Muslims as, 202, 206n22, 207n23, 260, 315, 318n7; reducing to the body, 70–76; repression of, 289–392; social benefits for, 354
naturalization, 125, 200, 213, 259–61
NDiaye, Marie, 327
Ndiaye, Pap, 326
negationism, 269, 271n18
nègre, term of, 324, 326
Nemmouche, Mehdi, 32n25, 286
néo-Parti colonial, 386
neutrality, 43–44, 205
new right, 305, 332, 345
NGOs, 138–42
Nice memorials, 398
Nicolaïdis, Dimitri, 99, 100, 102
Nizan, Paul, 285
Noiriel, Gérard, 18, 19, 237
Non au changement de peuple et de civilisation (Camus), 296
nondiscrimination policies, 187–88

Nora, Pierre, 8, 21, 23, 409n17; memory and, 89, 90, 100, 263, 397, 398
norms: colonial, 74; gender, 75–76, 273–74, 275–76, 280, 282n8, 283n15; of indigenization, 75–77
Norway, 292
nostalgerians, 387
nostalgia, colonial, 7, 22, 156, 395–96, 399–400
Notre-Dame-d'Afrique, 399
Nouveau Parti anticapitaliste (NPA), 334
Nouvelle Droite, 305, 332, 345
Nouvel Observateur, 107, 116, 226
nudity, 274–75

OAS (Organization of the Secret Army), 20, 82, 307, 387, 398, 400, 401
Obama, Barack, 29, 195–96
Occidentalism, 337, 338
Odunlami, Stella, 321
Œuvre Française, 335–36, 339nn13–14
Offenstadt, Nicolas, 95, 404
Officers' Ward, The, 92
Oïs, Mostefa, 389
Onfray, Michel, 24
"On n'est pas couché," 324
Opinionway polls, 212, 352, 368, 376n1
Orban, Viktor, 379
Ordre Nouveau, 339n14, 343
Organization for Economic Cooperation and Development (OECD), 354
Organization of the Secret Army (OAS), 20, 82, 307, 387, 398, 400, 401
Orientalism, 10, 253, 337, 338
Orientalism (Said), 246
Orientals, 227
"Orphée noir" (Sartre), 25
Ortiz, Jean, 213
Ory, Pascal, 3–4
"other": as an alter ego, 281; fear of, 227, 297, 355, 395; images of, 161, 202; popularism and, 357; in school curriculum, 86
Ottoman Empire, 312, 359
"Oublier nos crimes" (Nicolaïdus), 99
oulemas, 128, 200
outsourcing migration management, 383–84
Overseas France, 165–71, 175–85; about, 165–67; anthropological and political specificities, 176–78; historical overview, 178–81; political struggles of, 179, 181–85; social struggles of, 180, 181, 182–83; unrest in, 175–76, 183; as a vestige of colonial utopia, 167–71

Pages africaines (Demangeon and Maurras), 224
Palais des Colonies of the Porte Dorée, 103, 410n29
Palestinians, 26, 289, 333, 355, 421–22
Paoli, Paul-François, 10
Paon, Marcel, 224
Parisien, 119
Paris Première, 360n15
Paris terrorist attacks, 1–2, 3, 337, 412, 413–14, 417, 423, 425n4
Paroles de Français, 216
Parti Chrétien Démocrate, 355
Parti Nationaliste, (PNF), 336, 339n14
Parti Populaire Français (PPF), 14, 288, 342, 346
Party of the Indigènes de la République (PIR), 307, 334, 373
Passing of the Great Race, The (Grant), 223
paternalism, 166, 201–202, 327, 371
patriarchal hierarchy, 70–72
Pauwels, Louis, 296
Paxton, Robert, 153, 155, 164n7
pedagogy, 233–34, 235, 239–43
Péninque, Philippe, 334, 347
Perpignan memorials, 399, 400–401, 405, 409n22, 410n23, 410n37
Perse, Saint-John, 178
personless identity, 274, 282n9
Petit Bleu, 215
philo-Semitism, 334, 374
pieds noirs, 6, 53, 58, 60n3, 313, 396, 398
pieds rouges, 60n5
pilot center, refugee, 384
Pitti, Laure, 193
Pluyette, Jean, 224
Poitiers, 134, 293, 359
Poland, 381
police: killings by, 216, 420–21; management of Islam, 124–25; security and, 282n4
Politique africaine, 250

polls, public opinion: on Algerian independence, 342; on authoritarianism, 336; on citizenship, 6; on Front National, 347; on globalization, 352; on immigration, 9, 33n46, 193, 212, 337, 351, 352–53; on Islam, 311, 333, 336–37; on race and racism, 209, 305, 368, 376n1; on state of France, 9
poor whites, 13–14, 35n71
Popular Front, 211, 227
population management policy, 414–15
Populations Registration Act (South Africa), 325
populism, 3, 5, 6, 351–59; about, 351–52, 356–58; globalization of, 352–54; hodgepodgeness of, 355–56; Muslims and, 358–59
Portuguese, 190, 191, 193
positive colonization, 295, 306, 309n13, 401, 404, 406. *See also* Loi Debré
positive discrimination, 49
postcolonial France, overview of, 132–33
postcolonial interpretation, 190
postcoloniality, 167, 168
Postcolonial Melancholia (Gilroy), 19
postcolonial studies, 61, 246–54, 267; academia's rejection of, 65–67, 249–51; defined, 62–63; need for scientific convergence on, 251–54; scholarship on, 247–49
Pouchepadass, Jacques, 253
Poujadist Movement, 342
Powell, Colin, 141–42
Powell, Enoch, 11
prejudice, 188, 306. *See also* racism
prison population, 423–24
privatizing cultural identity, 203–204
progressives, 224, 290–91, 355, 357–58, 359
Progress Party, 292
Prohibition of Mixed Marriages Act (South Africa), 325
prohibition strategy on race, 187–88, 190
protection of national labor law, 211
prototyping, 273
public schools, 134, 158, 161, 304, 356, 391. *See also* education
public space: banning of headscarves, veils, and burqas in, 28, 121, 134, 147, 198, 205n3,290, 294; Islam and, 124, 198–99, 203–204
Pudal, Bernard, 95
pure French stock, 23, 118, 184, 239, 315, 387
purpose of book, 3
Puy du Fou theme park, 102, 103

Quai Branly Museum, 320, 396–97, 407, 408n5
qualification, 147, 200
Quand l'Algérie était française, 107
quenelle, 336, 339n13
Que sais-je? (Vallois), 225
Qu'est-ce qu'on a fait au bon dieu (de Chauveron), 221
Qu'est-ce qu'un Français (Weil), 258
quotas, immigration, 211, 257, 380–81
quotas on products, 353

Ra, 248
race: acknowledgment of, 195–96; biological notion of, 307; mixing of, 10, 13, 71, 220, 224, 247 (*see also* interracial marriage); return of, 220–22, 229n8; term of, 187–88. *See also* racism
Race Relations Act (UK), 15
Races, racisme et antiracisme dans les années 1930 (Reynaud-Paligot), 225
racial hierarchy, 81, 131, 187, 214, 225, 303, 416
racialization, 189, 195, 221, 228, 326. *See also* ethnicization
racial terminology, 189
racism, 13, 14, 23–24; antiwhite, 306, 375; in *banlieues,* 145, 147; biological, 330, 359; CERD and, 303–304; cultural difference and, 227–28; differentialist, 305–306; *Exhibit B* and, 323; Finkielkraut on, 387; hydraulic, 364–65; identity and, 306–308; institutional, 27, 145, 373, 414; Islamophobia and, 374, 415–16; media and, 215, 368; memory and, 306–307; nanoracism, 363–67; polls on, 209, 305, 368, 376n1; postcolonial migration and, 190–94; in school curriculum, 83, 84, 235; scientific, 247; in twenty-first century, 209, 215–17, 228, 363–67; "without race," 187–90. *See also* antiracism
racist wounds, 364
radicalization, 6, 414, 423–24, 427nn33–34
Radicalization in the West (Silber and Bhatt), 298n3

Raffarin, Jean-Pierre, 403
Ramadan, Tariq, 125–26
Rana, Aziz, 262–63
Raoult, Éric, 327
rape, 73, 74–75
Raspail, Jean, 295–96, 299nn27–28
Rassemblement bleu Marine (RBM), 14
Rassemblement Populaire, 291
Ravier, Stéphane, 331
Ray, Nicolas, 55
Raymond, Michel, 220
Réaction, 223
recognition demands, 133, 135–36
Réconciliation Nationale party, 335
Reconquista, 312
Red Cross, 138
Reding, Viviane, 216
refugee camps, 217, 382, 384
refugee crisis, 336–37, 378–84, 385n3, 385n5
Régions d'Outre-Mer (ROM), 165
religion: in France, 315–16; millennials and, 59; populism and, 351–52; power of, 26; separation of church and state, 123–24, 125, 127–28, 136, 200, 203, 204–205. *See also* Christianity; Islam
religious symbols, law banning, 123, 203, 205
relocating *banlieue* minorities proposal, 415
relocation of migrants, 381–82
Rémond, René, 263
Renan, Ernest, 48, 157, 393
Renault, 193
reparations, 78, 167, 373
repentance, 18, 21, 94, 306–307, 395, 397, 405, 408n2
replacement myth, 330, 331
repression: colonialism and, 388–91; in Overseas France, 166–67, 180
Republic: about, 130; colonial fracture and (*see* Republic and the colonial fracture); colonial memory and, 156–58, 163; colonization and, 130–31; integration model of, 133–35, 161–62, 163, 204; Muslim policies of, 198, 200–202, 206–207nn22–23, 207n25; new debates within, 135–36; Overseas France and, 167–69; post colonial historic periods, 132–33; separation of church and state, 123–24, 125, 127–28, 136, 200, 203, 204–205
Républicains (LR), 10, 407
Republic and the colonial fracture, 43–51; civilizing mission and, 47–49; identity politics and, 43–44, 49–50; origins of, 44–46, 52n8, 52nn4–5
Republican feminism, 283n11
republicanism: American revolution and, 262–63; French, 45–46, 51, 182, 184, 204–205, 263; values of, 131, 133–34, 163, 200, 312, 316, 347–48
Résistance Républicaine, 293
Resnais, Alain, 56
responsibility, 58–59, 72–73
Retour d'URSS (Gide), 286
Réunion, 131, 165, 166, 175
reverse colonization, 8, 359, 360n15
Ricœur, Paul, 104, 242
Rif War, 291
right of blood, 258, 344
right of the soil, 192, 258, 267, 277, 344
Rigouste, Mathieu, 289–90, 298n12
Rioufol, Ivan, 296
Rioux, Jean-Pierre, 402, 404, 410n28
Riposte Laïque, 292, 293, 339n12
Rivarol, 349n8
"Rivers of Blood" (Powell), 11
Robert, Fabrice, 293
Rocard, Michel, 227
Roma, 18, 209, 213, 216, 304, 358, 359
Romains, Jules, 225
Romier, Lucien, 223
Rousso, Henry, 90, 92, 103, 104
Roy, Olivier, 424
Royal, Ségolène, 21
RTL radio, 226, 228
rules of behavior, 205, 208nn46–47
Ruptures postcoloniales, 3, 31n9
Ruscio, Alain, 155, 398, 400
Rushdie, Salman, 294

Sahlins, Peter, 259
Said, Edward W., 151, 246, 250–51, 253, 267
de Saint-Arnaud, Achilles Le Roy, 57
Saint-Domingue, 179
Saint-Michel RER station attack, 118
Salafism, 276, 285, 294, 313–14
Salan, Raoul, 398, 399
Salon de l'agriculture (Agricultural Fair), 216
same-sex marriage, 355–56, 358

Sansal, Boualem, 10
Sans Frontière, 371
de Sardan, Jean-Pierre Olivier, 138
Sarkozy, Nicolas, 5, 21, 194, 209, 387, 407; on being French, 18–19; on the burqa, 272; on colonialism, 36n101, 399–400; immigration and, 18, 212, 216, 217; Marseille museum project and, 401, 404; memory and, 89, 101, 102, 103; on repentance, 395, 408n2; speech in Dakar, 13, 86, 102, 224, 306–307; on women, 277, 278
Sarraut, Albert, 217, 224, 297, 391
Sarrazin, Thilo, 11
Sartre, Jean-Paul, 24–25
Satanic Verses, The (Rushdie), 294
saucisson-pinard, 292, 293
Saudi Arabia, 289, 312
Saurel, Philippe, 402
Sayad, Abdelmalek, 7, 70, 76, 240
Schengen, 382
Schnapper, Dominique, 98
scholars, race, 226–27. *See also specific scholars*
scholarship: on decline of France question, 8–11, 34n52; postcolonial studies and, 246; on race, 220, 222–23, 225–26; textbooks, 79–82; on West's decline, 223–25
Schor, Paul, 96
Schor, Ralph, 209
Schweitzer, Albert, 389
Schweitzer, Louis, 421
scientific racism, 247
"second Algerian War," 9
Second Empire, 127, 130
second generation immigrants, 53, 191
Second Republic, 127, 130–31, 263
sectarianism, 251, 276, 415
secularism, 28; French left and, 332–33; Front National and, 333, 347, 348, 357; Islam and, 123, 198, 200–205; polls on, 336; racism and, 27, 365, 376; rise in, 128; school system and, 242, 413; veils and headscarves and, 274, 279, 290–91
security: burqas and, 272, 273–74, 282n4, 282n10; discrimination and surveillance and, 125, 127; threat of Muslim Arab and, 116, 117, 119, 120–21, 295, 297, 314
segregation, 12, 56, 187, 194, 325
Seine-Saint-Denis, 415
Senegal, 47, 383
Sennep, 286
separation of church and state, 123–24, 125, 127–28, 136, 200, 203, 204–205
separatism, 71, 73–74
September 11 attacks, 120, 147–48, 295, 422
Serre, Philippe, 214
Service de la main-d'œuvre (Department of Foreign Labor), 210
"Sexes et races: Deux réalités" (Huston and Raymond), 220
sexual assault, 17, 73, 74–75, 277–78, 283nn25–26, 283n29
sexual equality, 74, 203, 275, 276–78
sexualization, 71–72, 73
sexual roles, 73–76
Shakespeare, William, 247–48
shared narratives, 168
sharia law, 254, 291
Shepard, Todd, 317n3
Siegfried, André, 220, 223, 225, 228
Silber, Mitchell D., 298n3
Simenon, Georges, 390
Simon, Patrick, 15, 43–44
Simon-Nicaise, Suzy, 410n23
Simonpiéri, Daniel, 400
situational apartheid, 12–13, 325
Skirt Day, 274
skirts, 274–76
slavery: abolition of, 130, 169–70, 179–80, 261, 266, 269, 406; about, 44, 52n5, 177, 178–79, 189; commemoration of, 117, 170, 271n19, 406; education of history of, 234, 235–36, 239, 241, 244n13; identity and, 263; impact of on public policy, 261–62; Taubira Law, 103, 105, 236, 245n32, 269–270, 271n19, 406
slave trade, 104–105, 135, 169, 235–36, 239, 244n13, 271n19
Slim, Hugo, 142
Smouts, Marie-Claude, 246, 266–67
social benefits, 354, 415
social foundations of Overseas France, 176–77, 178–79, 182–84, 185
social français Parti, 14
social housing, 415
Socialist Party, 217, 398, 410n24
socialization of colonial memory, 153, 154, 160, 161

social personality, 272–73
societal shift of France, 315–17
Société générale d'immigration (SGI), 210
Society of Nations, 214
Sofres survey, 117
Soral, Alain, 334–35, 347
Sorbonne, the, 64
SOS Enfants d'Iraq, 349n12
SOS Racisme, 305, 355, 371, 372, 375
Soumission (Houellebecq), 10
sous-direction de l'information générale (SDIG), 272
South Africa, 12, 22, 187–88, 325, 414
Soviet Union, 285, 288, 344
Spanish, 138, 191, 193, 210
Spanish Civil War, 297
Spengler, Oswald, 223
Spire, Alexis, 265
Stalin, Joseph, 286, 288
Stavo-Debauge, Joan, 203–204
Stelae, 400, 409n22
stereotyping, 86, 148, 287
stigmatization, 202–203, 364
Stoezel, Jean, 193
Stop le Contrôle au Faciès, 375
Stora, Benjamin, 12, 21, 31n11, 96, 98, 107, 238, 396, 407
studies, public opinion. *See* polls, public opinion
subaltern studies, 250, 266–67
Sudan, 383–84
sugar, 235
superiority: French academia, 249, 252; race, 22, 131, 247, 252; of the West, 224
al-Suri, Abu Musab, 5, 32n21
surveillance, 126, 127
Sweden, 381
Swiss Confederation, 353
Swiss People's Party, 353, 360n8
Syria, 5, 414, 422, 423, 427n33
Syrian refugees, 379–80, 381, 384, 385n5

Tabarot, Michèle, 404, 410n30
Taguieff, Pierre-André, 332, 333
Tasin, Christine, 292–93, 298n17
Taubira, Christiane, 23, 215, 228, 308, 324, 405, 418
Taxi, 221
Tears of the White Man, The (Bruckner), 92
Téchiné, André, 56
television: "Arab" representation on, 115; memory and, 91–92, 94, 155
Télévision, nouvelle mémoire (Bruckner), 92
TeO study, 33n46
Terminal: Blood Diamonds (Bailey), 322
Terres australes et antarctiques françaises (TAAF), 165
terrorism, Islamist, 27–28, 134; anxiety over, 27–28, 286, 314–15, 336–37; attacks of, 1–2, 337, 413–14, 417, 423, 425n4 (*see also specific attacks*); citizenship and, 412, 418; colonialism connection to, 412–14, 418, 423, 424–25; origins of, 6–7, 32n25, 417–18, 421–24; stigmatization and, 118–19, 124–25, 147, 148, 286–87; strategies of, 5
Tevanian, Pierre, 18
textbooks: Black France and, 322; colonization in, 79, 80–84, 160, 234–35, 237; immigration in, 237; Islam in, 124; memory and, 94, 97; overseas France in, 87; role of, 79, 400, 409–10n17; slavery in, 235–36, 239
TF1, 212, 216
Thénault, Sylvie, 100
Théoule-sur-mer memorials, 399
There Ain't No Black in the Union Jack (Gilroy), 19
Third Republic, 44–49, 52n4, 127, 130, 135, 161, 166, 324
Thorez, Maurice, 213, 286
Thou Shalt Not Kill (Autan-Lara), 56
Tillion, Germaine, 392
time and memory, 91, 104, 107
Tixier-Vignancour, Jean-Louis, 342, 343
Todd, Emmanuel, 178
torture, 21, 83, 159, 337
totalitarianism, 345, 355
Toubon, Jacques, 410n29
Toulon memorials, 399
Tous nés en 1848, 169
Trajectoires et origines study, 15
Traverso, Enzo, 90
treaties targeting discrimination, 188–89, 229n8
Tremolet de Villers, Vincent, 409n17
Trente Glorieuses, 19, 132–33, 233, 348, 418
Trintignant, Marie, 278

Trois femmes puissantes (NDiaye), 327
Trotskyist Fourth International, 332
Trump, Donald, 25
Tunisia, 25, 265, 289, 390, 410n26
Turkey, 379, 380, 384
Two Faces of American Freedom, The (Rana), 262–63
2084 (Sansal), 10
two-tier citizenship, 6

ulemas, 128, 200
Ultras, 50
understanding, 3–4, 6, 29, 31n16
unemployment, 13, 27, 212, 314, 343, 353, 419–20
UNESCO, 187, 370
UNICEF, 140
Union des organisations islamiques de France (Union of Islamic Organizations of France, UOIF), 355
Union for a Popular Movement (UMP), 10, 211–12, 217, 324, 396, 407, 416–17
uniqueness, French, 47
United Kingdom, 11, 15, 132, 359, 385n3
United Nations, 139–40, 141, 306–307; Committee on the Elimination of Racial Discrimination (CERD), 216, 303–304; High Commission for Refugees (UNHCR), 379–80, 385n3; UNESCO, 187, 370
United States, 65, 105, 332, 419; Afghanistan and Iraq Wars and, 344, 422; American Revolution, 262–63; Front National and, 344, 346; immigration and, 25, 210, 257, 380; racial segregation and discrimination in, 12, 187–88, 262, 326, 373; slavery in, 186, 263
universal citizens, 43–44
Universal Declaration of Human Rights, 187
Universal Declaration of the Rights of Man, 254
universalism, 334, 345; colonialism and, 45, 46, 51; education and, 240–41; memory and, 91, 161; postcolonial studies and, 251, 254; racism and, 14, 204, 372, 376
Urban, Yeri, 258
urban unrest, 5, 11–12, 116, 292, 295, 372, 420
Usages et mésusages de l'histoire (Offenstadt), 95
utopia, colonial, 48, 156, 159, 169, 170

Valeurs Actuelles, 296
Vallaud-Belkacem, Najat, 405
Vallin, Charles, 215
Vallois, Henri Victor, 225
Valls, Manuel, 209, 290, 291; apartheid and, 12–13, 324, 325; immigration policy and, 213, 414–15; Paris attacks response of, 1, 2, 3, 412, 417–18
values of republicanism, 131, 133–34, 163, 200, 312, 316, 347–48
Vanneste, Christian, 282n10, 400, 404, 409n19
Vaulx-en-Velin, 116, 420–21
Veil, Simone, 194
veils. *See* burqas
Vergès, François, 49, 103
"Vichy and the Modernization of Algeria" (Lefeuvre), 98
Vichy France, 14, 291; antisemitism of, 330, 396, 416; memory and, 57, 58, 85, 155, 164n7, 396, 397; policies of, 210, 258, 261
victimhood, 132, 135, 306; identity-based, 308, 373; memory and, 58–59, 96; in pedagogy, 239, 240; sectarianism, 415–16
Vidal-Naquet, Pierre, 90, 99, 235, 248, 249
Vingtième siècle: Revue d'histoire, 98, 101
violence against women, 277–78, 283n25
Viollette, Maurice, 260
Viollis, Andrée, 389
virtue leagues, 369–70
vocabulary of threats, 18

Wahhabism, 316
Wahnich, Stéphane, 27
Wallerstein, Immanuel, 254
war, 1–2, 4, 30n4
Wars of Religion, 316
water, 140
"We are all French monkeys," 308
Weil, Patrick, 350n22; interview with, 257–70
welcome centers for asylum seekers, 384
welfare, 336
West: contempt for, 23–24; fear of decline of, 222–25, 286, 296, 337; postcolonial studies and, 247, 251, 253–54; superiority of, 224
"White Man's Burden, The" (Kipling), 281
Wieviorka, Michel, 18, 228

Wieviorka, Olivier, 95
Wild Reeds (Téchiné), 56
women, 261; assault against, 17, 73, 74–75, 277–78, 283nn25–26, 283n29; colonized, 71, 73; dress and, 272–77, 278–81; equality and, 74, 203, 275, 276–78; imputed roles of, 73–75; norms of indigenization of, 75–77; "ours" versus "theirs," 277–78, 283n29
word clouds, 27
words, 149–51
World Health Organization, 140
World War I, 158, 192, 264

xenophobia, 161, 331; French law on, 204, 309n4; Front National and, 348; immigration and, 210, 213–15, 217, 296; public opinion on, 305; state, 17, 206n10

Yersin, Alexandre, 389, 394n13
Yerushalmi, Yosef H., 99
Yugoslavia, 332

Zancarini-Fournel, Michelle, 97–98
Zappi, Sylvia, 43–44
al-Zarqawi, Abu Musab, 5
Zelensky, Anne, 222
Zemmour, Éric, 8, 9, 227–28, 296, 360n15, 387, 393n4, 397
Zidane, Zinedine, 119, 120, 121, 202, 203
Zionism, 335, 338, 339n8, 413. *See also* anti-Zionism
Zitrone, Léon, 92
Z&N, 360n15
Zucca, André, 93
Zytnicki, Colette, 62